Living in
Norway

Patricia Crinion Bjaaland's
classic guide for new residents

Now in a completely new third edition by
Michael Brady and Belinda Drabble

P̄

Palamedes Press

Palamedes Press
Oslo, Norway

Living in Norway
First edition 1983, Second edition 1985, Second revised edition 1988
© Patricia Crinion Bjaaland
Completely new third edition 1999
© Palamedes Press

ISBN 82-91570-01-9

Printed in Norway
layout by Anne Andresen
editing by Sam Hall, Global Syndications, UK
cover photograph of Kongsvold Fjellstue by Rohny Kristensen
all other photographs by Frits Solvang
back cover map courtesy of The Norwegian Mapping Authoruty
printed by Grafisk Markeds Design AS

Contents

Preface

This book is a practical guide to living in Norway for new residents from other countries. It is not a tourist guide-book (though tourists may find it useful), because it presents all aspects of everyday life and work, not just holiday entertainment and sightseeing. The topics covered include the 170 some of the first two editions plus more than 700 selected in response to the needs of new residents from five continents and in many cases were chosen to answer specific queries.

The topics are arranged in alphabetical order, grouped by subject into 48 chapters, which also are in alpha-betical order. All the facts presented are available in Norway from the organisations and the printed and on-line sources mentioned in the topics. So this book may also be used as a starting point for finding further informa-tion.

The comparative rankings with other countries are extracted with permission from *Pocket World in Figures 1999*, ISBN 1-86197-110-9 and *Pocket Europe in Figures 1999*, ISBN 1-86197-093-5, published by The Econo-mist in association with Profile Books, London.

British English is the language of this book, as suits the majority of new residents from other countries. A Glossary of British English – American English is included on the last two pages for the convenience of Ameri-can readers who may be unfamiliar with the British variety of the language.

Norwegians and residents who can read Norwegian may be interested in two of the many reference books we used. The converse book to *Living in Norway* is *Flerkulturell Håndbok* by Gunnar Neegaard, Oslo, Kom-muneforlaget 1998, ISBN 82-446-0530-8. It is an encyclopaedic book of advice on dealing with peoples of other cultures who reside in Norway. A small, convenient and comprehensive reference is *Norsk Almanakk 2000*, published by Almanakkforlaget, Oslo, book no. 704511200100. In addition to the customary calendar and chronological tables, it contains a wealth of information on the country.

We humbly acknowledge the contributions of more than 500 experts who we consulted in writing this book. We are particularly grateful for the helpfulness of many people in the civil service, in local and national offices as well as in ministerial departments. In many cases, they not only supplied information and verified the texts we had written on topics in their fields, but made corrections and suggested additions. Without their co-operation, this book would have been less comprehensive.

October 1999
Michael Brady and Belinda Drabble

How to use this book

First, read the Check Lists before you depart for Norway or before you return from Norway to your home country. Then you may find information in at least two ways:
- by reading the chapters, each on a different subject, or
- by looking up and reading individual topics.

If you seek a specific topic, you may locate it:
- among the topics of the chapter to which it relates.
- in the English or Norwegian indexes, to find its page number(s).

All names of topics and other essential terms and names in English are followed by their equivalents in Norwegian in italics in parentheses: English term (*Norwegian term*). All English equivalents of Norwegian names and words normally not translated are listed in parentheses and quotes: *Norwegian word* ("Equivalent English word").

All Norwegian words are in *Bokmål*, the leading version of Norwegian. *Nynorsk* is used only in names that have no equivalents in *Bokmål*.

Cross-references to other topics are indicated by a pointer and the topic in bold: ☞ **Topic**, suffixed by the chapter name if the Topic is in another chapter: ☞ **Topic** (Chapter name).

Symbols indicate telecommunications and postal addresses:
℡ telephone number
☎ telefax number
✉ postal address
✉ E-Mail address
☻ Internet address

Telephone and telefax numbers are written as they are to be dialled in Norway; if you dial a number from abroad, add the international access indicator (00 in Europe) and the country code for Norway (47) to dial the numbers. The country codes for numbers in other countries are given, prefixed by the international standard plus sign, such as +44 for a number in the United Kingdom, which from Norway would be dialled 0044.

Street addresses are written using the common abbreviations: v or vn for *veien* ("way") and g or gt for *gate* ("street").

For local numbers and addresses, references are given to the Pink Pages (*Rosa sider*) or Yellow Pages (*Gule sider*) of the telephone directories for the country.

Prices vary with time and location. Consequently, typical prices valid at press time are included in the Prices chapter, but not in the individual topics, except when they refer to specific dates or are likely to stay fixed for many years.

If you find errors or feel that other topics should be included, please write Palamedes Press ✉ PO Box 8768 Youngstorget, 0028 Oslo, ✉ palamedes@online.no and suggest a correction or addition. If your suggestion is used in the next edition of *Living in Norway*, Palamedes Press will send you a complimentary copy of it, so be sure to include your ✉ postal address.

Check lists (*Huskelister*)

Before you arrive in Norway and before leaving Norway to live in another country, check the following lists to see if you have attended to essential matters. All the organisations named in the lists are described in this book.

Before arriving in Norway Except for passports, which must be originals, you may bring photocopies of all documents. In alphabetical order, the principal details and documents are:

Bank account (*bankkonto*) number, bank branch address and international transfer number, to ease transfer of funds if you elect to open an account with a Norwegian bank; see "Exchange transfer" below.

Baptism certificate (*dåpsattest*) if you have been baptised in a Christian church and wish to join a congregation in Norway.

Birth certificate (*fødselsattest*) for yourself and all members of your family; needed to apply for the National ID Number (NIN) used in all public registrations and many commercial matters.

Car import (*innførsel av motorvogn*) When you move to Norway, you may bring in a car without paying import duty or tax provided that at the time of entry you have owned it at least one year (52 weeks), it has been driven at least 5,000 km and you have resided abroad for at least five consecutive years. If your stay in Norway will be relatively short, less than one year, and you will maintain residence in your home country, you may bring in a car for temporary use and need not register it in Norway. If you fail to meet these conditions, such as by bringing in a car that you have owned only 50 weeks or by keeping a foreign-registered car in Norway for more than a year, you must pay import duty and tax on it.

Car insurance (*bilforsikring*) records, including the details of any rebates or discounts you have received by having a safe driving record, to assist you in obtaining similar discounts when buying car insurance in Norway.

Credit card (*kredittkort*) details that you may have used in obtaining credit cards; useful should you need to prove creditworthiness in Norway.

Curriculum vitae (*CV*) or résumé of your qualifications and experience; needed in applying for jobs.

Customs (*Toll*) Make a list, in English, of the belongings you will bring into Norway, principally for clearing Norwegian customs but also in case outgoing customs clearance is required in your country of departure.

Divorce (*skilsmisse*) papers, including any agreement on alimony payments by or to yourself; needed in application for a NIN as well as in filing income tax returns (*selvangivelse*).

Driving licence (*førerkort*) If you are a resident of and have a driving licence issued by an EEA (*EØS*) country, you may use that licence to drive in Norway; be sure it is valid for the duration of your stay. If you have a licence issued outside the EEA, you may use it to drive in Norway for a period of temporary residence of up to one year. But if you become a resident, you may use the licence for three months only. It should show the date of first issue, as if you can prove that you have held it more than one year, you may exchange it for a Norwegian licence.

Educational certificates (*attester, diplom*), including school, college or university diplomas, transcripts of marks if you intend to continue your education, trade certifications, professional organisation and union membership details. If possible, have these documents translated into Norwegian or into English.

Exchange transfer (*Valutaoverføring*) You may freely transfer or bring up to NOK 25,000 per person of your own funds in connection with moving to Norway. If you bring in or transfer more than NOK 25,000, you must fill out form F/2711. For cash or cash equivalents (bank drafts, cheques, travellers' cheques) carried with you, pick up a form at the border crossing where you enter Norway, and present it to Customs. For a bank transfer, fill out the form at the Norwegian bank to which the transfer is made.

Health and social insurance (*helse og trygd*) If you are a resident of an EU or EEA country and are covered by its National Insurance arrangement, you may have proof of coverage certified on an E111 form that will entitle you to services after you arrive in Norway and until you establish residence. The E111 form is also carried by Norwegians travelling to EU and EEA countries, so there is a Norwegian language version of it, entitled *Attest for rett til naturalytelser under opphold i en medlemsstat.*

Insurance policies (*forsikringspoliser*) which may remain in force and for which you may need to continue paying premiums, as with life assurance.

Mail redirection and return (*Post omadressering og retur*) Notify all correspondents and business connections of your change of address. Check with the post office that serves your home to ensure that post will be redirected. Most post offices will redirect several weeks or months and thereafter will return post to the sender. National post offices implement international redirection and charges for it in various ways; ask your post office for details.

Marriage certificate (*vigselsattest*) if you are married and particularly if your spouse moves with you; needed in public registrations and tax matters.

Medical record (*journal*), particularly if you are disabled or depend on a prescription drug and wish to transfer your medical status to Norway.

Military service (*militærtjeneste*) record, particularly if you are a young man intending to apply for Norwegian citizenship and thereby be subject to conscription.

Passport (*pass*) for yourself and all members of your family; needed to enter the country and to prove your identity thereafter, as in applying for a National Identity Number (NIN) or a driving licence. Be sure that your passport is valid on your intended arrival date and at least one year thereafter. Most foreign citizens can renew their passports at embassies, but renewal sometimes takes several days or weeks, and you will need your passport for identification when settling in Norway. Citizens of other Nordic countries (Denmark, Finland, Iceland and Sweden) are exempted from passport requirements.

Professional certification (*godkjennelse*), such as that of a medical doctor or dentist, should you wish to practise in Norway. If possible, have these documents translated into Norwegian or into English.

Proof of purchase (*kvittering*) including amount and date of purchase of expensive items, such as cars and professional equipment, upon which duty might be charged when you bring them into the country.

Social security (*trygd*) details, which may be necessary if you wish to have income in Norway credited to your social security account in your home country.

Unemployment benefits (*arbeidsledighetstrygd*) If you are a citizen of an EU or EEA country and are entitled to unemployment benefits in your home country, the benefits may be paid out in Norway for a period of three months. The relevant authority in your home country will issue an E303 form which you can deliver to a governmental employment office in Norway to initiate payments.

Vaccination (*vaksinasjon*) records or certificates, particularly for children, for filling in health records, as may be required by health services and schools. Ask for records to be transferred to international standard vaccination cards, which are recognised world-wide.

Visa (*visa*) if required from your own country to enter Norway.

Before leaving Norway to relocate in another country When Norwegian documents are involved, you may have to pay the costs of translating them into English or other languages. In alphabetical order, the principal details and documents are:

Antiques and valuable paintings by recognised Norwegian artists (*Antikvariske gjenstander og verdifulle malerier fra kjente kundtnere*) may be taken out of the country only by permit. Contact the National Gallery (*Nasjonalgalleriet*) concerning valuable paintings by recognised Norwegian artists and the Norwegian Folk Museum (*Norsk Folkemuseum*) for antique objects of Norwegian origin.

Bank account (*bankkonto*) Close your account or, if you wish, give your bank branch your new address; see "Exchange transfer" below.

Baptism certificate (*dåpsattest*) If you have had a child baptised in Norway, ask the church to issue an English translation of the baptism certificate, which you may need for the child to join a congregation in another country.

Birth certificate (*fødselsattest*) Retain the original birth certificate of any child born in Norway and ask the local National Registry office or hospital where the child was born for an English translation of the certificate.

Car (*bil*) If you have a car and sell it before leaving, be sure to notify the local Motor Vehicle and Driving Licence Inspectorate (*Biltilsyn*) and notify the company that insured the car. If you are taking a car with you, be sure that its insurance will be valid in the countries through which you intend to drive.

Child allowance (*barnetrygd*) Notify the benefit office of the date of your departure.

Co-op loyalty card If you have been a member of a co-op, remember to claim your refund before you leave.

Credit card (*kredittkort*) Close all credit card accounts, or, if you wish, notify the banks or companies involved of your new address.

Curriculum vitae (*CV*) If you have worked or studied in Norway, make a list of your new qualifications and experience and, if you wish, ask your immediate superior to write a certification (*attest*) of the work you have accomplished.

Customs (*Toll*) Make a list, in English, of the belongings you will take out of the country, principally for clearing customs in your destination country but also for clearing outgoing customs in Norway. For further information, contact the local customs district (*Tolldistrikt*).

Divorce (*skilsmisse*) If you have divorced in Norway, ask your embassy to issue an official translation of the Norwegian divorce papers.

Driving licence (*førerkort*) If you have a Norwegian Driving Licence, present it and two passport photos at one of the automobile association offices and request an International Driving Licence (*internasjonale-førerkort*) which you may need to drive abroad. The automobile associations will know which countries honour a Norwegian licence and which will require an international licence.

Educational certificates (*attester, diplom*) If you have attended a school, college or university in Norway and have completed a course of education, ask for a translation of the Norwegian certificate(s) into English.

Educational loans from the state (*Statens lånekasse for utdanning*) If you have an educational loan, send a notice of change of address to *Statens lånekasse for utdanning* at the address listed on your repayment slips (*innbetalingsslipp*). You may

then continue repayment from abroad.

Exchange transfer (*Valutaoverføring*) You may freely transfer or bring up to NOK 25,000 per person of your own funds in connection with moving to another country. If you take out or transfer more than NOK 25,000, you must fill out form F/2711, available at banks, post offices and border crossings, and present it to the bank making the transfer or to customs at your point of departure.

Guns (*Skytevåpen*) You must fill out a form for an export permit, available at customs, to take a gun out of the country. There are two types of permit, temporary export (*midlertidig utførsel*) and export for more than one year (*utførsel som gjelder over ett år*). For further information, contact the local customs district (*Tolldistrikt*).

Health and social insurance (*helse og trygd*) If you move to an EU or EEA country and have been covered by *trygd* in Norway, you can have proof of coverage certified on an E111 form that will be entitle you to services until you establish residence. The E111 form is also carried by Norwegians travelling to EU and EEA countries, so there is a Norwegian language version of it, entitled *Attest for rett til naturalytelser under opphold i en medlemsstat.*

Mail redirection and return (*Post omadressering og retur*) Notify all correspondents and business connections of your change of address. The simplest and cheapest way to do this is to use the postage-free address change cards (*Melding om ny postadresse*) in handy A6 format (10.5 X 14.8 cm) available at post offices. There are two versions. One in Norwegian may be sent to all Nordic countries (Denmark, Iceland, Finland, Norway, Sweden), and one in English and French may be sent to all other countries. While at the post office, also pick up and fill out a similar notification to Norway Post (*Melding om endring av postadresse*) and address it to the post office that serves your home. That post office then will forward for nine months and thereafter return items to their senders. Individual items are not re-addressed, but are collected and put in a larger envelope which when full is posted to your new address. For items with return addresses, the senders are billed for any additional postage; for items without return addresses, additional postage is collected upon delivery.

Marriage certificate (*vigselsattest*) If you married in Norway, ask your embassy for a certified translation of your marriage certificate.

Military service (*militærtjeneste*) Most countries which permit dual nationality have agreed that young men subject to conscription should serve in the country of residence only. So if you are a young man of dual nationality who has completed military service in Norway, ask your military organisation for an English translation of your service record, to prove service to the military authorities of your home country. In any case, you should contact the local police (*politikammer*) or conscription unit (*vernepliktsverket*) to clarify your status before leaving the country.

National Register (*folkeregister*) Complete a notice of moving (*Melding til folkeregister om flytting*), form RF-1400, with your dates of leaving Norway and arriving at your new address in another country. This information will automatically serve to notify all government organisations.

Passport (*pass*) for yourself and all members of your family: be sure that your passports are valid before you leave the country.

Professional certification (*godkjennelse*) If you have acquired professional certification in Norway, retain the original certificate and ask the issuing organisation to give you an authorised translation of it into English.

Proof of purchase amount and date of purchase of expensive items, such as a duty-free car.

Social security (*trygd*) details If you have worked in Norway, ask your employer for a record of your social security payments and ask how they will be treated when you leave the country.

Tax (*skatt*) Contact your local tax office (*ligningskontor*) and inquire about the rules applicable at your date of leaving the country. If you have worked only part of the year, you may be eligible for a tax refund. If you have worked an entire year and leave at the end of it, you may owe tax. In all cases, you should state your new address.

Telephone and mobile cellular phone companies (*telefon, mobiltelefon*) Cancel your subscription. In most cases, the company will ask for a date when your line is to be closed and an address to send a final bill. If you have made a deposit, ask for a refund or for it to be deducted from your final bill.

TV If you have had a cable or satellite TV subscription, cancel it, return any equipment leased and ask for a refund of any deposit.

Unemployment benefits (*arbeidsledighetstrygd*) If you are a citizen of an EU or EEA country and are entitled to unemployment benefits in Norway after being gainfully employed, your benefits may be paid out in your home country. Contact the local employment office and ask for an E303 form which you can submit in your home country.

Vaccination (*vaksinasjon*) records or certificates If you or members of your family have been vaccinated in Norway, ask for an international vaccination card for each person. These cards have multi-lingual texts and need not be translated.

Visa (*visa*) If you move to a country other than your home country, you may need a visa. If you are a citizen of a Nordic country, you need neither passport or visa to move to another Nordic country. If you are a citizen of an EU or EEA country, and move to another EU/EEA country, you may stay there up to three months before applying for a residence permit. Otherwise, check with the embassy of your destination country for visa requirements.

Frequently Asked Questions – FAQ Here are some FAQ (same abbreviation in Norwegian) on the country and its population. Most of the answers are to be found in this book.

Adult literacy? 99.0%
Area? mainland with Svalbard and Jan Mayen 385,364 sq km, mainland only 323,758 sq km.
Biggest company? Statoil (oil and gas).
Border length? total 2,542 km, with Sweden 1,619 km, Finland 727 km and Russia 196 km.
Coast line length? 21,465 km with fjords and bays and 2650 km without.
Constitution? 17 May 1814.
Currency? *krone* ("Crown")
Divorces per 1,000 population? 2.7.
Farms? 3% of land area.
Favourite holiday country? Norway, 7 of 10 on holiday.
Fertility rate (per woman)? 1.9.
Forests? 27% of land area.
Highest mountain? *Galdhøpiggen*, 2469 m.
Highest waterfall? *Kjellsfossen*, 804 m.
Households? 1.8 million.
King Harald and Queen Sonia wedding? 29 August 1968; took oath? 21 January 1991; coronation? 23 June 1991.
Largest city population? Oslo, 741,621.
Largest glacier? *Jostedalsbreen*, 487 sq km.
Largest island? *Hinnøya*, 2198 sq km.
Largest lake? *Mjøsa*, 362 sq km.
Life expectancy: men 75.45 years, women 80.97 years.
Longest fjord? *Sognefjord*, 204 km.
Longest river? *Glomma*, 600 km.
Marriages per 1,000 population? 4.6.
Median age? 36.2 in 1995, estimated 41.0 in 2020.
National animal? European elk, *alces alces* (*elg*).
National anthem? *Ja vi elsker.*
National bird? dipper or water ouzel, *cinclus cinclus* (*fossekal*).
National flower? heather, *caluna vulgaris* (*røsslyng).*
National folk costume? *bunad.*
National stone? zoisite (*thulitt*).
Nobel laureates? 10: Chemistry 2, Physics 1, Literature 3, Economics 2, Peace 2.
Number of men per 100 women? 98.5.
Olympic medals, summer games (1896-1996)? 25th with 124 (45 gold, 41 silver, 38 bronze)
Olympic medals, winter games (1924–1998)? 1st with 239 (83 gold, 87 silver, 69 bronze)
Population? 4,445,329 as at 1 January 1999.
Population in urban areas? 73%
Population per sq km? 13.
Population over 65? 15.9%
Population under 15? 19.4%
Principal exports? oil, gas and products.
Principal imports? machinery and transport equipment.
Tallest building? Plaza Hotel, Oslo, 37 floors, 117 m.

Arriving, settling, leaving (*Ankomst, innflytting, utflytting*)

Asylum (*Asyl*) If you are a refugee, you may apply for asylum. The policy on refugees complies with the United Nations Convention relating to the Status of Refugees, and the country works with the United Nations High Commissioner for Refugees (UNHCR) to help people who have left their homes to escape war, persecution and human rights abuse. Norway also has its own rules set forth in the Immigration Act (*Utlendingsloven*). The rules permit granting asylum on a case-by-case basis to refugees, who are defined as persons under threat of persecution in their home countries, due to race, religion, sex, nationality, political beliefs or social group. Moreover, asylum may be granted on humanitarian grounds to persons whose lives may be endangered by return to their home countries. Resettlement by voluntary repatriation to home countries is also supported in accordance with UNHCR practices. If you intend to apply for asylum, you must tell the immigration officials at your point of arrival. They will check your travel documents, make a record of your application for asylum, retain your passport and issue you a green registration certificate which certifies your application. You will then be lodged in a Transit Reception Centre for asylum applicants. Thereafter there are two phases in your status as a refugee. The first starts when you arrive, includes initial interviews by officials of the ☞ **The Directorate of Immigration** (Government and Social Services chapter) and formal application, and ends when you receive a decision on your application for asylum. The second involves actions taken on the decision on your application.

If you are granted asylum, you will receive a Norwegian ☞ **residence permit**, will learn Norwegian in classes and will be offered other training, such as in ☞ **water skills** (Sports, Recreation, Hobbies chapter), and then will be settled in the country. If your application is rejected, you will be deported. You may appeal any decision concerning your application. The appeal should be sent to the same office to which your initial application was made, and from there will be sent to the Directorate of Immigration.

If the Directorate cannot find sufficient grounds for reversing the original decision, the case is passed on to the Ministry of Justice, whose decision is final. For further details see the booklet *Are you applying for asylum in Norway?*, which is regularly updated and published for free distribution by the Directorate in Albanian, Arabic, English, French, Persian, Polish, Serbo-Croatian, Somali, Spanish, Tamil, Tigrinya and Turkish editions. You also can view the Norwegian government Internet site ☻ http://odin.dep.no for information in Norwegian and in English. The site has its own search engine, which you may use to search by keying in "Asylum" in English or "Asyl" in Norwegian. For general information on the UNHCR and refugees, view the UNHCR web site ☻ http://www.unicc.org/unhcr.

Customs Duties (*Toll*) When you move to Norway, you may import your household effects free of duty and value added tax (VAT, or *merverdiavgift – MVA* in Norwegian) provided you have resided abroad continuously for one year or more and can prove that all the items imported have been used and will continue to be used by yourself and your family during your stay in Norway. Your household effects will be accompanied by a written declaration that is usually submitted to the Customs Service (*Tollvesenet*) by the removal company working on your behalf. New articles and consumer goods (household effects, spirits, wine, beer and tobacco) may not be imported duty-free as removal goods. You will need to specify them on the importation of removal goods declaration form and duty will need to be paid on these items. Special regulations apply to ☞ **Car import and temporary import** (Cars, Roads, Traffic chapter) as well as to the importation of pleasure boats and professional effects, such as dental instruments. All international airports have red and green channels. You enter through the green channel if the goods you are carrying are bought duty and tax-free, the amount of spirits, wine and tobacco allowed depends on your point of departure. If you have more than the specified ☞ **duty-free quota** (Travel and Transport chapter), you should enter through the red channel. A comprehensive leaflet explaining the allowances are available at ports, airports and on board ferries travelling to Norway. If you live in Norway and travel abroad frequently with expensive items like a portable PC or camera equipment, you should request a special identification certificate from the customs authorities. On it, you can list the items you will carry out of and back into the country, and thereby be able to prove ownership should it be questioned at customs. Importation of spirits of more than 60% of alcohol is prohibited. You may bring spirits, wine and tobacco duty-free if you have been out of the country for at least 24 hours or the goods were purchased in the Nordic countries. If you have been out of Norway for less than 24 hours you may only bring in a specified amount of tobacco. You can also import 10 kg (15 kg, if entering from the Nordic countries) of agricultural products (dairy, fruit, vegetables, certain cut flowers and bulbs), up to 3kg of this allowance can be meat. You may bring with you into Norway notes and coins, in Norwegian and foreign currency to the value of NOK 25,000. This does not apply to traveller's cheques. To import, or re-import a dog or cat, a permit is required, see ☞ **Pet importation** (Pets & Animals chapter). Norway is a signatory of the Convention on International Trade in Endangered Species of Wild Flora and Fauna (CITES). Consequently, the importation or exportation of endangered species is regulated; contact the Directorate for Nature Management (*Direktoratet for Natur Forvalting*) ✆ 73580500 for details. Antiques or old objects of Norwegian origin that have artistic, cultural or historical value cannot be exported without special permission. Similarly, if you are moving to Norway and intend to bring back into the country an object of interest, obtain documentation before hand to prove that the item has come into the country with you. Call the closest office of Customs, *Tollvesenet* in the Pink Pages, for further details. If you order items abroad and have them sent to you directly you will be charged import duties, VAT and an administration charge. Gifts sent from abroad are delivered duty-free, provided they are not tobacco products, wine or spirits and have a value of NOK 500 or less. Updated customs and import information are available on-line at the Customs web site ⊕ http://www.toll.no with pages in Norwgian and in English.

Family reunification (*Familiegjenforening*) means that a family member abroad is granted a residence permit to be reunited with one or more members of his or her family already living in Norway, who must be:

- a citizen of Norway or another Nordic country (Denmark, Finland, Iceland or Sweden)
- a citizen of another country with a settlement permit in Norway. A settlement permit grants the right to live and work in Norway on a permanent basis.
- a citizen of another country with a work permit or residence permit which may be grounds for a settlement permit, as is the case for refugees that have been granted asylum.
- a citizen of another country with a residence permit to study in Norway.

Residence permits on the grounds of family reunification are granted principally to spouses or children under 18 years of age. The person seeking reunification must be a close relative of the person already in Norway. The Norwegian definition of "close relative" applies to fewer relatives than in some other countries. In some cases, cohabitants, parents and other close relatives may be granted residence permits or work permits to ensure family reunification. In general, the person seeking reunification must be guaranteed adequate financial support. If the conditions for family reunification are fulfilled, work permits are usually granted to persons over 18 years old, to permit them to be able to seek work and take jobs. Work permits are also granted for applicants between 15 and 18 years old, provided their parents or guardians have consented. For complete, current information, see the booklet entitled *Information on Family Reunification in Norway*, updated regularly and published for free distribution by ☞ **The Directorate of Immigration** (Government and Social Services chapter) in English, French, Norwegian, Serbo-Croatian and Somali.

Immigration (*Innvandring*) From the 1860s through the 1920s, so many Norwegians emigrated to other countries that the overall population grew more slowly than normal and even declined in some years. That trend has now reversed. Net migration, the number of persons immigrating to Norway minus the number emigrating to other countries, has been positive since the late 1960s. Current statistics indicate that without immigration, the population would decline. Despite bearing more children per capita than the women of most countries in Europe, Norwegians are not reproducing rapidly enough to sustain the population. With immigration at the current rate, the population is expected to rise from 4.45 million (1999 figure) to slightly more than 5 million by the year 2050. If you are a refugee and wish to immigrate to Norway, you may seek ☞ **Asylum**. If you are a citizen of another country and wish to live, study or work in Norway, you will need official permission, as granted by ☞ **Residence and Work Permits.** If you wish to settle permanently, you may apply for ☞ **Norwegian citizenship**. As of October 1998, simplified citizenship rules apply for citizens of other Nordic countries – Denmark, Finland, Iceland and Sweden.

Norwegian citizenship (*Norsk statsborgerskap***)** is described legally in the Citizenship Act (*Statsborgerrettsloven*) of 8 December 1950 and the amendment to it of 25 May 1979. Citizenship is based on descent, which means that children have their parents' citizenship. This means that you can acquire citizenship by birth (one or both of your parents are Norwegian citizens) or by application in one of three principal ways. You may apply for citizenship to the ☞ **The Directorate of Immigration** (Government and Social Services chapter) if you:
- are over 18
- have lived in Norway consecutively for the past seven years
- have no criminal record
- have no appreciable outstanding alimony payments to a divorced spouse,

You may acquire Norwegian citizenship by notifying the nearest office of the County Governor (*Fylkesmann*) of the county where you live (there are 18 Governors in the country), provided that you:
- have lived in Norway for more than five years before the age of 16 and permanently from age 16 to 21.
- are between 18 and 21 years of age and have lived in Norway for ten years and for at least five consecutive years at the time of application.
- were born in and lived in Norway until you were 18 years old, but subsequently lost your Norwegian citizenship.

You may apply for Norwegian citizenship at the nearest office of a County Governor (*Fylkesmann*) for:
- an adopted child less than 12 years old, provided that you and your spouse are Norwegian citizens and that the child lives in Norway.

Dual citizenship is not permitted. Consequently, if your application for Norwegian citizenship is granted, you must give up your former citizenship. However, there are exceptions, if you:
- have dual citizenship because you inherited two nationalities from your parents.
- were born of Norwegian parents in a country where citizenship is based on the territorial principle (you are a citizen of the country in which you were born).
- have applied for Norwegian citizenship, but cannot be released from your previous citizenship.
- have been granted Norwegian citizenship through notification through a County Governor's Office, as described above.

As a dual citizen, you will:
- have the right to hold two passports.
- be entitled to the protection of both countries.
- be considered a Norwegian citizen, equal to other Norwegian citizens in every respect.
- if you are a young man subject to ☞ **Conscription** (Defence chapter), you will be called to serve in the country where you permanently reside. Normally, you will not be required to serve in the other country of your citizenship.

The rules described above are the basic conditions affecting citizenship. There are many variations to them. For instance, if a woman who is not a Norwegian citizen gives birth to a child, but is not married to its father, who is a Norwegian citizen, the child will be granted citizenship if she and the father marry before the child is 18 years old. For complete, current information, see the booklet entitled *Information on Norwegian Citizenship* updated regularly and published for free distribution by Directorate of Immigration in English, French, Norwegian, Polish, Turkish, Urdu and Vietnamese editions.

Relocation services provide assistance in moving to and settling in a new country. Services vary from providing local orientation and contacts to comprehensive packages of familiarisation, training, guiding and housing location services. Typically, services are offered by specialist companies, usually with offices in major international business cities. They range in size from global networks to local bureaux. The global giant is Cendant International Assignment Services, whose GlobalNet™ destination services network spans almost 100 countries and 300 locations, ☺ http://www-cendantmobility.com. In

Europe, one of the larger relocation organisations is Outpost, affiliated with the Shell oil company and located in The Hague, Netherlands, ✍ http://www.euronet.nl/users/outpost_/ europe.html. Moreover, many larger international companies have their own or contract for services. If you are an employee being sent to Norway by an international company, your employer or a specialist company in your home country may offer relocation and orientation, either before you leave your home country or after you arrive in Norway. In Oslo and Stavanger, the two major international business cities in Norway, the relocation services are:

Oslo area

Doorway to Norway, Nancy Sandmæl's personalised relocation and orientation services for companies ✆ 66982519, 🖷 66982019, ✉ Sundveien 5, 1397 Nesøya, ✉ nancysan@online.no

SAS Relocation, a subsidiary of Scandinavian Airlines (SAS) and a member of the GlobalNet™, focuses on the corporate market in Scandinavian cities, ✆ 67598599, 🖷 67597977, ✉ Snarøyveien 57, 1330 Oslo Lufthavn

Stavanger area

Skagen Housing, an estate agent and housing rental service with associates in all related services, from tradesmen to furniture rental, ✆ 51549005, 🖷 51549006, ✉ Verksgt. 62, 4013 Stavanger.

SPIN – Stavanger Partner Information Network, helps with integration into the locality and publishes information on living and working in Stavanger, including an annual Information Guide, a Job Guide and a Guide to Medical Services, ✆ 51693210, 🖷 51693030, ✉ PO Box 40, 4056 Tananger, ✉ spin@shell.no

Removals (*Flyttetjenester*) Contact removal companies (*flyttebyråer*) as soon as you plan to move, either to or from Norway. The removal business is increasingly competitive, so you can shop around for both prices and services offered. In moving to Norway, be sure to engage a company that has a liaison agreement with a reputable Norwegian removals company. Likewise, in moving from Norway, engage a company that has a liaison agreement with a company in your destination country. For further information on the Norwegian companies and their international liaison agreements, you may contact the Norwegian Removal Companies Association (*Norske Flyttebedrifters Forbund*), ✆ 22465830, 🖷 22568252, ✉ PO Box 5003 Majorstua, 0301 Oslo, ✉ oslo@adamsexpress.no

Most removal companies with international business now standardise on ☞ **Containers** (Transport chapter), particularly whenever sea transport is involved. The contents of a typical house will fill a 20-foot container, though the 40-foot size may be needed for the contents of a large house. The removal company will bring the container to your house, most often on a truck fitted with a hydraulic lifter that can place the container alongside the truck bed, on the ground, and lift it back again when it is filled. The standard container is about 2.5 m wide, so the truck will need a width of at least 6 m to drive in and manoeuvre the container. In Norway, the lifter is on the left side of the truck bed; in some countries, it is on the right.

The Norwegian customs procedures for personal belongings brought when you move to the country are straightforward and simple. You may import your household effects free of duty and value added tax (VAT), provided that they are used and will continue to be used by you. However, you must declare and pay duty and VAT on any new items bought duty and tax-free for export from the country of shipping. Alcoholic drink or tobacco can be imported but is subject to ☞ **Customs duty**. But if you arrive at an international airport, you may bring in your duty-free quota provided that you hand carry it through customs. A television set may be included in your duty-free household effects, but it must be registered for a ☞ **TV licence** (Telecommunications & Broadcasting chapter). Special regulations apply to ☞ **Car import and temporary import** (Cars, Roads, Traffic chapter) and to ☞ **Pet importation** (Pets and Animals chapter), as well as to the importation of leisure craft (motorboats and sailboats) and professional effects, such as dental instruments. For any international removal to or from Norway, you should complete a Descriptive Inventory List (*Inventar liste*) of all goods handled by the removal company. For a removal to Norway, this List will be attached to an Import Declaration Form (*Innførselsdeklarasjon, RG0124*). You may, but need not be present to clear your goods through customs, because the Norwegian removals company will act on your behalf.

Residence and Work Permits (*opholdstillatelse, arbeidstillatelse***)** are issued by the Police in the place where you live. You are allowed to stay in Norway for up to six months and start work immediately without the necessary documents if you are a citizen of a member country of the EEA (*EØS*). If you intend to stay longer your employer should notify the Aliens office (*Utlendingsseksjon*) at the main Police station in your vicinity. You need to take a copy of your employment contract and a letter detailing your salary to the police in the place where you live. They will require three passport photographs. If you are granted a residence and work permit, it will be sent to you in the post. It is called an *arbeidstillatelse* and has your photograph on it. Once you receive the permit, you should go to the ☞ **National Register** (Registrations, Rights, Licences chapter) in your municipality (*kommune*) to apply for your ☞ **National Identity Number(NIN)** (Registrations, Rights, Licences chapter). You will need your NIN for all official business, including seeing a doctor, applying for a bank account, applying for child benefit, getting a driving licence, applying for a library card, to name but a few. The National Register (*folkeregister*) will inform the tax office (*ligningskontor*). Some employers apply for residence and work permits as a group, these can be granted for a period of up to 5 years. The personnel department of your employer will take care of most of the details. If you are a citizen of a country outside the EEA, you must apply for your residence and work permit from the Norwegian Embassy in your home country. You will require the permit before you are allowed residential entry into Norway. If you are married to, cohabiting with or in a ☞ **registered partnership** (Family and Children chapter) with a Norwegian, you do not need to apply for residency beforehand. You must report to the police station where you live in Norway within the first week of arrival. [Note, however, that a residence permit obtained on the grounds of a relationship may not be renewed if the relationship ceases, ☞ **divorce, separation or break-up of relationship, consequences for a residence permit** (Family and Children chapter)]. If you are seeking ☞ **asylum**, other rules apply. A residence permit is usually granted for one year. Special regulations apply to residence permits for foreign residents ☞ **studying in Norway** (Education chapter). For the details of residence and work permits, see the two free booklets on the subject published by ☞ **The Directorate of Immigration** (Government and Social Services chapter):

Work Permits and Residence Permits in Norway, in English, French, Norwegian, Polish, Russian and Serbo-Croatian editions, and *Residence Permits in Norway for Persons from EEA Countries*, in English, French, Norwegian and German editions.

Visa requirements (*Visumplikt***)** Citizens of other countries who wish to enter Norway must have a valid passport or other identification which is officially recognised as a valid travel document. Citizens of other Nordic countries – Denmark, Finland, Iceland and Sweden - are exempt from this requirement and may enter Norway without a passport or visa. You need a passport but do not need a visa if you are a citizen of one of the 78 EU, EEA and other countries with which Norway has an agreement on visa-free entry. However, citizens of some countries are required to have visas, which are intended for visitors and consequently are valid for up to three months. If you wish to reside and work in Norway, you will need ☞ **Residence and work permits**. If you need a visa, you must apply for it before departing for Norway. You also must have a valid passport or other identity document, be able to return to the country where the visa was issued and have enough money to cover your travel and living expenses for your trip to Norway. Special rules apply to refugees and to seamen. For a list of visa-free countries, visa applications and other details, contact the nearest Norwegian Embassy or Consulate or ☞ **The Directorate of Immigration** (Government and Social Services chapter).

Banking, finance, insurance (*Bank, finans, forsikring*)

Account, bank (*konto*) Most ☞ **Banks** offer both current accounts and savings accounts. A current account (*Personkonto, Brukskonto, Foliokonto*) is one on which cheques can be drawn and balance can be debited using ☞ **Payment cards** or ☞ **Giro** transfers. Most banks offer several varieties of current accounts, usually packaged with other bank services and aimed at specific user groups, including wage-earners (*lønnskonto*), young people (*ungdomskonto*), students (*studentkonto*) and retired persons (*honnørkonto*). Interest is paid on current accounts, usually at the lowest rate offered by a bank. Other services, such as an overdraft facility (*kassakreditt*), may be connected to a current account. Cheques are now used in fewer than 2% of all non-cash payments, and many current account holders have no chequebooks. Consequently, *sjekkonto* the equivalent of "checking account", the American expression for a current account, is no longer used. A savings account (*sparekonto*) is intended for long-term placement and accordingly usually pays a higher rate of interest than a current account in the same bank, but has a maximum number of withdrawals per year to attain that interest rate. For larger balances, most banks offer high interest accounts (*høyrentekonto*) and investment accounts (*plasseringskonto*). Account balance statements (*saldi*) are usually sent at the end of each month for a current account and less frequently for a savings account. There are no tax-free accounts, but most banks have accounts offering tax advantage. The young people's saving for housing purchase (*Bolig sparing for ungdom – BSU*) account permits 20% of a year's deposits to be deducted on a tax return, currently up to a maximum of NOK 100,000 saved through the years, for persons up to the age of 33. A ☞ **Share investment with tax relief** currently offers a NOK 750 reduction in assessed tax per person for each NOK 5000 invested in a share fund, or up to NOK 1500 tax reduction for NOK 10000 invested by a married couple, with the requirement that the shares must be held for four years from the date of purchase. An ☞ **Individual pension agreement** (Retirement chapter) offers 28% tax return deduction for yearly amounts of up to NOK 40,000 saved. By law, all commercial banks are members of the Commercial Bank Deposit Protection Fund (*Forretningsbankenes sikringsfond*) and all savings banks are members of the Savings Bank Deposit Protection Fund (*Sparebankenes sikringsfond*), which guarantee individual deposits of up to NOK 2 million in case of bank failure.

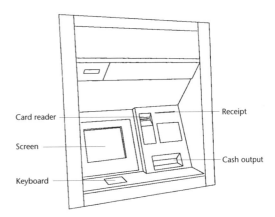

Card reader

Screen

Keyboard

Receipt

Cash output

Typical ATM; configuration varies from bank to bank and indoor and outdoor ATMs may be arranged differently. Drawing courtesy NCR Norge.

ATM (*Minibank*) There are about 2,000 automated-teller machines (ATMs) in the country. Some are located outdoors at bank branches and usually are identified by conspicuous signs reading *Minibank* and the name of the bank, whilst some are located indoors at banks, airports and shopping malls. The operating banks determine the cards acceptable at their ATMs. Visa/Barclay and Mastercard are the most commonly acceptable international cards at ATMs which feature choice of language, Norwegian or English for international credit card transactions. Some ATMs at gateway airports and city banks with international trade also offer foreign exchange services in several languages. All Norwegian bank account ATM services are coordinated so an account or cash card (*minibankkort*) issued by any bank may be used in any ATM throughout the country to withdraw cash against debiting an account. This service is supported in Norwegian only. The keypad is the international standard with Norwegian names on the three command keys: *Klar* Enter, *Feil* Clear and *Avbryt* Cancel. The order of interactive on-screen text varies from bank to bank, but almost all include eleven basic commands:

Velkommen sett inn kortet Please insert card
Tast inn koden Enter PIN
Velg beløp Choose amount
Velg tjeneste Choose service
Kontanter Cash
Kvittering ja/nei Receipt yes/no
Kontoutskrift Account summary
Ta kortet Please take your card
Ta kvittering Please take your receipt
Ta pengene Please take your money
Ta pengene og noter beløpet Please take your money and note the amount (printer out of order)

Banks (*Bank*) As elsewhere in Europe, banking in Norway is divided between the public and private sectors, and all bank and financial activities are regulated by the Banking, Insurance and Securities Commission (*Kredittilsynet*).

In the public banking sector there is one central bank (*Norges Bank*), which issues ☞ **Currency** and sets interest rates, and six lending institutions, which primarily are concerned with domestic and international business and industrial financing. However, two of the institutions offer private services. The State Educational Loan Fund (*Statens lånekasse*) offers loans to finance education at vocational schools, colleges and universities, and the housing bank (*Husbanken*) offers mortgages to finance housing built to prescribed standards.

The private banking sector consists of commercial banks and savings banks, both of which offer general banking services to the public. The names "commercial" and "savings" are historical. In years gone by, a commercial bank (*forretningsbank*) made loans to commerce, as for financing trade, and was itself a commercial business, whilst a savings bank (*sparebank*) accepted only the deposits of small savers. The difference in the form of organisation remains: today commercial banks are private companies owned by their shareholders, whilst savings banks are independent foundations permitted by law to use the word "savings" (*spare*) in their names. Otherwise, the services offered are increasingly similar. Both commercial banks and savings banks are becoming all-in-one banks, offering a range of finan-

cial services in addition to traditional banking business. The commercial banks and savings banks have jointly developed an integrated, secure payment system which also includes the Norwegian Postal Bank.

The commercial bank category consists of nearly 30 commercial institutions, which include both Norwegian banks and branches of foreign banks, the Postal Bank (*Postbanken*) and other specialised financial institutions. The two largest Norwegian commercial banks are *Den norske Bank (DNB)* and *Christiania Bank (Kreditkassen)*, each of which has branches (*filial*) throughout the country and offices abroad in London, New York, Singapore and other financial centres. The Postal Bank offers its services at post offices throughout the country. The foreign banks conducting business in Norway include other Scandinavian banks as well as international banks. Almost all banks and companies in the commercial category are members of The Norwegian Bankers' Association (*Den norske Bankforening*), ✆ 22014100, 🖷 22014190, ✉ Hansteensgt. 2, 0253 Oslo, 🖂 bankforeningen@bankforeningen.no.

There are 132 savings banks in the country. The largest, and third largest of all Norwegian banks, is Union Bank of Norway (*Sparebanken NOR*), with branches throughout the country and offices abroad in Stockholm, Copenhagen and Luxembourg. The other savings banks vary from smaller banks with one or two branches in a city or town to larger regional banks with up to 100 branches. The savings banks are members of The Norwegian Savings Banks Association (*Sparebankforeningen*), ✆ 22110075, 🖷 22362533, 🖂 Universitetsgt. 8, 0164 Oslo, 🖂 firmapost@sparebankforeningen.no ◉ http://www.sparebankforeningen.no

For general information on banking, contact the associations at the numbers listed above. For specific information on banks and their services, contact offices or branches at numbers listed under *Bank- og finanstjenester* in the Yellow Pages or under the name of the bank in the Pink Pages.

Basic sum (*Grunnbeløpet*) is a central reference point in all computations relating to National Insurance (*folketrygd*) payments, benefits and pensions (*pensjoner*) as well as in many taxation (*skatt*) matters. *Grunnbeløpet*, abbreviated G in computations, is an amount in kroner that is tied to the general cost of living and is set by Parliament at least once a year, usually on 1st May. It has risen through the years in step with the rising cost of living: in 1967, G was set at NOK 5,400, and on 1 May 1999 it was set at NOK 46,950. One G is the minimum annual National Insurance basic pension (*grunnpensjon*). There may be supplements to or reductions from the basic pension, such as a 25% reduction for each person of a couple when both receive a pension. In taxation, G enters in determining brackets. For instance, companies having employees earning more than 16G per year must pay a surtax on the amount of salary above 16G.

Budget, household (*Budsjett, husholdning*) The most recent ☞ **Statistics** (1998) show that the average Norwegian household consists of 2.3 persons who together spend NOK 204,268 (1995 kroner) a year, of which close to half is for housing and transport. The average percentages for the categories of consumption (*forbruk*) are, in the order of Table 181 in the Statistical Yearbook:

Food	13.8%
Beverages and tobacco	3.8%
Clothing and footwear	6.2%
Rent, fuel and power	24.0%
Furniture and household equipment	8.6%
Health care	2.4%
Transport	21.1%
Recreation and education	11.1%
Other goods and services	8.9%

Cheque (*Sjekk*) As in other countries, a cheque is a bill of exchange that is drawn on balance in a bank account and is payable on demand. As late as 1988, cheques were used in 17.5% of all non-cash payments, about as much as ☞ **Payment cards** were used at the time. Thereafter, payment card and automated ☞ **Giro** transactions became more common and cheque use dwindled, to less than 2% of all noncash payments in 1998. Nonetheless, cheques are convenient, particularly for personal transactions and for paying bills for which giro forms are not sent. Cheques may be drawn on a current account (*foliokonto*) as well as on some other types of account; ask your ☞ **Bank** for details and service charges. Cheque design varies from bank to bank, but all have spaces for the payee's name, the sum paid (*pålydende*) in words and numerals and your signature. If you are unsure of your ability to write the sum paid

in Norwegian, you may write it in English. But always be sure to write the numerals of it in the European format, with a decimal comma (separating kroner and øre) and, if you wish, a dot separating thousands. A properly filled-out cheque is regarded as an ordinary cheque (*vanlig sjekk*) which may be exchanged at a bank for cash. For additional security against theft, you may make it a crossed cheque (*krysset sjekk*) which can only be paid into a bank account. Do this by drawing two parallel lines across it, at an angle about at its midpoint. If you wish, you may insert '& Co.' between the lines, as is the practice in the UK. To cash an ordinary cheque or deposit a cheque in your bank account, countersign it on the reverse side, at the left end, or 'under the numbers' (on the front side), preferably at a teller's wicket in a bank. As you sign, show the teller your *Bankkort* (☞ **Payment cards**) which has your signature and photo, as well as a seven-character alphanumeric identification code, which the teller will write on the reverse of the check to authorise payment or deposit. You must also show your Bank card and follow the same procedure to pay by cheque in a shop. Accordingly, most blank cheques now have a small form box on their reverse sides, with spaces for your identification code and the signature of the person who viewed your Bank card. For ultimate security, such as in transferring a large sum for the payment on a house for which you need a receipt, ask your bank to issue a banker's draft (*bankremisse*), which is a certified cheque issued by the bank and drawn on your account.

Currency (*Valuta*) The unit of currency is the Crown (*Krone*), commonly abbreviated *kr*, but also NOK (by banks) and NKr (in international business). The abbreviations for Nordic currencies, along with the UK Pound and US Dollar for comparison, are:

Country	Unit of Currency	Abbreviations		
		ISO, used by banks	Everyday	Intern. business
Denmark	Krone	DKK	kr.	DKr
Finland	Marka	FIM	mk.	Fmk
Iceland	Krona	ISK	kr.	Ikr
Norway	Krone	NOK	kr.	NKr
Sweden	Krona	SEK	kr.	SKr
UK	Pound	GBP	£	£
USA	Dollar	USD	$	$

Sources: ISO 4217, The Economist Style Guide

The krone is divided into 100 øre. Until 1974, coins were minted in denominations down to 1 øre. But inflation and the rising cost of minting diminished the value of the øre coins, which were successively withdrawn. Today, only the 50 øre coin remains, and all sums, as at shop checkouts, are rounded off to the nearest 50 øre when settled in cash.

Five coins are in circulation: 50 øre (bronze 18.5 mm, 1996), 1 kr. (copper-nickel, 21.0 mm with 3 mm centre hole, 1997), 5 kr. (copper-nickel, 26 mm. with 4 mm centre hole, 1998), 10 kr. (copper-nickel, 24 mm, 1995) and 20 kr. (copper-zinc-nickel, 27.5 mm, 1994). The 10 kr and 20 kr coins bear a portrait of H.M. King Harald V; the 50 øre and 1 kr coins bear his monogram and the 5 kr coin features

the St. Olav Order. Three older coins with a portrait of King Olav V, 5 kr (29.5 mm), 1 kr (25 mm) and 50 øre (22 mm) remain in circulation.

Five bank notes are in circulation. Four in the current "Series VII" are of different sizes with uniform gradation of an increase of 5 mm in width and 8 mm in length between successive denominations, to ease identification by the blind and visually impaired: 50 kr (128 x 60 mm, green, Peter Christen Asbjørnsen portrait, 1997), 100 kr (136 x 65 mm, red, Kirsten Flagstad portrait, 1997), 200 kr (144 x 70 mm, grayish-blue, portrait of Kristian Birkeland, 1994) and 500 kr (152 x 75 mm, reddish brown, Sigrid Undset portrait, 1999). The older 1000 kr (155 x 78 mm, reddish-violet, Christian M. Falsen portrait, 1990) will be

20 kr, 10 kr, 5 kr, 1 kr and 50 øre coins

Photo: Frits Solvang

1000 kr, 500 kr, 200 kr, 100 kr and 50 kr banknotes

replaced in 2001 by a new Series VII banknote. All bank notes have watermarks, microlettering, security threads, register marks and screen traps to prevent counterfeiting. Three older banknotes, 500 kr (155 X 78 mm, blue, Edvard Grieg portrait), 100 kr (145 x 78 mm, reddish-brown, Camilla Collett portrait) and 50 kr (135 x 67 mm, green, Asmund O. Vinje portrait) remain in circulation.

Currency restrictions (*Valutaregulering*) are stated in *Norges Bank's* (central bank's) foreign exchange regulations of 27 June 1990, as amended, most recently on 11 December 1996. Upon arriving in or departing from Norway, you may carry up to a total of NOK 25,000 per person per trip in bank notes and coins, in Norwegian currency, foreign currency or both Norwegian and foreign currencies. This limit applies regardless of whether you are a resident of Norway or of another country. If you carry more than NOK 25,000 you must fill out Norges Bank form F/2711, available at all post offices and customs border crossings and present it to customs at your point of arrival or departure. The same rules apply to import and export shipments of bank notes and coins via postal or courier services. There is no limit on the denominations of Norwegian or foreign bank notes that you may carry, although you may find NOK 1000 bank notes sometimes difficult to exchange abroad. The complete foreign exchange regulations are available in Norwegian and in English translation, on Norges Bank's Internet site ⊛ http://www.norges-bank.no.

Debt collection (*Inkasso*) If you use credit cards, have outstanding bills or owe on a loan or mortgage, you are a debtor. Those to whom you owe are your creditors. If you fail to pay a bill by its due date, your are regarded to have defaulted (*misligholdt*) on it. Then you may be contacted by a debt collector. As in most European countries, debt collection is regulated by law. Creditors collect outstanding debts in four principal steps.

1. Notification (*varsel*): Most bills and loan agreements include a notice of penalty interest (*forsinkelsesrenten*) for late payment, such as "After due date, penalty interest is charged at the rate of 1% per month or part thereof" (*Etter forfall beregnes renter med 1% pr. påbegynte måned*).

2. Reminder and notification of imminent debt collection (*purring/innkassovarsel*): Once a payment is past due, a creditor may send a reminder and charge for sending it, as well as charge for the accumulated penalty interest, as well as give notice of debt collection proceedings to be initiated within 14 days.

3. Debt collection (*inkasso*): After 14 days from the date of a reminder, an unpaid debt may be sent to a debt collection organisation, which will initiate out-of-court collection (*utenrettslige inndriving*) by first sending a request for payment (*betalingsoppfordring*) within 14 days or more and then registering the unpaid debt in the debt register (*betalingsanmerkningsregister*). The debtor is responsible for the costs involved.

4. Legal collection (*rettslig inndriving*): After the due date of the request for payment, the debt collection organisation may initiate legal collection by the Conciliation Board (*Forliksrådet*) for unsecured debt, such as ordinary bills, or by the Bailiff (*Namsmannen*) who is empowered to attach or provisionally attach property (*utleggsforretning*), to initiate eviction (*utkastelse*) and to hold forced sales by auction (*tvangsauksjon*).

If you receive a reminder that is in error or if you owe less than the amount stated, you should immediately contact the creditor and the debt collection organisation. If there is reasonable doubt that you do not owe the sum stated, you are not responsible for debt collection costs. Likewise, if a creditor or a debt collection organisation fails to follow good collection practice (*inkassoskikk*), such as by misstating the facts or your rights or threatening you or setting due dates in national holiday weeks, you are not liable for collection costs. If you or your family have difficulty paying a legitimate debt (*betalingsproblemer*) and have received a request for payment, you may contact the debt collection organisation to negotiate a compromise on payment and halt listing in the debt register. By law, you cannot be deprived of belongings essential in your everyday life. But as you are responsible for the expenses of debt collection as well as for accrued interest, postponement often worsens a debt situation. Five types of organisation are involved in debt collection:

• debt collection agencies (*inkassobyråer*) in the financial sector, responsible to the Banking, Insurance and Securities Commission (*Kredittilsynet*)

• debt collection agencies (*inkassobyråer*) attached

to legal offices, responsible to the Supervisory Council for Legal Practice (*Tilsynsrådet for advokatvirksomhet*)

- Lawyers, auditors, bookkeepers (*Advokater, revisorer, regnskapsførere*)
- Banks, financial institutions, insurance companies (*bank, finans, forsikring*) with debt collection departments
- Governmental and municipal agencies (*Stat, kommuner*)

The ☞ **Consumer council** (Human Rights, Consumer Rights chapter) publishes and regularly updates a fact sheet (*Faktablad*) on debt collection. For a copy of it, or for advice should you believe you are unjustly treated in a collection matter, contact the nearest office of the council, see *Forbrukerrådet* in the Pink Pages.

Due date (*Forfallsdag*) Bills (*regning*) and invoices (*faktura*) almost always include a due date which is the last date on which the amount stated may be paid. The date is stated in several ways, all with the same meaning. An invoice may have a line labelled *Forfallsdag* or just *Forfall*, whilst *Betalingsfrist* is the label of the field in the upper right-hand corner of the standard ☞ **Giro** form. Late payment (*for sen betaling*) incurs interest on overdue payment (*morarente*) as stated on an invoice. A typical statement is: *Etter forfall beregnes renter med 1,00% pr påbegynte måned* ("After the due date, interest is charged at the rate of 1.00% for each month begun"). In general, Giro payments take two to three business days to clear. So to be sure that a bill or invoice is paid on time, you should initiate payment of it several days before its due date.

Insurance policies, bonds, retirement plans and the like will also have a *forfall*, which is the date of maturity, after which payments are no longer made and benefits or yields may be made available.

Euro Norway is not a member of the EU, but its ☞ **Exchange** and other international financial transactions are affected by the euro, which on 1 January 1999 at 00.00 a.m. became the official currency of 11 member countries of the European Union (EU) with a fixed conversion rate against their national currencies. From then on, the value of the euro against the dollar and all other currencies, including the Norwegian krone and those of the four EU member countries who stayed outside the Euro zone (Denmark, Great Britain, Greece and Sweden) will fluctuate according to market conditions. Initially, the Euro is a non-cash medium of transaction, as by cheques, bank transfers, credit cards and other electronic means, and may be used by consumers, shops, companies and public sector agencies. Euro bank notes and coins are scheduled to be put in circulation starting 1 January 2002. The graphic symbol for the euro was inspired by the Greek letter epsilon and looks like a lower-case letter "e" with two horizontal, parallel lines across it. The official abbreviation is EUR on the International Standards Organisation (ISO) currency designation list. The predecessor of the EUR, the European Currency Unit (ECU) computed from a basket of national currencies of the EU countries, was used in transactions and listed in tables of exchange rates up to 31 December 1998. The EUR rates from 4 January 1999 and the ECU basket rates up to 31 December 1998 are available on the Internet (daily, ten days backward, monthly and annual average rates) at ☞ http:// europa.eu.int/euro. The exchange rate between the Norwegian krone (NOK) and the euro is set by Norges Bank (the central bank) at 2:30 p.m. on weekdays and published in the financial pages of newspapers the day after.

 EUR

Euro conversion rates
One EUR equals

ATS, Austrian schilling	13.7603
BEF, Belgian franc	40.3399
FIM, Finnish markka	5.94573
FRF, French franc	6.55957
DEM, German mark	1.95583
IEP, Irish punts	0.787564
ITA, Italian liara	1936.27
LUX, Luxembourg franc	40.3399
NLG, Netherlands guilder	2.20371
PTE, Portugese escudo	200.482
ESP, Spanish peseta	166.386
NOK, Norwegian krone*	8.90
USD, US dollar*	1.17

Sources: EU web site for 11 national currencies,

* market rate on 31 December 1998.

Exchange (*Valuta*) of foreign currencies is regulated by Norges Bank, the central bank, currently according to guidelines of 1990 with amendments of 1996. In summary, you may freely exchange up to 25,000 Norwegian kroner (NOK) or its equivalent at almost all banks and larger post offices, which either buy (*kjøp*) foreign currency and give you Norwegian kroner, or sell (*salg*) foreign currency and accept payment in Norwegian kroner. Upon arriving in Norway from abroad, you must declare any amount above NOK 25,000 but may freely exchange up to NOK 40,000 provided that you show identification, such as a passport. Upon departing from the country, you may freely take up to NOK 25,000. If you exchange larger sums at a bank, you should have an account with it, and the bank is obliged to report the transaction to ☞ **Norges Bank**. The exchange rates (*valutakurs*) for the most commonly traded currencies are listed in the financial sections (*Økonomi*) of daily newspapers, usually for the previous business day and under the heading *Valuta* (Currency), and include the amount of Norwegian kroner needed to buy other currencies, including 1 US Dollar (USD), 100 German Marks (DEM). 100 Swedish Kroner (SEK), 100 Danish Kroner (DKK), 100 Netherlands Guilders (NLG), 100 Belgian Francs (BEF), 1 British Pound (GBP), 100 Swiss Francs (CHF), 100 French Francs (FRF), 100 Japanese Yen (JPY), 100 Austrian Shillings (ATS), 100 Finnish Marks (FIM), 1 Canadian Dollar (CAD), 100 Spanish Pesetas (ESP), 100 Portuguese Escudos (PTE), 100 Icelandic Kroner (ISK), 1 Irish Pound (IEP), 100 Greek Drachmas (GRD) and 1 Euro (EUR), as well as 1 Special Drawing Rights (SDR), the unit used by member countries of the International Monetary Fund (IMF) to extend rights in purchasing foreign currency from the IMF to increase their foreign exchange reserves. Rates for currencies not listed in newspapers are available at banks, which usually have daily lists of the buying (*kjøp*) and selling (*salg*) rates for all currencies traded. Norges Bank provides reference exchange rates, but individual banks set their own buying and selling rates for cash, checks, transfers and other exchange transactions. Through the years, the country has employed various currency policies, including linking to a trade-weighted basket of currencies in the 1980s, unilateral linking in the early 1990s to the European Currency Unit (ECU) that was computed from the national currencies of EU countries and valid through 31 December 1998 before the ☞ **Euro** became the EU currency on 1 January 1999.

Family expenditure (*Husholdnings utgifter*) Two organisations serve families as consumers. The ☞ **National Institute for Consumer Research** (Government and Social Services Chapter) is the centre for research, analysis and testing in fields related to personal consumption. The ☞ **Consumer Council** (Human Rights, Consumer Rights chapter) is dedicated to safeguarding the interests of consumers. Both are concerned with family expenditure. The Institute for Consumer Research regularly compiles a standard budget for after-tax consumption expenditure (*standardbudsjett for forbruksutgifter*). For instance, in 1998, the typical standard budget family of an adult couple with an eleven-year-old girl and a five-year-old boy spent NOK 180,300 a year in daily expenses, exclusive of housing, tobacco and alcohol, higher-level education, health services, expensive hobbies, holidays, celebrations and gifts. The Consumer Council publishes a consumer reports magazine (*Forbruker Rapporten*) as well as numerous booklets and fact sheets on consumer topics. The family account book (*Regnskaps bok*) has 35 pages of forms in which are designed to help a family keep monthly and annual budgets and records of expenses, and includes summaries of the major laws affecting consumer rights; it and other Consumer Council publications are stocked by larger book shops.

Funds (*Fond*) are increasingly in favour, perhaps because they permit individuals to invest without becoming directly involved in financial activities. Many types of funds are offered by banks, insurance companies and financial organisations, and involve investments in shares (*aksjer*), bonds (*obligasjoner*), the money market (*pengemarked*) or a combination of these (*kombinasjonsfond*). According to the Act on Securities Funds (*Lov om Verdipapirfond*), all funds must be approved by and monitored by the Banking, Insurance and Securities Commission (*Kredittilsynet*). By law, funds may invest only in securities which are:

- listed by securities exchanges in the EEA (European bourse), ☞ **EFTA, EU & EEA** (Government and Social Services chapter).
- traded in other regulated markets in the EEA.

- traded on other exchanges which are open to the public and are regulated by supervisory agencies.
- are new and backed by a conditions of issue including a commitment to apply for listing in one of the three markets listed above.

In terms of numbers of persons investing, the AMS funds offering ☞ **Share investment with tax relief** are among the most popular. Other funds offered on the Norwegian market include various broad-based funds (*breddefond*), indexed funds (*indeksfond*), foreign funds (*utenlandsfond*), exchange funds (*valutafond*) and umbrella funds (*parallyfond*) such as SICAV (*Socètè d'Investissement á Capital Variable*) in Luxembourg.

Giro (*Giro*) is a system whereby credits are transferred between accounts. As in other European countries, the post office developed its system (*postgiro*) and the banks developed theirs (*bankgiro*). The two systems now work together, and there is only one giro form for interbank transfers. Most bills now have giro forms attached. So to pay a bill, you need only fill in your account number and sign the form, as shown below, and submit it for debiting to your account. You may deliver the form to a teller at a branch of your bank. The teller will date stamp the giro receipt and send the form on for processing by the Banks' Central Clearing House (*Bankens Betalingssentral – BBS*). This is the most expensive way to

process a giro form, because it involves manual handling at a bank. You can eliminate teller handling and cut giro processing charges to your account by using one of the two systems for posting filled-in forms. More than 100 banks now offer *BrevGiro* (Letter Giro), a system in which you fill out and sign giro forms and post up to 40 forms in a single prepaid envelope to BBS for debiting to your account. The Post Office Bank, *Postbanken*, offers a similar system. Banks offering these systems also offer two automatic varieties of them, known as *AutoGiro* ("Automatic Giro") and *AvtaleGiro* ("Agreement Giro"), which are convenient for regular payments, such as rent, mortgage payments and electricity and telephone bills. *AutoGiro* is an agreement between you and the seller. It permits the seller to debit your account directly without your intervention. You may or may not receive notice of debiting, depending on the agreement. *AvtaleGiro* is an agreement between you and your bank. Each month, the bank sends you a notice of the bills that fall due the following month, with a stated deadline date for your reply to it. If you do not intervene by replying before the deadline, all the bills listed are debited to your account. You may intervene before the deadline to indicate that some or all of the bills on the list are not to be paid. You can initiate *AutoGiro* or *AvtaleGiro* by filling in forms available at your bank. You must, of course, ensure that your account always has sufficient balance to cover bills debited to it. Most banks that offer Brev-

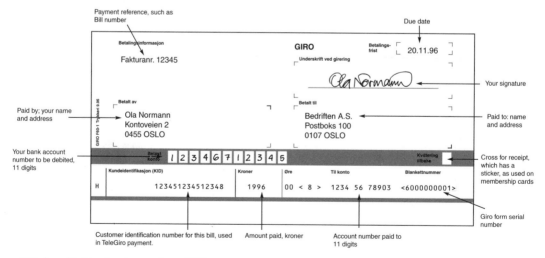

Giro form filled in, drawing courtesy of BBS.

Giro now also offer *TeleGiro*, a ☞ **Telebanking** service. Each year, private persons pay more than 100 million bills via the giro systems, and more than 1.7 million account holders have BrevGiro agreements. So unlike some countries, including Great Britain, where the giro system is used for, and consequently especially associated with social security payments, the Norwegian giro systems are the commonplace way to pay all bills and receive all payments.

Gold and silver (*Gull og sølv*) are the principal noble metals (*edelmetall*) traded and quoted in the financial pages of newspapers, usually under the heading Metals (*Metaller*). In 1891, a uniform metric measure of fineness replaced the carat (*karat*) proportional measure of one twenty-fourth for the fineness of gold and names such as sterling (*sterlingsølv*) for the fineness of silver. The metric measure is a three-digit number expressing the parts per thousand of the pure metal. For instance, pure gold has a fineness of 999, indicating a purity of 999/1000 and equivalent to the older 24 carat, whilst a metal of 750/1000 gold is equivalent to 18 carat. Likewise, 925/1000 silver is equivalent to the older sterling designation. To be designated "gold", a metal must have a fineness of at least 585/1000. Likewise, "silver" must have a fineness of at least 830/1000. Fineness is stamped on ingots of a metal and on some items worked from it, such as on silverware, as well as stated in the descriptions of gold and silver items, such as jewelry. There is no import duty on gold or silver other than value-added tax (*MVA*) which is charged on the invoiced purchase price plus shipping costs.

Insurance (*Forsikring*) Together, the 29 countries of the ☞ **OECD** (Government and Social Services chapter) account for about 95% of the world insurance market. Among them, Norway ranks 16th in spending on insurance premiums as a percentage of its GDP

The main types of insurance for individuals (as opposed to companies) are accident insurance (*ulykkesforsikring*), automobile/motor insurance (*bilforsikring*), fire insurance (*brannforsikring*), health insurance (*helseforsikring*), home insurance (*hjemmeforsikring*), life and retirement assurance (*pensjonsforsikring*), leisure craft insurance (*båtforsikring*) and travel insurance (*reiseforsikring*). The insurance

business is competitive and both Norwegian and foreign ☞ **insurance companies** offer policies. For specific details, contact one or more companies. For general information, see the publications of the Association of Norwegian Insurance Companies (*Norges Forsikringsforbund*), such as:

- *Hva er Forsikring?* ("What is insurance?"), a general handbook, January 1995, 180-page paperback, ISBN 82-91303-01-6, in Norwegian only.
- *Insurance in Norway*, a biennial overview of the insurance sector, 1998 edition, 28-page booklet A4 format, also on-line
  ⊕ http://www.forsikring.no along with other information in Norwegian and in English.

Most Norwegian insurance terms have equivalents in English. A helpful guide is:

- *Forsikrings ordbok* ("Insurance glossary"), Norwegian-English and English-Norwegian, by Åge Lind, Kunnskapsforlaget 1989, 58-page hardcover A5 format, ISBN 82-573-0314-3.

Insurance complaints (*Forsikringsklager*) If you are dissatisfied with an insurance company service, such as non-payment of a claim which you consider justified, you may write or call the company's complaints department (*klagenemnd*), which is obliged to give you a written answer. If you are dissatisfied with that answer, you may appeal to the Norwegian Bureau for Insurance Disputes -NBI (*Forsikringsklagekontoret*), which is affiliated with the ☞ **Consumer council** (Human Rights, Consumer Rights chapter) and acts as a consumer organisation ✆ 23131960, 🖷 23131970, ☞ Bygdøy allé 19, 0262 Oslo, ✉ firmapost@forsikringskontoret.no. NBI is the secretariat for two insurance boards, which it may consult in handling your complaint: the Insurance Agreements Board – IAB (*Forsikringsskadenemnda*) and the Board for Reduced Compensation – BRC (*Avkortingsnemnd*). The IAB principally is concerned with legal aspects, such as interpretation of laws and insurance contracts. The BRC principally is concerned with assessing the degree of negligence that may be involved. NBI will handle your complaint free of charge and advise you of the outcome.

Insurance: Home insurance (*Hus- og hjemforsikring*) There are three basic types of household insurance:

Home content insurance (*hjemmeforsikring*) is best if you rent or own an apartment or if you rent a house. It covers loss of furnishings (*innbo*) and possessions (*løsøre*) due to fire (*brann*), escape of water (*vannledningskade*), theft (*tyveri*) and natural disasters (*naturskade*).

Private house insurance (*villaforsikring*) is necessary if you own your house. In addition to offering the same coverage as home insurance, it also covers the building, usually with comprehensive building (*kasko bygning*) insurance that covers most sudden and unforeseen (*plutselig og uforutsatt*) damages.

Holiday home insurance (*hytteforsikring*) is advisable if you own a cottage or cabin. It offers coverage similar to private house insurance.

There are various extra insurance provisions, as for mildew and dry rot (*sopp og råte*), breakage of plumbing fixtures and windows (*bruddskader, sanirær porselen og vinduer*) and the like. Usually, these extra provisions are offered in combination with a main policy, which then might be called "combined" (*kombinert*), such as *kombinert villaforsikring*.

Most ☞ **Insurance companies** offer a schedule of discounts depending on how well your home is secured (*sikkerhetsrabatt*). Typically, the insurance company will give you a personal statement (*egenerklaring*) form to fill out listing the security provisions of your home, including a compulsory smoke detector (*røykvarsler*) on each floor, a compulsory fire hose (*brannslange*) long enough to reach all rooms, at least one 6 kg dry-powder fire extinguisher (*brannslokkingsapparat*) rated for use on live electrical equipment, burglar alarms (*innbrudsalarm*), drains (*sluk*) in rooms with washing machines or hot-water heaters and security locks on external doors. All alarms and security locks should be FG-approved (*FG-godkjent*) by the Norwegian Insurance Companies Approval Committee (*Forsikrings-selskapenes Godkjennongsnevnd*).

Insurance: Leisure craft insurance (*Fritidsbåtforsikring*) usually covers a boat and its accessories and is valid in Norway, Denmark, Finland and Sweden and their territorial waters up to 12 nautical miles from their coasts. All categories of leisure craft may be insured, including motorboats, rowboats, yachts and sailboards for windsurfing. There are three basic types of insurance:

Liability (*Ansvar*) insurance provides coverage for persons other than the one insured, who usually is the boat owner, and customarily is limited to a maximum amount of compensation for any one event. Liability for leisure craft differs from liability in ☞ **Motor insurance** in one vital aspect. A motor vehicle carries objective liability (*objektivt ansvar*), that is liability exists even if none of the persons involved in an accident are at fault. A leisure craft has fault liability (*skyldansvar*) but no objective liability. So when two boats are involved in an accident that can easily happen (*hendelig uhell*), neither are covered by their liability insurance.

Comprehensive (*Kasko*) insurance covers specified damages, such as due to theft (*tyveri*) or vandalism (*hærverk*).

Fire and theft (*Brann og tyveri*) insurance covers loss due to fire, explosion or lightning strike and can be extended to cover theft and vandalism. These three basic types are offered in four combinations: liability only; liability and comprehensive; liability and fire; liability, fire and theft.

Insurance: Life insurance (*Livsforsikring*) traditionally offers financial protection against the death of a person in the form of payment to a beneficiary, usually a family member. There now are many forms of life insurance, in part due to tax regulations governing allowable deductions. The three principal forms are:

Term life insurance (*dødsrisikoforsikring*) is the simplest and cheapest form of life insurance. It pays a beneficiary upon the death of the insured person and usually is valid for a few months up to a few decades, such as 20 or 30 years. After the validity period, the insurance is cancelled and no payment is made upon subsequent death of the person who had been insured. Young couples with children and mortgages often have term life insurance to cover expenses should one of them die.

Endowment with term insurance (*Sammensatt livsforsikring*) is the most expensive form of traditional life insurance. It provides the same coverage as does term life insurance, but also will pay out the insurance sum if the insured person survives the endowment period to a specified retirement age, such as age 67. People wishing to save for their retirement often elect endowment insurance.

Disability capital insurance (*Uførekaptial*)

is usually combined with term life risk insurance or endowment insurance, but sometimes is a separate policy. It provides income after a permanent disability and thereby supplements the National Insurance disability benefits. The disability covered usually is related to earning ability (*ervervsuførhet*) and not to injuries that may be covered by accident insurance (*ulykkesforsikring*) but may not affect earning ability.

There are numerous variations of these three basic forms of life insurance. Sometimes they are combined with other insurance, including:

Accident insurance (*Ulykkesforsikring*) provides compensation in case of injury. It has three common forms of coverage: individual (*individuell*), family (*familie*) and child (*barn*).

Credit life insurance (*Gjeldsforsikring*): issued to a creditor to cover the life of the borrower for an outstanding loan or mortgage. The borrower must pay the premiums and coverage stops when the loan or mortgage is repaid.

Pension/retirement assurance (*Pensjonsforsikring*) can cover a variety of payment plans including retirement (*alderspensjon*), disability benefit (*uførepensjon*), spouse pension (*ektefellepensjon*) and orphans (*barnepensjon*) or other beneficiary (*livsarvingpensjon*) benefits. If you are not covered by a collective pension plan (*tjenestepensjonsordning*) at your place of work, you should consider pension assurance to supplement National Insurance pension payments when you retire. Up to a set limit, premiums for private retirement assurance are deductible on your income tax returns.

Pension account assurance (*Engangsbetalte pensjonsbevis*) offers an estimated future retirement pension for a single lump-sum payment instead of regular premiums over time. Taxwise it is treated like ordinary pension/retirement assurance.

Insurance: Motor insurance (*Motorvognforsikring*), also called **automobile insurance (*bilforsikring*)** is of three general types:

Third party liability (*ansvar*) insurance covers sums which you may legally be obliged to pay due to having damaged others' property or injured people other than yourself or passengers in a car you drive. It is required by law and accordingly is called traffic insurance (*trafikkforsikring*). You must prove that you have traffic insurance in order to register or drive a car. If you fail to renew a traffic insur-

ance policy and it lapses, the insurance company will notify the ☞ **Motor vehicle and driving licence inspectorate** (Cars, Roads and Traffic chapter); your number plate will then be withdrawn and may be confiscated by the Inspectorate or the police.

Personal injury (*personskade*) insurance covers the driver (*fører*) of a car and the passengers (*passasjerer*) in it in case of injury in an accident. A specified minimum of personal injury insurance is required by law and considered part of traffic insurance, but most insurance companies offer additional coverages.

Comprehensive (*kasko*) insurance on your own car is voluntary. It may be relatively inexpensive partial (*delkasko*) insurance that covers only fire (*brann*), theft (*tyveri*), windscreen/window breakage (*glass*) and road assistance (*veihjelp*) or more expensive complete (*helkasko*) insurance that also covers collision damage (*kollisjonsskade*). Comprehensive rates depend on the amount of coverage provided, the age of the car, the amount deductible (*egenandel*) at your own expense and where you live in the country.

The rates for all types of motor insurance are higher for young people, up to age 25, than for older drivers. Rates also depend on how far a car is driven: there is a minimum rate that permits driving up to 8,000 km a year, and increasing rates for greater distances driven. A discount, or no-claims bonus (*bonus*) is granted in progressive steps according to the number of years the insured car has been driven without an insurance claim against it. The discount varies, but can be up to 75% five years or more with no claims. The percentage discount is reduced with each claim paid. Consequently, drivers occasionally elect to pay minor damages to other cars, such as in car parks, rather than forfeit bonus percentages.

Insurance: Private health insurance (*Helseforsikring, privat*) If you want private health insurance and intend to live in Norway, there are several ways to obtain coverage. Some European insurance companies offer private health insurance plans that are valid throughout the ☞ **EFTA, EU and EEA** (Government and Social Services chapter). So, if you will maintain insurance policies in your home country while living in Norway, you should check with your insurance company to see if it offers a suitable policy. Four Norwegian companies offer private health insurance that is intended to ensure ready access to health services, and coverage schemes are available for both companies and individuals.

Nordisk Helse Assistanse (Nordic Health Assistance) co-operates with the European division of Reliance National Insurance Company of the USA to offer company policies covering the patient share (*egenandel*) of the costs of treatment in public clinics and hospitals as well as the costs of private treatment. Contact the company for further details ✆ 64938990, ✉ 64938997, ✉ Sagav. 13, 1440 Drøbak, ❧ http://www.nha.no.

Norsk Helseforsikring (Norwegian Health Insurance), a subsidiary of International Health Insurance (IHI) of Denmark, offers company and individual policies in a range of coverages, from treatment in clinics and hospitals to all-inclusive policies covering the services of chiropractors, dentists, doctors, opticians, physiotherapists and surgeons, as well as ancillary expenses including medicines. Contact the company for further details: ✆ 22334280, ✉ 22411301, ✉ PO Box 1603 Vika, 0119 Oslo, ❧ http://www.norskhelse.no, or for information in English, view the IHI Internet site ❧ http://www.ihi.dk.

Storebrand, a general insurance company, co-operates with the German health insurance company, *Deutsche Krankenversicherung* to offer policies to companies and individuals, covering the patient share (*egenandel*) of the costs of treatment in public clinics and hospitals as well as the costs of private treatment. Contact the company for further details: freephone ✆ 80083313, ✉ 22311370, ✉ PO Box 1380 Vika, 0114 Oslo, ❧ http://www.storebrandhelse.no.

Vesta, a general insurance company, offers policies to companies covering the patient share (*egenandel*) of the costs of treatment in public clinics and hospitals as well as the costs of private treatment. Its private clinic working partners include *Volvat Medisinske Senter* in Oslo, *Bergen Medisinske Senter* in Bergen, *Vestfold Medisinske Senter* in Tønsberg and *Media3* in Ålesund. Contact the company for further details: ✆ 22964450, ✉ 22964001, ✉ PO Box 5220 Majuorstua, 0303 Oslo.

Insurance: Travel insurance (*Reiseforsikring*)

provides coverage when you are travelling away from home. Travel insurance policies may involve an annual premium and cover up to a total of one month of travel during any time of the year (*årsforsikring*), or may be bought for single trips (*enkeltforsikring*) and can be bought for an individual (*enkeltperson*) or a family (*familie*). Four principal coverages are offered:

Luggage insurance (*Reisegodsforsikring*) covers damage to or loss of luggage while travelling. As a rule, it does not cover documents, stocks or bonds, manuscripts, exposed film or the like. Some policies also cover theft or robbery of cash up to a limited amount.

Travel accident insurance (*Reiseulykkeforsikring*) provides coverage similar to ordinary accident insurance and is valid for travel abroad.

Travel health insurance (*Reisesykeforsikring*) covers the health care expenses of sudden illness or accident while travelling, including transport back home. Some policies also cover the additional expenses of unexpected travel back home should a member of your immediate family at home . suddenly fall ill, suffer an accident or die.

Travellers' liability insurance (*Reiseansvarsforsikring*) covers the legal liabilities that you may incur while travelling abroad.

These four types of travel insurance may be bought individually or in combination (*kombinert forsikring*). They do not cover cancellation insurance (*avbestillingsforsikring*), which provides a refund of an otherwise binding booking of tickets, as for charter trips or discounted airline tickets. Cancellation coverage provides a refund when you cannot travel as planned due to you or a member of your immediate family suffering a sudden illness or accident, death in your immediate family, or fire, burglary or other damage to your home or place of business that requires you to stay home. All travel agencies and transport companies selling tickets also offer cancellation insurance, which you may buy if you wish when you book discount travel. Some credit card companies include cancellation insurance whenever one of their credit cards is used to pay for tickets.

Interest (*Rente*) is money paid to a lender of cash for the use of it. It is usually expressed in terms of an interest rate (*rentesats*) in percentage of a sum borrowed for a period of one year. The central bank of Norway, ☞ **Norges Bank** sets the bank base rate (rentenivå) which reflects government economic policy. The bank base rate also acts as the minimum lending rate on which all other interest rates are set. As an individual, you most likely will be concerned principally with the current borrowing rate (lånerente), such as on a mortgage or loan, and interest paid (renteavkastnig) on investments, such as on savings accounts. In personal income tax, interest paid and interest earned are treated equally. That is, on your tax return, you may deduct interest paid on loans, but you must also must declare interest earned on savings or investments. When evaluating investment, you should consider interest yield after tax (avkasting etter skatt). All interest income (renteinntekter) is taxed at 28%. Any sum invested, as in a savings account or other financial instrument, is subject to an estate tax (formueskatt) of 1.1%. With time, inflation diminishes the value of money. Consider, for instance, an interest income of 8%:

Interest income	8.00%
Minus tax	- 2.24%
minus estate tax	- 1.10%
Yield after tax	4.66%

So if you invest a sum at 8% interest for a year, your yield at the end of the year is 4.66%. But during that year, the value of money has been diminished by inflation, which averaged 2.5% a year in the late 1990s. Consequently, your final real rate of interest (realrenten) would be about 2.06%. Nonetheless, investment is worthwhile, as long as the real rate of interest is positive.

Invoices (Faktura) are written or printed bills which give the details of goods or services ordered or delivered and state discounts, trade terms (betingelser) and applicable taxes, which usually are the computed ☞ **MVA** (Taxes, Duties, Excise chapter). Most invoices are now printed with a filled-in ☞ **Giro** form. You may fill in your bank account number, sign the form and return it by post. Or, if you have a relevant agreement with your bank, you may pay via dataphone or via the Internet. The date of invoicing (dato) and due date (forfall) will be stated. Penalty interest (morarente) at a stated rate usually is charged for late payment (for sen betaling) after the due date. As a rule, you should post a signed giro three bank days in advance to ensure payment by its due date.

Loans (Lån) are one of the few goods or services

for which you must submit an application for purchase. But if your finances are relatively solid – or even if they are not and you have solid security, such as a saleable house – the only difficulty you may have in borrowing is selecting among loans offered on a buyer's market. Many financial organisations loan to private persons, including ☞ **Banks** and ☞ **Insurance companies**, credit institutions (kredittforetak), pension plans (pensjonskasser) and public lending organisations, such as the Norwegian State Housing Bank (Husbanken).

If you need to borrow, you should start by inquiring about the loans offered by the organisations with which you have connections, such as your bank, the insurance company with which you have policies or the pension fund at your workplace. Compare their offerings, starting with the overall cost of borrowing (lånets kostnad).

Start your comparison by evaluating nominal interest (nominell rente) and true interest (effektiv rente). The nominal interest is the rate stated by the lender. The true interest is the percentage of the principal that you must pay to service the loan, and includes nominal interest, initial processing fees (etableringsgebyr) and instalment charges (termingebyrer). Because fees and charges usually are fixed, the difference between nominal interest and true interest is highest for smaller loans. If you borrow over a period of several years and your wages at least keep step with inflation, you should consider the real interest (realrente), which is the true interest minus inflation. It indicates the cost of servicing your loan in the future.

Loans are repaid in instalments (termin), each of which consists of repayment (avdrag), interest on the remaining principle and the instalment charge. There are many repayment plans (nedbetalingsprofil); the most common are the serial loan (serielån) and the amortised loan (annuitetslån). The serial loan has fixed repayments, so its instalments initially are large and then decline as the loan is paid off. The amortised loan has fixed instalments, so repayment initially is small and then increases as the loan is paid off.

Mortgage (Boliglån) For most people, a mortgage to buy a house or flat is larger and therefore more important than any other loan they may take out. A mortgage involves providing security (sikker-

het) for a loan in the form of an agreement to transfer the rights to a property (*pant*) should the amount borrowed not be paid as agreed. The agreement is valid after it has been signed by both the lender and the borrower and properly recorded by the local ☞ **Public registrar** (Rights, Registrations, Licences chapter). The lending institution, such as a bank, insurance company or pension fund, called the mortgagee (*panthaver*) usually will grant a mortgage for a certain portion of the purchase price (*kjøpesummen*) or valuation price (*verditakst*) as set by an assessor or valuation agency, as listed under *Taksering* in the Yellow Pages. Two figures are commonly used: loan value (*lånetakst*) and market value (*omsetningsverdi*). The loan value usually is 80% to 85% of the valuation price. Normally, the lending institution will grant a mortgage for up to 80% of the purchase price or up to 80% of the valuation price in refinancing. Full financing, up to 100% of the purchase price, usually is granted only if other security is offered, such as a mortgage on the home of the parents of a young couple buying their first home. An initial mortgage is called a first mortgage (*første prioritetelån*), because the borrower, called the mortgagor (*pantsetter*) has no previous mortgages on the property. If you need more money after taking out a first mortgage, such as to remodel an older house, you may consider taking out a second mortgage (*annen prioritetslån*). The term "second" means that the lender ranks behind the lender of the first mortgage in case the property should be sold to pay defaulted debt. If you have a first and a second mortgage on a house and pay off the first mortgage, the second mortgage advances to a first mortgage. Any mortgage you take out thereafter will be a new second mortgage.

Non-cash payments (*Betalingsformidling*) Individuals now increasingly shop and pay bills using one of three means of non-cash payments ☞ **Payment cards,** ☞ **Giro** and ☞ **Cheques**. Card use now is most common and accounts for more than half of the some 750 million non-cash transactions per year in the country. Giro is a close second, with slightly less than half of the total, whilst cheque use has dwindled to less than two percent. These payment statistics are compiled regularly by ☞ **Norges Bank** and are available at its web site.

Norges Bank is the Central Bank of Norway. Most countries have a Central Bank. Examples are the Bank of England in the UK, the Federal Reserve System in the USA, the Deutsche Bundesbank in Germany, the Banque de France and the Bank of Japan. Each differs slightly from the others in its scope of activities, in the powers it exercises, and in its relationship with its government. But each Central Bank serves both the government and the banking system of its country. The interplay of these two roles has resulted in Central Banks playing key parts in conducting monetary policies affecting the cost and availability of money and credit. This makes each Central Bank important in its domestic economy, and together with other Central Banks, influential in the financial markets of the world. Some Central Banks, such as the Bank of Japan, elect to translate their names when used internationally. Others, such as Deutsche Bundesbank – and Norges Bank – retain their names in their native languages. Norges Bank is a separate legal entity owned by the State. It is an executive and advisory body for monetary, credit and foreign exchange policy. It issues ☞ **Currency**, promotes domestic and international payment systems and monitors developments in the money, credit and foreign exchange markets. Its head office is in Oslo and it has 12 regional branches. The printing works are in Oslo and the Royal Norwegian Mint is in Kongsberg. For further information on Norges Bank, contact the ☞ **Central Information Service** (Media and Information chapter) or the Bank itself ✆ 22316000, ☎ 22413105, ✉ PO Box 1179 Sentrum, 0107 Oslo, ✉ central.bank@norges-bank.no, ⊕ http://www.norges-bank.no with pages in Norwegian and in English.

Payment cards (*Betalingskort*) are now used in more than half of the some 750 million automatic transactions a year in the country. There are three principal varieties of cards: debit cards, credit cards and charge cards.

Debit cards (*Bankkort*), also called cash cards (*Kontantkort*), are used in ☞ **ATM terminals** (*Minibank*) to withdraw money and in readers (*kortlesere*) to debit purchases made in shops equipped for Electronic Funds Transfer at the Point of Sale (EFTPOS). A debit card identifies the holder of a deposit account in a bank, which must have sufficient balance to cover the amount debited when the card is used. The

Banks' Central Clearing House (BBS), which operates the ☞ **Giro** system, also operates *Bank Axept*, a debit card offered by all ☞ **banks**. Commercial banks offer inter-bank and international debiting via the Visa network, and savings banks offer similar services via the Eufiserv network. The postal bank (*Postbanken*) has its own card. Cards issued by a bank can be used all its ATM terminals and in most other banks' ATM terminals as well; the logos of the acceptable cards are usually displayed on the ATM close to its instructions. Many ATMs at airports, major railway stations, larger banks and banks near border crossings also offer foreign exchange and issue foreign currency against debiting an account or credit facility.

Credit cards (*Kredittkort*) are used in the same way as debit cards, but provide a credit facility. Most credit cards are issued by banks in various plans that combine debit to a deposit account with a credit extension to it. The non-bank credit cards include the *Her & Nå (GE Capital), X-tra Kapital (GE Capital), Kjøpekort (Gjensidige/GE Kapital), Multikort (DnB Finans)* and *Bohus-kortet (DnB Finans)* domestic credit cards valid only in Norway, and the American Express, Cirrus, Diners Club and Master Card Eurocard international credit cards. Credit account cards (*Handlekonto*) are credit cards valid for purchases at a single chain of shops, such as *Ellos* and *Ikea*. Interest is charged on credit provided by credit cards, usually at rates that are considerably higher than ordinary bank loan interest rates. For instance, in July 1999, the effective interest rate on a credit card debt of NOK 10,000 ranged from 24.6% to 34.7% for domestic credit cards and 19.2% to 32.5% for credit account cards.

Charge cards (*Handlekort*) are valid at the outlets of specific retailers and require regular monthly settlement, usually against an invoice sent on a specified day of the month. The petrol station companies – Statoil, Hydro-Texaco, Shell, Esso, Fina and DuPont Jet – issue charge cards valid for purchases at their service stations throughout the country and, in some cases, throughout Scandinavia or Europe.

All debit and charge cards issued in Norway can be used in all shop card readers in the country, as can most international cards issued abroad. However, some international credit cards are valid only with a Scandinavian personal identity number (PIN). Almost all Norwegian payment cards are international standard 85 x 54 mm plastic cards with a black magnetic stripe on the reverse side. Debit cards and most credit cards are issued with the bearer's passport-sized photo and signature above the stripe. For further details on card services and costs, contact the issuing banks and payment card companies at addresses and telecommunications numbers listed in the Pink Pages.

Pawnshops (*Pantelåneforretninger*) lend money on the security of personal property such as jewelry, silver, sports equipment, high-end cycles and musical instruments. The way a pawnbroker (*pantelåner*) operates is strictly controlled by law. In general, a pawnshop will loan out a tenth to a fifth of a deposited object's value, usually with a minimum of NOK 100 and a maximum of NOK 200,000 for a single loan. When you take an object to a pawnshop as security for a loan (*håndpant*), you must show proper identification to prove that you are a legitimate pawnor (*lånetager*) and, for some objects, proof of ownership, such as a receipt for the purchase of a high-end cycle or a golf association card for pawning golf clubs. The pawnbroker (*pantelåner*) will record these details and then pay you the full amount of the loan in cash. The bookkeeping is necessary, as pawnshops work closely with the police and with insurance companies to hinder sale of stolen goods. If you are the genuine owner of the goods pawned, you have nothing to fear, as pawnshop records are confidential. After pawning an object, you have the remainder of the month plus the following four months to repay the loan and redeem the object. The current rate of interest is 2.75% per month, and a fee of NOK 20 – 60 is charged for the transaction. If you do not redeem the pawned object, the pawnbroker will notify you in writing of a deadline date for redeeming the object before it is sold at auction. You will receive a further notice if the object actually is auctioned. A very small percentage of pawned objects are auctioned; most are redeemed by their owners. Historically, pawnshops originally were under the jurisdiction of the police, but now they operate under concessions (*konsessjon*) issued by the Banking, Insurance and Securities Commission (*Kredittilsynet*). Banks have such concessions, so they may operate pawnshops. As this book goes to press, the only pawnshops in the country are a chain of three K-Pawnbrokers (*Lånekontoret*) shops owned by the oldest bank in the country, *Kreditkassen* of Oslo. In fact, in 1848 *Kreditkassen* got its start as a lending institution by accepting jugs of wine pawned as security. For further information or pawning, call or visit the main pawnshop ☏ 22484157, ✉ 22484402, ✉ Brugaten 12, PO Box 1166 Sentrum, 0107 Oslo, ⊕ http://www.lanekontoret.no

Personal finances (*Privatøkonomi*) Aside from ☞ **Taxation figures**, which are made public each year, personal finances were long a taboo topic, and consequently little information was available on them. This was in part reflected in the division of upper secondary schools (*gymnas*) into two groups, those with business-oriented curriculum (*handelsgym*) and those with all other curricula; either you studied business and thereby knew something about it, or you did not and were ignorant of it. That view has changed, triggered in part by the founding, in 1983, of ☞ **Dine Penger** (Media and Information chapter), the country's first magazine dedicated to private finances. Information is now readily available, from *Dine Penger* as well as from the ☞ **Consumer Council** (Human Rights, Consumer Rights chapter).

Saving (*Sparing*) in a bank remains one of the more common investments. This most likely is because bank deposits are safe: the State protects against bank failure through guarantees for up to NOK 2 million per account. There are more than 160 ☞ **Banks**, some with branches throughout the country, and most compete to attract savers by offering various plans for bank deposit (*bankinnskudd*). Provided other aspects, such as loyalty to a bank where you have other accounts or the convenient location of a nearby bank, are not more important, you should compare the interest schemes offered by competing banks. The schemes usually offer increasing interest for greater deposits, in stages. However, the offers vary from bank to bank. Consider two banks, A and B, both of which offer 3% interest on savings account balances up to NOK 50.000, but differ in their offerings for greater balances. Bank A offers 6% on amounts above NOK 50,000, whilst bank B offers 6% when overall balance exceeds NOK 50,000. The effect of interests they offer are shown below:

balance, NOK	Bank A	Bank B
25,000	3.0%	3.0%
50,000	3.0%	6.0%
150,000	5.0%	6.0%
300,000	5.5%	6.0%

In all cases, you should assess ☞ **Interest** in terms of the benefit you receive after tax and after inflation.

Most banks offer savings accounts (*sparekonto*) with special provisions, including:

Contractual young people's savings for housing (*Boligsparing for Ungdom – BSU*) includes a tax advantage and is offered by almost all banks and lending institutions to persons up to age 34 who will use the sum saved to buy housing. A BSU account permits you to save up to NOK 15,000 a year up to a maximum of NOK 100,000. Each year, one-fifth of the BSU sum saved is deducted from assessed tax. In all, you can save NOK 20,000 in taxes. You may use the funds saved in a BSU account for a purpose other than financing housing, but then you forfeit the tax deduction. Many banks offer borrowing advantages (*lånerett*) to BSU account holders.

Fixed rate of interest on deposits (*Fastrenteinnskudd*) is offered by a few banks and involves an agreement to fix interest paid over a period of one to several years. The advantage is that you gain if the interest rate falls. The disadvantage is that fees are usually charged for withdrawals before the end of the agreement period.

High-interest accounts (*Høyrentekonto*), including investment accounts (*kapitalkonto*) and growth accounts (*vekstkonto*) offer higher interest against restricted access (*bruksmuligheter*), such as limiting withdrawals at no charge (*gebyrfrie uttak*) and not providing check (*sjekk*) or card (*kort*) access.

Special condition accounts (*Særvilkår*) vary from bank to bank and may be aimed at particular depositors, such as retired persons. The conditions usually are similar to those for fixed rate of interest and high-interest accounts.

Securities register (*Verdipapirsentralen*) Established in 1986, the national securities register is The Norwegian Registry of Securities (*Verdipapirsentralen -VPS*) for shares (*aksjer*) and bonds (*obligasjoner*). It functions as do national securities registers in other countries, such as the Swedish Securities Register

Centre (*Värdepapperscentralen VPC*). Shareholders (*aksjonærer*) and bondholders (*obligasjonseiere*) open a securities account (*verdipapirkonto*) with a registrar (*kontofører*), usually a bank, which registers all changes in shares and bonds held in its accounts. All shares listed on the stock exchange (*børsen*) and all primary capital certificates (*grunnfondsbevis*) are registered in VPS, so share certificates (*aksjebrev*) are no longer issued. Most shares and bonds listed in accounts are held by their owners, but they may also be registered by a nominee (*nominell eier*) who acts on behalf of the beneficial (real) owner (*egentlige eier*). The investment consultant at your bank will be able to give you the full details of the relevant dealings. VPS also provides extensive information on its activities ✆ 22635300, 🖷 22635200, ✉ PO Box 6570 Rodeløkka, 0501 Oslo, ✈ http://www.vps.no

Share investment with tax relief (*Aksjesparing med skattefradrag – AMS*) has been in effect since 1982. It replaced the former savings with tax relief (*sparing med skattefradrag – SMS*) that had been instituted in 1975 and was phased out in the mid 1980s. AMS permits you to buy up to NOK 5,000 as a single person (*klasse 1*) or up to NOK 10,000 as a couple (*klasse 2*) in a ☞ **Fund** before 31st December of a tax year. The result will be a tax reduction of up to NOK 750 for a single person or up to NOK 1500 for a couple. If you take advantage of that tax reduction, you must keep the AMS investment for four years from its purchase date; thereafter you may sell it. You may sell before the four years have elapsed, but then you will lose the tax relief and a corresponding sum will be added to your taxes. Whatever the date of sale, you will be subject to ☞ **Capital gains tax** (Taxes, duties, excise chapter) on any gains realised in period that you held the AMS investment. Most AMS funds charge a subscription fee (*tegnings gebyr*) of about 3%, so you should purchase AMS shares for NOK 5154 or NOK 10,309 to realise the full AMS tax reduction. AMS has been increasingly popular, but has been debated by politicians. The tax reform of 1992 disbanded AMS and replaced it with ASG (*aksjespasring med skattefri gevinst*), but AMS was rapidly re-instated. In the late 1990s, two political parties – The Centre Party (*Senterpartiet*) and the Christian Democratic Party (*Kristelig folkeparti*) – put forth programmes calling for extended AMS and re-introduction of SMS.

The stock exchange (*Børs*) in Oslo is the *Oslo Børs*; it retains its name in English. It was founded in 1828 and now has a turnover of about NOK 1.5 billion per day of trading. It has three listings of companies:

- Main List (*Hovedlisten*) of major companies in property, finance, commerce, manufacturing, IT and communications, media and publishing, offshore, shipping, transport and other activities.
- SMB List, instituted in 1992 to offer Small and Medium-sized Companies (*Small og Mellomstore Bedrifter – SMB*) the advantages of a regulated market for trading their shares.
- PCC List, instituted in 1987, principally to permit savings banks to bring in equity capital from the market by issuing Primary Capital Certificates (PCC).

For complete details, including directory of the Norwegian securities market, fees, acts and regulations, the trading system, listing and membership, contact Oslo Børs ✆ 22341700, 🖷 22341925, ✉ PO Box 460 Sentrum, 0105 Oslo, ✉ info@ose.no, ✈ http://www.ose.no with pages in Norwegian and in English.

The stock market (*Aksjemarkedet*) is handled by the Oslo Børs, which is the country's ☞ **Stock exchange**. The activities of Oslo Børs are highly automated; for instance, all shares traded are listed with the ☞ **Securities register**, so share certificates are no longer issued. Only a registered securities firm (*verdipapirforetak*) with a seat on the exchange (*sete på børsen*) can trade there. The general procedure for private investors to start trading is:

1. Choose a registered securities firm, as listed under *Verdipapirhandel* or *Verdipapirmegling* in the Yellow Pages.
2. The firm will open a securities account (*verdipapirkonto* or *VPS konto*) as listed with the Securities register. The account is a list of the securities you hold and the trading in which you have been involved. It will be active as long as you have shares in it. Usually an account will be closed if it has had neither shares nor trading for 13 months.
3. When your account is activated, place an order (*handelsordre*) with the securities firm.
4. The securities firm will issue a receipt for the transaction.
5. Within four business days, you will receive a notice

of change (*endringsmelding*) in the post from the Securities register.

6. Your VPS account and your bank account will be credited/debited on the fourth day after the transaction is completed.

You can monitor the share price (*aksjekurs*) of your shares as well as others listed on the Oslo Børs in the financial pages (*Økonomi*) of major newspapers; *Aftenposten* and *Dagens Næringsliv* have the most comprehensive listings.

Telebanking (*Telebank*) allows you to carry out bank transactions, at any time of the day or night, from any fixed or mobile telephone with a ☞ **Telephone keypad**. The telebanking services offered by the commercial and savings banks vary, but are of two sorts. The customer account service (*Kontofon*) provides figures, such as account balance and recent transactions, and allows you to transfer funds between different accounts in the same bank. Some banks also offer printouts of Kontofon transactions via telefax. The interbank giro transfer service (*TeleGiro*) is part of the ☞ **Giro** system and permits you to pay a giro by keying in the details of it. Kontofon and TeleGiro both provide protection by requiring you to use your personal identity number (PIN) to gain access to services, and both operate using a menu system with voice prompts in Norwegian. Contact your bank branch for further details on its telebanking services and charges.

Transfer of funds (*Overføring av penger*) You can transfer funds between accounts in the same bank at the counter of any of its branches or remotely, by ☞ **Telebanking**. You can transfer funds between accounts in different banks at the counter of either bank or by using ☞ **Giro**. You can transfer funds to payees or accounts in other countries (*overføre penger til utlandet*) at the counter of your bank or by using the *ValutaGiro* for amounts up to NOK 60,000; for larger amounts, contact your bank for advice. In *ValutaGiro*, you fill out a form that resembles the Giro form, but has spaces for the currency to be transferred and for the receiving bank address code (*mottakerbanks kode*). For some 7,000 banks and other financial institutions world-wide, a bank's address code is its SWIFT code. SWIFT stands for Society for Worldwide Interbank Financial Telecommunications, which is an international Electronic

Data Interchange (EDI) network owned by some 1,600 member banks, including the central banks of most countries. (The US Federal Reserve is not a member, but it participates in some types of payments.) It is the most used global system for electronic transfer, carrying some three million transactions a day. So in everyday banking language, "wire transfer" usually means transfer via SWIFT. In Norway, most banks have SWIFT addresses (*SWIFT adresse*) and can both accept and expedite SWIFT transfers. If you have a *Brevgiro* facility on your Norwegian bank account, you may post a *ValutaGiro*; several banks now use the Postal Bank (*Postbanken*) for all such transfers; ask your bank for details.

Travellers cheques (*Reisesjekker*) are no longer used as much as they were in the days before ☞ **Payment cards** became commonplace. There are no country-wide statistics on travellers cheques. However, the combined figures of the leading commercial ☞ **Banks** indicate that the turnover in travellers cheques dropped steadily throughout the 1990s to half its level at the end of the 1980s. Another indication is that ☞ **Norges Bank** no longer lists travellers cheques in its annual statistics of foreign exchange transfers into and out of the country. The Eurocheque once was a much-used means of international payment and consequently was favoured by tavellers. But its use also dwindled through the 1990s, and effective 1 January 1999, Europay, the Eurocheque agent in Norway, suspended it. So if you receive a Eurocheque, you cannot cash it in Norway, and consequently should return it to the sender. Despite the overall trend, banks and travel bureaux recommend travellers cheques for travel to areas where payment card use is not yet commonplace, such as in Eastern Europe or some countries in Africa and Asia. The two leading travellers cheques are American Express and Thomas Cook/Master Card. American Express cheques are available in US dollars, Euros, German Marks, French Francs, British Pounds and Swiss Francs, and Thomas Cook/Master Card cheques are available in US Dollars, Euros, German Marks, British Pounds, French Francs and Japanese Yen. Travellers cheques in Norwegian Kroner are also available. Most larger banks in cities keep stocks of travellers cheques and expedite orders at their counters, whilst smaller banks may not keep stocks, but always can fill orders within two to three bank days.

Wills and inheritance (*Testament og arv*) The Inheritance Act (*Arveloven*) sets forth the requirements for wills and inheritance and covers a wide range of situations and personal relationships which may be involved. The principal provisions are summarised here.

A will (*testament*) is a document in which a person specifies the way that his/her estate (*formue*) is to be distributed to heirs (*arvinger*) after death. For a will to be valid, it must be in writing (*skriftlig*), and the person writing it, known as a testator (*arvelater*) must be at least 18 years old and must have the will signed by at least two witnesses (*vitner*), both of whom must be present at the same time.

There are four classes of heirs: relatives, spouses, designated beneficiaries and the State.

Relatives are divided into three classes that designate the order of inheritance (*arvefølge*), which means that heirs in the first class have first priority on inheritance. If there are no heirs in the first class, inheritance goes to heirs in the second class, and so on to the third class. In the first class are dependent heirs (*livsarvinger*) including children, grandchildren and great-grandchildren. The second class, which includes parents and, if the parents are dead, their children (the brothers and sisters of the testator). The third class includes grandparents and their children and their children's dependants, that is, aunts, uncles and cousins.

If a testator has dependent heirs (*livsarvinger*), they are entitled to a mandatory part of the inheritance (*pliktdelsarv*) which the will cannot take from them. This means, for instance, that a parent cannot write a will which deprives a child of inheritance. The mandatory part is equivalent to two-thirds of the total estate, and is limited to NOK one million from each parent for each child and NOK 200,000 for each grandchild.

A spouse also is entitled to a mandatory part of an inheritance. However, a separated (*separert*) or divorced (*skilt*) spouse has no such right. For instance, if a couple have joint property (*felleseie*) and have made no statement of separate property (*særeie*), when one of them dies, the survivor is entitled to half the joint estate or an amount equal to four times the ☞ **Basic sum**, whichever is greater, plus at least one-quarter of the remainder (half or less of the joint estate). The dependent heirs, such as the couple's children, are then entitled to two-thirds of one-half of the joint estate of their parents. The surviving parent may execute the estate or to postpone execution of it (*uskiftet bo*).

Designated beneficiaries may inherit amounts up to limits set by the provisions for dependent heirs and spouses.

The State inherits an estate if a deceased (*avdødde*) person has no relatives entitled to inheritance and has made no will.

A heir may relinquish the right to an inheritance (*avkall på arv*) by giving notice (*avslag på arv*) before the will is executed. For instance, parents with children may elect to relinquish an inheritance and transfer it to their children, in order to minimise inheritance tax (*arveavgiften*).

The execution of a will (*skifteoppgjør*) has two principal steps. First, the probate court (*skifterett*) in a city or town must be notified of the death (*dødsfall*) of the testator. In rural districts, notice can be given to the sheriff (*lensmann*). Then the heirs can elect the form of execution, which may be either private (*privat skifte*) or public (*offentlig skifte*). In practice, legal heirs who agree completely on the execution of a will usually prefer the private alternative, as public execution takes longer and entails a fee for the services of a public administrator of the estate (*bobestyrer*). However, if a will is challenged on any grounds, such as because it has not been properly executed or a rightful heir has not been included, the execution must be public, by the probate court.

If need be, you may consult a lawyer expert in inheritance law (*arverett*) to draw up your will or assist in the execution of an estate.

Business and work
(*Næringslivet og arbeid*)

A broad overview of business and work Norway has a mixed economy in which most companies are private, but many national services are provided by public corporations owned by the State. Moreover, health care and education are provided mostly by public sector organisations, though private health care and private education are increasing. As elsewhere in Europe, many nationalised business monopolies have recently been privatised and their markets opened to competition. For instance, in November 1994, the Telecommunications Administration was reorganised as a private company, Telenor AS, with the shares owned by the State, and in January 1998 the telecommunications market was deregulated. In December 1996, Norwegian Railways was reorganised into a private operating company, NSB BA, with the shares owned by the State, and a permanent way and fixed facilities agency, the Norwegian National Rail Administration (NNRA). Consequently, private companies may now compete with Telenor in telecommunications and private operators may now compete with NSB BA and operate trains on NNRA rails.

Today, less than a tenth of the workforce is employed in agriculture, forestry or fishing, the traditional occupations of centuries gone by. Most now work in the industrial sector or in the service sector, as in trade and transport, education and health service, or in industry. The service sector is gaining. In 1980, eight women in ten and five men in ten were employed in the service sector. Fourteen years later, in 1994, 84% of all working women were in the service sector, the highest percentage in Europe. The corresponding figure for men was 57%, for a second place in Europe, just one percentage point behind the Netherlands with 58%.

With few exceptions, all jobs are open to all persons qualified for them, regardless of sex, ethnic background or religious beliefs. Work permits are required for all foreign nationals, except for citizens of other Nordic countries (Denmark, Finland, the Faeroes, Iceland and Sweden), but otherwise all foreign nationals are treated equally with Norwegians in applying for work. Women and men have equal rights in work, education and care for children in the home. Increasingly, women work outside the home and mean take more responsibility for housework and child care and upbringing.

Unemployment is low. Consequently, in many parts of the country, finding work is difficult, particularly for inexperienced young people, women who have been at home for several years, older people or immigrants. However, numerous skills upgrading programmes are available to better equip people for the challenges of today's labour market.

Annual vacations are relatively long, four weeks plus one day for all employees and five weeks for all employees age 60 and older. The average work week is 37.5 hours, and the average work year is 1725 hours.

Child labour (*Barnearbeid*) Children less than 15 years old cannot be employed in ordinary work, such as performed by adults. They can take light jobs, such as delivering newspapers outside school hours. The ☞ **Working hours** for young persons 15 to 18 years old cannot include night work or overtime, and their employment is subject to specific safety regulations. School pupils up to 18 years old must have four weeks of ☞ **Vacation** each year, of which three weeks must be in summer.

Collective bargaining and labour disputes The ☞ **Employer organisations** and the ☞ **Unions** have a basic agreement (*hovedavtalen*) which sets forth the rules for collective bargaining and for resolving labour disputes, as well as specifies how management-labour relations are to be conducted at workplaces. Moreover, two laws deal with these matters, the Act relating to labour disputes (*Lov om arbeidstvister*) and the Act regarding wage boards in labour disputes (*Lov om lønnsnemd i arbeidslivet*).

The employer organisations and the unions negotiate wages and working conditions in a yearly National Agreement on Wages (*Tariffoppgjøret*). When negotiations are in progress, both the employers organisations and the unions may press their demands and take action if necessary. The agreement reached (*tariffavtale*) is valid for a contract period (*tariffperiode*) of two years but can be re-negotiated or terminated after one year.

The principal means of action are strikes (*streik*) by the unions and lockouts (*lockout*) by the employers. Strikes or lockouts during the contract period are considered unlawful, and any persons involved in them are legally responsible for compensatory claims which may be made by the other party, such as for loss of income. In practice, there are few unlawful strikes or lockouts. Moreover, in the ten year (1988-97) averages of working days lost each year per 1,000 employees for the 23 ☞ **OECD** (Government and Social Services chapter) countries, Norway is just the median country: 11 countries are more strike-prone and 11 are less.

Commerce and service (*Handel og service*) accounts for close to a fifth of the GDP of the country and employs three in ten workers. Alone, wholesale and retail trade employs a seventh of the workforce, about as much as does all of industry. The sector is expanding rapidly, and by the year 2030 is expected to account for nearly half the GDP and engage 45% of the workforce.

There are now some 34 branch organisations covering the A-Z of commerce and service, as well as its global aspects, such as the International Chamber of Commerce (ICC). Most are affiliated with the Federation of Norwegian Commerce and Service Enterprises (*Handels- og Servicenæringens Hovedorganisasjon – HSH*). For further information, particularly if you contemplate starting a business and seek the organisation for it, contact HSH ✆ 22541700, ☎ 22561700, ✉ PO Box 2900 Solli, 0230 Oslo, ✉ info@hsh-org-no, ⊛ http://www.hsh-org.no

Commercial terms The standard delivery terms first compiled by the International Chamber of Commerce (ICC) in 1936 are used in all international trade. They are called "Incoterms" in all languages and were updated most recently in 1990. There now are 13 Incoterms in four categories:

E-terms: a seller makes goods available to a buyer at the seller's own premises; one term, EXW (Ex Works).

F-terms: a seller agrees to deliver goods to a carrier designated by a buyer; three terms: FCA (Free Carrier), FAS (Free Alongside Ship), FOB (Free On Board). Note: Norway uses this international definition of FOB, which differs from that used in the USA and Canada, where FOB means 'Ex Works'.

C-terms: a seller contracts for transportation to a buyer but assumes no responsibility and bears no additional costs after despatch; four terms: CFR (Cost and Freight), CIF (Cost, Insurance and Freight), CPT (Carriage Paid To), CIP (Carriage and Insurance Paid To).

D-terms: a seller bears all costs and risks in transporting goods to the destination country; five terms: DAF (Delivered At Frontier), DES (Delivered Ex Ship), DEQ (Delivered Ex Quay), DDU (Delivered Duty Unpaid), DDP (Delivered Duty Paid).

Publications on Incoterms are available from the ICC Business Bookstore at the ICC head office ✆ +33 149532828, ☎ +33 149532942, ✉ 38, Cours Albert 1er, F-75008 Paris, France, ⊛ http://www.iccwbo.org or from any of the ICC national committees in more than 60 countries. The Norwegian Committee is *ICC Norge* ✆ 22541700, ☎ 22561700, ✉ PO Box 2900 Solli, 0230 Oslo.

Company organisation (*Foretaksform*) is similar to that of other countries in Europe. There are four general types of organisation.

Sole proprietorship (*Enkeltmannsforetak*): One person provides all the capital and bears all the risk. There is no distinction between the owner's private income and fortune and that of the company. Accordingly, the company profits are the owner's income and are so treated tax-wise. There is no specific designation in a company name to indicate that it is a sole proprietorship.

General partnership (*Ansvasrlig selskap*): Two or more persons provide the capital and bear all risk. As opposed to a sole proprietorship, a general partnership is a juristic person (*juridisk person*) with its own income and fortune. General partnerships may be undivided, in which all partners are individually and collectively responsible for all liabilities, or divided, in which the overall liability of the company is divided between the partners. The undivided form is simply called *Ansvarlig selskap*, abbreviated *Ans.* The divided form is called *Ansvasrlig selskap med delt ansvar*, abbreviated *DA*.

Limited liability company (*Aksjeselskap*): The capital for the company is provided by several people, with the liability of each limited to the amount of share capital invested. A limited liability company is a juristic person (*juridisk person*) with its own income and fortune and its own responsibility for liability. There are two principal forms of limited liability companies. In terms of numbers of companies, the most common form is private ownership, in which the persons who provided the capital to found the company own it and are entitled to share its profits. The share capital at the time of founding must be at least NOK 100,000. This form of company is called *Aksjeselskap*, abbreviated *AS*, *As*, or *as*, sometimes with a slash between the letters, as *A/S*. A public limited company is a limited liability company which can offer its shares to the public, as by trading on a stock exchange. Share holders share the profits of the company and are free to trade their shares. The share capital at the time of first public offer and stock exchange listing must be at least NOK 1,000,000. This form of company is called an *Allmenne aksjeselskap*, where the word *allmenne* means "the general public", and the name is abbreviated *ASA*. In other words, all Norwegian companies traded on the stock exchange are *ASA*.

Co-operative society (*Samvirkelag*): A co-operative society is a company owned and managed by a society of persons or groups of persons who intend not to make a profit but to provide benefits to the society's members, such as do ☞ **Co-operative shops** (Shopping chapter). The most common form is an *Andelslag* ("Share society"), abbreviated AL.

Discrimination (*Diskriminering*) in workplaces is illegal: there should be no job bias on the basis of sex (*kjønn*), religious belief (*trosbekjennelse*), race (*rase*), skin colour (*hudfarge*), ethnic background (*etnisk opprinnelse*), lifestyle (*leveform*) or homosexuality (*homofil legning*).

Nonetheless, discrimination exists. In 1996, a survey conducted by Norway Statistics reported that of the immigrants surveyed, one in six felt that discrimination was the cause of their not being offered jobs for which they had applied.

If you feel that you are subjected to discrimination at work, you should notify your immediate superior. If your supervisor does not act, you should contact the safety representative (*verneombud*), the union representative (*tillitsvalgt*), the ☞ **Unions** or the ☞ **Labour inspectorate**.

If you feel that you are subject to discrimination because of your sex – in most cases, because you are a woman – you also may contact the ☞ **Gender equality** (Human Rights, Consumer Rights chapter) ombudsman (*Likestillingsombudet*).

EEA nationals' work rights (*EØS arbeidsvilkår*)
The principal EEA provisions concerning individuals relate to work and residence. If you are a citizen of an EEA country, you may stay in Norway and seek work for a three-month period without having to obtain a work permit or a residence permit, provided that you can support yourself. If you find work within three months, you have the right to remain in Norway, but you must apply for a residence permit. As a job seeker from an EEA country, you are entitled to the same job placement services as are Norwegian job seekers. If you are entitled to unemployment benefit in your home country and have been registered there as wholly unemployed for four consecutive weeks, you may, before coming to Norway, apply to the employment service in your home country to have your unemployment benefits paid to you in Norway for up to three months. As a citizen of an EEA country, you also may study or set up business as a self-employed person in Norway under the same conditions and rules as Norwegian citizens. For further information, contact the nearest EURopean Employment Service (EURES) office (*Arbeidskontor* or *EURES* in the Pink Pages) or call the national freephone ✆ 80033166. There now are EURES services in Bergen, Bodø, Oslo, Stavanger, Trondheim, Tromsø and Ålesund and offices are planned in other cities; for current information in English, contact a EURES office or view the Directorate of Labour Internet site ✉ http://www.aetat.no with pages in Norwegian and in English.

Employer organisations (*Arbeidsgiverorganisasjoner*) represent employers in collective bargaining, promote legislation and policies conducive to business and advise and set standards for member companies, such as standard pension agreements. They are, so to speak, the employers' equivalent of the ☞ **Unions** to which their employees belong.

The largest employer organisation is The Confederation of Norwegian Business and Industry (*Næringslivets Hovedorganisasjon – NHO*), which has more than 15,500 member companies that together account for 40% of the country's GDP ✆ 23088000, 🖷 23088001, ✉ PO Box 5250 Majorstua, 0303 Oslo, ✉ http://www.nho.no with pages in Norwegian and in English.

The Ministry of Labour and Government Administration (*Arbeids- og administrasjonsdepartementet – AAD*) represents the State as an employer ✆ 22249090, ✈ 22242710, ✉ PO Box 8004 Dep, 0030 Oslo, ⊜ http://odin.dep.no/aad with pages in Norwegian and in English.

The Association of Local and Regional Authorities (*Kommunenenes Sentralforbund – KS*) represents municipalities and counties as employers ✆ 22947700, ✈ 22832222, ✉ PO Box 1378 Vika, 0114 Oslo, ✍ ks@kommorg.no, ⊜ http://www.ks.no with pages in Norwegian and in English.

The Norwegian Association of Publicly-owned Companies (*Norges Arbeidsgiverforening for Virksomheter med Offentlig Tilknytning – NAVO*) represents private companies owned by the State ✆22419600, ✈ 22419661, ✉ PO Box 1511 Vika, 0117 Oslo.

Franchising is the granting of rights to others to sell products or services: one company (the franchisor) grants a licence to another (the franchisee) which entitles the franchisee to conduct business under the trade name of the franchisor and to make use of all the support necessary to establish, maintain and promote business. The outlets and shops of many international chains, particularly in fast food services, actually are franchised and are owned and operated as local businesses. In Norway, there are more than 180 franchised trade name chains, including:

- Car hire: Rent-A-Wreck.
- Convenience shops: 7 Eleven.
- Estate agents: Postbanken Eiendomsmegling.
- Fast foods and restaurants: Big Horn Steak House, By the Way, Kaffebrenneriet, McDonalds, Piccolo, Subways and Veikroer.
- Fitness centres: SATS.
- Perfume and toiletry supplies: Bodyshop and Estetique.
- Photographic supplies: Chrono and Click.
- Supermarkets: Rema 1000.
- Textiles: Princess gardiner.

If you wish to start a franchised business, contact the head office of the company listed in the Pink Pages (most of the head offices are in the Oslo area). Other sources of information on franchising are:

Norwegian Franchise Association (*Norges Franchise Forening – NFF*), the national member of EFF to which most franchisors belong, head office

✆ 22541700, ✈ 22561700, ✉ PO Box 2900 Solli, 0230 Oslo.

FranchiseNet, an inter- Scandinavian information centre ✆ +46 31836936, ✈ +46 31811072, ✉ PO Box 5243, S-40224 Göteborg, Sweden, ✍ info@franchisenet.net, ⊜ http://www.franchisenet.net with pages in Danish, English, Finnish, Norwegian and Swedish.

European Franchise Federation – EFF, with European and global contacts, including to the World Franchise Council (WFC) and the International Franchise Association (IFA) in North America; head office in Brussels ✆ +32 25201607, ✈ +32 25201735, ✉ Bd. de l'Humanité, 116/2, B-1070 Brussels, Belgium, ✍ eff-franchise@euronet.be

Health, Safety and Environment – HSE (*Helse, miljø og sikkerhet – HMS*) is the collective name of all the professions concerned with occupational health and safety, the working environment and the environmental aspects of business and industry. Typical HSE measures include ☞ **Occupational health services**. Four governmental agencies are involved in monitoring adherence to the various rules and regulations involved: the Directorate for Fire Inspection and Explosion Prevention (*Direktoratet for brann- og eksplosjonsvern*), the ☞ **Labour inspectorate**, the Norwegian Directorate for Product and Electrical Safety (*Produkt- og elektrisitetstilsynet*) and the State Pollution Control Authority (*Statens forurensningstilsyn*). The ☞ **Employer organisations** and the ☞ **Unions** also have extensive HSE activities. All firms with more than 40 employees are required to have specific programmes for security, which involves all matters related to threats to business and industry, including espionage, sabotage, fraud, organised crime, computer crime and other crime, as well as preparedness and civil defence measures. Accordingly, the Norwegian Industrial Safety and Security Organisation (*Næringslivets sikkerhetsorganisasjon – NSO*) and the Norwegian Industrial Security Council (*Næringslivets sikkerhetsråd – NSR*) extend the HSE field to include security.

Jobs (*Jobber*) The ways of finding, applying for, starting and dismissing or resigning from jobs are similar to those elsewhere in Europe.

Finding a job You may look for work yourself by reading the job vacancy (*stilling ledig* or *stillings-*

marked) classified advertisements (*annonser*) of the daily newspapers or the ☞ **Norwegian Gazette** (Media and Information chapter) and then calling or writing the organisations offering jobs of interest. But if you have yet to learn Norwegian well enough to read the job vacancy advertisements or otherwise need help, you should consult the nearest office of the Public Employment Service, which is country-wide and free. It is so comprehensive and widely available that there are only a few private employment agencies, most for temps or jobs in specialist sectors. Both public and private services are listed under *Arbeidsformidling* in the Yellow Pages, and the Public Employment Service offices are listed under *Arbeidskontoret* or *Arbeidsformidling* in the Pink Pages. The Norwegian Labour Market Administration (*Arbeidsmarkedetaten*) has a freephone ☏ 80033166 that you can call to ask about job vacancies, educational courses, school and college vacancies and the like. It also has supports an extensive web site ⊕ http://aetat.no with pages in Norwegian and summary pages in English, and publishes two detailed pamphlets, *Norway, Access to Job Vacancies* and *Looking for Work in Norway*, both available at the offices of the Public Employment Service.

Applying for a job Most employers prefer written job applications, but some prefer direct contact. In either case, you should prepare a written application, preferably in Norwegian or in English. It should contain a resume (*resyme*) of your background and qualifications for the job, including your name, address, telecommunications numbers, date of birth, nationality, languages in which you are fluent, education and previous experience. You should attach photocopies of your educational certificates, such as school records and college or university degrees (*eksamenspapirer*), as well as records of previous jobs held (*attester*) and the details of your residence permit. If any of these certificates or records are not in Norwegian or English, you should have them translated; your embassy or consulate probably can advise you on how certified translations may be made. The local Public Employment Service Office will be able to advise you on your application. If you are called in for an interview, be sure to arrive before the appointed hour to give yourself time to find the person who will interview you. Normally, at the end of an interview, you will be told whether or not you will be considered for the job and when an offer may be made.

Starting a job For almost all jobs, you should have an employment contract (*arbeidskontrakt*). In it there should be a clear specification of your wages (*lønn*), working hours (*arbeidstid*), whether your are to be a permanent employee (*fast stilling*) or are only temporary (*midlertidig*), whether you are to work full time (*full stilling*) or part time (*deltidsstilling*), period of notice (*oppsigelsestid*) and other details of the job. If you are hired as a permanent, full-time employee, you usually will have a trial period (*prøvetid*) of up to six months. During the trial period, you may resign or may be dismissed on two weeks' notice.

Resigning or being dismissed from a job After successful completion of the trial period, the period of notice is longer, initially one month and increasing to three months after ten years of employment, and then longer after age 50. A dismissal or resignation (*oppsigelse*) must be given in writing. If you are dismissed, your employer must inform you of your negotiating rights and, if you so request, state the reason for your dismissal. If you feel that you have been unjustly dismissed, you may put in a complaint to the union representative (*tillitsvalgt*) at the company or the ☞ **Labour Inspectorate**. When you leave a job, you should ask your employer for a work record (*sluttattest*) which gives the details of your employment, including your job description, duration of employment and the employers assessment of your performance. You will need work records in applying for future jobs.

Labour costs (*Lønnskostnader*) are high, both because wages for time worked are high and because additional wage costs, including employer social security contributions and holiday pay are also high. In 1997, Norway ranked fourth highest in the world in labour costs, behind Belgium, Switzerland and Germany. In that year, Norwegian skilled industrial workers were the fourth best paid in Europe, school teachers the seventh best paid, department managers the seventh best paid and secretaries the fifth best paid.

The Labour inspectorate (*Arbeidstilsynet*) is a government agency under the Ministry of Local Government and Regional Development (*Kommunal- og regionaldepartementet*). It acts primarily to promote safety and prevent accidents in workplaces, to monitor working environments and to ensure that laws on the ☞ **Working enviornment** are compiled with. The Act on the Working environment has a broad scope, so the Labour inspectorate has numerous duties, ranging from monitoring and advising on the handling of hazardous materials to publishing guidelines and compiling statistics on workplace safety. It performs its tasks both centrally, at its head office in Oslo, and at the local level, in 13 offices around the country (*Arbeidstilsynets distriktskontorer*). At your workplace, you most likely will have a safety delegate (*verneombud*) elected by the employees who acts as the contact with the Labour inspectorate and consequently handles all working environment complaints from the employees. However, as a private person, you also may contact a district office directly should you have a legitimate complaint related to any aspect of the working environment. For instance, you might call a district office to complain of an inadequately fenced construction site that may pose a hazard to passing children or to report careless removal of asbestos siding that spreads toxic asbestos dust. The district office may then act by sending out an inspector, who has the authority to require corrective measures or to stop works if need be. The districts and the cities where their offices are located are: 1 Moss, 2 Oslo, 3 Hamar, 4 Drammen, 5 Tønsberg, 6 Kristiansand S., 7 Stavanger, 8 Bergen, 9 Ålesund, 10 Trondheim, 11 Bodø, 12 Tromsø, 13 Skien. For queries or complaints, contact the nearest district office at the address and telephone number listed in the Pink Pages. For overall information, contact the head office of the Directorate of Labour Inspectorate (*Direktoratet for Arbeidstilsynet*) ✆ 22957000, ☎ 22466214, ✉ PO Box 8103 Dep, 0032 Oslo, ✆ http://www.arbeidstilsynet.no

Norwegian titles and approval of foreign education (*Norske titler og godkjenning av utenlandsk utdanning*) Professional and vocational titles are important because they often are prerequisites for positions and usually are included in employment contracts. Most of them are legally protected. This means that you must have the recognised qualifications for a title in order to use it. For residents educated within the country, the matter is straightforward. For instance, if you are an engineering graduate of the Norwegian University of Science and

Technology (NTNU) you may use the title *sivilingeniør* which is equivalent to "Chartered Engineer" in English. But if you are a resident or a foreign citizen who was educated abroad, you must apply for approval of your education in order to use the relevant title. In principle, approval is straightforward and amounts to showing that your education meets the same requirements as the equivalent education in Norway. However, in practice, showing equivalence can be complex. Curricula vary from country to country and there are many international agreements on transfer of qualifications, not least those applying within ☞ **EFTA, EEA and EU** (Government and Social Services chapter). Moreover, curricula change and new agreements are continually made. Fortunately, the agencies responsible for approval keep comprehensive lists of curricula and agreements and consequently can readily assess applications or answer questions concerning titles. The requirements for approval vary by profession. So you should first contact the responsible agency to find out what you must do to file an application for approval. The agencies responsible for approval of higher education titles are listed below. For certification of a vocational title, contact the trade organisation involved.

Architects and Engineers: Chartered Architect (*Sivilarkitekt*) and Chartered Engineer (*Sivilingeniør*): Contact International Section, Norwegian University of Science and Technology (*Internasjonal seksjon, NTNU*) ✆ 73595700, ☎ 73595210, ✉ Gløshaugen, 7491 Trondheim.

Business: MBA or equivalent (*Siviløkonom*): contact the International office of the Norwegian School of Economics and Business Administration (*Internasjonalt kontor, Norges Handelshøyskole*) ✆ 55959300, ☎ 552548383, ✉ Helleveien 30, 5045 Bergen.

Education: Teacher, secondary-school teacher, lecturer (*Lærer, Adjunkt, Lektor*): contact Basic School Department, Ministry of Education, Research and Church Affairs (*Kirke-, utdannings- og forskningsdepartementet – KUF*) ✆ 22249090, ✉ PO Box 8119 Dep, 0032 Oslo.

Health services: Bioengineer (*Bioingeniør*), Chiropractor (*Kiropraktor*), Dentist (*Tannlege*), Ergonomist (*Ergoterapeut*), Medical Doctor (*Lege*), Midwife (*Jordmor*), Nurse (*Sykepleier*), Orthopaedic engineer (*Ortopedingeniør*), Physical Therapist (*Fysioterapeut*),

Psychologist (*Psykolog*), Radiologist (*Radiograf*) and Welfare Nurse (*Vernepleier*): contact Chief County Medical Officer in Oslo (*Fylkeslegen i Oslo*) ℡ 22003900, ℻ 22003910, ✉ PO Box 8041 Dep, 0031 Oslo.

Veterinary (*Veterinær*): contact Ministry of Agriculture, Department for Food Production and Health (*Landbruksdepartementet, Avdeling for matproduksjon og helse*) ℡ 22249426, ℻ 22249559, ✉ PO Box 8007 Dep, 0030 Oslo.

The Occupational health service (*Bedriftshelsetjeneste*) of an organisation aims to promote employee health at work. Larger organisations often have a company doctor (*bedriftslege*) who monitors the working environment and employee health. The occupational health service and the company doctor are concerned only with the working environment and not with general employee health outside the workplace. So for health matters not connected with your work, make an appointment with a general practitioner or specialist.

Occupational injury benefit (*Yrkesskadetrygd*)
If you are injured at your workplace, you may be entitled to an occupational injury benefit (*yrkesskadetrygd*). You need not have been paying National Insurance (*Folketrygd*) contributions to be eligible. Your employer is required to notify the National Insurance office and the ☞ **Labour inspectorate** of all injuries sufficiently serious to require medical attention.

Parental leave (*Foreldre permisjon*) applies principally to pregnancy and maternity but also to adoption. A woman is entitled to parental leave provided that she has been in paid employment for at least six of the ten months prior to giving birth. The father is also entitled to parental benefit provided that both he and the mother have been in paid employment for the same six of ten months. Before birth or adoption, parents may choose a benefit period of either 42 weeks at full pay or 53 weeks at 80% pay in connection with birth, or 39 weeks at fully pay or 49 weeks at 80% pay in connection with adoption. Parents may share the benefit period between them. However, specific weeks are designated for each. The mother must take three weeks of the benefit prior to birth or forfeit them. Six weeks after birth are reserved for the mother and four for the father. Moreover, parents are entitled to take up to one year of leave without pay in addition to the pregnancy and birth, adoption, or assuming care of foster children. For complete details, see *The rights of parents of small children in Norway*, booklet compiled by five government agencies and published in September 1997 for distribution by National Insurance offices (*Trygdekontor*) and available in Norwegian and English editions.

Salaries and wages (*Gasje og lønn*) are usually paid monthly to all permanent employees. Traditionally, a salary (*gasje*) is a fixed annual amount paid in monthly installments to a professional person, whilst a wage (*lønn*) is calculated on an hourly rate paid in weekly or monthly amounts to an industrial worker. However, that distinction has nearly disappeared, particularly in Norwegian, where almost all earnings are called *lønn*. There are three principal types: fixed earning (*fast lønn*), hourly rate (*timelønn*) and piecework (*akkordlønn*), as well as combinations of two of the principal types. If you have a permanent job with regular pay, you should open an earnings account (*lønnskonto*) in a bank and give your employer the account number, so you can be paid by direct deposit to it. The direct deposit to a *lønnskonto* is both quick, because you don't have to go to a bank branch with a cheque, and convenient, because your pay deposit is made even when you are away. With each payment of your earnings, you will receive a earnings slip (*lønnsslip*) with the details of earnings, tax and other deductions. Taxes are deduced according to your tax level, as stated on your tax card (*skattekort*). Other deductions may include tax previously due (*skyldig skatt*) or any child maintenance (*barnebidrag*) you may be required to pay if you are divorced. Your employer cannot deduct other expenses, such as rent or meal allowance, unless you have a written agreement that specifically permits the deductions.

Scale of travelling expenses (Reiseregulativ) almost always means the governmental scale for travelling expenses (*Regulativ for reiser på statens regning*). Compensation for travelling expenses according to this scale is accepted by tax authorities. Consequently the scale is widely used, both in the public and private sectors. It covers both domestic

travel (*reiser innenlands*) and travel abroad (*reiser i utlandet*), and the maximum amounts that can be charged without receipts for food (*kostgodtgjørelse*), lodging (*nattillegg*) and use of private car (*bruk av egen bil*) and other means of transport (*andre skyssmidler*) are set forth. The scale is periodically revised and available on-line at
⊕ http://odin.dep.no/aad/publ/reiser/

Self-employment (*Selvstendig nærings-drivende*) If you wish to work for yourself and not by employed by anyone else or any company, you have two alternative approaches to self-employment. First, you may freelance (same word in Norwegian), as do some writers, and submit your ☞ **Tax card** (Taxes chapter) to all companies for whom you work. Each company will then deduct taxes according to the rate specified on your tax card. From the tax viewpoint, at the end of the year, all the companies that paid for your services and deduced taxes from amounts paid to you have employed you. Second, you may find that ☞ **Starting a business**, such as a sole proprietorship, ☞ **Company organisation** may be more profitable. The general guidelines for starting your own business are outlined in a brochure published by the ☞ **The Directorate of Immigration** (Government and Social Services chapter), entitled *Work and Tax*, December 1994, ISBN 82-427-0276-4. The complete details of starting a business are given in a brochure published in Norwegian only by the Ministry of Trade and Industry (*Nærings- og handelsdepartementet*) *Formelle krav for foretaksetableringer* ("Formal requirements for establishing businesses"), publication K-0512B, July 1988.

Shadow economy (*svart økonomi*), also known as the underground economy, the parallel economy, the second economy, the black economy or just the black market, exists throughout the world. Although the shadow economy includes national and international criminal activities, most of it consists of transactions in ordinary goods and services that are off the books but otherwise are legal. High taxation and regulation of labour and product markets are believed to be its principal causes. Typically, if you pay a cleaner or a tradesman in cash without receipt or neglect to include some income received on your tax return, you participate in the shadow economy.

Estimates of the overall size of the shadow economy vary; the European Union (EU) believes that it may account for 7% to 16% of the total economic activity in Europe. In an official report released 1 February 1999, the Directorate of Taxes (*Skattedirektoratet*) revised its previous estimate of the Norwegian shadow economy of 5% – 6% of the GDP upwards, to at least double that figure. Professor Friedrich Schneider of the faculty of Social and Economic Sciences at Johannes Kepler University, Linz, Germany, has studied the shadow economies of Europe and other industrialised countries by comparing money in circulation, total expenditures, interest trends and other factors. His figures, which are higher than the EU estimates, are quoted in international magazines, including The Economist. In 1999 he estimated that the shadow economy in Norway accounted for about 20% of the country's GDP, less than in Italy, Spain, Belgium and Sweden, but more than in many other countries.

Sick leave (*Sykefravær*) You are eligible for paid sick leave after you have worked for at least two weeks for an employer. If you are ill and unable to work you should telephone or otherwise notify your employer as soon as possible, so you may receive sickness benefits (*sykepenger*) from the first day of your absence from work. If you anticipate being ill for no more than three calendar days, you need do no more, as you are deemed to have given self-certified notice (*egenmelding*) of your absence. You may use *egenmelding* up to four times a year. However, if you are ill for more than three calendar days, you must have a doctor's certificate of your illness (*sykemelding fra lege*), which you should give to your employer as soon as possible. Note that calendar days count; if you are ill and away from work on Friday, the following Saturday and Sunday count in the three days. Your employer is responsible for your paid sick leave for the first two weeks of an illness. Thereafter, ☞ **National Insurance** (Government and Social Services chapter) pays your wage. With few exceptions, paid sick leave is equal to your normal pay, and you pay normal taxes on it.

You are entitled to sick leave to care for an ill child for whom you are responsible, provided the child is age 12 or less, or age 16 or less if the child is chronically ill or handicapped. You can take up to 10 days sick leave per calendar year to attend to sick children, up to 15 days if you have two or more children, or up to 20 days if one child is chronically ill or handicapped and up to 30 days if two or more children are chronically ill or handicapped.

For further information on sick leave and sick pay, contact the nearest National Insurance Office, listed under *Trygdekontor* in the Pink Pages.

In the late 1990s, overall sick leave in Norway averaged 6.5% of all working hours.

Starting your own business (*Etablere din egen bedrift*) If you are at least 18 years old and are either a citizen of Norway or another Nordic country or a foreign citizen with a residence permit and a work permit, you may start your own business. Starting involves three steps:
1) Decide on the form of ☞ **Company organisation**.
2) Complete the required registrations. For details and forms, see the booklet, *Samordnet register-melding* (Co-ordinated registration), available from all agencies concerned:
- The business registry (*Foretaksregister*) at the ☞ **Brønnøysund Register Centre** (Registrations, Rights, Licences chapter). All *AS* companies and *Ans* companies in retail trade or with more than five employees must register and will be assigned an enterprise number. Other *Ans* companies are not required to register but may if they wish.
- The local tax office (*Ligningskontoret*). Depending on the nature of business, the tax office will calculate advance payment of tax or advance tax witholding.
- National Insurance Office (*Trygdekontor*) if the company has any employees, including yourself. The company will then have an employer number.
- The county tax office (*Fylkesskattekontor*) for all businesses whose activities involve VAT (*MVA*) and for all businesses with an annual revenue of more than NOK 30,000.
3) Complete any special registrations that may be necessary, such as with:
- Chief county medical officer (*Fylkeslege*) for a health services practice.
- Food control authority (*Næringsmiddeltilsyn*) for grocery shops and eating places.
- Motor vehicle inspectorate (*Biltilsynet*) for a car workshop.

Many municipalities (*kommune*) have business departments (*næringsetat*) which provide advice on the paperwork involved in starting a business. Oslo has a dedicated office, *Servicekontoret for næringslivet* ("Service office for business") ✆ 22860110, ✉ 22860130, ✉ Tollbugt. 27, 0157 Oslo, and publishes a guide for new businesses, *Hvem gjør hva for næringslivet* ("Who does what for business").

If you wish to start a business, you might consider ☞ **Franchising**, which offers the advantage of a recognised brand and a ready-made concept.

If you wish to farm and settle in the countryside, you might consider one of the many ☞ **Farms** (Housing chapter) that are for sale or lease.

Unemployment benefits (*Arbeidsledighets-trygd*) If you are dismissed from your job, you are entitled to unemployment benefits, provided you are a Norwegian citizen or have a valid work permit and have earned a certain minimum gross income in the last, or one of the last three calendar years before you apply for benefits. As soon as you are dismissed from a job, you should register as unemployed (*arbeidsledig*) at the local Employment Service office (*Arbeidskontor*) listed in the Pink Pages. First, the Employment Service office will try to find you a new job. You must be willing to take any job that the office finds suitable. If neither the office or you find a new job, you may apply for unemployment benefits, popularly called "day pay" (*dagpenger*). Special rules apply to citizens of EEA countries. In the late 1990s, Norway had an unemployment rate of less than 5% of the workforce, one of the lowest in Europe and below the averages for both the ☞ **EU** and the **OECD** (Government and Social Services chapter).

Unions (*Fag organisasjoner*) More than a million employees in the country are union members. There are more than 50 unions, in three groups: 28 trade unions allied in The Norwegian Confederation of Trade Unions (*Landsorganisasjonen i Norge – LO*), 22 professional unions allied in The Confederation of Academic and Professional Unions (*Akademikernes Fellesorganisasjon – AF*) and three independent unions.

LO is the largest, with more than 830,000 members in all, and oldest, being founded in 1899. It is involved in the international labour movement, principally through the Council of Nordic Trade Unions

(NFS), the European Trade Union Confederation (ETUC) and the International Confederation of Free Trade Unions (ICFTU). It is politically active, particularly in labour matters, and it maintains facilities dealing with unionism, including The Labour Movement Archives and Library (*Arbeidbevegelsens bibliotek*) in Oslo. It publishes extensively, both in print and on-line. For further information, contact any member union at addresses and telecommunications numbers listed in the Pink Pages, or LO directly ✆ 23061050, 📠 23061743, ✉ Youngsgate 11, 0181 Oslo, 📧 lo@loit.no, 🌐 http://www.lo.no with pages in Norwegian and in English. In alphabetical order by the names of their respective trades in English, the 28 LO unions are:

Cantors and organists *(Norsk Kantor- og Organistforbund – NKOF)*

Chemical industry workers *(Norsk Kjemisk Industriarbeiderforbund – NKIF)*

Construction workers *(Norsk Arbeidsmandsforbund – NAF)*

Electricians, electronics and IT technicians *(EL & IT forbundet)*

Food industry workers *(Norsk Nærings- og Nytelsesmiddelarbeiderforbund – NNN)*

Functionaries not in other unions *(Norsk Tjenestemannslag – NTL)*

Hotel and restaurant staff *(Hotell- og Restaurantarbeiderforbundet – HRAF)*

Military cadre *(Norges Offisersforbund – NOF)*

Municipal employees *(Norsk Kommuneforbund – NKF)*

Musicians and theatre workers *(Norsk Musikerforbund – NM)*

Office, service sector and shop employees *(Handel og Kontor i Norge – HK)*

Oil industry workers *(Norsk Olje- og Petrokjemisk Fagforbund – NOPEF))*

Penal system workers *(Norsk Fengsels- og Friomsorgsforbund – NFF)*

Postal functionaries *(Den norske Postorganisasjon – DnP)*

Postal workers *(Norsk Postforbund – NPF)*

Printed media editorial staff *(Arbeiderbevegelsens Presseforbund – APF)*

Printing and graphic arts workers *(Norsk Grafisk Forbund – NGF)*

Production industry workers *(Fellesforbundet)*

Railway engine drivers *(Norsk Lokomotivmannsforbund – NLF)*

Railway workers *(Norsk Jernbaneforbund – NJF)*

School teachers *(Skolenes Landsforbund – SL)*

Seamen *(Norsk Sjømannsforbund – NSF)*

Social workers *(Fellesorganisasjonen – FO)*

Supervisors and functionaries *(Forbundet for Ledelse og Teknikk – FLT)*

Team sport players *(Norske Idrettsutøveres Sentralorganisasjon – NISO)*

Timber industry workers *(Norsk Treindustriarbeiderforbund – NTIF)*

Translators *(Norsk Tolkeforbund)*

Transport workers *(Norsk Transportarbeiderforbund – NTF)*

AF has some 160,000 members who have higher education at the college and university level. About a third of its members are government civil servants, a third employed by local municipalities and a third in the private sector. It is a member of NFS and ETUC as well as the International Confederation of Trade Unions (ICT) and the Trade Union Advisory Committee to the OECD (TUAC). It organises continuing education courses and workshops to prevent its members from being outdated. It publishes extensively, both in print and on-line. Its member unions are active in professional matters, such as standardisation. For further information, contact any member union at addresses and telecommunications numbers listed in the Pink Pages, or AF directly ✆ 22823300, 📠 22424548, ✉ PO Box 506 Sentrum, 0105Oslo, 📧 af@af.no, 🌐 http://www.af.no with pages in Norwegian and in English. In alphabetical order by the names of their respective trades in English, the 22 AF unions are:

Air traffic controllers, broadcasters, meteorologists and maritime pilots *(Fellesorganisasjon for norsk Flygelederforening, norsk meteorologforening m.fl.)*

Church of Norway religious teachers *(Den norske Kirkes Kateketforening)*

Deacons *(Det norske Diakonforbund)*

Engineers *(Norges Ingeniørorganisasjon – NITO)*

Ergotherapists *(Norsk Ergoterapeutforbund)*

Folk high school staff *(Samnemnda for NF og NKF)*

Foreign Service professionals *(Utenrikstjenestens Forening)*

Librarians *(Bibliotekarforbundet)*

Local law enforcement officers *(Norges Lensmannslag)*

Midwives *(Den norske Jordmorforening)*
Military officers, academy graduates *(Krigsskoleut-dannede offiserers Landsforening)*
Nurses *(Norsk Sykepleierforbund)*
Pharmacists *(Norges farmaceutiske Forening)*
Physiotherapists *(Norske fysioterapeuters Forbund)*
Radiographers *(Norsk Radiografforbund)*
School supervisors *(Norsk Skolelederforbund)*
State automobile inspectors *(Statens Bilsakkyndiges Forening)*
Tax auditors *(Skatterevisorenes Forening)*
Tax inspectors and tax collectors *(Skattefogdenes Landsforening)*
Teachers *(Lærerforbundet)*
University and college graduates *(Universitet- og høyskoleutdannedes Forbund)*
Vinmopolet functionaries *(Overordnede funksjonærers Forening v/A/S Vinmonopolet)*

The independent unions are for professions in the performing arts and upper secondary school and college education. For further information, contact any member union at addresses and telecommunications numbers listed in the Pink Pages, or LO or AF, as both have liaison with the independent unions. Alphabetically, by profession in English, the unions are:

Actors *(Norsk skuespiller forbund)*
Ballet dancers, choreographers and instructors *(Norsk balletforbund)*
Teachers *(Norsk lærerlag)*

Work week and work year (*Arbeidsuke og årsverk*) By law, a job may require no more than nine hours of work a day and no more than 40 hours of work per week, although there are some exceptions. Shift workers *(skiftarbeidere)*, who must work evenings and nights, have a shorter work week, whilst some work weeks, as for offshore oil workers, are longer. Many union contracts call for no more than 37.5 hours a week. In the late 1990s, the average work week for all employees was about 35.5 hours a week. In some sectors, including farming, fishing and offshore oil work, the averages were higher, but still no more than 45.1 hours a week, the figure for oil industry workers. By law, employees are entitled to at least four weeks plus one day of ☞ **Vacation** (Holidays chapter). Consequently, when public holidays are deduced, the work year averages about 1725 hours. Most companies have both full-time and part-time employees, as well as temps hired for specific tasks. Accordingly, the total workforce of a company usually is stated in work-years *(årsverk)*, which is a number that may be equal to or less than the total number of employees.

The Working environment (*Arbeidsmiljø*) is governed by the regulations set forth in the Act on Working Environment *(Arbeidsmiljøloven)* which covers employer and employee rights and is intended to protect employees and to ensure safe and healthy working conditions. It is available in an unofficial translation into English: *Act No. 4 of 4 February 1997 Relating to Worker Protection and Working Environment amended last on 28 February 1997*, Oslo, Cappelen Akademisk Forlag, June 1997, 64 page booklet, ISBN 82-456-0387-2, which you may order from any book shop *(bokhandel)*. The Act has 17 chapters, each of which covers a specific aspect of the working environment:

Chapter I. Objectives and scope
Chapter II. Requirements
Chapter III. Duties of employer and employees
Chapter IV. Responsibility of manufacturers, suppliers etc.
Chapter V. Consent of Labour Inspectorate in construction works
Chapter VI. Reporting occupational accidents and diseases
Chapter VII. Safety delegates and working environment committees
Chapter VIII. Right to leave of absence
Chapter IX. Employment of children and young people
Chapter X. Working hours
Chapter XI. Wage payments and holiday allowance
Chapter XIA. Engagement (hiring)
Chapter XII. Notice of termination and summary dismissal, etc.
Chapter XIIA. Rights of employees in the event of change of ownership
Chapter XIII. The Labour Inspectorate
Chapter XIV. Penalties
Chapter XV. Entry into force; amendments

Working hours (*Arbeidstid*) vary. Most offices start work at 8 am and finish at 4 pm, though 9 am to 5 pm is increasingly common in some sectors, such as financial services. Industries tend to start earlier, 7 or 7:30 am and finish eight hours later.

Almost all public and private offices have Saturday off (*lørdagsfri*). Working hours in shops correspond to opening hours, which may include Saturdays. Whenever an activity requires longer hours or work round the clock – such as health services, transportation, offshore oil or hotels and restaurants – working hours are split up into shifts of normally no more than nine hours.

Many companies now offer flexible working hours (*fleksitid*) that allow you to come and leave as you wish, provided that you are at work during the period of core business for the day (*kjernetid*). Many workplaces require you to clock on and clock off (*stemple*) at a time clock (*stemplingsur*), both to ensure that you work the contractual number of hours and to aid bookkeeping on contracts.

Any hours you work exceeding 40 hours a week are considered to be overtime (*overtid*), for which you are entitled to at least 40% overtime pay in addition to your base hourly wage rate. However, if you are in a salaried management position or are self-employed, you usually are not entitled to overtime pay.

If you work more than five and a half hours a day, you are entitled to a meal break (*spisepause*). If you work at least eight hours a day, you are entitled to meal breaks totalling at least 30 minutes. Some companies, particularly larger companies with cafeteria services, include the 30 minutes in the day's business hours, such as being open from 8 am to 4 pm, with three or four half-hour lunch breaks for different divisions of the company, between 11 am and 1 pm.

You are entitled to at least 36 hours of continuous free time (*sammenhengende fritid*) each week. If your job involves weekend work, such as in a hospital, you are entitled to have a Sunday or public holiday free every second or third week.

If you work on shifts, you are entitled to at least ten hours free between successive shifts, unless the Labour Inspectorate (*Arbeidstilsynet*) has approved a shorter free time for your employer.

Night work (*nattarbeid*), defined as being work between 9 pm and 6 am, is permitted only for defined activities which cannot be performed at other times. Likewise, work on Sundays and public holidays is permitted only by special permission or agreement with a union (*etter særskilt tillatelse eller avtale*).

The full regulations governing working hours are stated in Chapter X of the Act on Working Environment, ☞ **Working environment**.

Cars, Roads, Traffic
(Biler, Veier, Trafikk)

About driving (om bilisme) Driving in Norway is much like driving elsewhere in Europe, on the right with increasingly international traffic regulations. A few things to remember (they are described in this chapter), particularly if you have no previous experience of driving in Europe:

- **Alcohol** Drink-drive limits are similar to those elsewhere in Europe. If convicted, usually on the basis of a breath test, you may be fined, jailed and lose your driving licence for a year or more.
- **Automatic traffic surveillance** is common throughout the country. Speed, and in some cases traffic light violations, are monitored.
- **Breakdown** Several emergency services as well as the automobile associations offer breakdown services. You must carry a red, reflecting warning triangle (varselstrekant) to set at roadside behind your car in case of breakdown.
- **Bridges and tunnels** are numerous, and many of them have tolls.
- **Driving lights** You must drive with dipped headlights on, even at midday.
- **Ferries** are commonplace, particularly along the west coast.
- **Main roads** are mostly the international European E-roads.
- **Right of way** At unmarked intersections between roads without priority, such as streets in cities and towns, the car on the right has priority.
- **Roundabouts** Traffic on roundabouts has priority over entering traffic. Triangular yield signs are posted on all entering roads to remind you of this.
- **Signs** follow European norms, though some are particular to Norway.
- **Speed** If not posted, the speed limit is 50 km/h in built-up areas and 80 km/h on open road.
- **Spot checks** may be made at any time, on any road, to check vehicles and drivers.
- **Tyres** Your car must be fitted with tyres that provide sufficient grip for the road conditions. For most drivers, this means winter tyres in winter and ordinary road tyres in summer.
- **Zebra crossings** Pedestrians have priority at zebra crossings, and cars must stop for them.

If you drive, you should learn the essential words in the vocabulary of cars and driving, which is large and changing, with new words continuously coming into the language, particularly from English. Fortunately, four good guides are available:

- *Aschehoug og Gyldendals Store Norske Leksikon Visuell Ordbok* (Pictorial encyclopaedia with texts in Norwegian, English, German and French), 1998, Kunnskapsforlaget, ISBN 82.573-0960-5, pp. 425-457 on road transportation, including vehicles.
- *Bil- og trafikk-teknisk ordbok* (Car and traffic glossary, Norwegian-English and English-Norwegian), 1979, Kunnskapsforlaget, ISBN 82-573-0079-9.
- *Bilteknisk Ordbok engelsk-norsk & engelsk-svensk* (English-Norwegian and English-Swedish automotive glossary), 1988, ScanBook, ISBN 82-991675-0-7.
- *Teknisk ordbok engelsk-norsk* (English-Norwegian automotive glossary), free booklet published by Haynes to accompany its Owners Workshop Manuals, available in shops selling ☞ **automotive books**.

In reading maps and city guides, as well as addresses in telephone directories, you will soon find that there are two spellings of the word for road, *vei* and *veg*. They are pronounced alike, rhyming with *jeg*, the pronoun equivalent to I in English. The reason for the two spellings lies in the history of the ☞ **Norwegian languages** (Language chapter) and their use varies throughout the country, though the ☞ **Public Roads Administration** consistently uses *veg*, in its name and all publications.

Annual vehicle tax (Årsavgift) is charged on all motor vehicles registered with valid ☞ **number plates** on 1 January and is due 15 March. In January and February, ☞ **Norwegian customs and excise** (Taxes, Duties, Excise chapter) sends bills for the annual vehicle tax to all registered vehicle owners. For new registrations, the full annual tax is charged for the first half of the year, until 30 June; thereafter half the tax is charged. Old cars delivered to ☞ **vehicle dismantlers** and taken off registry before 15 March are exempt from the annual vehicle tax. The tax varies by category of vehicle: NOK 1965 (in 1999) for cars, vans, recreational vehicles, minibuses and combi-vehicles up to 3.5 tons weight and NOK 1550 for motorcycles. The tax for trucks is less, but heavy trucks, weighing 12 tons and more, must pay an annual HGV (heavy goods vehicle) tax (*vektårsavgift*). In June, the ☞ **Public Roads Administration** posts a set of two small coloured validation stickers (*kontrollmerker*), sometimes called seals (*oblater*), to all owners who have paid the tax. The stickers have the same number as the vehicle's number plate and the four digits of the following year when tax must again be paid. The tax is zero for veteran cars (age 30 or more) and for electric cars, but the tax procedure is followed, with new validation stickers each year.

Automatic traffic surveillance (*Elektronisk overvåking*)

Automatic traffic surveillance (*Elektronisk overvåking*) cameras are installed alongside streets and roads throughout the country to detect and photograph cars that violate speed limits or ignore traffic signals. The cameras, popularly called "photo boxes" (*fotobokser*) because of their box-like shape on top of poles, are parts of automatic traffic control – ATC (*automatisk trafikkontroll* – *ATK*) systems intended to ensure adherence to traffic regulations and thereby cut accident rates. They have been as successful as they have in other countries, particularly along stretches of roads where speeding has contributed to higher accident rates.

Automobile associations (*Automobil foreninger*)

Automobile associations (*Automobil foreninger*) offer many services to their members, including breakdown assistance (*veitjenester*), discounts (*rabatter*), legal advice (*juridisk rådgivning*), technical advice (*teknisk rådgivning*), car testing (*testing*), camping grounds (*campingplasser*), trip services (*turservice*), international driving licence (*internasjonale førerkort*) issue and member magazines (*blad*). There are two automobile associations, the Royal Norwegian Automobile Club and the Norwegian Automobile Association.

The Royal Norwegian Automobile Club (*Kongelig Norsk Automobilklub* – *KNA*) was founded in 1907 and is the older of the two associations. As its name implies, it originally was exclusive and concerned with cars as a pastime. But it is now more egalitarian and open to all, though it remains involved in motor sports and is the Norwegian member of *Federation Internationale de l'Automobile (FIA)*, the international motor sports governing body

recognised by the International Olympic Committee. KNA now has some 19,000 members and 26 local associations throughout the country. For further details, contact the head office in Oslo ✆ 22561900, ✆ 22552354, ✉ PO Box 2425 Solli, 0201 Oslo, ✺ http://www.kna.no

The Norwegian Automobile Association (*Norges Automobil-Forbund* – *NAF*) was founded in 1924 and now is the larger of the two associations, with some 410,000 members and 75 local associations throughout the country. Its member benefits include the services of a countrywide 24-hour emergency centre (*alarmsentral*) local-call-rate help line ✆ 81000505. It is a member of *Alliance Internationale de Tourisme (AIT)*, the international federation of national automobile associations. It performs services for members of other national associations belonging to the AIT, including issuing *Carnets de Passages* (customs permits to take vehicles across borders for specified lengths of time) and issuing Letters of Credit when needed. For further details, look under *Norges Automobil-Forbund* in the Pink Pages if you live in a city where the local association may be large enough to have a staffed office. Otherwise, contact the head office in Oslo ✆ 22341400, ✆ 22331372, ✉ PO Box 494 Sentrum, 0105 Oslo, ✺ http://www.naf.no

The AIT was founded in 1898 as a motor touring association, a fact reflected in its name. The FIA was founded in 1904 and now has a touring and automobile branch and a motor sports branch. Together, the AIT and FIA have 212 member associations in 120 countries world-wide and represent more than 100 million members. They now share offices in Geneva, Switzerland. For further information, contact KNA or NAF in Norway, or view the web sites for the AIT ✺ http://www.aitgva.ch and the FIA ✺ http://www3.fia.com with pages in English and in French.

Automotive books (*Bøker om biler*)

Automotive books (*Bøker om biler*) may be hard to find, though some book shops, petrol stations and car parts dealers stock a few owner's workshop manuals for popular cars and the clubs for ☞ **Veteran cars** (Sports, Recreation, Hobbies chapter) have manuals for their makes. Fortunately, *Automobilia*, Scandinavia's largest speciality automotive book shop is in Oslo. It catalogues some 24,000 book titles every autumn and has more than 10,000 titles in stock, most in English and many in Norwegian and other European languages The subject categories include cars, motorcycles, cycles, aeroplanes, ships, trains, model railways, military and weapons. For further information, catalogues or ordering, contact *Automobilia* ✆ 22608660, ✉ 22608602, ✉ Uranienborgveien 25, PO Box 7035 Majorstua, 0306 Oslo, ✉ bookshop@automobilia.no, ✉ http://www.automobilia.no with pages in Norwegian and in English and a search engine for topics and book titles.

Bridges (*Broer*) There are about 17,000 bridges on the public road network. The Drammen Bridge on E18 is the longest, at 1892 metres, followed by the Nordhordlandsbrua on E39, 1614 metres long. Understandably, the technology of bridge building is well advanced, and Norway is the first country in Europe to build floating bridges, for roads along the west coast, employing technologies and experience from the building of North Sea offshore oil platforms.

Cars (*biler*) Norway has the world's 17th highest car ownership, 408 cars per 1,000 people. The number of cars now increases by 1.6% a year, and there are nearly 1.8 million cars in the country (1998). The average age of all cars is 9.9 years (1998), among the oldest in Europe. Each year, some 80,000 cars are delivered to ☞ **vehicle dismantlers** for recycling and destruction, and owners are refunded an ☞ **end of life deposit**. The average end-of-life age varies from 12.8 years for Skoda to 21.1 years for Mercedes and averages 17.3 years for all cars.

Car ferries (*Fergesamband*) Norway has a coastline of 21,925 km, the second longest in Europe, after Russia (37,653 km). So there are many waters to be crossed and consequently many ferry routes. Bridges and tunnels are gradually replacing the car ferries, but there are still more than 150 fixed ferry routes integrated into the road network, with a total capacity of more than 10,000 cars.

Car import (*Innførsel av motorvogn*) If you bring a car when you move to Norway, it will be subject to import duty and value-added tax. For instance, in its instructions (RG-193, 1 January 1999) for filling out the form to calculate duty and tax, Norwegian Customs and Excise gives the example of a Jaguar X.16

3.2 first registered abroad on 2 January 1995 and imported to Norway in 1999. Upon arrival, its declared value CIF ☞ **Commercial terms** (Business and Work chapter) is NOK 150,000. The total duties and taxes on it, computed on the basis of its weight (*egenvekt*) of 1750 kg, motor displacement (*slagvolum*) of 3239 cm^3 and motor power (*effekt*) of 149 kW amount to NOK 203,152. As this example shows, save for luxury cars, importing may not be financially worthwhile. But you may bring in a car without paying duty and tax, provided you fulfil the conditions summarised below (valid mid 1999). Before you move to Norway and import a car or other motor vehicle, you should read the most recent issues of the complete regulations, available in Norwegian and English versions, printed or on-line from Norwegian Customs and Excise (*Tollvesenet*) ✆ 22860300, ✉ 22175485, ✉ PO Box 8122 Dep, 0032 Oslo, ✉ http://www.toll.no with pages in Norwegian and in English. For all queries, submission of forms and other matters concerning import, contact the nearest Regional Customs Administration listed under *Tollvesenet* in the Pink Pages.

Importation as removal goods (*Innførsel ved flytting til Norge*) If you will take up residence you need not pay duty or tax on a car brought in when you arrive, provided:

- you have resided abroad for at least five consecutive years prior to arrival. If you have resided abroad for a shorter period of not less than two years, you will be allowed a partial reduction of duties and taxes.
- you have not been registered as a resident in Norway for those five years, or two years if you seek partial reduction of duties and taxes.
- the car has been registered in your name for at least one year (52 weeks) prior to entry
- the car has been driven at least 5,000 km
- the car is imported when you take up residence in Norway
- you will keep the car and you and your family will be the sole users of it for at least two years

The complete regulations are set forth in publication RG-0197 (Norwegian) and RG-1098 (English), and you should fill out form RG-131 and submit it to the nearest Regional Customs Administration after arrival.

Temporary importation (*Midlertidig innførsel*) If you will stay in Norway less than one year and will not take up residence, you may bring in a car for use during your stay and keep it registered on foreign number plates, provided that you:

- are a permanent resident of another country.
- have not resided in Norway for more than 365 days within the last two years.
- are not or have not been registered as a resident of Norway in those two years
- can document, such as by a copy of an employment contract, that you will be in Norway less than one year.
- bring the car with you when you arrive and notify the Norwegian Customs at the first border crossing of your intent to keep the car during your stay.

The complete regulations are set forth in publication RG-0195 (English) and RG-1096 (Norwegian), and you should fill out form RG-129 and submit it to the nearest Regional Customs Administration after arrival. In some cases, you may be allowed to keep the car for an additional year, provided you submit a request to Customs before the end of your first year in the country.

Car number plates (*Bilskilter*) identify cars listed in the motor vehicle register (*Motorvognregister*) maintained by the ☞ **Norwegian Public Roads Administration**. All number plates are made of aluminium, and the most prevalent numbering consists of two capital letters followed by five numerals. Colours designate category of use: black on natural aluminium, by far the most common, is for private cars; black on a green background is for delivery vans; yellow on a blue background is for diplomatic vehicles. Plates for motorcycles and trailers resemble private car plates and have two letters followed by four numerals. A small (2 x 5 cm) coloured validation sticker (*kontrollmerke*) with the vehicle registration and the year of expiration is fixed on both front and rear plates, just after the second identifier letter. It indicates that the ☞ **Annual vehicle tax** has been paid. Vehicles that are not yet registered may have one of two types of red temporary use plates with two letters followed by two numerals. Dealer plates, such as may be affixed for test driving a new car, have white letters and numbers and are fitted with straps for temporary attachment. New and used cars brought in from abroad, as by their owners, have self-adhering number signs with black letters

and numbers as well as an expiration date. The number plates on ☞ **Tax-free export cars** (*Tollskilt*) resemble the ordinary registration private car plates but have two black numerals on a red background at each end of the plate giving the month (left end) and year (right end) of expiration.

The first two letters of a number plate are the district of first registration identifier, as listed below, with two exceptions: EL for electric vehicles and GA for gas-powered vehicles. A car keeps its number as long as it is registered in Norway. The letters I, M, O, Q, W, Æ, Ø and Å are not used.

District of first registration identifiers:
AA-AC Halden
AD-AV Fredrikstad
AJ-AP Mysen
AX-BB Moss
BC-BK Drøbak
BL-CB Sandvika
CC & CE-CU Lillestrøm
CV-CZ Eidsvoll
DA-FR Oslo
EL Electric vehicle
FS-HA Hamar
GA Gas-powered vehicle
HB-HE Elverum
HF-HH Tynset
HJ-HR Kongsvinger
HS-HY Lillehammer
HZ-JB Otta
JC-JP Gjøvik
JR-JT Fagernes
JU-KA Hønefoss
KB-KD Gol
KE-KS Drammen
KT-KY Kongsberg
KZ-LF Horten
LH-LR Tønsberg
LS-NC Larvik
ND-NU Skien
NV-NZ Notodden
PA-PB Rjukan
PC-PL Arendal
PN-PV Kristiansand
PX-RD Mandal
RA-RB Flekkefjord
RE-RY Stavanger
RZ-SB Egersund

SC-SL Haugesund
SN-TE Bergen
TF-TK Voss
TL-TR Stord
TS-TU Odda
TV-TZ Førde
UA-UB Nordfjordeid
UC-UD Sogndal
UE-UL Ålesund
UN-UP Ørstra
UR-UV Molde
UX-VA Kristiansund
VB-VC Sunndalsøra
VD-VR Trondheim
VS-VV Støren
VS-VZ Orkanger
XA-XC Brekstad
XD-XJ Steinkjer
XR-XL Levanger
XN-XP Størdal
XR-XU Namsos
XV-XZ Mosjøen
YA-YD Mo i Rana
YE-YJ Bodø
YK-YL Fauske
YN-YS Narvik
YT-YY Svolvær
YU-YX Sortland
YZ-ZB Harstad
ZC-ZN Tromsø & Svalbard
ZD-ZJ Finnsnes
ZP-ZR Vadsø
ZS Kirkenes
ZT-ZV Alta
ZX Hammerfest

Old number plates: The above numbering system went into effect on 1 April 1971. Before then, the first registration identifier was a single letter designating the county as listed below; it was followed by one to five numerals. In 1958, the number of cars registered in Oslo outstripped the capacity of the numbering system, so six-digit numbers without a prefix letter were issued. Old number plates can still be seen on pre-1971 cars not re-registered and may be used on veteran cars 30 years old or more.

County of first registration identifier (up to 1 April 1971)
A Oslo (until 1958)
B Østfold

C Akershus
D Hedemark
E Oppland
F Buskerud
H Telemark
I Aust-Agder
K Vest-Agder
L Rogaland
O Bergen
R Hordaland
S Sogn og Fjordane
T Møre og Romsdal
U Sør-Trøndelag
V Nord-Trøndelag
W Nordland
X Troms
Y Finnmark
Z Vestfold

Diplomatic number plates: For the yellow-on blue diplomatic number plates, the first two numerals following the CD (*Corps Diplomatique*) identifier are the code for the embassy of registration:
10 USA
11 Argentina
14 Belgium
15 Brazil
16 UK
17 Bulgaria
20 Canada
21 Chile
24 Costa Rica
26 Denmark
28 European Union
29 Egypt
31 Estonia
33 Finland
34 France
37 Greece
40 India
41 Indonesia
42 Iran
43 Iceland
44 Israel
45 Italy
48 Japan
49 Yugoslavia
52 China
53 South Korea
55 Croatia

Car parts and accessories (*Bildeler og rekvisita*) New parts and accessories are sold by new car dealers and parts and accessories shops listed under *Bildeler og rekvisita* in the Yellow Pages. Used parts are available at ☞ **Vehicle dismantlers**. There are three chains of parts and accessories shops, all with printed catalogues and Internet web sites; look for their shop addresses and telecommunications numbers in the Pink Pages.

- Bilvarehuset has three shops in the Oslo area, three in the western part of the country at Rådal, Ulset and Loddefjord, and one in Trondheim ☻ http://www.bilvarehusene.no
- Torshov has shops in Oslo, Asker, Drammen, Ski, Strømmen and Trondheim ☻ http://www.torshovbil.no.
- Biltema is by far the largest car parts and accessories company in the Nordic countries, with shops in Sweden, Norway and Finland and mail-order service covering Denmark, Estonia and Russia. In Norway, its shops are located in Arendal. Bergen, Kristiansand, Oslo, Sandnes, Sarpsborg and Trondheim ☻ http://www.biltema.com with pages in English.

Car prices (*Bil priser*) are among the highest in Europe, principally because of taxes that account for about half the price of a car. Of the dealer price (1999) of NOK 200,000 for a VW Golf, nearly NOK 90,000 is tax. Of the price of NOK 270,000 for a Ford Mondeo, NOK 131,000 is tax. The tax on a car consists of one-time tax (*Engangsavgift*) and an ☞ **End-of-life vehicle deposit**, as well as VAT (*MVA*) on the sum of the import price, one-time tax and end-of-life vehicle deposit. In turn, the one-time-tax consists of three parts: weight tax, motor displacement tax and motor power tax. All are progressive: a heavier, higher-powered car pays a higher overall tax rate than a lighter, lower-powered car. Used cars are subject to the same tax schedule, with a reduction (*bruksfradrag*) of the one-time tax for the age of the car.

Example of imported used car Norwegian Customs and Excise illustrates its car tax schedule with the example of a 1995 model Jaguar XJ6 3.2 valued at NOK 150,000 upon import in 1999. The taxes on it, based on its weight, engine displacement and power, are:

weight tax	NOK	72,965
displacement tax		96,239
power tax		65,044
Total one-time tax	NOK	234,338
Minus 42% age discount		98,422
Final one-time tax	NOK	135,916
End-of-life deposit		1,200
Import value		150,000
Total value		287,116
23% VAT on total value		66,036
Total tax on car	NOK	203,152

Example of imported used motorcycle: The Norwegian Motorcycle Union (☞ **Motorcycle clubs**) gives a similar example of a 1998 Yamaha YZFR1 998 cc motorcycle imported from England in 1999. Its value upon import is its cost of £7,500 times the 12.8 exchange rate plus NOK 2,000 in freight, for a total of NOK 98,000. The total taxes on it amount to NOK 81,515.

Car registration (*Registrering*) If you buy a new car, the dealer will complete registration for you. Likewise, most used car dealers will complete registration. But in buying a used car, you should ask whether the price includes the re-registration fee (*omregistreringsavgift*) charged for transfers of ownership of registered vehicles and payable to the Oslo Customs House (*Oslo Distriktstollsted*), preferably using a prepared Giro form. The fee varies according to category of vehicle, year of first registry and vehicle weight. There is no re-registration fee for veteran cars, 30 years or more old, but the ownership transfer procedure must be followed. If you sell or buy a used car, you must fill out a notice of vehicle ownership change (*Melding om kjøretøy som skifter eier*), an A5 format form no. NA-0232, and submit it to the nearest ☞ **Norwegian Public Roads Administration** traffic station, which will have forms and can advise you on filling them in. With the form, you must submit the original receipts for payment of the re-registration fee and the ☞ **Annual vehicle tax** as well as the former owner's vehicle registration card (*Vognkort*). Upon submission, you must identify yourself, such as by showing your driving licence, passport or credit card with a photograph.

Car rental (*Bilutleie*), also called self-drive car hire, is commonplace and readily available throughout the country. Cars (*personbiler*), vans (*varebiler*), minibuses (*minibusser*) and trucks (*lastebiler*) are rented out. There are four major types of car rental companies, listed under *Bilutleie* in the Yellow Pages:
- International companies renting out new vehicles, including Avis, Budget, Europcar, and Hertz, with broad rental services, including counters at international airports.
- The international new vehicle rental and leasing divisions of car manufacturers, including Ford, Mitsubishi, Volvo and VW/Audi, and petrol station operators, including Esso and Statoil.
- Local companies renting out new vehicles, including car dealers offering rental and leasing.
- Local companies renting out used cars, sometimes under an international franchise, such as Rent-A-Wreck.

The international companies offer their respective booking and discount schemes. The local companies renting out new vehicles usually offer more uniform and often lower listed rates with fewer or no discounts. Most of the international companies and some local companies offer one-way and other city drop-off, but otherwise you should return a vehicle to the agency where it was rented; inquire upon renting if you need a one-way vehicle. The car rental market is competitive, so it pays to call several rental agencies and compare prices.

The conditions for car rental are similar to those in most other countries. You must have a valid ☞ **Driving licence** for the type of vehicle rented. Most rental agencies prefer that you have an international credit card (*kreditkort*) or Norwegian bank debit card (*bankkort*) as identification and means of payment. The standard and additional insurance offered upon renting are according to the national norms for ☞ **Motor insurance** (Banking, Finance, Insurance chapter). The Norwegian Association of Car Rental Companies (*Norges Bilutleieforbund*) recommends renting new vehicles, as according to road laws, the driver is responsible for the condition and safety of the vehicle.

For chauffeur-driven car hire, look for the word *privatsjåfør* ("private chauffeur") or look under *Limousineutleie* in the Yellow Pages.

Car repair (*bil service*) There are more than 4,000 car workshops in the country; look for them under *bilverksteder* in the Yellow Pages. New car dealers (*Bilforretninger*) also have workshops specialising in the makes of cars that they sell (*merkeverksted*). Some workshops offer a fixed price "menu" of common repairs, such as brake, clutch, electric, exhaust and suspension works. They are called *menyverksteder* ("menu workshops"). The specialist workshops, listed separately in the Yellow Pages, include body repairs (*biloppretting*), brakes (*bremseservice, bilbremseverksteder*), cleaning (*bilpleie*), diesel (*bildieselverksteder*), electrics (*bilelektriske verksteder*), instruments (*bilinstrumenter*), motors (*motoroverhaling*), painting (*billakkering*), tyres (*bilgummiverksteder*), undercoating (*bilunderstellsbehandling*) and windscreens (*bilglass*).

Cars, new (*nybiler*) Most major brands of American, European, Japanese and Korean cars and trucks are sold by dealers (*Bilforretninger* in the Yellow Pages) including Alfa Romeo, Audi, BMW, Chrysler (all brands), Citroën, DAF, Daihatsu, Ducato, Ferrari, Fiat, Ford, General Motors (all brands), Hino, Honda, Hyundai, Iveco, Jaguar, Jeep, Kia, Lada, Lancia, Land Rover, MAN, Mazda, Mercedes, MG, Mitsubishi, Nissan, Opel, Peugeot, Porsche, Renault, Rover, Saab, Scania, Seat, Setra, Skoda, Subaru, Suzuki, Toyota, Volvo and VW. Other brands not regularly marketed are imported by specialist dealers, usually identified by the word *importør* (importer) or *megler* (broker) in their corporate names. Should you fail to find a dealer for a specific brand, contact The Norwegian Automobile Importers' Association (*Bilimportørenes Landsforening*) ✆ 22646455, ✁ 22648595, ✉ PO Box 72 Økern, 0508 Oslo, for the names and addresses of authorised dealers. In shopping for a new car, first find the published list price (*listepris*) at any dealer and then compare dealer discounts (*rabatt*) and accessory packages (*utstyrpakke*) on the model of your choice. If you are shopping for one of the more popular cars, it may pay to consider a company version (*businessutgave*) with an accessory package, such as winter tyres, radio and air conditioner, at a total price lower than its list price. Company versions often are cheaper because company car taxation is based on delivered price in brackets of 50,000 kroner. For instance, a car with a list price of 267,000 kroner may be offered as a well-equipped company car at 249,900 kroner, just under the 250,000 kroner lower bound of the next highest company car tax bracket.

Cars, used (*Bruktbil*) are sold both by car dealers and by private persons. Car dealers, listed under *Bilforretninger* in the Yellow Pages, include used car dealers, used car departments of new car dealers, used car importers (*import* in name), car auctioneers (*bilauksjon* in name) and brokers (*megler* in name) selling for others. Companies, as well as private persons selling cars, advertise in the classified sections of newspapers; the larger newspapers have A-Z listings by make of car. The weekly *Autobørsen* ("Car trader") magazine sold by newsagents and available on subscription ✆ 22757500, ✁ 22757501, ✉ PO Box 131, 0611 Oslo, ⊕ http://www.autoborsen.no, regularly lists more than 2,000 cars, most with colour photographs. *Autobørsen* is 80% owned by the Guardian Media Group of the UK and consequently is similar to its Auto Trader magazines published in many countries. ☞ **Dine Penger** (Media and Information chapter), publishes an yearly index of cars made in the past ten years, usually with the April issue. In it, three prices are listed for each make, model and year of car: the net price (*Netto*) that a dealer will pay for a car, the average retail price (*Brukt*) and what the car cost when new (*Ny*). There also is a guide to price variation, depending on how far a car has been driven: 10,000 km a year is little

(*lite kjørt*) and 20,000 km is a lot (*Mye kjørt*). Unlike other personal chattels (moveable belongings), liens on cars are like mortgages on houses in that they are attached to the cars, not their owners. This means that a used car put up for sale may be burdened with debt, which might transfer to the buyer. Reputable dealers will clear debt in transferring ownership, usually by obtaining a letter of release from the lien holder when payment has been made. But no law requires that debt on a car be included in the description of it, so buyers can be deceived. There is a simple way to prevent that. All legal liens on cars must be registered by the chattels registry (*Løsøreregisteret*), part of the ☞ **Brønnøysund Register Centre** (Registrations, Rights and Licences chapter). You can access the car database of the registry from any keypad telephone, automatically 24 hours a day or operator assisted in business hours, in three steps. First, call the database ✆ 75007502, and wait for the instruction: *tast registreringsnummer, avslutt med firekant, eller tast firekant hvis du ønsker veiledning* ("key in the registration number, finish with the # key, or key in # for assistance").

Second, key in the registration number, consisting of two letters followed by five numerals. Norwegian keypads do not have letters, so all letters must be coded into numbers, each prefixed by an asterisk:

A = * 01	B = * 02	C = * 03
D = * 04	E = * 05	F = * 06
G = * 07	H = * 08	I = * 09
J = * 10	K = * 11	L = * 12
M = * 13	N = * 14	O = * 15
P = * 16	Q = * 17	R = * 18
S = * 19	T = * 20	U = * 21
V = * 22	W = * 23	X = * 24
Y = * 25	Z = * 26	Æ = * 27
Ø = * 28	Å = * 29	

For instance, the registration number AV 15342 is keyed in as * 01* 22 15342 #.

Third, the automatic voice message system of the database then repeats the registration number that you keyed in, using the ☞ **phonetic alphabet** (Media and Information chapter) for the letters, and tells you if the car is free of debt or if there is a lien on it and, if so, how much. For instance, if AV 15342 is free of debt, it will not be listed, so the voice message will have three parts. First, the number will be repeated: "*Alfa Victor en fem tre fire to*". Then non-registry will be stated: "*er ikke registrert i registeret*". Finally, the date of the last revision of the register will be stated: "*ajour per (date)*". If there is registered debt, the total will be stated along with the date when the lien was taken out, such as by the original owner upon purchase. The debt may be lower, if some of it has been paid. Should you have cause to believe that a loan was taken out on the car after the date stated, wait a few days and call back for new information. Printout certificates of lien are available upon paying a fee.

Diesel fuel (*Diesel*) is sold by almost all of the country's more than 2200 petrol stations (*bensinstasjoner*). Like ☞ **petrol**, its price includes motor vehicle fuel tax. Diesel engine-grade fuel for non-road uses, as in motorboats, tractors, forestry and construction machinery, power plants and the like, as well as for diplomatic vehicles is cheaper, as it is not taxed for road use. This low-tax (*lavavgiftsbelagt*) diesel is coloured green, to distinguish it from fully-taxed diesel, and it is sold by many petrol stations and by boat yards to qualified users. All diesel fuels and heating oils are now available in "environmental diesel" (*miljødiesel*) varieties that when burned release fewer particulates and nitrogen oxides than do the ordinary varieties.

Drink-driving (*Alkoholpåvirket kjøring*) is among the leading causes of road accidents. Accident statistics indicate that some 40% of all drivers killed in accidents were under the influence of alcohol or drugs at time of death, and the annual costs incurred by drink-driving are estimated at more than NOK 1.1 billion.

The legal blood alcohol limit (*promillegrense*) for driving is 50 milligrams of alcohol in 100 millilitres of blood (50mg%), customarily written in Norwegian as *0,5 promille*. This is the same limit as in many other continental European countries, but higher than in neighbouring Sweden (20mg%).

The law also sets a limit of 0.25 milligrams of alcohol in one litre of breath as equivalent to the 50mg% blood alcohol limit. Consequently, the breath test (*utandingsprøve*) is most common. The police can require a breath test:

1. If there is reason to suspect drink-driving.
2. If a driver has violated other traffic laws so as to imply drink-driving.

3. Of drivers involved in a traffic accident, regardless of who is at fault.
4. At ☞ **Spot checks**.

Blood tests are taken only in certain circumstances, such as when there is reason to suspect intoxication due to drugs, and may be taken only by doctors or other health care professionals.

The minimum punishment for a driver found guilty of drink-driving is a fine, a jail sentence of 21 days or more and loss of driving licence for at least one year. The fine, jail sentence and duration of loss of licence go up with the severity of the conviction.

In step with the greater number of cars on the road, anti-drink-driving measures are being intensified. The lower limit in Sweden, introduced in 1990, resulted in a decline in the number of drink-driving accidents. Consequently, the current Norwegian road and road traffic plan (*Norsk veg- og vegtrafikkplan*) for 1998-2007 calls for lowering the limit to 20mg%. Convicted drink-drivers, particularly those with alcohol problems, can be offered rehabilitation courses instead of jail, as have been problem drink-drivers since 1996 in a test project in five counties. Starting in 1999, the rules governing drink-driving have been extended to drink-boating, with a legal blood alcohol limit of 80mg%.

Driving licence (*Førerkort*) regulations are administered by the ☞ **Public Roads Administration**. They are summarised here; for full details, contact the nearest *Trafikkstasjon* at the address listed in the Pink Pages. The driving licence categories (*førerkort klasse*) are like those of EU and EEA countries:

A Motorcycle (*motorsykkel*), at least age 21 for heavy motorcycles or 18 for medium-weight motorcycles.

A1 Light motorcycle (*lett motorsykkel*) up to 125 cc, at least age 16.

B Motor car, light van (*personbil, varebil*), at least age 18.

C Truck (*Lastebil*) over 3500 kg with trailer up to 750 kg, at least age 21 or 18 with restrictions.

C1 Small truck (*liten lastebil*) up to 7500 kg, at least age 18.

D Bus (*Buss*) with more than 8 passenger seats, trailer up to 750 kg, at least age 21.

D1 Minibus (*Minibuss*) with 9-16 passengers, trailer up to 750 kg, at least age 21.

E Trailer (*Tilhenger*) for categories B, C, D or D1,

in combination, such as CE Road Train (*Vogntog*).

S Snowmobile (*Beltemotorsykkel – snøscooter*), at least age 16.

T Tractor (*Traktor*), at least age 16.

Category A, A1 and B, S and T licences are valid for 100 years from date of birth. However, from age 70 on, you must have a doctor's certificate that you are fit to drive and carry it whenever driving. Categoy C, C1, D and D1 licences are valid for 10 years.

You may use a valid licence issued by an EEA (*EØS*) country, subject to the age and validity rules for the corresponding Norwegian licence. You may use a valid licence issued by a country outside the EEA (provided it is a signatory of the Geneva Convention of 1949 or the Vienna Convention of 1968 on Road Traffic) to drive for up to one year of temporary residence. However, if you become a permanent resident, you may use a category A, A1 or B licence for three months only. Thereafter, you may exchange your licence for a Norwegian licence at the nearest *Trafikkstasjon*, provided you are age 19 or older and have held the licence for at least one year. Note that the licence should show the date of first issue, to prove how long you have held it. If it does not – some licences show date of expiration, but not date of issue, whilst others show the date of last renewal – you might ask the issuing authority to give you a written confirmation of how long you have held the licence. If you exchange your foreign licence and wish to have it back upon leaving the country at some later date, ask that it be kept on file and not discarded. Category C, CE, D, DE, D1 and D1E licences from outside the EEA are not valid for driving Norwegian-registered vehicles.

Diplomats may use their national licences for the duration of their posting.

When you have been a permanent resident for six months and if you meet the age requirements, you may apply for a Norwegian licence just as can any citizen. ☞ **Driving schools** offer courses of instruction to prepare for the driving licence examinations. You also may prepare in part by ☞ **practice driving** privately, such as with one of your parents in the family car. The Norwegian Driving School Association has published a well-illustrated book on the regulations and how to prepare for the examination, in Norwegian and English editions:

Norwegian: *Veien til førerkort*, by K. Borch, D. Moe, J. Nermark and K. Torsmyr, 1998, 294 pages softcover, ISBN 82-7310-092-8.

English: *How to Get Your Drivers Licence*, by K. Borch, G. Hole and K. Torsmyr, 1992, 258 pages softcover, ISBN 82-7310-049-9.

Driving schools (*Trafikkskoler*) are private training centres that are authorised by the Public Roads Administration to teach driving and prepare pupils for taking the examinations for ☞ **driving licences**. There are about 600 driving schools in the country. Most offer a broad range of courses for the various categories of driving licences as well as programmes co-ordinated with ☞ **practice driving**, but some specialise, as in training for motorcycles or bus and truck drivers. In addition to Norwegian, most driving school instructors (*trafikklærere*) will speak English, and many speak other languages. You may find a driving school by looking under *Trafikkskoler* in the Yellow Pages, or, if the school is one of the some 350 that are members of the Norwegian Driving School Association (*Autoriserte Trafikkskolers Landsforbund – ATL*), by contacting ATL or by viewing the interactive school locator map in its web site ☏ 22190520, ☏ 22673630, ✉ PO Box 144 Manglerud, 0612 Oslo, 🖰 http://www.atl.no

ELCIDIS is the abbreviation of ELectric vehicle CIty DIStribution systems, a project supported by the European Commission up to 31 August 2001 and involving six cities in Europe, as well as CITELEC, the European Association of Cities Interested in the Use of Electric Vehicles. Stavanger is one of the cities. The other five are Rotterdam, Netherlands; Stockholm, Sweden; La Rochelle, France; Erlangen, Germany and Milan, Italy. The purpose of ELCIDIS is to demonstrate the possibilities for more efficient, environmentally cleaner city distribution systems operating with electric vehicles. The cities have differing parts of the programme. In Stockholm, for instance, vans of up to 11 tons capacity are integrated into transport fleets. In Stavanger, the focus is on smaller delivery vans, of up to 500 kg capacity. Citroën, Peugeot and Mercedes electric vehicles are in service for Norway Post, the Public Roads Administration, Lyse Energy and for the Municipality of Stavanger, and recharging stations have been set up. For further details, contact SunLab Attn. H.N. Røstvik ☏ 51533442, ☏ 51524062, ✉ Alexander Kiellandsgt 2, 4009 Stavanger, ✉ sunlab@rl.telia.no, or view the

ELCIDIS web site ⊕ http://citelec.vub.ac.be/elcidis with pages in English.

Electric cars (*Elbiler*) are promoted through governmental measures favouring them, and Stavanger is one of six partner cities in the European electric vehicle project, ☞ **ELCIDIS** . There is no ☞ **annual vehicle tax** on an electric car. Starting in 1999, electric cars are identified by the initial letters EL on their ☞ **car number plates**. An electric car pays no toll on ☞ **toll roads** and parks free (for the posted time limits) in municipal car parks. At least five makes of electric car are now on the roads. Three are made by French car manufacturers, Citroen, Peugeot and Renault. Two are made by Norwegian electric car companies, Kewet and Pivco.

Kewet is the sales leader thus far, with two straightforward, simple models, the Citi-Jet and the Citi-Van. Originally developed and made in Denmark, Kewet cars are now made in Norway. Kollega Bil of Oslo sells and leases the cars. For further information, contact the Kollega Bil head office ✆ 22385615, ☎ 22385687, ☞ Marcus Thranesgate 2A, 0473 Oslo.

Pivco, now owned 51% by Ford, offers the Think, featuring a moulded plastic body on an aluminium space frame. The car was developed and is made in Norway. For further information, contact the Pivco head office ✆ 22252050, ☎ 22254120, ✉ Stanseveien 4, 0975 Oslo, ⊕ http://www.pivco.no with pages in Norwegian and in English.

End-of-life vehicle deposit (*Vrakpant*) The price of a vehicle under 3.5 tons sold in 1977 or later includes a deposit which is refunded when it is dismantled at the end of its life. Upon delivery to an authorised ☞ **vehicle dismantler**, a notice of dismantling (*vrakmelding*) is filled out with the vehicle's registry number (*kjennetegn*) and chassis number (*understellsnummer*). The vehicle dismantler sends the notice to Norwegian Customs and Excise, which then refunds the deposit, NOK 1500 (1999) by post to the owner.

Engine block heaters (*Motorvarmere*) are electrical heaters that warm the coolant in an engine block for easier wintertime starting, faster warm-up, less fuel use and lower battery drain. The typical heater has a capacity of about 400 watts and fits into a frost plug in the water-jacket; there also are models that will heat the oil pan of an air-cooled engine. Models are available to fit all current models of cars, vans and trucks. If you turn the heater on two hours before you intend to start your car – there are automatic timers for the purpose – you save about half a litre of petrol in starting and vastly reduce the wear on the engine. Moreover, in starting on a cold winter morning, a warmed engine emits some 60% to 80% less carbon monoxide than if it were cold, and catalytic converters function sooner after a warm start. Interior heaters (*kupévarmere*) and battery chargers (*batteriladere*) are also available and can be fitted with the engine block heater, so a car will be both comfortably warm and will start easily. All are made to operate from a standard household 220 volt, 50 Hz earth electrical outlet. Some employers fit electrical outlets in their car parks as an extra employee benefit. Car dealers sell and fit engine block heaters, interior heaters and battery chargers, and car parts shops sell them for DIY installation. The leading brands are Bosch, Calix and Defa.

E roads (*Europaveier*) are main international roads in Europe, uniformly numbered in white on rectangular green signs along the roads and on maps, with the letter E followed by a one to three-digit number. In Norway, the E-roads are the principal trunk highways of the ☞ **roads network**. By number and direction, south-to-north and east-to-west, they are listed below. If you have an older map, it may have some older road numbers, which were replaced by newer E numbers on 17 May 1997. The older numbers are listed in brackets (Rv = national road):

- E6 Swedish border at Svinesund – Oslo – Hamar – Trondheim – Narvik – Karasjok – Kirkenes
- E8 Finnish border – Tromsø (connects with E6)
- E10 Swedish border at Bjørnfjell – Sortland – Stokmarknes – Sørvågen (connects with E6)
- E12 Swedish border – Mo i Rana (connects with E6)
- E14 Swedish border at Teveltunet – Størdal (connects with E6)
- E16 Sandvika – Hønefoss – Fagernes (connects with E18)
- E18 Swedish border at Ørje – Oslo – Drammen – Kristiansand- Stavanger (connects with E6)
- E39 Danish ferry quay Kristiansand – Stavanger [old E18]- Bergen – Trondheim [old Rv1, Rv65,

Rv71] (connects with E18)
- E75 Finnish border at Roavvegeddi – Tana bru – Vardø [old Rv98](connects with E6)
- E105 Russian border at Storskog – Kirkenes [old Rv886] (connects with E6)
- E134 Drammen – Haugesund [old Rv11] (connects with E18)
- E136 Dombås – Ålesund [old Rv9] (connects with E6)

Fuel consumption (*Forbruk*) customarily is stated in litres consumed per *mil* (10 km). If you are accustomed to thinking in terms of miles per gallon, you may wish to convert. The UK and US gallons differ, so there are two conversion factors:
- miles per UK gallon = 0.354 km/litre
- miles per US gallon = 0.425 km/litre

Conversions to typical figures are:

consumption	litres/ mil	miles/ UK gallon	miles/ US gallon
low	0.5	56	48
average	1.0	28	24
high	1.5	19	16

Helmets (*Hjelmer*), also called crash helmets (*styrthjelm*) must be worn by motorcycle and moped drivers and their passengers, except:
- when a motorcycle or moped is at a standstill.
- when driving in garages, car parks, petrol stations, workshops or other limited areas.
- when a person has a medical certificate of inability to use a helmet.

Helmets should be approved for motorcycle use. Each current make and model of approved helmet has a number that begins with 04 indicating conformance to the European ECE R22-04 standard in effect since November 1997 as well as a serial number, printed on a label affixed to the retention system or comfort interior.

Helmets are recommended, but not obligatory for cyclists. Accident statistics show that a helmet substantially reduces the chance of serious or fatal head injury in a collision or spill. There are no mandatory standards for cycle helmets, but a good helmet meets the minimum requirements for ☞ **CE marking** (Measurements and Standards chapter). Conformance to various national standards, such as the UK BS6863 or the Swedish KOVFS 1985:6. indicates a reasonable level of protection.

Lights and headlights (*Billys og hovedlys*) Whenever a car or other motor vehicle is being driven, its lights, including headlights or driving lights (*kjørelys*), must be on, day or night. Consequently, many cars have been delivered with lights that turn on with the ignition switch, so they cannot be driven with their lights off. Parking lights may be used only when parked or standing still. All lights must conform to the vehicle construction regulations of the ☞ **ECE** (Government & Social Services chapter). So the lights of vehicles brought in from countries using other regulations may require modification before registration in Norway. For instance, sealed-beam headlamps, as used in the USA and made to Society of Automotive Engineers (SAE) standards, are not permitted, because they lack shielding of the low-beam filament, as required by ECE Regulation 37 for headlamps. Yellow headlamps, as used in France, are permitted, but white headlamps are recommended. The most common headlamp is the type H4 for 12 Volt car electrical systems, which has a power rating of 60 Watts on high beam and 55 Watts on low beam.

Medicines that affect driving (*Trafikkfarlige legemidler*) are marked with a red triangle, with its apex up, on the package. Typically they are tranquilisers (*nervemidler*), sleeping pills (*sovemidler*), travel sickness preparations (*midler mot reisyke*), allergy preparations (*midler mot allergi*), stronger analgesics (*smertestillende midler*), stronger cough suppressants (*hostestillende midler*) and relaxants (*muskelavslappende midler*). You should avoid these if you intend to drive. Even small amounts of alcohol usually will amplify the effects of many of these medicines and further degrade the ability to drive or perform any other activities requiring co-ordination and judgement. Depending on the person, other medicines also may affect driving; consult your doctor if in doubt.

Motorcycles (*Motorsykler*) There are about 70,000 registered motorcycles in the country, and each year, some ten thousand new motorcycles are sold. Six in ten of them are heavy motorcycles and four in ten are light motorcycles and mopeds, with engines of 125 cc or less. The ten leading makes that account for 95% of all new heavy motorcycle sales are BMW, Ducati, Harley Davidson, Honda, Jawa,

Kawasaki, Moto Guzzi, Suzuki, Triumph and Yamaha. The leading makes in new light motorcycle sales are Honda, Jawa, Peugeot, Piaggio, Simson, Suzuki and Yamaha. Look in the Yellow Pages under *Motorsykler og Mopeder* to find the nearest dealer of a particular make. If you fail to find a dealer or seek a dealer for a make of motorcycle not advertised in the Yellow Pages, contact the Motorcycle Importers Association (*Motorsykkelgrosistenes forening*), which maintains an updated list of dealers ✆ 66849711, ✉ 66849788, ⊠ Østre vei 76, 1315 Nesøya.

Motorcycle clubs (*Motorsykkelklubber*) There are some 550 clubs in the country for road motorcyclists. Most of the clubs, 440 in all, are members of the Norwegian Motorcycle Union (*Norsk Motorcykkel Union – NMCU*). In turn, the NMCU is a member of the Nordic Motorcycle Council (NMR) and the Federation of European Motorcyclists Associations (FEMA). In addition to furthering the interests of motorcyclists, the NMCU and its member clubs work with the Public Roads Administration (*Statens Vegvesen*) to promote motorcycle safety and ensure quality training of motorcyclists. The NMCU has regional committees in 18 of the country's 19 counties as well as a staffed head office, which you may contact for information and addresses of clubs ✆ 69256864, ✉ 69256869, ☞ PO Box 5126, 1503 Moss, ✉ nmcu-off@bdsnett.no, ➂ http://www.nmcu.org with pages in Norwegian and summary pages in English, as well as links to the International Riders' Rights Directory (IRR) and other English and multilingual web sites.

Parking (*Parkering*) There are two groups of rules for parking, general rules that apply on all streets and roads, and specific rules that apply in signed and marked areas.

General parking rules state that you may not stop (and, of course, not park):
- Along blind stretches of road (*uoversiktlige steder*).
- In intersections (*veikryss*).
- On walkways or cycle paths/lanes (*gangfelt og sykkelfelt*) or closer than 5 m to them.
- Along motorways (*motorvei*).
- On level crossings (*planovergang*) or rail lines or 5 m from them.
- At public transport stops (*holdeplasser*).

You may stop, but not park:
- In front of a driveway (*inn- og utkjøring*).
- At a lay-by (*møteplass*).
- At pedestrian precincts (*gågater*).
- Along a priority road (*forkjørsvei*), including all national roads and most country roads.

Specific parking rules for signed and marked areas, as in cities and towns:
- No stopping: marked by round blue sign with red border and diagonal slash from upper left to lower right.
- No parking: marked by round blue sign with red border and crossing diagonal slashes.
- Parking allowed: white letter P on rectangular blue background, usually with validity hours below, such as *08-17 (09-15) maks 3 timer mot avgift* which means "8am to 5pm Mon-Fri and 9am to 3pm Sat, maximum 3 hours against fee paid (as in a parking meter or vendor)".
- Car parks: white letter P on rectangular blue background at entrance.

The major cities publish their parking rules in folders, with texts in Norwegian, English, French and German, available at tourist offices, police stations and some car parks.

Pedestrian reflectors (*Personreflekser*) are small plastic figures that people wear at night to be better seen by cars. In the dark, a pedestrian, jogger or cyclist is first visible to a car with dipped headlights at a distance of 30 metres. At a speed of 50 km/h, the driver then has just two seconds to react, and less time at higher speeds. However, if the person is wearing a reflector, it seems to flash in the lights of the car. The distance of first visibility goes up to 150 metres, which gives the driver more time to react. Indeed, Nordic country statistics show that persons not wearing reflectors are eight times more likely to be involved in night-time accidents than those wearing reflectors. Consequently, all Nordic traffic safety organisation recommend their use.

Pedestrian reflectors are technically known as retroreflectors, which means that they reflect light back in the direction from which it comes, irrespective of the angle involved. They actually are high-tech devices and are used in advanced applications such as laser surveying. A retroreflecting cube was left on the moon to allow accurate measurement of its distance from the earth using a laser. The more down-to-earth applications include car rear reflectors, traffic signs and road markings.

There are many shapes and sizes of pedestrian retroreflectors. The most popular variety is fitted with a string and a safety pin, so it may be pinned into a pocket and taken out at night to dangle and move as you walk, which improves its reflection. The most common shape is a circle, about six centimetres in diameter. But there are many other shapes: square, rectangular, snowflake, teddy bears and other animals familiar to children. Some are fitted with clips to attach to bicycle spokes or tape to adhere to jogging clothing. All pedestrian retroreflectors conform to the International Commission on Illumination (CIE) standards and to the various Nordic country standards, such as Norwegian standard NS9370.

Pedestrian retroreflectors are sold in petrol stations, sports shops and supermarkets. But by far, most are given away free, as advertising for shops and companies as well as public agencies, including schools and the police. Each year, several hundred thousand free advertising retroreflectors are given away and used in the Nordic countries.

The leading manufacturers of the pedestrian retroreflectors available in Norway are Grønneviken Industrier of Norway ✆ 55948820, 🖷 55348101, ✉ Herman Grans vei 5, 5162 Laksevåg and Talmu of Finland ✆ +358 277551, 🖷 +358 27755500, ✉ FIN-24100 Salo, Finland, ✇ http://www.talmu.fi with pages in English.

Periodic car inspection (*Periodisk kontroll av personbiler*) All registered motor vehicles must be periodically inspected for roadworthiness and emissions. The inspection is in accordance with EEA agreements and EU directives, so it is commonly called *EØS kontroll* ("EEA inspection") or *EU kontroll* ("EU inspection"). Private cars and vans up to 3,500 kg are inspected first when four years old and thereafter every other year. Buses, taxis regardless of weight and all other motor vehicles and trailers over 3,500 kg are inspected once a year. Private cars registered before 1 January 1960 are exempt from inspection. The last figure of a car's number plates determine the year and last month for inspection:

Even figure: 0 in October, 2 in February, 4 in April, 6 in June and 8 in August of even-numbered years (2000, 2002 etc.)

Odd figure: 1 in January, 3 in March, 5 in May,

7 in November and 9 in September of odd-numbered years (1999, 2001 etc.).

Two months before its inspection month, the nearest traffic station (*Trafikkstasjon*) will send you a written notice calling your car in. So you then have three months to call and make an appointment and have the car inspected. Inspection may be performed by the local *Trafikkstasjon* or by any one of 1800 authorised car repair shops (*bilverksteder*) throughout the country. There is a charge for inspection, which varies among the car repair shops but is the same for all *Trafikkstasjoner* throughout the country. The results of the inspection are reported on a standard inspection form (*Kontrollseddel*) to the *Trafikkstasjon* where the car is registered.

The form is a check list of 84 items (not all applicable to passenger cars) in eight categories: 1 Identification (*Identitet*), 2 Brake system (*Bremseanlegg*) and Brake function (*Bremsevirkning*), 2 Steering (*Styring*), 3 Visibility (*Sikt*), 4 Lights, Reflectors and Electrical system (*Lys/Refleks/Elektrisk*), 5 Axles, Suspension, Springs, Shock absorbers, Wheels and Tyres (*Aksler/Hjulopph/Fjærer/Støtdempere/Hjul/Dekk*), 6 Support structure and Bodywork (*Bærende konstruksj/Karosseri/Påbygg*), 7 Other Equipment (*Annet utstyr*) and 8 Emissions (*Miljø*).

If a car passes the inspection, it is recommended for approval (*godkjenning*) and the original *Kontrollseddel* is given to the owner to keep with the registration (*vognkort*) in the car. A car that fails the inspection must be repaired and then taken to the *Trafikkstasjon* for inspection.

Petrol (*Bensin*) is sold in three principal varieties, none leaded:
- 98 octane with lubricating additives (*98 Bensin*), with red signs and hose nozzle collars on pumps.
- 98 and 95 octane with no additives (*Blifri*), with green signs and hose nozzle collars on pumps.

Sale of leaded petrol ceased throughout the country on 31 December 1995. So the word *Blifri* ("Unleaded") is outdated. But it persists, both in everyday language and in signs on pumps in ☞ **petrol stations**. So when you see *Blifri*, regard it to mean "no additives".

The price of petrol is among the highest in the world, principally because taxes account for about 80% of the price you pay at a petrol station pump. Nonetheless, there is competition and prices differ by location and time of the year. Occasionally there are petrol price wars (*bensinkrig*). In general, the unattended stations have the lowest prices, which are often matched, or nearly so, by competing attended stations nearby. So to save most when tanking, look for an unattended station or an attended station near it.

Petrol stations (*Bensinstasjoner*) Eight companies together have 2217 petrol stations in the country: Esso and Statoil have the most, with 525 each, followed by Shell with 429, Hydro-Texaco with 412, Fina (now owned by Shell) and including Smart with 279, Conoco Jet with 28 and Rema with 19. Most petrol stations are manned and have convenience shops, and some are open day-round. All petrol stations are self-serve and accept credit cards, bank debit cards or their own proprietary charge cards, often at the pumps, and cash at the till during opening hours. The Conoco Jet and Smart unattended stations accept cards and bank notes. Almost all petrol stations in the country sell ☞ **Diesel** and three varieties of ☞ **Petrol**, and many also sell paraffin oil and tax-free diesel for non-road use. For locations of stations, look under the names of the companies in the Pink Pages or view their Internet sites:
Esso ✉ http://www.esso.no,
Statoil ✉ http://www.statoil.no,
Shell and Fina ✉ http://www.shell.no,
Hydro-Texaco ✉ http://www.hydrotexaco.no,
Conoco Jet ✉ http://www.jet.no

Practice driving (*Øvelseskjøring*) for taking the test for the common category B (**driving licence** is allowed for persons 16 and older. There are four ways to prepare for taking the test:
1. All training at a driving school (*kjøreskole*).
2. Practice driving, as with one of your parents.
3. Some practice at a driving school and some private.
4. Co-operative training between a driving school and your parents.

Regardless of which of these four alternatives you may choose, you must complete the mandatory minimum of 9.5 hours of training at a driving school, consisting of driving:
• in traffic (*i trafikk*).
• on snow and ice (*glattkjøring*).
• at night (*mørkekjøring*).

You may drive only when accompanied by a qualified driver in the car. That driver must be at least 25 years old and must have a valid driving licence held for at least five consecutive years. The car used must have a hand brake between the front seats, be fitted with an extra mirror and carry a square white sign with a red letter L, clearly visible from behind the vehicle, whenever the practice driver is driving. The extra mirror and the L signs are sold by the ☞ **automobile associations** and many ☞ **petrol stations**. For further details, contact the nearest Traffic Station (*Trafikkstasjon*) listed under *Statens vegvesen* in the Pink Pages.

The Public Roads Administration (*Statens vegvesen*) is an agency of the Ministry of Transport and Communications (*Samferdselsdepartementet*). It has district offices (*vegkontor*) throughout the country, one in each of the 19 counties. Each district office administers one or more road depots (*vegstasjon*) and traffic stations (*trafikkstasjon*). In all, there are 92 road depots and traffic stations in the country, some of them joint depots and stations. You can find them listed in the Pink Pages under *Statens vegvesen*. You may contact the road depots for information on road works, road traffic and weather conditions and the like. If you drive a car, you probably will deal most often with the traffic stations, which inspect vehicles, process vehicle sale and transfer documents and issue ☞ **car number plates**, and examine for and issue ☞ **driving licences.**

Road maps (*Vei kart*) are sold by book shops, kiosks and petrol stations. Book shops usually have the best selection. The two leading map publishers are the Norwegian Mapping Authority (*Statens kartverk*), a government agency, and Cappelen, a domestic publisher with its own map-making division. The Statens Kartverk selection of road maps includes:
• maps in 1:400,000 scale for the country in four sections: South (*Sør*), Mid (*Midt*), Nordland county and Troms and Finnmark counties.
• map of entire country in 1:1,000,000 scale.
• atlas book in 1:300,000 scale with cities in 1:20,000 scale.
• city maps and street plans.
• *Veiviseren* ("Road guide") CD-ROM for Windows 3.x, 95 and NT, with driving route, time and cost

information.

Moreover, Statens Kartverk offers a quadrangle map series covering the entire country (*Norge 1:50000*), recreational maps (*Turkartserien*), the Explore Norway (*Opplev Norge*) CD-ROM for Windows 95/98 & NT4.0, nautical charts of several types (*Sjøkart, Båtsportkart, Den norske los*), as well as imported maps including:

- Hallwag (Switzerland) road maps of Europe.
- Berndtson & Berndtson (Germany) road maps, geographic maps, recreational maps, city guides and road atlases for Europe, the USA and Australia.

On-line lists of map may be viewed at ☞ http://www.statkart.no

Cappelen road maps include:

- maps in 1:325,000 scale for counties and regions to 1:1,000,000 for the whole country.
- city guides for Ålesund, Bergen, Drammen, Haugesund, Moss, Oslo, Sandefjord and Sarpsborg,

Moreover, Cappelen offers mountain recreation maps (*Fjellkart*) in 1:100,000 scale, as well as a selection of imported maps, including:

- GeoCenter (Germany and the UK) road and other maps of the world.
- Geodætisk Institut (Denmark) road maps of Denmark.
- Kümberly+Frey (Switzerland) road maps of European and other countries.
- Lanmäteriet (Sweden) road maps of Sweden.
- Michelin (France) road touring maps of Europe and some countries in Africa.

For a complete list of all road and outdoor maps, see the annual Cappelen catalogue (*katalog*) available free at book shops, or view the map list on-line at ☞ http://www.cappelen.no by selecting *Faktabøker* and then *Alle faktabøker*. The abbreviations of the map publishers used in the catalog and on the web site are: CK Cappelen, FA Falk, GEO GeoCenter International, GI Geodætisk Institut, KF Kümberly+Frey, LAN Lanmäteriet and MI Michelin.

The Road Patrol (*Utrykningspolitiet – UP*) is the part of the ☞ **Police** (Crimes, Wrongs, Countermeasures chapter). It originally was a countrywide mobile police force intended to support local police, but now it is primarily responsible for reducing traffic accident rates and ensuring adherence to traffic rules. Its functions include monitoring traffic, including performing ☞ **spot checks**, controlling the transport of hazardous goods, monitoring traffic noise and pollution, monitoring adherence to trucking regulation and keeping an eye on all vehicles and persons suspected of illegal use, transport or trade in narcotics.

Roads network (*Veier*) In all, there are 90,471 km of roads in the country. Of the total, about 40% are local authority roads (*kommunale veier*), 30% county roads (*fylkes veier*) and 30% national roads (*riksveier*). About 7,600 km of the national roads, including the international ☞ **E-roads**, are classified as trunk roads (*stamveier*), which, though they make up only 8.4% of the roads network, carry about half of all traffic. In all, 570 km of the trunk roads are motorways. A motorway is a highway with restricted access from other roads. It is for motor vehicles only; pedestrians and cyclists are not allowed. There are two types of motorway in Norway:

- Class A motorway (*Motorveg klasse A*) has no level intersections with other roads, has two or more lanes in each direction and has a median strip or barrier dividing the directions.
- Class B motorway (*Motorveg klasse B*) may have level intersections with minor roads, has one lane in each direction and has no physical separation between the directions.

In all, there are 128 km of Class A motorway and 442 km of Class B motorway. Compared even to some smaller countries, the total network is modest, the 18th longest in Europe. But though the cities are congested as are cities elsewhere, the overall road network is the least congested in Europe, just 18 cars per kilometre of road.

Road maps are sold in the ☞ **petrol stations** that have convenience shops and by kiosks and book shops throughout the country. The ☞ **automobile associations** publish updated maps and touring guides. Two good reference books on roads are:

Veg i Norge/Roads in Norway, compiled by Geir Hasle, Public Roads Administration, 1993, 88 pages hardcover, Norwegian and English text. An authoritative guide to the road network and road building.

Adventure Roads in Norway by Erling Welle-Strand, NOTRA Books 1996, 256 pages hardcover, in English, ISBN 82-90103-71-9. A well illustrated guide to day tours or extended touring.

Road user information centre (*Vegmeldingstjenesten*) The Public Roads Administration maintains an information centre that continuously monitors and provides information on roads and road conditions throughout the country, including driving distances and national highway ferry timetables. Call its countrywide, 24-hour helpline ✆ 175.

Seat belts (*Bilbelter*) must be used whenever they are fitted in a car, except:
• when a car is at a standstill.
• in reversing.
• when driving in garages, car parks, petrol stations, workshops or other limited areas.
• in low-speed driving with frequent stops, such as to deliver mail or newspapers, pick up refuse and so on.
• when a person has a medical certificate of inability to use a seat belt.
• for drivers of taxis in service.
Infants and children should be seated in a carrier or portable child restraint seat (CRS) fitted to the adult diagonal and lap seat belt of a car and approved to the European ECE R44-03 standard in effect since late 1998. There are five categories:
• Group 0: age 0 – 9 months, weight 0 – 10 kg.
• Group 0+: age 0 – 18 months, weight 0 – 13 kg.
• Group 1: age 9 months – 4 years, weight 9 – 18 kg.
• Group 2: age 4 – 7 years, weight 15 – 25 kg.
• Group 3: age 6 – 11 years, weight 22 – 36 kg.
Some of the Group 0 carriers and seats are designed to travel rearward facing in the front seat (unless a passenger airbag is fitted) or in the rear seat. Children age 12 and younger or shorter than 140 cm should not sit in a seat where an airbag is fitted. However, if a child must sit in a seat with an airbag, the airbag legally may be disabled and then enabled at some later date, provided the disabling and enabling are entered in the car's registration card (*vognkort*). Check with the car brand dealer for the procedure as well as with the nearest traffic station (*Trafikkstasjon*) for details.

Speed limits (*Fartsgrenser*) Unless posted, the countrywide speed limits are 50 km/h in built-up areas and 80 km/h on open roads. The open road limit is posted down to 70 km/h on many roads, to reduce road accident rates. The first trunk road with the reduced limit was the E18 highway on the west side of the Oslofjord, identified as a high accident stretch (*ulykkesstrekning*) throughout Vestfold County and consequently now posted for 70 km/h.

A posted limit is given by a black number on a white background on a circular sign with a red border. The end of a posted zone is indicated by a circular sign with the same number in gray on a white background with diagonal slash lines through the number. Some motorways and other roads of high standard are posted for 90 km/h. Residential areas are usually posted for 30 km/h or 40 km/h. Some thinly built up areas are posted for 60 km/h.

There are a few exceptions. Even on roads posted for 90 km/h, caravans and cars towing trailers without brakes and weighing more than 300 kg are limited to 60 km/h, cars towing trailers with brakes as well as buses and trucks are limited to 80 km/h.

Spot checks (*Trafikkontroll*) of motor vehicles may be made at any time along any road by the ☞ **road patrol** or by Public Roads Administration personnel or both. Customs officers may also spot check vehicles close to the borders with Sweden and Finland and on either side of them. Spot checks are made by uniformed officers, usually wearing yellow reflecting vests with their functions on the back, such as *Politi* ("Police") or *Toll* ("Customs").

A spot check may be of all vehicles or selected vehicles, such as just heavy trucks. If you are stopped, you will be asked to show your ☞ **driving licence** and the ☞ **car registration**, which the law requires that you have in the vehicle when driving. If your car is registered in Norway, the ☞ **annual vehicle tax** stickers on the number plates and the latest ☞ **periodic inspection** certificate carried with the registration will also be checked. If the spot check is for ☞ **drink-driving**, all drivers will be given breath tests. If the spot check is for roadworthiness, Public Roads Administration officers may check the car. Roadworthiness checks as well as truck weight and hazardous goods transport checks usually are made at permanent roadside scales, which are open only when checks are made.

A spot check may be only of vehicles that have violated a traffic regulation, in most cases speeding. These checks usually are made by two groups of police. The first uses radar or laser speed meters to check the speed of all vehicles passing a point. They radio the registration of speeding vehicles further along the road to the second group, who stops the offenders.

Close to borders, customs officers may spot check vehicles for goods in excess of ☞ **duty-free quotas** (Travel and Transport chapter) as well as for illegal goods such as narcotics.

In 1999, some police districts extended the powers of *UP* officers at spot checks to conduct general search of suspicious vehicles or their passengers.

Tax-free export cars (*eksport biler*) If you will be in Norway temporarily, for less than a year, you may buy a tax-free car for export to your home country. Most major international makes of cars have tax-free export programmes in which you can order a car in advance, to the specifications of your home country, drive it for less than a year and take it home when you leave. It will be fitted with tax-free number plates (*Tollskilt*) which resemble ordinary ☞ **Car number** plates but have two black numerals on a red background at each end of the plate giving the month (left) and year (right) of expiration. Tax-free registration is permitted in Oslo, Bergen, Kristiansand, Larvik, Trondheim and Tromsø. Dealers in those cities will have the details. You also may inquire at a major dealer in your home country before departure. Saab and Volvo, which are made in neighbouring Sweden, offer extensive programmes that include home shipping from selected ports for cars made to Canadian or US specifications.

Saab International and Diplomat Sales (IDS) has its head office in Gothenburg ✆ +46 52085000, 🖷 +46 31630126, ✉ Saab International and Diplomat Sales, PO Box 1545, S-40150 Göteborg, Sweden, 🖳 http://www.saab.com with pages in English. The Saab IDS representative in Norway is SAAB Norge ✆ 22064600, 🖷 22064608, ✉ PO Box 314 Skøyen, 0212 Oslo.

Volvo Tourist and Diplomat Sales (TDS) has its head office in Gothenburg ✆ +46 31590000, 🖷 +46 31535535, ✉ Volvo Car International AB, S-40508 Göteborg, Sweden, 🖳 http://www.car.volvo.se with pages in English. The Volvo TDS representative in Norway is Isbergs Personbiler ✆ 22882500, 🖷 22645517, ✉ PO Box 240 Økern, 0510 Oslo.

TIR plates (*TIR skilt*) Large blue plates with the letters TIR in white, at the front and back of a truck, indicate that it is qualified to carry goods internationally between countries without being subject to customs inspection in countries of transit along its route. TIR is an abbreviation of *Transport Internationale Routier*, the shortened name in French of the Customs Convention on the International Transport of Goods, which is administered by the Transport Division of the ☞ **ECE** (Government & Social Services chapter). A TIR qualified vehicle has a carnet, which is a customs permit that allows it to remain abroad from its home country for an limited period of time.

Toll roads (*Bomveier*) Tolls (*bompenger*) are collected on some roads, bridges and ferries (*veier, bruer og fjergsamband*). As a general rule, cyclists, pedestrians, emergency vehicles, funeral processions and road maintenance vehicles are exempt from tolls. Motorcycles are exempted from toll on some toll roads. Larger plazas (*bomstasjoner*) have several lanes, usually marked for vehicles with toll subscriptions (*abonnement*) and for automatic and manual toll booths. Three cities, Oslo, Bergen and Trondheim, charge tolls for entering the city from outside a ring of roads around it (*bompengering*). The other toll plazas along national roads are listed below by the road number (E for European highway, Rv for National Road), station name and county.

E6, Lierfjorden road, Nordland and Troneheim-Stjørdal road, Sør-Trøndelag

E10, Nappstraumen tunnel, Nordland

E16, Sollihøgda-Vik road, Buskerud

E18, Eidanger peninsula roads, Telemark and Drammen through road, Buskerud

E39, Kristansund mainland road, Møre og Romsdal, Nordhordaland bridge, Hordaland and Rennesøy ferry, Rogaland

E69, Kåfjord-Honningsvåg ferry, Finnmark

E134, Åkrafjorden road, Hordaland

Rv1, Mortevika-Arsvågen ferry, Rogaland and ferries to/from Valevåg, Hordaland

Rv5, Fjørland-Sogndal road, Fodnes-Mannheller ferry and Naustdals tunnel, Sogn og Fjordane

Rv17, Helgelands bridge, Nordland

Rv47, Mekjarvik-Skudeneshavn ferry, Rogaland

Rv64, Skålavegen tunnel/bridge, Møre og Romsdal

Rv108, Hvaler tunnel, Østfold

Rv354, Kulltangen bridge, Telemark

Rv457, Flekkerøy tunnel, Vest-Agder

Rv545, Valevåg-Skjersholmane ferry and Sagvåg-
Siggjarvåg ferry, Hordaland
Rv562, Askøy bridge, Hordaland
Rv653, Eiksund ferry, Møre og Romsdal
Rv658, Ålesund-Giske/Vigra road, Møre og Romsdal
Rv714, Hitra mainland road, Hitra-Fjellværøy road
and Kjerringvåg-Flatval ferry, Sør-Trøndelag
Rv755, Skasrnusund bridge, Nord-Trøndelag
Rv863, Kvalsund mainland road, Troms

Traffic accidents with personal injury
(*Trafikkulykker med personskade*) are more frequent than in the other Nordic countries. In 1997,
there were 275 injuries, 7 of them fatal, per 100,000
population, compared to 247 (6 fatal) in Sweden,
192 (9 fatal) in Denmark and 183 (9 fatal) in Finland. Nonetheless, in Europe, Norway ranks 24th in
the number of road accidents and not even in the
top 30 in the number of persons killed. For the ten-
year period, 1989–1998, an average of around
12,000 persons a year were injured in traffic, 314
fatally. Nonetheless, driving is increasingly safer. In
1939, when there were less than 120,000 motor
vehicles in the country – against 1.8 million today –
nearly 2600 persons were injured in accidents, 116
of them fatally.

Traffic fines (*Bøtesatser ved trafikforseelser*) can,
if the police so elect, be on-the-spot optional fines
(*forenklet foelegg*). Fines are set by local police departments and must be paid within 14 days of acceptance. The arresting police officer will write out a
form with an attached ☞ **Giro** (Banking, Finance,
Insurance chapter) form for payment. For extremely
serious or multiple violations, the police may confiscate a driving licence and initiate prosecution, with
no option for on-the-spot fines. For further information on traffic offences and fines, contact your local
police department (*Politi*), and for information on the
details of payment, the State Agency for the Recovery of Fines, Damages and Costs (*Statens Innkrevn-
ingssentral*) ✆ 75124200, ☎ 75155502, ✉ PO Box
455, 8601 Mo i Rana. For an overview of on-the-spot
optional fines, see the ☞ **Road patrol** folder in Norwegian or the international version in five languages
(English, German, French, Italian and Spanish), which
is available from police departments. The following
condensed Code of Offences is extracted from the
1998 edition of the folder.

- Excessive speed in 60 km/h or lower speed-limit
zone: varying from NOK 500 or three days imprisonment for up to 5 km/h over limit, up to NOK
2500 or 11 days imprisonment for 21-25 km/h
over limit.
- Excessive speed in 70km/h or higher speed-limit
zone: varying from NOK 400 or three days imprisonment for up to 5 km over limit, up to NOK
3500 or 15 days imprisonment for 31-35 km/h
over limit.
- Driving through a red light: NOK 2500 or 11 days
imprisonment.
- Failure to comply with traffic signs: NOK 1900 or
seven days imprisonment.
- Crossing solid centreline, driving on pavement,
turning from wrong lane or driving without proper registration: NOK 1300 or five days imprisonment.
- Illegal overtaking: NOK 2500 or 11 days imprisonment.
- Failure to give way: NOK 2500 or 11 days imprisonment.
- Driving with defective or improper lights, failure
to give proper signals, improper light use, carrying more people than allowed by vehicle certification: NOK 600 or three days imprisonment.
- Riding a motorcycle or moped that has been
altered to have more power or attain a higher
speed than for which it was registered: NOK 1200
or five days imprisonment.
- Driving a car with a defective hand brake: for
vehicle less than 3.5 tons: NOK 1200 or five days
imprisonment; for vehicle over 3.5 tons: NOK
2500 or 11 days imprisonment.
- Driving a moped or a tractor legally incapable of
more than 40 km/h on a motorway: NOK 600 or
three days imprisonment.
Cycling in violation of traffic signs and signals: NOK
400 or three days imprisonment.

Traffic signs (*Trafikkskilt*) use internationally
recognised symbols, so you can get the message,
even if you don't know the language. There are three
main groups of signs.
Circular signs are orders that you must obey.
Red circles are prohibitive (*forbudsskilt*), telling you
what you must not do. For instance, a black number
on a white background in a red circle is the maximum allowable speed. Blue circles give positive

instructions (*påbudsskilt*) telling you what you must do. For instance, a bent white arrow pointing to the right in a blue circle means that your lane must turn right at the next intersection.

Rectangular signs provide information. A blue sign is for general information. E road numbers are in white on a green background, other road numbers in black on a white background. Yellow signs with black lettering give road directions. Yellow chevrons on a black background mark a sharp deviation.

Triangular signs give advance warning of hazards (*fareskilt*), give way (*vikepliktskilt*) and right-of-way (*forkjørsskilt*). They give you information on the road ahead and what you must prepare to encounter. If you have driven in Europe, you most likely will recognise all of them, save two silhouettes: a running moose warns of an animal crossing and a skier warns of a ski trail crossing.

If you take a course of instruction for a ☞ **driving licence**, you will learn the signs. Otherwise, colour folders with all current signs are available free at all ☞ **Public roads administration** traffic stations and are listed in many maps and road guidebooks. Some signs, particularly temporary information signs for diversions, may use abbreviations, of which the most common are:

E, Ev Europaveg E-Road
F, Fv Fylkesveg County Road
Fk Ferjekai Ferry quay
Gr Grense Border
kl klokke hour of the day
Kv Kommunal veg Municipal Road
Omkj. Omkjøring Diversion
R, Rv Riksveg National Road
X kryss Crossing

Transport of dangerous goods (*Transport av farlig gods*) Norway is one of 34 contracting parties to the European Agreement concerning the International Carriage of Dangerous Goods by Road (ADR), which is administered by the Transport Division of the ☞ **ECE** (Government & Social Services chapter). ADR aims to increase the safety of international transport by road, and contains provisions on:
• types of packing which may be used
• consignment procedures
• transport equipment (vehicles and their construction and equipment)

• operations (driver training, supervision, emergency procedures, loading and unloading, signs on vehicles)
The ADR provisions concerning flammable and explosive materials are administered by the Directorate for Fire and Explosion Prevention (*Directoratet for Brann og Ekxplosjonsvern*). The ADR provisions concerning radioactive materials are administered by the Norwegian Radiation Protection Authority (*Statens Strålevern*). Vehicles carrying dangerous goods are marked with conspicuous signs, red with a flame for flammable goods and yellow with a radiation symbol for radioactive goods.

Trygg Trafikk is the Norwegian society for traffic safety. Founded in 1958 at the initiative of the Ministry of Transport (*Samferdselsdepartementet*) and other agencies and organisations, including the ☞ **automobile associations**, it now is a countrywide organisation with local offices in all 19 counties and 315 member organisations, institutions, associations, companies and county agencies. It works closely with sibling organisations in the other Nordic countries, such as the National Society for Road Safety (*Nationalföreningen för Trafiksäkerhetens Främande*) in neighbouring Sweden. Internationally, it is a member of the International Road Safety Organisation – PRI (*La Prévention Routière Internationale*). Trygg Trafikk's major mission is to promote road safety with the goal of decreasing road fatalities and injuries and raising people's awareness of road dangers. It does this in many ways, principally through long-term public awareness campaigns, such as the Children's Traffic Club (*Barnas Trafikklubb*) for children ages 3 to 6 plus and through acting as a central clearinghouse for all topics related to road and traffic safety. It publishes safety booklets, often in cooperation with the Public Roads Administration, as well as a regular professional periodical, *Trafikken og Vi* ("Traffic and Us").

For further details and the addresses of local offices and member organisations, contact the Trygg Trafikk head office in Oslo ✆ 22209215, ☎ 22110195, ✉ PO Box 2610 St. Hanshaugen, 0131 Oslo, ✺ http://www.tryggtrafikk.no, or for further information on road safety organisations throughout Europe and the current issue of the European Road Safety News, contact the PRI head office ✆ +352 318341, ☎ +352 311460, ✉ PO Box 40,

L-8005 Luxembourg, ✉ int.road.safety@pri.lu, ⊕ http://www.restena.lu/pri with pages in English, French and German.

Trucking (Veitransport) The allowable sizes and weights of trucks are limited according to the carrying capacity of roads and bridges. There are five road use classes (bruksklasser), abbreviated Bk and a numeral indicating the maximum axle load, from six to ten tons. The heaviest, Bk10, permits an axle load of up to 10 tons or up to 11.5 tons if it is a single driving axle. The entire main road network (stamvegnett) is now classified to Bk10 and for total truck weights of up to 50 tons, the same as in the Netherlands, less than Finland (53 tons) but more than most other European countries. Some 1730 km of roads in the national network (riksvegnett) are limited to lower axle load use classes; about half of the limitations are due to the limited carrying capacities of bridges. The maximum allowable width is 2.55 m, or 2.6 m for a built-on van body (påbygg) for refrigerated transport. The maximum allowable length is 18.75 m, or up to 22 m for timber transport (tømmertransport). The weight class restrictions on roads are listed in a booklet and drawn on a map published by the ☞ **Public Roads Administration**:

- Vegliste, Riksveger ("Road list, National Roads) is a booklet with tables of the weight capacities of all national roads.
- Tungtrafikk på riksveger i Norge ("Heavy traffic on national roads in Norway") is a map with all details on weight, width and length restrictions, with texts in Norwegian, English, Finnish, French and German.

Tunnels (Tunneler) There are some 820 road tunnels (vegtunneler) in the country, which together have a total length of some 600 km. Many are short, about one kilometre or less in length. But there also are many long tunnels: of the 100 longest road tunnels in the world, 25 are in Norway, and the world's longest, 24.5 km on the new E16 motorway between Aurland and Lærdal in Sogn og Fjordane county is now being built and is scheduled for opening in 2001. There are 17 tunnels under waterways or parts of fjords, and five more are under construction, including the North Cape Tunnel which, at 6.8 km, will be one of the world's longest. There are also many shorter road underpasses (vegunderganger)

and railway underpasses (jernbane underganger). Tunnels are posted ahead of each entrance with a triangular advance warning sign with a red border and a black drawing of a tunnel entrance. The vertical height clearance in most tunnels is 4.5 m. Tunnels with lower clearances are posted ahead of each entrance with a round prohibited sign with a red border and the restricted height of vehicle in black on a white background. Tunnel data are stated in two free publications of the ☞ **Public Roads Administration**:

- Tunneler og underganger på riksveger i Norge ("Tunnels and underpasses in Norway") is a booklet with texts and tables in Norwegian and summary texts in English.
- Tungtrafikk på riksveger i Norge ("Heavy traffic on national roads in Norway") is a map with all details, including the restrictions on the transport of dangerous goods (farlig gods) in some road tunnels.

Tyres (Dekk) for cars and other motor vehicles are available in as many brands and types as elsewhere in Europe; look under Bilgummi ("Car tyre dealers") or Bilgummiverksteder ("Car tyre services") in the Yellow Pages.

Studded tyres (piggdekk) were developed in the 1960s and rapidly became popular in the Nordic countries, prompted in part by road laws requiring that a car have sufficient grip for the road conditions. A studded tyre usually has 80 to 120 steel studs, each projecting about 1.5 mm out from the running surface of the tyre. The purpose of the studs is to increase grip on ice and snow. So they have been permitted for winter use, but prohibited in the summertime, from the first Monday after Easter until 1 November in most of the country, and from 1 May to 15 October in the three northernmost counties. This requirement prompted car owners to have two sets of tyres, usually mounted on hubs to simplify changing twice a year.

However, studded tyres were soon found to have several serious drawbacks. Most obviously, the studs abrade roads. Asphalt surfaces wear three times as fast when wet than when dry. So the combination of a long winter and a high percentage of vehicles fitted with studded tyres accelerated road wear. In the late 1990s, some two hundred thousand tons of asphalt a year were worn off the roads of the country. Aside from expense of road repair – some NOK 250 million a year – the pulverised asphalt dust in the air became a serious health hazard, particularly in cities, where the roads were clear of ice and snow for most of the winter. Another drawback was that the noise generated by studded tyres bothered both drivers and those who lived along roads. Moreover, the grip of new studded tyres diminishes as the studs wear, and worn studded tyres were found to give drivers a false sense of security – which, in turn, contributed to increasing the chances of collisions in winter. Consequently, the Public Roads Administration (*Statens Vegvesen*) now advises against studded tyres, and the cities of Oslo, Bergen, Trondheim and Stavanger may impose an extra duty on cars fitted with them. Oslo elected that option and starting 1 December 1999, now imposes a duty of NOK 1,000 a year or NOK 350 a month for short-term use within the city limits. Bergen and Trondheim expect to impose a duty in 2000 or later, and Stavanger perhaps in 2002.

Because studded tyres have been so popular, the alternatives to them are called "studless" (*piggfrie*). Studless winter tyres are not the same as all weather M+S (Mud and Snow) tyres. The designs of most M+S rated tyres emphasise high-speed highway performance ahead of grip on snow and ice. True studless winter tyres usually are made of softer rubber than are ordinary road tyres or M+S tyres, for better grip at low temperatures. But the softer rubber will wear more quickly in higher speed summertime driving. So if used in summer, studless winter tyres may be less safe than ordinary road tyres in braking and manoeuvring at high speeds. Consequently, just as for studded tyres, car owners usually have two sets of tyres, one for winter and one for summer, mounted on hubs, and a set of chains (*kjettinger*) for grip on icy stretches of road when needed.

Vehicle dismantlers (*Biloppsamlere*) Each year, more than 80,000 cars and other motor vehicles are scrapped. The companies involved usually are listed in the Yellow Pages under *Bilopphogging* ("Car breaking") and often use that word in their names. But other terms are also used, including *Bildemontering* ("Car dismantling") and *Bilskroting* ("Car scrapping"). The dismantlers authorised to accept vehicles for refund of the ☞ **End-of-life vehicle deposit** are also called *Biloppsamlingsplass* ("Car collection depot"), and may be so listed in the Yellow Pages or may mention that status in their advertisements in listings under *Bilopphogging*. Most dismantlers now operate according to regulations based on the proposed EU Directive on End of Life Vehicles, COM(97)358, and accordingly sort the dismantled materials for re-cycling or safe destruction. The sale of used car parts (*brukte bildeler*) is part of the re-cycling and is a major service of most dismantlers. So if you need used car parts, look under *Bilopphogging* in the Yellow Pages. More than 60 dismantlers, all authorised as car collection depots, coordinate their used parts sales through the Norwegian Car Dismantlers Association (*Norges Biloppsamlers Forening – NBF*), which publishes a catalogue of some 100,000 used parts (*Delebilkatalogen*) in ten issues a year. The NBF is a member of the European Group of Automotive Recycling Associations (EGARA) and thereby has access to vehicle dismantlers throughout Europe. For further details on vehicle dismantlig or a subscription to the used parts catalogue, contact the NBF office ✆ 22598894, ✇ 22567575, ✉ Parkveien 9, 0350 Oslo, ✍ lnyboe@online.no, ⊕ http://www.lokalnett.com/Nbf

Wintertime road restrictions apply whenever roads either are closed for the winter (*vinterstengte veger*) or may in adverse weather be open only to traffic in convoys of vehicles (*kolonnekjøring*), to prevent lone vehicles being stranded by drifting snows. Most of the affected roads are in the high mountain plateau region in the central, southern part of the country or close and along the coast in the northern part of the country, including the northern part of Nordland county, Troms county and Finnmark county. For instance, in the wintertime, convoy driving is often required along stretches of the E6 south-north highway. In all cases, closed roads or convoy conditions are posted alongside the road, usually at the last junction or town open to road traffic. For the latest information for the entire country, call the road conditions service (*Vegmeldingstjenesten*), a 24-hour countrywide helpline ✆ 175. The ☞ **automobile associations** and the district offices of the ☞ **Public Roads Administration** also have continuously updated information.

Character, Customs, Country
(Væremåte, Skikk, Land)

About Norway (Om Norge) Norway is a constitutional monarchy. This means that the King rules according to powers granted in the Constitution and that the monarchy is sustained by law. It can, by vote of Parliament, be abolished by an amendment to the Constitution. Proposals for such an amendment have been put forth, but all have been tabled in Parliament, which underscores the popularity of the Royal family. One reason may be that Parliament itself had a hand in establishing the current Royal line, when in 1905 it asked Prince Carl of Denmark to ascend the throne, which he did as King Haakon VII – the grandfather of King Harald V now on the throne.

In principle, the King is one of the three pillars of government – the other two are the legislature and the judiciary. But in practice, that is a formality only, as the ministerial Government exercises the powers granted to the King by the Constitution. It does this through the Cabinet of Ministers, of which the King is the formal head.

These and other matters, the A-Z of the country's character and customs, are the topics of this chapter.

Americanisation (Amerikanisering) As elsewhere in Europe, the popularity of American culture – principally films, TV shows and pop music – is viewed with mixed feelings. Sceptics fear that it may erode the native culture. Yet many imitate it: country and western music has been popular since the days of Hank Williams and Jim Reeves, there is a national Elvis impersonator contest and Norwegian-made serial "soap operas" are among the most popular of prime-time TV shows. In a mid 1990s survey that ranked young people in Europe in terms of an "Americanisation index", Norway was on top, followed by Switzerland and Sweden, and far above Italy and France.

Nonetheless, other social aspects outweigh the culture of the young in reflecting the extent of Americanisation of the country. The overall urban living pattern is perhaps the most obvious. Throughout Europe, the status of the inner cities is increasing. Paris is the best example: fully 95% of the population with the highest incomes live in the central parts of the city. The trend is similar elsewhere – Berlin, London, Rome – a wealthy city surrounded by less well-off areas. But in Norway the trend is more toward the suburbs, as in the USA. Bærum, the adjoining municipality south-west of Oslo, has a higher average per-capita income than the city. Likewise, better roads are being built to serve the suburbs, as in the USA. The underlying causes may lie in the histories of cities. In 1800, London was a city of more than a million, and other cities in Europe were populous well before 20th century technologies changed cities. In Norway, as in the USA, urban concentrations of population are more recent, and nostalgia for country life correspondingly stronger than elsewhere in Europe.

Politically, the country is closer to the USA than are many other countries in Europe. In part that may be due to Norway having been one of the original members of ☞ **NATO** (Government and Social Services chapter), and for having a major NATO facility throughout the cold war. Many aspects of religious life also are closer to those of the USA than to those of central European countries. While Catholicism is strong in central and southern Europe, Norway is predominantly Protestant with a strong fundamentalist movement, as in the USA.

Roots may underlie all the trends. The population of Norway now is about 4.5 million, including all residents of foreign extraction. The Norwegian-American population of the USA now is some 3.9 million. In short, there are almost as many persons of Norwegian heritage in the USA as there are in Norway.

Baptism and confirmation (Dåp og konfirmasjon) are Christian rites practised by the ☞ **Church of Norway** (Church and Religion chapter). Baptism (dåp) signifies admission to the Church and consists of sprinkling the forehead of an infant with water, usually at a regular Sunday church service, with the parents, other family members and at least two godparents (faddere) attending. Confirmation (konfirmasjon) reaffirms baptism at age 15 and consists of a course of religious instruction followed by a special Sunday church service, usually held twice a year, once in the spring and once in the autumn.

Despite dwindling church attendance, some 82% of all infants are baptised and about 75% of all youth are confirmed in Church of Norway churches and chapels. The ceremonies have become socially significant, and are occasions for family gatherings and the giving of presents to the baptised infant (*dåpsbarn*) or confirmed youth (*konfirmant*), as well as for reports in local newspapers. Starting in 1951, secular confirmation (*borgerlig konfirmasjon*) has been offered by the Human and Ethical Union (*Human-Etisk Forbund*) as an alternative to Christian confirmation.

Beggars (*Tiggere*) According to the Act on Vagrancy, Begging and Drunkenness (*Lov om Løsgjængeri, Betteri og Drukkenskab*) of 1900, repeated or annoying begging is illegal and subject to arrest and imprisonment. Nonetheless, there are beggars in the cities, particularly in downtown Oslo. Most of them are narcotics addicts who beg in the street rather than steal to support their habit. They are no more numerous and usually less obvious than beggars in some cities elsewhere, because they do not sit with signs and outstretched hands or hats, but rather walk shopping streets, pedestrian precincts and underground stations to ask passers-by for money. In mid 1999, a skilled ambulating street beggar could bring in as much as NOK 2,000 a day in Oslo.

Christmas (*Jul*) is celebrated on the eve (*juleaften*), 24th December. Preparations begin weeks in advance, usually on the first of the four Sundays in Advent, the period before Christmas observed in Christian faiths in commemoration of the coming of Christ. The celebration of Advent includes lighting a candle (*adventslys*) in an Advent candelabrum (*adventsstake*), one for each of the Sundays, the first candle on the first Sunday, the first and second candle on the second, and so on. A home with children will have an Advent calendar (*julekalender*), which is a card with flaps to open on each day, revealing a picture (and sometimes a sweet). The tradition of Christmas baking (*julebakst*) triggers the Christmas spirit (*julestemming*), though those who care not to bake can find a wide selection of cakes and biscuits in shops, as does the hanging of a Christmas sheaf of oats (*julenek*) to feed small birds, outside the front door of a house or on the balcony of a flat. Sales of evergreen ☞ **Christmas trees** (Housekeeping chapter) begin weeks in advance, and most families will decorate their tree the day before Christmas eve (*lillejuleaften*). In families with small children, Father Christmas (*julenissen*) comes at a convenient time after dinner, announcing his arrival by knocking on the veranda door of a house or main door of a flat and carrying gifts (*julegaver*) in a sack. Neighbours with small children often trade *julenisse* roles and packed sacks of gifts. In one house, father will disappear "to go for an after-dinner walk", put on a *julenisse* mask and costume, including the traditional red stocking cap, and visit the neighbours. Afterwards, he puts the costume at a pre-arranged place, and returns home, to await the visit of the neighbouring father. Families without children simply place gifts under the tree, to be opened after dinner, usually when coffee and cakes are served. As in many other countries, shops start off Christmas trade (*julehandel*) by decorating streets and pedestrian precincts (*julegata*) weeks in advance, often in late November. In December, most shops, particularly those in centres and malls, will be open longer than usual, up until midday on Christmas Eve. Christmas day and the day after, the 26th, are public holidays and most shops are closed, though petrol stations and some convenience shops will be open. Most shops reopen on the 27th (if it is not a Sunday) and keep ordinary business hours through midday on New Years Eve, the 31st. However, some shops, as well as many offices, remain closed from Christmas to New Year's Eve (*romjulen*). For more information on Christmas in Norway, view the *julenisse* web site ☺ http://www.julenissen.no with pages in Norwegian and in English.

Christmas feast (*Julebord*) Scandinavian tradition calls for sumptuous meals on major holidays, including Christmas. The traditional *julebord* (in Danish and Norwegian) or *julbord* (in Swedish) is a large serving table, spread with Christmas dishes served once a year. Now a *julebord* may be either a self-serve Christmas dinner table at a restaurant or an annual company party held during the Christmas season and featuring such a table. In alphabetical order by their names in Norwegian, the items on a *julebord* menu may include *aspik* fish or vegetables in aspic, *baconfett* bacon fat, *fisk* fish, *flatbrød* unleavened wafer bread, *geitost* goat cheese *grønn erterstuing* creamed dried peas, *julepølse* Christmas sausages, *kalkun* turkey, *kålrotstappe* mashed rutabaga (the Swedish turnip, called "Swede" in England), *karamellpudding* caramel pudding, *lefse* potato pancakes, *lutefisk* boiled lye-steeped codfish, *medisterkaker* pork sausage patties, *pinnekjøtt* steamed mutton ribs, *ripsgele* currant jelly, *riskrem med rød fruktsaus* creamed rice with red fruit sauce, *rødbeter* pickled beets, *rødkål* red cabbage, *rødvinsaus* red-wine gravy, *rosenkål* Brussels sprouts, *saus* gravy, *sennep* mustard, *surkål* sour cabbage, *svineribbe* spareribs, *syltagurk* pickles, *tyttebær* wild cranberries and *vossakorv* boiled dinner sausages. *Julebord* menus have become so large that few private homes attempt them, and most now are served by restaurants or caterers. Alcoholic drink is increasingly a part of the *julebord* tradition, and in the late 1990s, distressingly so, when some company *julebord* turned into drunken brawls. Moreover, *julebord* season drink driving has become an annual problem. The police have reacted with spot checks of drivers on heavy *julebord* evenings (*julebordkontroll*) starting in late November.

Clog almanac (*Primstav*) The *primstav*, literally "new-moon staff" is the oldest known form of calendar in the Scandinavian countries. Like the clog almanac of medieval England, it was carved of wood, with notches for the days of the year. So it is called "clog almanac" in English. But whilst the English clog almanac was a square block or stick, the Norwegian *primstav* was long and thin, in the shape of a sword, with carved symbols for the important holidays and events of the year. It was a perpetual Julian calendar with two sides, one for summer (14 April – 14 October) and one for winter (14 October – 14 April). After the Gregorian calendar was adopted in 1700, the *primstav* fell into disuse, though the best preserved *primstav* in the collections of the *Norsk Folkemuseum* was carved in 1707. Today, the *primstav* is a collector's item, and replicas of it are sold as souvenirs and as rustic interior decorations.

Competitiveness (*Konkurranseevne*) Each year, the Institute for Management Development (IMD), a Swiss business school, compiles the World Competitiveness Yearbook, which ranks countries according to 228 criteria. On the 1999 World Competitiveness Scoreboard, Norway ranked 13th, a drop from 6th in 1998 and 5th in 1997. For complete details and the rankings of other countries, see the Yearbook, available from IMD and summarised on-line ✆ +41 216180111, ✉ +41 216180707, ✉ PO Box 915, CH-1001 Lausanne, Switzerland, ✉ info@imd.ch, ⊕ http://www.imd.ch

Constitution day (*Grunnlovsdag*) Visitors and new residents often are astonished at the country's national pride and the yearly outpouring of it, on the 17th May. Norway most likely has more flag poles on which the flag is flown more often than in any other country. And on 17th May, there's certain to be a flag on every pole. Wherever there are more than two Norwegians, there's a parade. Many in the parades and many watching them wear *bunads*, the ☞ **Folk costume**, and carry flags. The national anthem and other patriotic songs are sung. Bands play and speeches are given. Countrywide, the graduating upper secondary-school pupils (*russ*) wake their teachers at the break of dawn, and then join in the parades. Restaurants and cafes do a booming business. Transport workers and taxi drivers are among the few who appear to be at work. It's the sort of celebration that breaks out elsewhere only upon the cessation of prolonged hostilities. That's part of the cause in Norway, as 17th May commemorates not the attaining of independence 1905, but rather the 1814 termination of 434 years of Danish rule and the writing of the country's ☞ **Constitution** (Government and Social Services chapter). The freedom was short-lived. By late July, Norway and Sweden were at war. By August, Norway had lost and found itself in a union with Sweden. It then answered to the Swedish crown, represented by Jean-Baptiste Bernadotte, also known as Crown Prince Karl Johan, first as the emissary of King Karl XIII of Sweden and then, after his ascension to the Swedish throne four years later, as King Karl XIV of the union. One of the measures Karl Johan, as Norwegians still called him, enacted was to forbid celebrations on the 17th of May. Many Norwegians ignored that command. In 1829, Karl Johan indicated his displeasure with the civil disobedience, and dispatched infantry and cavalry to disperse a crowd that had congregated to celebrate the day at the Stortorvet marketplace in Christiania, as Oslo was then named. Military might won, but Karl Johan lost the day. *Torvslaget* (The Marketplace Battle) became part of the legend that rooted the 17th in Norwegian consciousness. Patriotism flourished. The national anthem, *Ja vi elsker*, was first sung in public on 17th May 1864, some 20 years after Karl Johan died. Children first joined public processions on 17th May, 1870. By 1900, the 17th was firmly established as an annual opportunity for Norwegians to collectively show their individuality. And that they do, wherever they are, throughout the world. But nowhere do celebrations match those in Norwegian cities. The record festivities are in Oslo. Downtown streets are closed off, and the parade up the main street to royal review at the palace takes hours. The Royal Guards march, but otherwise there is hardly a uniform to be seen: most of the marchers are Oslo school children, each carrying a flag. In the city where celebrations were once forcefully quelled, they now grow by the year, under the stony gaze of a statue of a mounted horseman, looking down the main street that bears his name – Karl Johan.

Corruption (Korrupsjon) Norway is one of the least corrupt countries of the world but is slightly more corrupt than its Scandinavian neighbours, according to the annual Corruption Perceptions Index (CPI) compiled by Transparency International (TI), an anti-corruption organisation based in Berlin. The CPI averages the results of several different polls of businessmen, risk analysts and the general public to arrive at a score ranging from ten (very clean) to zero (highly corrupt). In the 1998 ranking of 85 countries, Norway scored 9.0 and shared eighth place with the Netherlands, behind Denmark in first place with a score of 10.0, Finland second with a score of 9.6, Sweden third with a score of 9.5 and Iceland fifth with a score of 9.3. The complete CPI is available at the TI web site
🕸 http://www. transparency.de

Creativity (Kreativitet) is both obvious and elusive. It is obvious because though small, Norway has produced more than its share of creative people. It is elusive because nobody can fully explain why this is so.

Arguably, the ☞ **Vikings** were the first creative Norwegians, with their superbly designed long ships and establishment of international trade. More recently, Fridtjof Nansen stands tall in the heroic age of polar exploration. He explored the Northwest Passage from Siberia toward Greenland drifting with the polar ice, using a special ship, the *Fram*, designed so the ice would lift but not crush it. The voyage was completed in 1893-1896 and, for its time, was as audacious and risky as the Moon landing of 1969. Later, the *Fram* took explorer Roald Amundsen to Antarctic, where he became the first to reach the South Pole in December 1911. Back home, Mr. Nansen turned his attention to other matters, including diplomacy. He was Norwegian Ambassador in London 1906-1908, and in 1922 he was awarded the Nobel Peace Prize for his Russian relief work. In 1947, ethnographer Thor Heyerdahl built a balsa raft, the *Kon-Tiki* and floated across the Pacific Ocean to show that commonly-held theories of global settlement might well be wrong.

The great names of 19th century arts included many Norwegians, such as composer Edvard Grieg, playwright Henrik Ibsen and painter Edvard Munch. In 1891, Fredrich Engels went from England to Norway to find out how so small and poor a country, only recently independent, could rank along with the British, French, Germans and Russians. He returned to England without an answer.

The trend remains evident in contemporary Norway. Jostein Gaarder is one of the most popular writers of the 1990s, with *Sophie's World* and other books translated and sold round the world. Pianist Leif Ove Andsnes and cellist Truls Mørk perform on world concert stages and are sought by recording studios, as is jazz saxophonist Jan Garbarek. Liv Ullman, known for her many roles in Swedish films, now is a film director. International building projects of the 1990s were designed by Norwegian architects, including the *Snøhetta* group of Oslo, which designed the library at Alexandria, and Niels Torp, also of Oslo, who designed the British Airways complex in London.

International diplomacy is still a strength. Thorvald Stoltenberg was the UN High Commissioner for Refugees. The Oslo peacemaking efforts built on the efforts of Jan Egeland of the Ministry of Foreign Affairs. Knut Vollebæk, also of the Ministry, was appointed chairman of the Organisation for Security and Co-operation in Europe (OSCE). And as others have shown, one need not be a diplomat to be internationally concerned. After a sweep of speed skating medals at the 1994 Olympic Winter Games at Lillehammer, Johan Olov Koss used his celebrity status to raise funds for Third World causes.

Cultural and natural heritage protection (Kulturminnevern og kulturlandskapsvern) refers to buildings and sites with historical, aesthetic, archaeological, scientific, ethnological or anthropological value and to outstanding physical, biological and geological formations.

World-wide, the United Nations Educational, Scientific and Cultural Organization (UNESCO) promotes the protection of cultural and natural heritage. There are four UNESCO World Heritage Sites in Norway: the Urnes Stave Church, the *Bryggen* buildings in Bergen, the mining town of Røros and the rock pictographs at Alta. For information on protection round the world, contact the UNESCO World Heritage Centre ✆ +33 145681889, ✉ +33 145685570, ⊠ 7, place de Fontenoy, F-75352 Paris, France, ✉ wh-info@unesco.org, ⊛ http://www.unesco.org/whc with pages in English and in French. For information on protection in the Nordic countries, contact the Nordic World Heritage Office (NWHO), a project operating through the end of 2001, with its head office in Oslo ✆ 22940580, ✉ 22940581, ⊠ PO Box 8196 Dep, 0034 Oslo, ✉ nhwo@ra.no, ⊛ http://www.grida.no/ext/nwho/ with pages in English.

In Norway, most cities have departments of cultural heritage; look under *Byantikvaren* in the Pink Pages. The Directorate for Cultural Heritage (*Riksantikvaren*) is responsible at the national level ✆ 22940400, ✉ 22940404, ⊠ PO Box 8196 Dep, 0034 Oslo, ✉ riksantikvaren@ra.no, ⊛ http://www.riksantikvaren.no with pages in Norwegian and in English. At either the local or the national level, a building or site may be listed (*fredet*) as being historically or culturally important and thereby be protected against major alterations or demolition.

The Directorate for Nature Management (*Direktoratet for naturforvaltning*) is responsible for natural heritage throughout the country and accordingly lists landscapes to be protected. Its head office is in Trondheim ✆ 73580500, ✉ 73580501, ⊠ 7485 Trondheim, ✉ direktoratet@naturvorvaltning.no, ⊛ http://www.naturforvaltning.no with pages in Norwegian and lists of publications, some in English.

Two associations are concerned with cultural and natural heritage protection. The Society for the Preservation of Norwegian Ancient Monuments (*Fortidsminneforening*) was founded in 1844 and arguably is the world's oldest cultural heritage society. It owns historic sites throughout the country, publishes a magazine and a yearbook and arranges historical site activities. Moreover, the benefits of membership include free admission to the Urnes stave church listed by UNESCO and other sites owned by the association, and rental of a flat in Røros. It has affiliated groups throughout the country, and a head office in Oslo ✆ 22422732, ✉ 22421984, ⊠ Dronningensgt 11, 0152 Oslo, ✉ fortidsminneforeningen@hovedadm.no. Norwegian Cultural Heritage (*Norsk Kulturarv*) focuses on preservation through active use (*vern gjennom bruk*) ✆ 61232033, ✉ 61232089, ⊠ Klones, 2680 Vågå, ✉ kulturar@online.no, ⊛ http://www.kulturarv.no with pages in Norwegian only.

Many books are available on the individual cultural and natural heritage sites of the country, in Norwegian and in other languages. The best overview book to date is a small, 260-page handbook, richly illustrated with colour photos and featuring sites in alphabetical order indexed to a locator map. Originally published in German in 1989, it has since been republished: *Knaurs Kulturführer in Farbe, Norwegen*, Augsburg, Germany, 1998, Bechtermünz Verlag, ISBN 3-8289-0674-5, and it is also available in Norwegian translation: *Norge, en kulturguide i farger*, Oslo, 1989, NKS-forlaget, ISBN 82-508-1010-4.

Drinking bout (Utdrikningslag) Traditionally, friends will hold a drinking party for a bride or groom on the eve of the wedding, to signify the end of single status. The party usually starts with a meal at a favoured restaurant or at the home of a close friend, suitably decorated for the occasion, as with old photos, the more embarrassing the better. Dress is seldom formal and often outlandish; the evening's entertainment usually includes songs and the giving of ridiculous gifts; and the high point of the evening is a practical joke on the guest of honour. Throughout the evening, alcoholic drink is liberally served. Hence the name *utdrikningslag*, literally "drinking-out party".

Drunkenness (Fyll) Compared to other countries, ☞ **alcohol consumption** (*Drink, Drugs, Tobacco* chapter) is low. Nonetheless, drunkenness is a conspicuous aspect of national behaviour. That has long been recognised and questioned. Ludvig Holberg (1684-1754), the outstanding Scandinavian author of his time, claimed both by Norway (where he was born) and Denmark (where he died), commented upon it in Jeppe of the Hill (*Jeppe paa Berget*), a parody play on Norwegian character first performed in 1722. In it, a character remarks *folk siger vel i Herredet at Jeppe drikker, men de siger ikke, hvorfor Jeppe drikker* ("the people of the township say that Jeppe drinks, but they don't say why Jeppe drinks").

There are many speculations as to "why Jeppe drinks". One holds that there is no tradition of daily consumption, as of wine in France, so drinking is done in sporadic bouts on festive occasions. Indeed, binges are a habitual part of the ☞ **Christmas feast** and of the annual routine for the ☞ **secondary school graduating class**, and tradition dictates that a party held on the eve of a wedding should be a ☞ **drinking bout**.

Be that as it may, attitudes on drunkenness are changing from customary tolerance to more frequent disdain. In 1996, a man was fired after punching his boss at the company Christmas feast. He sued to reclaim his job, contending that drunken attack was a minor matter. The court did not agree and upheld the boss' right to fire the man. On airline flights in 1998, wildly drunken passengers became so dangerous that the pilots emergency landed to have them arrested and subsequently heavily fined. In 1999, incidents involving drunken Norwegian young people on holiday in Mediterranean countries made headlines at home.

The economy (Økonomien) of the country is a mix of free market capitalism and government intervention. The government controls key sectors, including ☞ **oil**, through State enterprises and subsidises otherwise unprofitable sectors such as farming and fishing. In several sectors, such as railways and telecommunications, government monopolies have been disbanded and privatised and markets have been deregulated. The country has the world's fourth highest GDP (Gross Domestic Product) per head, but also the world's fourth highest cost of living. The GDP growth was a heady 4% a year through most of the 1990s, but slowed to an estimated 2.3% in 1999 and 1.8% in 2000 according to estimates by the ☞ **OECD** (Government and Social Services chap-

ter). The slowdown was due mostly to declining prices for oil, the country's major export. Nonetheless, the country had a considerable surplus in its balance of payments, and forecasts indicate that both the trade surplus and the current-account surplus will grow through 2000.

An extensive ☞ **National insurance scheme** (Government and Social Services chapter) and other welfare measures contribute to public-sector expenditure being more than half the GDP, which in turn results in one of the world's highest levels of taxation. The country has long depended on international trade and in addition to oil, is a major exporter of raw materials and semi-processed goods and an importer of more than half its food. It has a maritime tradition that dates back to the time of the ☞ **Vikings** and now ranks among the leading shipping nations of the world. It is rich in natural resources, including oil, fish, forest, minerals and hydroelectric power.

Through the 1990s, unemployment hovered around 4%, about half the 8% average for OECD countries. Inflation, however, is about 3.5%, nearly triple the OECD average of 1.2%. The OECD has urged the country to streamline its economy by reforming its welfare system and further deregulating its markets.

Elections (Valg) are held every four years, on a Monday in September. To vote, you must be at least 18 years old by 31 December of an election year and must be registered in the election roll (*manntall*) kept by the office of the ☞ **National Register** in the municipality in which you live. After the year 2000:

- The parliamentary elections (*Stortingsvalg*) will be held in 2001, 2005 etc.; all citizens may vote.
- The county and municipal elections (*Fylkestingsvalg og kommunestyrevalg*) will be held in 2003, 2007, etc.; all citizens and foreigners resident in the country for at least three years may vote.
- The Sámi parliamentary elections (*Sámetingsvalg*) will be held in the same years as parliamentary elections; Sámi citizens may vote.

The ☞ **Parliament** (Government and Social Services Chapter) is elected by proportional representation. This means the 165 members of Parliament are elected on the basis of the proportion of votes cast for their parties in the election, in 19 electoral districts, each of which is a county. In each district, the voter picks one party list, but can vary the order of candidates on it. The district seats are shared according to each party's vote, starting with the top names on each list. The number of seats allocated to each district is in proportion to its number of registered voters, with one modification: the sparsely populated districts are given more seats in Parliament in proportion to population than are the more populous districts. For instance, one vote in Finnmark, the northernmost county, counts twice as much as one vote in the far more populous Akershus or Oslo counties. Consequently, both territorial fairness and demographic fairness are nearly ensured. Nonetheless, in the basic system, larger parties may be over-represented and smaller parties underrepresented in an election. Consequently, eight seats are withheld from the basic computation and allocated among the parties who gain too few (or no) seats in relation to the total number of votes they receive country-wide. However, parties must receive at least four percent of the overall vote to be eligible for the eight seats at large. County and municipal elections are similar to national elections, except that there are no sub-divisions into geographic areas.

Energy (*Energi*) Despite its relatively small size, Norway is the world's thirteenth largest producer and fourth largest exporter of energy. ☞ **Oil** accounts for the bulk of the energy produced and exported, but the country also is a leading producer of electric power, almost all of it hydroelectric.

There are electric power generating plants in all 19 counties, and together they produce nearly 112 TWh (thousand million kilowatt-hours) a year, nearly all of it consumed within the country. Norway has a power sharing agreement with its Nordic neighbours, Sweden, Finland and Denmark, and starting in 1992, electric power is exported to other countries, principally Germany. About a third of the country's hydro-electric potential has not yet been exploited. But developing it is expensive, so other means of generation are being considered, including thermal generation using gas from offshore fields in the North Sea.

For comprehensive information on the energy sector, see the *Fact Sheet Energy Sector and Water Resources (Faktaheftet Energi- og vasdragsvirksomhet i Norge)* in English and Norwegian editions, as well as the other publications of the Ministry of

Petroleum and Energy ☏ 22249090, ☏ 22249565, ✉ PO Box 8148 Dep, 0033 Oslo, ✉ postmaster@oed.dep.telemax.no, ⊕ http://www.oed.dep.no with pages in Norwegian and in English.

Flag and coat of arms (*Flagg og Riksvåpen*)
The design of the flag is based on the Christian cross, as are the designs of the flags of all Nordic countries, and has a blue on white cross on a red background. The national flag (*handelsflagg*) is rectangular, of proportions 16 to 22 in height to width. The colour fields also have set proportions, in height 6 red, 1 white, 2 blue, 1 white and six red, and in length 6 red, 1 white, 2 blue, 1 white and 12 red. The state flag (*statsflagg*), has the same design but has a swallow-tail and tongue. It is flown only by public agencies and only on flag days, ☞ **public holidays and flag days** (Holidays chapter). The national coat of arms (*riksvåpen*) is gold on a red background and depicts a lion facing left under a crown, and holding an axe in its forepaws.

The national flag.

Folk costumes (*Bunad*), like the habits of religious orders, are throwbacks to the everyday clothing of the past. The Norwegian *bunad* is evidence of that: the word originally meant "clothes". But unlike habits, *bunads* did not retain their original utilitarian simplicity. They evolved to a wide range of costumes, varying in style, cut, colouring and accessories, according to locale and the skills and tastes of their makers. There were *bunads* for men, women and children, for dress and for everyday wear. Almost every area of the country had its own styles. But in the 19th century, manufactured cloth and garments replaced home-made products. The growing cities weakened bonds to rural roots. Emigration took its toll. The *bunad* seemed doomed to extinction, when it was single-handedly rescued by author Hulda Garborg (1862-1934). In her fellow city dwellers, Garborg saw a need for preserving the traditions slowly smothering in cities. In the late 1890s, she started a *leikarring*, or folk dance group, in Oslo. Folk dances should, of course, be done in folk costumes, which led Garborg to compile the first anthology on *bunads*, published in 1903. It was a best seller. Garborg and one of her *leikarring* dancers, Klara Semb, started the folk dance movement that sparked the *bunad* renaissance. Today the result is that there are more known types and varieties of *bunads* than ever before. Some, like those from Setersdal, until recently one of the more isolated valleys, date back 300 years or more. Others, like the *bunad* from Bærum, a suburban township south-west of Oslo, were first designed in the late 1940s. Women's *bunads* characteristically have skirts or dresses of double-shuttle weave wool, bodices or jackets of contrasting material over blouses and scarves. Sashes, purses, ornamental silver and traditional shoes and stockings complete the costume. Men's *bunads* are three-piece knickerbocker suits, with matching or contrasting vests, knee-socks and traditional shoes. Fewer men than women own or wear *bunads* on the festive occasions for which they are now used. While the dark suit remains the standard formal attire for men, women still face the dilemma of what to wear for formal occasions; in Norway, a *bunad* is always correct. The widespread appeal of the *bunad* is matched by the range of opinions on it. Traditionalists maintain that *bunads* from a particular district are properly owned and worn only by persons born and bred there: a *bunad* should match the dialect of its wearer. Moderates maintain that correct *bunad* style outweighs the circumstances of the wearer's birth and upbringing: anyone can wear a *bunad*, provided that its style is correct. Radicals view the *bunad* as a style to be copied piecemeal into modern garments. Whether or not you are concerned with wearer identity, you may see and buy the real thing at home crafts and specialist clothing shops; look under *Husflid* or *Bunader* in the Yellow Pages.

Geography (*Geografi*) The Kingdom of Norway consists of the mainland on the Scandinavian peninsula as well as the archipelago of Svalbard and the island of Jan Mayen in the Arctic. The country has three dependencies in the Antarctic: Queen Maud's Land on the mainland, Peter I's Island and Bouvet Island, which are not part of the Kingdom. The geographical features are:

- Area: mainland 323,758 km^2, Kingdom 385,364 km^2.
- Border: with Finland 727 km, with Russia 196 km, with Sweden 1619 km, total 2542 km.
- Delimitation of the mainland including islands: Latitude: 57°57'31"N at Pysen to 71°11'09"N at Knivskjelodden; Longitude: 31°10'07" E at Vardø to 04°29'57" E at Holmebåen.
- Highest mountain: Galdhøpiggen 2,469 m.
- Highest waterfall: Kjelsfossen 840 m.
- Largest glacier: Jostedalsbreen 487 km^2.
- Largest island: Hinnøya 2,198 km^2.
- Largest lake: Mjøsa 362 km^2.
- Length of mainland without islands (S-N): 1752 km.
- Longest fjord: Sognefjord 204 km.
- Longest river. Glomma 600 km.
- Width (E-W): 6 km least, 430 km greatest.

Geology (*Geologi*) The country is rich in oil and in minerals. Almost all known minerals have been found, though not all are financially worth extracting. Nonetheless, each year, products of bedrock, minerals and deposits (*berggrunn, mineraler og løsmasser*) are exported in quantity. Alone, crushed stone and gravel account for a respectable NOK 2.4 billion in exports, and olivine is exported to meet 70% of the world's industrial needs. Understandably, geology is advanced, particularly as the exploration for and exploitation of offshore ☞ **oil** depends on accurate geological surveys. The Geological Survey of Norway (*Norges geologiske undersøkelse – NGO*) has recently finished a major mapping effort that produced a Bedrock Map of Norway (1:1 million scale) and a map of Norway and the Continental Shelf (1:3 million scale) in printed and digital form. For further information on geology and geological maps, reports, publications and databases, contact NGO ✆ 73904011, 🖷 73921620, ✉ Leiv Erikssons vei, 7491 Trondheim, ✉ ngu@ngu.no, 🌐 http://www.ngu.no with pages in Norwegian and in English and links to other geological web sites.

Hávamál, literally "Words of the High One", is a collection of 164 poems that sum up the wisdom of Odin, the warrior-wizard god of Nordic mythology. It is the second of 29 parts of the Poetic Edda, the first of the two books of ancient Icelandic literature. It is frequently quoted, and schoolchildren learn about it as part of their Viking heritage. Much of the wise advice is as valid today as it was when it was composed around AD 700 – 900. The first poem, for instance, could be a warning to all who engage in business or diplomatic negotiations. In translation into English, it reads:

When passing
a door-post,
watch as you walk on,
inspect as you enter.
It is uncertain
where enemies lurk
or crouch in a dark corner.

If you wish to gain an appreciation of the culture of the Vikings, read Hávamál. It is now available in popular editions published by Gudrun Publishing of Oslo, Göteborg and Reykjavik, including the original Icelandic and translations into Norwegian (ISBN 82-91522-00-6 hard cover, 82-91522-01-4 paperback) and English (ISBN 9979-9070-0-2 hard cover, 9979-9070-1-0 paperback) as well as into Chinese, Danish, Dutch, Finnish, French, Italian, Japanese, German, Russian, Spanish and Swedish.

Honesty and lawfulness (Ærlighet og lovlydighet) Norwegians are traditionally viewed as honest, law-abiding folk. One of the classic travelogues, Norway* , expresses the favourable opinion that "the points about them (the Norwegians) that impressed me the most were their absolute honesty and the complete absence of servility." This characteristic can still be found. In 1998, Prime Minister Kjell Magne Bondevik took sick leave due to the psychological stress of the pressures of his post, and admitted so publicly. He was praised at home and abroad for his forthright honesty. Unfortunately, recent studies indicate that the old honesty and lawfulness are declining, notwithstanding the PM's recent example. In 1975, there were some 30,000 crimes registered in Oslo; in 1995 the total was 70,000. Finders of valuables and money once turned their finds in to the lost-and-found at police stations and railway stations. That no longer is the case; by late 1997, fewer than two of 100 pocketbooks turned in to Oslo lost-and-found contained any money. Regrettably, lack of everyday honesty has reached teenagers: figures published in early 1999 indicated that 76% of 15 and 16 year-olds would keep excess change given them at shop and supermarket cash points. Even the scrupulously honest Norwegian businessman may also become an artefact of the past. In 1997,

some 900 business administration students in Norway, Spain, the Czech Republic and the USA were asked if they would sacrifice ethics to attain or maintain success. Slightly more than a tenth of the women students answered "yes". Of the men students, the Norwegians were the least bound by ethics: fully 42% answered "yes", compared to 25% of the Americans, 22% of the Spanish and 18% of the Czech men.

* Beatrix Jungman (author) and Nico Jungman (illustrator), Norway, London, A&C Black, April 1905, page 193. Mr. and Mrs. Jungman had previously gained recognition for their first book describing Holland in colour drawings and text. The book on Norway was their second, and was sold internationally.

Inventions (Oppfinnelser) Through the years, many Norwegian inventions have gained world use. Many are specialised, perhaps out of necessity. Nautical historians recognise the styrboard ("steering-board") at the aft right of a Viking ship as one of the first practical rudders as well as the origin of the word "starboard" for the right side of a ship. Chemists may know that the first commercially feasible fixation of atmospheric Nitrogen in 1906 employed the process developed by physicist Kristian Birkeland and engineer Sam Eyde and spawned the modern fertiliser industry. Ski historians know that in 1923, ski racer Peter Østbye invented the first practical cross-country ski wax. But what of the common, everyday things that we all use? Ask almost any Norwegian, and you will learn of two, the cheese plane (ostehøvel) and the paper clip (binders). Indeed, in January 1999 Norway Post confirmed that belief by issuing two commemorative postage stamps, one for each of these great inventions, the cheese plane outlined on a blue background, the paper clip on a red background. Regrettably, as historians soon pointed out, the public and Norway Post were only half right. The cheese plane rightfully was invented in 1927 by Thor Bjørklund at his carpentry shop in Lillehammer, as he sought a better way to thinly slice the goat cheese in his daily packet lunch. Even the Dutch, who now produce and export as many cheese planes as do the Norwegians, admit that Norway was first. The paper clip is another matter. An invention commonly cited as first is that of Norwegian Johan Vaaler, who took out a patent in 1899 in Germany and in 1901 in the USA. The design was impractical; it was never manufactured. Its technical flaw was that the wire did not complete two full loops as in most of today's paper clips and in the clip on the commemorative stamp, which is the feature that enables them to hold papers together. The earliest patent depicting the modern paper clip was issued in 1899 to William Middlebrook of Waterbury, Connecticut, USA. But this patent was not for the clip itself but rather for a machine to make it, which indicates that the design was widely known at that time. Although never patented, the design may have been introduced as early as 1883 by the Gem Manufacturing Co. Ltd. of England. Hence the trade name Gem, which persists to this day. [For a detailed history of the development of the paper clip, see *From Pins to Paper Clips*, Chapter 4 of *The Evolution of Useful Things* by Henry Petroski, New York, Alfred A. Knopf publishers, 1993, 290 pages hardcover, ISBN 0-679-441226-3.]

Vaaler's patented clip.

Postage stamps: kr. 3.60 lauding, kr. 4.00 misleading

Jante Law (*Janteloven*): the most-known quote from the works of Axel Sandemose (1899-1965), a Danish-born Norwegian experimental novelist. He went to sea in his youth, jumped ship in Newfoundland, and worked in a lumber camp before returning to Denmark to take up writing. He settled in Norway in 1929. Published in 1933, *En flyktning krysser sitt spor* (A Fugitive Crosses His Tracks) contains the 'Jante Law' that regulates the citizenry of Jante, the fictional small town symbolic of the conventional society of his childhood: 'You who have grown up elsewhere can never fully appreciate the inevitability of the Jante Law. You will find it funny and will never know its deadly oppression of a working-class youth in Jante. With the ten Jante Rules of the Jante Law, Jante holds its people down'. Here they are (author's italics retained in translation):

1. You shall not believe that you *are* something.

2. You shall not believe that you are equal to *us*.
3. You shall not believe that you are wiser than *us*.
4. You shall not imagine yourself better than *us*.
5. You shall not believe that you know more than *us*.
6. You shall not believe that you can rise above *us*.
7. You shall not believe that *you* are capable.
8. You shall not laugh at *us*.
9. You shall not believe that anyone cares about *you*.
10. You shall not believe that you can teach *us* anything.

Scandinavian social psychologists and management theorists now quote the Jante Law as an example of self-imposed restraints on human progress. The applicability of its ten rules is perhaps more widespread.

The labour movement (*Arbeiderbevegelsen*) is strong in Norway as it is throughout Scandinavia. In the mid 1990s, union membership as a percentage of wage and salary earners was 58% in Norway, lower than the ☞ **OECD** and world high of 91% in Sweden, but far higher than in other industralised countries, such as Great Britain (33%), Japan (24%) and the United States (14%). This strength is due to three factors. The first is political strength. The labour movement began in 1848. In 1899 it founded the first ☞ **Unions** (Business and Work chapter). But 12 years previously, in 1887, it initiated the founding of the Labour Party (*Arbeiderparti*), which was in power for 44 of the 69 years between 1928 and 1997. The second is national collective bargaining under the provisions of two laws and in which annual negotiations proceed according to a basic agreement (*hovedavtalen*) between the unions and the ☞ **Employer organisations** (Business and Work chapter). Finally, national ☞ **Unemployment benefits** (Business and Work chapter) are paid to workers dismissed from their jobs, and each union has a conflict fund (*kampfond*) to support its members in cases of prolonged strikes or lockouts. These three factors – political strength, national collective bargaining and ensured unemployment benefits – have contributed to the strength of the unions and the labour movement.

The National Budget (*Budsjett*) is a formal plan for future national revenue and expenditure as well as economic policy which the ☞ **Government**

(Government and Social Services chapter) puts before Parliament (*Storting*), usually once a year in October, and including proposals for changes in taxation which later become law. After a national budget for the following year has been released, it usually is featured in newspaper reports, and copies of it may be bought in book shops. A summary in English may be downloaded from the ODIN official documentation web site ☞ http://odin.dep.no/html/english

National character (*Den norske væremåten*)
Most portrayals of Norway, from the journey of Pytheas in 330-325 BC on, have been travelogues. Even in the words of the national anthem, written by Nobel prize-winner Bjørnstjerne Bjørnson, aspects of the country are more frequently mentioned than are attributes of its citizenry. Characterising Norwegians is more recent, starting in the late 20th century. That may be why there still is no agreement on the national character.

Yet, some traits can be singled out. In its booklet welcoming new residents from other countries, ☞ **The Directorate of Immigration** (Government and Social Services chapter) begins by observing that "the variations between people are less than in many other countries. This means that there is a lesser difference between rich and poor or between city dwellers and country folk". Despite this egalitarian view, Norwegians have gained international renown in almost all walks of life; ☞ **creativity** seems to be a national trait.

The action of individuals against an egalitarian background has fascinated foreign businessmen, most likely one of the keener groups of observers of a country's habits. In the late 1980s, two Norwegians collected observations made by some 80 business executives from 18 countries in a book that is both informative and entertaining: *Norwegians as Others See Them*, compiled by K. Habert and A. Lillebø, Norwegian School of Management Press, 1988, 180 pages hardcover, ISBN 82-7042-282-7.

Indeed, the view of the outsider often is the most revealing. According to a study made by G. Prakash Reddy, Professor of Anthropology at Sri Venkateswara University in India, the apparently opposing traits of individuality and likeness may be more general to Scandinavia. He studied Hvilsager, a small village in Denmark, yet the findings humorously reported in his book apply well to Norway, perhaps because the country was ruled by Denmark for 400 years. English edition: *Danes Are Like That!*, Grevas, 1993, 175 pages softcover, ISBN 87-7235-624-3. Danish edition: *Sådan er Danskerne!*, Grevas, 1991, 208 pages softcover, ISBN 87-7235-622-7.

More directly relevant to Norway are the views of cultural historian Nina Witoszek, who spent some 10 years pondering the national character, after arriving in Oslo in 1983 from her native Poland. She contends that the roots of national character do not lie in 19th century romanticism, as is popularly believed. Instead, she sees a more earthy "pastoral enlightenment" as the shaping force, as put forth in her book *Norske naturmytologier, fra Edda til økofilosofi* ("Nature Mythologies: From the Eddas to Ecophilosphy"), Pax Forlag, 1998, 184 pages hardcover, ISBN 82-530-1979-3.

Oil (*Olje*) from offshore fields in the North Sea is the driving force behind the prosperous economy of the country. Norway is the world's fourth largest exporter of energy in all forms and second only to Saudi Arabia in the export of oil. With one exception, the offshore fields on the Norwegian continental shelf are named after the gods of Norse mythology who figure so strongly in the sagas of the ☞ **Vikings**. The exception is the *Ekofisk Feld*, the first to come on stream in 1971. Its name reflects the history of North Sea oil activities. In 1962, the Phillips oil company became the first to apply for permission to conduct oil surveying offshore in the North Sea. Surveys began, and finds were made. Philips followed its tradition of naming them in an alphabetical order. As the finds were at sea, the names of fishes were used; hence the Brisling and Cod Fields. The fifth find on the Norwegian continental shelf challenged the naming system. Norway wanted the name to be Norwegian, but had no fish name beginning with the letter E. So a linguistic compromise was made by combining *Eko*, the name of an electric eel in the Indian Ocean, with *fisk*, the Norwegian word for fish. For comprehensive information on offshore oil activities, see the *Fact Sheet Norwegian Petroleum Activity 1999 (Faktaheftet 1999 Norsk petroleums-virksomhet)* available in English or in Norwegian, in printed versions or on-line from the Ministry of Petroleum and Energy ✆ 22249090, 🖷 22249565, ✉ PO Box 8148 Dep, 0033 Oslo, ✉

postmaster@oed.dep.telemax.no,
⊕ http://www.oed.dep.no with pages in Norwegian and in English.

Population (*Befolkning*) As at 1 January 1999, the population of the country was about 4.45 million. The overall population density is 14.5 people per square kilometre, one of the lowest figures in the world and less than a tenth of that of many countries in central Europe. Yet more than six in ten residents live in densely populated areas, the most in metropolitan Oslo, which now has a population of nearly 750,000. Other urban centres include Bergen with a population of more than 225,000, Kristiansand with nearly 72,000, Trondheim with nearly 150,000, Stavanger with nearly 110,000 and Tromsø with 58,000. About one resident in 16 is foreign born, either a naturalised Norwegian citizen or the citizen of another country. About half the population has never been married; 38% are married and 14% have been married and now are either divorced or surviving widows or widowers. The current life expectancy is 80.87 years for women and 75.45 years for men.

Poverty (*Fattigdom*) Despite being very real for those who suffer it, poverty is not entirely understood. At the outset, poverty may be said to be of two types, absolute and relative. Absolute poverty is defined in economic terms, usually as the inability to acquire an accepted minimum of goods and services. Relative poverty depends on the society in which one lives. Relative poverty in a city in Norway differs considerably from relative poverty in a farming village in a more southerly country. Within a single country, poverty may be viewed as indirect or direct. Indirect poverty is the lack of income, whilst direct poverty is the lack of essentials, such as a place to live.

In an industralised country, indirect poverty is usually assessed, because money is needed to acquire essentials. According to official ☞ **statistics** (Statistics and Polls chapter), poverty in Norway is increasing rapidly, from 3.1% under the poverty threshold (*fattigdomsgrense*) in 1985 to 5.6% in 1994. This figure and other statistics on poverty are included in Statistics Norway's annual report, *Kronisk fattigdom i Norge, 1986-1995, Kap. 3 i Inntekt, skatt og overføringer 1999* ("Chronic poverty in Norway, 1986-

1995, Chapter 3 of Income, Taxes and Transfers 1999"). The poverty threshold is set according to the European Union (EU) definition of half the average after-tax income for the country. Family compositions vary and families share resources so family needs are based on a unit of one for the first adult, 0.7 for the second adult or child age 16 or more, and 0.5 for younger children. For instance, in 1994, the average single-person after-tax income was NOK 124,900. Consequently, a single person with an after-tax income of half of NOK 124,900 = NOK 62,450 was considered poor. Likewise, for a family consisting of a couple and a young child, an after-tax income of half of NOK 124,900 x (1.0 + 0.7 + 0.5) = NOK 137,390 was considered poor.

The poor are becoming more evident, particularly in the cities. In 1998 in Oslo, there were 2,000 to 3,000 homeless persons and 200 down-and-outs, and some 135 families with 300 children spent Christmas in hostels. In a country with more than 90,000 millionaires, this underscores the trend seen elsewhere, that the gap between rich and poor is widening.

Private consumption expenditure (*Privat konsum*) per capita has risen steadily and is now more than NOK 97,000 per person per year. Of that sum, the average person spends 22.1% on travel and transport (*reiser og transport*), 21.8% on housing, electricity and heating (*bolig, lys og brensel*), 13.3% on food (*matvarer*), 12% on leisure and education (*fritidssysler og utdannelse*), 9.4% on miscellaneous goods and services (*andre varer og tjenester*), 8.6% on furniture and household articles (*møbler og husholdningsartikler*), 6.5% on clothing and shoes (*klær og skotøy*), 3.6% on drink and tobacco (*drikkevarer og tobacco*) and 2.9% on health care (*helsepleie*).

Racism (*Rasisme*) is the theory that human abilities and characteristics are determined by race. It is not the same as ☞ **discrimination** (Business and Work chapter). Racism involves personal opinion, which may or may not result in action. So it may remain unseen. Discrimination, on the other hand, involves action, which can be seen, such as refusing to employ an otherwise qualified person because of his or her race. Consequently, there are laws against it in the workplace, in schools and the like.

Racism is a problem, not only because it can cause

discrimination but also because it triggers harassment and violence. The results have ranged from annoyance to tragedy. Black people often complain that they are checked more frequently at immigration and by the police than are people of ethnic Norwegian appearance. In 1998, Oslo police stopped a teenage boy of African extraction some 17 times in three weeks because they suspected that he had stolen the new, high-end offroad bicycle he was riding, even though he carried the receipt proving that he had bought it. In 1999 in a rural town, a teenage boy of Indian birth, adopted as an infant and raised Norwegian, was racially harassed by classmates at school, increasingly violently and ultimately to death. Fortunately the media have highlighted these and other similar incidents, and the public is increasingly aware of the blot of racism. In 1998, the ☞ **Centre for Combating Ethnic Discrimination** (Government and Social Services chapter) was founded to deal with the relevant problems. Even the royal family is concerned: in June 1999, Crown Prince Haakon returned home to announce that he would build on what he observed while a student at the University of California and would work to combat racism and to promote ethnic diversity.

Reading habits (*Lesevaner*) Norway is a country of readers. The spending per head on books is the highest in the world, well ahead of second-place Germany and nearly twice as high as in the UK (14th place). In part this may be due to the relatively high price of books, but it is also due to reading being a prime pastime. Women are the country's leading bookworms, on the average spending twice as much time as men in reading. The pervasive reading habit is reflected in the sales of ☞ **newspapers** (Media and Information chapter): every day, six are sold for every ten people in the country, the third highest rate worldwide.

The Royal family (*Kongehuset*)

King Harald V, born 21 February 1937, ascended the throne 17 January 1991, crowned in Nidaros Cathedral 23 June 1991.

Queen Sonja, born 4 July 1937, originally a commoner when married on 29 August 1968 to Harald when he was Crown Prince.

King Harald V and Queen Sonja have two children:

Crown Prince Haakon Magnus, born 20 July 1973.

Crown Princess Märta Louise, born 22 September 1971.

King Harald V has two sisters:

Princess Astrid Maud Ingeborg, born 12 February 1932, married 12 January 1961 to Johan Martin Ferner, born 22 July 1927.

Pricess Ragnhild Alexandra, born 9 June 1930, married 15 May 1953 to Erling Sven Lorentzen, born 28 January 1923.

For further information, visit a library or bookshop, as there are dozens of books about the Royal family and its individual members, in Norwegian and in other languages.

The Sámi are the indigenous people of northern Scandinavia and the Kola Peninsula of Russia. They are sometimes called Lapps, but they prefer the name Sámi, which comes from Sámpi, their name for themselves and the land that they have inhabited for thousands of years. The size of the Sámi population is not known, but is conservatively estimated at 70,000, of which about half live in Norway. Their native languages are related to Finnish, Hungarian and Estonian and have little in common with Norwegian. Traditionally, the Sámi have been hunters, fishermen and reindeer herders. Some still follow the traditional callings, whilst others practise more modern trades. One of the more famous of them is film director Nils Gaup, whose Pathfinder (1987), the first feature-length Sámi film, was nominated for an Academy Award (Oscar).

As has been the fate of indigenous peoples elsewhere, the Sámi have been subjected to discrimination under regulations that aimed to enforce assimilation and loosen their ties with their ethnic origins. Until the early 1960s, Sámi pupils at Norwegian-Sámi school were forbidden to speak their mother tongue, even during breaks. Moreover, the singing of *joik*, the native Sámi song, also was forbidden. Many children were obliged to attend boarding schools from age seven, to separate them from their parents. People with Sámi names were not allowed to own land in Finnmark, Norway's northernmost county.

Matters are better now. The Sámi have their own flag, acknowledged in 1986, and their own Parliament (*Sámeting*), opened in 1989. The Sámi language is encouraged at schools, and colleges have programmes of Sámi studies. The traditional *joik* song form has gained international recognition: Mari Boine Persen has sung on stages round the world; Nils-Aslak Valkepää sang *joik* at the opening ceremony of the 1994 Olympic Winter Games at Lillehammer; Wimme Saari mixes *joik* with techno backgrounds.

For further information, contact the Centre for Sámi Studies at the University of Tromsø (*Universitetet i Tromsø*) ✆ 77645535, ℻ 77676672, ✉ Breivika, 9037 Tromsø, ☞ http://www.uit.no/ssweb with pages in English, Norwegian and Sámi, or the Sámi Parliament (*Sámediggi*) ✆ 78467100, ℻ 78466155, ✉ PO Box 144, 9730 Karasjok.

Secondary school graduating class (*Russ*) In the final weeks of upper secondary school, for a few weeks in the spring, around ☞ **Constitution Day**, the graduating pupils celebrate in a way that has become uniquely Norwegian. They dress in red or blue costumes with matching visored caps, travel in old buses or vans in the same colour, all adorned with risqué texts, sometimes in English and loudly party. These are the *Russ*. Though their deeds are new, their roots are historical. Before the University of Oslo was founded in 1812, Norwegians who wished to study at a university went abroad, most of them to Copenhagen. The University there required applicants to stand an *Examen Artium*, or admittance examination. After the *Examen Artium* and before its results were made known, the applicant was given an animal horn to wear on his (there were no women students at the time) forehead, and was thereafter teased by the older students. When the results were made known, a "forsaking the horns" ceremony was held for those who passed. The horn was removed, to signify that they had left the realm of the wild and had become worthy of university studies. Like other academic terms of the time, the ceremony had a name in Latin: *Cornua depositurus*, of which the Norwegian word *Russ* is a contraction.

With time, particularly after universities were founded in Norway, the tradition changed. The *Examen Artium* shifted from being an entrance exam to university to being the final examination of upper secondary school, or *gymnasium*, as it was then known. Likewise, the *Russ* celebration (*Russefeiring*) moved back, from the first year at university to the last year at *gymnasium*.

The visored caps (*Russelue*) became the usual attire, starting in 1905, when students in Oslo copied the red caps worn by German students on visit the year before. The custom spread rapidly throughout the country. In 1916, the business studies *gymnasium* adopted a cap of the same design, in blue. Thereafter, one spoke of the red and blue varieties of *Russ*: *Rødruss* and *Blåruss*. *Russ* 'business cards' (*Russekort*) came in the 1950s, each bearing a portrait photo and a personal motto for celebration, also often risqué. The celebrations for a class include creating a din early in the morning of Constitution Day, the 17th of May, to wake its teachers.

Finishing upper secondary school and going on to university is no longer restricted to the select few, but now is increasingly commonplace. Nonetheless, a wild tradition acquired by the intellectual elite of times gone by lives on, as ever greater numbers of *Russ* celebrate in the springtime, in repainted buses fitted with multi-hundred watt stereos and with uninhibited partying, sometimes 24 hours a day. The celebrations are tolerated but increasingly questioned. The significance of being a *Russ* seems to have given way to party excesses that have become an annual social hazard. The noise during and litter after all-night, multi-bus *Russ* parties (*Russefest*) has annoyed neighbourhoods and brought out the police. In May 1998, some 150 *Russ* from Oslo on a weekend trip to Gothenburg, Sweden turned their party there into a rowdy, drunken brawl and were expelled from the city and country. Back home in Norway, the incident made headlines, and Minister of Education Jon Lilletun called for an end to *Russ* drunkenness (*Russefylla*) and contemplated measures to constrain it, such as changing the dates of examinations in order to cut back the time available for partying.

Sexual activity (*Seksual aktivitet*) According to a 1997 survey conducted for Durex, a manufacturer of condoms, the average couple has sex 100 times a year, which is more than the averages for the other Nordic countries but less than the averages for many countries farther south. The age of consent is 16 for having legal heterosexual or homosexual relations with a person of the same age or older.

Stress (same word in Norwegian) is a common term for the psychological and physiological changes that may result from adverse circumstances. In small amounts, stress can be physically and mentally stimulating. But prolonged, high levels of stress are believed to among the contributing causes of some illnesses, including high blood pressure, ulcers and coronary thrombosis. Chronic mental overstimulation and burden can cause psychological disturbance. Consequently, stress management is a factor in health care, particularly as stress is second after overload maladies as a cause of sick leave. Despite a decreasing workweek – now 35 hours, compared to more than 40 hours in the 1960s – and more labour-saving devices in the home and the workplace, reported cases of stress are increasing. However, stress scientist Holger Ursin at the University of Bergen believes that the stress levels may be overstated. Many people may be stressed because stress is in fashion, a part of the increasingly hectic lifestyle.

Suicide (*Selvmord*) has been declining but remains one of the leading causes of violent death. In 1995, for instance, there were 548 suicides, some 60% more than the number of traffic fatalities (341) and 12 times the number of murders (45). Depression is believed to be the leading cause of suicide, particularly among young men, for which the suicide rate is high and nearly double that of 1970. In 1997, the *Bergens Tidende* newspaper compiled data from police, road authorities and road transport organisations and concluded that about one traffic fatality in ten probably is a suicide, so the actual number of suicides in a year may be higher than statistics indicate.

Tipping and charges (*Driks og avgifter*) vary. Restaurants add service charges (*service*) into bills, so you should tip only if the service has been superior. Most cloakrooms and left-luggage rooms post fixed charges (*avgift*) for their services, but some do not, so you must ask what is expected. Porters at airports will tell you their charges upon request. Taxi drivers, barbers, hairdressers and others who provide personal services do not expect tips, but you can round off a bill upwards to the nearest NOK 10 if you feel you have been well served. Doormen usually expect tips for services provided, such as for calling or hailing a taxi. Rates vary widely, by location – city or town – and by service – hotel or entertainment, so your best guide to tipping tradition is to ask someone who has been to the place before.

Values (*Verdier*) As elsewhere, the globalisation of the media and the economy and the onrush of new technologies, such as the Internet, has left people feeling uncertain about life in the modern world. Accordingly, in January 1998, the Values Commission (*Verdikommisjonen*) was set up. The Commission is headed by a judge and has in all 49 members, including social workers, religious leaders and university and college faculty members. Its goal is not to preach morality, but to help people reflect over the issues they face and seek answers themselves.

The Vikings (*Vikingene*) were the adventuresome Scandinavian peoples of medieval times. Their age of prominence, the Viking Era (*Vikingtiden*), began in 793 with the sacking of the monastery at Lindisfarne and ended in 1066 at the Battle of Stanford Bridge, in which King Harald Harråde was killed. Though relatively short, the Viking Era is vital in the history of Scandinavia in general and Norway in particular. Before it, the country was pagan and was divided into innumerable chiefdoms and small kingdoms. When it ended, the country was united under a King and the Christian Church.

The origin of the word *Viking* remains a mystery. Scandinavians regard it to have been derived from *Vik*, the word for bay or inlet, with the suffix *ing* meaning "hailing from", so the *Vikings* were the people who 'came from the bays'. However, the word may be older, as it appears in Anglo-Saxon glossaries of the early eighth century. If so, the Vikings owed their name to those they met abroad.

Written records in Europe describe the Vikings as warlike pirates who committed depredations on land. But they also were exceptionally skilled seafarers who developed the long ships, the most advanced of their day. Modern marine architects have run the vital measurements of the long ships through a computer and have found that the Vikings got it right: the ships are not only graceful, but also have the optimum combination of two conflicting concepts, maximum stability and minimum friction. Vikings voyages crossed the oceans to discover Iceland, Greenland and North America, as well as southward and eastward, to the Mediterranean Sea and up the Russian rivers to the Black Sea and the Caspian Sea. As they went, the Vikings traded and set up international commerce; cities afar, such as Dublin and York, were Viking trading ports.

The crucial thing about the Vikings is that they were essentially farmers. Forests in those days grew to the water's edge so there was much less agricultural land available (it's still only 4% of Norway's land mass today!) While this was helpful in terms of easy access to timber for building houses and ships – it also meant that as the population grew, there was an acute shortage of agricultural land.

If a Viking farmer died, his eldest son inherited the farm. The second and third sons thus had no hope of ever owning their own farms. And if a Viking youth wanted to marry, he had to pay the girl's father a house bond — the origin of the word "husband". If he had no farm, he certainly wouldn't be able to afford such a bond – and therefore couldn't marry.

So it was primarily for these reasons that the Vikings took to the seas. They needed land and raided other countries (monasteries provided good pickings) but in almost all cases they eventually integrated with the local populations and became farmers again. Indeed, they never really had empirical ambitions. Nonetheless, they did become feared raiders – not least because plunder from foreign shores enabled them to marry and eventually live comfortable farming lives.

There are Viking burial mounds and historical sites throughout Norway. Two museums are devoted entirely to the Vikings. The Viking Ship Museum (Vikingskiphuset) at Bygdøy in Oslo features three exceptionally well preserved and restored long ships found at Gokstad, Tune and Oseberg as well as extensive collections of Viking artefacts ✆ 22438379, ☎ 22445581, ✉ Huk Aveny 35, 0287 Oslo. The Lofotr Viking Museum at Borg (Vikingmuseet på Borg) in the Lofoten Islands is a reconstruction of a Viking chieftain's homestead, the largest of its kind ever found. The displays include objects that connect Viking trade to England, France, Germany and southern Europe ✆ 76084900, ☎ 76084910, ✉ 8360 Bøstad, ✉ http://home.sol.no/~perkaa/what/vestvaag/lofotr.html with pages in English.

Viking themes are also part of entertainment. The Tusenfryd amusement park south of Oslo includes the Vikingland theme park. The annual Vikingfestival held in June at Kopervik on the west coast features an extensive programme of activities and exhibitions ✆ 52857375, ☎ 52857360, ✉ 4250 Kopervik, ✉ http://gjedde.interpost.no/karmoy/kkviking.html with pages in Norwegian. In the summertime, there are Viking markets (Vikingmarked) and Viking plays (Vikingspillene) at several locations. Replicas of Viking jewelry are popular, and some rock music groups have taken Viking names, most notably Ragnarock, from Ragnarok the ultimate and final battle in Norse Mythology (Norrøn mytologi). Other names from Norse Mythology are widely used, in company names as well as in the names of offshore oil platforms in the North Sea. The Vikings are historical, but their legacy is very much a part of contemporary life.

War history (Krigshistorie) principally means the history of the Second World War, when the country was invaded and occupied by Germany from 9 April 1940 until final liberation on 8 May 1945. Many books have been written about the period; arguably the best overview in English is "Norway and the Second World War" (Oslo, Aschehoug "Tokens of Norway" series, 1996, 174 pages hardcover, ISBN 82-03-22163-7). Several films have been made on events during the occupation, particularly on the sabotage of the heavy water plant of the Vemork power station at Rjukan in Telemark county on 27 February 1943. And author John Steinbeck early paid tribute to the spirit of the occupied people in "The Moon is Down", a novel first published in March 1942. In it, the occupiers and the occupied are not identified. But the story is so clearly of Norway that copies of the book printed in the original English in neutral Sweden in 1942 were circulated in Norway by the home front, each clearly rubber stamped Denne bok tilhörer det norske folk. Send den vider når du har lest den. ("This book belongs to the Norwegian people. Read it and pass it on.").

Church and Religion
(*Kirke og religion*)

The Bible (*Bibelen*) in Norway has a history entwined with that of the country. The first Bible available in the vernacular was the Danish translation of 1530, used throughout the period of Danish rule, until 1814. Thereafter, the Bible was translated into Norwegian in several stages. A Norwegian edition of the New Testament, re-worked from the Danish, appeared in 1819. The first independent translation into Norwegian was published in 1904. Thereafter, there have been several modifications, in step with changes in the language and in part to suit the Bible to changing times. The most widespread edition, now used in churches throughout the country, was first published in 1978 and reprinted several times since. A modernised version of the New Testament, *Godt nytt*, was first published in 1975. A new translation of the Bible as well as a dual-language Norwegian-English version of The New Testament and The Book of Psalms (*Det Nye Testamente og Salmenes bok*) were published in 1988. A Norwegian translation of the English King James version was published in 1997. A simplified, extracted Bible for children, *Utvalgte fortellinger*, has been periodically published through the years, last in 1993. There are Bibles in Norway's minority languages, Sámi and Nynorsk. There are Bibles in Braille for the blind, Bibles on CD-ROM and on-line on the Internet. The ☞ **Books of the Bible** (this chapter) are the same as those of the King James version of the Bible in English. All other works related to the Bible and its use are available in Norwegian editions. The current standard Concordance (*Ord i Bibelen*) was published in 1987. The latest edition of the Apocrypha (*Apokryfene*), the collection of books excluded from the Hebrew Bible, was published in 1988. The current edition of the Book of Hymns (*Norsk Salme Bok*) was published in 1985. These and numerous other Christian works are available from several publishers. Most larger publishers offer selections of Christian literature, and three specialise in Bibles and other Christian works. For further details or titles of books available, contact a book shop (*bokhandel*), as most now have on-line search and ordering facilities. For complete overviews as well as on-line services, contact:

- The Norwegian Bible Society (*Det norske Bibelselskap*), an interdenominational organisation founded in 1816, and its affiliates Verbum Press (*Verbum Forlag*) which specialises in hymnals and music, and Christian Films (*Kristen Filmtjeneste*) which specialises in films and videos ✆ 22932700, 🖷 22697313, ✉ bibel.forlag@bibelselskapet.no ✉ verbum.forlag@bibelselskapet.no ✉ kristenfilm@bibelselskapet.no ● http://www.bibelselskapet.no
- Norwegian Bible (*Norsk Bibel*) was founded in 1986 and is owned by several Christian publishers ✆ 38199330 or 22007380, ✉ nb@norsk-bibel.no, ● http://www.norsk-bibel.no
- Bible Press (*Bibelforlaget*), the independent publisher of the Norwegian translation of the King James version of the Bible ✆ 63803099, 🖷 63816922, ✉ hermon@online.no

Books of The Bible (*Bibelens skrifter*) The Norwegian ☞ **Bible** has the same Books as the King James version in English. Most of the titles of the Books in Norwegian are similar to their equivalents in English. But some differ. The Norwegian titles, as now used in the media, and their English equivalents are listed below. Only abbreviated versions are listed; for instance, in the New Testament, the Norwegian "*Paulus' første brev til tessalonikerne*" is listed as "*1. Tessalonikerbrev*" and the English "Epistle of James" is listed as "James".

Bibelen Norwegian version of 1978 Det Gamle Testament	The Bible King James version The Old Testament
1. Mosebok	Genesis
2. Mosebok	Exodus
3. Mosebok	Leviticus
4. Mosebok	Numbers
5. Mosebok	Deuteronomy
Josva	Joshua
Dommerne	Judges
Rut	Ruth
1. Samuelsbok	I Samuel
2. Samuelsbok	II Samuel

1. Kongebok	I Kings	Hebreerbrevet	Hebrews
2. Kongebok	II Kings	Jakobs brev	James
1. Krønikebok	I Chronicles	1. Peters brev	I Peter
2. Krønikebok	II Chronicles	2. Peters brev	II Peter
Esra	Ezra	1. Johannes' brev	I John
Nehemja	Nehemiah	2. Johannes' brev	II John
Ester	Esther	3. Johannes' brev	III John
Job	Job	Judas' brev	Jude
Salmenes bok	Psalms	Johannes' åpenbaring	Revelation
Salomos ordspråk	Proverbs		
Forkynneren	Ecclesiastes		
Høysangen	Song of Songs		
Jesaja	Isaiah		
Jeremia	Jeremiah		
Klagesangene	Lamentations		
Esekiel	Ezekiel		
Daniel	Daniel		
Hosea	Hosea		
Joel	Joel		
Amos	Amos		
Obadja	Obadiah		
Jona	Jonah		
Mika	Micah		
Nahum	Nahum		
Habakkuk	Habakkuk		
Sefanja	Zephaniah		
Haggai	Haggai		
Sakarja	Zechariah		
Malaki	Malachi		

Det Nye Testament	**The New Testament**
Matteus	Matthew
Markus	Mark
Lukas	Luke
Johannes	John
Apostlenes gjerninger	The Acts
Romerbrevet	Romans
1. Korinterbrev	I Corinthians
2. Korinterbrev	II Corinthians
Galaterbrevet	Galatians
Efeserbrevet	Ephesians
Filipperbrevet	Philippians
Kolosserbrevet	Colossians
1. Tessalonikerbrev	I Thessalonians
2. Tessalonikerbrev	II Thessalonians
1. Timoteus' brev	I Timothy
2. Timoteus' brev	II Timothy
Brevet til Titus	Titus
Brevet til Filemon	Philemon

Catholicism (*Katolisisme*) Christianity came to Norway starting about 900 AD. In 1030, a missionary king, Olav, died a martyr's death at the battle of Stiklestad, and was canonised as Saint Olav. Thereafter, Norway was regarded as a Christian country, responsible to the Pope. In the centuries that followed, monasteries, convents, churches and cathedrals were built, and the Church became a major force in the life of the country. In 1537, during the Reformation, the King of Denmark (who then ruled Norway) imposed Lutheranism and suppressed Catholicism. All monasteries and convents were closed and their property confiscated, and churches and cathedrals were either made Protestant or fell into disuse. Despite threat of punishment, Catholic groups survived until the 18th century. In 1814, when Norway declared independence from Denmark, the Constitution then drafted barred Jews, monks and Jesuits (a Catholic order) from the country (rescinded for Jews in 1857, for monks in 1891 and for Jesuits in 1956). That history is much in evidence today. The ☞ **Church of Norway** is Evangelic Lutheran, a Protestant faith, and Catholicism a minority faith. Nonetheless, there are nearly 40,000 Catholics in the country, which makes Catholicism statistically the second largest Christian faith in Norway. The country is divided into three Church districts, the diocese of Oslo and the prelatures of Trondheim and Tromsø, and there are 31 parishes. There is now a variety of religious communities in the country, both active and contemplative. The Dominican and Franciscan orders are well established. There are three Catholic schools: St. Franciskus in Arendal, St. Paul in Bergen and St. Sunniva in Oslo. In the diocese of Oslo there are ancillary Catholic services, including an information agency, the St. Olav Press (*St. Olav Forlag*), the St. Olav book shop (*St. Olav Bokhandel*). Spiritual guidance (*sjelesorg*) is offered by native speaking priests to the capital city's many Catholics from abroad, in Croatian, Polish, Portugese, Spanish, Tagalog, Tamil and Vietnamese, and there are centres for Croatians, Filipinos and Vietnamese. For further information, call the nearest Catholic facility listed under *Katolske Kirke* in the Pink Pages or contact the central organisations in Oslo ✆ 22207226, 📠 22204857, ✉ Akersveien 5, 0177 Oslo, ⊕ http://www.katolsk.no with pages in Norwegian, English, French, German, Polish, Portuguese and Spanish.

The Church of Norway (*Den norske kirke*) has belonged to the Evangelical Lutheran branch of Christianity since 1537 and has been a state church since 1660. Today, Norway is one of six countries in Europe to have a Protestant state church; the others are the United Kingdom and the other Nordic countries: Denmark, Finland, Iceland and Sweden. About 87% of all Norwegians belong to the Church of Norway, and it has some churches and chapels in the country. Parish (*menighet*) work is conducted by a council under the leadership of a pastor (*prest*). The country is divided into 1,310 parishes, 98 deaneries and rural deaneries and 11 dioceses. The clergy numbers more than 1,200, of which about 12% are women, who have been ordained since 1961. The first woman bishop of the church was appointed in 1993 to the See of Hamar. Services (*gudstjenester*) are held on Sundays, usually at 11 a.m., and several times a day on major holidays, such as Christmas Eve and Easter Sunday. Programmes of services are announced two or three days in advance, usually under *Gudstjenester* or *Kirker* in the classified pages of local newspapers, as well as for entire months or seasons of the year in leaflets in the vestibule (*våpenhuset*) of most churches. The liturgy (*liturgi*) is Evangelical Lutheran and varies from high mass (*høymesse*) to less formal services for families with small children (*familiegudstjeneste*). Most parishes support other religious activities, such as YMCA (*KFUM*) and YWCA (*KFUK*) groups, Sunday Schools (*søndagsskoler*), youth activities (*ungdoms aktiviteter*) and care for the elderly (*eldre omsorg*), often in a building near the church. Parishes also support mission work abroad. Regrettably for the Church, attendance is low: according to current Statistics Norway figures, some half the population attend neither services nor other church activities in the course of a year, and only 10% attend ten times or more a year.

Nonetheless, awareness of the Church remains high: some 82% of all infants are baptised and about 75% of all youth are confirmed in Church of Norway churches and chapels, and church weddings are commonplace. For further details, contact the nearest church (look under *Kirken, den norske* in the Pink Pages) or the Church Information Service (*Kirkens informasjonstjeneste*) in Oslo ✆ 22932750, 📠 22932828, ✉ dag.stange@kirken.no, ⊕ http://www.kirken.no with pages in Norwegian, in English and in Sámi.

Islam In terms of numbers of people belonging to various religions in Norway, Islam is the second most practised faith (after the Church of Norway), with some 65,000 residents of the country either being practising Muslims or hailing from Muslim countries. According to the latest (1998) figures, the largest group of Muslims in Norway are the immigrants (*innvandrere*) and their families and descendants who coame from the 1970s on, in all some 19,000 from Pakistan, 7,800 from Turkey and 4,500 from Morocco. In the 1980s and 1990s, many refugees (*flyktninger*) of Muslim faiths came from the areas of Europe ravaged by war, including 10,000 from Bosnia and 4,500 from Kosovo. Other Muslim faith groups include 7,600 from Iran, 5,000 from Somalia and 3,200 Kurds and others from Iraq. More than half the Muslims in the country live in the metropolitan Oslo area. Accordingly there are 15 Mosques and Muslim organisations in the city. Otherwise, there are Muslim organisations in eleven counties: Buskerud county including metropolitan Drammen has six; Hedemark county has one in Elverum; Hordaland county including metropolitan Bergen has three; Nord-Trøndelag county has one in Levanger; Oppland county has one in Lillehammer; Rogaland county including metropolitan Stavanger has seven ; Telemark county including metropolitan Skien has five; Troms has one in Tromsø; Vest-Agder county including metropolitan Kristiansand has seven ; Vestfold county including the cities of Tønsberg and Larvik has two; and Østfold county including the cities of Fredrikstad; Halden and Sarpsborg has six. The Koran is sold in major book shops (*bokhandel*), and there is a Norwegian translation of the first two Suras: *Koranen på norsk*, Oslo, Urtehagen, 1996, ISBN 82-91695-00-8. A comprehensive overview book in Norwegian on Islam in Norway was published in 1998: *Islam i Norge* by Mohammed Bouras, Millennium in co-operation with the Islamic Council, 1998, ISBN 82-517-8907-9. The *Oslo-Net* provides an Internet service of Muslim resources for the metropolitan Oslo area ✉ oslo@muslimsonline.com, ⊕ http://salam.muslimonline.com/~oslo with pages in English. The Islamic Council in Norway (*Islamsk Råd Norge*) co-ordinates Muslim affairs in the country and interacts with other Muslim organisations and information services ✆ 22357613, ⌧ PO Box 658 Sentrum, 0106 Oslo, ✉ inra@online.no, ⊕ http://www.uio.no/~tayyabr/irn with pages in Norwegian. To find Islamic organisations, look under Islamic, *Islamsk* and *Islamske* in the Pink Pages, view the *Oslo-Net* web pages or contact the Islamic Council.

Judaism (*Jødedom*) historically must be the most repressed religion in the country. The ☞ **Constitution** (Government and Social Services chapter) of 1814 barred Jews from the country, but in 1851 the ban was rescinded. In 1852, the first Jew, Abraham Vollman from Lübeck, came to Oslo (Christiania as it was then called) and opened a shop. Thereafter, the Jewish population grew slowly through the years, to about 1800 in 1940, at the time of the German invasion. In 1942, the Germans demanded that Norwegian Jews be sent to Nazi concentration camps. The collaborationist government complied. (The King and Parliament had fled to England and comprised the true government in exile during the war.) Some 770 Jews were deported, of whom 758 were killed in death camps. The Norwegian home front successfully smuggled 900 Jews across the Swedish border to safety. In 1996, after media exposure of wartime history, the Ministry of Justice appointed a commission to examine the issue of restitution of Jewish property confiscated by the collaborationist regime. There are now about 1500 Jews in the country. Most are in the greater Oslo area. There also is a small community of about 120 in Trondheim, which boasts the northernmost Synagogue in the world. It also is the only Synagogue known to have once served as a railway station. The Mosaic Community (*Det Mosaiske Trossamfund*) represents the Jews of Norway. There is one Rabbi (*Rabbiner*), who officiates at the Synagogue in Oslo and also supervises the shop selling ☞ **Kosher food** (Food and Eating chapter). The Oslo Community runs a kindergarten

and an after-hours Hebrew school for primary and secondary school pupils. Numerous Jewish organisations are active. The Community owns a country estate that is used for summer camps and Shabbat seminars, and publishes a magazine entitled *Hatikwa*. For details, contact the Mosaic Community ✆ 22696570, ⊠ 22466604, ⌧ Bergstien 13, 0172 Oslo, ✉ kontor@dmt.oslo.no, ⊕ http://www.dmt.oslo.no with pages in Norwegian and in English.

Religious denominations and other ideological associations (*Tros- og livssynssamfunn*)
Though most Norwegians are members of the ☞ **Church of Norway** (this chapter), more than one resident in 15 belongs to another religious denomination or ideological association. There are no accurate overviews, because official ☞ **Statistics** (Statistics and Polls chapter) are kept only for denominations and associations which receive central government subsidies. The following list may not be complete, but includes the principal denominations and associations active in Norway and listed in readily available public and private sector sources. To find a denomination or association, look for its name in Norwegian in the Pink Pages or under *Kirker og trossamfunn* in the Yellow Pages. If you have Internet access, you may find further information, in Norwegian and in English, on "Theology Online", the web site maintained by the Faculty of Theology of the University of Oslo ⊕ http://www.tf.uio.no. Alphabetically by everyday name in English (*everyday name in Norwegian*), the denominations and associations are:

- American Churches (*Amerikanske kirker*): Baptist and Lutheran
- Anglican-Episcopal (*Det engelske Kirke*)
- Adventists (*Adventistsamfunnet*)
- Bahá´í (*Bahá´í*)
- Baptists, including Norwegian Baptist Union (*Det norske Baptistsamfunn*)
- Buddhists (*Buddhistforbundet*)
- Christian Centres (*Kristne senter*)
- Christian Scientists (*Kristen vitenskap*)
- Church of England (*Den Engelske Kirke*)
- Church of Jesus Christ of Latter-Day Saints (*Jesu Kristi Kirke av Siste Dagers Hellige*)
- Church of God International (*Syvende dags kristne*)

- Evangelic Lutheran Church Community (*The evangelisk-lutherske kirkesamfunn*)
- Free Evangelic Congregations (*De frie evangeliske forsamlinger*)
- Friends (*Kvekere*)
- Greek Orthodox Church (*Den greske ortodokse kirke*)
- Hindus (*Hinduer*)
- Human and Ethical Union (*Human-Etisk Forbund*)
- Islam (*Islam*)
- Janinism (*Jainismen*)
- Jehovah's Witnesses (*Jehovas vitner*)
- Lutheran Free Church of Norway (*Den Evangelisk Lutherske frikirke*)
- Methodists (*Metodistkirken*)
- Missionary Alliance (*Det Norske Misjonsforbund*)
- Orthodox Jews (*Det Mosaiske Trossamfund*)
- Pentecostalists (*Pinsemenigheter*), including Norwegian Pentecostalist Congregations and the International Church of the Foursquare Gospel (*Josvakirken*)
- Rinzai Zen (*Zen Rinzai*)
- Roman Catholic Church (*Den romersk-katolske kirke*)
- Salvation Army (*Frelsesarmeen*)
- Sikh (*Sikh*)
- Taoism (*Taoismen*)
- Unification Church (*Den Forente Familie*)

Cities (*Byer*)

Cities (*Byer*) The country is increasingly urban. When the Constitution was signed in 1814, only one person in ten lived in a town or a city. By 1900, the figure was just one in three. Half the population lived in urban areas in 1950, and three-quarters in 2000. Most of the urban areas are metropolitan areas centred on a city and which may include other towns. A rural area may be considered to be an urbanised area (*tettsted*) if it has a population of more than 200, is less than one-quarter dependent upon farming and has an average distance between houses of less than 50 metres. In turn, an urbanised area may be considered to be a town (*bygd*) or city (*by*) if it has a population of more than 2000. The distinction between city and town is made in several ways. One is historical: as in the UK, a city is a larger town with a cathedral, the seat of a bishop of the Church of Norway. Indeed, there are cathedrals in the 11 largest cities: Bergen, Bodø, Fredrikstad, Hamar, Kristiansand, Molde, Oslo, Stavanger, Tønsberg, Tromsø and Trondheim. One common belief reflects seagoing tradition: a port town may be a city. However, that definition fails for Hamar, which has a cathedral, and for Lillehammer, which has no cathedral but in 1994 was the country's most famous city with the staging of the Olympic Winter Games. Another distinction is in the language. Two prepositions, *i* and *på*, equivalent to the English "in" are used when describing a person's place of residence: "she lives in Oslo" is *hun bor i Oslo*, but "she lives in Lillerstrøm" is *hun bor på Lillestrøm*. However, that distinction also fails, most notably for Hamar. Moreover, opinion and usage vary; one way to start a trivial but lively discussion at a party is to ask the native speakers whether it should be *i Hamar* or *på Hamar*. Perhaps the safest definition of "city" is a large town that administratively has the status of a city. By all definitions, the six largest cities in the country, in clockwise order starting with the capital, are Oslo, Kristiansand, Stavanger, Bergen, Trondheim and Tromsø.

Bergen

Location: on the west coast, in Hordaland county, at 60°20'N latitude.
Year founded: 1070
Population (1999): 227,276

Area: 465 square kilometres
Normal midday temperature in mid January: 1.5 °C and mid July: 14.5 °C
Normal yearly precipitation: 2250 mm
First digit of postcode: 5
First two digits of telephone numbers: 55

Bergen is the country's second most populous city and the principal port on the west coast. Tourists from round the world will remember the city as the gateway to the fjords of western Norway, as it is the homeport for many fjord cruises as well as the southernmost port for the coastal express liners. Indeed, it was sea trade that built the city, and from the 13th to the 16th centuries, Bergen was a principal port in the Hanseatic trade league. The Hanseatic Quay – *Bryggen* – remains, and now is one of the four UNESCO World Heritage Sites in Norway.

The name Bergen derives not from German, but from the old Norse *Bjørgvin*. Until the railway line eastward over the central mountain plateau to Oslo was opened in 1909, Bergen was isolated from the rest of the country. Scotland was closer by ship than Oslo, England less distant than Copenhagen. Centuries of being international before becoming national left their mark on the city. Many local traditions as well as expressions differ from those elsewhere in the country.

One is the *Buekorps* ("Crossbow corps"), an organisation for 10 to 20 year-old boys. Corps boys are easily recognised by their natty tunics and tam-o-shanter caps dating to the 1850s, when the organisation was founded in emulation of the home guards. Their activities consist of marching drills, shouldering rifles and crossbows, to the roll of double-headed drums. It is a tradition unique to Bergen.

Relics of history abound. *Håkonshallen*, a gothic festival hall built in 1261, arguably is the best example of medieval profane architecture remaining in Scandinavia. And there's *Bryggen*. Throughout the city there are venerable buildings, many centuries old. Consequently, the *Bergenser*, as the natives are called, have endeavoured to preserve their city, principally by saving it from highway blight. That often has meant boring road tunnels through solid rock. There now are 13 tunnels, a total of 13.5 km, in and around the city, the costs offset by toll charges.

Kristiansand

Location: on the south coast in Vest-Agder county,

at 58°10'N latitude.
Year founded: 1641
Population (1999): 71,498
Area: 276 square kilometres
Normal midday temperature in mid January: –0.9 °C
and mid July: 15.7 °C
Normal yearly precipitation: 1380 mm
First digit of postcode: 4
First two digits of telephone numbers: 38

Kristiansand is the fifth largest and southernmost major city in the country. It is called the "capital" of *Sørlandet*, which means the strip of coastal towns and villages that have become favourite summer holiday destinations. The city was the first and is still one of few in Norway to have a rectangular street plan, with seven streets parallel to the Otra River and eleven streets perpendicular to it. Most of the older buildings are masonry, as they were built after a fire destroyed the city in 1892.

The port of Kristiansand has been busy with national and international traffic ever since the steamships of the London–St. Petersburg line first called there in 1839. It was the last westward, and first eastward port of call for liners in the heyday of passenger travel by ship across the North Atlantic. It remains one of the busiest ports for international ferry traffic.

The Kristiansand Zoo and Amusement Park (*Kristiansand Dyrepark*) is the only large zoo in the country. In the city park (*Byparken*) there is a statue of Norway's national poet and Kristiansand's native son Henrik Wergeland (1808-45), by Gustav Vigeland, the country's most known sculptor.

Oslo

Location: in southeastern part of country at head of Oslo Fjord, 59°55'N latitude.
Year founded: 1048
Population (1999): 502,867
Area: 454 square kilometres
Normal midday temperature in mid January: –4.3 °C
and mid July: 16.5 °C
Normal yearly precipitation: 763 mm
First digit of postcodes: 0 and 1
First two digits of telephone numbers: 22 and 23

Oslo is the capital and the most populous city in the country. It was founded as an administrative and trades centre and later became an industrial centre as well. It has changed names twice: once to Chris-

tiania – with a short 50-year period of respelling to *Kristiania* – and then, three centuries later, back to Oslo. It is a city of contrasts.

The downtown area retains the convenience of a medieval capital: the Palace, Parliament, courts and government offices, older university buildings, central railway and bus stations and largest shops and pedestrian precincts are all within convenient walking distance of each other. Yet the city is spread out: more than three-quarters of its area is open space. Including the *Oslomarka* woodlands on the hills surrounding the city to the north, the city and its environs are larger than London. It is the only capital in the world in which an Olympic Winter Games (1952) have been held. Yet it also is a major port, where container ships and cruise ships alike call. It is the only city in the country with trams and an underground. Yet it has an extensive network of cycle paths and, in parks and woodland areas, footpaths and trails.

Oslo has one of the most enduring legends of the country. In the eleventh century, Hallvard Husaby, a man widely known for fairness, attempted to rescue a young, pregnant girl being pursued by three men. He took her in his boat on the Drammensfjord, but the villains caught and shot them both, tying a millstone around his neck and tossing the bodies into the fjord. A few days later, Hallvard's body was found floating in the fjord, despite the millstone, still securely tied to his neck. A saint was born. City shields depicting St. Hallvard have been used since the 14th century. The current version, designed in 1924, shows Hallvard on a lion throne, the three lethal arrows in his left hand, the millstone in his right – and the nude girl he attmpted to save at his feet. Around the periphery is the Latin motto: *Unanimiter et Constanter* ("Unanimous and Eternal").

Stavanger

Location: on the southwest coast, in Rogaland county, at 59°N latitude.
Year founded: 1125
Population (1999): 108,109
Area: 66 square kilometres
Normal midday temperature in mid January: 1.2 °C
and mid July: 14.0 °C
Normal yearly precipitation: 1250 mm
First digit of postcode: 4
First two digits of telephone numbers: 51

Stavanger developed as a trade and industrial town, known for its shipping and export products, of which canned fish was among the more prominent. It might have continued that trend, but in 1966, it became the base for offshore oil exploration in the North Sea. Then, when oil was discovered, it became the base for offshore activities some 300 km to the south-west. As more offshore oil fields came on stream, oil companies established head offices in Stavanger.

The oil business triggered other businesses, including the helicopter airline that grew to be one of the world's largest of its kind. Building, fitting and supplying the offshore platforms and systems connected to them, such as undersea pipelines and onshore facilities, became a major industry. Stavanger now is the oil capital of Norway, which is second only to Saudi Arabia in oil exports.

Despite the bustle of the modern, high-tech city, Stavanger has retained many of its traditional attractions. *Gamle Stavanger* ("Old Stavanger") has 170 white wooden houses that are some of the best preserved in the country. The impressive "Pulpit" rock outcropping overlooking the nearby Lysefjord remains one of the major tourist attractions of the west coast.

Tromsø
Location: on an island in the northern branch of Straumsfjord, at 69°40'N latitude.
Year founded: 1250
Population (1999): 58,121
Area: 2558 square kilometres
Normal midday temperature in mid January: –4.4 °C and mid July: 11.9 °C
Normal yearly precipitation: 1031 mm
First digit of postcode: 9
First two digits of telephone numbers: 77

Tromsø can claim to be the biggest city in Norway in terms of its area, which is larger than all of Vestfold county in the southern part of the country. The built-up part of the city is on an island between the mainland and the larger coastal island of Kvaløya. The sheltered location early made it an ideal home-port for commercial operations in Arctic waters as well as the last port of call for polar expeditions.

The city's high latitude has made it a world centre for Arctic research, such as on the Aurora Borealis (Northern Lights) at an observatory built in 1927.

The University of Tromsø was opened in 1972, and remains the most northerly university in the world. The Tromsø Satellite Station is a world leader in acquiring images from polar-orbit meteorological satellites; the satellite weather map you see on TV most likely first came to Earth at Tromsø.

The city is the cultural centre of the North. The *Nordnorsk Kunstmuseum* has fine collections of contemporary art, and *Tromsø Museum* has one of the world's best collections of Sami art. Just over the bridge on the mainland, is the Tromsdalen church, a daring and impressive modern work by architect Jan Inge Hovig. Its entire east wall, 23 metres high and covering an area of 140 square metres, consists of a dalle (French for "flagstone") technique glass window by artist Victor Sparre.

In one respect, Tromsø is Arctic. From 21 May to 23 July, the sun shines 24 hours a day and there is no night; from 25 November to 21 January, the sun stays below the horizon and night lasts 24 hours. Yet the climate is mild. The average midday temperature in January is the same as in Oslo and summer temperatures are about the same as in Trondheim.

Trondheim
Location: on the south shore of Trondheimsfjord in Sør Trøndelag county, at 63°25'N latitude.
Year founded: 997
Population (1999): 147,187
Area: 342 square kilometres
Normal midday temperature in mid January: –3.3 °C and mid July: 13.0 °C
Normal yearly precipitation: 850 mm
First digit of postcode: 7
First two digits of telephone numbers: 73

Trondheim was founded as Nidaros, in the tenth century. In the eleventh century, work started on a cathedral, built over the grave of St. Olav, the King who christianised the Vikings. Later, the Pope made the Bishops of Greenland, Iceland, the Isle of Man, the Orkney Islands and the Faeroes, as well as Bishops in Norway, responsible to the Archbishop of Nidaros. The cathedral there then became one of the holy sites of Europe and the goal for many pilgrimages.

The cathedral became known as *Nidarosdom*. But the city that grew up around it became Trondhjem, a name rooted in Nordic mythology. From 1030 until the early 13th century, Trondhjem (Nidaros) was the principal residence of Kings, and thereby the country's capital. But with the Reformation, the city lost its religious prominence, and the last Archbishop fled the country in 1537.

Nonetheless, the *Nidarosdom* still is a goal for pilgrimages, as one of the five cathedrals in "European Pilgrimage 2000". Its size and Romanesque-Gothic architecture have made it the most magnificent church in Scandinavia, and it is the cathedral in which Norwegian kings are now crowned. Accordingly, in everyday speech, it is spoken of as the only *katedral* (cathedral) in the country, whilst the other ten cathedrals – defined in the liturgical sense as the seats of bishops – are *Domkirker*, from *Dom*, the Scandinavian and German word for cathedral.

Modern Trondheim is a cultural and educational centre; the Norwegian Institute of Technology was founded in 1910 and the university incorporating it in 1973. Cultural monuments abound, such as the 18th century *Stiftsgården*, the largest and most richly decorated wooden building in the Nordic countries. In the centre of the city square there is a statue on top of a tall column, of Olav Tryggvason, the Viking King who founded the city in 997.

Climate and environment (*Klima og miljø*)

Banned chemical products (*Forbud mot kjemiske produkter*) There are more than 7,000 chemical products available to consumers, and many of them are toxic or environmentally hazardous. The most dangerous have been banned, including:

- Azo dyes (*Azo-farvestoffer*) in ☞ **chemicals in clothing** (Clothing chapter), banned in 1995.
- Chlorofluorocarbons – CFCs (*KFK*), environmentally harmful, banned in 1991 in aerosol spray cans and thereafter in other products.
- Halogenated hydrocarbons (*Halon*), highly toxic, banned in 1993 in fire extinguishers and thereafter in other products.
- Lead (*Bly*) in ☞ **petrol** (Cars, Roads, Traffic chapter), highly toxic, banned in 1995.
- Mercury (*Kvikksølv*) in ☞ **thermometers** (Health Care chapter), toxic and environmentally hazardous, banned in 1998.

For further information, contact the ☞ **Norwegian Pollution Control Authority.**

Climate (*klima*) Despite its northerly location, Norway has a mix of three of the main types of climate: temperate like Britain, cool continental like northeastern Europe and polar, like the Arctic regions and the interiors of northern Canada and Siberia. Yet, Norwegian weather has comparatively few extremes and none of them rate mention as a weather record in the *Guinness Book of Records*. This is because the Gulf Stream of the North Atlantic current warms the long coast, elevating the country's temperatures well above the global averages for other regions at equal latitudes. Alaska, for instance, also has a long coast warmed by currents in the Pacific Ocean, but is far colder than Norway. Only in the Matanuska Valley north of Anchorage is fruit grown commercially, whilst in Norway, orchards abound in the southern part of the country and fruit is grown as far north as Trondheim. Broad-leaved deciduous trees grow as far as 64°N, and pine, fir, spruce and birch trees grow as far as 70°N. In comparison, on the east coast of North America, there are no forests north of 54°N. The Norwegian west coast climate is benign and wet. Seldom do temperatures go below –10 °C in the winter or over +25 °C in the summer. Of the west coast cities, Bergen has the greatest precipitation, some 2250 mm per year, about double the average for the UK. The inland weather is subject to greater extremes of temperature, from –35 °C in the winter to +30 °C in the summer, but has less precipitation. In some winters, there is no snow in Bergen, whilst inland snows may stay on the ground through April or May. The few truly polar regions of mainland Norway are the inland mountain plateaus and the highest peaks. Starting about 1990, winters have become milder, due to changes in the Gulf Stream caused by the North Atlantic Oscillation (NAO), a cousin of the El Niño of the Pacific Ocean. Climatologists have yet to understand NAO, but believe that it is responsible for the more pronounced long-term variations of climate of the past century. If that is so, the current trend is now toward colder winters through the year 2010. At Norway's northern latitudes, the cycles of day and night vary more than they do in countries farther south. In Oslo, the length of the day, reckoned from sunup to sunset, varies from about six hours in midwinter to nearly 19 hours in midsummer. In Tromsø, north of the Arctic Circle, the sun is above the horizon from mid May through late July, and there is no night, whilst from late November through mid January, the sun is below the horizon and there is no daylight.

Cold (*kulde*) A scientific, non-theological inquiry into why the Hells of many religions are depicted as hot places might conclude that suffering from heat was known to and dreaded by the peoples of warm climates, where most of the world's religions began. The same inquiry might uncover exceptions, one of which certainly would be from the pre-Christian Viking Age. The Vikings knew, respected and sometimes feared cold weather. According to the Edda Saga, one of the major legends of the Viking Age, "The way to Hell is northwards and downwards" (*Nor og ned går helvetes veg*). The Viking Hell was a cold place, from which one did not return. Were a reincarnated Viking to reappear today, would he view a household freezer as a place where one keeps the Devil locked up? Legend notwithstanding, compared to other countries at the same latitude, Norway has a relatively mild ☞ **Climate.**

Environment (*Miljø*) is a major concern, and the

country's efforts in environmental management and protection have been praised by the ☞ **OECD** (Government and Social Services chapter). Indeed, in Norwegian, the name of the Ministry of Environment is *Miljøverndepartementet*, literally "Ministry of environmental protection". Five subordinate institutions of the Ministry, the Directorate for Nature Management (*Direktoratet for Naturforvaltning*), the Directorate of Cultural Heritage (*Riksantikvaren*), the Norwegian Mapping Authority (*Statens Kartverk*), the Norwegian Polar Institute (*Norsk Polarinstitutt*) and the Norwegian Pollution Control Authority (*Statens Forurensningstilsyn*) are either partly or wholly concerned with environmental matters. For further information, contact the local offices of these institutions listed in the Pink Pages. Statistics Norway has published a comprehensive overview of environmental matters in English: *Natural Resources and the Environment*, Oslo and Kongsvinger, Statistics Norway, 1997, 216 pages softcover, ISBN 82-537-4394-7.

Jellyfish (*Maneter*) swim in waters along the coast and in saltwater bays and fjords. The two most common varieties are the moon jellyfish (*glassmanet*), *Aurelia aurita* biological name in Latin, up to 40 cm in diameter, and the giant pink jellyfish, also known as the lion's mane jellyfish (*rødgule brennmanet*), *Cynea capillata* biological name in Latin, up to one metre or more in diameter. The stings of jellyfish (*manetforbrenning*) found in Norwegian waters are considered not to be lethal, as can be the stings of some jellyfish found in tropical waters. But a jellyfish sting can be painful and frightening. Lidokain anaesthetic salve, available over-the-counter at ☞ **Pharmacies** (Health care chapter), is the recommended medicine for soothing stings.

The Norwegian Meteorological Institute (*Det norske meteorologiske institutt – DNMI*) provides meteorological services to the public and private sectors and to the general public. It is most known as the source of all data for ☞ **weather forecasts**. But it also compiles meteorological data from the mainland as well as from adjacent sea areas and the Svalbard archipelago, conducts research and development and provides special service for public and private sector clients on a commercial basis. In addition to its head office at Blindern in Oslo, it has two regional offices (*regionkontorer*) and meteorological offices (*Værtjenestekontorer*) at 12 airports throughout the country. For further information, contact the Oslo head office ℡ 22963000, ℻ 22963050, ✉ PO Box 43 Blindern, 0313 Oslo, ✉ met.inst@dnmi.no, the western region office ℡ 55236600, ℻ 55236703, ✉ Allégaten 70, 5007 Bergen, ✉ meteovest@dnmi.no or the northern region office ℡ 77684044, ℻ 77689003, ✉ Kirkegårdsveien 60, 9005 Tromsø, or view the DNMI web site ⊕ http://www.dnmi.no with pages in Norwegian and in English.

Noise (*Støy*) is unwanted sound. The word noise comes from the Latin *nausea*, which means seasickness. Indeed, noise causes illness, including loss of hearing, stress, and high blood pressure, as well as loss of sleep at home and reduced productivity at workplaces. As in most industrialised countries, noise is the most widespread form of pollution. One resident in four is subjected to traffic noise that is higher than the recommended limit of 55 decibels. Aircraft, construction works, industries and railways also create noise that bothers those who live nearby. Moreover, noise from neighbours, such as from high-power audio systems, bothers many people. Consequently, there are regulations and measures to limit noise. For instance, noise baffles (*støyskjerm*) are common along highways and railway lines that pass through residential areas and hearing protectors are obligatory in noisy construction and industrial work. For further information on noise and noise abatement measures, contact the ☞ **Norwegian Pollution Control Authority**.

Pollution (*Forurensning*) The geographical location of the country makes it particularly vulnerable to trans-border pollution, such as acid rain and the fallout from the Chernobyl atomic power plant disaster of 1986. Current activities contribute to pollution: in a 1995 comparison of countries world-wide, Norway ranked fifth in carbon dioxide released per head, principally because of its offshore oil activities but also because of high road traffic levels. In the late 1990s, diesel vehicle exhausts and particles of asphalt pulverised by studded tyres combined to raise air pollution to hazardous levels in many cities. Public and private sector organisations are aware of these problems and steps are being taken to remedy them. Pollution is now controlled by law: the Act relating to protection against pollution and relating to waste (*Lov om vern mot forurensninger og om avfall*) was enacted in 1981 and has been updated since. ☞ **Recycling** is widespread and in the mid 1990s, Norway ranked seventh in the world in percentage of glass recovered and sixteenth in the percentage of paper recovered. Waste management is now incorporated in countrywide regulations, including ☞ **end of life vehicle deposits** (Cars, Roads, Traffic chapter) and ☞ **Green fees** (Electrical and Electronics Goods chapter) on appliances and consumer electronics. There are many ☞ **banned chemical products**. Environmental management is a concern throughout industry, and companies now routinely report on their environmental activities in their annual reports. Norway Statistics (*Statistisk Sentralbyrå*) now routinely compiles environmental statistics and publishes an annual report of them entitled "Natural Resources and the Environment" in Norwegian and English editions. For further information on pollution and related topics, contact ☞ **The Norwegian Pollution Control Authority**.

The Norwegian Pollution Control Authority (*Statens forurensningstilsyn – SFT*) is the national regulatory agency that works to combat pollution in all forms, to promote waste management, and to regulate uses of environmentally hazardous materials. Its tasks include combating industrial pollution, supervising the national emergency response system for acute pollution by oil and other substances and for monitoring air and water pollution. It works with the Directorate of Nature Management (*Direktoratet for Naturforvaltning*) to oversee the activities of each County Department for Environmental Affairs (*Fylkesmannens miljøvernavdeling*), which, in turn, support environmental activities by the municipalities (*kommunene*) at the local level. Moreover, it offers a range of publications aimed to combat pollution and to promote environmental awareness. For further information, contact the local environmental affairs office, listed under *Miljøvern* under the municipality in the Pink Pages. Or contact the SFT head office ✆ 22573400, 🖷 22676706, ✉ PO Box 8100 Dep, 0032 Oslo, ✉ postmottak@sft.telemax.no, ✉ http://www.sft.no with pages in Norwegian and in English and on-line ordering of publications at ✉ http://www.sft.no/skjema.html

Recycling (*Resirkulering*) is the reuse of waste materials through collection (*innsamling*) or receiving (*mottak*) and subsequent reuse (*gjenbruk*) or reclamation (*gjenvinning*).

Two countrywide recycling programmes involve a fee paid on new goods to finance their recycling: the ☞ **end-of-life vehicle (ELV) deposit** (Cars, Roads, Traffic chapter) on cars and the ☞ **green fee** (Electrical and Electronics Goods chapter) on electrical and electronics goods. Some programmes are international, such as the return and recycling of laser toner cartridges: a prepaid parcel post label is packed in the box with each new toner cartridge, so you may post the old cartridge to the nearest recycling station.

Most municipal ☞ **refuse** (Housekeeping chapter) collection services now include source sorting (*kildesortering*). Paper is collected in special sacks, usually twice a month, and containers are placed out at convenient locations, such as municipal car parks and larger petrol stations, for glass, batteries, metal and hazardous materials. Homeowners with gardens are encouraged to compost organic waste. For further information, contact the refuse service in your municipality, listed under *Renholdsverket* or *Renovasjonsavdelingen* in the Pink Pages.

A countrywide free lottery for NOK 1 million each month encourages the return of milk and other liquid food paperboard cartons. To take part, you write your name and telephone number on an empty carton and pack folded empty cartons into it. When you have several packed cartons, you put them in a plastic bag on top the sack of paper to be collected for recycling. At the sorting plants, packed cartons are picked out at random, and a winner is drawn and notified. For information, contact *Norsk returkartong* ("Norwegian Return Carton") ✆ freephone 80031500, ✉ http://www.returkartong.no. For further details on recycling countrywide, contact the ☞ **Environmental Home Guard** (Non-government Organisations chapter).

Snakes (*Slanger*) There are only three species of snake in Norway and the rest of Scandinavia:

adder, or common European viper (*huggorm* or *hoggorm*)(*Vipera berus* biological name in Latin), the only one of the three that is poisonous, found throughout continental Europe and east to the Pacific coast of Asia. Can be recognised by the zigzag dark pattern the length of its back, against a dark brown or red-brown background for the female, and a grey-brown background for the male. Length commonly 50 to 70 cm, and sometimes up to 90 cm.

grass snake, also called the ringed snake (*buorm*)(*Natrix natrix*), found throughout continental Europe and one of the few snakes that can be found north of the Arctic Circle. Can be recognised by a zigzag pattern on its back. Sometimes mistaken for the adder, but can be distinguished from it by its bright orange or yellow collar, which the adder lacks, and the round pupils of its eyes, whilst those of the adder are vertical slits. Length commonly 70 to 80 cm.

sooth snake (*slettsnok*)(*Coronella austriaca* in Latin), found in northern, central and southern Europe, as far east as the Caucuses. Can be recognised by two to four rows of dark spots along its back. Length commonly about 75 cm.

Fortunately, the poisonous adder fears people and will flee if possible, and equally fortunate, its bite seldom is lethal. However, if bitten, the Red Cross advises that a person bitten:

- rest, to prevent the venom spreading in the body.
- contact a doctor for treatment.
- call the emergency number ✆ 113 if he/she feels unwell or dizzy.

Snow (*Snø*) The peoples of the north have lived with snow for centuries. Yet throughout the world, snow and cold historically have slowed the settling of high latitudes and have thwarted armies. Major team sports, such as football, often suffer when early snows cancel autumn games. Yet the winter sports in which Norway excels depend on snow and cold. For those who deal with it, snow has a far greater impact than any other aspect of winter weather. Consequently, scientists have long studied snow and there are many books about it. If you are interested in snow research, contact the Norwegian Polar Institute (*Norsk Polarinstitutt*) ✆ 77750500, 🖷 77750501, ✉ Polarmiljøsenteret, 9296 Tromsø, ✉ info@npolar.no, 🖳 http://www.npolar.no/npi with pages in English only.

Snow affects everyday life both less and more than it does in countries further south. Its affects are lesser, because the ☞ **climate** is comparatively mild and snowfalls modest compared to other areas at similar latitudes. Moreover, ☞ **snow clearing** (Housekeeping chapter) is efficient, so even heavy snowfalls seldom disrupt for very long. The impact of snow is more strongly felt, because winters are long and snow may be expected at least six months of the year. Moreover, once snow falls, it often stays, for two reasons. First, temperatures usually drop below 0 °C and the ground freezes before the first snowfall. Snow stays longer on frozen ground than on unfrozen ground, which warms the snow and hastens melting. Second, at the northern latitude of the country, the winter sun is low in the sky. So it does not melt snows as quickly as it does when higher in the sky, as in countries further south. Even in late winter, a snowfall on a road in Norway melts more slowly than on a comparable road in central Europe.

Water (*Vann*) The amount of fresh water available is equivalent to 112,500 cubic metres per year per person, five times as much as in neighbouring Sweden and 60 times as much as in Germany. The high figure is due both to the high annual rainfall and snowfall of some 1400 mm, 40% greater than the world average, and to a low population density, just 13 people per square kilometre. Inland lakes, rivers, streams and waterfalls are prominent in the landscape. Understandably, Norwegians have long believed that they are blessed with ample quantities of pure water. Unfortunately, that belief is partly outdated: there still is an enormous amount of fresh water, but it is decreasingly safe to drink. An official study conducted in 1980 traced outbreaks of waterborne illnesses back to 1931. In 1999, one resident in seven in the country had substandard drinking water, and an average of 550 people a day suffered water-borne illness, principally diarrhoea and nausea. There are many causes of the pollution, including agricultural runoff into reservoirs, trans-border acid rain and leakage between older water supply mains and sewerage in cities and towns. Consequently, some 1200 of the country's 1600 water-supply works deliver substandard water. The National Institute of Public Health (*Statens institutt for folkehelse*) has both studied the problems involved and has proposed improvements, including disinfection of drinking water supplies. For further details and lists of Public Health publications on water quality, contact the main offices in Oslo ✆ 22042200,

☎ 22353605, ✉ PO Box 4404 Torshov, 0403 Oslo, 🖂 folkehelsa@folkehelsa.no, 🌐 http://www.folkehelsa.no with pages in Norwegian and selected pages in English.

Weather forecasts (*Værvarslinger*) are printed in newspapers and are part of radio and TV news programmes. The printed and TV forecasts use symbols, such as drawings of clouds and raindrops to indicate rain, a snow crystal to indicate snow, clouds partly obscuring a sun to indicate partly cloudy and a sun to indicate clear skies. Forecasts usually are for the next 24 hours or for the following day as well as for the next five days (*5 dagers varsel*). In forecasts for the public, the country is divided into six weather regions:

- *Østenfjells*: east of the central mountain ranges and south of Trøndelag county.
- *Fjelltraktene i Sør-Norge*: the central mountain ranges.
- *Vest-Norge sør for Stad*: the west coast and immediate areas south of the Stad peninsula, which is the point on land in Sogn og Fjordane county that marks the demarcation between the North Sea and the Norwegian Sea, areas of the Atlantic Ocean distinguished from each other in part by differing currents and weather patterns.
- *Trøndelag og Møre og Romsdal*: the midland counties.

- *Nordland*: county at the Arctic Circle.
- *Troms og Finnmark*: the northern counties.

Forecasts for mariners and fishermen include other information, such as wind strengths, wave heights and storm warnings. Temperatures (*temperatur*) and precipitation (*nedbør*) are often compared against normal (*mot normal*), which is the average for the day or season over the previous thirty-year period of meteorological observations. The current normals are the averages for the period from 1961 to 1990 and are valid for the period from 1991 to 2020.

The ☞ **Norwegian Meteorological Institute** supports countrywide weather forecast billed service telephone helplines:

Today's and tomorrow's weather ✆ 82053000 (NOK 5/min) voice prompt menu for selecting one of 12 district forecasts.

Long-term forecast ✆ 82073000 (NOK 12/min) voice prompt menu for selecting one of three regional forecasts.

Coastal and maritime forecast ✆ 82073015 (NOK 12/min) voice prompt menu for selecting one of three maritime area forecasts.

Consultation with meteorologist ✆ 82090001 Oslo, 82090002 Bergen, 82090003 Tromsø (NOK 22/min).

Consultation with weather staff ✆ 82072022 Bodø Airport, 82072040 Sola (Stavanger) Airport (NOK 22/min).

Clothing (*Klær*)

Clothing for men (*herreklær*), women (*dameklær*), young people (*ungdomsklær*) and children (*barneklær*) is mostly of European design and labelling, and accordingly has European ☞ **Clothing sizes**. However, as in other countries, the garments you buy in shops actually may be manufactured anywhere in the world, and increasingly in Asian or third-world countries. If you wish to know the origin of a garment, check on the label, as international trade laws require that the country of manufacture be stated.

All global brands, such as Levis®, are widely sold in shops, and there are numerous international brands, including those sold by brand-name ☞ **Chain stores** (Shopping chapter). If you buy but are not quite sure that you will keep a garment, such as buying for a child and wishing to ensure it fits, ask if you may deposit (*deponere*) its purchase price in the event that you elect to return. Health regulations dictate that some garments, such as underwear, are not returnable. Likewise, prevailing shop practice permits return on items sold at regular prices, but not on items sold at discounted price in sales. Upon return of a garment, some shops may issue a credit

Basic symbol	Care		Warning
Wash	⎍₉₅	Hot (95°C) Normal setting, normal rinse, normal centrifuge	Do not wash
	⎍₆₀	Warm (60°C) Normal setting, normal rinse, normal centrifuge	
	⎍₆₀	Warm (60°C) Reduced agitation, cooling rinse, gentle centrifuge	
	⎍₄₀	Lukewarm (40°C) Normal setting, normal rinse, normal centrifuge	
	⎍₄₀	Lukewarm (40°C) Reduced agitation, cooling rinse, gentle centrifuge	
	⎍₄₀	Lukewarm (40°C) Little agitation, normal rinse, normal centrifuge, do not hand wring	
	⎍₃₀	Cool (30°C) Little agitation, normal rinse, gentle centrifuge	
	⎍	Lukewarm (40°C) hand wash	
Bleach	△	Can use chlorine bleach	Do not bleach
Dry	◎	Hot (60°C) tumble dry	Do not tumble dry
	◎	Warm (40°C) tumble dry	
Iron	⟿	High (200°C)	Do not iron
	⟿	Medium (150°C)	
	⟿	Low (100°C)	
Dry clean	Ⓐ	Any solvent	Do not dry clean
	Ⓟ	Any solvent except trichloroethylene	
	Ⓟ	Any solvent except trichloroethylene, gentle programme	
	Ⓕ	Petroleum solvent only	
	Ⓕ	Petroleum solvent only, gentle programme	

note (*tilgodelapp*), whilst others will reimburse in cash. Some chain stores offer a 30 day return on all items sold at regular prices. So always check return policy when buying.

Clothing care symbols (*Vaskesymboler*) on garment labels indicate the best care procedures. They are based on an international system of five basic symbols, for washing, bleaching, drying, ironing and dry cleaning. If you follow the procedures indicated by the symbols on a garment, it should not shrink, stretch or change colour unduly.

Clothing for children (*barneklær*) Standard sizes for children's clothing in Europe and Norway are in centimetres length/height up to two years, and by age in years thereafter: 56cm (newborn to 2 months old), 62cm (2–4 months), 68cm (4–6 months), 74cm (6–9 months), 80cm (9–12 months), 90cm (2 years), 3 years, 4 years, 5 years, 6 years, 7 years, 8 years, 9 years, 10 years. So for children less than two years old, use a measuring tape (*målebånd*) and the child's age to select sizes. Most children's clothes are bought from ☞ **Chain stores** (shopping chapter), where there is a good selection of

Men's sizes		
European	**American/British numerical**	**American/British name**
46	36	Small
48	38	Small
50	40	Medium
52	42	Large
54	44	Large
56	46	Extra Large
58	48	Extra Large

Men's shirt sizes		
European	**American/British, by collar in inches**	**American/British name**
36	14	Small
37	$14^1/_2$	Small
38	15	Medium
39	$15^1/_2$	Medium
41	16	Large
42	$16^1/_2$	Large
43	17	Extra Large
44-45	$17^1/_2$	Extra Large
46	18	Extra Large

Women's sizes				
European	**American Misses' numerical**	**American Women' numerical**	**British Women's numerical**	**American/British name**
38	6		8	Small
40	8		10	Medium
42	10	34	12	Medium
44	12	36	14	Large
46	14	38	16	Large
48	16	40	18	Extra Large
50	18	42	20	Extra Large
52	20	44		Extra Large

Children's sizes		
European (height in cm)	**American numerical**	**British (height in inches)**
125	4	43
135	6	48
150	8	55
155	10	58
160	12	60
165	14	62

casual, sturdy and fashionable clothes. Second hand clothes shops ☞ **Used clothing** (this chapter) are another good source. There are specialist shops importing clothes, especially party wear, from EU countries, but these tend to be expensive. If you prefer to sew your own clothes, patterns, fabrics and notions are available, see under *tekstiler* or *syartikler* in the Yellow Pages. Some useful words: bathrobe (*badekåpe*), blouse (*bluse*), boots (*støvler*), cap (*lue*), cardigan (*jakke*), dress (*kjole*), gloves (*hansker*), jacket (*jakke*), mittens (*votter*), nightdress (*nattkjole*), overcoat (*frakk/kåpe*), pants (*bukser*), scarf (*skjerf*), shirt (*skjorte*), shoes (*sko*), shorts (*kort bukser*), skirt (*skjørt*), slippers (*tøfler*), snowsuit (*bobledress*), socks (*strømper/sokker*), sweater (*genser*), swimsuit (*badedrakt*). tights (*strømpebukser*), T-shirt (*T-skjørte*), underpants (*underbukser*), underwear (*undertøy*), vest (*undertrøye*).

Clothing sizes (*Størrelse på klær*) are mostly European sizes, although some labels also have British and American sizes. Size conversions are given on page 101, but actual garment size may vary according to manufacturer and country of origin. Stocking sizes are the same as ☞ **Shoe sizes**.

Cold blocker cream (*Kuldekrem*) is a high fat-content preparation that can be used by both children and adults to protect the face in cold weather. Three brands widely sold by ☞ **Pharmacies** (Health Care chapter) are *Apobase fet (Alpharma multinational, Norway)* containing 60% fat, *Ceridal lipogel (Preval Dermatica, Germany/Stiefel, UK)* containing 65% fat and *Locobase (Yamanouchi, Japan/Europe)* containing 70% fat. Rub the cream on your face about half an hour before you go outdoors, which is enough time to let the water in it evaporate and prevent frost damage to the skin. If you ask for *kuldekrem*, beware the similarity of the word to *koldkrem*, which is "cold cream", a common cosmetic cooling cream for the face.

Dressing for the cold (*Bekledning mot kulden*)
A Norwegian saying maintains that there is no bad weather, only bad clothing. Ordinary clothing shops stock a selection of cold-weather garments that are found only in speciality shops in warmer countries. The six basic rules for dressing for the cold are:
• Match clothing to activity: When standing still, the average adult produces 85 Watts of heat. Even moderate exercise increases that heat, such as to around 625 Watts when cross-country skiing. Vigorous exercise, such as cross-country ski racing, can turn up the heat to 1400 Watts. The more you move, the less clothing you need.
• Stay dry: Water is a good heat conductor, so wet clothing quickly loses its insulating value. Clothes may be wet from without, from snow or rain, or from within, from absorbed perspiration. Dry out and in is the rule.
• Layers are best: Still air is a good insulator. The more air that is trapped in clothing, the better it insulates. As a rule, several thin layers trap more air than a single thick layer.
• Overlap to prevent gap: Trapped, insulating air can leak out when garments fail to meet, or, worse still, bare skin can be exposed. Be sure that upper and lower body garments are long enough to overlap at the waist and that stockings overlap legs of long underwear.
• Wind chills: Winter wind cools the body, just as a breeze or blast from a fan in your home feels cool in the summertime. Outdoor clothing which may keep you comfortably warm at freezing, 0 °C, may be inadequate with a moderate breeze at the same temperature, because the movement of air depresses the effective temperature to −11°C. So you should dress not just for temperature, but for temperature and wind conditions.
• Cut down cotton: Cotton fibres can retain about 25 times their own dry weight in moisture, which is why cotton is used for towels. But wet cotton insulates poorly, which is why you should avoid high cotton content (50% or more) garments for winter wear.

Most children live in their snowsuits and winter boots outside, leaving ordinary shoes for indoors. To ensure that your child is warm and dry while playing outdoors, purchase an all-in-one snowsuit (*parkdress*). This is made from fabric called Beaver Nylon with half the front leg and the entire back leg from the waist down covered in rubberised fabric. The lining of the suit is removable for ease of washing, and is either made of a fleecy material or padded nylon. The suit can also be worn without the lining in the autumn or early spring. The largest size available is 140cm (age 10). Snowsuits for older children and adults do not have the rubberised fabric or the removable lining. Most snowsuits have some form of reflective material, either tape sewn on the garment (at arm, calf, chest or back) or a motif. You can add reflective material to outdoor clothing, by buying reflecting tape (*tekstilrefleks*) from shops selling fabric and sewing notions. *Cherroux* is a popular brand of rubber boot lined with fleece. For dry and warm feet, Goretex® and similar waterproof, breathable fabrics are becoming more popular in the manufacture of footwear. Popular brands are *Ecco, Elefanten* and *Footi*. The advantage with these is that you can wash them (in water only; don't use soap). Moreover, if your child suffers from sweaty feet, the fabric allows the foot to breathe. Some brands now incorporate reflective material on their boots. Most of the heat lost from the clothed body escapes from your head, therefore it's best to wear a hat that covers the ears, or a balaclava and a scarf or neck gaiter made from a fleecy material. Mittens are warmer than gloves, and small clips (*votteholdere*) help hold the mitten to its sleeve. You will even find children wearing their hats or balaclavas under their skiing helmets. Woollen underwear is still popular, but synthetic fibres, which transport perspiration, are more comfortable to wear when you are active outdoors. Traditionally Norwegian children wear full-length undergarments, but today with heated homes and classrooms, this can make them uncomfortable when indoors. *Helly Hansen* sells a two piece fleecy suit that children can wear over their clothes and under their outdoor clothes, but is too bulky to wear as underwear. The same rules apply for adults. You will be wearing more practical clothes, a waterproof and windproof shell over thin layers, hats, gloves and thermal underwear. You will find that the cold

Your body produces more heat when you exercise moderately or vigorously than when you stand still.

creeps through your boots and soles of your shoes. When purchasing new footwear for the winter keep in mind whether you want to add woollen innersoles, and take them with you when trying out new shoes and boots. *Pertti Palmroth* ladies shoes and boots from Finland are made of 100% waterproof material and fur-lined. Being visible while walking along dark roads is vital, ☞ **Pedestrian Reflectors** (Cars, Roads and Traffic chapter).

Dry-cleaning (*kjemisk rensing*) Look under *Renserier* in the Yellow Pages for dry-cleaners and laundries. Dry-cleaning is expensive, most cleaners offer economy bulk cleaning (*kilorens*) which is charged by the kilogram of garments cleaned, regardless of colour and type of fabric. If you want your clothing to be pressed after *kilorens*, an additional charge is payable. Clothes cleaned as individual items are pressed afterwards. If a garment has been cleaned according to the manufacturers care-label and it is damaged in the process, the cleaner will advise you to return the item to the shop where it was bought. However, if a garment is damaged through negligence of the cleaner, you are entitled to reimbursement. Buttons, however are not replaced. Items that need particular attention, for example, bridal gowns, curtains, leather, sheepskin and down filled duvets (*dyne*) are sent away to specialist cleaners.

Ice and snow, walking on (*Gå på glattføre*) You can make your foothold more secure on ice and snow by fitting your shoes or boots with *brodder*, which are metal studs somewhat like calkins, the turned-down ends and front projection on horseshoes that prevent slipping. There are several designs. The simplest design resembles the crampons used in mountain and glacier climbing: a metal plate, with sharp studs, is held under the ball of your foot with a strap over the toe of your shoe and a strap or elastic around the heel, so it is easy to put on and take off. A slightly more advanced design features studs fixed to a rubber slip-over that fits the sole snugly. Another design features a serrated ceramic plate held under the toe by rubber straps over the toe and around the heel. A robust type, called *Ola-brodder* or *Skomaker-brodd* attaches permanently to the front edge of the heel (at least 5 cm high) of a winter boot and has a hinge, so the studs may swing back, under the heel, for grip, or forward so they are hidden, for walking on pavement or indoors. *Brodder* are sold by sports shops (*Sport og fritidsutstyr* in the Yellow Pages), shoemakers (*skomakere*) and by some shoe shops (*sko*).

Knitting (*strikking*) is taught to children, boys as well as girls, at kindergarten. Although the beautiful Norwegian jumpers look very intricate in their design, the beauty is you only need to know how to knit (and not how to purl, as well) because the jumper is knitted in a circle, using a circular needle (*rundpinne*) made of two small knitting needles held together by a length of nylon tubing. The sleeves are knitted in a similar fashion and when all three components are complete, a cut is made down either side of the body tube and the circular sleeves are sewn in. Yarn (*garn*) is displayed on racks inside and sometimes outside shops that sell wool and patterns. All patterns (*mønster*) are in Norwegian, but some shops catering to tourists sell a small selection of knitting kits, each having a pattern in English and the yarn needed to make one garment. So, in most cases, if you wish to knit a jumper from a pattern, have the pattern translated by a Norwegian friend who knits. Alternatively you can ask in the shop whether they know of anyone who would knit the jumper for you for payment. Some useful words: knitting needle (*strikkepinne*), knitwear (*strikkevarer*), pattern (*mønster*), yarn, wool (*garn*).

Name tapes (*navnebånd*) The first time you may need these is when your enrol your child in a kindergarten (*barnehage*) or primary school (*barneskole*) where all children have nearly identical play suits (*parkdress*) and wellingtons (*gummistøvler*). Name tapes are ordered by post; ask at your local *barnehage* for the form to send off. Shops selling bedding and textiles often provide a similar service; see under *Utstyrsforretninger* in the Yellow Pages.

Rainwear (*Regntøy*) Rain does not deter children, or anyone else from being outside. The secret is to have the right clothes. Helly Hansen offers two piece rubberised rainsuits for children. The 'trousers' are bibbed, with adjustable, elastic shoulder straps and squeeze-and-release buckles, and elastic on the bottom cuff to keep the trousers over rubber boots, with an elastic strap to keep them firmly over your boot.

Buy trousers big enough to go over clothing. You may even find that the trousers will be worn over snow-suits when the snow is wet. The rubber boots are mid-calf length and wide-mouthed so normal indoor trousers can be stuffed into them. A pair of rubber boots for spring and summer and a pair of fleece-lined boots for the winter are sufficient. There are numerous manufacturers of performance rainwear for adults, sold in most clothing and sports shops.

Shoes and footwear (*Sko og fottøy*) are sold in a wide variety in shoe shops (*Skotøy* in the Yellow Pages), as suits the variations of climate in the country. ☞ **Shoe sizes** are mostly European, but some imported athletic shoes and boots are sold in British and American sizes. A shoemaker (*skomaker*) or shoe repair shop (*skokreparasjon*) will repair shoes, handbags, briefcases and other leather goods in the traditional way. A heel bar (*flikkbar*) executes quick repairs. These shops also sell shoe polish (*skokrem*) and other accessories. Sturdy winter shoes (*vintersko*) and boots (*støvler*) are popular for wintertime outdoor wear. But custom dictates that they not be worn indoors, so when visiting, take along a pair of indoor shoes and change upon arriving. Most Norwegian shoe and boot designs are variations on commonplace international designs, but two are unique to the country. The Nesnalobben wool felt boot with an upturned toe, simple lacing and a plastic sole is warm and practical for outdoor wear at temperatures well below freezing, but not practical for temperatures above freezing, as the felt may then absorb water. Felt slippers (*filttøfler*) with a metal clasp are ideal for indoor wear whenever floors are cold. Some helpful words are: bootee (*skolett*), casual shoe (*dagligsko*), counter (*hælkappe*), court (*pumps*), cuff (*kantebånd*), flip-flop (*strandsandal*), galosh (*kalosje*), heels (*hæler*), high heels (*høyhæler*), inner soles (*inleggsåler*), jogging shoes (*joggesko*), laces (*lisser*), lace-up (*snøresko*), ladies boot (*stovlett*), mountain boot (*fjellstøvel*), outsole (*yttersåle*), oxford shoe (*snøresko*), plimsoll (*tennissko*), pump (*ballarinasko*), sandal (*sandal*), shoe polish (*skokrem*), slip-on (*mokasin*), slipper (*tøffel*), sole (*såle*), toe-strap (*tåsandal*), tongue (*pløse*), vamp (*overlær*), waist (*gelenk*) and waterproofing (*impregnering*).

Shoe sizes (*Størrelse på sko*) Most shoes and footwear are sized according to the European Paris

Point System, in which sizes are 1.5 times the inside length in centimetres of a shoe. For instance, a shoe with an inside length of 28 cm is a size 42. Each whole number increase in size corresponds to 2/3 centimetre increase in inside length. Some shoes and boots, particularly those made by multinational athletic shoe makers, are sized in American, English and European systems. American and English sizes are not as conveniently related to length as are European sizes: whole-size number differences correspond to 1/3 inch, with women's size numberings starting at a length of slightly more than 8 inches and men's size numberings starting at a length of about 8 3/4 inches. Conversions between European, UK and US sizes are listed below.

European Paris Point size	UK size	US men's size	US women's size	US children's size
18	2			2.5
19	3			3.5
20	4			4.5
21	4.5			5
22	5.5			6
23	6			6.5
24	7			7.5
25	7.5			8
26	8.5			9
27	9.5			10
28	10			10.5
29	11			11.5
30	11.5			12
31	12.5			13
32	13			13.5
33	1			1.5
34	2		3.5	2.5
35	2.5		4	3
36	3.5		5	4
37	4		5.5	4.5
38	5	6	6.5	5.5
39	6	7	7.5	6.5
40	6.5	7.5	8	7
41	7.5	8.5	9	
42	8	9	9.5	
43	9	10	10.5	
44	9.5	10.5	11	
45	10.5	11.5		
46	11.5	12.5		
47	12	13		

Textile chemical content (*Kjemikaler i tekstiler*) Chemicals are used in dyeing, preserving, softening and in other ways to alter the basic properties of textiles, as used in clothing. Many of the chemicals used are toxic, principally formaldehyde and the azo dyes. Formaldehyde is derived from methyl alcohol and is frequently used in textiles in clothing manufacture, to strengthen and dye fibres and to impart characteristics such as no-iron and wrinkle-free. But it is toxic, as it may cause or worsen allergies, and is potentially carcinogenic (cancer-causing). Azo dyes are based on azo chemicals, which contain nitrogen and impart colours. They are widely used, particularly in brilliantly-coloured clothing made in Asia. But some azo dyes are hazardous, because the azo chemicals they contain can break down to other chemicals known as arylamines, many of which are carcinogenic. Consequently, the Norwegian Pollution Control Authority (*Statens forurensningstilsyn – SFT*) regulations limit the chemical content of textiles used in clothing and other articles sold in Norway. Azo dyes that can break down to any one of the 20 known carcinogenic arylamines are banned. Formaldehyde is regulated at levels depending on garment use: for infants less than two years old, for clothing in direct contact with skin and for clothing not normally in direct contact with skin. Moreover, the Norwegian Textile Institute (*Norsk Teknoinstitutt*) is one of a group of textile institutes in 13 European countries that together support *Oeko-Standard 100* ("Ecological standard 100"), a voluntary industry standard that limits the amounts of toxic substances used in textile manufacture. Products meeting the *Oeko-Standard 100* may be marked with a label featuring a stylised sunflower and the words "Confidence in Textiles" or *Trygge Tekstiler* in Norwegian.

Used clothing (*Brukte klær*) is sold by used clothing shops and at various markets. Most used clothing shops are listed in the Yellow Pages (see *Brukte klær* under *Klær*). Some shops specialise, such as in women's fashions (*Dametøy*) or youth trends (*Ungdomsklær*), whilst others offer a broad selection.

The Fretex shops, operated by the ☞ **Salvation Army** (Non-government Organisations chapter) are the most numerous and offer the broadest selection. There are 57 in the country, located in Arendal, Bergen, Bodø, Bryne, Drammen, Egersund, Fredrikstad, Halden, Haugesund, Hjelmeland, Indre Arna,

Jørpeland, Karmsund, Kragerø, Kristiansand, Levanger, Lillesand, Lillestrøm, Molde, Mørkved, Moss, Nesttun, Nyborg, Oslo, Rådal, Sandnes, Sandvika, Sarpsborg, Skien, Stavanger, Stord, Straume, Tønsberg, Tromsø, Trondheim, Voss, Ølen and Ålesund; look for the nearest shop in the Pink Pages under Fretex. Some Fretex shops have a second name designating a region: Fretex-Elevator in the east, Fretex Vest-Norge in the west and Fretex Midt Norge in the middle of the country. The Fretex shops are simple, but successful: together, the shops in the Oslo area sell a ton of clothing a day.

In the Oslo area, the UFF (U-landshjelp fra Folk til Folk) ("Development Aid, People-to-People") shops specalise in used clothing. UFF is part of The International Humana People to People Movement that has organisations in 26 countries in Europe, Asia, North America and Africa ☺ http://www.humanapeople-topeopole.org with pages in English. In Norway UFF collects some one thousand tons of clothing a year, mainly from containers located throughout the Oslo area. Part of the clothing is sold in shops to fund support development projects listed under UFF in the Pink Pages.

In the autumn and in the spring, ☞ **flea markets** (Shopping chapter), usually held by sports clubs, parent support groups for school bands and the like, often offer used clothing; look for announcements under Kunngjøringer in the classified section of the local newspaper for dates and locations. Parishes, schools and benevolent organisations also arrange used clothing markets, often for particular types of clothing, such as infants and children's wear (Barnetøy) and usually announce them in parish or school newspapers or in placards at local markets.

Crime, wrongs, counter-measures (*Kriminalitet, ugjeringer, mottiltak*)

Arrests (*Arrestasjoner*) are made by the police (*politi*) in criminal cases (*straffesaker*), which differ from civil cases (*sivilesaker*) in which the police usually are not involved. If you are arrested by the police, you cannot be held for more than four hours without being formally charged (*siktet*) of a crime. But if you are accused of a crime for which the prison sentence may be more than six months, you may be held on remand in custody (*varetektsfengslet*) pending investigation (*etterforskning*) and subsequent trial (*sak*). To hold you in custody, the police must first take you to a preliminary examination court (*forhørsretten*) within 24 hours of your arrest, unless it was on a Friday or Saturday, in which case you will be taken to the court the following Monday. The court may either release you or allow the police to retain you in custody for a period of time depending on the severity of the crime of which you are accused. While you are in custody, the police may interrogate you (*politiforhør*) and make a record of anything you say, for subsequent prosecution (*tiltale*). If you are guilty of the crime of which your are charged, you may wish to plead guilty (*tilstår*) and be sentenced (*dømt*) at the preliminary examination. But if you are innocent, the speed of your release depends on how well you convince the police that you have been falsely arrested. For further information on arrests and your rights if arrested, contact one of the ☞ **free legal advice** (Law, Lawyers, Courts chapter) organisations or read Chapter 2: The Arrest, in *The Prisoner's Handbook* (English edition) or *Fangehåndbok* (Norwegian edition), a 186 page, inexpensive softcover book published by *Juss-Buss*, a free legal advice organisation, which you may visit during consultation hours, Monday 10 am to 3 pm and Thursday 5 to 8 pm ✆ 22851850, 🖷 22851870, ✉ St. Olavs gt. 29, 0166 Oslo, ✉ http://www.jus.uio.no/jussbuss/ with pages in Norwegian and in English.

Crime (*Kriminalitet*) There are now slightly more than 9,000 reported offences per year per 100,000 population, the fourth highest figure in Europe. However, alone that figure is deceptive, because report-ing procedures and perceptions of illegality vary from country to country. The figure for Norway includes misdemeanours (*forseelser*) which, if excluded, would cut the offence figure by a third. Moreover, offence reporting has varied through the years. Until the mid 1960s, for instance, parking violations were considered to be offences and accordingly were reported.

Nonetheless, the overall offence and crime rates are rising and now are about six times as high as they were in the mid 1950s. Theft is the most common crime, accounting for nearly two of every three crimes reported. As in many other countries, narcotics violations are increasingly a part of overall crime, not only because of their number – nearly one in ten of all crimes – but also because the trade in and use of illicit narcotics drives other crime, including theft. White collar crime and environmental violations are rising and now account for nearly one in 20 of reported offences. Many trends lie behind the increasing crime rate, such as increasing urbanisation – fully a quarter of all reported offences are committed in the city of Oslo, which has only a tenth of the country's population.

However, there are opposing trends. Violence, though increasing, remains low compared to other countries. The rate of serious assault is lower than that of most other countries in Europe and far lower than the top 20 in the world. The murder rate is one of the world's lowest, considerably less than one murder per 100,000 population, arguably due in part to strict laws on ☞ **guns and gun controls** (Sports, Recreation, Hobbies chapter).

For a complete overview of crime in Norway, see the overview books that are available to the general public: *Kriminalitet i Norge* ("Crime in Norway"), a series now in its sixth volume, compiled by the Norwegian Narcotics Police Association (*Norsk Narkotikapolitiforening – NNPF*) and published by *Norske Publikasjoner* ✆ 22237910, 🖷 22337965, ✉ Rådhusgt. 28, 0151 Oslo, and *Kriminalitet og rettsvesen* ("Crime and Law"), Oslo, Statistics Norway, 3rd edition 1997, ISBN 82-537-4414-5.

Exploitation of women and children (*Utnyttelse av kvinner og barn*) ranges from violating accepted morals to breaking laws, and includes incest, paedophilia, prostitution and rape.

Incest (*Incest*) is broadly defined as sexual abuse

within the close family. In most cases, incest is the exploitation – physical, psychological or both – of the sexual integrity of children and adolescents by someone – usually an adult – with whom they have a relationship of trust. The sexual abuse may take many forms, from being forced to view pornographic material to forced oral sex and rape. More than one child in ten experiences such sexual abuse. Accordingly, there are public and private sector centres dedicated to combating incest, both through helping victims and through promoting public awareness of it; "incest must be revealed, not concealed" is their motto. Many centres are staffed by women who themselves were abused as children and consequently are able to offer true sympathy in addition to advice and aid. If you are a child, adolescent or adult victim of incest, or if you observe and fear it, you may contact the nearest centre, listed under *Viktige telefonnummer* in the preface to the White Pages, usually under *Støttesenter mot incest* or under *Incestsenteret*. No Abuse, an on-line clearinghouse for information on and links to organisations dealing with problems of abuse, lists all the centres ☻ http://www.privat.telnett.no/~noabuse with pages in Norwegian only. The Support Centre against Incest (*Støttesenter mot incest* – SMI) in Oslo is one of the largest in the country and offers pamphlets and brochures with advice to children and to mothers, in Norwegian and in English ✆ 22331193 as well as text telephone 22335474 for deaf persons, ☎ 22330296, ✉ PO Box 8895 Youngstorget, 0028 Oslo.

Paedophilia (*Pedofili*) is the abnormal, especially sexual love of young children. The abnormal aspect might be a psychological condition that should be treated, whilst sexual abuse (*utukt*) of young (younger than 14) children is illegal. Anyone who sexually abuses a child or incites to such abuse, as by spreading child pornography (which itself is illegal), is subject to prosecution, no matter where the act took place.

The number of convictions for paedophilia was slightly more than 500 in 1998 and is rising, perhaps because the police are more diligent and because the public are increasingly aware of the extent to which perversion can destroy childhood. One consequence is that the police in some cities and towns now take precautions and warn the residents of a neighbourhood with small children when-

ever a convicted paedophilic person moves in.

Care for abused children is widely available. The facilities for raped and abused women (listed below) also aid their children. In 1995, a National Resource Centre for Sexually Abused Children (*Nasjonalt ressurssenter for seksuelt misbrukte barn*) was opened at the Aker Hospital (*Aker sykehus*) in Oslo ✆ 22894400 countrywide helpline Monday-Friday 8 am – 3:30 pm.

Norwegian organisations are internationally active in combating child pornography and paedophilia. In August 1996, in connection with the first World Congress Against Sexual Exploitation of Children, the Ombudsman for Children (*Barneombudet*) and ☞ **Save the Children** (NGOs chapter) initiated a programme to identify paedophilic networks and the methods used by criminals involved in the sexual exploitation of children. The programme set up a child abuse warning service with an E-Mail address which was announced in newspapers round the world. Reports received at it are passed on to the Norwegian Police, who in turn channel the information to the relevant international authorities. So if you find any form of child pornography or networking among child abusers on the Internet, you may E-Mail the details of it to Save the Children at ✉ children@risk.sn.no or for a description of the programme, view its web site ☻ http://childhouse.uio.no/redd_barna with pages in English.

Prostitution (*Prostitusjon*) Public brothels were part of city life up until the late nineteenth century. Opinion leaders of the time opposed the practice; Christian Krogh's painting "Albertine in the Police Doctor's Waiting-room" (*Albertine i politilegens Venteværelse*) of 1886-87 and his novel *Albertine* published at the same time helped prompt the abolishment of public prostitution in 1888. Since that time, prostitution has been a private affair of uncertain legal status. The vice law of 1902 prohibits soliciting but not the act of prostitution itself. A subsequent law prohibits procuring. So, from a purely legal viewpoint, the prostitute of today can ply her or his trade, but can do nothing to acquire customers. Nonetheless, the trade exists, as it does elsewhere, in its varieties, including streetwalking, call girls, massage parlours, escort services and male prostitution. New in the 1990s is the influx of foreign-born prostitutes, Russians in the north and

Asians and Central Americans in the larger cities in the south. Except for paedophilia involving the sexual abuse or exploitation of children, which is illegal, the current view is that both prostitutes and their clients are people, entitled to full rights according to the United Nations Universal Declaration of Human Rights of 1948. Consequently, public and private organisations dealing with prostitution are dedicated to counselling and support, both for prostitutes and their clients. The national Prostitution Centre in Oslo (Pro-sentret) is staffed by social service professionals and volunteers ℡ 23100200, ℻ 22410544, ✉ Tollbugt. 24, 0157 Oslo, ✉ prosntrt@online.no ☻ http://home.sol.no/~prosntrt with links to other on-line resources. Pro-sentret assists other social services organisations throughout the country, offers counselling for individuals, operates the national helpline ℡ 23100200, publishes brochures and pamphlets and has programmes to help prostitutes quit the trade. All services and publications are in Norwegian only, but the helpline and office personnel speak English and other European and Asian languages. Public and private organisations throughout the country also offer counselling and support; look for Kirkens Bymisjon (City Mission), Natthjemmet (Overnight Hostel) or Utekontakten (Street Contact) in the Pink Pages of the phone directory. Pro-Sentret can also supply the names and telephone numbers of other centres.

Rape (Voldtekt) Statistics indicate that rape is no more common than are crimes that are committed in civil service, just 456 convictions a year (1998). However, women's organisations and social workers believe that conviction figures fail to reflect prevalence, as many rapes and attempted rapes go unreported. That need not be so, as there are more than 50 rape crisis centres throughout the country, at least one in each county. If you are a woman who has been abused or raped, you may call the nearest centre at the helpline number listed for Krisesenteret for mishandlede og voldtatte kvinner listed under Viktige telefonnummer in the front of the White Pages. You may call anonymously if you wish, and in addition to counselling and medical aid, the centre can provide refuge for you and your children if you need to escape your home. Outpatient clinics (legevakt) and the gynaecological departments of regional hospitals (regionsykehus) and central hospitals (sentralsyhkehus) have reception facilities for rape victims

(voldtektsmottak). If you report a rape to the police, you are entitled to legal support by a qualified lawyer (bistandsadvokat) appointed by the court (retten). If you want a specific lawyer, the court will try to accommodate your wish. In addition to representing you in court, the lawyer has the right to be present during any questioning (avhør) and may protest improper (utilbørlig) questions. In each of the 11 dioceses of ☞ **The Church of Norway** (Church and Religion chapter) there is a Christian Resource Centre for Abused Women (Kirkelig Ressurssenter for mishandlede kvinner) that offers spiritual, psychological and health service counselling; call the nearest church, listed under Kirken in the Pink Pages, for the names and numbers of the contact persons to call. There is a countrywide rape victims support group, DIXI, Landsforeningen for voldtatte ℡ Stavanger 51520360 Wednesdays 6 to 9 pm and Oslo 22114320 Tuesdays 6 to 9 pm, ✉ PO Box 407, 4067 Stavanger, ✉ waldow@rl.telia.no, ☻ http://home.sol.no/~dixi with links and lists of addresses of reception centres and other facilities countrywide.

Fines for misdemeanours (Bøter for forseelser) vary. In a 1998 survey of fines levied by police in nine cities – Bergen, Fredrikstad, Kragerø, Kristiansand, Oslo, Sandefjord, Tønsberg, Tromsø and Trondheim – the fines for disorderly drunkenness (fyll og bråk) ranged from NOK 1500 to 10,000, for drinking (alcoholic) in public (drikking på offentlig sted) from NOK 1000 to 4000, for refusal to move when requested by police (ikke etterkomme politiets pålegg om å fjerne seg) from NOK 1000 to 5000 and for urinating in public (urinering på offentlig sted) from NOK 1000 to 3000.

Lawbreaking (Lovbrudd) is reported in ☞ **statistics** (Statistics and Polls chapter) for the whole country and detailed in the annual Statistisk årbok in Norwegian and "Statistical Yearbook of Norway", its English edition, and on-line by Statistics Norway (Statistisk sentralbyrå). In alphabetical order, some of the more familiar crimes, with the numbers reported in 1998 in parentheses, are: arson (164), assault (10,216), attempted murder (48), attempted rape (107), counterfeiting (1185), drink driving (9330), forgery (3285), housebreaking and burglary (4967), incest (143), motor vehicle theft (21,672), murder

(38), narcotics violations (16,180), perjury and false evidence (596), petty larceny (15,802), racial discrimination (45), rape (456), robbery (1034), smuggling (53), speeding (10,419), spreading pornography (209), tax violations (1955), telephone harassment (2,710), theft, all types (193,630) and vagrancy (4477).

Police (*Politi*) are organised in 54 Police Districts (*Politidistrikt*), each headed by a Chief of Police (*Politimester*), who also is in charge of adjacent rural police districts (*lensmanndistrikt*). The principal tasks of the police are to maintain law and order and to prevent and investigate crime. The police also perform other services, such as issuing passports, organising search and rescue parties and granting permits for public events and lotteries. Moreover, the police administer and provide services relating to the legal aspects of foreigners in the country, such as issuing ☞ **residence and work permits** (Arriving, Settling, Leaving chapter). Contact the nearest police, listed under *Politiet* in the Pink Pages, for further information. Larger city Police Districts have full information services as well as Internet web sites, such as the Oslo Police District's ✆ http://www.opol.no with its own search engine. There are four major countrywide police services:

- *Kripos* (National Bureau of Crime Investigation) assists the Police Districts and acts in international police work through the International Criminal Police Organisation (Interpol).
- *Politiets overvåkningstjeneste – POT* (Norwegian Police Security Service), responsible for preventing terrorism, espionage and threats to national security.
- *Økokrim* (National Authority for Investigation and Prosecution of Economic and Environmental Crime) acts in matters concerning "white-collar crime" and violations of environmental laws.
- *Utrykningspolitiet – UP* (Central Mobile Police Force), the country's ☞ **Road patrol** (Cars, Roads, Traffic chapter).

Moreover, the Norwegian Police Academy (*Politihøgskolen*) offers a three-year curriculum in basic police methods at its main school in Oslo ✆ 23199900, ☎ 23199901, ✉ PO Box 5027 Majorstua, 0301 Oslo, and at its school in Bodø ✆ 75588000, ☎ 75588030, ✉ Slekkåsveien, 8016 Mørkved, ✆ http://www.politihs.no for both facilities.

Prison and probation (*Fengsel og friomsorg*) In proportion to its population, Norway imprisons few people, just 58 per 100,000 population, the third lowest rate among countries in Europe, hardly 60% of the rate in the UK (100) and a mere tenth of the rate in the USA (600). And Norwegian prisons are not crowded, as occupancy averages 84 prisoners per 100 available places. In an average year, some ten thousand persons are imprisoned, and the average length of stay in prison is 89 days.

There are 43 prisons with a total capacity of slightly more than 2,800 places, of which nearly 900 are in open facilities. There are five central prisons (*landsfengsel*): Bastøy at Horten, Bergen at Nyborg, Bretvedt at Oslo, Ila at Oslo and Ullersmo at Klofta. There are four prison regions – East, West, North and South – each with regional prisons (*kretsfengsel*) and auxiliary prisons (*hjelpefengsel*). Sentences of up to 30 days are usually served in a regional prison or an auxiliary prison. Sentences of up to six months are usually served in a regional prison, while longer sentences usually are served in a central prison. The Prison Board (*Fenmgselsstyret*) can make exceptions to these general rules and can, upon application, meet a prisoner's wish for serving in a specific prison. If you are sentenced to prison, you may wish to learn more about prison matters. Juss-Buss, a ☞ **Free legal advice** (Law, Lawyers, Courts chapter) organisation operated by University of Oslo law students [Monday 10 am to 3 pm and Thursday 5 to 8 pm ✆ 22851850, ☎ 22851870, ✉ St. Olavs gt. 29, 0166 Oslo, ✆ http://www.jus.uio.no/jussbuss/ with pages in Norwegian and in English] has published a comprehensive prisoner's handbook, most recently in the third edition of 1998: *Fangehåndboka* (Norwegian edition, 164 pages) and *The Prisoner Handbook* (English edition, 184 pages), softcover, available at the office or on order for NOK 50.

The Probation Service (*Friomsorg i Frihet – KIF*) executes municipal sanctions and measures, including service orders, drink-driving and other supervision programmes, early release and suspended sentence supervision. KIF facilities are located in all 19 counties, and there are some 50 in the country.

Security services (*Vakttjenester*) include the providing of private guards (*vekter*), alarm systems (*alarmsystemer*), reception staff (*resepsjonstjenester*), valuables transport (*verditransport*), personal protection (*personbeskyttelse*) and other services involved in protecting people and property. The security services sector is expanding rapidly, in part due to an increasing need for protection as rates of ☞ **crime** rise. The largest company in the sector is Securitas, founded in 1934 in Sweden and now offering services in 19 countries in Europe and North America, including Norway. In all, more than 100 companies offer security services; you can find them listed under *Vaktselskaper* in the Yellow Pages. In contacting a company, be sure that it is established and reputable, as the rapid expansion of the sector has attracted many unqualified firms. You may ask the police (*politi*), who certify security services and thereby know their operations. You also may contact the Norwegian Security Services Association (*Norske Vaktselskapers Landsforening – NVL*) ✆ 23088650, 🖷 23088659, ✉ Essendropsgt 6. 0368 Oslo, ✉ firmapost@sbl.no, or view the NVL list of member companies via the *vakt* link on the *Servicebedriftenes Landsforening* web site ⊜ http://www.sbl.no

Victim support (*Støtte til voldsofre*) There are many forms of support for victims of ☞ **violence**.
If you are the victim of a violent act, you may call the national association for victim support (*Landsforeningen for voldsofre*) ✆ 22655455. The number is listed in the front pages of the Pink and White Pages of all telephone directories and is answered by persons who themselves are survivors of violence. When you call, the person answering will advise you in Norwegian, or in English if you prefer, where to go or which organisation to call nearby for immediate assistance. The association is represented in the European Forum for Victim Services.

If you are the victim of a crime, you may seek advice from one of the *Rådgivningskontorene for kriminalitetsofre* ("Advisory offices for victims of crimes") located in Drammen, Fredrikstad, Haugesund, Oslo, Tromsø and Trondheim. Call the police department (*Politi*) listed in the Pink Pages for the phone number, address and consultation hours of the nearest office.

If you wish to learn more about victim support and the measures that promote it, you may contact *Norsk Forbund for Voldsofre – NFV* ("Norwegian alliance for victim support") ✆ 22108150, 🖷 22108657, ✉ Vestlisvingen 94, 0969 Oslo or read its magazine, *Voldsoffer*.

If you have been the victim of reported criminal violence, you may apply for Criminal Violence Compensation (*Voldsoffererstatning*), by filling out a form available at police stations and submitting it to the offices of the County Governor (*Fylkesmann*). Compensation is intended to offset loss and varies from NOK 1000 to NOK 200,000, and is co-ordinated on the national level by the Criminal Violence Compensation Board (*Erstatningsnemnda for voldsofre*) of the Ministry of Justice and the Police.

Violence (*Vold*) is increasing. Each year, some 13,000 incidents of violent crime are reported to the police, equivalent to 342 per 100,000 population, a level six times as high as in the late 1950s. Moreover, crime statistics alone reflect only part of the problem, as each year an estimated 110,000 persons are victims of violence. One of five incidents of violence occurs in the home, and one of eight young persons is now subjected to violence or threat of violence. Young women, 16 to 24 years old, are the most vulnerable: in 1997, some 14% were the victims of violence or threat of violence. These figures are not from the sensationalist media, but from an official report compiled and released in 1999 by Statistics Norway. Understandably, the public is alarmed. The public and private sectors are involved in preventing and combating violence. There is a national Resource Centre for Information and Studies on Violence (*Kompetansesenter for voldsofferarbeid*) ✆ 22452720, 🖷 22452725, ✉ PO Box 8178 Dep, 0034 Oslo, ✉ vos@hioslo.no, ⊜ http://www.hioslo.no/annet/voldsoffer. There are ☞ **victim support** measures and organisations and a countrywide helpline listed in all telephone directories. Major organisations, including the ☞ **Red Cross**, the ☞ **Salvation Army** (Non-government Organisations chapter), church groups and youth organisations have anti-violence activities. An organisation in Oslo is dedicated to working with young people to prevent their becoming criminal and violent: Youth Against Violence (*Ungdom mot Vold*) ✆ 22113111, 🖷 22676666, ✉ PO Box 4769 Sofienberg, 0506 Oslo, ✉ ungdommotvold@2ci.net, ⊜ http://www.ungdom-mot-vold.no

Defence (Forsvar)

The Air Force (Luftforsvaret), or Royal Norwegian Air Force, became an independent service in 1944. Air power is essential in Norway's Total Defence Concept and in establishing and maintaining air superiority in time of crisis or war. In peacetime, the Air Force has nearly 9,000 personnel, and in time of war, some 33,000. For further details, contact the nearest Air Force unit listed under *Luftforsvaret* in the Pink Pages, or the Press and Information Branch at the ☞ **Headquarters Defence Command**.

Air-raid shelters (Tilfluktsrom) throughout the country can accommodate a total of some 2.6 million people. Public air-raid shelters, mostly in larger cities, have a total capacity of some 280,000 people. Since the second world war, building regulations have required that air-raid shelters be built in all buildings open to the public, as well is in larger private buildings, such as office complexes and blocks of flats. The total capacity of these private building air-raid shelters is 2.3 million. In peacetime, these air-raid shelters may be fitted with temporary interiors and thereby be used for other purposes, such as for storage lockers for blocks of flats or clubs in university and college buildings. However, should international tension increase and war threaten, the temporary interiors must be removed to free the shelters for their original purpose. In 1998, research studies concluded that the usefulness of air-raid shelters might be questioned in a modern, high-tech war. However, Norway's long coastline and harbours mean that the country must be prepared to defend itself against attack by conventional weaponry. Consequently, air-raid shelters remain important, particularly in the northern part of the country. So the current strategy is to maintain existing air-raid shelters through the year 2048 and to build new shelters in the northern counties of Finnmark and Troms.

Alarms (Varsling) are sounded to warn the public of imminent danger or air raid. There are 1,200 warning facilities (*varslingsanlegg*) throughout the country, mostly in cities and larger towns. Each facility has sirens (*sirener*) or hooters (*tyfoner*) that can be heard throughout its coverage area. There are three warnings:

Urgent warning, listen to your radio (Viktig melding – lytt på radioen): A five-minute sequence of three sets of three tone blasts each; about one minute between successive sets. Church bells give warning to areas lacking warning facilities.

Air raid, seek cover! (Flyalarm, søk dekning!): A one-minute sequence of short tone blasts.

All clear (Faren over): A continuous tone for about half a minute.

Alarm facilities are periodically tested, usually at midday, on dates and at times announced in advance in the *Kunngjøringer* (Announcements) section of the classified advertisements in newspapers.

Armed forces (Forsvaret) Norway spends approximately 2.3% of its annual GDP on defence, about the same level of expenditure as other member countries of ☞ **NATO** (Government and Social Services chapter). As in other member countries of the ☞ **OECD** (Government and Social Services chapter), military spending has gone down in recent years, from 7.4% of the corrected national budget in 1990 to 5.9% in 1998. The strength of the forces in peacetime (*styrke i fred*) is some 35,000, of which about 11,800 are cadre (*befall*) and 22,700 are conscripts (*vernepliktige*). Moreover, there are some 9,000 civilian employees (*sivilt tilsatte*). The strength under full mobilisation (*mobilisering*) is about 234,000. The individual services are described in this chapter. For a more complete overview, see the comprehensive, pocket-sized booklet published by the Ministry of Defence (*Forsvarsdepartementet*) with editions in Norwegian *Fakta om Forsvaret* ISBN 82-90390-76-9 and English *Norwegian Defence, Facts and Figures* ISBN 82-90390-77-7, available from offices of the forces (*Forsvaret* in the Pink Pages).

The Army (Hæren) is the largest of the services, with some 22,000 personnel in peacetime. It is currently undergoing extensive restructuring. The mobilisation Army of the future will be smaller and have an improved personnel and material standard. In wartime, it will be organised into six brigades, of which three will be part of the 6th Division in Troms county. Moreover, it will deploy 22 field battalions spread throughout the country. For further details, contact the nearest Army unit listed under *Hæren* in the Pink Pages, or the Press and Information Branch at the ☞ **Headquarters Defence Command**.

Cadre training schools (*Befalsskoler*) All three services, the Army (*Hæren*), the Navy (*Sjøforsvaret*) and the Air Force (*Luftforsvaret*) have schools (*Befalsskoler*) for training non-commissioned and commissioned officers. Men or women applicants must be Norwegian citizens, at least 18 years old, have no criminal record, pass a physical examination and an acceptance test. There are 16 schools in the country. The Army has eleven, for Infantry in Trøndelag county (*Infanteriet – BSIT*), Infantry in North Norway (*Infanteriet – BSIN*), Cavalry (*Kavaleriet – BSK*), Field Artillery (*Feltartilleriet – BSFA*), Light Anti-Aircraft (*Lett luftvernartilleri – BSLV*), Engineers, (*Ingeniørvåpenet – BSIV*), Signals (*Hærens Samband – BSHSB*), Ordnance (*Trenvåpen – BSHT*), Medical Services (*Sanitet – BSHS*), Technology (*Ingeniørhøgskole – HIS*) and Espionage and Security (*Etterretnings- og sikkerhetstjeneste – FSES*). The Navy has two, for the Coast Artillery (*Kystartilleriet – BSKA*) and the Navy in general (*Marinen – BSMA*). The Air Force has three, for the Air Force in general (*Luftforsvaret – LBSK*), for pilots (*Flygeskole – LFS*) and for continuing education (*Skolesenter Kjevik – LSK*). For further information, contact the Defence Forces Recruitment and Media Centre (*Forsvarets rekrutterings- og mediesenter*) in Oslo ✆ 81000222, 🖷 23093466, ✉ Oslo Mil Akershus, 0015 Oslo, 🖳 http://www.frm.mil.no or the nearest recruitment office, look under *Forsvarets rekruttering* in the Pink Pages.

Civil preparedness (*Sivilt beredskap*) is part of the country's concept of total defence (*totalforsvaret*). This means that civilian agencies and the ☞ **Armed forces**, as well as the ☞ **Home guard** act together to manage emergencies by complementing each other at local, regional and central levels. Civil Defence (*Sivilforsvaret*) is organised in 40 districts throughout the country, each headed by a police commissioner (*Politimester*). The mobilisation organisation consists of some 50,000 men and women trained in civil defence. An additional 33,000 industrial safety and emergency workers can be called upon in case of national emergency. There are Peacetime Contingency Teams – PCT (*Fredsinnsatsgrupper – FIG*) in more than a hundred municipalities (*kommune*). Each PCT consists of 20 or more persons who can be mobilised on one hour's notice and are fully equipped for fire-fighting, rescue and paramedical services. In addition to Civil Defence itself, the national emergency preparedness encompasses administration (*administrativ beredskap*), supply and provisions (*Økonomisk beredskap*), police (*Politi*), health services (*Helseberedskap*) and information (*Informasjonsberedskap*). For further local information, contact the nearest Civil Defence unit listed under *Sivilforsvaret* in the Pink Pages. For comprehensive information for the whole country, contact the Directorate for Civil Defence and Emergency Planning (*Direktoratet for sivilt beredskap*) ✆ 22358400, 🖷 22351781, ✉ PO Box 8136 Dep, 0033 Oslo, ✉ postmottak@dsb.dep.no, 🖳 http://www.dsb.no with pages in Norwegian and in English.

Conscription (*Verneplikt*) If you are a man and a Norwegian citizen, you are subject to compulsory military service. In most cases, you will receive notice (*innkalling*) to report for your first medical examination and classification (*sesjon*) in the first half of the year of your 18th birthday. Thereafter, usually in the autumn of that year, you will be called up to basic training (*Førstegangstjenesten*), usually for about 12 months, in one of the three ☞ **Armed forces**. After basic training, you may elect to continue in the military, in which case you may wish to apply to a ☞ **Cadre training school**. If you return to civilian life, you will either become part of the reserve forces and will periodically be called up for refresher training (*Repetisjonstjeneste*) or to be assigned to the ☞ **Home guard**. If you are a dual citizen, as of Norway and another European country or the USA, you normally are called up only in the country of your permanent residence upon your 18th birthday. If you are a conscientious objector, after finishing *sesjon*, you may apply for exemption from military service due to conflict with your convictions (*søknad om fritak for militærtjeneste av overbevisningsgrunner*). You should submit your application to the nearest board of the National Service Administration (*Vernepliktsverket*), which will register it and send it to the Department of Justice (*Justisdepartementet*) for review and decision. If exemption is granted, you must perform civilian service (*siviltjeneste*) instead of military service, for a period of about 16 months. For further information on all aspects of conscription and military service, contact the nearest board of the National Service Administration; there are six in the country, at Bergen, Kristiansand, Hamar, Harstad,

Oslo and Trondheim; look under *Vernepliktsverket* in the Pink Pages for addresses and telecommunications numbers, or contact the head office in Oslo ☏ 23093805, 🖷 23093394, ✉ Oslo Mil Aksershus, 0015 Oslo, ✉ verneplikt@vpv-stab.mil.no, ⊕ http://www.vpv.mil.no

Construction (*bygning*) of defence facilities, as well as their management, maintenance and administration, is performed by the Norwegian Defence Construction Service (*Forsvarets bygningstjeneste*). It is one of the oldest military agencies in the country, with roots dating back to 1688. Today it has a staff of some 350, with its head office in Oslo and regional offices in Hamar, Sola, Trondheim and Harstad. For further details, contact the Press and Information Branch at the ☞ **Headquarters Defence Command**.

Headquarters Defence Command (*Forsvarets overkommando*) The ministerial ☞ **Government** (Government and Social Services chapter) is the highest executive authority responsible for military and civilian preparedness in peacetime and for the command of the total defence in time of war. The military command authority is delegated to the Chief of Defence. The relevant administration is performed by the Headquarters Defence Command, which has its headquarters at the Huseby Base in Oslo. In addition to its military functions, the Headquarters Defence Command maintains a comprehensive Press and Information Branch (*Pressetjeneste*) that acts as a central agency for all information on the Armed Forces and other military matters in the country ☏ 23098236, 🖷 23098483, ✉ Oslo mil/Huseby, 0016 Oslo, ✉ presse-info@fo.mil.no, ⊕ http://www.mil.no

Home guard (*Heimevernet*), or Territorial Army, was established in 1946. It is decentralised, with units in all 435 municipalities, divided into 18 districts throughout the country. Though principally a military auxiliary, it also acts as an emergency service in times of natural or other non-military disasters. Home Guard officers, non-commissioned officers and servicemen are recruited from the local community, so as to be familiar with local conditions. For best operational efficiency, each Home Guard unit has contacts with the civilian sector and makes use of the civilian expertise of its members. Overall, the Home Guard is divided into three branches that correspond to the three military services: Land corresponding to Army, Naval corresponding to the Navy, and Air Defence Artillery corresponding to the Air Force. Together, Home Guard units can mobilise a strength of up to 83,000 and have more than 1,000 permanent facilities throughout the country. Accordingly, the Home Guard is well financed, by about 2.2% of the national defence budget. For further information, contact the nearest Home Guard unit listed under *Heimevernet* in the Pink Pages, or the Press and Information Branch at the ☞ **Headquarters Defence Command**.

Matériel Commands (*Forsyningskommando*) Each of the three major armed forces has its Materiel Command: The Army Materiel Command (*Hærens forsyningskommando*) which also serves the Home Guard, the Navy Materiel Command (*Sjøforsvarets forsyningskommando*) and the Air Force Materiel Command (*Luftforsvarets forsyningskommando*). The mission of each Materiel Command is to provide the materiel necessary to achieve credible combat capability. For further details, contact the Press and Information Branch at the ☞ **Headquarters Defence Command**.

Military academies (*Krigsskoler*) There are three military academies for higher-level education of officers, one each for the Army (*Hæren*), Navy (*Sjøforsvar*) and Air Force (*Luftforsvar*). Men or women applicants must be Norwegian citizens and must have successfully completed an officer training course, as at a ☞ **Cadre Training School** for non-commissioned and commissioned officers and must have served at least one year in the Army, Navy or Air Force. The course of studies is divided into two levels. After completing the first level of two or three years, cadets must serve for one or two years in the forces before being eligible to apply for the second and final level of two years. After graduation, officers are required to serve a minimum of two years. For further information, call the Defence Forces Recruiting and Media Service (*Forsvarets Rekrutterings- og mediasenter*) ☏ 81000222 or call or visit the nearest recruiting office, see under *Forsvarets rekruttering* in the Pink Pages.

Army: The national Military Academy

(*Krigsskolen*) was founded in 1750 and is the oldest college in Norway as well as being one of the world's oldest military academies. The upper level of studies offers three elective programmes, in tactics and operations (*taktisk/operativ linje*), military technology (*Militærteknologisk linje*) and international co-operation (*Internasjonalt samarbeid*). The Academy has exchange programmes with other military academies in Europe and frequently arranges study trips within Norway and to other countries. The campus is located at Linderud in Oslo and adjoins the *Oslomarka* forest recreation preserve. ℗ 23099000, 🖷 23099410, ✉ Utfartsvn 2, 0593 Oslo, 🖂 webmaster@ks.mil.no, ⊕ http://www.ks.mil.no

Navy: The Naval Academy (*Sjøkrigsskolen*) was founded in 1817. The focus is on theory and practice, and the Academy co-operates with naval academies in other countries, including the Royal Military College of Science in England, the US Naval Postgraduate School, the Amphibious Warfare School in the USA and Führungsakademie der Bundeswähr in Germany. The campus is located in mod-

ern facilities at Laksevåg near Bergen. ℗ 55502000, 🖷 55505004, ✉ 5078 Haakonsvern, ⊕ http://www.icon.no/bsma/userhtml/sksks

Air Force: The Air Force Academy (*Luftkrigsskolen*) was founded in 1949. It co-operates extensively with air force academies abroad, and pilots and navigators are trained in the USA. It also provides the initial training for careers in civil aviation. The campus is located in Trondheim. ℗ 73995423, 🖷 73995424, ✉ 7004 Trondheim, ⊕ http://www.lksk.no

Military Ombudsman Board (*Ombudsman-nsnemda for Forsvaret*) The military forces consist of people, so the purpose of the Military Ombudsman Board is both to ensure general human rights in the armed forces and to contribute to efficient defence of the country. The Board acts both for military cadre and conscripts and for conscripts who elect civilian service (*sivile tjenestepliktig*) ℗ 23356470, 🖷 22410008, ✉ PO Box 1453 Vika, 0159 Oslo.

Military ranks (*Militære grader*) The Norwegian military ranks and their equivalents in British English and American English are listed below.

Army (*Hæren*)

Norway	UK	USA
General	General	General
Genaralløytnant	Lieutenant-General	Lieutenant General
Generalmajor	Major-General	Major General
Brigader	Brigadier	Brigadier General
Oberst	Colonel	Colonel
Oberstløytnant	Lieutenant-Colonel	Lieutenant Colonel
Major	Major	Major
Kaptein	Captain	Captain
Løytnant	Lieutenant	1st Lieutenant
Fenrik	2nd Lieutenant	2nd Lieutenant
Sersjant	Sergeant	Sergeant
Korporal	Corporal	Corporal
Menig	Private	Private

Navy (*Skøforsvaret*)

Norway	UK*	USA
Admiral	Admiral	Admiral
Viseadmiral	Vice-Admiral	Vice Admiral
Kontreadmiral	Rear-Admiral	Rear Admiral
Flaggkommandør	Commodore	Commodore
Kommandør	Captain (N)	Captain

Kommandørkaptein	Commander Senior Grade	Commander Senior Grade
Orlogskaptein	Commander	Commander
Kapteinløytnant	Lieutenant-Commander	Lieutenant Commander
Løytnant	Lieutenant	Lieutenant
Fenrik	Midshipman	Ensign
Matros	Seaman	Seaman

*Royal Navy only, not Royal Marines

Air Force (*Luftforsvaret*)

Norway	UK	USA
General	Air Chief-Marshal	General
Generalløytnant	Air Marshal	Lieutenant General
Generalmajor	Air Vice-Marshal	Major General
Oberst I	Air Commodore	Brigadier General
Oberst II	Group Captain	Colonel
Oberstløytnant	Wing Commander	Lieutenant Colonel
Major	Squadron-leader	Major
Kaptein	Flight Lieutenant	Captain
Løytnant	Lieutenant	1st Lieutenant
Fenrik	2nd Lieutenant	2nd Lieutenant
Sersjant	Sergeant	Sergeant
Korporal	Corporal	Corporal
Menig	Private	Private

The Navy (*Sjøforsvaret*), or Royal Norwegian Navy as it is known in English, is responsible for monitoring and securing Norwegian interests in sea areas under Norwegian jurisdiction. These waters cover an area almost seven times that of the mainland. The ships of the regular Navy give the Coast Guard credibility in handling minor crises and they will support the Coast Guard if required. In peacetime, the Navy has some 7,800 personnel, and in time of war, some 22,000. For further details, contact the nearest Navy unit listed under *Sjøforsvaret* in the Pink Pages, or the Press and Information Branch at the ☞ **Headquarters Defence Command**.

Research (*Forskning*) in fields related to defence is conducted by the Norwegian Defence Research Establishment (*Forsvarets forskningsinstitutt – FFI*), which was established in 1946. There now are five divisions, four at Kjeller near Oslo and one, for underwater defence, at Horten on the Oslo Fjord. FFI is an interdisciplinary institute covering most engineering fields as well as biology, medicine, political science and economics. It now has a staff of about 530, of which 350 are engineers and scientists. For further details, contact the FFI Information Office ☎ 63807000, ☒ 63807115, ✉ PO Box 25, 2007 Kjeller, ◉ http://www.ffi.no with pages in Norwegian and in English.

Telecommunications and information technology (*telekommunikasjon og datateknologi*) are provided to all defence services by the Norwegian Defence Communications and Data Services Administration (*Forsvarets tele- og datatjeneste*). In addition to its military tasks, the Administration also supports civilian navigation systems and provides services to some governmental agencies. For further details, contact the Press and Information Branch at the ☞ **Headquarters Defence Command**.

Drink, drugs, tobacco (*Alkohol, narkotika, tobakk*)

Alcohol consumption (*Omsetning av alkohol*) is low compared with other countries. In statistical terms of equivalent litres of pure alcohol consumed per year per capita, Norway's figure of 5.35 litres per year per capita ranks it well below the top 20 in the world as well as below the top 20 in Europe. Even with the addition of an estimated 1.62 litres per year per capita to account for smuggling, home brewing and tourist import, alcohol consumption is about half that in Luxembourg, Portugal or France, the leading consumers in Europe as well as the world. Alcohol consumption is less than it has been in past years, though towards the end of the 1990s it began to rise. Drinking habits are changing, apparently in step with increasing internationalisation. In 1997, sales of wine were twice as much and distilled liquor half as much as in 1980. Moreover, alcohol is becoming more readily available. In 1980, close to half of the country's 454 municipalities had no shops licensed to sell alcoholic drink and 91 municipalities were completely dry, with neither sales nor serving of alcohol. In 1997, only 6 of the country's 435 municipalities had no licensed shops and only one was completely dry. For further information and statistics on consumption, see the most recent edition of the annual report, *Rusmidler i Norge, Alcohol and Drugs in Norway 98*, Oslo, Rusmiddeldirektoratet and SIFA, Norwegian and English texts, 107 pages A4 format, ISBN 82-90594-85-2.

Anti smoking (*Mot tobakkskadene*) There are two private anti-smoking organisations:

The Anti Smoking Injury Association (*Landslaget Mot Tobakkskadene – LMT*) ✆ 22593000, ⌧ PO Box 5327 Majorstua, 0304 Oslo, which is supported by The Norwegian Cancer Association (*Den norske kreftforening*).

Smoke-free Environment Norway (*Røykfritt Miljø Norge*) ✆ & ✆ 22111253, ⌧ PO Box 8701 Youngstorget, 0028 Oslo, a member of the European Union of Non-Smokers (*Union Europeenne des Non-Fumeurs*) is completely independent.

The two organisations jointly publish a quarterly newsletter, Smoke-Free (*Røykfritt*), with news and overviews of restaurants and other public places where smoking is banned, principally in Norwegian with extracts and reports to sister organisations in other countries in English.

The National Council on Smoking and Health (NCSH) (*Tobakksskaderåd*) is a governmental bureau. It publishes brochures and pamphlets on the risks of smoking and using snuff, compiles data on the nicotine and tar content of cigarettes and provides tobacco health risk information to schools ✆ 22248990, ✆ 22248991, ⌧ PO Box 8025 Dep, 0030 Oslo, ✉ post@tobakk.no, ✆ http://www.tobakk.no with pages in Norwegian and key pages, such as laws, in English.

The NCSH co-operates with Tobacco Free Initiative, the World Health Organisation project that was founded in July 1998 to focus on tobacco as an important public health issue world-wide. For further information, contact the Regional Office for Europe ✆+45 39171248, ✆ 39171854, ⌧ Scherfigsvej 8, DK-2100 Copenhagen, Denmark, ✉ pan@who.dk, ✆ http://who.int/toh/TFI with pages in English, in French and in Spanish.

Problems with alcohol and drugs (*Alkohol og stoff misbruk*) According to estimates made by public and private organisations, about one in twenty-five adults is dependent on alcohol (*alkohol*), medicinal drugs (*medikamenter*) or illicit drugs (*stoff, narkotika*). In alphabetical order by their names in English, the principal organisations dealing with alcohol and drug problems are:

Agency for the Prevention and Treatment of Alcohol and Drug Problems, The Municipality of Oslo (*Rusmiddeletaten, Oslo kommune*) funds and co-ordinates 55 institutions and other services for alcoholics and drug addicts, including six detoxification units, five treatment units mainly for alcoholics, nine treatment institutions mainly for drug addicts, three smaller treatment communities for drug addicts, 18 half-way houses, seven institutions for care of elderly and disabled alcoholics and seven other specialised services ✆ 23213300, ✆ 23213380, ⌧ Grensen 5/7, 0159 Oslo, ✉ postmottak@rusmiddeletaten.oslo.kommune.no, ✆ http://www.rusinfo.no with pages in Norwegian and in English.

Alcoholics Anonymous – AA (*Anonyme alkoholik-*

er), the international organisation that helps alcoholics cure themselves, some 165 groups, some English-speaking, in country ℗ 91177770 countrywide information line listed under *Viktige telefonnummer* in White Pages of telephone directory, head office ℗ 22468965, ℻ 22468177, ✉ PO Box 205 Sentrum, 0103 Oslo, ✉ aa_tjeneste@hotmail.com, ⊕ http://home.sol.no/~aanor with pages in Norwegian and in English.

Bergen Clinics Foundation (*Stiftelsen Bergensklinikkene*) provides narcotics treatment and counselling and conducts research ℗ 55908600, ℻ 55908610, ✉ PO Box 297, 5804 Bergen, ✉ bergenclinics@bergenclinics.hl.no, ⊕ http://hotell.nextel.no/bergenclinics with pages in Norwegian and in English.

Marita Foundation (*Maritastiftelsen*), a Christian organisation working with addicts and prostitutes ℗ 22992950, ℻ 22992960, ✉ Christian Kroghs-gate 34, 0186 Oslo, ✉ marita@marita.no, ⊕ http://www.marita.no with links to other organisations.

Narcotics Anonymous – NA (*Anonyme narkomaner*), the international organisation that helps drug addicts cure themselves, several groups in country ℗ 90529359 countrywide helpline listed under *Viktige telefonnummer* in White Pages of telephone directory, head office ✉ PO Box 5257 Majorstua, 0301 Oslo, ⊕ http://www.wsoinc.com World Services in English.

National Institute for Alcohol and Drug Research (*Statens Institutt for Alkohol- og Narkotikaforskning*) conducts research and publishes findings on all aspects of alcohol and drug addiction ℗ 22040870, ℻ 22719059, ✉ Dannevigsveien 10, 0463 Oslo, ✉ postmaster@sifa.no, ⊕ http://www.sifa.no with links to publications.

Norwegian Directorate for the Prevention of Alcohol and Drug Problems (*Rusmiddeldirektoratet*), a government agency, oversees use of alcohol, including its manufacture and wholesaling, and problems associated with alcohol and drug abuse; has wide range of publications and a library ℗ 22246500, ℻ 22246639, ✉ PO Box 8152 Dep, 0033 Oslo, ✉ nn.nn@rusdir.dep.telemax.no, ⊕ http://www.bibsent.no/rusdir with details of how to access library.

Phoenix House Oslo (*Veksthuset*) is modelled on the Phoenix House in London and is a non-profit drug abuse community providing treatment for adult addicts ℗ 22923560, ℻ 22923542, ✉ PO Box 3867 Ullevål Hageby, 0805 Oslo, ⊕ http://home.sol.no/~alaoui/vekst.html

Tyrili Foundation (*Tyrilistiftelsen*), an independent organisation working with drug abuse, particularly with teenagers and also with prisoners in the Pathfinder programme, has a centre and living communities ℗ 22675850, ℻ 22675930, ✉ Sverres gate 4, 0652 Oslo, ✉ info@tyrili.no, ⊕ http://www.tyrili.no with pages in Norwegian and in English.

Union of Drugfree Youth (*Ungdom mot narkotika*) encourages young people to say no to drugs on their own account and now has more than 8,000 members throughout the country ℗ 22671616, ℻ 22681044, ✉ PO Box 4773 Sofienberg, 0506 Oslo, ✉ umnpost@online.no, ⊕ http://www.nettinfo.no/umn with pages in Norwegian and in English.

Vang Centre (*Vangseter*) is a private rehabilitation facility for alcoholics and addicts based on the Minnesota Model ℗ 62598400, ℻ 62598017, ✉ Vangseter, 2323 Ingeberg, ⊕ http://www.vangseter.no

Quit smoking (*Røykeavvenning*) The National Council on Smoking and Health ☞ **anti smoking**, operates a helpline freephone ℗ 80040085 and publishes various aids, such as 10 and 12-day diaries to help smokers quit, in Norwegian only. Pharmacies (*apotek*) stock several types and brands of quit-smoking preparations, such as *Nicorette* nicotine chewing gum intended to replace cigarettes and thereby ease withdrawal from smoking.

The smoking law (*Røykeloven*) and its related regulations are intended to limit the damages to health caused by the smoking, snuffing, sucking or chewing of tobacco products. The principal provisions are:

- Advertising is banned, both direct – as for tobacco products, pipes, cigarette papers and cigarette rollers – and indirect, as for other products bearing the brand names of tobacco products.
- Health warnings are obligatory on packaging as well as are concise statements of the tar and nicotine yield of cigarettes.
- The minimum age for buying tobacco products

is 18.
- Vending machine sale of tobacco products is prohibited.
- No smoking on public transport vehicles or in facilities for public use, such as cinemas, theatres, shops, public offices and schools.
- No smoking in at least half the seats in an eating place.
- No smoking in areas of workplaces frequented by many persons, including public service facilities, rooms where two or more persons work and all corridors, stairwells, toilets and lifts.

The relevant law is the Act Relating to Prevention of the Harmful Effects of Tobacco (*Lov om vern mot tobakkskader*), enacted 9 March 1973, no. 14. It is available in print and on-line, in the original Norwegian and in English translation, from many sources, including the ☞ **translated laws** (Laws, Lawyers, Courts chapter) and the National Council on Smoking and Health, ☞ **anti smoking**.

Temperance organisations (*Avholds organisasjoner*) The Norwegian Temperance Alliance (*Avholdsfolkets Landsråd*) is the Norwegian member of Eurocare, the international advocacy for the prevention of alcohol-related harm in Europe. It is the co-ordinating body for 16 temperance organisations in the country, including affiliates of the ☞ **IOGT** (Organisations, Societies, Clubs chapter). The Alliance and its member organisations work in accordance with the World Health Organisation European Charter on Alcohol and through its own actions and those supported by Eurocare. For further informa-

tion on temperance activities in Norway, contact the Alliance ☏ 23214500, ✆ 23214501, ✉ Torggata 1, 0181 Oslo, ✉ al@avhold.no,
⊕ http://www.avhold.no for temperance affairs and ⊕ http://www.alkoholfornuft.org for all matters related to alcohol consumption. For information on international activities in Europe, contact Eurocare ☏ +44 1480466766, ✆ +44 1480497583, ✉ 1 The Quay, St. Ives, Cambridgeshire, PE17 4AR, UK, ✉ eurocare@bbs.eurocare.org,
⊕ http://www.eurocare.org with pages in English and selected topics and downloadable files in French, German, Italian, Portugese and Spanish. In 1999 and with the support of the European Commission, Eurocare and the Confederation of Family Organisations in the European Union (Coface) jointly compiled a report *Alcohol Problems in the Family*, which may be ordered from Eurocare or the Norwegian Temperance Alliance or downloaded in English or French from the Eurocare web site.

Tobacco consumption (*Bruk av tobakk*) is higher than in the other Nordic countries. In 1997, 34% of the adult population were daily smokers, compared to 23% in Denmark, 24% in Finland and 19.3% in Sweden. However, men apparently are quitting smoking more rapidly than women: in 1973, more than half the men and a third of the women, 16 to 74 years old, were daily smokers. Thereafter, smoking declined steadily among men, to 34% daily smokers in 1998, but not among women, 32% in 1998. An additional one adult in ten is an occasional smoker.

Education and Research
(*Utdanning og forskning*)

About education (*Om utdanning*)   Norway spends more on education than do most countries, some 7.6% of its gross domestic product (GDP), compared to less than 5% average for the ☞ **OECD** (Government and Social Services chapter). On the average, one resident in five is undergoing some form of education or training and as many are taking adult education courses. The formal education system is similar to that of other European countries and is divided into three levels:

- Primary and lower secondary schools, compulsory for 6 to 16 year-olds
- Upper secondary schools and apprenticeship training programmes, elective for 16 to 19 year-olds
- College and universities, elective and selective, for young adults

The adult education system offers courses parallel to these three levels. Most educational institutions are public; private education is a small yet growing sector. Most teaching is in Norwegian, but primary schools offer mother-tongue instruction for children from other cultures. Some upper secondary schools, colleges and university departments offer courses in other languages, principally English, and, in the far north, in Sámi. These and other facets of education are briefly described in this chapter. For complete details, see one or both of two overview booklets:

- Education (*Utdanning*), one of five booklets in the "For you – an immigrant in Norway" (*Til deg som er innvandrer i Norge*) series published in 1995 by ☞ **The Directorate of Immigration** (Government and Social Services chapter), 50 pages, A5 format, English edition ISBN 82-427-0278-0, Norwegian edition ISBN 82-427-0277-2.
- More Education? (*Mer Utdanning?*), an overview for vocational guidance (*Yrkesorientering*) published by the Directorate of Labour (*Arbeidsdirektoratet*) in 1998, 180 pages, A4 format, English edition number HA0022e, Norwegian edition number HA0022.

These booklets are available for reading at many schools, colleges, universities, public libraries and municipal public services offices. If you wish to order free copies, contact the ☞ **Central information service** (Media and Information chapter).

The Adult Education Association (*Folkeuniversitetet*) is one of the country's leading organisers of adult education. Each year, about 125,000 people sign up for one or more of its 13,000 courses offered by its 162 local departments. There are *Folkeuniversitetet* in all counties of the country. The basic principle is that of the open university in that there are no formal prerequisites for admission. However, *Folkeuniversitetet* also offers courses of formal study at the upper secondary school and college levels. If you are a newly-arrived resident from another country, you may be most interested in the extensive range of courses offered in Norwegian as a second language as well as in other languages. *Folkeuniversitetet* co-operates with the University of Bergen in giving the Norwegian language test (*Norsk språktest*) for those who wish formal certification of fluency in Norwegian, ☞ **Norwegian language instruction** (Language chapter). *Folkeuniversitetet* has the sole right in Norway to give International Certificate Conference (ICC) foreign-language examinations. and acts as the Local Secretary for Cambridge University (UCLES) in holding English examinations under the aegis of the University. For further details and course catalogues, contact the nearest *Folkeuniversitetet* listed in the Pink Pages. Or you may contact the head office in Oslo, *Studieforbundet Folkeuniversitetet* ✆ 22988800, ☏ 22988801, ✉ Christian Kroghs gate 34, 0186 Oslo, ✉ landssekr@sentralt.funorge.no, ☻ http://www.funorge.no with pages in Norwegian and in English.

ANSA is the acronym for the Association of Norwegian Students Abroad, which was founded in 1956 to assist Norwegians who elected to study at colleges and universities in other countries. The choice of a name in English was prophetic, as through the years, more students have studied abroad in English than in any other language. Each year, some 13,000 Norwegians students study abroad at more than 1000 educational institutions in 60 countries worldwide. Consequently, ANSA supports an extensive international education information center at its head office in Oslo, which has a staff of five to handle the some 700 or more inquires that come in every week. The ANSA Membership Department (*Medlemsservice*) deals both in recruiting new members and in providing current members with benefits, which include numerous travel discounts in Norway, inexpensive insurance at home and while studying abroad and a wide range of academic and professional counseling services. ANSA maintains databases on educational institutions abroad and on the current rules for transfer of academic credentials and transcripts and consequently functions as a non-government organisation in matters pertaining to international education. When ANSA was founded, there were few foreign students in the country, so its initial intent was to assist Norwegians who study abroad. But none of its statutes require Norwegian citizenship, so it is open to any resident of the country with a Norwegian upper secondary school or college degree. For further information, contact the ANSA head office in Oslo ✆ 22477600, ☎ 22335177, ✉ Storgata 3, 0155 Oslo, ✉ sentralt@ansa.no, ☞ http://www.ansa.no with pages in Norwegian and in English.

Approval of foreign education (*Godkjenning av utenlandsk utdanning*) in order to continue college or university studies in Norway depends on
*   whether it was taken within the EEA or elsewhere. Within the EEA, the transfer of academic credentials has been eased by numerous agreements and international systems, including the ☞ **ECTS – European Credit Transfer System**.
*   the academic discipline. Some professions may put forth additional requirements, such as fluency in Norwegian being required of school teachers.

These and other details concerning approval of foreign education are available from the offices of admission of colleges and universities. The National Academic Information Centre ☞ **NAIC** has the best overview of current Norwegian and international regulations and practices.

Art schools and academies (*Kunstskoler og kunstakademier*) There are numerous schools of art, of which five offer a two-year curriculum at a level between upper secondary school and national academy. There are three national academies of art. Students at the schools or the academies are eligible for state ☞ **Educational grants and loans**.

Art schools: four of the five schools are private with partial state support, which cuts tuition costs, and one is public.
*   Asker Art School (*Asker Kunstskole*) is a private foundation. It is located in a large, refurbished industrial building about 30 km southwest of Oslo near a greater Oslo area commuter train station ✆ 66796304, ☎ 66796895, ✉ PO Box 4, 1380 Heggedal,
    ☞ http://www.næringsnett.no/bedrift/asker_kunstskole
*   Mølla Art School (*Mølla Kunstskole*) is private and is located in an art centre in downtown Moss, a city southeast of Oslo on the fjord ✆ 69256955, ☎ 69256959, ✉ PO Box 179, 1501 Moss, ☞ http://home.sol.no/~mkunstsk/om
*   Rogaland Art School (*Kunstskole i Rogaland*) is private and is located in Stavanger on the southwest coast of the country ✆ 51893320, ☎ 51893117, ✉ Nedre Dalgt. 4-6, 4013 Stavanger, ✉ krogalan@online.no,
    ☞ http://www.bang.no/kir
*   Nordland Art and Film School (*Nordland Kunst- og Filmskole*) is public and is located at Kabelvåg in the Lofoten islands in Nordland county ✆ 76066360, ☎ 76066366, ✉ PO Box 49, 8310 Kabelvåg, ✉ artfilm@lofotposten.no,
    ☞ http://www.kunstfilm.no
*   Oslo School of Drawing and Painting (*Oslo tegne og maleskole*) is private and is located in downtown Oslo ✆ 22677063, ☎ 22681645, ✉ Alnagaten 11, 0192 Oslo,
    ☞ http://www.tegneogmaleskole.no

Art academies are public and aim to provide students with the qualifications to become professional artists. Teaching is in the form of individual instruction, over a period of up to four years, and exchange programmes are offered between the three academies.
*   National Academy of Fine Arts (*Statens kunstakademi*) is the largest and oldest of the three academies, having been founded in 1909 in Oslo. It has one of the largest libraries of art books in the country and is located near the National Gallery ✆ 22995530, ☎ 22995533, ✉ St. Olavs gate 32, 0166 Oslo, ✉ berit.andresen@khio.no, ☞ http://www.statkunst.no with pages in Norwegian and in English.
*   Trondheim Academy of Fine Art (*Kunstakademiet*

i Trondheim) is part of the faculty of Architecture, Planning and Fine Art at the Norwegian University of Science and Technology ✆ 73597900, ✉ 73597920, ✉ NTNU, 7491 Trondheim, ✉ see web site, ⊕ http://www.kit.ntnu.no with pages in Norwegian and in English.

• Vestlands Art Academy (*Vestlandets Kunstakademi*) is part of the Bergen College of Art and is located in downtown Bergen ✆ 55902560, ✉ 55902570, ✉ C. Sundtsgt. 53, 5004 Bergen, ⊕ http://users.aol.com/ianrsmith/photonet with pages in Norwegian and summaries in English.

The Centre for International University Co-operation (*Senter for internasjonalt universitetssamarbeid – SIU*) manages programmes for international co-operation on behalf of the ☞ **Norwegian Council of Universities**. There are five major programmes:

• **NUFU** is the Norwegian Council of Universities´ Committe for Development Research and Education. NUFU is also a co-operation programme between university institutions in Norway and in developing countries aiming to build up research capacity and competence at the partner institutions in the South.

• **SOCRATES** is the European Community action programme for co-operation in the field of education. SOCRATES facilitates international co-operation at all educational levels from kindergarten to universities through part programmes like COMENIUS (schools), LINGUA (languages) and ERASMUS (higher education). It is applicable to the 15 member countries of the European Union (EU) as well as to three EEA countries, Iceland, Liechtenstein and Norway.

• **Central and Eastern Europe** This programme supports co-operation projects between academic and research institutions in Norway and corresponding institutions in Central and Eastern Europe. Private sector institutions and organisations may also participate. The general purpose of the programme is to build up institutional competence and thereby contribute to secure a democratic and sustainable development of the reformed countries in Central and Eastern Europe. Northwest Russia and the Baltic States are given priority.

• **The NORAD Fellowship Programme** is part of the overall development efforts of ☞ **NORAD** (Government and Social Services chapter). It provides fellowships and scholarships for students from developing countries to study at master level in Norway.

• **NORDPLUS** is the programme for network co-operation and for mobility of university students and faculty members within the Nordic countries. NORDPLUS has the long-term goal of promoting a Nordic educational community.

SIU also acts as a central repository for printed and electronic information on academic education and schools. For instance, it maintains databases of the names, addresses and telecommunications numbers of Norwegian schools and higher education institutions world-wide; it provides search facilities for faculty members seeking contact with peers on other faculties; and it keeps a database of external resources. For further details on SIU or its programmes or services, contact the head office in Bergen ✆ 55546700, ✉ 55546720, ✉ Harald Hårfagres gt 20, 5020 Bergen, ✉ siu@siu.no, ⊕ http://www.siu.no with pages in Norwegian and in English.

Colleges and universities (*Høgskoler og universiteter*) The 12 institutions of higher learning at university level – four universities, six university colleges and two colleges of art – are listed below along with their telephone numbers and post addresses of their offices of admissions. Contact an institution directly for its catalogue and details of its curriculum. Contact ☞ **The Universities and Colleges Admission Service** for application procedures and details. In addition to these 12 institutions, there are ☞ **State colleges** and ☞ **Private colleges**.

Universities
• The University of Oslo (*Universitetet i Oslo*) ✆ 22857844, ✉ PO Box 1148 Blindern, 0137 Oslo.
• The University of Bergen (*Universitetet i Bergen*) ✆ 55584300, ✉ Parkveien 9, 5007 Bergen.
• The Norwegian University of Science and Technology (*Norges teknisk-naturvitenskapelige universitet*) ✆ 73597700, ✉ 7034 Trondheim.
• The University of Tromsø (*Universitetet i Tromsø*) ✆ 77645590, ✉ 9037 Tromsø.

University colleges
• The Norwegian University of Agriculture (*Norges landbrukshøgskole*) ✆ 64947550, ✉ PO Box

5003, 1432 Ås.
- The Oslo College of Architecture (*Arkitekthøgskolen i Oslo*) ☎ 22997000, ✉ PO Box 6768 St. Olavs plass, 0130 Oslo.
- The Norwegian School of Economics and Business Administration (*Norges handelshøgskole*) ☎ 55959595, ✉ Helleveien 30, 5035 Bergen-Sandviken.
- The Norwegian College of Physical Education and Sport (*Norges idrettshøgskole*) ☎ 22185600, ✉ PO Box 4014 Ullevål Stadion, 0806 Oslo.
- The Norwegian College of Music (*Norges musikkhøgskole*) ☎ 23367000, ✉ PO Box 5190 Majorstua, 0302 Oslo.
- The Norwegian College of Veterinary Medicine (*Norges veterinærhøgskole*) ☎ 22964515, ✉ PO Box 8146 Dep, 0033 Oslo.

Colleges of Art
- The Oslo National College of the Arts (*Kunsthøgskolen i Oslo*) ☎ 22995580, ✉ Ullevålsvn. 5, 0165 Oslo.
- The Bergen National College of the Arts (*Kunsthøgskolen i Bergen*) ☎ 55587300, ✉ Strømgt. 1, 5015 Bergen.

In many respects, the studies offered by colleges and universities are similar to those offered elsewhere in Europe. But there's one aspect of Norwegian higher education which undeniably is first in the world: the extent and variety of it available north of the Arctic Circle, where the sun shines 24 hours a day in midsummer and not at all in midwinter. Here there are thriving academic communities at latitudes where there are only barren wastelands in most of the Eurasian continent. So unique are these offerings in the world of education that they comprise an individual entry in this book ☞ **Higher education in Northern Norway**.

Degrees (*Grader*) As in many countries, there are three levels of college and university studies: undergraduate, graduate and doctoral. However, the names of the degrees awarded at the three levels differ in name from those awarded in many countries, in part because many of them are in Latin. The degree of *candidatus magisterii* (literally "candidate school master", it's original purpose), abbreviated *cand.mag.*, is awarded after three and a half to four years of undergraduate studies in history, philosophy, mathematics, natural sciences or social sciences.

Further study, of one and a half or more years, leads to other *cand.* degrees that have suffixes indicating the topic studied: economics (*cand.oecon.*), education (*cand.ed.*), engineering (*siv.ing.*), health sciences (*cand.san.*), humanities (*cand.philol.*), law (*cand.jur.*), mathematics, natural and applied sciences (*cand.scient.*), medicine (*cand.med.*), odontology (*cand.odont.*), pharmacy (*cand.pharm.*), psychology (*cand.psychol.*), social sciences (*cand.polit.*) and theology (*cand.theol.*). The *Magistergrad*, abbreviated *Mag.art.* is similar to a Master's degree and is awarded in some disciplines in the humanities and social sciences. The *Doktorgrad*, abbreviated *Dr.philos.*, is equivalent to the Ph.D. awarded by universities elsewhere and is the highest academic degree. Understandably, the differences in programmes of study from those of other countries combined with the Latin names of degrees have caused increasing difficulties as more and more students transfer their academic credentials between countries. For instance, the engineering degree of *sivilingeniør* (literally "civil engineer" in the original English sense, meaning "non-military"), abbreviated *siv.ing*, is sometimes claimed by holders of it to be equivalent to the Master of Science (M.Sc.) awarded in other countries. However, a holder of a foreign degree of Bachelor of Science (B.Sc.) in engineering from an internationally-recognised university, can, upon application, have it certified as equivalent to *siv.ing.* and thereby be permitted to use that title. Moreover, holders of *siv.ing.* degrees awarded in Norway are advised to equate them to the B.Sc. level when applying for graduate studies abroad. These and similar difficulties led in 1998 to the Minister of Education putting forth a parliamentary proposal that the Latin names of the undergraduate and first-level graduate degrees be dropped in favour of Bachelor and Master.

Distance education (*Fjernundervisning*) involves learning with the teacher and the student(s) physically separated. It includes traditional correspondence courses by post as well as on-line interaction via the Internet. There is no open university, so distance education, particularly of adults, has thrived. Since 1948, it has been regulated by law, and a sector organisation, the ☞ **Norwegian Association for Distance Education (NADE)** promotes and co-ordinates distance education. Both independent organisations and traditional academic institutions offer a variety of courses, as listed below. Most of the courses are in Norwegian, but some are in English and other languages. Contact the organisations or institutions listed for further details. When no general E-Mail address (✉ symbol) is listed, view the web site (✆ symbol) which will have a list of the E-Mail adresses of staff members.

Agruculture
- The Norwegian Agricultural Correspondence College ☎ 23158920, ✉ 23158921, ✉ PO Box 9303 Grønland, 0135 Oslo,
  ✉ post@landbruksforlaget.no,
  ✆ http://www.landbruksforlaget.no

Aviation
- The Correspondence School for Aviation (*Luftfartsbrevskolen – NAK*) ☎ 23102904,
  ✉ 23102901, ✉ PO Box 383 Sentrum, 0102 Oslo, ✉ ifb@nak.no,
  ✆ http://www.nif.idrett.no/luftsport/motor/ifb

Banking
- The Norwegian College of Banking (*BI – Senter for finansutdanning*) ☎ 67545030, ✉ 67540530, ✉ PO Box 580, 1302 Sandvika, ✉ ba@ba.no,
  ✆ http://www.bi.no/ba

Bible studies
- Biblia Distance Education (*Biblia fjernundervisning*) ☎ 22007275, ✉ 22007203, ✉ Sinsenveien 25, 0572 Oslo, ✉ biblia@nlm.no,
  ✆ http://www.nlm.no/biblia

Defence
- The Norwegian Armed Forces Distance Education (*Forsvarets fjernundervisning – FFU*) ☎ 23403886, ✉ 23093502, ✉ Oslo Mil, Akershus, 0015 Oslo, ✉ info@ffu.mil.no,
  ✆ http://www.ffu.mil.no

Diaconal training (nursing, social work, deacons)
- Diakonhjemmet College (*Diakonhjemmets køgskolesenter*) ☎ 22451945, ✉ 22451950, ✉ PO Box 184 Vinderen, 0319 Oslo,
  ✆ http://www.diakonhjemmet.no with pages in Norwegian and in English.

Electrical contracting
- Electrical Sector Development Centre (*Elektrobransjens utviklingssenter – ELBUS*) ☎ 22955650, ✉ 22605006, ✉ PO Box 23 Blindern, 0313 Oslo, ✉ elbus@elbus.no, ✆ http://www.elbus.no

General college, school and vocational studies
- FB Distance Education (*FB Fjernundervisning*) ☎ 22396000, ✉ 22396001, ✉ PO Box 343 Sentrum, 0101 Oslo, ✉ info@fb.no,
  ✆ http://www.fb.no/fb
- NKI Distance Education (*NKI Fjernundervisningen*) ☎ 67588800, ✉ 67530500, ✉ PO Box 111, 1319 Bekkestua, ✉ info@nki.no,
  ✆ http://www.nki.no/fj
- NKI Electronic College (*NKI Nettskolen*) ☎ 67588800, ✆ Hans Burums vei 30, 1357 Bekkestua, ✆ http://www.nettskolen.com with pages and, upon enrollment, on-line courses in Norwegian and in English.
- NKS Distance Education (*NKS Fjernundervisning*) ☎ 22596000 or freephone 80080400, ✉ 22596090, ✉ O Box 5853 Majorstua, 0308 Oslo, ✉ stud.info@nks.no, ✆ http://www.nks.no with pages in Norwegian and summaries in English.

Insurance
- The Norwegian Academy of Insurance (*Forsikringsakademiet*) ☎ 22048660, ✉ 22440079, ✉ PO Box 2555 Solli, 0202 Oslo,
  ✉ firmapost@forsakad.no,
  ✆ http://www.forsakad.no with pages in Norwegian and summaries in English.

Languages
- The Norwegian Language Institute (*Norsk Språkinstitutt – NSI*) ☎ 23100110, ✉ 23100127, ✉ Kongensgt. 9, 1053 Oslo,
  ✉ caisa.lie@online.no,
  ✆ http://www.norsksprakinstitutt.no

Lumber trades
- The Norwegian Lumber School (*Norges Byggskole*) ☎ 63892560, ✉ 63803500, ✉ PO Box 293, 2001 Lillestrøm,
  ✉ norges.byggskole@online.no,
  ✆ http://www.byggskolen.no

Management
- The Norwegian School of Management (*BI Fjernundervisning*) ☎ 67545030, ✉ 67570805, ✉ PO Box 580, 1302 Sandvika,
  ✉ fjernundervisning@bi.no,
  ✆ http://www.bi.no/bifu

Metalworking and woodworking trades
- National Institute of Technology, Distance Education (*TI Fjernundervisning*) ☎ 22865000,

☎ 22204680, ✉ PO Box 2608 St. Hanshaugen, 0131 Oslo, ⊕ http://www.teknologisk.no

Penology

- Prison and Probation Staff Education Centre (*Kriminalomsorgens utdanningssenter – KRUS*) ✆ 22651660, ☎ 22641958, ✉ PO Box 6138 Etterstad, 0602 Oslo, ✉ firmapost@krus.no, ⊕ http://www.krus.no

Plumbing and heating trades

- VVS Distance Education (*VVS Fjernundervisning*) ✆ 22805060, ☎ 22805065, ✉ PO Box 6726 rodeløkka, 0503 Oslo, ✉ vvsfu@vvsfu.no, ⊕ http://www.vvsfu.no

Pulp and paper industry trades

- Institute for Vocational Traning within the Pulp and Paper Industries (*PIL-skolen*) ✆ 23087800, ☎ 23087899, ✉ PO Box 5478 Majorstua, 0305 Oslo, ✉ pil@pil.no, ⊕ http://www.pil.no with Norwegian and English texts on pages.

State college curricula

- Bergen College (*Høgskolen i Bergen*) ✆ 55587500, ☎ 55326407, ✉ Nygårdsgt. 112, 5008 Bergen, ✉ post@hib.no, ⊕ http://www.hib.no with pages in Norwegian and in English.
- Gjøvik College (*Høgskolen i Gjøvik*) ✆ 61135100, ☎ 61135170, ✉ PO Box 191, 2815 Gjøvik, ⊕ http://www.hig.no
- Lillehammer College (*Høgskolen i Lillehammer*) ✆ 61288000, ☎ 61288200, ✉ PO Box 1004, 2626 Lillehammer, ⊕ http://www.hil.no

University studies

- Norwegian University of Science and Technology (*Norges Teknisk-Naturvitenskapelige Universitet – NTNU*) ✆ 73586690, ☎ 73595237, ✉ Studieavdeling, 7491 Trondheim, ⊕ http://www.ntnu.no/etterutdanning with pages in Norwegian and summaries in English.
- University of Bergen (*Univedrsitetet i Bergen, Senter for etter og videreutdanningstilbud – SEVU*) ✆ 55582040, ☎ 55589646, ✉ Universitetet, 5020 Bergen, ✉ sevu@sevu.no, ⊕ http://www.uib.no/sevu
- University of Oslo (*Universitetet i Oslo, Seksjon for etter- og videreutdanning og fjernundervisning – UNIVETT*) ✆ 22856700, ☎ 22854458, ✉ PO Box 1135 Blindern, 0318 Oslo, ✉ fjernu@admin.uio.no, ⊕ http://www.uio.no/sfa/univett

Educational-psychological service (*Pedagogisk-psykologisk tjeneste*) Pupils with learning difficulties have the right to assessment of their needs by the educators and psychologists of the Educational-psychological service (*PP-tjenesten*) associated with each local school department (*skoleetaten*). When *PP-tjenesten* has identified the special needs of a pupil, it prepares a suitable teaching programme in co-operation with the parents and the school. The principal intent is to permit the pupil to take part in the social, educational and cultural community of the school. For further details, contact the local *PP-tjenesten* listed in the Pink Pages.

ECTS – European Credit Transfer System was developed by the European Commission (EC) to provide consistent procedures that ensure recognition of academic qualifications transferred between countries. It includes means of measuring and comparing learning, including uniform guidelines for:

- credits: For normal workloads, 60 ECTS credits represents one year of study, 30 ECTS credits a semester and 20 ECTS credits a trimester. One Norwegian credit point (*vekttall*) is equivalent to three ECTS credits.
- marks: The ECTS Grading Scale of six letters, from A for best through F for failing. University and college faculties translate the Norwegian academic scale of 1 (best) through 6 (failing) to ECTS letters ☞ **Marks**.
- recognition: Specific ECTS courses in international programmes are recognised at all institutions with similar programmes. Many Norwegian colleges and universities offer courses specifically for international students and are accordingly taught in English and marked according to the ECTS Grading Scale.

All universities and most colleges in Norway offer ECTS programmes; contact the international office at the university or college for details.

Educational level (*Utdanningsnivå*) Norway is a well-educated country. Of the 3.5 million persons older than age 16 in the country, more than half have completed upper secondary school and one in five has college or university education. City dwellers tend to be better educated than people who live in rural districts. The greater Oslo area leads the country in the frequency of higher education: more than three residents in ten have college or university degrees, and in suburban Bærum, the number is more than four in ten. MBAs are also more commonplace in Bærum than elsewhere in the country, some 14 for every 1000 inhabitants, whilst in neighbouring Asker, the percentage of chartered engineers is the highest in the country, more than 33 per 1000 inhabitants. Industrial centres understandably lead in certification in the trades: in Årdal, the site of a major primary metals industry, one in six inhabitants is fully qualified in an industrial trade.

Educational grants and loans (*Stipend og lån til utdanning*) are given by the State Educational Loan Fund (*Statens lånekasse for utdanning*, abbreviated *Lånekassen*), an agency of the Ministry of Education and Church Affairs. Each year, the Ministry provides the Loan Fund with detailed regulations on how financial aid is to be administered and allocated. These regulations are published in February-March and come into effect the following August for the next academic year. The Fund is administered from Oslo and has regional offices in Bergen, Stavanger, Tromsø, Trondheim and Østra, and each year it gives a total of some NOK 10 billion in financial support to more than 230,000 upper secondary, college, university and continuing education students. The basic financial aid package is intended to meet a student's needs during a ten-month academic year, and may be supplemented with travel aid or, for studies abroad, a tuition grant. No interest is charged on a loan as long as a student studies and qualifies for support. Interest starts to accumulate after a student completes or interrupts a course of study. Thereafter, the principal and interest on the loan must be repaid in quarterly installments over a period of up to 20 years. Financial support is principally intended for citizens of Norway, but there are provisions for supporting certain categories of students from other countries who have been accepted by Norwegian educational institutions, including political refugees and asylum seekers, immigrants and students from the Nordic countries, from the EEA countries and from developing countries. For further details, contact the nearest *Statens lånekasse for utdanning* offices listed in the Pink Pages or the head office in Oslo ✆ 22726700, ☎ 22642636, ✉ PO Box 195 Økern, 0510 Oslo, ✆ http://ww.lanekassen.no with pages in Norwegian and in English.

Entrance requirements abroad (*Opptakskrav i utlandet*) If you have completed upper secondary school in Norway and wish to study abroad, your approach to application depends on the sort of school you attended and where you wish to study. If you have studied at one of the ☞ **Foreign schools** you will be guided by its relationships with higher education in the country whose curriculum it follows, and the school most likely will have advised you on the opportunities for further study. If you have completed studies at a Norwegian upper secondary school, such as in an ☞ **International baccalaureate** programme, you will need advice in applying for admission and meeting the entrance requirements of colleges and universities abroad. Many upper secondary schools have advisers who deal with international studies. However, ☞ **ANSA** specialises in such matters and arguably is the best single source of information and assistance. If you wish to study in the USA, you will need to take one or more of the ☞ **Standardized tests for study in the USA** which are given in Norway. ANSA also has updated information on these tests.

Eurydice is the Information Network on Education in Europe. Originally set up in 1980, its role is to promote the exchange and the compiling of accurate, comparable information on educational systems and on national educational policies. The 15 member countries of the EU and the three member countries of the EEA participate, and starting in 1996, the Network has been extended to Eastern European countries and to Cyprus. The Network comprises National Units, each of which is a Ministry of Education or its equivalent. The National Unit in Norway is the Eurydice Unit of the Administration Division of the Ministry of Education, Research and Church Affairs (*Kirke-, utdannings- og forskningsdepartementet*) which maintains and updates the Eurydice dossier for Norway ✆ 22247494, ☎ 22242730, ✉ PO Box 8119 Dep, 0032 Oslo. The European Unit of the Network, established by the European Commission, co-ordinates activities and supports comparative studies. Its services and products include the EURYBASE database on educational systems and various comparative documents and studies. For further information, contact the European Unit head office ✆ +32 2 2383011, ☎ +32 2 2306582, ✉ Rue d'Arlon 15, B-1050 Brussels, Belgium, ✆ http://www.eurydice.org.

Folk high schools (*Folkehøgskoler*) are schools for adults, usually 18 and older, in Nordic countries (Denmark, The Faeroes, Finland, Greenland, Iceland, Norway, Sweden and the Åland Islands). The designation "high school" is the best translation into English, but may mislead. The schools are neither "high schools" in the American sense nor colleges (*Hochschule*) in the German sense. They are schools which through their curricula, teaching methods and environments, seek to promote lifetime skills. The schools of each Nordic country have developed to meet its needs, but all share common traits. One is that almost all *folkehøgskoler* are boarding schools, as social interaction at school is seen as a vital part of education. Another is that there is no set curricula that applies to all *folkehøgskoler* or even to groups of them; each school sets its own curricula and schedule of activities and thereby determines its own profile. The concept of *folkehøgskoler* evolved in Denmark in the mid 19th century. It was an age which produced four great men, for which Denmark arguably is most remembered: philosopher Søren Kirkegaard, fairy-tale author Hans Christian Andersen, neoclassical sculptor Bertel Thorvaldsen and clergyman and poet Nikolaj Frederik Severin Grundtvig. It was Grundtvig (1783-1872) whose concepts resulted in the founding in 1844 of the first *folkehøgskole* at Rødding in the northern part of Danish-speaking Slesvig. There are now some 400 *folkehøgskoler* in the Nordic countries. Their activities are co-ordinated by the Nordic Folk High School Council (*Nordisk Folkehøgskoleråd*), which is associated with the European Association for the Education of Adults (EAEA), which has its head office in Barcelona, Spain. There are 83 *folkehøgskoler* in Norway. Most are run by private organisations, foundations, religious denominations and ideological associations, though some are run by county councils and municipalities. In each county, the *folkehøgskoler* are partly supported by state grants, and students may receive scholarships. The customary minimum age for application is 17, though 16 year-olds are occasionally accepted. Each year, some 11,000 students attend a full school year at the country's *folkehøgskoler*, and some 17,000 attend short courses. Overall, six of ten students are women. All *folkehøgskoler* offer general curricula and most offer vocational subjects. There are programmes for the deaf at several *folkehøgskoler*, and one offers special curricula. There is a *folkehøgskole* dedicated to Sámi culture, and two with extensive programmes for retired persons. The principle language of teaching is Norwegian, though many schools offer courses in English and other languages. For a complete catalogue of all 83 *folkehøgskoler* and application details, contact the Information Centre for Folkehøgskolen (*Informasjonskontoret for Folkehøgskolen*) in Oslo ☎ 22416675, 🖷 22415268, ✉ Karl Johans gate 12, 0154 Oslo, 🖃 admin@info-folkehogskolen.no, 🖳 http://www.info-folkehogskolen.no with pages in Norwegian, English and German.

Foreign schools (*Utenlandske skoler*) Many foreign cultural groups and clubs offer courses, often in language and religion, for their expatriate citizens living in Norway. For details, contact the cultural attaché at the relevant embassy. There are private schools that follow the school plans and teach in the languages of other countries. They may be more expensive than Norwegian ☞ **Private schools**, depending on whether or not they receive Norwegian school subsidies or are supported by the school systems of their home countries. There are many schools in the Oslo area, because it is the capital with a diplomatic and large foreign population, and in the Stavanger area, due to the large number of foreigners working in the oil industries there, but there also are schools in Bergen and Trondheim. The schools having upper secondary levels offer the ☞ **International Baccalaureate** programme. Many, but not all of the schools are members of the European Council of International Schools (ECIS), the world's largest association of its sort, with offices in Australia, Spain, the UK and the USA; for addresses and further information, contact the ECIS Secretariat ☎ +44 1730 268244, 🖷 +44 1730 267914, ✉ 21 Lavant Street, Petersfield, Hampshire GU32 3EL, UK, 🖃 ecis@ecis.org, 🖳 http://www.ecis.org

Foreign schools in Bergen

American/British The International School of Bergen is located 3 km form the centre of the city and provides English-language schooling based on US and UK curricula for children age 3 to 16 and now with children from 20 countries ☎ 55287716, 🖷 55271488, ✉ Vilhelm Bjerknesvei 15, 5081 Bergen, 🖃 murison@iosb.gs.hl.no

Foreign schools in Oslo

British The Oslo International School follows

the British school plan and accepts pupils 3 to 19 years old. It is truly the most international school in the country; its pupils come from 40 countries. The school is located at Bekkestua, a suburb of Oslo and school bus service is provided ☎ 67532303, ℻ 67591015, ✉ Gamle Ringeriksvei 53, 1357 Bekkestua, ◉ http://www.home.sol.no/~ois-it

French The French school (*Den franske skole – Lycée Français René Cassin*) is one of 414 schools associated with *l'Agence pour l'Enseignement Français à l'Etranger* (The French School Directorate for Education Abroad) and accepts pupils 3 to 18 years old. About half the pupils are French or part French, a quarter Norwegian and a quarter of other nationalities. English, German, Spanish, Norwegian and Latin are taught as foreign languages. The school is located in the Frogner district of Oslo near many of the embassies ☎ 22443609, ✉ Skovveien 9, 0257 Oslo, ✉ mdupont4@yahoo.com, ◉ http://www.france.no/lycee/lycee-no.

German The German School (*Den tyske skole i Oslo – Max Tau*) follows the German school plan and accepts pupils in kindergarten and the first ten years of school. Pupils of some 12 nationalities attend the school, many of them bicultural. The school is located just north of the downtown sector of the city ☎ 22931220, ℻ 22931230, ✉ Sporveisgaten 2, 0354 Oslo.

Foreign schools in Stavanger

American/British The International School of Stavanger offers curricula leading to an American High-School Diploma, a British General Certificate of Secondary Education (GCSE) and has classes for ages 3 to 19. It has some 600 pupils from 34 countries, which makes it the largest foreign school in the country. It is located in nearby Hafrsfjord ☎ 51559100, ℻ 51552962, ✉ Treskeveien 3, 4043 Stavanger, ✉ intschol@iss.stavanger.rl.no, ◉ http://www.iss.stavanger.rl.no.

British The Stavanger British School offers the National Curriculum for ages 4 to 13 as well as international playgroup programmes for ages 2 to 4 ☎ 51575599, ℻ 51571516, ✉ Gauselbakken 107, 4032 Stavanger.

Dutch The Netherlands School (*Den nederlandske skole*) offers the Dutch school plan for children 4 to 12 years old. It also provides *Nederlandse Taal en Cultuur – NTC* ("Dutch language and culture") classes in Stavanger and in Sandnes for chil-

dren 6 to 16 years old. The school is located at the Tjensvoll primary school ☎ 51872530, ℻ 51872529, ✉ Tjensvollveien 54, 4021 Stavanger.

French The French school (*Den franske skole – Lycée Français*) follows the French school plan and accepts pupils 3 to 18 years old. The school is located in Stavanger ☎ 51533841, ✉ PO Box 370, 4002 Stavanger.

Foreign schools in Trondheim

British The Birralee International School follows the National Curriculum for children age 4 to 13 and adjusts curriculum for children from other countries. It shares facilities with the Kalvskinnet primary school in the centre of the city ☎ 73521644, ℻ 73520375, ✉ Bispegata 9C, 7012 Trondheim, ✉ biralee@online.no, ◉ http://www.wave.no/edu/birralee

Higher education in Northern Norway (*Høgre utdanning i Nord-Norge*) On the map, the northern strip of the country – the counties of Nordland, Troms and Finnmark – seems thin. But the map deceives. Together the three counties cover a land area equal to a third that of Norway and about thrice that of Switzerland, much of it as rugged as that country's famed Alps. Most of Northern Norway (*Nord-Norge*) lies north of the Arctic Circle (*Polarsirkelen*) at 65° 33' north latitude; the southern border of southernmost Nordland county runs almost along the 65th parallel. It's a place of space – the population density is only four persons per square kilometre. Distance travel is mostly by air or sea. But here there are thriving cities and towns, as well as seven state colleges and a university, understandably the world's most northerly institutions of higher education. Moreover, the country's four universities jointly have a facility for arctic studies on the island of Spitzbergen in the high Arctic. The Council for Higher Education in Northern Norway (*Råd for høgre utdanning i Nord-Norge*) co-ordinates the activities of the institutions and acts as a centre for information on education in Northern Norway ☎ 77645743, ℻ 77644900, ✉ University of Tromsø, Department of Studies, 9037 Tromsø, ✉ rhu@adm.uit.no, ◉ http://www.adm.uit.no/rhu. In alphabetical order by their names in English, the eight institutions are:

Bodø College (*Høgskolen i Bodø*) is the largest of the colleges, with about 3,600 students. It has six faculties: business, social sciences, fishery and natural science, humanities, nursing and teacher education ℗ 75517200, ℻ 75517457, ✉ 8049 Bodø, ✉ postmottak@hibo.no, ⊛ http://hibo.no with pages in Norwegian and in English.

Finnmark College (Høyskolen i Finnmark) is located at Alta and consequently is the world's northernmost college. It also has an extension facility in Hammerfest. There are four faculties: business and administration, recreation and culture, teacher training and health services ℗ 78450500, ℻ 78434438, ✉ Forums vei 31, 9509 Alta, ✉ postmottak@hifm.no, ⊛ http://www.hifm.no

Harstad College (Høgskolen i Harstad) was founded in 1983 and now offers 17 programmes of studies of one to three years in duration. There are two faculties: business administration and social sciences, and health and social services. The college is small, with a staff of 90 and about a thousand students, but it co-operates extensively with colleges in other countries ℗ 77058100, ℻ 77058100, ✉ Havnegata 5, 9404 Harstad, ✉ postmottak@hih.no, ⊛ http://www.hih.no with pages in Norwegian and in English.

Narvik College (Høgskolen i Narvik) is the newest college. In 1954, it was founded as an amalgamation of smaller colleges in the city, and in November 1997, it moved all facilities into a new building complex. It also has an extension faculty at Alta. There are seven technical curricula: civil, environmental, electrical, electronics, space technology, mechanical and computer engineering, as well as interior design and nursing ℗ 76966000, ℻ 76966810, ✉ PO Box 385, 8505 Narvik, ✉ postmottak@hin.no, ⊛ http://www.hin.no

Nesna College (Høgskolen i Nesna) is the southernmost of the colleges, just half a degree north of the Arctic Circle. It offers a programme of general studies as well as curricula for pre-school teachers, English, sports, social studies, information technology and natural sciences ℗ 75056770, ℻ 75057900, ✉ 8701 Nesna, ✉ by departments, see web site, ⊛ http://www.hinesna.no with pages in Norwegian and in English.

Saami College (Samisk Høgskole) is one of the world's few colleges specialising in Sámi studies, and consequently is known by the name *Sámi Allaskuvla*. It offers a broad range of studies in Sámi language and culture, as well as traditional college subjects, taught in Sámi ℗ 78487700, ℻ 78487702, ✉ Hánnoluohkká 45, 9520 Kautokeno, ✉ adm@samiskhs.no, ⊛ http://www.samiskhs.no

Tromsø College (Høgskolen i Tromsø), along with the University, make Tromsø a centre of higher education. The College was founded in 1994 and now offers four lines of study, in health studies, the arts, engineering and business and teacher training ℗ 77660300, ℻ 77689956, ✉ Mellomveien 110, 9293 Tromsø, ✉ postmottak@hitos.no, ⊛ http://www.hitos.no

University of Tromsø (Universitetet i Tromsø) is the world's northernmost university. It has five faculties and The College of Fishery Sciences. The faculties are Social Science, Science, Humanities, Medicine and Law. The University supports five centres: The Roald Amundsen Centre for Arctic Research, the Centre for Development and Environmental Studies, the centre for Sámi Studies, the Centre for Women's Studies and Women in Research and the Centre for Teacher Education, Further Education and Distance Education. Moreover, it supports The Tromsø Museum. ℗ 77644000, ℻ 77644900, ✉ 9037 Tromsø, ⊛ http://www.uit.no with pages in Norwegian and in English.

University Courses on Svalbard (Universitetsstudiene på Svalbard) is a private foundation established by the Norwegian government and owned by the country's four universities. It is located in the high Arctic, in the village of Longyearbyen on Spitzbergen Island in the Svalbard archipelago, and offers 35 courses of studies and supports research in arctic topics, including geology, geophysics, biology and technology. It now has about 100 students, about half of whom are from abroad. Consequently, English is the teaching language ℗ 79023300, ℻ 79023301, ✉ PO Box 156, 9171 Longyearbyen, ✉ postmottak@unis.no, ⊛ http://www.unis.no with pages in English only.

Home schooling (Hjemmeundervisning) is on the upswing. Though still at a modest level – some 400 children throughout the country as this book goes to press – current growth amounts to a doubling each year. As elsewhere, religious and ideological convictions differing from the mainstream lie behind the efforts of many families to school their children at home. However, two recent developments have accelerated the trend in Norway. First, the number of ☞ **Schools** is declining steadily as schools become more centralised, which means that some children are no longer schooled near home. Second, education is becoming increasingly efficient and consequently more centrally controlled, as through ☞ **Reform 97**, which some parents find dehumanising. Nonetheless, the rules and regulations concerning schooling are liberal in that ten years of education (*utdanning*) are required, not ten years of schooling (*skolegang*). That difference permits education in the home. As in other countries, home schooling, also called home education, is organised chiefly through liaison between families practising and educators promoting it. For further details, contact the information service supported by educators and families: Education Otherwise – Norway (*Opplysningstjenesten for hjemmeundervisning og skoleutvikling – OTH*) c/o Christian W. Beck ✆ 22371177, ✉ Fjellgt. 25, 0566 Oslo, or c/o Marta B. Straume ✆ 55241797, ✉ Londalsflaten 41, 5267 Indre Arna, OTH Internet ✉ oth@bdd.no, ☻ http://bdd.no/oth in Norwegian with summary in English.

The International Baccalaureate Diploma is a rigorous, two-year, pre-university course of studies, leading to examinations, for upper-secondary school students between 16 and 19. It is based not on the educational system of any one country, but reflects a compromise between the specialisation required in some national systems and the breadth preferred in others. The general objectives of the International Baccalaureate (IB) are to provide the student with a balanced education, to facilitate geographical and cultural mobility, and to promote international understanding through shared academic experience. Since it was founded in the 1960s, the IB Diploma has become a symbol of academic achievement and intellectual promise. Consequently, it has become a recognised asset in gaining admission to prominent colleges and universities throughout the world, which regard it as proof of capability and commitment to learning. Only upper-secondary schools approved by the International Baccalaureate Organisation (IBO) in Geneva, Switzerland, are authorised to offer the IB programme and to present candidates for examination. IBO curriculum and assessment activities are based in Cardiff, Wales, UK. A network of regional offices in Buenos Aires, Geneva, New York and Singapore provides services to member school, assisted by representatives in eight other cities round the world. There are now some 800 member schools in nearly 100 countries, offering IB programmes in English, French or Spanish. In Norway, the IB programme is taught in English at selected upper-secondary (*videregående*) schools throughout the country, as well as at private schools, such as the Oslo International School and the International School of Stavanger ☞ **Private schools**. The IB curriculum comprises:

• One subject from each of six subject groups: 1) First language (including literature), 2) Second language, 3) Humanities, 4) Experimental sciences, 5) Mathematics, 6) Electives in art and design or an additional subject from the first four groups.
• Theory of knowledge (TOK)
• An extended essay of 4000 words
• Creative, action and Service (CAS), creative and social activities

For the details of IB availability near your home, contact the local school department (*skoletaten* under the name of the municipality in the Pink Pages). For information on the global IB programme, contact the nearest of the IBO offices in Amman, Buenos Aires, Cardiff, Geneva, Mexico City, Moscow, Mumbai, Nairobi, New York, Singapore, Stockholm, Sydney and Yokahama. The head office in Geneva provides information on all IB matters ✆ +41 22 791 7740, ☏ +41 22 791 0277, ✉ Route des Morillons 15, CH-1218 Grand-Saconnex, Geneva, Switzerland, ✉ IBHQ@ibo.org, ☻ http://www.ibo.org with complete pages in the three IB languages, English, French and Spanish.

The International Summer School (ISS) at the University of Oslo is a centre for learning in an international context. Since it started in 1947, it has drawn students from more than 150 countries worldwide. It now accepts some 550 students every summer, from the last week of June to the first week of August, for a programme of studies in Norwegian language, Norwegian and Scandinavian literature, folklore, history, history of art, culture and society, politics and international relations and economics. Courses for graduate students and professionals are offered in special education, peace research, international development studies, energy planning and the environment, medical care and health services.

Students earn a minimum of six semester-hour credits and are awarded the School's Certificate of Achievement. There is no tuition fee. Students pay for room, board, registration and their own personal expenses. Some scholarships are available. Each year in November, ISS issues a prospectus for the forthcoming summer, with the details of entry requirements, courses, housing, financial aid and extra-curricular activities. The deadline for application is 1 February. For further information, contact the head office at the University of Oslo ✆ 22856385, ✇ 22854199, ✉ PO Box 3, Blindern, 0303 Oslo, ✉ iss@admin.uio.no, ✇ http://www.uio.no/iss. Applicants living in Canada and the United States may contact the ISS office at Saint Olaf college ✆ +1 507 6463269, ✇ +1 507 6463732, ✉ ISS N. American Branch Office, St. Olaf College, 1520 Saint Olaf Avenue, Northfield, MN 55057-1098, USA, ✉ iss@stolaf.edu.

Marks (*Karakter*) of proficiency are given in schools, colleges and universities, with the exception of primary school (*barneskole*), school years 1–7,

where teachers confer with parents or guardians twice a year but do not record marks. In lower secondary school (*ungdomsskole*), school years 8–10, and upper secondary school (*videregående skole*), school years 11–13, numerical marks on a scale of 6 (best) down to 1 (poorest) are assigned. Lower secondary schools previously used names for marks on a five-level scale: *Særdeles god (S)* "exceptional", *Meget god (M)* "above average", *God (G)* "average", *Nokså god (NG)* "below average" and *Lite god (LG)* "lacking". In the educational reform of 1997, these names for marks were abandoned in steps following school years, such that the outgoing tenth-year pupils of 1999 were the last to whom they were assigned. However, the lowest three name marks, *God (G)*, *Noksa god (NG)* and *Lite god (LG)* are retained for evaluations of neatness and behaviour (*orden og oppførsel*). Colleges and universities also assign numerical marks on a scale of six, but the order is the opposite of that used in schools: 1 is best and 6 is poorest. Numerical marks are averaged and then divided into five rankings, which have names in Latin.

numerical average	abbreviation	full name	translation
1.0 – 1.5	Laud	Laudabilis prae ceteris	"praiseworthy above others" – first-class with special mention
1.6 – 2.5	Laud	Laudabilis	"praiseworthy" – first-class honours
2.6 – 3.2	Haud	Haud illaudabilis	"not without praise" – second-class honours
3.3 – 4.0	Non	Non contemnendus	"worthy of contempt" – third-class
4.1 – 6.0		Immaturus	"imperfect" – failed

The ☞ **ECTS –European Credit Transfer System** has standardised on the ECTS Grading Scale used to transfer college and university marks between countries. It uses the first six letters of the alphabet as marks, A best and F failed. The correspondence between the ECTS Grading Scale and the Norwegian numerical scale vary according to the faculty of a college or university. A typical equivalence used by several college and university faculties is:

numerical average	ECTS scale letter	ECTS scale name
1.0 – 1.4	A	Excellent
1.5 – 2.1	B	Very Good
2.2 – 2.9	C	Good
3.0 – 3.6	D	Satisfactory
3.7 – 4.0	E	Sufficient
4.1 – 6.0	F	Fail

Montessori schools (*Montessoriskolene*) offer education based on the approaches developed by Maria Montessori (1870-1952), the first woman medical doctor in Italy. In her work in Rome at a free clinic for the children of the working class and the poor, she became convinced that intelligence is not rare and that most newly born children have a human potential that only needs to be developed. Accordingly, she involved principles, practices and teaching methods aimed to elicit that inborn potential. The ideas spread, and there now are Montessori schools and foundations world-wide. In Norway, there are four Montessori foundations and 25 Montessori kindergartens and schools. The kindergartens are most numerous, 19 in all. Of them, seven are in Oslo and an additional five in the adjoining suburbs. The remaining six are at Alversund, Baråker, Bergun-Nesttun, Drøbak, Rasta, and Tønsberg. One of the kindergartens at Sandvika, a suburb southwest of Oslo, is an international pre-school. The are six primary schools, three in the greater Oslo area and one each at Baråker, Bergen-Paradis and Drøbak. One of the Oslo schools also offers lower-secondary education. Montessori education is partly state supported, so tuition fees are lower than in many countries where the schools have no state support. For further details, contact the nearest *Montessoriskole* or *Montessoribarnehage* (kindergarten) listed in the Pink Pages. There is no head office for the schools and kindergartens, but the main Norwegian Montessori Foundation (*Norsk Montessoriforbund*) acts as a central facility for Montessori activities in the country ✆ 22681141, 📠 22674029, ✉ Odalsgt. 19, 0658 Oslo, 🖥 http://www.home.sol.no/~montessori.

Music and cultural schools (*Musikk- og kulturskoler*) There are music schools in nearly all of the country's 435 municipalities. Almost all the schools are public (*kommunale musikkskoler*), because the teaching of music is part of general education made available to all children. Music classes differ in three minor respects. They are voluntary, not compulsory as is the classes of primary and lower-secondary schools. They involve minor costs and are not free as is municipal schooling. And they usually are taught in a facility separate from other municipal schools. In Europe, and in fact in the world, only the Netherlands has so comprehensive a programme of music education. Each year, some 5,200 music teachers in music schools throughout the country teach close to 100,000 children. Many municipal music schools also teach other performing arts, such as drama and dance, and consequently are known as "Music and cultural schools" (*Musikk- og kulturskoler*). Admittance to a music school is by application only; there are no prerequisites, auditions or entrance examinations, and all levels are taught, from beginner on. Together, the State and the municipality cover nearly 75% of the costs of a school, leaving parents to pay only about a quarter of the cost of music teaching. Moreover, municipalities offer music school scholarships, usually based on financial need, so all children can attend, regardless of the wealth of their parents. A result of the widespread availability of music teaching is that talent is recognised early and encouraged. This may be one reason why though small, Norway produces many world-class musicians. One of the leading young pianists of the 1990s concert stages is Leif Ove Andsnes, who started his career at the Karmøy Municipal Music School, just as violinist Arve Tellefesen started his the generation before at the Trondheim Municipal Music School. And it may be one reason why Trondheim, Norway is the venue for the Sixth European Youth Music Festival, the first of the 21st century. The European Youth Music Festivals are hosted by the European Music Union (EMU), an alliance of European music schools in 21 countries comprising 120,000 music teachers and more than 3.5 million pupils. The EMU member association in Norway is the Norwegian Council of Schools of Music and Culture (*Norsk Musikk- og Kulturskoleråd – NMoK*). For further information, contact the nearest school, listed in the Pink Pages under the name of the municipality, usually as *Musikkskole*. NMoK periodically publishes the *Musikk & Kultur Guiden* ("Music and Culture Guide"), a 160-page, A5 format book listing all the schools as well as the music academies, festivals, publishers and other organisations, as well as the principal music schools in Denmark and Sweden. For general information as well as the names and addresses of NMoK liaison offices throughout the country, contact the head office ✆ 73562000, 📠 73562001, ✉ Byns vei 60, 7018 Trondheim, 📧 nmok@nmok.no, 🖥 http://www.nmok.no.

NAIC – The National Academic Information

Centre was set up in 1991 with its principal name in English; the Norwegian translation is *Informasjonssenter for Internasjonal utdanning*. NAIC is a part of the Department of International Relations at the University of Oslo and has five key national functions.

- Act as an information centre on international education and academic recognition.
- Advise on the admission of foreign students to Norwegian colleges and universities.
- Respond to enquiries and provide relevant information concerning higher education in Norway.
- Facilitate and co-ordinate the evaluation of individual applications for ☞ **Approval of foreign education**. Receive and review applications for academic recognition and forward them to the appropriate colleges/universities.
- Act as the country's National Academic Recognition Information Centre (NARIC) and European Network of Information Centre (ENIC) within the framework of the European Community (EC), the Council of Europe and the United Nations Educational, Scientific and Cultural Organisation (UNESCO).

For further details, contact NAIC in Oslo ✆ 22858860, ☏ 22858869, ✉ PO Box 1119 Blindern, 0317 Oslo, ✉ NAIC@admin.uio.no, ⊕ http://www.admin.uio.no/sfa/sip/naic with pages in English.

The National Centre for Educational Resources (*Nasjonalt læremiddelsenter – NLS*) is, as its name implies, a central resource facility for educational materials expertise and products. Its principal commitment is to primary and secondary schools. It initiates and supports research into the development of educational resources. It does not compete with commercial textbook publishers, but does approve textbooks published by them for use in schools. Its own publications fill the gaps not covered by commercial publishers. For instance, NLS distributes educational resources for mother-tongue teaching. It also develops teaching aids used in foreign language instruction. Arguably its most widely known service is *Skolenettet* (The School Network) on the Internet, a result of the national commitment to fully exploiting the benefits of information technology (IT) in education and teaching. *Skolenettet* has material for teachers and other educational professionals, school pupils, parents and others concerned with schools ⊕ http://skolenettet.nls.no with pages in Norwegian and pages on selected topics in English, French and German.

NLS co-ordinates Internet resources, including *Skolenettet*, with those of other Nordic countries and with the European Schoolnet (EUN) ⊕ http://www.en.eun.org. NLS maintains a large library of educational resources ✆ 22476500, ☏ 22476551, ✉ Bankplassen 3, 0151 Oslo, open to the public and used by researchers, students, teachers and pupils. NLS has national tasks for primary and lower secondary school libraries. At the international level, NLS supplies data on Norwegian education and educational research to European Council databases and conducts research in specialised education and distance learning. For further information, contact NLS at its head office in Oslo ✆ 22476500, ☏ 22476552, ✉ PO Box 8194 Dep, 0034 Oslo, ✉ nls@nls.no

NORDLIKS is an acronym for *NORDisk Litteratur, Kultur og Språk* (Nordic Literature, Culture and Language) and is a forum for co-operation among universities in Denmark, Finland, the Faeroe Islands, Greenland, Iceland, Norway and Sweden, and for association with Baltic area Universities in Estonia, Latvia and Lithuania as well as in St. Petersberg, Russia. The principal activities include the exchange of faculty members and students the arranging of intensive courses and workshops. In Norway, the Nordic studies departments of the Universities of Bergen, Oslo, Tromsø and Trondheim participate. If you are in Norway and interested in Nordic literature, culture and language, you can contact the Nordliks programme at one of these four universities. Otherwise, information in Norwegian is available at the Nordliks web site maintained by the University of Oslo ⊕ http://www.hf.uio.no/inl/nl

The Norwegian Association for Distance Education (*Norsk Forbund for Fjernundervisning*) plays an active role in promoting and developing distance education. Within the country, it is a consultative and co-operating body for the Ministry of Education, Research and Church Affairs (*Kirke-, utdannings- og forskningsdepartementet*). Internationally, it maintains liaison with several international organisations, including the International Council for Distance Education (ICDE), the European Association for Distance Teaching Universities (EADTU), the Association of European Correspondence Schools (AECS), the European Distance Education Network (EDEN) and the European Federation for Open and Distance Learning (EFODL). Moreover, it is active in a Nordic network of distance education organisations. The combination of national and international activities is reflected in it having both a Norwegian identity – *Norsk Forbund for Fjernundervisning (NFF)* and an English identity – Norwegian Association for Distance Education (NADE), as well as publications and materials in English as well as in Norwegian. Contact the individual ☞ **Distance education** organisations for the specific details of courses and services. Contact NADE/NFF for general or professional information on the distance education sector ✆ 22028160, 🖷 22028161, ✉ Gjerdrums vei 12, 0486 Oslo, ✉ nade@nade-nff.no, 🖳 http://www.nade-nff.no with pages in Norwegian and in English and with links to web sites maintained by international and other national organisations.

The Norwegian Council of Universities (*Det norske Universitetsråd*) is a co-operative and coordinating body for four universities and six university colleges:

- University of Bergen (*Universitetet i Bergen*)
- University of Oslo (*Universitetet i Oslo*)
- University of Tromsø (*Universitetet i Tromsø*)
- Norwegian University of Science and Technology (*Norges teknisk-naturvitenskapelige universite'*), Trondheim
- Norwegian School of Economics and Business Administration (*Norges Handelshøyskole*), Bergen
- Norwegian College of Sport and Physical Education (*Norges idrettshøgskole*) at Oslo
- Norwegian State Academy of Music (*Norges musikkhøgskole*), Oslo
- Norwegian School of Veterinary Science (*Norges veterinærhøgskole*), Oslo
- Agricultural University of Norway (*Norges landbrukshøgskole*), Aas
- Oslo School of Architecture (*Arkitekthøgskolen i Oslo*)

The Council has permanent committees for university research, for university studies and for international co-operation, as well as for selected special topics. The Secretariat in Bergen also includes ☞

The Centre for International University Cooperation. For further details, contact the Council at its head office in Bergen ✆ 55589830, 🖷 55589840, ✉ Harald Hårfagresgt. 17, 5020 Bergen, ✉ ur@uib.no, 🖳 http://www.uib.no/ur.

Private colleges (*Private høgskoler*) There are 25 private colleges with approved curricula. They are listed below by major course of study, along with their telephone numbers and post addresses. Nineteen of the colleges have state support (*statsatilskudd*). Six are completely independent of state support and accordingly are marked (*indep.*).

Anthroposophic education
- Rudolf Steiner College of Education (*Rudolf Steinerhøgskolen*) ✆ 22449565, ✉ Prof. Dahlsgt. 30, 0260 Oslo.

Architecture
- Bergen School of Architecture (*Bergen arkitektskole*) ✆ 55314692, ✉ Sandviksboder 59-61A, 5035 Bergen.

Basic medicine
- Encefalon School of Basic Medicine (*Encefalon*) (*indep.*) ✆ 22180312, ✉ PO Box 3922 Ullevål Hageby, 0806 Oslo.

Christian media, missionary activities and teaching
- Fjellhaug Mission Seminary (*Fjellhaug skoler*) (*indep.*) ✆ 22377090, ✉ Sinsenvn. 15, 0572 Oslo.
- Media College at Gimlekollen Media Centre (*Medieskolen Gimlekollen Mediesenter*) (*indep.*) ✆ 38145000, ✉ PO Box 4100 Kongstård, 4689 Kristiansand.
- Norwegian Missionary College (*Misjonshøgskolen*) ✆ 51516210, ✉ Misjonsvn. 34, 4024 Stavanger.
- Norwegian Teacher Academy for Religion and Education (*Norsk Lærerakademi*) ✆ 55325650, ✉ PO Box 5812, 5812 Bergen.

Dance
- Norwegian College of Ballet (*Den norske Ballethøyskole*) ✆ 22572410, ✉ PO Box 2956 Tøyen, 0608 Oslo.
- College of Eurhythmics (*Den norske Eurytmihøyskole*) ✆ 22443290, ✉ Prof. Dahls gt. 30, 0260 Oslo.

Diaconal activities including nursing
- Norwegian Lutheran Hospital and College

(*Diakonhjemmets høgskolesenter*) ✆ 22451945, ✉ PO Box 184 Vinderen, 0319 Oslo.

- Deaconess Nursing School (*Diakonissehjemmets Høgskole*) ✆ 55575780, ✉ Ulriksdal 10, 5009 Bergen.
- College of Deaconia and Nursing (*Høgskolen for diakoni og sykepleie*) ✆ 22358300, ✉ Lovisenberggt. 15, 0456 Oslo.
- Parish Sisters' Hospital College of Nursing (*Menighetssøsterhjemmets sykepleierhøgskole*) ✆ 22466840, ✉ PO Box 5223 Majorstua, 0303 Oslo.
- Norwegian Deaconia College (*Norsk Diakonihøyskole*) ✆ 22358300, ✉ Lovisenberggt. 15, 0456 Oslo.

Management and marketing
- Norwegian School of Management (*Handelshøgskolen BI*) ✆ 67570500, ✉ PO Box 580, 1302 Sandvika.
- OMH Business School (*Oslo Merkantile Høgskole*) (*indep.*) ✆ 22596000, ✉ PO Box 5853 Majorstua, 0308 Oslo.
- Rogaland School of Management (*Rogaland Markedshøyskole*) (*indep.*) ✆ 51529990, ✉ PO Box 128, 4001 Stavanger.

Music
- Barrat Due's Conservatory of Music (*Barrat Dues Musikkinstitutt*) ✆ 22465878, ✉ Lyder Sagens gt. 2, 0358 Oslo.

Nursing and welfare nursing
- Betanien College of Nursing (*Betanien sykepleierhøgskole*) ✆ 55162000, ✉ Vestlundvn. 19, 5145 Fyllingsdalen.
- Rogaland College of Welfare Nursing (*Rogaland vernepleierhøgskole*) ✆ 51435099, ✉ Nærlandsheimen, 4365 Nærbø.

Polytechnics
- Polytechnical College (*Den Polytekniske Høgskolen*) ✆ 67588800, ✉ PO Box 111, 1319 Bekkestua.

Pre-school teaching
- Queen Maud's Memorial Foundation College of Education for Pre-School Teachers (*Dronning Mauds Minne Høgskole for forskolelærerutdanning*) ✆ 73512477, ✉ Th. Owesens gt. 18, 7044 Trondheim.

Retail trade
- Norwegian School of Trade and Management (*Varehandelens Høyskole*) ✆ 66903555, ✉ PO Box 53, 1371 Asker.

Theology
- Free Faculty of Theology (*Det teologiske menighetsfakultet*) ✆ 22590500, ✉ Gydas vei 4, 0363 Oslo.

Tourism
- Norwegian College of Tourism (*Norsk reiselivshøgskolen*) (*indep.*) ✆ 22889188, ✉ Grensevn. 86C, 0661 Oslo.

Private schools (*Private skoler*) offer an alternative to the public schools. Private schooling began in the nineteenth century, when congregations outside the Church of Norway started their own schools. In 1926, the first of the ☞ **Steiner schools** opened in Oslo. Through the years, lack of financing constrained most private schools and consequently limited the availability of private schooling. Some schools were partly supported by the municipalities in which they were located, but most relied on funding by their founders, such as congregations, or by tuition paid by parents, or by both. Today's situation is far better, arguably due to the efforts of Jens Bjørneboe (1920-1976), an author and Steiner School teacher. In 1955, Bjørneboe published *Jonas*, a novel about a boy wrongly judged unfit by a rigidly authoritarian school system. *Jonas* shook the educational establishment to its very roots and triggered debate that initiated reforms. That process culminated in 1970, with the passing of the Act on Private Schools (*Privatskoleloven*) which not only permitted greater latitude in schooling but also provided 85% state support to schools offering educational alternatives in Norwegian schooling on the basis of religion, ethnic background or teaching methods. Today, there are 209 private schools in the country, with a total of nearly 20,000 pupils. A third of the schools receive state support on the grounds of religion whilst nearly a quarter are supported because they offer alternative teaching methods. For instance, the two largest groups of private schools, the ☞ **Steiner Schools** and the ☞ **Montessori schools**, are state supported and consequently less expensive than corresponding schools in other countries which are not supported. For further information, contact the private school of your choice listed under *Skoler* in the Yellow Pages.

Recognition of foreign education (*Godkjenning av utenlandsk utdanning*) If your education is from another country, you may need to have it recognised, such as if you intend to continue your education or if you need proof of your qualifications in a trade or profession. As in other countries, recognition of upper secondary or higher education obtained abroad involves showing how it relates to the corresponding levels in the national educational system. For a complete overview, see the brochure published by the Ministry of Education, Research and Church Affairs: "Recognition of Foreign Education in Norway: Upper Secondary Education and Higher Education" (English edition, no. F-4051E) or *Godkjenning av utenlandsk utdanning, videregående oppløring og høgre utdanning* (Norwegian edition, no. F-4051), most recently updated May 1998 and available from all educational offices or on-line at ✉ http://www.odin.dep.no/kuf/publ/1998/godkjenning/ with links between the Norwegian and English editions.

Reform 97 One of the principals that guide education is that schools must change to meet the needs of an ever changing society. Consequently, the primary and secondary school system is periodically reformed. The most recent reform took effect on 1 July 1997 and is known as Reform 97 in both Norwegian and English.

Religion classes (*Undervisning i religion*) Religion is a compulsory subject in all schools. Evangelical Lutheranism, the faith of the ☞ **Church of Norway** (Church and Religion chapter), is taught in all public schools and non-sectarian private schools. Accordingly, the subject is entitled Christianity (*kristendom*). Upon parental request, children of other faiths may be excused from Christianity class. The school may then substitute another subject, such as alternative beliefs (*alternativ livsynsorientering*), which deals with religions and beliefs in general and also teaches ethics (*etikk*). If you are of another faith and object to your child being taught Evangelical Lutheranism, you should ask the school about the options offered.

Research institutes (*Forskningsinstitutt*) There are several hundred research institutes and other facilities, most governmental and many in ☞ **colleges and universities**. The principal institutes are listed under *Forskning og utvikling* in the Yellow Pages.

Residence permits for studying in Norway (*Oppholdsstillatelse for utdanning i Norge*) may be granted provided that you
• will be a full-time student during your stay,
• have been admitted as a student to a recognised college or university,
• submit a plan for your studies,
• can support yourself,
• have a place to live,
• return to your country of origin upon completing your studies.

Otherwise, the general rules for ☞ **Residence and work permits** (Arriving, Settling, Leaving chapter) apply. You should request course overviews or catalogues and admission materials from the college or university you will attend; in most cases, you should apply for admission to the ☞ **University and College Admission Service – UCAS**. You may finance your studies by one of the ☞ **Educational grants and loans**. For complete details, see the 20-page booklet entitled *Residence Permits for Studying in Norway*, published by ☞ **The Directorate of Immigration** (Government and Social Services chapter) and available in Norwegian, English, French and Spanish editions (the English edition has ISBN 82-427-0291-8) available at most college and university admissions offices and many public libraries (*folkebibliotek*).

Scholarships (*stipend*) More than 2,000 grants of various sorts are available. Most are awarded on an annual basis and consequently have one application deadline each year, but many are awarded two or more times a year and have a corresponding number of application deadline dates. Notices of most grants along with their application deadlines are published under *Kunngjøring* in the classified advertising section of newspapers, but many are not widely publicised. Fortunately, there is an annual guide to all grants throughout the country: *Legathåndboken* ("Legacy handbook"), published each January and sold by book shops. The current (as this book goes to press) 1999 edition has an ISBN number 82-90571-13-5. In it, available grants are divided into seven major groups: Educational, by Discipline (*fagorientert*), Educational, Geographically Specified (*geografisk begrenset*), Educational, Institution Specific (*lærestedsorientert*), Study Abroad (*utlandet*), Research (*Forskningsstipend*), Social Services (*Sosiale*) and Miscellaneous (*Diverse*). With the exception of the geographically-specified scholarships, which often are for persons hailing from a specific district or town, there seldom are any restrictions on the citizenship of the applicant, although almost all applications require residence. In other words, if you are a foreign national residing in Norway, you may apply for almost any grant, provided you fulfil its stated conditions for applicants. Many grants require application on a form, so always contact the grant administrator before applying.

Schools (*Skoler*) Ten years of basic schooling (*grunnskolen*) are compulsory (*opplæringsplikt*), divided into seven years of primary school (*barneskolen*) and three years of lower-secondary school (*ungdomsskolen*). All children have the right to, but are not required to an additional three years of upper-secondary school (*videregående skolen*). As in most industrialised countries, schools have recently become more centralised: there are now some 4000 primary, lower secondary and upper-secondary schools in the country, down from about 4250 in 1990. Most schools are public, although there are a growing number of ☞ **private schools**, many of them state-supported and consequently inexpensive compared to private schooling in many other countries.

All schools are mixed with boys and girls studying together in the same classes. Primary and lower-secondary schools supply schoolbooks (*skolebøker*), and primary schools supply writing materials (*skrivesaker*). Parents need only supply a school bag (*veske*) or knapsack (*ransel*) and a small pencil case (*pennal*), make a packed lunch (*matpakke*) each school day, and ensure that a child has the proper clothing whenever there are lessons in physical education (*kroppsøving*), including swimming (*svømming*). In primary school, physical education classes are mixed: boys and girls are together in a class, but have separated changing rooms and showers. Ordinary clothing is worn at school; there are no school uniforms.

One of the overall aims of public schooling is that it should be egalitarian, with equal rights and opportunities for all children. Consequently, children with learning difficulties (*særlige vansker*) and handicapped (*funksjonshemmede*) children have the same right and obligation to schooling as do other children, and to the extent possible for each child, are integrated (*integrert*) in ordinary classes through special programs provided by the ☞ **Educational-psychological ser-**

vice. Likewise, classes are not divided by ability, and there is no ☞ **streaming** in public schools.

Children usually attend the school nearest home. If you have school-age children and settle in a municipality (*kommune*), you should contact the local school department (*skoletaten* under the name of the municipality in the Pink Pages) to enrol them. If a child does not speak or understand Norwegian, notify the school department who can arrange for ☞ **mother tongue education** (Language chapter) and enrol the child in classes for Norwegian as a second language (*Norsk som andrespråk*). During the school year, you should notify the school whenever you must keep a child at home due to illness or injury or whenever a child cannot participate in physical education or other outdoor activities. Apply for permission in advance if you intend to travel abroad and take a child with you. Be sure to notify the school department if your child moves to another municipality, to another school district within a municipality or out of the country, so its name may be taken off the school roll.

School year schedule (*Skolerute*) The school year starts the latter half of August and finishes before midsummer day in late June. In that period, there are 38 weeks of school and six weeks of holidays, including an autumn holiday (*høstferie*), Christmas holiday (*juleferie*), winter holiday (*vinterferie*) and Easter holiday (*påskeferie*). The summer holiday lasts eight weeks. Schools are closed on all public holidays. Most public holidays are included in the holiday weeks, but three are not: two fixed holidays, the 1st of May, Labour Day (*1. mai*) and the 17th of May, Constitution Day (*Grunnlovsdag*), and one variable church holiday, Ascension Day (*Kristi himmelfartsdag*).

Science parks (*Forskningsparker*) are areas of land devoted to research and development or to enterprises connected with the physical sciences. More than 350 companies and scientific organisations have facilities in science parks, of which there are nine in the country: one in Aas Science Park (*Forskningsparken i Ås*); one in Bergen: Bergen High-Technology Center (*Høyteknologisenteret*); one in Kjeller near Oslo: *Campus Kjeller*; one in Oslo: Oslo Research Park (*Forskningsparken*); one in Stavanger: Rogaland Science Park (*Rogaland Forskning*); one in Tromsø: Tromsø Science Park (*Forskningspasrken*); and three in Trondheim: Trondheim Innovation Centre (*Teknostallen*), Leiv Eiriksson Innovation (*Leiv Eiriksson Veksselskap*) and *Nyfotek*. For further information, contact the Science Parks listed (names in italics here) in the Pink Pages, or contact the Norwegian Science Park Association (*Forskningsparkene i Norge – FIN*) ✆ 77679760, 📠 77679750, ✉ c/o Forskningsparken, 9005 Tromsø, ⊕ http://www.fin.no with pages in English and an on-line access to a database of the activities of all the Science Parks.

Social services financial support for students (*økonomisk sosialhjelp i studietiden*) If you need financial aid for your college or university studies, you should apply for one of the ☞ **Educational grants and loans** offered by the State Educational Loan Fund (*Lånekassen*). However, as a student you can receive social assistance in acute situations, both while a student and afterwards, when you repay your student loan. Likewise, in some cases, parents who cannot afford to meet their child's upper secondary school expenses may also receive support. For further details, contact the social security office (*Trygdekontor*) in the municipality (*kommune*) where you reside and accordingly are registered with the National Register (*Folkeregister*).

Space-related activities (*Romvirksomhet*) are more extensive than meets the eye, principally because being a small country, Norway is not active in space ventures that gain international media attention. Nonetheless, in some sectors, its space activities are of world rank.

In the commercial sector, Telenor Satellite Services is second in Europe in satellite broadcasting and seventh in the world in satellite communications turnover. Norway has the third greatest investment share in INTELSAT (world's leading communications satellite operator), after the USA and the UK. The satellite communications ground station at Eik on the west coast has more communications traffic than any other station in the global INMARSAT systems. NERA, a telecommunications firm near Oslo, is the world's leader in mobile satellite telephony, with 40% of the market for mobile terminals and half the market for INMARSAT ground earth stations. Alcatel Space Norway (formerly AME Space), a maker of components for electronic circuits on board satellites, is among the world leaders in its field.

Global services are strong. The Tromsø Satellite Station is an integral part of the global COSPAS/SARSAT satellite search and rescue system. It also acquires data from remote sensing satellites and makes them available to national and international users. The SvalSat satellite ground station on Spitzbergen island in the Svalbard archipelago in the Arctic is unique, as no other station in the world is so well located to access data from satellites in polar orbits. The Andøya Rocket Range, located at 69°N latitude, is one of the world's leading facilities for studies of northern lights and other arctic atmospheric phenomena.

Education is another strength. The Andøya Rocket Range is the national centre for space-related education and training, and hosts a variety of courses. The Andøya Space Camp for upper secondary school pupils, under the auspices of the Young Scientists Association, is an example. SAREPTA – The Internet School Forum on Satellites and Environment – features a satellite image bank, with daily updates from the Tromsø Satellite Station, that provides a unique tool for teaching topics related to weather and the environment ⊕ http://www.sarepta.org with pages in English for use by schools world-wide.

Space-related activities in the country are co-ordinated by the Norwegian Space Centre (*Norsk Romsenter*), a foundation that co-operates closely with the Ministry of Trade and Industry and conducts the country's liaison with the European Space Agency (ESA). For further information, contact the head office in Oslo ✆ 22511800, 📠 22511801, ✉ PO Box 113 Skøyen, 0212 Oslo, 📧 space.centre@spacecentre.no, ⊕ http://www.spacecentre.no with pages in English.

State colleges (*Statlige høgskoler*) The 26 state colleges offer semester and year courses in basic and intermediate subjects as well as some major curricula. They also offer two to four year programmes of vocational training, including business administration, engineering, nursing and teaching. Many teach courses in English and, in the north, in Sámi. The colleges are listed below in alphabetical order of their names in English (location town/city listed when not incorporated in name); for addresses, telecom numbers, web site addresses and other details, see the *Søkerhandboka* (Applicant's handbook) published by ☞ **The Universities and Colleges**

Admission Service, or look in the Pink Pages for the town/city where a college is located : Agder College (*Høgskolen i Agder*), Kristiansand, Akershus College (*Høyskolen i Akershus*) at Bekkestua, Bergen College (*Høgskolen i Bergen*), Bodø College (*Høgskolen i Bodø*), Buskerud College (*Høgskolen i Buskerud*) at Kongsberg, Finnmark College (*Høgskolen i Finnmark*) at Alta, Gjøvik College (*Høgskolen i Gjøvik*), Harstad College (*Høyskolen i Harstad*), Hedemark College (*Høgskolen i Hedemark*) at Elverum, Lillehammer College (*Høgskolen i Lillehammer*), Molde College (*Høgskolen i Molde*), Narvik College (*Høyskolen i Narvik*), Nesna College (*Høyskolen i Nesna*), Nord-Trøndelag College (*Høyskolen i Nord-Trøndelag*) at Steinkjer, Oslo College (*Høgskolen i Oslo*), Sámi College (*Sámi allaskuvla/Samisk høgskole*) ast Kautokeino, Sogn og Fjordane *College* (*Høgskolen i Sogn og Fjordane*) at Sogndal, Stavanger College (*Høgskolen i Stavanger*), Stord/Haugesund College (*Høgskolen Stord/Haugesund*) at Rommetveit, Sør-Trøndelag College (*Høgskolen i Sør-Trøndelag*) at Trondheim, Telemark College (*Høgskolen i Telemark*) at Porsgrunn, Tromsø College (*Høgskolen i Tromsø*), Vestfold College (*Høgskolen i Vestfold*) at Tønsberg, Volda College (*Høgskolen i Volda*), Østfold College (*Høyskolen i Østfold*) at Halden, Ålesund College (*Høgskolen i Ålesund*).

Standardised tests for study in the USA If you wish to study at a college or university in the USA, you will be required to take one or more standardised tests, as administered by the Educational Testing Service (ETS) of Princeton, New Jersey, USA during the academic year, from August to June. First, you should obtain the application forms and information from the admissions office of the college or university you wish to attend, and from it determine which tests you must take. If English is not your mother tongue, you will be required to take one or more tests of proficiency in English in addition to the entrance tests. All the ETS tests are arranged and administered in Norway by Test Information of the University of Oslo at Test Centres in Bergen, Oslo, Kristiansand, Trondheim, Tromsø and Ålesund. There are two main types of test:

- Language: Test of English as a Foreign Language (TOEFL), Test of Written English (TWE) and Test of Spoken English (TSE).
- Entrance: Scholastic Aptitude Tests for general

studies (SAT I) and specific studies (SAT II) or American College Test (ACT) for undergraduate studies; Graduate Record Exam (GRE) for most graduate studies and Graduate Management Admission Test (GMAT) for management and business studies.

Test Information, as its name implies, is an information centre. It does not register applicants for examinations. However, it publishes a Bulletin of Information with the details of registration procedure. For further details, contact Test Information at the University of Oslo International Summer School ✆ 22854028, ✇ 22854199, ✉ PO Box 3 Blindern, 0313 Oslo, ✇ http://www.uio.no/iss/test.

Steiner schools (*Steinerskolene*) offer education based on the concepts put forth by Rudolf Steiner (1861-1925), the Austrian philosopher, scientist, artist and educator who inaugurated anthroposophy, the movement to develop cognition and the realisation of spiritual reality. The Steiner schools are part of the educational movement based on Rudolf Steiner's principles. In some countries, the movement is known as Waldorf education, after the first such school founded in 1919 in Germany, for the children of the workers at the Waldorf-Asoria cigarette factory. There are now Steiner or Waldorf schools world-wide; there are anthroposophical societies in many countries and a world head office in Dornach, near Basel, Switzerland. In Norway, there are some 28 Steiner Schools and more than 30 kindergartens throughout the country, located at Asker, Askim, Bergen-Paradis, Bærum, Fredrikstad, Gjøvik, Haugesund, Jevnaker, Klokkarstua, Kristiansand, Lillehammer, Lørenskog, Moss, Nesodden, Nesttun, Oksvoll, Oslo, Ottestad, Stavanger, Tofte, Tromsø, Trondheim, Vestskogen, Ålesund and Ås. Most of them offer primary and lower secondary schooling, whilst two are upper secondary schools. The Rudolf Steiner College (*Rudolf Steinerhøyskolen*) at Oslo offers teacher training. The schools publish *Steinerskolen*, a quarterly magazine. Steiner school education is partly state supported, so tuition fees are lower than in many countries where the schools have no state support. For further details, contact the nearest *Steinerskolen* listed in the Pink Pages or the head office in Oslo ✆ 22445655, ✇ 22444760, ✉ Professor Dahlsgate 30, 0260 Oslo, ✇ http://www.steiner.no

Streaming (*Kursplandeling*) is the practice of dividing pupils in a school into streams according to ability. It involves differentiation (*differensiering*) and grouping by level (*nivågruppering*). Though it is a general principle, it almost always applies to above-average pupils: a school that offers streaming has special measures for gifted children. In 1960, a variety of streaming involving curricula division (*kursplandeling*) was introduced in public secondary schools, first in Bergen and then elsewhere in the country. Three levels were offered in Norwegian, English and mathematics classes, and two levels were offered in German and Science classes. The practice was abandoned in 1974, because it conflicted with the principle of egalitarian public schools. However, some private schools offer streaming.

Transfer to/from a Norwegian school (*Skifte til/fra en norsk skole*) involves transfer of credentials. The procedure involved for primary and lower-secondary schools depends on whether a child moves from another country and seeks admittance (*opptak*) in a Norwegian school or leaves a Norwegian school to move abroad.

Transfer from abroad to a Norwegian school: In general, the school will place a child in a class with pupils of the same age, particularly in primary school, for which there are no marks. Nonetheless, you should bring a certificate of previous schooling, in Norwegian or in English, to submit upon enrolling a child. The school will then send the certificate to the appropriate office of the Ministry of Education for evaluation and approval.

Transfer from Norway to a school abroad: You should notify the school well in advance and request a transcript certificate (*vitnemål*), in English if you will move outside the Nordic countries. The school will then prepare the certificate and have it authorised by the National Education Office (*Statens utdanningskontor*) in the county (*fylke*), so you can take it with you when you leave.

The Universities and Colleges Admission Service – UCAS (*Samordna opptak*) is a centralised service that processes most applications to undergraduate studies at public colleges and universities as well as to some private colleges, some 40 institutions in all. Each year, it processes more than 80,000 applications for some 600 study programmes. The application procedure is simple and straightforward. First, you should obtain a copy of the application form for Admittance to Universities and Colleges (*Søknad om opptak til universiteter og høgskoler*), fill it in, and submit it to UCAS Norway before 15 April or before 1 March for some application groups, including students with foreign secondary education. At UCAS, your application will be registered and then processed along with other applications. Your application will then be forwarded to the relevant colleges or universities, and by 1 June you will be notified accordingly and asked to submit any additional information if needed. You will receive notice by 25 July on the status of your application, and must then respond immediately if you have been admitted. The application forms, as well as the guideline *Søker-handboka* ("Applicant Handbook") are available at upper secondary schools, colleges and universities, and at some municipal offices. For further details, contact UCAS Norway at the University of Oslo ☏ 22858800, ✉ 22858801, ✉ PO Box 1133 Blindern, 0317 Oslo, ✉ postmottak@so.uio.no, ✉ http://www.so.uio.no with pages in Norwegian, English and Sámi.

Vocational training (*Yrkesopplæring*) is provided in a joint effort by the school system and business and industry. Pupils who finish the compulsory ten years of primary and lower-secondary school qualify for three years of full-time vocational training at the upper-secondary level. There are many combinations of formal schooling and on-the-job apprentice training; the most common is "two plus", in which the first two years are at school and the third year is in business or industry. The first school year comprises a broad foundation course (*grunnkurs*) of studies. There are 13 foundation courses, 11 of which lead to qualification in one of 200 recognised trades. The second school year comprises an advanced course, which is more specialised than the foundation course. More than 100 advanced courses are available. The third year consists of on-the-job training as an apprentice (*lærling*). Some trades require a fourth apprentice year. A journeyman (*svenn*) may combine schooling, apprenticeship and, for some trades, test or examination, to attain vocational certification (*svennebrev*). For further information, contact the nearest upper secondary school (*videregående skole*) which offers vocational coursework (*yrkesfaglig utdannelse*) or the Vocational Training Board (*Yrkesopplæringsnemnda*) in the county (*fylke*) in which you live.

Electrical and Electronics Goods
(*Elektriske og Elektoniske Artikle*r)

Appliances or "white goods" (*Hvitevarer*) originally meant larger electrical equipment for household use, but now also include smaller kitchen apparatus. The typical home will have several, such as a coffee mill (*kaffekvern*), cooker/stove (*komfyr*), dishwasher (*oppvaskmaskin*), food processor (*kjøkkenmaskin*), freezer (*fryseboks*), iron (*strykejern*), microwave oven (*mikrobølgeovn*), refrigerator (*kjøleskap*), tumble dryer (*tørketrommel*), vacuum cleaner (*støvsuger*), waffle iron (*vaffeljern*) and washing machine (*vaskemaskin*). As a rule, appliances are not included in housing sales or rentals, though they may be included in furnished rentals. All appliances are made for 220 V or 230 V, 50 Hz ☞ **electricity** (Housekeeping chapter), as is common throughout Europe. Appliances made for other electricity supplies, such as the 110 V, 60 Hz common in North America, will not work without a transformer. And even with a transformer, an appliance with a motor, such as a refrigerator or washing machine, will run more slowly and may seriously overheat. Moreover, as electrical connection regulations differ, a 110 V appliance may be dangerous in use on a 220V circuit. Consequently, it's wise to leave any 110 V 60 Hz appliances behind when you move. In most cases, it's cheaper to leave any larger appliances behind and buy new when you arrive. Most appliances are sold by ☞ **chain stores** (Shopping chapter), which rely on volume sales of internationally traded brands to keep prices low in a highly competitive market. Moreover, many shops sell factory seconds, overstocks and display goods at reduced prices; look for *B-varer* in advertisements and on signs in shops.

Green fee on electrical and electronics goods (*Miljøgebyr på elektriske og elektroniske produkter*) On 1 March 1999, Norway became the first country to levy a green fee on all new electrical appliances, consumer electronics and computers. So consumers now take part of the responsibility for the damages caused by goods they use and discard. In paying a fee upon purchase, you help offset the cost of cleaning up afterwards. The fee, typically from NOK 10 for a cellular telephone, to NOK 100 for a 21 inch or larger TV to NOK 350 for a 400 litre or larger freezer, covers the cost of collection, transportation and safe destruction of discarded products. In destruction, potentially polluting materials are removed and metals and plastics are sorted for recycling. The household appliance, electronics and computer trades co-operate with environmental authorities in the return and recycling program, called *El-Retur*, which consists of two recycling companies. More than 100 companies co-operate in *Hvitevareretur AS* for recycling electrical goods, and more than 350 companies co-operate in *Elektronikkretur AS* for recycling electronics goods. In practice, you now can deliver used appliances, consumer electronics and computers to retail shops or dumps, free of charge, because the costs of handling them have already been paid. The full list of green fees is available on-line at the *El-Retur* web site ☞ http://www.elretur.no

Radio, TV, video and hi-fi (same in Norwegian) are sometimes called *brunvarer* ("brown goods") to distinguish them from *hvitevarer* ("white goods"), which are appliances and kitchen apparatus. You will find shops listed under *Radio og TV* in the Yellow Pages. The market is keenly competitive and sales are frequent, so prices are comparable with and sometimes lower than prices elsewhere in Europe. In comparing prices, check to see if the ☞ **Green fee** is included in the prices stated. If you buy a TV, you must either have a ☞ **TV licence** (Telecommunicatins and Broadcasting chapter) or submit payment for one upon first purchase. If you intend to bring in a TV from abroad, be sure that it complies with the European ☞ **TV standards** (Telecommunications and Broadcasting chapter). Most radio, TV, video and hi-fi goods now are sold by ☞ **chain stores** (Shopping chapter), which rely on volume sales of internationally traded brands to keep prices low. Moreover, many shops sell factory seconds, overstocks and display goods at reduced prices; look for *B-varer* in advertisements and on signs in shops.

Telecommunications equipment (*Telekomutstyr*) for consumers includes all devices which may be connected to telephone lines, such as telephones, telefax terminals, modems and ISDN boards for computers, as well as all wireless equipment, including mobile phones. You will find the names of specialist shops listed under *Telefonapparater og –systemer* in the Yellow Pages. Competition is fierce, particularly for mobile telephones, and sales are frequent. In comparing prices, check to see if the ☞ **Green fee** is included in the prices stated. An item of fixed-line equipment, such as a telephone or telefax terminal, bought in another country may be used only if it meets the requirements of the ☞ **Norwegian Post and Telecommunications Authority** (Telecommunications and Broadcasting chapter). Equipment sold in EEA countries usually will meet the requirements, but equipment sold elsewhere may not comply with the requirements and consequently may not function properly when connected.

Emergencies
(Nødsituasjoner)

Ambulance Services (*ambulanse*) Call 113 in medical emergencies (*medisinsk nødhjelp*) if you need an ambulance immediately. The telephone will be answered by a paramedic who is supported by an ambulance coordinator. If the problem is not acute, but you are not sure what you should do next call the outpatients clinic (*legevakt*), their number can be found in the Pink Pages. The *legevakt* is a 24 hour medical service, they will assess your needs over the telephone and ask you to come to their clinic or arrange for a home visit, ambulance or other specialized service. If you are on a leisure craft (motorboat or sailboat) request help on VHF channel 16.

Drowning (*Drukning*) is one of the leading causes of accidental death. In 1996 the last year for which complete figures are available, there were 114 deaths due to drowning, about a third as many as due to traffic accidents (341), the leading cause of accidental death. The country has a long coastline and a seafaring tradition, and boating is popular, so drowning is a threat for many. Yet bathing and inadvertent falls into water are the leading causes of drowning. Consequently, ☞ **Norwegian People's Aid** (*Non-government Organisations chapter*) supports an extensive programme of preventive measures, including annual bathing awareness actions (*badevettaksjoner*) for children in kindergartens and schools, compiles monthly drowning statistics and publishes brochures on drowning dangers. Moreover, ☞ **Fire brigades** rent out life-jackets, and ☞ **First aid courses** (Health Care chapter) teach artificial respiration, life saving and water safety. The police and ☞ **Rescue services** may search for a drowning victim who cannot be located. And the folklore of centuries of seafaring sometimes helps. In 1998, a conventional search for a teenage boy who had drowned in a lake at the head of the Hardanger Fjord failed and was abandoned. A retired sheriff knew that roosters had long been used in searches for the drowned and had used one to successfully locate a drowned diver in 1984. So he rowed systematically back and forth, with an Italian rooster under a cardboard carton in the centre of the rowboat. After three hours, the rooster began to crow loudly; the sheriff looked around the boat and spotted the drowned boy floating alongside.

Emergency numbers (*Nødtelefon*) are listed in large type in red, blue and yellow coloured backgrounds on the verso (back side of the cover) and page 1 of all Pink and White Pages telephone directories. **Call these numbers in critical situations only.** When you call, speak slowly, particularly if you have yet to speak Norwegian well or must speak in English. Give information in the following order (*gi opplysninger i denne rekkefølge*).
1. Name, address and municipality (*navn, adresse og kommune*)
2. Telephone number from which you call (*Telefonnummer du ringer fra*)
3. Describe the situation (*Beskriv situasjonen*)

    Call 110 for fire and acute pollution (*brann og akutt forurensing*) Should you discover a fire, the first thing to do is close doors, windows and other openings, call the fire brigade and warn anyone else who is in danger. Help anybody in need of it and get away from the source of the flames. Also call 110 if you see acute pollution, as leakage from an oil tank truck damaged in a collision.

    Call 112 for the police and rescue services (*politi og redningssentral*) Call if you are the victim of a violent crime or you have observed a crime. If you see an accident on the road, take control, secure the accident site and use the emergency triangle in your car to warn others.

    Call 113 for medical emergencies, doctor, ambulance (*medisinsk nødhjelp, lege, ambulanse*) When there has been an apparent heart attack or someone is choking, the paramedic answering the telephone will tell you what to do until the ambulance arrives. It is wise to go on a ☞ **First aid course** (Health Care chapter) so you can learn to give aid in medical emergencies.

    When the situation is not critical and you can wait for assistance (*når hjelpen kan vente litt*), call the ordinary eight-digit numbers for *Brann*, *Politi* and *Legevaktsentral* listed on page 2 of the telephone directory.

Fire brigades (*Brannvesen*) Call 110 in an emergency, and the local number listed under *Brannvesen* in the Pink Pages for all other calls. Fire brigades rent out life-jackets to fit people from newborn weight up to 120 kg. Some brigades offer extended services to the community including installation of fire and burglar alarms with direct connection to the fire brigade, security alarms for individuals in the home, lift alarms and technical alarms for registering water leaks and temperature changes in refrigeration rooms and units. There are charges for these additional services. If you inadvertently have locked yourself out of your house or car, the brigade can gain access for you free of charge. As in many other countries, if your cat is stuck up a tree or your hamster down a drainpipe, the brigade will come to your aid.

Helplines (*Hjelpetelefon*) are listed under General Information (*Generell Informasjon*) in the front pages of the Pink and White Pages telephone directories under *Viktige telefonnummer* ("Important telephone numbers") and *Nyttige telefonnummer* ("Useful telephone numbers") as well as under various listings in the ☞ **Yellow Pages** (last chapter). In alphabetical order by their equivalent names in English, the principal help lines are listed below. Three-digit numbers and numbers starting with 8 are countrywide; those starting with 9 are to mobile phones. Calls to freephone numbers (*Grønt nummere*) starting with 800 are free; calls to numbers starting with 810 are at local rates; calls to numbers starting with 820 – 829 involve costs, which usually are stated by the service provided; all other calls are charged at prevailing rates.

Age/senility concern (*Nasjonalforeningen for folkehelse, pårørende telefonen til aldersdemente*) ✆ 81533032.

AIDS helpline (*AIDS Informasjonstelefon*) ✆ 81003200.

Alcoholics Anonymous (*Anonyme alkolikere*) day-round crisis ✆ 91177770; local contact listed under *Viktige telefonnummer*.

Bank/credit card loss/theft reporting (*Bankenes meldingstjeneste*) ✆ 80030250.

Cancer information centre (*Kreftlinjen*) ✆ 81001210.

Casulty clinic (*Legevakten*) local number listed under *Viktige telefonnummer*.

Central governmental information service (*Statens informasjonstjeneste*) ✆ 80030300.

Child care watch (*Barnevernsvakten*) local number listed under *Viktige telefonnummer*.

Children and youth contact (*Barn og unges kontakttelefon*) ✆ 80033321.

Childrens' Ombudsman (*Barneombudet*) ✆ 80031700.

Consumer Council (*Forbrukerrådet*) local number listed under *Forbrukerrådet* in Pink Pages.

Dental emergency clinic (*Tannlegevakt*) local number listed under *Viktige telefonnummer*.

Drug concerned parents (*Narkotikarådgivning og støttetelefon for pårørende*) ✆ 81500205.

Drug concerned relatives counselling (*Veiledningssenteret for stoffmisbrukeres pårørende*) Oslo head office ✆ 22209508.

Enquiries, foreign and maritime telephone and telefax numbers ✆ 181.

Enquiries, Norwegian telephone and telefax numbers ✆ 180.

Herpes information (*Herpes informasjonstelefon*) ✆ 80049066.

Homosexual youth information(*Homofiles ungdomstelefon*) ✆ 81000277.

Incest advice for men (*IFM – Incestsenteret for menn*) Oslo head office ✆ 22424202.

Incest victim support (*Støttesenteret mot incest*) local number listed under *Viktige telefonnummer*.

Intoxicated parents; childrens' counselling (*Tele-Bamsen*) ✆ 80030350.

Men's crisis centre (*Krise/rådgivningstelefonen for menn*) Oslo head office ✆ 22419016.

Mental health counselling (*Mental helses hjelpetelefon*) countrywide ✆ 81003339.

Narcotics Anonymous (*Anonyme narkomane i Norge*) crisis ✆ 90529359.

Narcotics watch (*Tollvesenets narkotikatipstelefon*) ✆ 80031212.

Outdoor recreation information (*Friluftstelefonen*) local number listed under *Nyttige telefonnummer*.

Parents' friend (*Organisasjonen for voksne for barn*) ✆ 81003940.

Pharmicists after hours(*Apotekvakt*) local numbers listed under *Viktige telefonnummer*.

Poison centre (*Giftinformasjonssentralen*) Oslo head office ✆ 22591300.

Post customer services (*Postens kundeservice*) ✆ 81000710.

Pregnancy care (*Alternativ til Abort i Norge*) Oslo head office ✆ 22478000.

Prostitution counselling (*Prostitusjon*) local number listed under *Viktige telefonnummer*.

Psychiatric patient support (AURORA) evenings at Oslo head office ℗ 22410350.

Public transport information (*Ruteopplysningen*) local number listed under *Nyttige telefonnummer*.

Quit smoking (*Røyketelefon*) ℗ 80040085.

Radio and TV interference reporting (*Radiostøykontrollen*) local number listed under *Radiostøykontrollen* in Pink Pages.

Rape crisis centre (*Krisesenteret for mishandlede og voldtatte kvinner*) local number listed under *Viktige telefonnummer*.

Road conditions (*Vegmeldingstjenesten*) day-round ℗ 175.

Samartians (*Kirkens SOS*) ℗ 81533300.

Security alarm (elderly) service (*Trygghetsalarmtjenesten*) local number listed under *Viktige telefonnummer*.

Security services (*Vakttjenester*) including services for homes and private persons: Falken day-round Oslo central ℗ 22232585; Viking ℗ 80032900; other companies and services listed under *Vaktselskaper* in Yellow Pages.

Sexual health (*Telefonen for sexuell helse*) ℗ 81002244.

Sexually abused children counselling (*Nasjonalt ressurssenter for seksuelt misbrukte barn*) Oslo centre 8 am – 3:30 pm at Aker Hospital ℗ 22894400.

Suicide crisis (*OmsorgSenteret*) preventative centre at Sandefjord ℗ 33464290.

Time of day (*Telfonuret*) ℗ 170.

Train schedules and booking (*NSB billettbestilling og ruteopplysning*) ℗ 81500888.

Victim support (*Landsforeningen for voldsofre*) Oslo head office ℗ 22655455.

Weather forecasts (*Værmeldingen*) short-term forecast (*korttidsvarsel*) ℗ 82053000, long-term forecast (*langtidsvarsel*) ℗ 82073000.

Welfare emergencies (*Sosial vakttjeneste*) local number listed under *Viktige telefonnummer*.

Women's aid (Church of Norway) (*Kirkelig ressurssenter for mishandlede kvinner*) Oslo head office ℗ 22548656.

Women's eating disorder counselling (*IKS – Interessegruppa for kvinner med spiseforstyrrelser*) Oslo head office ℗ 22422222.

Youth advice (*SUSS – Senteret for Ungdom, Samliv og Seksualitet*) ℗ 80033866.

Poisoning (*forgifting*) Should a child ingest household cleaning liquids, suspicious mushrooms, touch chemical compounds or be bitten by a snake, the first point of contact is the Poisons Information Centre (*giftinformatjonstelefon*) ℗ 22591300. They will tell you what you need to do next.

Rescue services (air) (*Luftambulanse*) Emergency medical cover using medical helicopters, planes and cars is provided by *Norsk Luftambulanse AS* (NLA), which is a subsidiary of the *Stiftelsen Norsk Luftambulanse* (Norwegian Air Ambulance Foundation), founded in 1977. NLA aims to improve standards of emergency medicine throughout the treatment chain, ensuring that the critically ill receive rapid and skilled assistance, no matter who provides the service, both in Norway and abroad. Great emphasis is placed on training lay people, emergency services personnel, doctors and nurses. NLA also offers industry advice on health and safety for employees working abroad. The Foundation contributes to research and further training in emergency medicine. Funding is by both membership and a grant from the Ministry of Social Affairs. There are 15 bases throughout the country which provide air ambulance services. Not all of them are operated by NLA, but the majority of medical personnel are NLA employees. The Foundation operates an educational subsidiary (*Norsk Luftambulanse Undervisning*) offering courses on Acute First Aid, Specialized First Aid (for industries like construction, chemical production, hotel and electrotechnical), Paramedic training, Pharmacology, Self defence, Survival, CPR and Disaster planning. For further information contact the head office ℗ 64904444, 🖷 64904445, ✉ PO Box 94, 1441 Drøbak.

Rescue services (sea) (*Redningstjeneste*) are coordinated by the Norwegian Lifeboat Association NSSR (*Norsk selskap til skibbrudnes Redning*), which is a nationwide humanitarian organisation that aims to save lives and property at sea. The NSSR was established in 1891 and is financed mainly through members subscription, donations and fundraising campaigns which include an annual lottery and many gaming machines installed in shopping centres, airports and on ferries. The NSSR also receives a grant from the Ministry of Fisheries. Some 113 sea rescue cutters (lifeboats) have been built since the first timber hull sailing boat "Colin Archer" was launched in 1893, this lifeboat is now owned by the Norwegian Maritime Museum in Oslo. Today the NSSR operates more than 30 purpose-built lifeboats stationed along the 2650 kilometre coastline.

A lifeboat's period of duty is 4 weeks during which a continuous 24-hour monitoring service is operated. When a lifeboat is called out, it operates under the local police authorities and rescue actions are directed from one of the main co-ordination centres (HRS Bodø in the North and HRS South Norway near Stavanger). The lifeboats are all equipped with up-to-date communications equipment. They also carry a MOB boat or inflatable, rescue harness, towing lines, pumps, fire extinguishers and diving equipment. There is at least one qualified diver on each lifeboat.

Although the primary purpose of the lifeboats is to provide sea rescue services, when time permits they perform others duties. They help transmit requests for pilots, carry pilots and personnel, post and provisions to manned lighthouses.

The NSSR 'Coastal Patrol' is a 'service package' for leisure boat owners. This includes towing the boat to the nearest port in the event of engine failure, assistance from a diver in the event of propeller snagging, hull leakage or damage, a discount scheme for boat insurance and organized escort convoys across certain exposed stretches of coastal waters from mid-June till mid-August. For further information contact NSSR ✆ 67577777, ✉ 67577750, ✉ Veritasv. 14, 1322 Høvik, ◉ http://www.nssr.no

Entertainment and night life (*Underholdning og natteliv*)

Amusement parks (*Fornøyelsesparker*) offer a variety of summertime entertainment and activities for children and families. They are located throughout the country, and their offerings range from small zoos and rustic activities to bathing pools and apparatus to larger parks, with rides and staged productions, such as at TusenFryd, the country's largest, at the junction of the E6 and E18 motorways just south of Oslo. There are nine larger parks: *Hardanger feriepark* at Kinsarvik ☎ 53663288, *Hulder- og trollparken* at Skaland ☎ 77858864, *Hunderfossen familiepark* at Fåberg ☎ 61277222, *Namsskogan familiepark* at Trones ☎ 74334105, *Skarnes lekeland* at Skarnes ☎ 62961003, *Snilsberg familieparken* at Gaupen ☎ 94365172, *Telemark lekeland* at Skien ☎ 35529293, *Telemark sommarland* at Bø ☎ 35951699 and *TusenFryd & Vikingland* at Vinterbro ☎ 64976401.

Children's theatre (*Barneteater*) is popular throughout the country, and both amateur and professional theatrical groups perform plays for children and youth. Most professional performances are during the Christmas season, and since 1907, the National Theatre in Oslo has had a regular Christmas programme of comedies for children. Plays based on Thorbjørn Egner's children's books, including "When the Robbers Came to Cardamom Town" (*Folk og røvere i kardemmome by*) and "The Animals of Chopping Hill Wood" (*Dyrene i hakkebakkeskogen*) are among the favourites. "Journey to the Christmas Star" (*Reisen til julestjernen*) by Sverre Brandt, with incidental music by Johan Halvorsen was first performed in 1924 and since has become a classic, part of growing up in Norway. Throughout the country, theatres put on *Reisen til julestjernen* at Christmas; the National Theatre has performed it several hundred times through the years. Puppet shows (*dukketeater*) are put on by more than 30 amateur and professional groups, and the *Oslo Nye Dukketeater* at *Frogner Hovedgård* in Oslo offers a year-round programme of puppet shows. Professional children's theatre performances and puppet

shows are advertised in newspapers, along with other entertainment, whilst amateur performances, as by school theatrical groups, usually are locally posted in schools and community centres as well as on supermarket bulletin boards. If you are interested in children's theatre, you may contact the Norwegian Association of Theatre for Children and Young People (*Norsk Barne og Ungdomsteaterforum*) ☎ 22678606, 🖷 22689634, ✉ PO Box 2838 Tøyen, 0608 Oslo. It is affiliated with the ASSITEJ (*Association Internationale du Théâtre pour l'Enfance et la Jeunesse*), or, if you wish, the ASSITEJ head office ☎ +46 86598633, 🖷 +46 86598901, ✉ PO Box 6033, S-12106 Johanneshov, Sweden, ✉ niclas.malmcrona@swipnet.se, ⊕ http://www.assitej.org with pages in English, in French and in Spanish.

Cinema (*Kino*) In all, there are nearly 250 cinemas in the country. The films they show are listed in the entertainment (*underholdning*) section of newspaper classified pages, under *kino* (cinema), or in Oslo and in Stavanger, under *kinematografer*. (In Norwegian, the everyday word *kino* is an abbreviation of *kinematograf*, as in English 'cinema' is an abbreviation of 'cinematograph'.) Until TV became commonplace in the mid 1960s, cinemas had as many as 1000 to 1500 seats, and the average resident visited the cinema five times a year. Thereafter, competition from TV cut cinema attendance; the average resident now visits the cinema 2.5 times a year, slightly more than in other European countries such as France (2.3), Spain (2.2) and the United Kingdom (2.0). Accordingly, cinemas typically now have several smaller theatres, such as Saga in Oslo with six theatres, Filmteatret in Trondheim with nine, Konsertpaleet in Bergen with thirteen and Filmteatret in Stavanger with twelve. Norway is the only country in which the local governments in cities and towns are the leading owners of cinemas; two of three cinemas are owned by the municipalities in which they are located, and together the municipally-owned cinemas account for 90% of the cinema attendance per year. Films shown are classified by the National Board of Film Classification (*Statens Filmtilsyn*) into five viewer age categories, all, seven, eleven, fifteen and eighteen (adult), ☞ **Film and video controls**. Seating in theatres is numbered, and tickets may be bought in advance, usually at the cinemas, or ordered by phone by calling numbers listed along with film adver-tisements in newspapers or under *kino* or *kine-matografer* in the Pink Pages. Showings are at specif-i© times; viewers are not admitted once the showing of a feature film has started, though they may be admitted as the initial advertising films and trailers are being shown. Smoking is not permitted in cinemas or in their foyers. Almost all cinemas have counters sell-ing sweets and refreshment, but not alcoholic drinks. Some cinemas, particularly those located in commu-nity centres (*samfunnshus*), also function as concert halls and live theatres, and their foyers feature spaces for walk-through art and craft exhibitions.

Circus (*Sirkus*) With its roots in ancient Rome, the modern circus is a travelling show featuring animals and feats of human skill and daring. In 1835, Fredrik Barthel started the first circus in Norway, and since then, his family has operated a circus, from 1927 named *Sirkus Benny* after Rudolf Benny Barthel. There are three other circuses in Norway: Agora, Arnado and Merino. Four Danish circuses – Arena, Arli, Ben-neweis (formerly Schumann of Copenhagen) and Flik-Flak – occasionally tour Norway, as does Circus Cikör of Sweden. Many circus acts are performed by foreign artists and are similar to the acts of other cir-cuses in Europe, with the exception that fewer ani-mals are used, in accordance with regulations on animal import. Posters advertising a circus will be posted in prominent places around the city or town the circus will visit, and advertisement will appear in the local newspaper. The circus season is short in step with the short summer. Winters are spent at a fixed home location, practising new routines for the following season. One of the ☞ **Folk high schools** (Education chapter), the *Fjordane Folkehøgskule*, offers courses of instruction in circus arts including acrobatics, juggling, dance, trick cycling, clowning, theatre and language. Contact the school for further details © 57860422, ☎ 57861630, ✉ PO Box 130, 6771 Nordfjordeid, ✉ fjordane.fhs@sf.telia.no, ⊛ http://www.info-folkehogskolen.no/skoler/fjo

Discos (*Diskotek*) The word "disco" originally was an American abbreviation of the French *discothèque* ("record library") and meant a dance hall where records were played by a "disk jockey" (DJ), as opposed to live music played by a band. But now a disco (*diskotek*) may play any sort of music – record-

ed, electronic or synthesised. There are hundreds of discos in the country, of two kinds. Youth clubs, municipal centres and the like often have disco evenings, usually on weekends. These discos will be announced on local bulletin boards and sometimes advertised in local papers. As a rule, they are held in places that serve no alcoholic drink and consequently may be open to younger teenagers. Commercial dis-cos, as listed along with night clubs under *Diskotek og nattklubber* in the Yellow Pages, are entertain-ment businesses, usually open throughout the week. Most serve alcoholic drink, and consequently have a minimum age of 18 to 21 for admittance. Business-es selling and renting disco equipment, lighting, karaoke equipment and disc jockeys are listed under *Diskotekutstyr* in the Yellow Pages.

Film and video controls (*Forskrift om film og videogram*) are exercised by the Norwegian Board of Film Classification (*Statens Filmtilsyn*) in two ways. First, all ordinary cinema films (features, short films and trailers) for public showing are viewed by the Board before release and accordingly classified. There are five viewing age categories, which are list-ed in cinema advertisements:

tillatt for alle universal (permitted for all ages).

7 år seven and upwards; may be viewed by chil-dren of age 4 or more when accompanied by an adult.

11 år, eleven and upwards; may be viewed by children of age 8 or more when accompanied by an adult.

15 år fifteen and upwards; may be viewed by chil-dren of age 12 or more when accompanied by an adult.

18 år eighteen and upwards (adult).

Classification depends on potential harm to the view-er. Banning is rare.

Second, videos are not viewed and classified before release, but must be registered by the Board before they can be sold or rented to the public. Prop-er registration is signified by a small red sticker affixed to the label of a video cassette case. The viewing age classifications that may appear on video labels are set not by the Board, but by the video distributors, following general video industry practice. However, in some cases, the age classifications may be similar to those set by the Board, as on cinema films subse-quently released as videos. In all cases, should the

Board have cause to suspect that the content of a video violates law, it can act to classify and, if necessary, ban it. The legal status of videos for private viewing, such as for videos bought from abroad by mail order, remains less restrictive; only child pornography is forbidden and subject to criminal law. For complete details in Norwegian and English versions, see the *Statens Filmtilsyn* Internet website
⊕ http://www.filmtilsynet.no

Film, TV and video soundtracks (*lyd*) Most cinema films shown, TV films broadcast and videos sold and rented are imported from other countries, so their original soundtracks are in other languages, with English leading by far. The soundtracks of some cartoon films and videos, particularly those for children too young to read, are dubbed in Norwegian (*Norsk tale*). Otherwise, most soundtracks are the originals, and dialogue is subtitled in Norwegian (*Norsk tekst*) at the bottom of the screen. So if you understand English, you can see the latest from Hollywood in its original form and simply ignore the subtitles. However, posters and newspaper listings and advertisements for films and the texts on video cases are in Norwegian. Some titles are translated, so you may need to consult a Norwegian-English dictionary to work back to the title of the original, if it is not listed in parentheses below the Norwegian translation. Norwegian films, of course, have Norwegian soundtracks, except for those with English soundtracks made for festivals abroad, such as the Golden Rose Television Festival held in the spring at Montreux, Switzerland.

Gambling (*Pengespill*) expenditure amounts to about NOK 20 billion a year, or an average of NOK 4,300 per resident. There is no destination gambling; that is, there are no gambling resorts or casinos. All gambling is one of three forms of convenience gambling:

Gambling machines (*spilleautomater*), such as electronic slot machines, video poker machines and the like, located in shopping centres and malls, in petrol stations and on board some ferries. There are some 30,000 in the country, and together they account for more than 41% of all gambling. Most of the machines are operated to generate income for humanitarian organisations, of which the Red Cross leads with some 10,000 machines.

Norwegian Pools (*Norsk Tipping*), so named because it started in 1948 to run football (soccer) pools, is a limited company wholly owned by the State. *Norsk Tipping* now offers seven games, which together account for more than 38% of all gambling, the most of any organisation:
- *Tipping* (the football pools): a weekly game to guess the results of 12 football matches, home team win, guest team win, or draw. The pools are by far the most popular game, accounting for 5% of all gambling, and the overall play rate (per-capita gambling per year) is greater than that of any other country.
- *Oddsen* ("the odds"): a daily quiz based on sport, with bets placed on the probability of certain results.
- *Lotto* (lottery): a weekly game of guessing seven correct numbers out of 34. According to Inter-loto, the international trade organisation, the *Norsk Tipping Lotto* has the world's highest per-capita turnover.
- *Viking Lotto* (Nordic lottery): a weekly game in the five Nordic countries of guessing six correct numbers out of 48.
- *Extra*: a TV-based game of chance broadcast during prime-time viewing on NRK 1 TV every Saturday; players must have a special player card.
- *Flax* ("Chance"): instant scratch tickets, with both year-round and seasonal varieties.
- *Pengelotteriet* ("passive lottery"): a simple, monthly numbers game.

You can play at any of the some 3,500 commission-agents (*kommisjonære*) in the country, of which 3,200 have on-line gaming terminals that accept player cards, valid for a year and sold by the agents.

Norsk Rikstoto ("Norwegian National Bookmakers"), which is jointly owned by the Norwegian Trotting Association (*Det norske Travselskap*) and the Norwegian Jockey Club (*Norsk Jockeyklubb*), operates all betting at the country's 14 trotting tracks and one flat racing track. It offers seven automatic totalisator wagers (*totalisatorspill*):
- *V5*: pick the winners in five races.
- *V75*: pick the winners in seven races, which may be at different tracks.
- *Dagens Dobbel* ("Daily Double"): pick winners in two races.
- *Duo*: pick first and second places in a race.
- *Trippel*: pick first, second and third places in a race.

- *Vinner* ("Winner"): pick the winner of a race.
- *Plass* ("Place"): pick the three best in a race.

You can wager at the tracks on race day or at any of the some 1,000 commission-agents (*klommisjonære*) in the country, of which 200 have on-line totalisator terminals.

Hardanger fiddle (*Hardingfele*) is the native Norwegian violin, named for the first such instrument, made around 1650 in the Hardanger area in the western part of the country. Unlike other members of the violin family, it has four active strings and a set of four sympathetic strings, lying closer to its belly. It is the only surviving member of a scattered, small and now mostly obsolete family of stringed instruments. In late Elizabethan times, English lyra-viols were briefly made with sympathetic strings. In the 18th century, similar instruments, known as *viola d'amour* in French and *Liebesgeige* in G erman, had a short and unimportant musical life in Central Europe. But in Norway, the *gigja* lived on, through its offspring, the *Hardingfele* Music on the *Hardingfele* is like that of no other violin; it is a second sort of fiddle. Nobody knows why it did not slide into oblivion along with its English and Continental cousins, but Norway's relative isolation until the mid 19th century probably contributed to its survival. It was then that Norway began to build the railways which were to foster greater mobility and eventually erode the music traditions of the more fixed peasant societies. But is was also the apex of the romantic era, in which Norwegians sought their national identities in their peasant roots. World-renowned Norwegian concert violinst Ole Bornemann Bull had discovered *Hardingfele* virtuoso Tarjei Augundsson. Known as *Myllarguten*, as his father had been a miller, Augundsson accompanied on concert stages throughout Scandinavia. The effect was far-reaching, as it brought traditional tunes to the cities. To this day, it lives on. The modern *Hardingfele* differs little from the first instrument. Its bridge is almost flat, which permits playing a variety of polyphony, the simultaneous sound of several notes of different pitch. When played, the active strings, usually tuned to A, D, A and E, cause the underlying sympathetic strings, usually tuned to D, E, F sharp and A, to vibrate. The effect can be compared to that of the drone pipes of a bagpipe. The *slåtter* ("peasant dances") that *Myllarguten* popularised were the model for Norwegian

national melody that first gained classical clothing under the pen of composer Edvard Grieg, as in his Opus 72, *Slåter – Norwegian Peasant Dances Arranged for Pianoforte Solo*. Naturally, Grieg's music is popular in Norway, but so are the original peasant melodies. *Spelemenn* (fiddlers) still play, although their national association, *Landslaget for Spelemenn*, is no longer as important as it once was on the cultural scene. But there are regular *spelemenn* contests, and there are frequent radio and TV programs featuring *spelemenn* players. Out in the countryside there are still many of them. And there's a statue of one of them, *Myllarguten*, in the village of Nordagutu in Telemark county.

Jazz is one of the most popular forms of music. There are jazz bands and clubs throughout the country. You can locate them on-line at ⊕ http://www.bgnett.no/nattjazz/Nojazz/info.html with pages in English and links to other jazz sites. For information on jazz throughout the country, contact the Norwegian Jazz Association (*Norsk Jazzforum*) ✆ 22412010, 📠 22412004, ✉ Tollbugt 28, 0157 Oslo, ⊕ http://www.notam.uio.no/nojf with pages in Norwegian and in English. There are many jazz festivals; the four largest have international programmes and accordingly have web sites in Norwegian and English:

Late May, Bergen: Nattjazz ("Night jazz") ✆ 55320976, 📠 55560070, ✉ PO Box 1957 Nordnes, 5817 Bergen,
⊕ http://www.bgnett.no/nattjazz

Late June – early July, Kongsberg Jazz Festivalc 32733166, 📠 32731366, ✉ PO Box 91, 3601 Kongsberg,
⊕ http://www.kongsberg-jazzfestival.no

Mid July: Molde Jazz Festival ✆ 71203150, 📠 71253635, ✉ PO Box 261, 6401 Molde, ⊕ http://www.moldejazz.no

Mid August: Oslo Jazz Festival ✆ 22429120, 📠 22429125, ✉ Tollbugt 28, 0157 Oslo, ✉ info@oslojazz.no, ⊕ http://www.oslojazz.no

Opera is one of the most universal words in music; other terms are translated, but opera is not. Opera lovers worldwide may know that Norway was the country of birth of legendary soprano Kirsten Flagstad (1895-1962) and the setting of just one opera, The Flying Dutchman (*Der Fliegende Hollän-*

der) by Richard Wagner. True cognoscenti will also know that Norway has a relatively young opera, founded in 1958, that now has gained world rank. The Norwegian Opera (Den norske Opera) now has a full programme in season and works with other opera groups throughout the country as well as with the National Ballet (Nasjonalballetten) with which it shares a home state in the Folketeater building in downtown Oslo. A building project has started for a new opera house to be completed in 2007 at Bjørvika, a waterside location similar to that of the Sydney opera house. For further information, contact the Opera ℗ 22427700, ℻ 22427877, ⊠ PO Box 8800 Youngstorget, 0028 Oslo, ✉ info@norskopera.no, ◉ http://www.wit.no/NorskOpera and for tickets ℗ 81544488.

Party entertaining (Selskapelighetet) Are you throwing a party and need anything? Look in the ☞ **Yellow Pages** (chapter). There you can find all you need, from the location (selskapslokaler) to marquees (telt) to caterers (selskapsarrangement og servering) who also can supply tables, chairs, dinner services and cutlery or maybe a motivational after-dinner speaker. Are you at a loss for what to wear? You can rent bunad, the ☞ **folk costumes** (Character, Customs, Country chapter) of Norway, or ball gowns, tuxedos, morning coats, wedding dresses, bridesmaids dresses, christening gowns or fancy dress (selskapsklær).

Symphony orchestras (Symfoniorkestre) are located in larger cities. The oldest is Harmonien, founded in 1765 in Bergen. The Oslo Philharmonic Orchestra (Oslo Filharmoniske Orkester), founded in 1919, is younger but now better known. Under the direction of Mariss Jansons since 1979, the Oslo Philharmonic has gained recognition world-wide for its recordings, concert performances and tours, as well as radio and television appearances. Director Jansons is also known for his directing and conducting with the Philharmonic Orchestras of St. Petersburg, London and Pittsburgh. At home in Oslo, the Philharmonic performs regularly in the Oslo Concert Hall (Konserthuset) and other venues. For further information, contact the Philharmonic office ℗ 22832355, ℻ 22014202, ⊠ PO Box 1607 Vika, 0119 Oslo, ◉ http://www.pluto.no/OFO with pages in Norwegian and text pages also in English.

Theatre (Teater) has long been a national pastime. Indeed, the country's most famous author is Henrik Ibsen, the dramatist known world-wide for the social criticism and symbolism of his plays. There are now professional and amateur theatrical groups in all cities and many larger towns. You will find the professional groups and theatres listed under Teater in the Yellow Pages, and you can contact the amateur groups through the schools, colleges and universities with which they are usually associated. However, you are unlikely to appreciate Norwegian theatre until you become sufficiently fluent in Norwegian to understand what is said on stage.

There is one professional foreign-language theatre, The English Speaking Theatre Oslo (TESTO), which is mainly a theatre in education (TIE) touring company, which also produces plays for the general public in Oslo and other cities. For details, contact TESTO ℗ 22466248, ℻ 22466249, ⊠ Åsavn 11A, 0362 Oslo, ◉ http://home.sol.no/~testo-no/ with pages in English. Otherwise, amateur foreign-language theatrical groups put on plays throughout the country. There are many groups; ☞ **embassies and consulates** (Foreigners chapter) and ☞ **foreign schools** (Education and Research chapter) most likely will know whom to contact for information on their activities.

Zoos (Dyreparker) There is one large zoo, the Kristiansand Zoo and Amusement Park. It covers an area of 60 hectares and features large areas, where animals are free to roam, yet has paths that permit visitors to observe them. It also has amusements, including Cardamom Town (Kardeommme by), based on the children's story of the same name by Torbjørn Egner, and a large pool and bathing area ℗ 38049700, ℻ 38043367, ⊠ 4609 Kardemomme by, ✉ booking@kristiansand-dyrepark.no, ◉ http://www.dyreparken.com with pages in Norwegian and in English. There are also several smaller mini-zoos, each with a few animals, usually in connection with other activities, including Lund's Gartneri at Fredrikstad ℗ 69349266, Namskogen Familiepark at Trones ℗ 74333700, Polar Zoo at Bardu ℗ 77184114 and Vassfaret Bjørnepark at Flå ℗ 32053510.

Family and children
(*Familie og barn*)

Adoption (*adopsjon*) If you are 25-45 years old, of good health and sound financial circumstances and preferably in a stable relationship of two or more years duration, you may apply to adopt a child. Applications for adoption by single parents are considered in special circumstances. Your first point of contact, whether or not you are a Norwegian citizen, should be the Governmental Office for Youth and Adoption (*Statens ungdoms- og adopsjonskontor – SUAK*). Of the 700-900 applications for adoption each year, about 95% are approved. In 1998 1,094 children were adopted, 805 from abroad (31 countries) and 289 from within the country. There are three approved adoption organisations:

- *Adopsjonsforum* ☎ 22557860, ✆ 22446260, ✉ PO Box 2364 Solli, 0201 Oslo
  ⊕ http://www.adopsjonsforum.no with pages in Norwegian, in English and in Spanish.
- Children of the World (*Verdens Barn*) ☎ 22933000, ✆ 22698555, ✉ Bogstadveien 27B, 0355 Oslo, ⊕ http://www.verdensbarn.no
- *InorAdopt* ☎ 38024620, ✆ 38024257, ✉ PO Box 266, 4601 Kristiansand S,
  ⊕ http://www.inoradopt.no

You need to obtain pre-consent for adoption from SUAK, which is then valid for a period of 2 years, with a further one year extension. Usually a child is adopted within one to two years of obtaining pre-consent. As a parent of a new baby or an adopted child you are entitled to a one-time payment which for 1999 is NOK 32,138, in addition if the child is adopted from overseas you are entitled to NOK 22,000. You are also entitled to take adoption leave, details of eligibility and payments are outlined in a brochure, in English, entitled 'Benefits in connection with pregnancy, birth and adoption', which is available from your local benefit office, look under *Trygdekontor* in the Pink Pages. For further details contact the SUAK head office ☎ 22242593, ✆ 22249523, ✉ PO Box 8036 Dep, 0030 Oslo, ⊕ http://www.suak.no with pages in Norwegian and in English.

Age factors (*Aldersgrenser*) A person is considered to be a minor (*mindreårig*) until age 18 and an adult when 21. Otherwise, the principal age factors are:

6 years old: starts school.

7 years old: can be held liable for damages.

12 years old: can express own wishes in matters of personal choice, such as religion; can decide on suitability of adoptive parent(s) required; should, along with parent(s) or guardian(s), be fully informed by doctor of any illness or injury.

13 years old: can start work by taking light, non-hazardous jobs that do not interfere with schooling; must submit tax return for own income.

14 years old: may be an apprentice or take work in connection with schooling; has right to own views in financial matters administered by guardian; allowed to take hunting test; allowed to choose home if parents do not live together.

15 years old: may be arrested and punished for crime; can choose own education; can decide on own to join or leave a religion or other organisation; may accept work that does not interfere with schooling and meets working environment rules; can sign on board a fishing vessel with parent(s) or guardian(s) permission; can hunt small game when accompanied by an adult.

16 years old: mandatory schooling ends; has right to upper secondary schooling; parents no longer receive child allowance; age of consent for having legal heterosexual or homosexual sex with person of own age or older; must have own passport when travelling abroad; may initiate legal proceedings; may hire on board a Norwegian ship; may hunt alone for small game; may own rifle or shotgun.

18 years old: voting age; can have full responsibility for own personal affairs and finances; may buy beer, wine and tobacco; may have hunting licence; eligible for social benefits; has right to continued financial support for education by parents provided that they can afford it and other financing is unavailable; may make out a will.

19 years old: military conscription for men.

20 years old: may buy liquor; may hunt big game.

21 years old: fully adult; all child support services cease; may own a pistol or revolver.

67 years old: retirement, both men and women.

Arranged marriage and forced marriage (*Arrangert ekteskap og tvangsekteskap*) are approaches to marriage in which the partners usually do not choose each other of their own free will.

The first may be inopportune; the second is illegal.

An arranged marriage is one in which parties other than the wife or husband-to-be, such as parents or other family members propose the partners. Arranged marriage is a widespread practice, throughout history and throughout the world, to this day. A form of it practised in Europe is the *mariage de convenance*, or "marriage of convenience", which is contracted or arranged for some advantage, such as money or social position. Either of the proposed partners in an arranged marriage is free to accept or reject the other, so the marriage is entered on the basis of mutual willingness.

Initially, a forced marriage may be similar to an arranged marriage in that a partner is chosen by parties other than the wife or husband-to-be. However, it differs in that there is no opportunity to reject the marriage or the partner chosen. Should a girl or boy object to the marriage or reject the partner chosen, they may be impelled through force, including threats and violence. So at least one of the partners, usually a girl or young woman, is forced into the marriage, sometimes when on holiday with her parents in their home country. Because she has no choice whatsoever and may have been subjected to threats or violence, a forced marriage constitutes a violation of her rights and therefore is illegal according to the Act on Marriage (*Ekteskapsloven*) of June 1991, applicable from January 1995 on. The law allows a woman forced into such a marriage to take legal action to have it annulled.

If you are a woman who has been or is being forced into a marriage, either in Norway or abroad, you may seek advice and counselling at the head office or one of the networks of ☞ **The MiRA Resource Centre** (Non-government Organisations chapter).

Au pair, trainee (*Au pair, praktikant*) If you wish to have someone to help look after your children, you may employ a young person – a Norwegian trainee (*praktikant*) or a foreign *au pair* – to live in your home. Your choice depends in part on your nationality. If both you and your spouse are foreigners in Norway, you may employ either a Norwegian *praktikant* or an *au pair* only from an EU or EFTA country. If either you or your spouse or both are Norwegian citizens, you may employ either a Norwegian *praktikant* or an *au pair* from any other country.

In most cases, a Norwegian *praktikant* will be a young student, often a woman in training to become a kindergarten or nursery teacher. You can find a *praktikant* by contacting the nearest employment office (*Arbeidsformidling* in the Pink Pages) or by advertising in the classified pages of the local newspaper. In employing a Norwegian *praktikant*, you must pay according to the current wage scale and otherwise observe prevailing employment practices; contact the employment office for details. As indicated by the name (from French), an *au pair* is a person who helps with the housework and cares for the children in exchange for room, board and pocket money, usually as a means of learning a language. An au pair from an EU or EFTA can enter the country and stay for three months; thereafter a residence permit and a work permit for the period of employment are required. An *au pair* from outside the EU/EFTA area must apply for a work permit from his/her home country. Work permits are granted for one year at a time, and the maximum stay is two years. The rules for employing an au pair are set forth in ☞ **The Directorate of Immigration** (Government and Social Services chapter) Circular (*Rundskriv*) no. 11/98, sent to all chiefs of police (*politimestere*) in the country and all foreign service facilities abroad (*utenriksstasjoner*). In summary, the person employed as an au pair must be at least 18 and not more than 30 years old and not a direct relative. Your family should consist of a married or cohabiting couple, with or without children, or a single parent with children. A single person does not qualify. Only one au pair is allowed per family. The daily language of your household must be Norwegian and your family should represent Norwegian culture. If one or more members of your family are of foreign origin or citizenship, you cannot employ an au pair from that country. However, exceptions can be made to this rule, provided the family member involved has long been a resident of Norway. You should have daily contact with the au pair. Your terms of employment must be stated in a written contract with the au pair and at least provide for a maximum work day of five hours, and no more than 30 hours a week and every other Sunday off, as well as one evening a week off duty. After 26 weeks of service, an au pair is entitled to a one-week holiday. You must ensure the au pair employment in your home for the entire contract period, provide him/her with a private room and pay a wage of at least NOK 2,500 a month in addition to free lodging and board. For full details, contact the nearest police station (*Politi* in the Pink Pages) or the Directorate of Immigration (*Utlendingsdirektoratet – UDI*) ✆ 67530890, ✉ 67125436. Most families prefer au pairs to commence work either at the beginning of a calendar year or the school year, so start the process a few months ahead of time. You can advertise overseas for an au pair, but it is easier to engage an agency that is in touch with agencies in other countries. Or you can contact The International Au Pair Association (IAPA) for the names, addresses and telecommunications numbers of its member agencies in 31 countries ✆ +45 33339600, ✉ +45 33939676, ✉ Bredgade 25H, DK-1260 Copenhagen K, Denmark, ✉ mailbox@iapa.org, ☞ http://www.iapa.org with pages in English. Note that the IAPA does not arrange au pair placements, but its member agencies do. In all cases, be sure that the agency you engage is approved by the Directorate of Labour (*Arbeidsdirektoratet*), to ensure that you comply with all relevant laws and practices. Four approved agencies are:

- Atlantis Youth Exchange ✆ 22626060, ✉ 22626061, ✉ post@atlantis-u.no, a non-profit organisation; IAPA full member.
- Au Pair and Trainee Agency Norway ✆ 94138657, ✉ 63973560, ✉ Rolf Hofmosgt. 18, 0655 Oslo, ✉ capion@online.no, specialises in au pairs who are youth in training for careers in import/export; IAPA full member.
- Butterfly & Papillon – Norway ✆ 55964028 or 24-hour mobile 95125914, ✉ 55964028, ✉ Gl. Algardsheimsv. 40, 2051 Jessheim, ✉ butterfly@online.no, focuses on au pairs to the Bergen, Oslo and Stavanger areas.

Norsk pratikant-formidling ✆ 66849829, PO Box 800, 5807 Bergen, ✉ PO Box 272, 1379 Nesbru, specialises in Nordic trainees for families in the Oslo area.

Baby equipment (*barneutstyr*) Prams (*barnevogner*) are sturdy and usually well insulated against the cold winters. Some prams are multifunctional and convert to a pushchair/stroller as the child grows up. It may be difficult to catch a glimpse of a baby in a *barnevogn* because they are so well wrapped up. If you peel back the layers one by one you will notice that a warmly dressed baby with a hat on is bundled up in a duvet with draw strings (*sovepose*), they may also be lying on a sheepskin or covered by one. When a child is old enough to sit up, you may see that they sit in a sheepskin-lined sack (*baby-pose*). Some useful words: baby bed (*barneseng*), baby walker (*gåstol*), bassinet (*babykurv*), car seat (*bilsete*), changing table (*stellebord*), crib (*krybbe*), highchair (*barnestol*), playpen (*lekegrind*), pram/carriage (*barnevogn*), pushchair/stroller (*sportsvogn/trillevogn*), scales (*vekt*), umbrella stroller (*klappvogn*).

Babysitters (*Barnevakter*) are usually found by word of mouth. Ask your neighbours or parents of other children at the local kindergarten or school if they know of anyone who might be suitable and what they might charge. If you are recently arrived, a young neighbour girl may knock on your door and ask to take your baby out for a walk; she is called a *passepike* ("minding girl"). For a small charge she will take your baby out for walk in the pram. If you are looking for daytime babysitting on a more regular basis, advertise for a child minder (*dagmamma*) either in the local newspaper or by placing ads on supermarket bulletin boards. You will also find *dagmammas* advertising their services on boards in supermarkets.

Bigamy (*bigami*) is the practice of having two spouses. It is the most frequent form of polygamy, which is having two or more spouses. The person with two spouses, most often a man with two wives, is called a bigamist (same word in Norwegian). Bigamy is illegal in Norway. Moreover, Article 12 of the European Convention on Human Rights states that "Men and women of marriageable age have the right to marry and to found a family, according to the national laws governing the exercise of this right". Consequently, a bigamist living in Norway violates the law, no matter where the multiple marriages took place.

Nonetheless, bigamy exists, particularly among Muslim immigrants. It is practised in several ways. A bigamist may marry a woman abroad and then another in Norway, or marry two abroad or two in Norway. Often, he may divorce his first wife in Norway in order to be able to marry again under Norwegian law, yet regard himself as still married to her according to Islamic tradition. He may have many motives, not least financial, as a divorced woman with young children and no job receives liberal welfare support. Aside from being illegal and offending Norwegian sensibilities, such practices deprive women of their dignity and deny them their individual freedom.

If you are a woman married to a bigamist or if you have had legal problems because of it, you may seek counselling and help from two organisations, the ☞ **MiRA Resource Centre** and the International Centre of the ☞ **Norwegian Red Cross** (Non-government Organisations chapter). MiRA works mostly within the country and at the Nordic level, whilst the Red Cross provides international assistance, such as when women married in Norway have been deprived of their rights when abroad.

If you are a man and are a bigamist or are contemplating bigamy, you should know that you are committing a crime. According to Norwegian law, bigamy is punishable by up to four years in prison or up to six years if you also deceived your second wife into believing that you were single and not already married.

Birth statistics (fødselsstatistikk) In 1997, 59,801 live births were recorded; 30,724 babies were boys and 29,077 were girls; 960 were the result of a multiple birth; 931 were twins and 29 were triplets. Some 41.2% were first-born, 33.3% the second child, 18.7% the third child, 6.7% the fourth child and 0.1% a fifth or more child. In all, 29,133 of the live births were out of wedlock. The average number of live-born children born to a woman of child-bearing age is slowly declining. In 1971-1975, the average woman bore 2.24 children; by 1997, the average had fallen to 1.86.

Burial ground, churchyard (gravlund, kirkegård) Most burial grounds are consecrated by ☞ **The Church of Norway** (Church and Religion chapter). However, any religious denomination or ideological association that is registered and active in a municipality may consecrate a local burial ground or part of it. Contact the clerics of your faith for the details of consecrated burial grounds. You can purchase up to two plots in a burial ground, next to each other or one on top of the other; the funeral director (begravelsesbyrå) will organise this for you. Citizens are given a free plot for 20 years. Thereafter, relatives may retain the plot if they wish

by paying rent to the municipal funeral department (gravferdsetaten in the Pink Pages). Also apply for a permit from them if you wish to have a tombstone. These can be ordered from a monumental mason (gravmonumenter in the Yellow Pages). Most graveyards are well maintained; should you wish for flowers or plants to be put on the grave on special days, you can order the service from gravferdsetaten. On Christmas Eve a candle is lit at the graveside, it is called a gravlys and you can purchase them from the florist and in supermarkets.

Charities (Veldidige organisasjoner) There are many charities, but no laws regulating how they collect money or how the money they collect is to be used. As elsewhere, this situation has been exploited and some ostensible charities have been keener on making money than on serving any cause of public-interest. And as elsewhere, there is a national accrediting body that monitors fund-raising organisations and consequently acts as the public watchdog against abuse of the willingness to give. The Norwegian Control Committee for Fund-raising (Innsamlingskontrollen – IK) was established in 1991 and is state certified for its task. It operates in a manner similar to that of national monitoring agencies in some 20 countries world-wide, all members of the International Committee on Fund-raising Organisations (ICFO). It both certifies charities and monitors their activities to ensure continued good practice. It accredits both one-time collections (enkeltinnsamlinger), such as those to finance aid to specific disaster areas, and established charities that have ongoing collections throughout the year (innsamlingsorganisasjoner). So whenever you consider contributing to a charity, look for a statement of its having been accredited by Innsamlingskontrollen. As this book goes to press, the accredited charities are Amnesty International Norge, Barne i våre hjerter, CARE Norge, Caritas Norge, Delta Internasjonalt KFUK-KFUM, Den norske kreftforening, Det norske baptistsamfunn, Flyktningerådet, Fondet for forsking om muskelsykdommer, FORUT, Kirkens Nødhjelp, Landsforeningen til støtte ved krybbedød, Marys Venner, Miljøstiftelsen Bellona, Nasjonalforeningen for folkehelsen, Norges Blindeforbund, Norges Diabetesforbund, Norges Røde Kors, Norsk Nødhjelp, Norsk Revmatikerforbund, Pastor Strømmes Minnestiftelse, Redd Barna, Redningsselskapet, Rådet for psykisk helse,

Skandinavisk Fjernadopsjon Forening, Stiftelsen Kirkens Bymisjon Oslo, Stiftelsen Norsk Luftambulanse, Stiftelsen Pinsevennenes Evangeliesenter, Stiftelsen Regnskogsfondet, Stiftelsen SOS-Barnebyer Norge, Stiftelsen Vida Nova, U-Landshjelp fra folk til folk, Utviklingsfondet and Verdens Barn.

Child benefit (*Barnetrygd*) is a tax-free benefit paid to the carer of a child under age 16 who is or will be resident in the country for 12 months or more. The carer may be one parent of a couple, a lone parent, a foster parent or a children's home or institution. It is not a social security benefit in the usual sense, but rather a means of compensating for the expenses of providing for children. It does not depend on the income of the carer to whom it is paid. Child benefit is paid monthly, starting one month after the child is born or takes up residence in the country and ceases at the end of the month of its 16th birthday. There are two basic ordinary rates: for the first and second child and for the third and subsequent child. An additional benefit is paid if you live in Finnmark county or the six northernmost municipalities in Nord-Troms. An additional infant benefit is paid for children one to three years old. An extended benefit equal to the rate for one more child than you actually have is paid if you are a widow or widower, are divorced or separated or are a lone parent. Special rules apply within the EEA for children whose providers live in another country. For instance, if you are resident and earn income in Norway and provide for a child living in another EEA country, child benefit will be paid. Likewise, if you are employed in another EEA country and provide for a child in Norway, the child benefit will be paid in that country. The local social security office will notify you and begin paying child benefit for a child born in Norway. Otherwise, you should apply to the social security office to initiate benefits. You also should contact the local social security office for rates, complete details and rules applying to citizens of other countries who take up residence; look under *Trygdekontoret* in the Pink Pages. For further information, see the *Child Benefit* brochure published in Norwegian and in English, last on 1 January 1999, by the National Insurance Administration (*Rikstrygdeverket*), or view the Administration's web site ⊕ http://www.trygdeetaten.no with pages in Norwegian and in English.

Childcare department (*barnevernsnemnd*) is found in each municipality. Its primary function is to help children and young people under the age of 18 who find themselves in difficult situations. They try to ensure acceptable living conditions for children in their own homes. Its staff makes home visits and offer help and advice where necessary. Help may be in the form of placing the child in a day-care centre, finding a place at school or to getting them a job. Help can also come from a support person or financial assistance. If you are aware of children or young people who find themselves in a difficult situation at home, you can voice your concerns to your nearest childcare department. In some situations, the daily care of children under 18 will be assumed by the authorities and where there is evidence of gross negligence, abuse or ill treatment, or the child's mental and physical welfare would suffer by living at home. A county board for social welfare cases (*fylkesnemnd for sosiale saker*) takes the decisions in these cases and a lawyer and an interpreter represent the parents, if required.

Children's games   Most of the traditional children's games played throughout Europe, North America and elsewhere, are played in Norway. In alphabetical order, the most popular games are, with their descriptions in English from the second edition of the complete Oxford English Dictionary:

- Cops and robbers or cops and thieves (*Gjemsel* or *Titt-tei*) play 'police' hunt 'robbers'.
- Cowboys and Indians (*Indianer og hvit*) players imitate the actions of, and especially battles between, cowboys and Indians.
- Follow my leader (*Hermegåsa*) players follow a leader, and each must do what the leader does, or pay forfeit.
- Hide-and-seek (*Gjemsel* or *Titt-tei*) one or more of the players hide, and the rest, at a given signal, set out to find them.
- Hopscotch (*Paradis* or *Hoppe paradis*) a player hops on one foot and drives forward with it a flat stone, fragment of a slate or tile, etc., from one compartment to another of an oblong figure traced out on the ground, so as always to hop over or clear each scotch or line.
- London bridge (*Bro-bro-brille*) a singing game with various actions.
- Marbles (*Klinkekuler*) a number of marbles are

arranged in a ring (or sometimes in a row), from which the players attempt to dislodge them by 'shooting' a marble at them with the finger and thumb.

* Tug of war (*Dragkamp* or *Tautrekking*) a contest between two teams who haul at the opposite ends of a rope, each trying to drag the other over a line marked between them.

Children's rights (*Barn og unges rettigheter*) are ensured in several ways. In January 1991, Norway ratified the United Nations Convention on the Rights of the Child. There is now a Childrens' Ombudsman, one of the three ombudsmen in the Ministry of Children and Family Affairs (*Barne- og familiedepartementet*); the other two are the ☞ **Consumer Ombudsman** (Human Rights, Consumer Rights chapter) and the Equal Status Council (*Likestillingsombudet*) ☞ **Discrimination** (Business and Work chapter). Legislation enacted in 1998 empowered the Childrens' Ombudsman to ensure that the provisions of the UN Convention are observed at all levels and throughout the society of the country. In practice, five basic groups of rights and freedoms (*rettigheter*) are involved: civil (*sivile*), political (*politisk*), financial (*økonomisk*), social (*sosial*) and cultural (*kulturell*). The complete details are given in Norway's initial report to the United Nations Committee on the Rights of the Child, entitled *The Rights of the Child*, Ministry of Children and Family Affairs and Ministry of Foreign Affairs joint publication Q-0827, 1993, 115 pages, A4 format, in Norwegian and English editions. The Childrens' Ombudsman has a contact network of teachers (*Kontaktlærernettverket*) in schools throughout the country. For further details as well as for current news, contact *Barneombudet* ✆ 22242630 and freephone 80031700, 🖷 22249524, ✉ PO Box 8125 Dep, 0032 Oslo, 🌐 http://www.barneombudet.no with pages in Norwegian.

Children's toys (*leketøy*) are sold in toys shops and larger department stores. Like other goods, toys are more expensive than in many other countries. So if you wish, you may find good quality used toys at flea markets (*loppemarked*), usually held in the spring and in the autumn, by school bands (*skolekorps*), church parishes (*menighet*) or other volunteer organisations. Children spend a lot of time out of doors, consequently popular toys are those that can resist the rigours of life outdoors and sports equipment. Some useful names: blocks (*klosser*), boat (*båt*), book (*bok*), bow and arrow (*pil og bue*), building set (*byggesett*), car (*bil*), cassette player (*kassettspiller*), bicycle (*sykkel*), blackboard (*tavle*), crayons (*fargeblyanter*), cash register (*kasseapparat*), doll (*dukke*), doll's pram (*dukkevogn*), doll furniture (*dukkemøbler*), doll's house (*dukkehus*), electric train (*elektrisk tog*), fire engine (*brannbil*), jungle gym (*klatrestativ*), kite (*drage*), marbles (*klinkekuler*), paper (*papir*), glue (*lim*), pencils (*blyanter*), piggy bank (*sparegris*), rattle (*rangle*), rocking horse (*gyngehest*), sandbox (*sandkasse*), scissors (*saks*), scooter (*sparksykkel*), skipping rope (*hoppetau*), sledge (*kjelke, akebrett, fiskekjelke*), slide (*rutsjebane*), soft toys (*kosedyr*), swing (*huske*), tea set (*te servise*), teddy bear (*bamse*), tent (*telt*), tricycle (*trehjulssykkel*), truck (*lastebil*). All the popular, international classical brands like Barbie®, Lego®, Fisher Price®, Playmobile® are sold here too. Toy shops also stock electronic toys like Gameboys and children's CD-roms.

Cohabitation (*Samboerforhold*) is an increasingly popular alternative to ☞ **marriage**. One of its attractions is that it lacks the formal bonds of marriage, yet lets a couple live together as husband and wife. Indeed, nearly half of all children now are born out of wedlock. Cohabiting couples also enjoy other advantages of marriage, such as being entitled to family discounts on airline tickets, provided cohabitation for two years can be proven. However, because it lacks a formal bond, cohabitation is not the legal equivalent of marriage, no matter how long an unmarried couple lives together.

The bond is informal. Unlike marriage and divorce, there are no rules for entering into or terminating a cohabitant relationship.

Financial relationships are not defined, as they are for marriages and for ☞ **registered partnerships**. Cohabitants are considered financially independent, though they may formally agree to share expenses, such as in buying housing.

Parental responsibilities for joint children are not automatic as they are for a married couple. The mother is considered the sole parent unless the couple otherwise notifies the ☞ **National register** (Registration, Rights, Licences chapter).

Adoption is restricted. A cohabitant couple cannot adopt a child, and single-parent adoptions are infrequent.

Inheritance is not automatic as it is for a married couple, though a cohabiting couple may make out individual wills with each other as beneficiaries. The welfare system views cohabitants as single persons, so they are not entitled to the same benefits as are married couples.

Taxation regards cohabitants as single persons who must file individual tax returns. The taxable income and estate of joint children cannot be put on one tax return, but must be shared between the two returns.

Cremation (kremasjon) is more common than burial in the cities. All arrangements can be made by a ☞ **Funeral director**. There are about 20 authorised crematoria (godkjente krematorier) in the country, most in the more densely-populated urban areas. The ashes are stored in a zinc urn because it is biodegradable. Urns are stored in a storeroom at the crematorium and in the summer a simple ceremony is held for the burial of the urn. You may request that you be cremated upon death, provided that you are 15 or older and that you make a written, signed and dated statement of your wish (erklæring om kremasjon). If you wish that your ashes be scattered after cremation, you should apply to the fylkesmann (County governor) of the county (fylke) in which the ashes are to be strewn.

Custody of a child or children (Foreldreansvar) usually is considered to be the mutual responsibility of a married couple. However, custody must be agreed upon in a ☞ **divorce**. The mother is considered the sole parent of a child born to a couple who live in ☞ **cohabitation**, unless the couple otherwise notifies the ☞ **National register** (Registration, Rights, Licences chapter). Parents who disagree on child custody may settle their disagreement in court or by application to the County Governor (Fylkesmann). The ☞ **Child care department** can act to assume custody of children of extremely negligent parents.

Day care centres (barnehager) are mainly run by the municipality (kommune), though some are private (privat). There are four types. Helsdagsbarnehager open from 07.30 until 17.00 five days a week.

Usually for children from 1-5 years old, held in a purpose built location, places can be shared. Familiebarnehager open from 07.45 until 16.15 five days a week, specially for children under 3, usually held in a private home. Halvsdagbarnehager take children 6 hours a day, normally from 09.00 to 15.00 and åpen barnehager where mothers or child minders can join their charges for a few hours per week.

You need to apply for a place, application forms are available from the health station (helsestasjon) where you take your child for their regular check ups, or from the municipality's Child and Youth section (Barn- og ungdomsavdeling). Telephone numbers for both of these are in the Pink Pages under your local municipality. Places are allocated in the spring for up take in August. There may be a waiting list. The municipality sets the cost. There is a rebate for siblings. If you are in a low-income bracket, it is possible to pay reduced rates or even to have a fully subsidised place. Children with special needs, or from single parent families or from families where there is severe illness in the immediate family will usually receive priority for places. ☞ **babysitters** for alternatives to day care centres.

Death (dødsfall) If a death occurs at home, call a doctor (lege) who can issue a death certificate (dødsattest). If a death occurs in a hospital (sykehus), the staff will ensure that a death certificate is issued. Norwegian Foreign Service Stations (utenriksstasjoner) will assist with the details involved in the death of a Norwegian citizen abroad. If a foreigner dies in Norway, his/her passport should be sent to the appropriate embassy and they will issue a form reporting death of a citizen abroad; usually a fee is charged for both the registration and the certificate itself. In most countries, death certificates are necessary to settle estates. The embassy can also recommend ☞ **Funerals directors** who can assist in shipping the deceased's body home, if the family so wishes. This may require special paperwork. Norwegians citizens register death with the local probate office (skifteretten in the Pink Pages) or sheriff's office (lensmannen in the Pink Pages), depending on where they lived. If you are a member of the National Insurance Scheme contact your municipal Social Services Office (sosialkontor) for information concerning widow's (widower's) payments, pensions, death payments. Brochures are available outlining the benefits.

Death notices (*Dødsannonser*) and obituaries (*nekrologer*) are printed in newspapers, usually in a fixed place; in Aftenposten, they appear on the penultimate page of the first section of the morning edition, Monday-Saturday. When a person dies, the family and friends usually insert a death notice within days. It usually is the only notice given, and contains the name of the surviving spouse, children and their spouses, and grandchildren and their spouses, in that order, as well as the details of the ☞ **funeral**. One of the 15 small symbols shown below appears at the top of the notice, to indicate the faith or wishes of the deceased. If the family so wishes, a friend or a colleague may write an obituary, which may appear several days or weeks later.

†   Latin cross (*Latinsk kors*)

☦   Greek Orthodox cross (*Gresk-ortodoks kors*)

☦   Russian cross (*Russisk kors*)

✡   Star of David (*Davidstjernen*)

⁂   Baha'i (*Bahai*)

❧   Flower (*Blomst*)

⚖   Amnesty International

✠   Freemasonry (*Frimurerlosje-emblemet*)

✿   Liturgical rose (*Liturgisk rose*)

⚓   Faith, hope and charity (*Tro, håp og kjærlighet*)

⚘   Human and Ethical Union (*Human-Etisk*)

⚜   Fleur-de-lis (*Fransk lilje*)

🕊   Dove of peace (*Fredsduen*)

○   Eternity (*Evighetssymbol*)

☸   Buddhism (*Buddhisttegn*)

☬   Sikh (*Sikh-symbolet*)

Symbols courtesy of Aftenposten.

Divorce (*skilsmisse*) More than four marriages in ten now end in divorce. That trend is new. At the end of the 1800's there were less than 100 divorces per year. This corresponds to 0.2 divorces per 1,000 married women as compared to 11.3 today. In the early 1930's, the number of divorces rose above 1,000. Since then, it has steadily increased, to 9,982 in 1996, of which 16,044 involved couples with children and 2,053 involved couples without children.

Either one or both persons of a married couple may seek a divorce. First, they must have lived apart for at least two years. Second, for at least one year, they must have had a legal separation (*separasjon*) granted by the County Governor (*fylkesmannen*). A separation is intended to give a couple time to review their marriage before taking the final step of divorcing. It requires that they live apart and be financially independent, but regards them legally to be still married.

If a couple has children less than 16 years old, before applying for a separation, they must partake in arbitration (*mekling*) at a ☞ **family counselling** office to reach agreement concerning custody of the children. When an agreement is reached, the office will issue a certificate of arbitration (*meklingsattest*) to be enclosed with the application for separation and with any subsequent application for divorce. A separated, but not divorced, person cannot remarry.

After being separated for one year or more, either person may be granted a permit of divorce (*bevilling*) by the County Governor. If a couple has no formal separation but simply split up and moved away from each other, after two years, either person may apply for a divorce on a form available at the municipal Social Welfare Office (*Sosialkontor*) or the County Governor's Office. A person who has been separated or divorced abroad may apply to the County Governor to have the status recognised as valid in Norway.

A separated couple has separate finances. However, if one person of a separated couple has worked in the home for many years and cannot find employment, he/she may claim financial maintenance (*økonomisk støtte*) from the other. In particular, a spouse with custody of the children can claim child support maintenance (*barnebidrag*) from the other. Child support maintenance is required by law and can be deducted from wages.

In some cases, a person may be granted a divorce without going through separation. For instance, a woman subjected to extreme brutality or attempted murder of herself or her children may be granted a divorce by decree (*skilsmisse ved dom*). Either person may apply for immediate dissolution (*oppløsning*) of a marriage in which one of the spouses is guilty of ☞ **bigamy** or in which the spouses are found to be closely related.

For further details, contact the nearest County Governor's office, listed under *Fylkesmann* in the Pink Pages.

Divorce, separation or breakup of a relationship, consequences for a residence permit (*Skilmisse, separasjon, samlivsbrud, konsekvenser for oppholdstillatelse*) If you have been granted a ☞ **residence permit** (Arriving, Settling, Leaving chapter) on the basis of your marriage to, cohabitation with or ☞ **registered partnership** with a Norwegian citizen or a foreign citizen with a valid residence or work permit, the renewal of your permit usually depends on whether or not the relationship continues and you still live together with your spouse or mate. This means that if the relationship ceases, your permit may not be renewed. However, even if the relationship ceases, your permit might still be renewed, provided you meet one or more of three conditions:

- you have one or more children under age 18 in Norway and both have and use the right of access to them.
- you are a woman with ties to Norway who, if you leave the country, will encounter unreasonable difficulties in your country of origin due to social or cultural attitudes.
- you are a woman who has broken out of a relationship because you or your children have been abused.

For further information, contact ☞ **The Directorate of Immigration** (Government and Social Services chapter).

Family counselling (*familievern*) is offered at more than 90 offices throughout the country. You may seek free help at one of these offices, as for

- marital problems
- dealing with difficult children
- family members in crisis
- individuals having difficulty relating to their family, friends or colleagues
- couples seeking advice in connection with separation or divorce
- the required arbitration for couples seeking separation who have children less than 16 years old

Professionals, including social workers, psychologists and psychiatrists, staff the offices. Interpreters usually can be provided when needed. All matters are

confidential. The offices are operated by two organisations.

Family Affairs Offices (*Familievernkontorer*) are run by the municipalities in liaison with the Public Family Affairs Offices Organisation (*Offentlige familievernkontorers Organisasjon – OFO*). You may contact the nearest office listed under *Familievernkontor* in the Pink Pages; the OFO head office has an updated list of the 62 offices in the country ✆ 22806130, 🖷 22806131, ✉ Markveien 35A, 0554 Oslo, 🖃 ofo@online.no

Family Counselling Offices (*Familierådgivningskontorer*) are run by the Family Affairs Office of the Church of Norway (*Kirkens Familievern – FK*). You may contact the nearest office listed under *Familierådgivningskontor* in the Pink Pages; the FK head office has an updated list of the 31 offices in the country ✆ 22170998, 🖷 22179936, ✉ Storgt. 20, 0184 Oslo, 🖃 kirkens.familievern@online.no

Funeral directors (*Begravelsesbyråer*) In the country as a whole, there are fewer than 250 funeral directors, who together handle about 44,000 ☞ **Funerals** a year. To locate a funeral director, look under *Begravelses- og kremasjonsbyråer* in the Yellow Pages. Most of the country's funeral directors are small or family businesses, although there are a few affiliation groups, such as the *Gruppen av samarbeidende Begravelsesbyråer – GSB* (The Affiliated Undertakers Group) of 11 independent funeral directors in smaller cities around the Oslo Fjord. In the late 1990s, international funeral companies – including Fonus, based in Stockholm, Sweden, and Service Corporation International (SCI), based in Houston, Texas, USA – entered the Norwegian market. Funerals are regulated by the Funeral Act (*Gravferdloven*) of 1996. Families unable to pay for a funeral can apply to the local municipality for support, contact the Social Services Office (*Trygdekontoret* in the Pink Pages) for details. The Norwegian National Association of Funeral Directors (*Begravelsesbyrånes Forening – Norge*) can provide details on the profession ✆ 22643977, 🖷 22654469, ✉ Ole Deviks vei 4, 0666 Oslo.

Funerals (*begravelse, bisettelse*) All arrangements for a funeral can be made by a ☞ **Funeral director**. In Norwegian, one speaks of two types of funeral. The traditional *begravelse* is the ceremony for a person to be buried and translates directly to "burial" in English. *Bisettelse* is the ceremony for a person not to be buried, but rather cremated or transported to another place for burial. In English its closest translation is "obsequies", which now is seldom used and is most associated with pompous memorial services. Should you wish that the body be repatriated to another country, the funeral director will make the necessary arrangements, including contacting the police to apply for permission to send the body overseas. In this case he will also contact the embassy where the death will be registered and a certificate issued. Current Norwegian rules require burial or cremation within eight days of death. Muslims require the body to be buried before the next dawn. In cities ☞ **Cremation** now is more common than burial. In Oslo 80% are cremated, whereas in the countryside only 5% are cremated. The basic coffin is white painted pine. A body may be viewed at the hospital or at the crematorium a few days before the cremation. During the winter, in order to bury the coffin, the ground is warmed up and dug by machinery. In the past, the coffins used to lie along the perimeter of the church in what was called a *svalegang* (cooling gallery). A funeral service ☞ **The Church of Norway** (Church and Religion chapter) involves at least the services of a priest and an organist. You may arrange more extensive services with the funeral director.

Guardianship (*Vergemål*) is administered by the Public Guardian's Office (*Overformynderi*), which is an institution that exercises superintendence and control of the assets of minors (*mindreårige*) less than 18 years old and of dependent adults legally incapable of doing so themselves (*umyndiggjorte*). In every town and district there is a Public Guardian's office, usually with two Public Guardians chosen by the Municipal Executive Board (*Formannskapet*). The principal law is the Act of 22 April 1927 relating to guardianship for persons who are legally incapable (*Lov om vergemål for umyndige*) as most recently amended on 9 January 1998. Excerpts from the original Act (but not its more recent amendments) are translated into English, pages 844-850 in *Norwegian Laws Etc. Selected for the Foreign Service*, published in 1980 by the Ministry of Foreign Affairs (*Utentiksdepartementet – UD*). According to paragraph 63 of the Act and a Ministry of Justice (*Justisdepartementet – JD*)

decision of 1988, the Public Guardian's Office shall control assets of NOK 30,000 or more belonging to children, minor heirs, senile, mentally ill and other incapable persons. According to paragraph 70, the sums held shall be invested to yield interest. In late 1998, *Aftenposten*, the country's leading newspaper, surveyed the Public Guardian Offices in the country and found that they together control NOK 4.5 billion in assets, and that the interest rates earned were low and varied from office to office, from 1.8% to 8%.

Handicapped (*Handikap*) people are those who lack some physical or mental abilities. There are many interpretations of the various words used. But in general use, handicapped persons are spoken of as being disabled (*funksjonshemmede*) from birth or as the result of disease or injury, or retarded (*utviklingshemmede*) in mental or physical development.

The routine development checks of infants and children at municipal ☞ **health stations** (Health Care chapter) help identify handicaps at an early age. If your child is handicapped, the health station will advise you on contacting the relevant specialists (*spesialister*) and institutions (*institusjoner*). There are three centres for disabled children and their parents:

Frambu is the national information centre dedicated to promoting the quality of life for persons and families afflicted by one of about 40 disorders and disabilities known to be so rare as to affect only one person in ten thousand. The centre is located in Akershus county about 20 km south-east of Oslo, and its activities principally focus on in-house, multidisciplinary, diagnosis-based educational courses of one to two weeks. For further information, contact *Frambu* ✆ 64856000, ☎ 64856099, ✉ Sandbakkv 18, 1404 Siggerud, ✉ info@frambu.no, ⊕ http://www.frambu.no with pages in Norwegian and in English.

Beitostølen Helsesportsenter ("Beitostølen Health Sports Centre") provides physical medicine and rehabilitation through planned activities. It is located north-west of Fagernes at the gateway to the Jotunheimen National Park and offers an extensive programme of summer and winter recreation and sports, including the annual *Ridderuke* week of competitive snow sports events that now draws participants from 36 countries. For further information, contact the Centre ✆ 61340800, ☎ 61341116, ✉ 2953 Beitostølen.

Valnesfjord Helsesportsenter ("Valnesfjord Health Sports Centre") provides physical medicine and rehabilitation through planned activities. It is located at Valnesfjord east of Bodø and serves the middle and northern part of the country. For further information, contact the Centre ✆ 75602100, 📠 75602450, ✉ Østerkløft Øvre, 8215 Valnesfjord.

☞ **Day care centres** give priority to handicapped children, provided that they can benefit from being with other children. Contact the municipal social services (*Sosialtjeneste*) or day-care centre office (*Barnehagekontor*) for further information. Many municipalities have a *lekotek* ("toy library") which has toys, books and special toys for disabled children available on loan and can advise on their use. Contact the local ☞ **Educational-psychological service** (Education and Research chapter) for the location of the nearest *lekotek*.

Financial support (*Økonomisk ytelser*) is available to parents of handicapped children. For details, contact the local *Trygdekontoret* listed in the Pink Pages. Parents may also be eligible for ☞ **respite care** (Health Care chapter) services.

Long-term ☞ **care of the retarded** (Health Care chapter) is now at the municipal level.

Marriage (*Ekteskap*) If you intend to marry, you may choose either a civil marriage (*borgerlig vigsel*) or a church marriage (*kirkelig vigsel*); from a legal viewpoint, the two are equal. A ☞ **city recorder or district recorder** (Registrations, Rights, Licences chapter) can perform a civil marriage. A minister of the ☞ **Church of Norway** or of one of the other registered ☞ **religious denominations** (Church and Religion chapter) can perform a church marriage. After the solemnisation ceremony (wedding), you will receive a marriage certificate (*vigselsattest*). Before you marry, you should be able to show that you fulfil the conditions for a valid marriage (*ekteskapsvilkårene*), which require that each of you:
- be at least 18 years old. Younger persons may marry with the consent of their parent(s) or guardian(s) and the permission of the County Governor (*Fylkesmann*).
- have full legal capacity (*være myndig*). A person declared without legal capacity (*umyndiggjort*), such as due to being retarded or addicted, can marry only by permission of his or her parent(s) or guardian(s).

- be unmarried; any previous marriage must have been terminated by a ☞ **divorce**; separated persons cannot remarry until they are fully divorced.
- not be closely related to the other.
- fully inform the other in case you have a venereal (sexually-transmitted) disease.
- have a valid ☞ **residence permit** (Arriving, Settling, Leaving chapter) if you are a citizen of another country.

You may show that you fulfil these conditions on a form entitled *Erklæring fra brudefolkene før prøving av ekteskapsvilkårene* ("Statement of the bridal couple prior to proving the conditions for a valid marriage"). Both of you must have a witness (*forlover*), who should be a person who knows you well. Each of them must fill out and sign a *Forlovererklæring* ("Witness statement"). With these forms completed, you can apply to have the marriage performed. You must also choose the surnames that you will have when married. You have three options: either one of you can take the other's surname (except for a surname taken in a previous marriage), or one of you can take the other's surname but keep your own surname as a middle name, or both of you can retain your surnames unchanged. At the ceremony, you must have at least two witnesses, usually, but not always, the bridesmaid and the best man.

Marriage settlement (*Ektepakt*) If you and your spouse or intended spouse so wish, you may specify how property is to be divided between you in marriage. The most common form of marriage settlement is separate property (*særeie*), in which property that belongs to one spouse is held outside the property held jointly (*felleseie*) with the other spouse. A marriage settlement is most often made before marriage but may be made thereafter. It is valid only if signed by both spouses and by two witnesses. It must be entered in the Marriage Contract Register (*Ekteskapsregisteret*) at the ☞ **Brønnøysund Register Centre** (Registrations, Rights, Licences chapter) to be valid in financial matters. A lawyer can help you draw up a marriage settlement and properly register it.

Name changes (*Endring av navn*) You may change your name once, by application at the nearest office of the ☞ **National register** (Registrations, Rights, Licences chapter) listed under *Folkereg-*

ister in the Pink Pages. Two forms are available for the purpose: *Melding om endring av navn* ("Notice of name change") and *Melding om endring av navn til barn under 18 år* ("Notice of name change of child younger than 18"). If you have changed your name once, you may change it again only through application for permission to the County governor listed under *Fylkesmann* in the Pink Pages. The general rules for ☞ **personal names** apply to name changes. Some specific rules apply to changes of family name (*slektsnavn*). You may change to a common (*vanlige*) family name unless there are special grounds that prohibit it. Updated lists of common family names are available at National register and County governor offices. However, you can change to a protected (*beskyttet*) family name only by consent of the families having that name. Nonetheless, change can be granted if one of your parents or step-parents have or had the name or if you had the name before a previous marriage.

Nappies (*bleier*) Popular disposable brands available in supermarkets are Libero and Pampers, for babies from 2kg in weight up to toddlers of 25kg, disposable pants for toddlers from 9kg. Popularity of washable nappies has declined in recent years, enquire in baby shops (*barneutstyr*) who may stock or be able to order them.

The night ravens (*Natteravnene*) are voluntary groups of adults, usually parents of schoolchildren, who walk streets at night to provide the adult presence that helps prevent violence, drug abuse and crime among the young. The night ravens are not police and do not interfere in incidents. But they co-operate with local police departments and have procedures to use their mobile phones to call the police if needed. The concept started in the early 1990s and now has spread to most cities and towns throughout the country. Local night raven groups usually are organised through the parents' associations of the local schools and often have contact persons, telephones, addresses and Internet web sites and brochures for new members, supported in part by the Vesta insurance company. The general philosophy is that parents should not sit at home and worry about their kids out on the town, but should go out themselves as night ravens. Usually, three to five night ravens, 18 years old or older, walk togeth-

er on Friday and Saturday evenings, from 9 or 10 in the evening to 1 or 2 in the morning, to see and be seen in risky areas. For further information on the night ravens, who always need more volunteers, call the local police department (*politi* in the Pink Pages), who will have the names of the *Natteravnene* contact persons.

Personal names (*Personnavn*) By tradition, most Norwegians have two names: a first name (*fornavn*) and a surname (*etternavn*). Up to about 1970, few children were given middle names. Thereafter middle names became increasingly common, and by the mid 1990s, more than four children in ten were give three names. The most common combination of three names is a first name, one parent's surname as a middle name (*mellomnavn*) and the other parent's surname. This reflects the prevailing practice according to the Name Act (*Navnloven*) of 1964. Upon marriage, a couple may choose between both retaining their names unaltered, the wife taking her husband's surname, as is the custom in many countries, or the husband taking his wife's surname; the person taking the other's surname may retain his/her surname as a middle name. If you have a child in Norway, you should register its birth and name with the ☞ **National register** (Registrations, Rights, Licences chapter) before it is six months old, to obtain a ☞ **National ID Number** and an official birth certificate, as is needed to obtain a passport as well as register birth abroad at an embassy. The hospital or attending midwife will issue a birth statement (*fødselsmelding*) which you then use in registering the birth. Registration of a name is subject to the Name Act, which affects both surname and first name. Children born to a couple with a common surname will have that surname. Children born to a married or cohabitant couple with differing surnames may be given either or both surnames. However, only the last of the names is regarded to be the child's family name (*slektsnavn*). If a surname is not chosen before a child is six months old, it automatically will be given the mother's surname. Almost any first name may be chosen, provided that it will not be inconvenient or embarrassing for the person named and provided that it is not or has not been a family name. However, family names that are or have been first names are excepted from this rule. The interpretation and enforcement of the Name Act is increasingly liberal, in accordance with the increasing internationalisation of Norway and an ever larger resident foreign population. If one or both of a child's parents are of foreign origin and both so wish, a foreign name tradition can be observed upon registry, provided it can be substantiated. Moreover, should a local office of the National register reject a first name application by Norwegian or foreign parents, they may appeal via the County Governor (*Fylkesmann*).Three first name dispute cases of the mid 1990s illustrate the current workings of the Name Act.

A girl's first name of Embla was rejected in Oslo, on the grounds that it had been used as a surname. The parents pointed both to a current successful registry of the same name in Trondheim and to its roots in Nordic mythology, where Ask and Embla are the first two people, the equivalents of Adam and Eve. Their appeal was granted.

In 1994, a boy's first name of Gesher, the Hebrew word for "bridge", was rejected in Hurdal, on the grounds that it sounded foreign and that it resembled the surname Geser. Appeals were overruled, and the mother was ordered to register another name. She refused, and consequently was fined NOK 1600. She refused to pay the fine, and therefore was jailed for two days in December 1998, an event reported in the New York Times. However, today the interpretation of the rules for first names is more liberal than in 1994.

A girl's first name of Kiri was rejected in Bærum, a suburb of Oslo, on the grounds that it seemed not to be a recognised name. The parents, who were English, called the British Embassy and requested substantiation of their citizenship and their choice name, in honour of Kiri te Kanawa, the famed operatic soprano from New Zealand. The Embassy complied and sent a telefax to the National Registry office in Bærum, and the name registration was completed the next day.

Pregnancy (*Svangerskap*) Pregnant women are entitled to free antenatal and childbirth care provided by the National Insurance Scheme. Pregnancy test (*graviditetstest*) kits for home use are sold at pharmacies (*apotek*), or a test can be performed by at the local health station (*helsestasjon*). AAN (Abortion Alternatives Norway) also offers tests, ☞ **Abortion** (Health Care chapter). Once pregnancy has been confirmed (usually at around 12 weeks), antenatal care and clinics are provided by a doctor (*lege*) or midwife (*jordmor*) at the health station. Upon first visit to a health station, a pregnant woman is seen by a doctor and by a midwife. The midwife is responsible for antenatal care but the doctor will see the woman a further 3 times during the pregnancy. Initially visits to the clinic take place once a month and as the pregnancy progresses the visits will be fortnightly and then weekly from week 34 onwards. A woman is responsible for her own medical notes during her pregnancy and will have to take them with her to all visits. Ultrasound (*ultralyd*) scans are offered from the 17th/18th week, about 95% take up this offer. Blood is screened for HIV, Rubella and Rhesus. If the pregnant woman comes from a country where Hepatitis B is common, they will be tested for it. Babies are delivered in hospital by a hospital midwife. Eight weeks after delivery, a mother may return to the antenatal clinic for a postnatal checkup. A mother who has worked for six of the previous 10 months is entitled to full maternity benefits under the ☞ **National Insurance Scheme** (Government & Social Services chapter). Maternity leave must commence between 12 weeks and 3 weeks prior to the due date. Four weeks of the benefit period is reserved for the father. The father can also take some or all of the maternity benefit period. Should a mother decide to return to work earlier, her maternity benefits will be correspondingly reduced. New mothers who haven't been working and therefore do not qualify for maternity leave are given a single payment. Most benefits from the National Insurance Scheme are adjusted annually. Information about maternity benefits, the basic amount and the current levels of payment can be obtained from the National Insurance Office, see *Trygdekontor* in the Pink Pages.

Amniocentesis (*fostervannsprøve*), the sampling of the amniotic fluid by the insertion of a hollow needle to determine the condition of an embryo, is also available free to women of age 37 or older and at a modest fee to younger women.

Chorionic Villus Sample – CVS (*Morkakeprøve*), a test on the placenta (*morkake*) to detect any chromosomal abnormalities in the foetus is offered at major hospitals.

Giving birth (*fødsel*) Almost all births are in public hospitals, which provide everything for the baby and the new mother. The mother does not need to bring her own nightgown or sanitary items, just personal items like a hairbrush, her toothpaste and brush and anything else that will make her stay in hospital comfortable. Up to five people can accompany the pregnant woman into the delivery suite, even children are welcome. A normal confinement is two to three days in major cities and four to five days elsewhere. A new mother can leave the hospital after two hours. Fewer than one birth in a hundred is at home, and accordingly there are few midwifes available to assist home delivery.

Privileges of parents of small children
(*Småbarnsforeldres rettigheter*) are included in regulations administered by five government agencies. For instance, pregnancy and birth are health matters subject to the regulations administered by the Ministry of Health and Social Affairs. Likewise, the aspects of raising small children are covered by the regulations administered by the Ministry of Children and Family Affairs. Parents who work are affected by the regulations administered by the Directorate of Labour Inspection; parents on military duty are subject to the regulations administered by the Ministry of Defence; and parents who have borrowed to support studies may be subject to the rules of the State Educational Loan Fund. Together, these regulations ensure:

- Financial benefits and grants during pregnancy and birth or in adoption, including paid leave for working mothers and fathers.
- Unpaid leave of absence from work, including daily leave for breast feeding mothers and up to two weeks for fathers.
- Leave of absence if a child or child-minder is ill.
- Reduced working hours when needed.
- Financial support, including ☞ **child benefit**, pension contributions for parents who stay at home and benefits for single parents.
- Educational Loan Fund maternity grants and postponement of loan repayments in connection with pregnancy, birth and adoption.
- Military leave for conscripts and postponement of service for single providers.
- Health care services and work reductions for pregnant women.
- Protection against dismissal during pregnancy or leave of absence.

- Health and education services, including clinics, day care, special education, family counselling and the like.

For further information, see the overview brochure "The rights of parents of small children in Norway" (*Småbarnsforeldres rettigheter*), Oslo, 1997, 32 pages, brochure number Q-0867 (Norwegian) and Q-0867E (English), available at National Insurance offices listed under *Trygdekontor* in the Pink Pages, as well as at the employee services offices of larger companies. The Norwegian edition is available on-line at
☞ http://odin.dep.no/bfd/publ/foreldre/sm.html

Registered partnership (*Registerert partnerskap*) is an officially recognised relationship between same-sex persons. As at 1 January 1999, 1370 residents were in registered partnerships, about one-third of them women and two-thirds of them men.

A registered partnership affords the same rights as ☞ **marriage**, except for adoption and church wedding, and involves the same procedures, including separation and divorce to terminate a relationship. Similar registered partnership rules are in effect in Denmark, Iceland and Sweden. Both partners must be at least 18 years old; at least one must be a Norwegian citizen and at least one must be resident in Norway. A foreign citizen entering a registered partnership in Norway must have a valid residence permit. A same-sex couple wishing to enter a registered partnership should contact the ☞ **Notary public** (Registrations, Rights, Licences chapter) in the municipality in which one or both of them lives, for an appointment for registration. Both must bring birth certificates, as issued by the ☞ **National register** (Registrations, Rights, Licences chapter). If one is a foreign citizen, he/she must bring an official statement of civil status to prove that he/she is not married or in an existing registered partnership. If both partners so wish, one may take the other's surname. A Norwegian registered partnership should be regarded as valid in Norway only, as it may not be recognised in other countries not having similar legal provisions. Likewise, practical difficulties may arise when registered partners travel abroad. For instance, Norwegian family travel insurance policies, which also are valid for registered partners, may not be recognised in some countries unless they carry the names of all persons insured. For further details on all current aspects of registered partnerships, contact the ☞ **Lesbian and gay organisation** (Organisations, Societies, Clubs chapter).

Surnames (*Etternavn*) By tradition, most Norwegians have two names: a first name and a surname. Up to about 1970, few children were given middle names. Thereafter middle names became increasingly common, and by the mid 1990s, more than four children in ten were given three names. The most common combination of three names is a first name and two surnames, one from each parent. This reflects the prevailing practice under the provisions of the Name Act (*Navnloven*) of 1964. Upon marriage, a couple may choose between the wife taking her husband's surname, as is the custom in many countries, or the husband taking his wife's surname, or both retaining their surnames. Children born to a couple with a common surname will have that surname. Children born to a married or cohabitant couple with differing surnames may be given either or both surnames. However, only the last of the names is regarded to be the child's proper family name (*slektsnavn*). In all cases, the choice of name for child should be registered with the ☞ **National register** (Registrations, Rights, Licences chapter) before the child is six months old, otherwise the child will automatically be given the mother's surname.

Voluntary work (*Frivillig innsats*) is common and sorts into two major groups.

First, as in other countries, voluntary organisations, including many ☞ **Non-government Organisations** (chapter) historically were started by and still rely upon unpaid work. In many sectors, such as health, social services and environmental conservation, voluntary organisations were the predecessors of governmental agencies. Conversely, many organisations that are supported by public funds, such as the Norwegian Confederation of Sports (*Norges Idrettsforbund*), rely on volunteer work in their operations. Consequently, the Ministry of Health and Social Affairs supports liaison between public agencies and some 35 private organisations that rely upon voluntary work, in the Norwegian Centre for Voluntary Work (*Frivillighetens samarbeidsorgan – FRISAM*) ✆ 22248547, ☎ 22248544, ✉ PO Box 8155 Dep, 0033 Oslo, ✉ frisam@oslonett.no, ⊕ http://www.dep.no/shd/imderet/frisam.

Second and far more commonplace is local-level collective work (*dugnad*), a descendent of the rural tradition of do-it-yourself (with the help of your neighbours). In Scandinavia, *dugnad* is particularly Norwegian; neither Danes or Swedes have the tradition or even a word for it. Arguably this may due to Norway never having had a feudal system or a nobility; farmers and fishermen were free, while their counterparts in other countries were more ruled by their lords. The only other instance of a similar tradition is that of barn raising in the pioneer USA, when neighbours would get together to put up the frame of a barn. In modern Norway, *dugnad* is pervasive. Day care centres and private schools rely on the *dugnadstimer* ("*dugnad* hours") of parents to maintain facilities. Social and sports clubs depend on *dugnad* in their daily activities. If you are a member of any club or organisation – and the average family belongs to at least six – you can expect a call to *dugnad* at least once a year, usually in the spring. Blocks of co-operative flats rely on *dugnad* to keep stairwells clean, cut grass and tidy grounds. If you live in a co-operative block, you will be assigned your turn at *dugnad*. Some housing projects were even built with a helping of *dugnad*, a fact reflected in the names of the streets on which they are located: there is a *Dugnadveien* at Årvoll in Oslo as well as at Gjettum in Bærum. Each year, residents of the country contribute more than 50 million hours of *dugnad*. And some events depend on *dugnad*: the Molte International Jazz Festival relies on some 600 volunteers for 30,000 hours of work each year. For the 1999 Norwegian Review Festival, a record 800 of the 1350 inhabitants of the village of Høylandet in Nord Trøndelag contributed *dugnadstimer*. Though *dugnad* often involves hard work, it can be enjoyable. Every major *dugnad* undertaking is also a social gathering, traditionally with coffee, tea, sandwiches and pastries served by relatives of the working *dugnad* crew (*dugnadsgjeng*).

Youth information (*Ungdomsinformasjon*) is a network of offices dedicated to providing young people with a broad range of information on city and town life, entertainment, schools, further education, job opportunities and the like. There are three *UngInfo* offices in Oslo: city centre, Furuset and Stovner, and one each in Alta, Bodø, Karasjok, Kautokeino, Kirkenes , Kristiansand, Porsanger, Stavanger, Steinkjer and Tana; you can find their addresses and telecommunications numbers listed under *UngInfo* in the Pink Pages for these cities and towns. There are five *UngInfo* web sites on the Internet, listed in links from the main Oslo site ⊛ http://www.unginfo.oslo.no with pages in Norwegian and summary pages in English. *UngInfo* is the Norwegian member of the European Youth Information and Counselling Agency (ERYICA) ⊛ http://www.alli-fi/euro/eryica with pages in English.

Food and eating
(*Mat og spising*)

Additives (*Tilsetningsstoffer*) to liquid and solid foods have been used for hundreds of years. For instance, there are historical records of colouring being added to wine more than 2000 years ago. Modern food additives have many purposes and sort into five major classes: preservatives (*konserveringsmidler*), antioxidants (*antioksidanter*), sweeteners (*søtstoffer*), colours (fargestoffer) and other additives (*andre tilsetningsstoffer*).

Throughout Europe, food-labelling regulations require specification of the ingredients. This includes additives, which now are specified according to uniform E-number codes, which have the advantage of being independent of language: the same E-number means the same additive, regardless of the country of origin or sale of a product or the language on its label. Nonetheless, some food manufacturers designate additives by their chemical names rather than their E-numbers. Both types of labelling – chemical name and E-number – are permitted in Norway, but in all cases, the additives must be on the list of some 300 approved for use in foods sold in the country. That number may increase to about 340 as a consequence of increasing conformity with rules within the European Union (EU).

Chemical names and E-numbers may sound very modern, but many of them designate products long in use. For instance, E330 is citric acid, which was originally obtained from lemon juice and has been used as a food additive since the 1890s, and ordinary baking powder is a blend of several E-number additives, principally E500 (bicarbonate of soda), E450 (tetrasodium diphosphate) and E341 (dicalcium phosphate). All additives are scientifically evaluated to ascertain if they pose health hazards. Scientists in the EU and the World Health Organisation (WHO) analyse each additive and set an Acceptable Daily Intake (ADI) for it. The ADI for an additive sets the maximum amount of it that a human can safely consume per day for an entire lifetime.

In Norway, the Norwegian Food Control Authority (*Statens næringsmiddeltilsyn* – SNT) is responsible for monitoring the use of additives in foods sold in the country and periodically issues lists of additives

approved for use in specified groups of foods. Together with the Consumer Council (*Forbrukerrådet*), SNT has published an explanatory booklet for consumers: *Tilsetningsstoffer i maten, trenger vi dem?* ("Additives in foods, do we need them?"), publication M-0686B, Oslo, May 1998 (Norwegian only). The list of E-number additives, with their chemical names, as approved for use in Norway is continuously updated and periodically published by SNT under the title *E-kodenøkkel* (E-number key). These publications are available free from SNT ✆ 22246722 (12-15 hours, Monday-Friday), 🖷 22246699, ✉ PO Box 8147 Dep, 0034 Oslo, or from local control authorities, see *Næringsmiddeltilsyn* in the Pink Pages. SNT points out that if you wish, you can carefully control your consumption of E-number additives. First, you can read the labels of all foods that you buy. Second, as a general rule, the more processed a food, the more additives it contains. So if you wish, you can reduce or even eliminate additives in your diet by making dishes from raw ingredients such as fresh fruit and vegetables, eggs, milk, untreated meats and fish.

Additives, Halal and Kosher aspects (*Tilsetningsstoffer, Halal og Kosher aspekter*) Interna-
tional and national directives concerning E-number ☞ **Additives**, including those administered by the Norwegian Food Control Authority, relate to chemical composition and purity and health risk, but not to source or method of preparation. Most E-number additives are derived from a single raw material, whilst others may be derived from various raw materials, some of which may be animalic and contrary to the religious requirements of Muslim *Halal* or Jewish *Kosher*. The principal E-number additives, which might be made from animalic raw materials, are listed below. Note that the list may not be complete; for Halal or Kosher approval, always consult a suitably authorised cleric.

- **Additives produced from fats:** E322, E422, E431, E433, E435, E436, E445, E470a, E470b, E471, E472a, E472b, E472c, E472d, E472e, E472f, E473, E474, E475, E476, E477, E479b, E481, E482, E483, E491, E492, E493, E494, E495, E570.
- **Additives produced from non-fats:** E630, E631, E632, E633, E634, E635, E1105.
- **Additives produced from insect products:** E120, E901, E904.

Baby food (*barnemat*) is sold in supermarkets and in ☞ **health food shops** (Shopping chapter), where organic food with the Debio label is sold. The variety of ready made food includes: Fruit purees : apricot (*aprikos*), blueberry (*blåbær*), peach (*fersken*), rosehip (*nype*), strawberry/apple (*jordbær/eple*). Fruit juices: blueberry, pear (*pærer*), prune (*svisker*). First foods (*barnegrøt*): rice with bananas (*ris med banan*), rusks (*kavring*), mixed cereal (*kornblanding*), corn (*mais*). First foods with milk (*barnegrøt med melk*): oats with banana and apricot (*havre med bannan og aprikos*), wheat (*hvete*), wheat and fruit (*hvete med frukt*), wholemeal (*sammalt hvete*). Baby food in jars: chicken (*kylling*), fish with lemon (*fisk med sitron*), lamb (*lam*), lasagne, pasta, liver (*lever*), rice pudding (*risgrøt*), roast lamb (*lammestek*), roast veal (*kanlvestek*), spaghetti with ham (*spaghetti med skinke*), turkey (*kalkun*), Baby formula (*morsmelkerstatning*) is produced by Nestlé and Collett and is also sold in ☞ **pharmacies** (Health Care chapter). Supermarkets stock baby hygiene supplies. Ask the pharmacy for medicinal supplies. Other useful terms: breast pads (*ammeindlaeg*), drinking beaker (*babykopp*), dummy/pacifier (*narresmokk*), feeding bottle (*tåteflask*), teething ring (*bitering*).

Baking (*baking*) recipes written in Norwegian use metric measures, so you will need metric scales (g and kg) and a metric measuring jug (cl, dl, l). These can be purchased from a kitchen shop, household department in a department store or home furnishings hypermarket. Norwegian recipes written in English usually state both metric and English measures; choose one method of ☞ **measures in cooking** and stick to it throughout a recipe. If you use recipes in English or American cookbooks, you may find ☞ **converting between measurement systems** (Measurements and Standards chapter) useful. You can mix and bake completely by hand or by using a bread machine, which you can buy, in shops selling ☞ **appliances** (Electrical & Electronic Goods chapter).

The most common types of flour used in baking are *siktet hvetemel* (sieved wheatmeal), *sammalt fin* (wholemeal, finely ground), *sammalt grovt* (wholemeal, coarsely ground), *byggmel* (barley flour), *havremel* (oat flour), *rugmel* (rye flour, both in coarse and finely ground varieties). You may find that your tried and tested recipes turn out slightly different with the flour types sold here, experiment and annotate your recipes accordingly. *Byggmel* is the main ingredient of flatbread (*flatbrød*) ☞ **bread**. *Havremel* is used in the porridge. Most ☞ **health food shops** (Shopping chapter) stock other flour types like soya (*soja*) and millet (*hirse*). Dried yeast (*tørrgjær*) is sold in packets containing 5 x 12g sachets, usually in the baking goods section of the supermarket. One sachet of dried yeast is equivalent to a 50g cube of fresh yeast (*gjær*) which is in the chill counters of the supermarket with dairy products. One sachet of dried yeast or one cube of fresh yeast is enough for one 450g loaf. If a recipe calls for self-raising flour, you may make it by adding one teaspoon of baking powder (*bakepulver*) to every 50 g of flour. Many cake mixes (*kakemiks*) are available. Frozen puff pastry (*butterdeig*) is available in packets of 5 sheets. Filo pastry is available in ☞ **foreign/ethnic food shops** (Shopping chapter).

The most popular type of celebration cake sold and made is *bløtkake*, made from layers of sponge cake with juice or liqueur, whipped cream (*kremfløte*) and fruit. Often a thin layer of marzipan, which can be bought ready rolled or in a sausage shape covers the cake. The layers of sponge cake (*kakebunn*) are available ready-made. The cake can then be decorated with *kakepynt*.

Cake fillings (*kakefyll*) in powder form (made with cornstarch, sugar and flavourings), yield a vanilla, chocolate, fruit or rum-flavoured custard. They are also available ready-made in small cartons and called vanilla cream (*vanilje krem*) or rum cream (*rom krem*).

During the pre-Christmas baking period you will find ready-made gingerbread (*pepperkake*), *kransekake* (for macaroon ring cake) and other biscuit doughs in 1kg portions. They are usually displayed near the delicatessen section.

Most mothers of small children bake buns (*boller*), which have cardamom as a flavouring. You will find recipes for *boller* on the packet of flour.
Pancakes (*pannekaker*) are popular, ready made mixes are available, but try making thick pancakes (*lapper*), made with butter milk and served similar to waffles with sour cream and jam.

Waffles (*vafler*) are served everywhere with jam and sour cream or even brown ☞ **goat cheese**. Ready-made mixes are available, but everybody has a favourite recipe, ask your neighbour or look in a ☞ **cookery book**.

Other things you might need when baking: baking parchment (*bakepapir*), baking powder (*bakepulver*), baking soda, bicarbonate of soda (*natron*), bran (*hvetekli*), cooking chocolate in tablet form (*kokesjokolade*), dark and light syrup (*mork og lys sirup*), fat in spray form (*formfett*), food colouring (*mat farge*), glace cherries (*kirsebær*), icing sugar (*melis*), preserved citron rind (*sukat*), lemon peel (*sitrokat*), mixed peel (*fruktblanding*), orange peel (*apsikat*), unsweetened cocoa in powder form (*kakao Regia*), vanilla-flavoured sugar (*vaniljesukker*), wheat-germ (*hvetekim*), various cake decorations come under the name *kakepynt*, coloured jelly in tubes for writing on cakes and biscuits (*pynte gele*).

Bars and Pubs (*barer og puber*) are found in most town and city centres and are similar to bars and pubs elsewhere. They serve alcoholic and non-alcoholic beverages, sometimes food and entertainment. Opening hours are regulated by the local municipality, with last orders usually half an hour before closing time. Look in the Yellow Pages under *barer og puber*.

Berry picking (*Bærplukking*) is a popular pastime in the autumn, and the ☞ **public right of access** (Sports, Recreation, Hobbies chapter) permits you to pick in most woodland and marsh areas where wild berries grow. The favoured berries are blackberries (*bjørnebær*), bilberries (*blåbær*), cloudberries (*multer*), mountain cranberries (*tyttebær*), raspberries (*bringebær*) and strawberries (*jordbær*).

Bread (*brød*) is sold by bakeries (*bakeri*), supermarkets and other food shops. Most bread is sold unsliced, does not contain preservatives and therefore does not keep well. The supermarkets also sell partially baked rolls and baguettes, pita bread, and Italian breads like ciabatta and focacia. In the frozen section you will find rolls, bagels, baguettes, garlic bread and pita bread. Breads from other countries are sold in ☞ **ethnic shops** (Shopping chapter). Gluten-free (*glutenfri*) bread is sold in ☞ **health food shops** (Shopping chapter) and in some supermarkets, and gluten-free bread mixes are widely available. There are four main types of bread:
- *Kneippbrød*, a whole-wheat bread made from ground wheat and named after a German priest, father Sebastian Kneipp (1821-1897) who first

baked it as part of natural healing. It is the most common coarse bread, and its ingredients can differ from baker to baker, related bread types *grahambrød* (graham bread), *vitabrød* (vitamin-enriched bread), *sigdalsbrød* (named for the Sigdal Valley where in 1935 it was baked as part of school lunch programme) and *helkornbrød* (whole-wheat bread), some bakers produce a coarser variation often called *fiberkneipp* (coarse-fibre whole wheat).
- *Loff* is plain white loaf, made from bleached white flour. There are several varieties of it, including *spiralloff*, "twist loaf", *Pariser* (baguette) and *formloff* (white tin loaf or sandwich loaf). *Rundstykker* are rolls made of the same ingredients as *loff*, though there are coarser versions of them.
- *Husholdningsbrød* (household bread) was originally made with rye flour, but now with more plain flour. A common variant is *Alminnelig* (ordinary) bread.
- *Grovbrød* (coarse bread) is a variety of rye originally baked in Denmark.

Moreover, there are two major types of unleavened crisp bread, which has a longer shelf life and consequently is sold mostly by markets and supermarkets, but not by bakers:
- *Knekkebrød*, a thicker rye crisp bread originated in Sweden and sold in packages of small rectangular wafers or larger circles. It is a popular lunch packet bread.
- *Flatbrød*, thin unleavened bread, traditional through the centuries, like the Indian chapati or the Jewish matzah, and sold in packages of small rectangular wafers. A "home-made" variety is sold in larger boxes containing pieces broken off large baked sheets. Both types are served with soups, cold smoked fish and cured meats.

Breakfast (*Frokost*) differs from that of many other countries. The basic is ☞ **bread**, usually hand-sliced, filling, dark breads with full textures still showing their links to the parent wheat and rye grains. On top of the slices go *pålegg* (literally "lay-on", a generic term for everything put on top of bread). ☞ **Goat cheese** (*geitost*), yellow cheeses, canned fish, sliced meats, liver sausage and jams and marmalades are the most commonplace in homes. Hotels will offer greater variety at breakfast cold tables (*kaltbord*), supplemented with soft-boiled eggs and a selection of warm cereals and dry cereals (*korn*), often eaten with butter milk (*kulturmelk*). The meal can be as hefty as taste dictates and time allows. The ingredients are usually placed on the table, and you make your own selection. When everything is there on the table on work or school days, most people also make the day's packed ☞ **lunch** (*matpakke*), using the breakfast *pålegg*, except for the slippery jams and marmalades. Warm cereals, like oatmeal, and processed dry cereals are increasingly popular, particularly with school children, but the bread-based breakfast remains the champion of morning ☞ **meals**. Warm breakfasts, with bacon and eggs and sometimes fried fish, are served in some farm homes, but usually after morning chores, such as milking cows and feeding farm animals.

Cafés , cafeterias and restaurants (*kafe, kafeteria og restauranter*) are ubiquitous. Cafés serve popular beverages and traditional pastries like *skyllingsbrød*, *berlinerboller* and *skolebrød*. Restau-rants to suit every pocket from fast food outlets, to haute cuisine. Eating out is not a cheap alternative to home cooking. Look in the Yellow Pages under *resatuaranter* for a café, cafeteria or restaurant. ℗ 80036000 to book a table at a restaurant anywhere in Norway.

Cheese (*Ost*) The average resident consumes some 15.3 kg of cheese per year. Most of the cheese is made in Norway, though many types are imported, principally from Denmark and France. Arguably, the most Norwegian of all cheeses sold is ☞ **goat cheese**, which is eaten in almost all homes and accounts for about a fifth of all cheese sales. The other leading cheeses are listed below. Many ☞ **cookery books** have overviews of cheese as well as cheese recipes. One of the best current reference books on cheese is *The Cheese Companion* by Judy Ridgeway, London, Apple Press 1999, 224 pages hardcover, ISBN 1-84092-081-5, sold by larger city book shops.

Norwegian	English	Fat content	Uses
Fresh cheeses			
Cottage cheese	Cottage cheese, skimmed milk	4.3%	On bread, in cooking, salads, desserts or straight out of the tub
Kesam		1%	Desserts, baking, sauces, dressings and dips
Norwegian national cheeses			
Norvegia	Gouda	27% (light 16%)	On bread, in pizza, quiches and other warm cheese dishes
Jarlsberg	Norwegian version of Emmental	27% (light16%)	On cheeseboard, on bread, pizza, sauces, cooking
Nøkkel	Cheese with cloves	27% (light16%)	On bread, in salads
Sveitser	Swiss cheese (Emmental)		On bread, for cold buffets
Ridder	Scandinavian version of Port Salut	38%	On bread, a dessert cheese, on cheese board
Norbo	"no-hole Swiss"	28%	On bread
Taffel	Table cheese	24%	On bread, in salads, as a snack, flavoured with tomato/pimento, ham/parsley, bacon or natural

Norwegian	English	Fat content	Uses
Cooking cheeses			
Burgerost	Hamburger cheese, combination of Jarlsberg and cheddar	30%	On hamburgers, eggs, cheese toasties, cheese waffles
Cheddar	Cheddar	32% – 48%	Blends well, no 'threads'
Matlagingsost	Cooking cheese, finely grated Norvegia, Jarlsberg and cheddar	29%	Vegetable gratin, in soups, sauces, fish and meat dishes
Mozzarella	Mozzarella	23% (light 16%)	Pizza, other warm cheese dishes
Pizza	Cooking cheese, coarsely grated Norvegia and cheddar	27%	Pizza, omelettes, soufflés, fondue
Soft cheeses			
Smørbar ost	Spreadable soft white cheese	16-19% (light 5-6%)	On bread, in soups, in sauces, on warm toast, in omelettes, flavours: prawn, bacon, tomato, ham. Light variety in ham and bacon
Kremost	Cream cheese	28% – 33%	Flavours: natural, pineapple/mandarin, hazlenut/cognac, herbs, spices, pepper, onion/leek and garlic
Norwegian specialities			
Gamalost	Mouldy cheese, whose roots lie in Viking times, crumbly	1% – 3%	On bread, usually with butter and jam or syrup
Pultost	Soft, sharp cheese	1%	On bread, with potatoes, on flat bread
Kvit geitost	White goat cheese	26%	On bread, or with brown cheese in lefse or on flat bread
Namdalsgomme	Soft whey cheese	12%	Lefse, , waffles, lomper (potato pancake) or on bread
International Specialities			
Brie	Brie	32% – 60%	Dessert, snack, deep fried brie with jam
Camembert	Camembert	27% – 60%	As above
Normanna	Blue-veined cheese	28% – 32%	On bread, in salads, soups, sauces
Norzola	Blue-veined	35%	On bread, in cheese dishes
Royal Blue	Blue-veined	44%	Dessert, cheese dishes
Gräddost	Gräddost	38%	On bread, snacks, in cheese dishes
Saint Paulin	Saint Paulin*	28% – 45%	On bread, in salads, desserts
Port Salut	Port Salut	24% – 45%	On bread, in salads, desserts
Edamer	Edam	27% – 40%	On bread, with fruit.
Crème Cherie	Flavoured cream cheese	23% (light 16%)	Desserts, on bread

* Saint Paulin was one of the first French imitations of Port Salut, tradenamed in 1938.

Coffee (*kaffe*) is popular and is served at any time of day. On average, every Norwegian drinks about 160 litres a year. Eight of ten residents drink coffee, most of them women, but men drink more of it. Most coffee is drunk at home. When you visit someone for coffee it will be kept hot in a thermos flask and will be accompanied with home-baked cakes and biscuits.

Most supermarkets sell coffee in two grinds, coarse *kokemalt* and finer *trakte* or *filter*, in tins and in foil packs, usually 250 g. If you use a coffee maker, percolator or cafétière, buy the *trakte* or *filter* grind. The coarser *kokemalt* grind is for traditional boiling in a coffee pot, where it is added to boiling water, stirred gently and left to stand for six to eight minutes. Markets with more extensive selections offer varieties, including mocha (*mokka*) and organically grown coffee (*organisk*). Specialist coffee shops and some of the larger supermarkets have grinders where you can select the type and amount of coffee and grind it there. Instant coffees, including decaffeinated (*koffeinfri*) are sold in jars and in foil packs, and instant flavoured coffees such as amaretto, espresso and cappuccino are also available in sachets.

Cookery books (*Oppskriftsbøker*) with Norwegian recipes are available in a wide variety in book shops (*bokhandel*). Most of these books are in Norwegian, but many are in English, German or French, translated from Norwegian originals. Many ☞ **Supermarkets** (Shopping chapter) offer cookery books, and some periodically feature displays of ring binders and recipe insert pages, usually based on the foods they sell. These books and ring binder pages are almost always in Norwegian.

If you are a new or temporary resident from abroad, you may have brought your favourite cookery books. If you have forgotten to bring them, you may be able to find them in the cookery book sections of major city book shops, which usually stock a wide range of foreign books. If you seek Norwegian recipes, you may be interested either in translated books or in books in Norwegian, depending on your proficiency in the language. The most popular books are listed below.

Books in English

The Norwegian Kitchen, Kjell E. Innli (editor), Kristiansand, Kam Forlag 1997, 224 pages hardcover, ISBN 8290-823-23-1

Norwegian Menus, Gunnar Jerman (editor), Oslo, Index Publishing, 1998, 158 pages hardcover, ISBN 82-7217-092-2.

Norway's Delight, Elise Sverdrup, Oslo, Aschehoug, 1988, 95 pages hardcover, ISBN 82-03-15954-0.

Books in Norwegian:

Den nye smårutete kokeboken, Ingrid Espelid Hovig, Oslo, Gyldendal, 3rd printing 1999, 317 pages hardcover, ISBN 82-05-20219-2.

Gyldendals nye store kokebok, Ingrid Espelid Hovig, Oslo, Gyldendal Fakta, 2nd edition 1998, 734 pages hardcover, ISBN 82-05-25531-8.

Norsk kokebok, Aase Strømstad, Oslo, Teknologisk Forlag, 1998, 717 pages hardcover, ISBN 82-512-0507-7.

Norsk mat til alle tider, Marit Bjerkås & Ingeborg Thoressen, Oslo, Gyldendal, 1996, 160 pages hardcover, ISBN 82-05-22788-8.

Glossary:

Kjøkken-ordbok, André Engh, Stavanger, Norges Kokkemesteres Landsforening, 1994, 371 pages hardcover, ISBN 82-990585-1-1; brief recipes of most dishes served in restaurants with names in Norwegian, French and German, as well as a glossary of terms in Norwegian, French, English, German, Danish, Finnish and Swedish.

Cookery terms (*Ord i matlaging*) are as numerous as they are in other languages. You will see them on food labels in the instructions for preparation (*tilberedning*). Alphabetically in Norwegian, the most common terms are:

arbeid (deigen) work (dough)
avkjøl cool
bland inn blend in
bland mix
bløte soften
brun i panne brown in a pan
dampe steam
dele divide
drysse sprinkle
elt knead
finhakket finely chopped
fritere deep fry
fryse freeze
garnere garnish
gni rub
grovhakket coarsely chopped
hell pour

hvelve turn out
kjevle ut roll out
knuse crush
kok boil
la let
legg på bunnen place in bottom
legg put (as in oven), cover (as with cloth)
løse seg dissolve
oppskåret cut up
øse baste
pensle med brush with
pisk whip
prikk prick
pynte decorate
rive grate
rør stir
server serve
sett set or put
sikte sieve
skille seg separate
skrelle peal
skylle rinse
smake til season to taste
småkoke simmer
smøre og strø grease and flour
smuldre crumble
snu turn
stek fry, bake
strimler strips
strø sprinkle
tilsett add
tine thaw
tøm vannet av drain
trill roll
under omrøring stirring continuously
varm warm
visp beat

Covers (Lokk) for opened food containers are fitted to the tops of some containers, such as the snugly fitting plastic lids on the tops of cans of ground coffee as well as the plastic lids supplied separately but free with cans of liver paste (leverpostei). Three useful covers are sold separately. The 8.5 by 15 cm rounded-end rectangular lid fits a can of mackerel; the 8 by 11 cm rounded-corner rectangular lid fits a can of sardines; and the deep 7 by 9.5 cm rectangular cap fits a block of ☞ **goat cheese**. They usually are made of red plastic and are solid either along with the items they fit or in blister packs hanging on displays along with other utensils.

Cream (Fløte) is sold in three varieties, in square paperboard cartons, usually 1/3 litre, but also 1 litre in some shops, each with the name of its type in a different colour and with the percentage fat marked on all sides of the carton:

Half cream (Kaffe fløte), "Kaffe" in blue, 10% fat, a thin pouring cream suitable for coffee (hence its name in Norwegian) or sauces. It cannot be whipped. It is ultrapasteurised, packaged in aseptic containers and has a long refrigerated shelf life, up to three months if unopened.

Single cream (Mat fløte), "Mat" in green, 22% fat, is used in cooking, especially in soups. It will whip thick, but not stiff. It is ultrapasteurised, packaged in aseptic containers and has a long refrigerated shelf life, up to three months if unopened.

Heavy or whipping cream (Kremfløte), "Krem" in orange, 38% fat, whips to double its original volume, suiting it for dessert toppings, cakes, pastries and soufflés. It is pasteurised and has a refrigerated shelf life of up to a week after the "best before" date stamped on its top seal.

Dairy products (Meireiprodukter) are popular: in 1998, the average resident drank nearly 130 litres of milk and more than 5 litres of cream, as well as ate some 6.6 litres of yoghurt, 15.4 kg of cheese and close to 4 kg of butter. In Europe, this puts Norway third in milk drinking, behind first-place Finland (149 litres) and fourth in cream consumption, behind first-place Denmark (9.3 litres), but only 11 in cheese eating and 12th in both Yoghurt and butter consumption. Various types of ☞ **milk**, ☞ **cream** and butter, nearly 70 different types of ☞ **cheese**, and other products including yoghurts, sauces, puddings and flavoured milk drinks are produced and sold throughout the country. The country is a net exporter of dairy products. Cheese leads in exports: in 1998, more than 27 thousand tons were exported, some 60% of it the increasingly popular Jarlsberg. Cheese is also imported from other countries, principally from Denmark, France and Switzerland, but in lesser quantity, some 2775 tons in 1998. That level, about a tenth as much as exports, is due in part to there being a high protective import duty on cheese.

Norwegian Dairies (Tine Norske Meierier) produce most of the domestic dairy products sold in stores under the Tine trademark, a co-operative organisation owned by some 90 dairies and 25 thousand milk producers in the country. For further information, contact the Tine Customer Service (*Tine Forbrukerservice*) ✆ 22938800, ✉ Breigt 10, 0187 Oslo, ⊕ http://www.tine.no with pages in Norwegian and in English. There are also many independent, local dairies and trademarked products, such as the *Synnøve Finden Meirier*, which produces and sells *Synnøve* cheeses in the greater Oslo area.

Desserts (*Desserter*) Packaged family favourites include compote (*kompott*), which is stewed fruit, either apricot (*aprikos*) or prunes (*sviske*) eaten with custard, over ice cream or just by itself, however it is not firm enough to use as a pie filling. Jelly (*gele*) in powder form, flavours include gooseberry (*stikkelsbær*), lemon (*sitron*), orange (*appelsin*), raspberry (*bringebær*), strawberry (*jordbær*). Rødgrøt, a red coloured jelly-like dessert made from thickened fruit juices of grapes (*druer*), cherries (*kirsebær*) and blackcurrants (*solbær*).

Sweet souffle (*fromasj*), lemon flavoured, ready to eat in the dairy section or in ready to mix packets. Cream (*kremfløte*) contains 35% fat and is suitable for whipping. Artificial whipped cream made from vegetable fat in spray cans or pouring 'cream', popular brands are *tastou krem topping, merikomel cuisine whipping.*

Puddings are available ready to eat in the dairy section, or in ready to pour packets. Flavours include almond (*mandel*), caramel (*karamell*), chocolate (*sjokolade*), mocha (*mokka*), rum (*rom*), vanilla (*vanilje*). Vanilla and caramel puddings are also sold frozen in a presentation mould, so when thawed, they can be turned out on a plate and decorated. When served, puddings are usually covered by a sauce (*puddingsaus*), for example strawberry or raspberry. Try chocolate or caramel sauce for pouring over ☞ **ice cream**. These sauces are available in squeezable plastic bottles or in sachets for mixing.

Sour cream porridge (*rømmegrøt*) and rice pudding (*risgrøt*) are delicious and can be made from scratch or bought ready to serve from the chill counters in the supermarket. Rice cream pudding (*riskrem*) is found in the freezer section.

Yoghurts made from full fat milk are popular and are sold flavoured and unflavoured with other ☞ **dairy products**.

Diabetic diet (*Kosthold for diabetikere*) Very few special diabetic food products are sold. This is because specific products for diabetic diets are no longer regarded as necessary. Instead, persons with diabetes are advised to learn the basic facts about foods and to read and interpret food labels, as many ordinary products meet the requirements of a normal healthy diet (*spis sunt*) following the guidelines set forth by the ☞ **National Council on Nutrition and Physical Activity**. The basic rules are that a diet should be high in starch (*stivelse*) and fiber (*fiber*), moderate in fat (*fett*) and low in salt (*salt*) and sugar (*sukker*). For dietary and other information on diabetes, contact The Norwegian Diabetes Association (*Norges Diabetesforbund*) ✆ 23051800, ☏ 23051801, ✉ PO Box 6442 Etterstad, 0605 Oslo, ✍ norges.diabetesforbund@dianet.no, ⊕ http://www.dianet.no with pages in Norwegian and in English. The Association is a member of the International Diabetes Federation ✆ +32 25385511, ☏ +32 25385114, ✉ 1 rue Defacqz, B-1000 Brussels, Belgium, ✍ idf@idf.org, ⊕ http://www.idf.org with pages in English and links to diabetes web sites world-wide.

Fats and oils (*Fett & olje*) Most butter is sold in blocks of 250g or 500g wrapped in gold foil or tubs. There are four varieties:
- *ektemeriesmør* ("ordinary dairy butter") containing 82% fat and 1.2% salt.
- *setersmør* ("mountain pasture butter") 80.5% fat and 2.5% salt.
- *usaltet meriesmør* ("unsalted butter") containing 83% fat.
- *fjell og gårdssmør* ("mountain and farm butter") containing 81% fat and 2.5% salt.

Tine is the most popular countrywide brand; look for packages with a flower design and the names of the types in different colours; the most-sold *ektemeriesmør* has green lettering, the lettering of the other types is in shades of brown.

Block margarine (*margarin*) is made up of 80% fat, 16% water and 2.5% salt, skimmed milk, vitamins A and D, betacarotene (*betakaroten*) and flavouring. The most popular cooking and baking margarine brand is *Melange*, it can be spread on bread and used in baking, frying and in biscuit recipes. *Soft* margarine contains about 40% fat, water, skimmed milk vitamins A, D and E and about 1.3% salt. It is not suitable for frying or making biscuits. There are new varieties of margarine being introduced, so look at the packaging when buying. *Bremykt* is a spread containing 70% butter and 30% soya oil. Harder fats like *Flott* (100% fat), *Delfia* (100% coconut fat) are used for deep fat frying and batters like doughnuts. *Delfia* is used in a very popular cake, the recipe is written on the packaging. Soya oil (*soyaolje*), corn oil (*maisolje*), olive oil (*olivenolje*), safflower oil (*solfrøolje*) and readily available in supermarkets. Less common oils like ground nut oil (*jordnøttolje*) and walnut oil (*valnøttolje*) are available in fruit and vegetable shops, larger supermarkets and ☞ **foreign/ethnic food shops** (Shopping chapter). *Formfett* is vegetable oil in spray form, used for greasing waffle irons, cake tins and baking trays. Unlike other fats, the spray can should be stored at room temperature. Another oil that you will hear a lot about is cod liver oil (*tran*) although this is not used for cooking, but traditionally is taken in the wintertime, usually in the morning, in liquid form by the tablespoon or in gelatine-coated capsules to promote health in winter.

Fish and shellfish (*fisk og skalldyr*) are sold fresh by fish mongers (*fiskehandler*) and the seafood counters of supermarkets and frozen by most food shops. "Fresh" is no longer expressed in days, as it was before refrigeration became common. Freshness is now an expression of quality and means that fish is not processed, salted or smoked. Fish retains its fresh quality for many days, provided it is continuously refrigerated in storage and transport at temperatures of 0° to 1°C, but preferably not over 1°C. Consequently, frozen whole fish can also be regarded as fresh. Some fish are canned: mackerel is sold fresh, frozen or canned in tomato paste, while sardines are sold only in cans, as is tuna (*tunfisk*), which is imported. Some fish, principally cod, salmon and trout, are also sold cured, smoked, salted or dried. Many saltwater and freshwater fish are available, led by the North Atlantic varieties caught by commercial fishermen, with cod being the leading fish, today as throughout history. From Viking times on, dried cod was the prime provision for ships. Norway's maritime trade was built in the middle ages. Bergen then

was a pivotal city of the Hanseatic league and exported split cod, salted and dried on wooden racks, called flakes, on rocky flats (*klippfisk*) and salted cod (*sprengt torsk*) to Great Britain and the Continent and imported salt to salt the cod that it exported. Throughout Europe, from the mid 16th to the mid 18th centuries, cod accounted for more than half of all fish consumed. So common was the fish, that the word acquired other meanings in the language. As in English, in which the word "cod" means a hoax or prank, the word *tosk*, a variant of *torsk* in Norwegian, means "fool". Cod remains so important that Norwegian commercial fishermen and fish shops and counters throughout the country distinguish between nine principal species – *torsk, kolmule, sei, brosme, kolje* or *hyse, lysing, lange, lyr* and *hvitting* – and for Atlantic cod, between coastal cod (*kysttorsk*) and winterspring cod (*skrei*). Cookbooks distinguish between the varieties of fishes as well as between saltwater fish (*havfisk*) and freshwater fish (*ferskvanns fisk*) and between fat fish (*fett fisk*) such as herring and mackerel and lean fish (*mager fisk*), such as those of the cod family. Most of the fish sold is caught by fishermen and is now called "wild", to distinguish it from farmed fish (*oppdrettsfisk*), which now accounts for about a tenth of the annual Norwegian production of some three million tons. The principal farmed fish are Atlantic salmon and rainbow trout. Although fish farming is commercially competitive and is a thriving export industry, farmed and wild fish are not identical, mostly because a growth environment contrived by humans is not the same as that of nature. Consequently, opinion on farmed fish varies. Gourmets prefer the wild varieties. As author Mark Kurlansky observed in *Cod*, "Gastronomically, a wild salmon and a farmed salmon have as much in common as a side of wild boar has with pork chops"*. Nonetheless, farmed salmon and trout are cheaper and more consistently available in shops than their wild counterparts. A comprehensive brochure with large colour drawings of the principal fish and shellfish and extensive tables of nutritional content, entitled *Facts About Fish* is published in English, French, German and Norwegian editions for free distribution by the Norwegian Seafood Export Council (*Eksportutvalget for fisk*) in Tromsø ✆ 77603333, ⊠ 77680012, ✉ Skippergt 35/39, 9005 Tromsø, ✉ postmottak@nsec.dep.telemax.no, ⊕ http://www.seafood.no with pages in Norwegian,

English and Japanese. Alphabetically, by their names in English, the most common fish and shellfish are:

Atlantic cod *torsk*
Atlantic salmon *laks*
blue whiting *kolmule*
bream *brasme*
burbot *lake*
capelin *lodde*
catfish, wolf-fish *steinbitt*
clam *musling*
coalfish, saithe *sei*
crab *krabbe*
crayfish *kreps*
cusk *brosme*
picked dogfish, spiny dogfish *pigghå*
dogfish *rødhå*
eel *ål*
flounder *flyndre, skrubbe*
haddock *kolje, hyse*
hake *lysing*
halibut *hellefisk, kveite*
herring *sild*
ling *lange*
lobster *hummer*
mackerel *makrell*
monkfish, anglerfish *breiflabb*
blue mussel *blåskjell*
Norway lobster *bokstavhummer, sjøkreps*
perch *abbor*
pike *gjedde*
plaice *rødspette*
pollack *lyr*
redfish, rosefish *uer*
sardine *sardin*
scallop *kammusling*
shrimp, prawn *reke*
silver bream *flire*
sole *sjøtunge*
spiny lobster *languster*
sprat *brisling*
squid *akkar*
trout *ørret*
turbot *piggvar*
whitefish *sik*
whiting *hvitting*

*Cod, by Mark Kurlansky, Penguin Books 1997, ISBN 0-14-027501-0, page 196.

Food control & inspection (*Næringsmiddeltilsyn*) is undertaken by the Norwegian Food Control Authority (*Statens Næringsmiddeltilsyn-SNT*). SNT supervises the work of the food industry, promotes Norwegian interests in international commissions and the UN organ Codex Alimentarius, incorporates EEA regulations into the national regulations; develops national regulations and initiates programs for charting and controlling unknown substances, infectious substances and natural poisons in foodstuffs. SNT also handles applications regarding laws and rules and deals with complaints as decided in the municipality. It notifies the public after consultation with experts whenever a foodstuff can endanger health. The exercising of SNT's broad spectrum of activities is done at a municipal level (*kommunale næringsmiddeltilsynet-KNT*), represented by 80 local offices dealing with compliance regarding the laws and regulations governing the production and sale of foodstuffs. The type of functions undertaken at municipal level is dictated by the size of the local food industry. They approve the facilities that import, produce, pack, store, serve and sell foodstuffs. They oversee and control the production and trade of all food and beverages (including milk). They test the ☞ **water quality** (Climate and Environment chapter) for both drinking water and bathing water. They follow up tips and complaints from the public, as for example in food poisoning. They run laboratories to test the bacteriological quality of foodstuffs and beverages, analysis of food additives and packaging in relation to food contamination. They control the meat before and after slaughtering, and since Chernobyl in 1986, they systematically check for radioactive content of meat from sheep and reindeer in the areas affected by the fallout. They supervise imported foodstuffs. They also have a mussel warning (*blåkjellvarsel*) service on their web site, which tells you by area, whether the mussels found there are safe to eat. For further information contact SNT ✆ 22246650, 🖷 22246699, ✉ PO Box 8187 Dep, 0034 Oslo, ✉ postmottak@snt.dep.telemax.no, 🌐 http://www.snt.no with links to rules, regulations and other information, as well as a search engine for food topics.

Fruits, berries and vegetables (*Frukt, bær og grønnsaker*) Consumption of fresh produce is low compared to other European countries. In a typical year, the average resident consumes 82 kg of fruit and berries and 102 kg of vegetables, of which 42 kg are potatoes. The average resident of a country in the European Union (EU) consumes slightly more fruit and berries and twice as much vegetables. The independent Information Centre for Fruit and Vegetables (*Opplysningskontoret for frukt og grønnsaker*) points to six causes of the relatively low consumption:

- Lack of tradition
- Custom of only one warm meal a day
- Northerly climate and relatively short growing season
- Limited availability outside of larger cities
- Varying quality
- High prices

Potatoes once were the basis of a warm meal, but consumption is declining and now is half of what it was in the 1950s. The decline is due in part to a rise in the consumption of pasta and processed potato products and to changing eating habits, as the daily family dinner is less and less regular. Fruits are more popular than vegetables, partly because they are eaten as convenience foods between mealtimes. Apples are the most popular fruit; some 20 kg per year per person are consumed in the country. Eating habits are gradually changing, as more Norwegians travel abroad, citizens of other countries immigrate to and settle in Norway and ethnic restaurants have opened in cities and towns throughout the country. The most commonly sold fruits, berries and vegetables are listed below. For further information, contact *Opplysningskontoret for frukt og grønnsaker* ✆ 23249400, 🖷 22644163, ✉ PO Box 187 Økern, 0510 Oslo, ✉ post@ofg.no, ☻ http://www.ofg.no

English	Norwegian	Botanical name
apple	*eple*	Malus domestica
apricot	*aprikos*	Prunus armeniaca
artichoke	*artiskokk*	Cynaro scolymus
asparagus	*asparges*	Asparagus officinalis
aubergine (eggplant)	*aubergine*	Solanum melongena
avocado	*avocado*	Persea americana
banana	*banan*	Musa paradsiaca
bean, green	*brekkbønner*	Phaseolus vulgaris
beet, red	*rødbete*	Beta vulgaris rubra
black currant	*solbær*	Ribes nigrum
blackberry	*bjørnebær*	Rubus fruticosus
blueberry	*blåbær*	Vaccinium corymbosum
broccoli	*brokkoli*	Brassica oleracea italica
brussels sprouts	*rosenkål*	Brassica oleracea gemmifera
cabbage	*hodekål*	Brassica oleracea var. alba
cactus pear	*kaktusfiken*	Optunia ficus indica
carrot	*gulrot*	Daucus Carota
cauliflower	*blomkål*	Brassica oleracea botrytis
celeriac	*knollselleri*	Apium graveolens var. rapaceum
celery	*stilkselleri*	Apium graveolens var. dulce
cherimoya	*cherimoya*	Annona cherimola
cherry	*kirsebær*	Prunus cerasus
chinese cabbage	*kinakå*	Brassica pekinensis
chives	*gressløk*	Allium schoenoprasum
clementine	*klementin*	Citrus reticulata
cloudberry	*multer*	Rubus chamaemorus
corn, sweet	*maiskolbe*	Zea mays var. rugosa

English	Norwegian	Botanical name
cranberry	tyttebær	Vaccinium vitisidaea
cucumber	agurk, slange	Cucumis sativus
currant	rips	Ribes rubrum
date	daddel	Phoenix dactylifera
dill	dill	Anethum graveolens
fennel	fennikel	Foeniculum vulgare
fig	fiken	Ficus carica
gooseberry	stikkelsbær	Ribes uva-crispa
grape	drue	Vitis vinifera
grapefruit	grapefrukt	Citrus paradisii
kiwi	kiwi	Actinidia chinensis
kumquat	kumquat	Fortunella japonica
leek	purre	Allium porrum
lemon	sitron	Citrus limon
lettuce, iceberg	isbergsalat	Lactuca sativa capitata
lime	lime	Citrus aurantifolia
lychee	litchi	Litchi chinensis
mango	mango	Mangifera indica
melon, honey	melon, honning	Cucumis melo var. melitensis
morello	moreller	Prunus avium
mushroom	sjampinjong	Agaricus bisporus
nectarine	nektarin	Prunus persica var. nectarina
onion	løk	Allium cepa
orange	appelsin	Citrus sinensis
papaya	papaya	Carica papaya
parsley root	persillerot	Petroselinum hortense
parsley	persille, krus	Petroselinum crispum
passion fruit	pasjonsfrukt	Passiflora edulis
pea, green	sukkererter	Pisum sativum
peach	fersken	Prunus persica
pear	pære	Pyrus communis
pineapple	ananas	Ananas comosus
plum	plomme	Prunus domestica
pomegranate	granateple	Punica granatum
potato	poteter	Solanum tuberosum L
radish	reddik	Raphanus sativus
radicchio (chicory)	sikorisalat	Cichorium intybus
raspberry	bringebær	Rubus idaeus
red pepper	paprika	Capsicum annuum
rutabaga (Swede)	kålrot	Brassica napus rapifera
spinach	spinat	Spinacia oleracea
strawberry	jordbær	Fragraria x ananassa
tomato	tomat	Lycopersicon esculentum
turnip	nepe	Brassica rapa rapifera
watermelon	vannmelon	Citrullus vulgaris
zucchini squash	squash	Cucurbita pepo

Game (vilt) is sold by game dealers (vilt in Yellow Pages) and by butchers that deal in it (kjøtt og vilt). The hunting of wild animals and the farming of tame animals supply it. European elk (elg in Norwegian, Alces alces in Latin), red deer (hjort, Cervus elaphus) and roe deer (rådyr, Capreolus capreolus) are hunted in the autumn. Reindeer (rein, Rangifer tarandus) is farmed in Finnmark county and is hunted in the winter. In season, meat is sold fresh, and out of season it is sold frozen in larger markets. The more common game birds include willow grouse (lirype, Lagopus lagopus), ptarmigan (fjellrype, Lagopus mutus), black grouse (orrfugl, Lyrurus tetrix), large European grouse, or capercaillie (storfugl, Tetrao urgallus) and hazel grouse (jerpe, Testrastes bonasia). Some wading birds, including duck (ender), geese (gjess) and sea birds (sjøfugl) are hunted, as are small mammals such as hare (hare) and beaver (bever).

Goat cheese (Geitost) is in a class by itself. In its various varieties and offspring cheeses, geitost is an indelible a part of everyday life; few homes are without it. It travels to work and school in packed lunches the country over. It is a standby on cold tables in mountain lodges and city hotels. Sometimes it appears at teatime, and often is served with waffles. By far, it is the leading cheese, accounting for a fifth of all cheese sold. Unlike other goat cheeses, such as the French chevret or rigottes, geitost is semi-soft and brown, as well as sweet. The consistency, colour and sweetness are due to the way it is made. All cheese making begins by separating milk into semisolid curds and watery liquid whey, high in milk sugar. Traditionally, the curds are used to make cheese, while whey has either been discarded or used to feed livestock. But in Norway, goat milk whey was boiled down to make "whey-butter" (prim) and lean whey cheese, both perishable and nearly tasteless.

Then, in the Gudbrandsdal Valley in the mid 19th century, budeia (farm maiden) Anne Haav working a seter – a summer pasture farm like a croft in Scotland – added cream to a vat of boiling goat milk whey and let it solidify to a solid mass at one-tenth its original volume. The result was a tasty, fat cheese that kept well and therefore could be sold. The recipe spread, and soon other seter were making their own varieties of geitost. Modern dairy processes have long since replaced the seter farms as the country's prime source of dairy products, and more productive cows

have replaced goats as milk producers. Yet the seter tradition lives on. Norwegians continue to boil whey down to a brown, sweet cheese while in other countries it is regarded as a by-product of cheese making and, aided by modern chemistry, turned into milk sugar, lactic acid, glycerine and alcohol. There are three types of geitost that differ by their content of goat's milk and in hue of the finished cheese, from a dark, coffee brown to a creamy, almost yellow tan. The colour is governed by the degree of caramelisation of the lactose. Real goat cheese (ekte geitost) is the darkest, sharpest variety, and as the name states, is made completely from goat's milk. Next in percentage and lighter and milder is Gudbrands Valley cheese (Gudbrandsdalost), made from 10% goat's milk and 90% cow's milk and named for the valley where geitost was first made. Cream whey cheese (fløtemysost) is lighter and milder yet, and is made wholly from cow's milk. Properly speaking, the three varieties classify as brown cheese (brunost), as only one is made wholly from goat's milk, but geitost persists in the everyday language. The cheeses are made in varieties differing by percentage fat content in dry matter, indicated by a two-digit number after a cheese identification letter. In order of increasing fat percentage: BG20 (blandet geitost, mixed goat and cow milk cheese, 20% fat in dry matter), H20 (halvfet, half-fat cream whey cheese, 20%), F33 (fløtemysost, cream whey cheese, 33%) and G35 (Gudbransdalost, 35%). Moreover, there are slight local variations of all types of brown cheese, mostly by shade. On the west coast, a darker cheese is preferred, while a lighter, almost yellow cheese is favoured in the north. Eastern and central preference lies between these two extremes. G35 Gudbrandsdalost is biggest seller in supermarkets and is exported under the Ski Queen label. All the varieties are sold in plastic-wrapped, uniform rectangular blocks of one-half and one kilogram weight. You can open the wrapper at the top and close it again to keep the cheese fresh. But ☞ **covers** made for the purpose seal better and keep the cheese fresher.

With the tradition of geitost goes the custom of how it is eaten. It is best enjoyed wafer-thin, on slices of coarser-grain breads or on rye or wheat biscuits, or alternatively as a sweet, in folded, buttered waffles. The wafer-thin slices are most easily produced with a cheese plane, one of the better-known ☞ **Norwegian inventions** (Character, Customs,

Country chapter). Skilled users can cut 175 slices from a one kilogram block of *geitost*.

Grains, nuts and pulses (*Korn, nøtter og belgfrukter*) are found in the baking and health food sections of supermarkets as well as in ☞ **Foreign/ethnic food shops** or ☞ **Health food shops** (Shopping chapter).

English	Norwegian
Grains	**Korn**
buckwheat	bokkhvete
corn	mais
graham	hvetegrøpp
guinea corn	durra
millet	hirse
oats	havre
pasta	pasta
pearl barley	byggryn
rice	ris
rye	rygg
wheat	hvete
Nuts	**Nøtter**
almond	mandel
Brazil	brasil
cashew	cashew
chestnut	kastanje
coconut	kokos
hazelnut	hasselnøtt
macadamia	macadamia
peanut	peanøtt
pecan	pecan
pine nut	pinjenøtt
pistachio	pistasj
walnut	valnøtt
Pulses	**Belgfrukter**
broad beans	snittebønner
butter/lima beans	limabønner
chick peas	kikerter
haricot/french beans	hagebønner
lentils	linser
peas, yellow or green	erter, gule eller grønne
soya beans	soyabønner
urd/mung beans	mungbønner

Halal meat (*Halal kjøtt*) comes from animals that meet the requirements of and have been slaughtered in the manner prescribed by Muslim law. In Norway, Halal beef, lamb and chicken are sold by butcher shops (*kjøttforretninger*) and by grocers (*dagligvarer*) in the areas of Oslo and other cities where Muslims live. Halal beef and lamb are slaughtered by Muslim butchers at Norwegian abattoirs and thereafter shipped to Halal shops. Halal chicken is slaughtered under Muslim supervision at chicken processing plants and is packed in distinctive plastic shrink-fit plastic bags and then frozen and distributed to shops. Fish is considered Halal but is not subject to Muslim practice in slaughter, so it may be bought fresh or frozen, at any fish shop (*fisk, detalj*) or supermarket. Proper Halal meat is stamped or marked, usually with the word Halal twice, once in Latin letters (as here) and once in Arabic letters. There are two ways to find shops selling Halal meats. First, look for the word Halal in the names of shops listed under *kjøttforretninger* in the Yellow Pages. Second, and in most cases quickest, inquire at the nearest Mosque (*Moské*), which will have information specific to the needs of newly arrived Muslims.

Herbs & Spices (*urter & krydder*) are sold, dried, in supermarkets, butchers, fishmongers and ☞ **Foreign/ethnic food shops** (this chapter) in glass jars and foil packets. Ground spices have the word *malt* on the packaging, while whole spices have *hel*. Popular herbs like parsley, coriander, dill, basil, mint and chives are sold fresh in greengrocers and most supermarkets. See the table on the following two pages.

HERBS AND SPICES

English	Norwegian	Botanical name
alfalfa	*lucedrne*	Medicago sativa
allspice	*allehånde*	Pimenta officinalis
anise	*anis*	Pimpinella anisum
basil	*basilikum*	Ocimum basilicum
bay	*laurbærblad*	Laurus nobilis
camomile	*kamille*	Matricariae flos
caper	*kapers*	Capparis spinosa
caraway	*karve*	Carum carvi
cardamom	*kardemomme*	Elettaria cardamomum
carob	*johannesbrød*	Ceratonia siliqua
cayenne	*kajennepepper*	Capsicum annum
chervil	*kjørvel*	Anthriscum cerefolium
chilli powder	*chilipulver*	Capsicum annum var. frutescens
chives	*gressløk*	Allium schoenoprasum
cinnamon	*kanel*	Cinnamomum zeylanicum
cloves	*nellik*	Eugenia aromatica
coriander	*koriander*	Coriandrum sativum
cumin	*spisskarve*	Cuminum cyminum
curry leaf	*karriblad*	Chalcas koenigii
curry powder	*karri*	None: a mix of spices
dill	*dill*	Anethum gravoelens
dill seed	*dillfrø*	Anethum gravoelens
fennel	*fennikel*	Foeniculum vulgare
fennel seed	*fennikelfrø*	Foeniculum vulgare
fenugreek	*bukkehornkløver*	Trigonella foenumgraecum
garlic	*hvitløk*	Allium sativum
ginger	*ingefær*	Zingiber officinale
horseradish	*pepperrot*	Armoracia rusticana
juniper	*einebær*	Juniperus communis
lemon balm	*sitronmelisse*	Melissae herba
lemon grass	*sitrongres*	Cymbopogon citratus
linseed	*linfrø*	Linum usitatissimum
liquorice	*lakris*	Glycyrrhiza glabra
marjoram	*merian*	Organum majorana
mint	*mynte*	Mentha
mustard (seed)	*sennep (frø)*	Brassica nigra juncea
nutmeg and mace	*muskatnøtt/blomme*	Myristica fragrans
oregano	*oregano*	Organum vulgare
paprika	*paprika*	Capsicum tgetragonum
parsley	*persille*	Petroso
pepper, black/white	*pepper, sort/hvit*	Piper nigrum
peppercorns	*hel pepper*	Piper nigrum
peppermint leaves	*peppermynteblad*	Menthae peperitae folium
poppy seed	*valmuefrø*	Papaver somniferum
pumpkin seed	*gresskarfrø*	Curcurbita maxima
rosemary	*rosmarin*	Rosmarinus officinalis

English	Norwegian	Botanical name
saffron	*safran*	Crocus sativus
sage	*salvie*	Salvia officinalis
salt	*salt*	Sal
savoury	*sar*	Saturejae folium
sesame seed	*sesam*	Sesamum indicum
sunflower seed	*solsikkefrø*	Helianthus annuus
tamarind	*tamarind*	Tamarindus indica
tarragon	*estragon*	Artemisia dracunulus
thyme	*timian*	Thymus vulgaris
turmeric	*gurkemeie*	Curcuma longa
vanilla	*vanilje*	Vanilla planifolia
wild marjoram	*bergmynte*	Origani herba

Ice cream (*Is*) Yearly ice cream sales amount to 59 million litres, equivalent to 13.5 litres for every person in the country. There are three major producers with countrywide distribution. Norsk Iskrem leads, having slightly more than half the market with its popular Diplom-Is brand and high-end Mövenpick Swiss and Bertelli Italian brands. Hening-Olsen has about a quarter of the market, Nestlé-Drammens Is 13% and several smaller, local producers together about 2.5%. Most food shops sell ice cream in one-litre and two-litre containers, as well as ice cream bars, sandwiches, cones and the like, which also are sold by kiosks and petrol stations. Food industry regulations set requirements for ice cream ingredients. For instance, a product labelled "ice cream" (*fløteis*) must contain at least 8% butterfat and 35% nonfat milk solids by weight, and one litre of it must weigh at least 500 grams. The contents list on a typical *fløteis* package might read:

Melk, fløte, sukker, mysepulver, vegetabilsk emulgator: mono-diglycerider av spisefettsyrer (E-471), stabilisatorer: natriumkarboxy-metylcellulose (E-466), johannesbrødkjernel (E-410), guarkjernemel (E-412), karragenan (E-407), natriumalginat (E-5401). Vanillin, etylvanillin, aroma

which in English translation reads:

"Milk, cream, sugar, powdered whey, vegetable emulsifier: Glyceryl monostearate, distearate (E471), stabilisers: Carmellose sodium (E466), Carob bean gum (E410), Guar flour (E412), Carrageenan (E407), Sodium alginate (E401). Vanilla, vanillin, flavour."

In alphabetical order by their names in Norwegian, *fløteis* and the other principal varieties are:

Fløteis Ice cream, containing at least 9% butterfat and 34% nonfat milk solids by weight.

Fløteis mykis Soft ice cream, containing at least 9% butterfat and 34% nonfat milk solids by weight (or 8% butterfat if it contains fruit or berries), as well as glycerol to make it softer to ease serving at freezer temperatures.

Fromasj Mousse, containing sweetened and flavoured whipped cream or cream and gelatine.

Fruktis Fruit ice, containing at least 10% fruit material and 20% nonfat solids by weight.

Lett is Light ice cream, with an energy content (in calories) at least 30% lower than *fløteis*; usually contains less fat than does *fløteis*, but can contain sugar.

Melke is Ice milk, containing 4% – 9% butterfat and at least 27% nonfat milk solids by weight.

Luksus iskrem Premium ice cream, containing more butterfat than *fløteis*, typically 11% – 18%.

Sherbet sherbet, containing at least 10% fruit material, 20% nonfat solids and 1% butterfat by weight.

Sorbet Non-dairy sherbet, containing at least 10% fruit material and 20% nonfat solids by weight.

Vannis Light fruit ice, containing less than 10% fruit material by weight.

Yoghurtis Frozen yoghurt, similar to *lett is*, but made from yoghurt instead of milk, and usually containing about 3% butterfat by weight.

Knives and forks (*Kniv og gaffel*) are used in eating in the continental European manner. Throughout a meal, the fork is held in the left hand, the knife in the right. The knife is used to move food onto the fork and to cut one piece of food for each bite. Holding only the fork in the right hand and moving it to the left to hold meat or fish while cutting many pieces, as is the custom in some countries outside Europe, is considered bad manners. But it is acceptable at home and in casual eating, such as in fast food restaurants when only a plastic fork is provided.

Kosher foods (Kosher mat) are those fit or allowed to be eaten according to the *Kashruth* dietary rules of ☞ **Judaism** (Church and Religion chapter). *Kosher* comes from Yiddish and is the term in English and in most European languages. *Kasher*, the Hebrew word, is also used. Muslims dietary rules also permit eating Kosher foods. *Shechitah*, the slaughtering of animals by a certified person in the prescribed manner, is prohibited in Norway. Consequently, Kosher meats are imported, mostly from Canada. Likewise, Norwegian cheese is not Kosher, but Kosher cheese is imported from Denmark. Kosher meats, cheeses and other items are imported from Israel. Some Norwegian foods, such as the traditional *King Oscar* Brisling Sardines, are authorised as Kosher. Some supermarkets sell Kosher products, usually placed on shelves near the dietary foods. The *Kosher Senter Hatikwa* in Oslo sells a complete selection of Kosher foods ✆ 22609166, 📠 22609206, ✉ Wm Thranes gate 36, 0171 Oslo, open Tuesdays, Wednesdays and Thursdays from 4 p.m. to 6 p.m. and Fridays from noon to 2 p.m.

Lunch (Lunsj) Visitors and new residents, even those from neighbouring Sweden, find the lack of accustomed midday meals perplexing. They see Norwegians getting along at midday on what appear to be picnic snacks. Lunch as it's known internationally remains rare on the eating scene. How can Norwegians survive their school or working days? Easy, say Norwegians, who have learned to anticipate the question, overstating the national habit by remarking that "we eat no lunch here". What most Norwegians eat away from home at midday are their packed lunches (*matpakke*), home-made snacks of open-faced sandwiches (*smørbrød*). The *matpakke* or *skolemat* ("school food") or *nistepakke* ("travel provisions") is no second-rate substitute. Unlike the packed lunches of the U.K or the brown bags of the USA, the *matpakke* connotes neither lack of rank in a

company nor lack of time to eat lunch. The *matpakke* is a bulwark of daily nutrition. It consists of slices of bread, decked with cheese, sliced meat or spreads, collectively known as *pålegg* (literally "lay-on"). Preparation includes stacking the *pålegg*-decked slices of bread, each covered with a small rectangle of sandwich paper called *mellomleggspapir* ("in-between paper"), and the whole wrapped in *matpapir* (sandwich paper). The bread and *pålegg* are much like the fare at ☞ **breakfast**. Indeed most *matpakke* are made at the breakfast table, with the result that lunch often is a packaged version of breakfast. In consuming the *matpakke*, the wrapping paper is folded out in lieu of a plate, and the small sheets of *mellomleggspapir* are plucked off, one-by-one. The *matpakke* tradition is acknowledged in regulations that oblige employers to furnish lunchroom facilities and offer beverages, usually coffee, tea and milk, at reduced prices. (Serving alcoholic beverages is prohibited in workplaces.) One of the perquisites offered by larger employers is a well-appointed lunchroom, often a cafeteria selling cold and warm meals to *matpakke*-less employees. The *matpakke* has become the very symbol of everyday school and working life. Conservationists, traffic experts and irritated motorists alike decry *matpakke kjørere* (*matpakke* drivers), cars carrying only their commuting drivers, clogging roads at peak hours. Literature documents the *matpakke*: Agnar Mykle, known for powerful description, details "the industrial worker's scepter, the valise containing a *matpakke* and a thermos". Humorist Kjell Aukrust maintains that party sandwiches differ from the *matpakke* variety only by being cut on a diagonal instead of straight across. There are even *matpakke* jokes. One standby is the tale of a gruff fellow who always opens his *matpakke* with a curse and gives away or discards a slice of bread decked with pungent *gammelost* cheese. "If you cannot stand *gammelost*, why not tell your wife to use another cheese?" his lunchmates ask. "Mind your own business," he growls: "I make my own *matpakke*!"

Meals (Måltid) Though eating habits are changing and fast food is increasingly popular, tradition prevails, and most Norwegians have four meals a day, three light and one major. The language reflects the pattern: it does not distinguish between 'meal' and 'mealtime' as does English, but makes do with one word, *måltid* (literally "time for food"). Breakfast (*frokost*) starts the day. Heavier than the European 'continental breakfast' but lighter than the U.K. variety, it needs an early sequel. Lunch (*lunsj*) is a late-morning snack, usually taken to and eaten at school or one's workplace. Dinner (*middag*) is the main and often only hot meal of the day, traditionally served sometime between 4 and 6 o'clock in the afternoon, at the end of the working day. With dinner that early, there's usually a light follow-up supper (*aftens*) later in the evening, prudently before bedtime. At weekends, the pattern changes insignificantly, though supper may be replaced by a longer after-dinner coffee (*ettermiddags kaffe*) and cake session, particularly when there are dinner guests.

Measures in cooking (*Mål og vekt i matlaging*) are in the metric system, usually volumes for liquids and grains and weights for all other ingredients. So you will need a graduated measure (*mål*) and a kitchen scale (*kjøkkenvekt*). Some foods are sold with quantity divisions on the package. For instance, butter (*smør*) has 50 gram and 100 gram increments marked on the wrapper, so you can cut off the right amount. The common measurements are:

g gram, the basic unit of weight.
hg hectogram, one hundred grams or one-tenth of a kilogram, unit of weight for fine foods sold in shops.
kg kilogram, one thousand grams, the basic unit of weight in shops.
l litre, the basic unit of volume in shops.
cl centilitre, one-hundredth of a litre.
dl decilitre, one-tenth of a litre, the most common unit of volume in recipes.
ml millilitre, one-thousandth of a litre or one-tenth of a centilitre, seldom used directly in recipes.
ss or spsk *spiseskje*, table spoon, equivalent to nearly 15 ml.
ts or tsk *teskje*, tea spoon, equivalent to nearly 5 ml.
kopp cup, 2.5 dl or $1/4$ litre, sometimes used in recipes.
If you use English or American recipes in Norway, you will need to convert from the English system to the metric system. Remember that the unit of weight, the pound, is the same in the UK and the USA, but the unit of volume, the quart, differs.
cup 3 dl UK or 2.4 dl. USA
pint 5.6 dl UK or 4.8 dl USA
quart 11.3 dl UK or 9.5 dl USA
teacup 1.5 dl UK
tablespoon usually 15 ml, but may vary
teaspoon usually 5 ml, but may vary
ounce 28.5 g
pound 454 g

In American and British recipes, oven temperatures may be given in degrees Fahrenheit, in relative terms, or, in the UK, in gas oven Regulo® thermostat marks. The conversions are:

Relative term	Gas oven Regulo® mark	Degrees Fahrenheit	Degrees Celsius
very slow	$1/4$	240°	116°
		250°	121°
	$1/2$	275°	135°
slow	1	290°	143°
		300°	149°
	2	310°	154°
		325°	163°
moderate	3	340°	171°
		350°	177°
	4	360°	182°
fairly hot		375°	191
	5	380°	193°
hot	6	400°	204°
		425°	218°
	7	435°	224°
very hot		450°	232°
	8	460°	238°
		475°	246°
extremely hot	9	480°	249°
		500°	260°
		525°	274°

Meat (*kjøtt*) Slightly less than a third of all meat is sold as fresh cuts. The rest is processed meat in the form of sausage (*pølse*), minced meat (*kjøttdeig*) and cold cuts (*pålegg*). Available at all supermarkets and butchers (*slakterier*). Butchers and supermarket meat counters provide well-illustrated cookery booklets for beef (*storfekjøtt*), barbecuing (*grill mat*), lamb (*lammekjøtt*), pork(*svinekjøtt*), reindeer (*reins-dyrkjøtt*) and sausages (*pølser*) issued by *Opplysningskontoret for kjøtt*, showing you the different cuts and suggesting ways to cook and serve, and how to freeze raw meat. For further information contact the Meat Information Office (*Opplysningskontoret for Kjøtt*) ☎ 22092100. 🖷 22150220, ✉ PO Box 395 Økern, 0513 Oslo ✉ post@ofk.no, 🖰 http://www.ofk.no

Beef (*Storfekjøtt*) For roast beef or dishes prepared in a frying pan, choose cuts from the hind quarters, for casseroles choose cuts from the fore quarters. These cuts are generally cheaper than the more tender hind quarter cuts. Cuts of up to 1.5kg can be prepared in the microwave, ensure that the cut has an even shape. *Karbonadedeig* is ground beef, free of sinew and up to 6% fat, is the leanest of meat and is used in hmaburgers, beef tartar and making minced steak. *Kjøttdeig* is ground beef with up to 14% fat, used in meat sauces for spaghetti, *kjøttkaker* (rissoles) and hamburgers. *Kjøttfarse* (sausage meat) made of beef, maybe prok and beef and pork fat. It is like *kjøttdeig* but with added salt, seasoning, starch and milk or water. Used in *kjøttboller* (meatballs) and meat rissoles.

Pork (*svinekjøtt*) Pork sold today is considerably leaner, it's fat content being 2-5 %. The fat is concentrated, so can be removed from the cut of meat. *Medisterdeig* is a mixture of beef and pork containing up to 25% fat and used in *medisterpølser* (chipolata sausages) and *medisterkaker* (sausage meat rissoles). *Medisterfarse* (pork sausage meat) sometimes with beef and beef or pork fat, which cannot be more than 23%. Used in sausage meat rissoles and *kålruletter* (stuffed cabbage leaves).

Sausages (*pølser*) are extremely popular, made with meat, potato and wheat flour. Well known varieties are *kjøttpolse*, *wienerpølse*, *grillpølse* containing not more than 20% fat, leaner varieties contain up to 14% fat, the only exception being *medisterpølse* (chipolata sausages) where the fat content is 25%.

New coarser varieties such as *løkpølse* (onion), *lammepølse* (lamb) and *brattwurst* are gaining popularity. 70 to 100 years ago most farms made their own sausages, very few do that today, although regional varieties still exist made with natural gut, high percentage of meat, coarse in texture and very tasty. Skin free 'straight' *grillpølse* are a relatively new invention. They are made with skin, but it is removed at the end of the production process. Do not boil sausages.

Mutton and lamb (*sau- og lammekjøtt*) Får is a common name for both lamb and mutton, with *fårikål* (lamb and cabbage stew) a national favourite that it even has its own fanclub, *Fårikålens venner*.

Offal (*Innmat*) sold in shops is strictly controlled by vets and comes from young animals to guarantee freshness. As it does not keep well, it is frozen soon after slaughter. Once purchased, use as soon as possible.

Cold cuts (*kjøttpålegg*) *Kokt skinke* (boiled ham), *lammerull* (press lambed interleaved with pork fat, *servelat* (beef, pork and binding agents. Cured (*speket*) cold cuts are called *spekemat* (å speke- to dry) literally means cured (dried) meat. The meat is salted and hung up to dry. It is eaten as a snack, in soups, salads and in sandwiches. Varieties include *spekeskinke* (leg of pork, both smoked and unsmoked), *westfalerskinke* (either smoked or unsmoked boned ham), *skinkerull* (boned, smoked back of bacon), *fenarull* (coarsley chopped lamb with added seasoning), *pinekjøtt* (flank of lamb or mutton, lightly salted), a favourite at Christmas. Cured sausage (*spekepølse*) salami, *stabbur* (horsemeat and mixed meat, fat and seasoning), *fårepølse* (mutton, goat and beef), *reinsdyrpølse* (reindeer and pork), *morrpølse*.

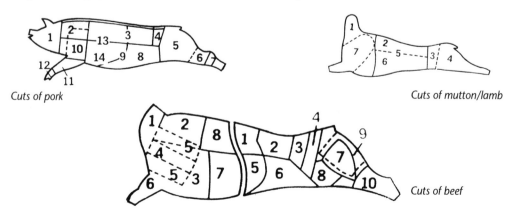

Cuts of pork

Cuts of mutton/lamb

Cuts of beef

Norwegian	English	Uses
Beef, fore quarter cuts		
1. Nakke	Neck end	*kjottdeig* (minced beef), *karbondadedeig* (lean minced beef), *kokekjøtt* (stewing meat)
2. *Høyrygg*	High ribs, blade	*grytteretter* (casseroles)
3. *Bryst*	brisket	"
4. *Bog med kuleben*	clod and brisket	"
5. *Bog uten kuleben*	Shoulder, chuck	", *stek* (pan fry, younger cuts)
6. *For-knoke*	Fore-shank	*Kraft* (stockmaking), minced beef
7. *Bibringe*	plate	*Grytteretter, kokekjøtt*
8. *Entrecote-kam*	Loin, wing rib	Entrecote, *biff* (steak), *kamstek* ☞), *koteletter* (beefsteak chops)
Beef, hind quarter cuts		
1. *Kotellet-kam*	beefsteak	*Kamstek* (loin), *koteletter* (beefsteak chops)
2. *Filet-kam*	Short loin	*Stek* (pan fry), *koteletter* (beefsteak cutlet), *T-benstek* (T-bone steak)
3. *Mørbrad*	tenderloin	*Ovnstek* (roast), casseroles, fondue
Benfri mørbrad	Fillet end of sirloin	"
4. *Mellommørbrad*	sirloin	as above
5. *Bibringe*	plate	Casseroles and stews (*kokekjøtt*)
6. *Slagside*	flank	*Rull* (beef roll, cold cuts)
7. *Flatbiff*	heel	Roast beef, fondue, casseroles and pan fry
8. *Rundbiff*	Round steak	*Bankebiff* (stewing steak), *rullebiff* (beef roll), pan fry or casserole
9. *Bankekjøtt*	Rump, stewing steak	*Bankebiff,rullebiff, stek, gryteretter*
10.*Bak-knoke*	Hind shank	Making stock, roast beef, fondue and casseroles
indrefilet	Inner rib steak	Pan fry whole or in medallions
ytrefilet	Outer rib steak	Roast beef
Cuts of pork (*svinekjøtt*)		
1. *Hode*	head	brawn
2. *Nakke*	butt	*Nakkestek* (back of bacon), *nakkekoteletter* (neck of pork) great for BBQs, casseroles
3. *kotelett-kam*	centerloin	*Svinekoteletter* (pork chops), *sommerkoteletter* (smoked pork chops for BBQ)
4. *mørbrad*	sirloin	*Grytestek* (pot roast), casseroles
5. *skinke*	leg (ham)	*Skinkestek* (roast leg of pork), *skinkebiff* for stir frying, *svineschnitzel*
6. *bak-knoke*	hind shank	Boiling, *ertesuppe* (pea soup)
7. *bak-labb*	hind foot	*Syltelabb* (pig's trotter)
8. *buklist*	belly	*Sylte* (brawn)
9. *sideflesk*	flank	Bacon, *stekeflesk* (frying ham), *ribberull* (rib roulade)
10.*bog*	shoulder	*Lettsaltet kokekjøtt* (lightly salted stewing meat), *bogstek* (shoulder steak)

Norwegian	English	Uses
11.*for-knoke*	fore shank	Boiling and in pea soup
12.*for-labb*	fore foot	Pig's trotter
13.*midtribbe*	blade end	
14.*flatribbe*	spareribs	BBQ
lever	liver	*Leverpostei* (liver paste)

Cuts of veal

1. *Nakke*	Neck	*Renskåret til deiger* (clean-cut ground), casseroles
2. *Kam*	Loin wing rib	Medallions, cutlets
3. *Mørbrad*	Tenderloin	Pan fry, casseroles
4. *Stek*	Rump	Roast, weinerschnitzel
4. *Bak-knoke*	Hind shank	*Kraft* (Soup stock), *renskåret til deiger*
5. *Side*	Flank	Boned veal roll, casseroles, roulade
1. *Bryst*	Brisket	Grilled brisket, boned roulade, casseroles
7. *For-knoke*	Foreshank	Soup stock, *renskåret til deiger*
7. *Bog*	shoulder	Pan fry, casseroles
5. *Nyrestykke*	saddle	*Rullestek*(roast beef), casseroles

Organs (*innmat*)

storfelever/lever av kalv	liver beef/calfs	Pan fry, liver pate
storfenyrer/nyrer van kalv	kidneys beef/calfs	Any kidney dish
kalvhjerte	Calves heart	Stuffed with prunes, apples or forcemeat
tunge	tongue	Boiled, served warm or cold and as cold cuts

Cuts of mutton/lamb (*sau- og lammekjøtt*)

1. *bryst med nakke*	neck	Lightly salted stewing meat, *fårikål* (mutton and cabbage stew), casseroles
2. *kotelett-kam*	rib	*Lammekoteletter* (chops)
3. *mørbrad*	sirloin	*Grytestek* (stewing steak), casseroles, *fårikål*
4. *stek*	Leg/shank	*Sau-/lammestek* (steak in slices for grilling)
5. *nyrestykke*	saddle	Casseroles, Ribs, *fårikål*
6. *side*	Flank, spare rib	Casseroles, Ribs, *fårikål*
7. *bog*	shoulder	Casseroles, *fårikål*, pan fry (boned)
2. *sadel*	centerloin	Saddle of lamb, rack of lamb,
lammelever	liver	Liver dishes
lammenyrer	kidneys	Kidney dishes

Milk and yoghurt (*Melk og yoghurt*) The yearly milk production is nearly 1.7 billion litres, of which more than a third is drunk as milk and close to half is made into cheese. Tine is the country's leading brand in ☞ **dairy products** including milk, which is sold in supermarkets, convenience shops and newsagent's kiosks.

Norwegian	English	Fat content	Uses
H-melk	homogonsied	3.9%	drink, food
Lettmelk	semi-skimmed	1.5%	drink, food
Dalsgården lettmelk	organic semi-skimmed	1.5%	drink, food
Skummet melk	skimmed	0.1%	drink, baking
Kulturmelk	full fat, acidified butter milk	3.8%	drink, baking, dishes requiring soured milk
Skummet kultur	skimmed, acidified butter milk	0.4%	diet uses
Kefir	full fat butter milk	3.8%	drink, baking, dishes using soured milk
Cultura	semi-skimmed butter milk	1.5%	drink, over cereal, also with fruit flavouring
Milkshake	semi-skimmed, flavoured	1.6%	strawberry, chocolate or vanilla flavoured
Yoghurt	yoghurt	3.2%	food, also with fruit flavouring
Lett yoghurt	low-fat yoghurt	0.5%	food, also with fruit flavouring
Drikkeyoghurt	liquid yoghurt	1.3%	Drink, food

Mushrooms (Sopp) can be either cultivated (*dyrket*) or wild (*viltvoksende*). The most common cultivated mushroom (*dyrket sjampingjong*), sold fresh and canned in markets, is the *Agáricus bisporus* by its generic Latin name. Picking wild mushrooms is a popular pastime. But it can be hazardous. Although edible wild mushrooms are delicious, the poisonous varieties can be toxic or lethal. The popular edible wild mushrooms include the field mushroom (*Beitesjampinjong, Agáricus campéstris*), which resembles the cultivated variety and the chanterelles (*kantarell* in Norwegian, *cantharéllus cibárius* in Latin). The poisonous varieties include the Cortinarius species, particularly the deadly poinsonous *Cortinárius rubéllus* (*spiss giftslørsopp*) found in mature conifer forests, the death cap (*grønn fluesopp, amantia phalloides*), rare in Norway but found in oak and beech woods and the most deadly of all mushrooms, involved in 90% of all deaths by mushroom poisoning worldwide, the all-white destroying angel (*hvit fluesopp, amanita virosa*) found in woodlands in the summer and autumn and deadly poisonous, and the fly agaric (*rød/brun fluesopp, amanita muscaria/regalis*), which was used as an insecticide in the middle ages and is commonly but wrongly believed to have been eaten by the Vikings as a hallucinogenic before battle (there is no historic or scientific evidence of such use, but the story persists and has even been cited in references). The best way to enjoy wild mushrooms and not be poisoned by them is to learn to recognise and pick only the edible varieties. Almost all book shops stock illustrated field guides to mushrooms: an extensive list of Norwegian and generic Latin names of mushrooms is given in *Norske soppnavn*, edited by Gro Gulden, 3rd edition 1996, Oslo, Fungiflora, ISBN 82-90724-17-9, and one of the more extensive British field guides includes the English names of many mushrooms found in Norway: *Mushrooms and Other Fungi of Great Britain and Europe*, by Roger Phillips, 1981, ISBN 0-330-26441-9. The more common poisonous mushrooms are illustrated in colour in a free brochure, *Giftige sopper* ("Poisonous mushrooms") published by the National Poisons Information Centre (*Giftinformasjonssentralen*) and available at health stations (*helsestasjon*) and often at pharmacies (*apotek*). Moreover, if you wish to pick wild mushrooms but are unskilled in distinguishing the poisonous from their edible look-alikes, it is best to pick in the autumn, on a day when you can have your pick checked by experts at a mushroom control (*soppkontroll*) station, at a location announced in advance in the classified section of the local newspaper. The Poison Information Centre recommends four measures if you suspect that you or someone you are with has eaten poisonous mushrooms:

1. Keep the remains of the mushroom – raw, cooked or in vomit – and take it with you to the health

station or hospital, as it will help identify the poison involved.

2. Try to identify the exact area or general location where the mushrooms were picked, as it will further aid identification of the variety of mushroom.

3. Contact *Giftinformasjonssentralen*, ℗ 22591300 (24-hours a day) for advice.

4. After eating a meal which you suspect may have contained poisonous mushrooms, you can take a few tablespoons of activated charcoal (*medisinsk kull*), available at pharmacies, as first-aid, but you should always contact a doctor. If you have small children and a garden or lawn, keep some activated charcoal on hand, to give them should they find and eat one of the varieties of poisonous mushrooms that may grow there, such as the clitocybes (*lumsk traktsopp, clitocybe dealbata*). As a preventive measure, it is of course best to mow down or otherwise remove all lawn and garden mushrooms before children can pick them.

If you are interested in mycology (the study of fungi) or pursue mushrooms as a hobby, you may wish to join the Norwegian Mycological Society (*Norsk soppforening*) ℗ 67547803, ☎ 67564613, ✉ Preståsen 11, 1337 Sandvika, ✉ soppforening@online.no, ⊕ http://alun.uio.no/botanisk/ sopp/nsf/OmNSF.html. The Society also sponsors guided mushroom picking tours on autumn weekends and co-operates with local mushroom associations and clubs throughout the country.

The National Council on Nutrition and Physical Activity (*Statens råd for ernæring og fysisk aktivitet*) is the country's centre of expertise on all aspects of nutrition, diet and physical activity and their affects on health. It advises government agencies, research communities, health and social services, schools, places of employment, voluntary organisations, the catering trade, the food industry, the grocery trade, the media and consumers. Its regularly publishes both professional reports and consumer brochures with hints (*tips*) on foods, dieting and physical activity ℗ 22249061, ☎ 22249091, ✉ PO Box 8139 Dep, 0033 Oslo, ✉ post@ser.no, ⊕ http://www.ser.no with pages in Norwegian and summary pages in English, as well as links to nutrition and health web sites world-wide.

Pizza is popular. There are pizza restaurants throughout the country. Most offer take-away as well as serving, and larger restaurants have delivery services. Pizza is a category under *ethnisk indelt* ("ethnic indexed") in the Yellow Pages for cities. There are chains of pizza restaurants, including Peppes, Pizza Hut and Mr. Pizza.

Pizza now is the leading convenience food for home preparation: three out of four people in the country eat it, on the average 17 times a year, and consumption is high, equivalent to 10 kg per person per year. Accordingly, frozen pizza is prominent in the selection of frozen foods in supermarkets, food shops and convenience shops. The leading brand is *Pizza Grandiosa*.

Poultry (*Fjærfe*) Chicken (*kylling*) and turkey (*kalkun*) are sold fresh year-round in butcher shops (*slakteri*), frozen and sometimes fresh in supermarkets and fresh in ☞ **foreign/ethnic food shops**. Raw whole chickens tend to be around 850g to 1200g in weight. Most chicken is bought as chicken breast (*bryst*), which is found prepacked near the other prepacked meat products. In the freezer section you can find hen chicken (*høns*) which is best for boiling. Frozen foil packs with chicken wings or chicken pieces, flavoured with chili, garlic or herbs are ideal for popping in the oven. Larger supermarkets also sell grilled chicken and chicken wings that are put into foil-lined paperbags to keep them warm until you get home. During the hunting season grouse (*rype*) are available in the shops selling ☞ **game** and year round in the freezer section in larger supermarkets.

Snacks (*Snack*) Norway is second only to the USA in per-capita yearly spending on savoury snacks. Accordingly, supermarkets, grocers and convenience shops offer a wide selection of crisps and other processed snacks.

Social mixing (*Selskapsliv*) was once formal. Most families had fixed daily routines, with dinner as early as four in the afternoon, and there were few foreign customs because the foreign-born population was small. Entertaining at home was infrequent and, by today's norms, overdone. As recently as 1986, a book on everyday etiquette, *Skikk og bruk*, devoted two chapters to entertaining and being a guest. The rules laid down then have fallen into disuse. Entertaining has become less formal, in step with more varied daily routines and, of course, with greater internationalisation of lifestyles. Arguably, only five customs survive. First, be on time. Being more than 15 minutes late, the "academic quarter of an hour" (*akademisk kvarter*) is considered rude. Second, beware the laws concerning ☞ **drink driving** (Cars, Roads, Traffic chapter): if you drink, don't drive; if you drive, don't drink. So if you are a host, provide non-alcoholic drinks for the drivers. Third, at a dinner, you may eat before the hostess or host, but not drink until one of them says *velkommen til bords* ("welcome to this dinner table"). Fourth, if you are seated at a table and have something to say that you wish all to hear, tap your glass to gain attention, but only after the meal is finished. Finally, express thanks. If you are a man seated with the hostess to your right, then it is your privilege to rise when the meal is over and give thanks for it in a short talk (*takk for maten*). The day after being a guest in someone's home, telephone them to express thanks (*takk for i går*), and the next time you see the hosts, recall their hospitality by saying *takk for sist* (literally "thanks for the last time"). Otherwise, the few remaining rules of etiquette depend on the company and the occasion, on whether a party is "pure Norwegian" or a mix of nationalities, whether it is inside in the winter or around an outside grill in the summer, for dinner, coffee and cakes or beer and pizza, and so on. If in doubt as to dress or custom, ask your hosts in advance.

Soft drinks (Leskedrikker) The consumption of carbonated soft drinks, including natural mineral waters, has grown in step with the rising affluence of the country. In 1950, the total annual consumption was equivalent to 9 litres per head, equivalent to one bottle every other week. In 1996, consumption had grown to 124 litres per head, equivalent to more than a bottle a day. Per-capita consumption of carbonated soft drinks in Norway, excluding natural mineral waters, leads in Europe, being more than in Germany or Denmark and close to three times as much as in France. Most breweries also bottle soft drinks, and there are more than 10 producers that bottle soft drinks only. Cola drinks account for half the Norwegian consumption, and the major international brands, such as Coca Cola and Pepsi Cola lead the market. Other international brands are available, but the domestic brands, such as Solo, an orange drink, and Farris, a natural mineral water, are sales leaders in their sectors. Soft drinks and mineral water are sold in supermarkets, grocery shops, kiosks and take-away shops, as well as by vending machines in offices, factories and railway and bus stations. The standard bottle sizes are 0.33 litre glass or plastic, 0.5 litre and 1.5 litre plastic, as well as 0.5 litre cans. There is a ☞ **deposit** (Shopping chapter) on all bottles and cans, which may be returned for refund in all shops that sell soft drinks and mineral water.

Sweets (Søtsaker) The average resident consumes more than 12 kg of chocolate and sweets per year, which puts Norway third, behind the Netherlands and Switzerland, among the leading countries in sweets consumption. Accordingly, supermarkets, grocers, kiosks, petrol stations and convenience shops have counters with wide selections of chocolate and sweets, often located near the cash point.

Foreigners (*Utlendinger*)

Embassies and consulates (*Ambassader og konslulater*) Norway maintains diplomatic relations with some 150 countries through their embassies; for details, see *The Oslo Diplomatic List* issued once a year by the Ministry of Foreign Affairs; the most recent at press time for this book was the October 1998 edition, ISSN 0808-2766. Nearly 70 countries maintain embassies or consulates in the Oslo area, while some 80 countries maintain embassies or other diplomatic offices elsewhere in Europe, but not in Norway.

Countries with embassies or consulates in Norway: The Embassies and consulates (with location of nearest embassy) in the Oslo area, with telephone and telefax numbers to Chancery or other principal office. See Yellow Pages under *Ambassader og konsulater* for addresses and other telecommunications numbers:

Argentina ✆ 22552449, ✉ 22441641.
Austria ✆ 22552348, ✉ 22554361.
Belgium ✆ 22552215, ✉ 22443808.
Brazil ✆ 22552029, ✉ 22443964.
Bulgaria ✆ 22554040, ✉ 22554024.
Burkina Faso (embassy in Copenhagen) consulate ✆ 22447112 ✉ 67144340.
Canada ✆ 22995300, ✉ 22995301.
Chile ✆ 22448955, ✉ 22442421.
China ✆ 22493857, ✉ 22921978.
Costa Rica ✆ 22425823, ✉ 22330408.
Croatia ✆ 22442233, ✉ 22443990.
Cyprus (embassy in Stockholm) consulate ✆ 67900079 ✉ 67970130.
Czech Republic ✆ 22430022, ✉ 22553395.
Denmark ✆ 22540800, ✉ 22554634.
Ecuador (embassy in Stockholm) consulate ✆ 67581013 ✉ 67581079.
Egypt ✆ 22447767, ✉ 22562268.
Estonia ✆ 22599802, ✉ 22599804.
Finland ✆ 22430400, ✉ 22430629.
France ✆ 22441820, ✉ 22563221.
Germany ✆ 22552010, ✉ 22447672.
Greece ✆ 22442728, ✉ 22560072.
Guatemala ✆ 22556004, ✉ 22556047.
Honduras (embassy in London) consulate ✆ 22021600 ✉ 22021601.
Hungary ✆ 22552418, ✉ 22447693.

Iceland ✆ 22833435, ✉ 22830704,
India ✆ 22552229, ✉ 22440720.
Indonesia ✆ 22441121, ✉ 22553444.
Iran ✆ 22552408, ✉ 22554919.
Ireland (embassy in Copenhagen) consulate ✆ 22122000, ✉ 22127071.
Israel ✆ 22447924, ✉ 22562183.
Italy ✆ 22552233, ✉ 22443436.
Jamaica (embassy in London) consulate ✆ 22140926, ✉ 22494490.
Japan ✆ 22551011, ✉ 22442505.
Jordan (embassy in Bonn) consulate ✆ 22683860, ✉ 22683886.
Republic of Korea ✆ 22552018, ✉ 22561411.
Latvia ✆ 22542280, ✉ 22546426.
Lithuania ✆ 22558150, ✉ 22556730.
Luxembourg (embassy in Copenhagen) consulate ✆ 22088000, ✉ 22670804.
Madagascar (embassy in Bonn) consulate ✆ 32893060 ✉ 32896364.
Malaysia (embassy in Stockholm) consulate ✆ 22400500 ✉ 22423750.
Mali (embassy in Bonn) consulate ✆ 22414895 ✉ 22414895.
Mauritius (embassy in Bonn) consulate ✆ 22925500, ✉ 22925513.
Mexico ✆ 22431165, ✉ 22444352.
Monaco consulate ✆ 22128030, ✉ 22562301.
Morocco ✆ 23197150, ✉ 23197151.
Nepal (embassy in London) consulate ✆ 22835510 ✉ 22830443.
Netherlands ✆ 22602193, ✉ 22569200.
New Zealand (embassy in The Hague) consulate ✆ 66849530, ✉ 66848909.
Pakistan ✆ 22555470, ✉ 22555097.
Poland ✆ 22555536, ✉ 22444839.
Portugal ✆ 22606225, ✉ 22564355.
Romania ✆ 22441512, ✉ 22431674.
Russia ✆ 225453278, ✉ 22550070.
Singapore consulate ✆ 67579760, ✉ 67579765.
Slovakia ✆ 22555590, ✉ 22555019.
South Africa ✆ 22447910, ✉ 22443975.
Spain ✆ 22447122, ✉ 22559822.
Sudan (embassy in Stockholm) consulate ✆ 22284849, ✉ 22284849.
Sweden ✆ 22443815, ✉ 22551596.
Switzerland ✆ 22430590, ✉ 22446350.
Thailand ✆ 22128660, ✉ 22049969.
Tunisia ✆ 22831917, ✉ 22832412.

Turkey ✆ 22449920, 📠 22556263.
United Kingdom ✆ 23132700, 📠 23132741.
United States of America ✆ 22448550,
📠 22430777.
Venezuela ✆ 22430660, 📠 22431470.
Yugoslavia ✆ 22448105, 📠 22431620.

Countries with no embassies or consulates in Norway: location of nearest facility given in parentheses:

Afghanistan (London).
Albania (Lidingö).
Algeria (Stockholm).
Angola (Lidingö).
Azerbaijan (London).
Australia (Stockholm).
Bahrain (London).
Bangladesh (Stockholm).
Barbados (London).
Benin (Bonn).
Bhutan (Geneva, Switzerland).
Bolivia (London).
Bosnia and Herzegovina (Stockholm).
Botswana (Stockholm).
Brunei Darussalam (Brunei Darussalam, Bandar Seri Begawan).
Burundi (Stockholm).
Cape Verde (Stockholm).
Colombia (Stockholm).
Congo (Brazzaville, Congo).
Democratic Republic of the Congo (London).
Côte d'Ivoire (Hellerup).
Cuba (Stockholm).
Dominican Republic (Stockholm).
El Salvador (London).
Eritrea (Stockholm).
Ethiopia (Stockholm).
Gabon (Libreville).
The Gambia (London).
Ghana (Hellerup).
Guinea (Rome, Italy).
Guinea-Bissau (Brussels).
Guyana (Brussels).
Holy See (Vedbæk).
Kazakhstan (London).
Kenya (Stockholm).
Democratic People's Republic of Korea (Lidingö).
Kuwait (Stockholm).
Laos (Stockholm).
Lebanon (Stockholm).

Lesotho (Hellerup).
Libya (Copenhagen).
Macedonia (FYROM) (Stockholm).
Malawi (London).
Malaysia (Stockholm).
Malta (Brussels).
Mauritania (Bonn).
Mongolia (London).
Mozambique (Stockholm).
Myanmar (London).
Namibia (Stockholm).
Nicaragua (Stockholm).
Niger (Bonn).
Nigeria (Stockholm).
Oman (The Hague).
Panama (Stockholm).
Paraguay (London).
Peru (Stockholm).
Philippines (Stockholm).
Qatar (London).
Rwanda (London).
Saudi Arabia (Stockholm).
Senegal (London).
Sierra Leone (London).
Slovenia (Stockholm).
Sri Lanka (Stockholm).
Swaziland (Copenhagen).
Syria (Bonn).
Tanzania (Stockholm).
Togo (Bonn).
Trinidad and Tobago (London).
Uganda (Hellerup).
Ukraine (Helsinki).
United Arab Emirates (Bonn).
Uruguay (Stockholm).
Vietnam (Älvsjö).
Yemen (London).
Zambia (Stockholm).
Zimbabwe (Stockholm).

Foreign citizens (*Utenlandske statsborgere*)

About one resident in 16 is foreign born. As at 1 January 1999, more than 165,000 citizens of other countries were permanent residents. Fully two-thirds of them were citizens of European countries, the most from Sweden (24,024) followed by Denmark (19,101) and the UK (11,204). Nearly one in five were citizens of Asian countries, the most from Pakistan (6931), followed by Iraq (4172) and Sri Lanka

(3662). Citizens of North and Central American countries accounted for slightly more than 6% of the total, with the most from the USA (8596). Citizens of African countries also accounted for about 6% of the total, with the most from Somalia (4117). Otherwise, there were 4075 citizens from South American countries, 730 from countries in Oceania and 376 stateless persons. More than 100,000 Norwegian citizens are naturalized, having been born in other countries, nearly half in Asia, followed by slightly less than a third in Europe, about 9% in Africa, 7% in South America and 2.5% in North and Central America.

Foreign culture organisations (*Kulturelle foreninger*) There are many foreign-language clubs, associations and religious groups. You can find them by inquiring at the relevant ☞ **embassies and consulates**. Those with fixed offices and telecommunications numbers include:

American Intercultural Student Exchange ✆ 22331800, ✉ Øvre Slottsgt 12B, 0157 Oslo.

American Pot Luck Club (Kristiansand) ✆ 38095112, ✉ egilhp@online.no or ✆ 38015399, ✉ bmoen@sn.no

American Women's Club of Oslo ✆ 22297195, ✉ PO Box 3101 Elisenberg, 0207 Oslo, ◉ http://www.AWCOslo.org

Association of International Professional and Business Women ✆ 22599192, 🖷 22599303, ✉ Harald Hårfagresv 17, 0363 Oslo, ◉ http://www.bi.no/aipbw/

Centre Culturel Francais d'Oslo ✆ 22605960, 🖷 22606816, ✉ Holtegt 29, 0355 Oslo, ◉ http://www.france.no

Dansk Samfund ✆ 67125215, ✉ Skogv 70, 1368 Stabekk.

Fondet for dansk-norsk samarbeid ✆ 22142390, 🖷 22494306, ✉ PO Box 109 Holmenkollen, 0324 Oslo.

Foreningene Nordens Forbund ✆ 22114060, 🖷 22110212, ✉ Akersgt 67, 0180 Oslo, ✉ fnf@norden.no ◉ http://fnf.norden.no with links to associations throughout the country.

Nordisk klubb ✆ 22430224, ✉ Eckersbergsgt 43, 0266 Oslo.

International Forum ✆ 22243513, 🖷 2243800, ✉ PO Box 1505 Vika, 0117 Oslo.

Norge-Amerika Foreningen ✆ 22447716, ✉ Drammensveien 20C, 0255 Oslo.

Norsk Bangladesh Forening ✆ 22413182, ✉ Dronningensgt 23, 0154 Oslo.

Norsk-Cubansk Forening ✆ 22203981, 🖷 22206051, ✉ Osterhausgt 8A, 0183 Oslo.

Petroleum Wives Club of Stavanger ✆ & 🖷 51890804, ✉ PO Box 521 Madla, 4040 Hafrsfjord.

Petroleum Women's Club, Oslo ✉ PO Box 196, 1322 Høvik.

Sambandet Norge-SUS ✆ 22302794, ✉ PO Box 4782 Sofienberg, 06506 Oslo.

Government and Social Services (*Statsfsorfatningen og trygdesystemet*)

About the system of government (*Om statsforfatningen*)

Norway is a parliamentary monarchy with a constitution adopted in 1814. The organised government is divided into three branches: the legislative (*lovgivende*) Parliament (*Stortinget*), the executive (*utøvende*) King in Council and the judicial (*dømmende*) courts. The system of government determines how the country is managed from the national to the local level.

The ☞ **Parliament** has 165 members representing the people who exercise their will in regular elections in which they may choose from among candidates of 21 ☞ **political parties**.

The ☞ **Ministerial Government**, historically called the King in Council, is the executive branch of the government. It is elected from among the members of Parliament.

The ☞ **Courts** (Law, Lawyers, Courts chapter) are independent of the other branches of government and consequently may pass judgement on both public and private sectors.

The ☞ **Ministries and departments** provide the everyday administration, organisation and services of the permanent government, also called the State (*Staten*).

In each of the 19 counties, a County governor (*Fylkesmann*) co-ordinates and administers State activities affecting individuals, including ☞ **name changes** (Family and Children chapter), ☞ **free legal aid** (Law, Lawyers, Courts chapter), maintenance payments and the like. The County governor's offices also include special services, such as the County Chief Medical Officer (*Fytlkeslege*), social services head office (*sosialavdeling*) and the county preparedness office (*beredskapskontor*).

Each county has a County municipality (*Fylkeskommune*), which is an independent agency at a level between the State and the local municipalities. The County municipalities deal with regional tasks including health services, secondary schooling, energy supply and roads.

The 435 municipalities (*kommunene*) consist of cities, towns and districts having local government.

Each municipality has a board (*kommunestyret*) consisting of 11 or more members elected every four years. The board deals with finances, building plans and other municipal matters.

The Centre for Combating Ethnic Discrimination (*Senter mot etnisk diskriminering*)

works to prevent and combat discrimination on the basis of religious belief, skin colour, nationality or ethnic origin. It is freestanding and independent of government administration. Its major functions are to act as a watchdog in both the public and private sectors, to provide free legal aid to individuals and to document the extent of discrimination in the country. Consequently, political scientists and lawyers make up its staff. For more information or for aid if you feel that you are subjected to discrimination, contact the head office in Oslo ☎ 22246987, ✆ 22246972, ✉ PO Box 677 Sentrum, 0106 Oslo, ✉ s-m-e-d@online.no, ⊕ http://www.smed.no with pages in Norwegian, English, French, German, Spanish, Vietnamese and Urdu.

The Directorate of Immigration (*Utlendingsdirektoratet*)

deals with all matters concerning foreigners in the country, including asylum, immigration, naturalisation, visas and residence and work permits. It administers measures for newly arrived immigrants, principally refugees, and co-operates with other agencies and organisations to integrate immigrants into the increasingly multicultural society of the country. It publishes pamphlets, booklets and reports on topics of interest to newly-arrived residents, in Norwegian, English and many other languages, and makes them available at its own offices and the offices of agencies and services, such as municipal libraries. It supports an extensive Internet web site ⊕ http://www.udi.no with pages in Norwegian, in English and in French and links to other sites.

- Head office ☎ 23351500 general, ☎ 23351600 information, ✆ 23351507, ✉ Hausmannsgt. 21, PO Box 8108 Dep, 0032 Oslo.
- Eastern Region Office (*Regionkontor Øst* covering Østfold, Vestfold and Akershus counties, as well as Oslo) ☎ 22339200, ✆ 22339210, ✉ Youngstorget 1, PO Box 8789 Youngstorget, 0028 Oslo.
- Inland Region Office (*Regionkontor Indre Østland*

covering Hedmark, Oppland and Buskerud counties) ✆ 61170910, ✉ 61170895, ✉ Storgata 10, PO Box 445, 2803 Gjøvik.

- Southern Region Office (*Regionkontor Sør* covering Telemark, Aust-Agder and Vest-Agder counties) ✆ 38106060, ✉ 38020480, ✉ Slottssquartalet, Tordenskjoldsgt 9, PO Box 647, 4666 Kristiansand.
- Western Region Office (*Regionkontor Vest* covering Rogaland, Hordaland and Sogn og Fjordane counties) ✆ 55317055. ✉ 55319085, ✉ Bugården 8, PO Box 4048 Dreggen, 5835 Bergen.
- Central Region Office (*Regionkontor Midt Norge* covering Møre og Romsdal, Sør-Trøndelag and Nord-Trøndelag counties) ✆ 73892400, ✉ 73892401, ✉ Peter Egges plass 2, 7005 Trondheim.

Northern Region Office (*Regionkontor Nord* covering Nordland, Troms and Finnmark counties) ✆ 76965810, ✉ 76963839, ✉ Dronningensgt 49, PO Box 803, 8510 Narvik.

ECE is the abbreviation of the Economic Commission for Europe, a United Nations forum at which the countries of Europe, North America and central Asia co-operate on economic matters. Norway participates in almost all ECE activities in matters related to environment and human settlements, trade, industry and timber, and transport. The principal Ministries involved are Agriculture (LD), Environment (MD), Petroleum and Energy (OED) and Transport and Communications (SD), though the works of other Ministries are also affected. The impact of the ECE on daily life is most obvious in transport, environmental matters and international shipment of goods. For instance, cars and other motor vehicles conform to ECE regulations. Norway co-operates with other countries within the ECE on pollution matters, and the first international meeting under the ECE Convention on Environmental Impact Assessment in a Transboundary Context was held in Oslo in May 1998. Throughout the world, the paperwork involved in import-export operations has been simplified and replaced by an electronic system developed by ECE and known as UN/EDIFACT. Further details on ECE matters in Norway are available in the publications and press releases of the Ministries involved. For complete information on the ECE, contact its Information Office ✆ +41 22 9174444, ✉ +41 22 9170505, ✉ Palais des Nations, CH-1211 Geneva 10, Switzerland, ✉ info.ece@unece.org, ✉ http://www.unece.org.

EU, EFTA and EEA (*EU, EFTA & EØS*) Norway is a member of the European Free Trade Association (EFTA) but not of the European Union (EU). Consequently, Norway is a signatory of the European Economic Area (EEA) agreement, which extends the internal market of the 15 EU countries to the three EFTA countries and thereby creates an economic area of 18 countries with a combined population of some 380 million. Under the EEA agreement, free movement of goods, persons, services and capital applies across the entire area. It also provides for cooperation in environment, social policy, education and research and development. Most of the provisions are extensive and are still being formulated by national and international groups of politicians and experts. There are three principal differences that set Norway, an EFTA member, apart from EU member countries. First, the EEA is not a customs union, so there is no common external tariff outside the area. Goods imported into Norway from EU countries are subject to customs duty. Second, the EEA covers neither a common agricultural policy nor a common fisheries policy, so Norwegian farming and fishing are independent of EU policy. Finally, the EEA has no provisions for common foreign policy, security policy or home and justice affairs, so Norwegian practices and domestic law may differ from those of EU countries. The principal EEA provisions concerning individual persons are those relating to work and residence, ✆ **EEA nationals' work rights** (Business and Work chapter). Many standard EU forms, such as the E111 certification of national health insurance coverage and the E303 unemployment benefits voucher, are valid in Norway. For further information on EU matters in Norway, contact *Europakommisjonens delegasjon* ✆ 22833583, ✉ 22834055, ✉ PO Box 1643 Vika, 0119 Oslo. Complete details on the EU in eleven languages are available on-line at ✉ http://europa.eu.int

The European Social Charter (*Den europeiske sosialpakt*) sets forth rules and legal standards in work and working conditions, health care, social matters and social security. Norway ratified the Charter in February 1997. Norwegians rules and regula-

tions in accordance with the Charter are described in press releases, brochures and pamphlets issued by the Departments responsible for the matters involved; the ☞ **Central information service** (Media and Information chapter) can help you locate and order them. The complete Charter, revised in May 1996 in Strasbourg and listed as European Treaty ETS No. 163, is available in English or French from the Council of Europe and can be viewed at and printed out from its web site
☞ http://www.coe.fr

Lost property (*Hittegods*) consists of lost articles that have been found but not claimed by their owners. If you find an article, you are legally obliged to return it to its owner. If you cannot find the owner, you should deliver the article to the lost property office (*hittegodskontor*) at the nearest police station (*politi*) or sheriff's office (*lensmann*). Major transport services, such as the railways, and larger department stores and shopping malls will also have a lost property service. A lost property office will try to find the owner of an article received. However, it will sell articles received at auction if they are not claimed within three months. Provided you put in a claim within three months of an article being returned to its owner, you are entitled to a finder's reward, which for articles worth NOK 500 or more, is fixed at 10% of the article's value. If you lose an article and wish to have it back, you should fill out a notice of loss (*tapsmelding*) at the closest police station or sheriff's office, which will notify you if the article is delivered to its lost property office.

The Ministerial Government (*Regjering*) is appointed as the executive body of the country. It is called "Ministerial" to indicate its executive status, and Government is spelled with a capital G to distinguish it from the more general word, meaning the system of government. The Ministerial Government consists of the Prime Minister (*Statsminister*) and the 18 Ministers (*Ministere*) making up the King in Council, which is the Cabinet (*Statsråd*) and chosen from among the 165 Parliamentarians (*Stortingsmenn*). The Ministers are the appointed heads of the Ministries of the permanent government (*Staten*), ☞ **Ministries and departments**. Two of the 16 Ministries have two Ministers each, while 14 have one Minister each.

Ministries and departments (*Departementene og etater*) The ministries have permanent civil service staffs. Each is headed by a politically appointed Minister (*minister*). Within each ministry there are several departments, each headed by a director general (*ekspedisjonssjef*). Note that in Norwegian, the word departement means "ministry", while in English, "department" means a part of a ministry. In alphabetical order by their Norwegian names (and common abbreviations used in governmental administration and in the media), the ministries and their departments, along with their official translations into English are:

Arbeidsdirektoratet, Directorate of Labour

Fylkesmannkontorene, County Governors

Konkurransetilsynet, Norwegian Competition Authority

Statens Forvaltningstjeneste, Government Administration Services

Statens Informasjonstjeneste, Central Information Service

Statens Pensjonskasse, Norwegian Public Service Pension Fund

Statsbygg, Directorate of Public Construction and Property

Statskonsult, Directorate of Public Management

Barne- og familiedepartementet (BFD), Ministry of Children and Family Affairs

Barneombudet, Office of the Commissioner for Children

Forbrukerombudet, The Consumer Ombud

Forbrukerrådet, Consumer Council

Forbrukertvistutvalget, Consumer Disputes Committee

Kompetansesenter for Likestilling, Centre for Gender Equality

Likestillingsombudet, Office of the Gender Equality Ombudsman

Markedsrådet, Market Council

Produkt- og Elektrisitetstilsynet, Norwegian Directorate for Product and Electrical Safety

Statens Institutt for Forbrukerforskning (SIFO), The National Institute for Consumer Research

Finans- og tolldepartementet (FIN), Ministry of Finance (and Customs)

Folketrygdfondet, National Insurance Scheme Fund

Kredittilsynet, Banking, Insurance and Securities Commission of Norway

Norges Bank, Central Bank
Oslo Børs, Oslo Stock Exchange
Skattedirektoratet, Directorate of Taxes
Sentralkontoret for Utenlandssaker, Central Office – Foreign Tax Affairs
Sentralkontoret for Storbedrifter, Central Taxation Office for Large-sized Enterprises
Oljeskattekontoret, Petroleum Tax Office
Statistisk Sentralbyrå, Statistics Norway
Toll- og Avgiftsdirektoratet, Directorate of Customs and Excise
Fiskeridepartementet (FID), Ministry of Fisheries
  Fiskeridirektoratet, Directorate of Fisheries
  Fiskeridirektoratets Ernæringsinstitutt, Institute of Nutrition, Directorate of Fisheries
  Fiskeriforskning, Norwegian Institute of Fisheries and Aquaculture
  Garantikassen for Fiskere, Guarantee Fund for Fishermen
  Havforskningsinstituttet, Institute of Marine Research
  Kystdirektoratet, Coast Directorate
Forsvarsdepartementet (FD), Ministry of Defence
  AFNORTHWEST, HQ Allied Forces Western Europe
  Forsvarets Forskningsinstitutt, Norwegian Defence Research Establishment
  Forsvarets Overkommando, Headquarters Defence Command Norway
  Forsvarets Rekrutterings- og Mediesenter, The Armed Forces Recruiting and Media Centre
  Forsvarskommando Nord-Norge (FKN), Defence Command North Norway
  Forsvarskommando Sør-Norge, Headquarters Allied Forces North Europe
  Vernepliktsverket, National Service Administration
Justis- og politidepartementet (JD), Ministry of Justice (and the Police)
  Brønnøysundregisteret, Brønnøysund Register Centre
  Datatilsynet, The Data Inspectorate
  Direktoratet for Sivilt Beredskap, Directorate for Civil Defence
  Generaladvokaten, Judge Advocate General
  Regjeringsadvokaten, Office of the Attorney-General
  Riksadvokaten, Director General of Public Prosecutions
  Statens Innkrevingssentral, State Agency for the Recovery of Fines, Damages and Costs

Sysselmannen på Svalbard, Governor of Svalbard
Kripos, National Bureau of Crime Investigation
Økokrim, National Authority for Investigation and Prosecution of Economic and Environmental Crime in Norway
Kirke-, utdannings- og forskningsdepartementet (KUF), Ministry of Education, Research and Church Affairs
  Det Norske Meteorologiske Institutt (DNMI), Norwegian Meteorological Institute
  Høgskoler og universiteter, Colleges (34) and Universities (5)
  Kirkerådet, Church of Norway, National Council
  Mellomkirkelig Råd, Church of Norway, Council on Ecumenical and International Relations
  Nasjonalt Læremiddelsenter, National Centre for Educational Resources
  Norges Forskningsråd, The Research Council of Norway
  Norgesnettrådet, Network Norway Council
  Norsk Fjernundervisning, Norwegian State Institution for Distance Education
  Norsk Institutt for Forskning om Oppvekst, Velferd og Aldring (NOVA), Norwegian Social Research
  Norsk Voksenpedagogisk Forskningsinstitutt, Norwegian Institute of Adult Education
  Riksbibliotektjenesten (RBT), National Office for Research Documentation, Academic and Special Libraries
  Samisk Kirkeråd, Sami Church Council
  Samisk Utdanningsråd, Sami Education Council
  Samordna Opptak, Universities and Colleges Admission Service
  Statens Lånekasse for Utdanning, State Educational Loan Fund
  Statens Utdanningskontor, National Education Office
Kommunal- og regionaldepartementet (KRD), Ministry of Local Government and Regional Development
  Arbeidsforskningsinstituttet, Work Research Institute
  Direktoratet for Arbeidstilsynet, Directorate of Labour Inspection
  Den Norske Stats Husbank, Norwegian State Housing Bank
  Direktoratet for Brann og Ekxplosjonsvern (DBE), Directorate for Fire and Explosion Prevention
  Norges Kommunal Bank, Local Government Bank of Norway
  Produkt- og Elektrisitetstilsynet, Norwegian Direc-

torate for Product and Electrical Safety
Produktregisteret, Product Register
Riksmeklingsmannen, Office of the State Mediator
Statens Arbeidsmiljøinstitutt, National Institute of Occupational Health
Statens Nærings- og Distriktsutviklingsfond (SND), Norwegian Industrial and Regional Development Fund
Utlendingsdirektoratet (UDI), Norwegian Directorate of Immigration
Kulturdepartementet (KD), Ministry of Cultural Affairs
Eierskapstilsynet, Media Ownership Authority
Museet for Samtidskunst, National Museum of Contemporary Art
Nasjonalbibliotek-Avdelingen i Rana, National Library of Norway, Rana Division
Norsk Filminstitutt, Norwegian Film Institute
Norsk Kulturråd, Norwegian Council for Cultural Affairs
Norsk Museumsutvikling, Norwegian Museum Authority
Norsk Språkråd, Norwegian Language Council
Riksarkivet, National Archives of Norway
Rikskonsertene, Norwegian Concert Institute
Riksteateret, Norwegian National Touring Theatre
Riksutstillinger, National Touring Exhibition of Norway
Statens Bibliotektilsyn, Norwegian Directorate for Public Libraries
Statens Filmtilsyn, Norwegian Board of Film Classification
Statens Medieforvaltning, Mass Media Authority
Utsmykkingsfondet for Offentlige Bygg, National Foundation for Publicly Commissioned Art
Landbruksdepartementet (LD), Ministry of Agriculture
Norsk Institutt for Landbruksøkonomisk Forskning (NILF), Norwegian Agricultural Economics Research Institute
Norsk Institutt for Skogforskning, Norwegian Forest Research Institute
Planteforsk, Norwegian Crop Research Institute
Reindriftsforvaltningen, Norwegian Reindeer Husbandry Administration
Statens Dyrehelsetilsyn, Norwegian Animal Health Authority
Statens Kornforretning, Norwegian Grain Corporation
Statens Landbruksbank, State Bank of Agriculture

Statens Landbrukstilsyn, Norwegian Agricultural Inspection Service
Statens Naturskadefond, National Fund for Natural Damage Assistance
Statens Næringsmiddeltilsyn, Norwegian Food Control Authority
Miljøverndepartementet (MD), Ministry of Environment
Direktoratet for Naturforvaltning, Directorate for Nature Management
Norsk Polarinstitutt, Norwegian Polar Institute
Riksantikvaren, Directorate of Cultural Heritage
Statens Forurensningstilsyn, Norwegian Pollution Control Authority
Statens Kartverk, Norwegian Mapping Authority
Nærings- og handelsdepartementet (NHD), Ministry of Trade and Industry
Bergvesenet, Directorate of Mining
Garantiinstituttet for Eksportkreditt, Norwegian Guarantee Institute for Export Credits
Justervesenet (JV), Norwegian Metrology
Norges Eksportråd, Norwegian Trade Council
Norges Geologiske Undersøkelse (NGU), Geological Survey of Norway
Patentstyret, Norwegian Patient Office
Sjøfartsdirektoratet, Norwegian Maritime Directorate
Skipsregistrene, The Norwegian Ship Registers
Statens Nærings- og Distriktsutviklingsfond (SND), Norwegian Industrial and Regional Development Fund
Statens Veiledningskontor for Oppfinnere (SVO), Norwegian Government Consultative Office for Inventors
Teknologisk Institutt (TI), National Institute of Technology, Norway
VINN, North Norwegian Institute of Technology and Innovation
Olje- og energidepartementet (OED), Ministry of Petroleum and Energy
Norges Vassdrags- og Energidirektoratet, Norwegian Water Resources and Energy Directorate
Oljedirektoratet, Norwegian Petroleum Directorate
Samferdselsdepartementet (SD), Ministry of Transport and Communications
Luftfartsverket, Civil Aviation Administration
Jernbaneverket, Norwegian National Rail Administration

Statens Jernbanetilsyn, Norwegian Railway Inspectorate

Vegdirektoratet, Directorate of Public Roads

Statens Vegvesen, Norwegian Public Roads Administration

Sosial og helsedepartementet (SHD), Ministry of Health and Social Affairs

Folketrygdkontoret for Utenlandssaker, National Office for Social Insurance Abroad

Giftinformasjonssentralen, National Poisons Information Centre

Pensjonstrygden for Sjømenn, Pension Insurance for Seamen

Rikstrygdeverket, National Insurance Administration

Rusmiddeldirektoratet, Norwegian Directorate for the Prevention of Alcohol and Drug Problems

Etat for Rådssekretariater og Enkelte Helse- og Sosialfaglige Oppgaver, National Council for the Disabled and National Council for the Elderly

Statens Råd foir Ernæring og Fysisk Aktivitet, National Council on Nutrition and Physical Activity

Statens Helsetilsyn, Norwegian Board of Health

Statens Helseundersøkelser, National Health Screening Service

Statens Institutt for Alkohol- og Narkotikaforskning, National Institute for Alcohol and Drug Research

Statens Institutt for Folkehelse, National Institute of Public Health

Statens Tobakksskaderåd, National Council on Tobacco and Health

Trygdeetatens Innkrevingssentral, National Insurance Service Agency for the Recovery of Maintenance Payment

Trygderetten, National Insurance Appeals Court

Utenriksdepartementet (UD), Ministry of Foreign Affairs

Direktoratet for Utviklingshjelp (NORAD), Norwegian Agency for Development Co-operation

Norges Internasjonale Pressesenter, Norway International Press Centre

The National Institute for Consumer Research (*Statens institutt for forbruksforskning – SIFO*)

conducts research for the Ministry of Children and Family Affairs and for other consumer-oriented institutions and agencies. It is involved in Nordic projects and is a member of Consumers International (CI). Its principal fields of research are private finances and debt, consumption and the environment, ☞ **family expenditure** (Banking, Finance, Insurance chapter) and public services to individuals. SIFO also conducts extensive testing in product safety and usefulness, in accordance to Nordic, European and international standards. Textiles are tested for flammability, wear-and-tear, colour fastness and washability. Toys and child-care products are tested for fire hazard, and mechanical and physical safety. Household appliances, including kitchen and bathroom equipment, are tested for function, ergonomics, safety and environmental features. Detergents are tested for compliance with the requirements for ☞ **ecolabelling** (Shopping chapter). The results of SIFO research and testing are made available in reports in the fields of advertising, consumer finances, consumption, distribution environment, food and market, public services and testing. Most of the reports are in Norwegian with summaries in English, whilst some are completely in English. Contact SIFO for further information on its activities or for ordering reports ☎ 67599600, ✉ 67531948, ✉ PO Box 173, 1325 Lysaker, ✉ sifo@sifo.no, ⊕ http://www.sifo.no with pages in Norwegian and in English and with lists of reports available.

National insurance (*Folketrygden*) is part of the

welfare system, which arguably is one of the most comprehensive in the world. Indeed, the country is said to be a welfare state; the word *folketrygden* literally means "people's social insurance", and the root word, trygd also means "protection" or "security". In principle, everyone contributes and everyone benefits. If you earn income, you and your employer both pay National Insurance taxes on your earnings. If you are employed, you are taxed at 7.8% of your gross income, and your employer contributes from 14.1% to zero, depending on the zone within the country. If you are self-employed, the basic rate is 10.7%. Your benefits may include:

- Pension at retirement age of 67.
- Survivor's benefits, to widow or widower.
- Disability benefits.
- Rehabilitation benefits.
- Medical treatment including hospitalisation.
- Sick leave benefits.
- Unemployment benefits.
- Occupational injury benefits.

- Single parent benefits.
- Funeral grants.
- Child benefit.

The measures are extensive and there are clear brochures on the benefits listed above as well as on other aspects of National insurance, in Norwegian, English and other languages, available at social services offices throughout the country, listed under *Trygdekontor* in the Pink Pages. For a complete overview, see *Det norske trygdesystemet* (Norwegian edition) or The Norwegian Social Insurance Scheme (English edition) published by the Ministry of Health and Social Affairs in January 1999 in printed brochures and on-line at
⊕http://odin.dep.no/shd/pub/1999/norsk/ norsk_trygd/ (Norwegian version) or
⊕http://odin.dep.no/shd/pub/1999/norsk/ norsk_trygd/eindex.html (English version).

NATO is an acronym for the North Atlantic Treaty Organisation. It is named for the Treaty signed in Washington on 4 April 1949, creating an alliance of 12 countries committed to each other's defence. From 1952 to 1982, four more European countries acceded to the Treaty. The 16 member countries are Belgium, Canada, Denmark, France, Germany, Greece, Iceland, Italy, Luxembourg, Netherlands, Norway, Portugal, Spain, Turkey, United Kingdom and United States of America. Though originally a military alliance, since the end of the Cold War and of the division of Europe, NATO has been restructured to enable it to participate in the development of co-operative security structures for the whole of Europe. Norway has been a member of NATO since its start, and major NATO facilities have been located in the country. Consequently, extensive information is available on the military and the civil aspects of NATO, mostly in Norwegian but also in English and other languages of the NATO countries. For military matters, contact the Norwegian Defence Information Service (*Det norske Forsvarets offisielle informasjonstjeneste*) at the Huseby base in Oslo ✆ 23098000, 📠 23098312,
✉ forsvarsnett@fo.mil.no, ⊕ http://www.mil.no
For all other matters, contact the governmental ☞ **Central Information Service** (Media and Information chapter) ✆ freephone 80030300,
📠 22249519,
⊕ http://www.si.dep.no/oppltjen.html or search in

the pages of ODIN, the governmental central web server ⊕ http://odin.dep.no or the pages in English or French at the central NATO web site
⊕ http://www.vm.ee/nato

NORAD is an abbreviation for Norwegian Agency for Development Cooperation and is a directorate under the Ministry of Foreign Affairs (*Utenriksdepartement – UD*). It is represented in 17 developing countries, in which its aim is to promote lasting improvements: Bangladesh, Botswana, Eritrea, Ethiopia, Guatemala, India, Mozambique, Namibia, Nicaragua, Pakistan, Palestinian areas, Sri Lanka, South Africa, Tanzania, Uganda, Zambia and Zimbabwe. NORAD is well financed. Though a small country, Norway ranks eleventh among bilateral and multilateral donor countries and is one of four countries that meet the United Nations goal of contributing 0.7% of the Gross Domestic Product (GDP) to aid; the other three are Denmark, the Netherlands and Sweden. The NORAD head office is in Oslo, as is the NORAD Information Centre, which has permanent exhibits, brochures and other publications in Norwegian, English and other languages, as well as other relevant information such as job opportunities, grants, youth exchange programmes, partners in co-operation and lectures. For further details, visit or contact the Information Centre, which is open from 12 noon to 3 p.m. Monday – Friday ✆ 22314453, 📠 22314474, ✉ Tollbugaten 31, PO Box 8034 Dep, 0030 Oslo,
✉ informasjonssenteret@oslo.norad.telemax.no,
⊕ http://www.norad.no with pages in Norwegian and in English.

The Nordic Council (*Nordisk råd*) is a forum for co-operation between Nordic parliamentarians and between parliamentarians and governments of the Nordic countries (Denmark, Finland, Iceland, Norway and Sweden). Its affiliate, The Nordic Council of Ministers (*Nordisk ministerråd*) has many activities, including hosting meetings between Nordic ministers, civil servants or both and arranging meetings, conferences and seminars, as well as working in matters of policy. The activities of these two Councils are extensive, as is the information on them. Brochures and pamphlets on the Councils are available at many government offices, and the ☞ **Central information service** (Media and Information chapter) can help you locate and order them. For more specific information, contact the Secretariats in Copenhagen: Nordic Council ✆ +45 33960400, 📠 +45 33111870, ✉ PO Box 3043, DK-1255 Copenhagen, Denmark; Nordic Council of Ministers ✆ +45 33960200, 📠 +45 33960322, ✉ Store Strandstræde 18, DK-1255 Copenhagen, Denmark, ✉ initialer@nmr.dk. For general information, view the extensive web site supported jointly by the two Councils ⊕ http://www.norden.org with pages in English, Finnish, Icelandic and Swedish.

Norwegian Embassies (*Ambassader*), Consultates General (*Generalkonsulater*) and Consulates (*Konsulater*) with Norwegian personnel are listed below, alphabetically by country. You may look up their addresses and telecoms numbers, as well as those of honorary consulates not listed below, in the telephone directories of cities listed, or, if your have Internet access, view the Ministry of Foreign Affairs (*Utenriksdepartementet*) web site ⊕ http://odin.dep.no/ud/utenriks/ut-stasj. Moreover, the Embassies in Bonn, Copenhagen, Kuala Lumpur, London, Seoul, Tokyo and Washington have their own web sites ☞ **Embassies and mission on the Internet** (Media & Information chapter).

Angola, Embassy in Luanda
Argentina, Embassy in Buenos Aires
Australia, Embassy in Canberra
Austria, Embassy in Vienna
Azerbaijan, Embassy in Baku
Bangladesh, Embassy in Dhaka
Belgium, Embassy in Brussels
Bosnia and Herzegovina, Embassy in Sarajevo
Brazil, Embassy in Brasilia, Consulate General in Rio de Janeiro
Canada, Embassy in Ottawa
Chile, Embassy in Santiago
China, Embassy in Beijing, Consulates General in Hong Kong, Shanghai
Côte d'Ivoire, Embassy in Abidjan
Croatia, Embassy in Zagreb
Czech Republic, Embassy in Prague
Denmark, Embassy in Copenhagen
Egypt, Embassy in Cairo
Estonia, Embassy in Tallinn
Ethiopia, Embassy in Addis Abeba
Finland, Embassy in Helsinki
France, Embassy in Paris
Germany, Embassy in Bonn with office in Berlin, Consulate General in Hamburg
Greece, Embassy in Athens
Guatemala, Embassy in Ca-Guatemala
Hungary, Embassy in Budapest
Iceland, Embassy in Reykjavik
India, Embassy in New Delhi
Indonesia, Embassy in Jakarta
Iran, Embassy in Teheran
Ireland, Embassy in Dublin
Israel, Embassy in Tel Aviv
Italy, Embassy in Rome
Japan, Embassy in Tokyo
Jordan, Embassy in Amman
Kenya, Embassy in Nairobi
Korea, Republic of, Embassy in Seoul
Latvia, Embassy in Riga
Lithuania, Embassy in Vilnius
Malawi, Embassy in Lilongwe
Malaysia, Embassy in Kuala Lumpur
Mexico, Embassy in Mexico City
Morocco, Embassy in Rabat
Mozambique, Embassy in Maputo
Netherlands, Embassy in Den Haag, Consulate General in Rotterdam
Nicaragua, Embassy in Managua
Nigeria, Embassy in Lagos
Pakistan, Embassy in Islamabad
Philippines, Embassy in Manila
Poland, Embassy in Warsaw
Portugal, Embassy in Lisbon
Romania, Embassy in Bucharest
Russia, Embassy in Moscow, Consulates General in Murmansk, St. Petersburg
Saudi Arabia, Embassy in Riyadh
Scotland, Consulate General in Edinburgh
Singapore, Embassy
South Africa, Embassy in Pretoria
Spain, Embassy in Madrid
Sri Lanka, Embassy in Colombo
Sweden, Embassy in Stockholm
Switzerland, Embassy in Bern
Syria, Embassy in Damascus
Tanzania, Embassy in Dar Es Salaam
Thailand, Embassy in Bangkok
Tunisia, Embassy in Tunis
Turkey, Embassy in Ankara
Uganda, Embassy in Kampala
UK, Embassy in London

Ukraine, Embassy in Kiev
United Arab Emirates, Embassy in Abu Dhabi
USA, Embassy in Washington, Consulates General in Houston, Miami, Minneapolis, New York, San Francisco
Venezuela, Embassy in Caracas
Vietnam, Embassy in Hanoi
Yugoslavia, Embassy in Beograd
Zambia, Embassy in Lusaka
Zimbabwe, Embassy in Harare

The Norwegian Institute of International Affairs (*Norsk Utenrikspolitisk Institutt – NUPI*) was established in 1959 by ☞ **Parliament** to promote the understanding of international issues in Norway. Although it is partly funded by the government, NUPI is independent in its studies of matters relevant to foreign policy and economic relations. NUPI conducts numerous research activities, organised in two major cross-disciplinary programmes – European co-operation and Collective security – and two sections – International economics and Development research. NUPI also disseminates information on international issues, publishes books, periodicals and reports. For further information, contact the head office ✆ 22056500, ☎ 22177015, ✉ PO Box 8159 Dep, 0033 Oslo, ✉ info@nupi.no, ✇ http://www.nupi.no with pages in Norwegian and in English.

OECD (*OECD*) The Organisation for Economic Co-operation and Development (OECD) assists member countries to develop economic and social policies that promote sustained economic growth and financial stability. Its 29 member countries are Australia, Austria, Belgium, Canada, The Czech Republic, Denmark, Finland, France, Germany, Greece, Hungary, Iceland, Ireland, Italy, Japan, Korea, Luxembourg, Mexico, The Netherlands, New Zealand, Norway, Poland, Portugal, Spain, Sweden, Switzerland, Turkey, the UK and the USA. Each year, the OECD publishes more than 500 books and periodicals, most in English and French. The subjects covered include agriculture and fisheries; cities, regions and countryside; development co-operation; economics and long-term analysis; economies in transition; education, employment labour and social affairs; environmental affairs; financial, fiscal and enterprise affairs; public management; science, technology and industry; trade; transport. Further details are available from the OECD ✆ +33 145248200, ☎ +33 145248500, ✉ 2, rue André-Pascal, F-75775 Paris Cedex 16, France, ✇ http://www.oecd.org with pages in English and in French. In Norway, the Department of External Economic Affairs of the Ministry of Foreign Affairs co-ordinates OECD activities and provides information in Norwegian.

Ombudsman (*Ombudsmann*) An ombudsman is an official appointed to investigate the complaints of individuals against maladministration by public agencies or against violation of laws concerning individual rights. The word originated in Sweden, where the first *ombudsmann* was instituted in 1809. With the definite suffix *-en*, the word designates an office to which a person is appointed: *ombudsmannen* is both a position and the title of the person holding it. There are six principal *ombudsmann* offices:
Children (*Barneombudet*) ☞ **Childrens' rights** (Family and Children chapter)
Consumer rights (*Forbrukerombudet*) ☞ **Consumer ombudsman** (Human Rights, Consumer Rights chapter)
Gender equality (*Likestillingsombudet*) ☞ **Gender equality** (Human Rights, Consumer Rights chapter)
Patients (*Pasientombudet*) ☞ **Patient ombudsman** (Health Care chapter)
Public administration (*Sivilombudsmann*) ☞ **Parliamentary Ombudsman for Public Administration**
Military services (*Forsvaret*) including civilian service conscripts (*sivile tjenestepliktige*) ☞ **Military ombudsman board** (Defence chapter)
There are also ombudsman offices in the private sector, in unions, employer organisations, professional organisations and some larger companies.

Parliament (*Storting*) is divided into two chambers, the Lower House (*Odelsting*) and Upper House (*Lagting*). When a new Storting first convenes following an election, it elects one-quarter of the Parliamentarians (41) to the *Lagting* and the remaining three-quarters (124) to the *Odelsting*. General elections for all 165 seats are held in September of every fourth year. In contrast to practice in some other countries with parliamentary systems, a Storting cannot be dissolved, and elections cannot be called outside the normal years. The principal powers of the

Storting are to pass new laws and to amend or repeal existing laws; to adopt the Fiscal Budget including annual revenues and governmental expenditures; to supervise the ministerial Government and the public administration; and to authorise plans and guidelines for the activities of the government through discussion of a wide range of issues of public interest. For more complete details and other facets of the workings of the Storting, see the Storting's free booklet, available in Norwegian and in English: *Storting, the Norwegian Parliament*, Oslo, 1996, ISBN 82-91283-06-0. The material covered by the booklet is also available and continuously updated on-line at ☞ http://www.stortinget.no with pages in Norwegian and in English.

Parliamentarism (*Parlamentarisme*) is the basis of the ☞ **system of government**. This means that ☞ **Parliament** has authority over the ☞ **Ministerial Government**. In turn, the Ministerial Government is accountable to Parliament and depends on retaining its confidence. Numerous constitutional practices guide relations between the two. Breach of these practices may have political repercussions, which may trigger the resignation of a Minister or even of an entire Ministerial Government. These matters are not stated directly in the Constitution, but have evolved through political precedence and are considered just as binding as if they had been. This is called constitutional precedence. Under parliamentary rule, the majority in Parliament determines who will fill the offices of the Ministers who constitute the Ministerial Government and the Cabinet. A sitting Ministerial Government need not always be backed by a Parliamentary majority, but it cannot continue in office if opposed by it. Parliament can oppose a sitting Ministerial Government by a vote of no confidence. If the vote passes, the Government is obliged to resign. The Government may also challenge Parliament; it can threaten to step down if its proposal on an issue is not accepted, through calling for a vote of no confidence. In practice, a Government usually resigns in the event of an electoral defeat when the majority in Parliament shifts and creates an imperative for forming a new Government.

Parliamentary Ombudsman for Public Administration (*Stortingets ombudsmann for forvaltningen*) The Ombudsman acts on complaints from individuals on the actions of state, county and municipal agencies. You can submit a complaint if you believe that a public agency has decided wrongly, has been offensive or unjust or has failed to take action or respond to a query. To submit a complaint, just write a letter, as there are no specific requirements or forms. In the letter, you should briefly explain the reasons for your complaint and should attach copies of any relevant documents. The Ombudsman will deal with your case in writing, but will not conduct inspections or interview persons. You will be informed of the progress and outcome of your case. The Ombudsman's services are free. For further information on the services of the Ombudsman, contact the head office in Oslo ☎ 22828500, 📠 22828511, ✉ PO Box 3, Sentrum, 0101 Oslo, ✉ post@sivilombudsmannen.no, ☞ http://www.sivilombudsmannen.no

Political parties (*Politiske partier*) There are 21 registered political parties, listed below in alphabetical order by their names in Norwegian, in the format of *Party name (Abbreviation)* English translation (year of first registry).

Det norske Arbeiderparti (A) Labour Party (1897)
Det Liberale Folkepartiet (DLF) New Liberal Party (1989)
Fedrelandspartiet Fatherland Party (1991)
Folkets vilje Will of the People Party (1993)
Fremskrittspartiet (FrP) Progress Party (1973)
Fylkeslistene for miljø og solidaritet (FMS) County Lists for the Environment and Solidarity (1989)
Hvit valgallianse (Stopp Innvandringen/Hjelp fremmede hjem) White Electoral Alliance (Stop Immigration/Repatriate Aliens) (1973)
Høyre (H) Conservative Party (1897)
Kristelig Folkeparti (KrF) Christian Democratic Party (1933)
Kristent Konservativt Parti (KKP) Christian Conservative Party (1965)
Miljøpartiet De Grønne The Green Party (1989)
Naturlovpartiet Natural Law Party (1993)
Norges Kommunistiske Parti (NKP) Communist Party (1924)
Pensjonistpartiet Pensioners' Party (1985)
Rød Valgallianse (RV) Red Electoral Alliance (1973)
Samfunnspartiet Society Party (1985)
Samlingspartiet Ny Fremtid New Future Coalition Party (1993)

Senterpartiet (Sp) Centre Party (1924)

Sosialistisk Venstreparti (SV) Socialist Left Party (1975)

Tverrpolitisk Folkevalgte (Kystpartiet) Non-Partisan Coastal Party (1973)

Venstre (V) Liberal Party (1897)

The Labour Party (*Arbeiderparti – A*), as the country's Social Democrats are called, was the principal party of government for decades until it lost power in the 1997 election, the last held before this book went to press. In that election, only eight parties gained seats in ☞ **Parliament**, in order of the number of seats held: 65 Labour (A), 25 Christian Democratic (KrF), 25 Progress (FrP), 23 Conservative (H), 11 Centre (Sp), 9 Socialist Left (SV), 6 Liberal (V) and 1 Non-Partisan Coastal (Kystpartiet), for a total of 165 seats.

World Health Organization – WHO (*Verdens helseorganisasjon*) is a specialised agency within the United Nations that is dedicated to promoting the health of peoples of all countries. The WHO is principally concerned with the control of epidemic disease, vaccination, water supplies and world-wide sanitation, though it increasingly is involved in combating health hazards such as narcotics and tobacco. Norway has close ties with the WHO: it joined in 1947, and Dr. Gro Harlem Brundtland, Norway's first woman prime minister (1981), is now the WHO Director-General.

The WHO Regional Office for Europe is located in Copenhagen ✆ +45 39171717, 🖷 +45 39171818, ✉ Scherfigsvej 8, DK-2100 Copenhagen, Denmark, ✉ postmaster@who.dk, ☻ http://www.who.dk with

pages in English and on-line documents available in English, French, German and Russian. Its concern with health throughout Europe is reflected in a comprehensive plan, "Health 21 – health for all in the 21st century", available as a printed booklet, ISBN 92-890-1348-6, or on-line from its web site.

WHO affairs in Norway are conducted principally by the Ministry of Health and Social Affairs (*Sosial- og helsedepartementet – SHD*) ✆ 22249090, 🖷 22249575, ✉ PO Box 8011 Dep, 0030 Oslo, ☻ http://odin.dep.no/shd with pages in Norwegian and selected pages in English. Offices and agencies within the Ministry are responsible for various aspects of WHO matters:

- General liaison: Health division (*Helseavdeling*) ✆ 22248703.
- Specific health matters: Norwegian Board of Health (*Statens helsetilsyn*), Division of Social Medicine (*Avdeling for samfunnsmedisin*) ✆ 22248871 🖷 22249590, ✉ PO box 8128 Dep, 0032 Oslo ☻ http://www.helsetilsynet.no with pages in Norwegian and in English.
- WHO publications: Norwegian Board of Health library, address above, ☻ http://www.helsetilsynet.no/bibliote/who.htm with links to WHO databases abroad and to databases of WHO publications to date.

WHO publications may be ordered in Norway from *ABC fagbokhandel* ✆ 22207420, 🖷 22208971, ✉ PO Box 2728 St. Hanshaugen, 0131 Oslo, ✉ abc.fagbokhandel@os.telia.no

Health care
(Helsetjenester)

A broad overview of health care (Helsetjenester) Norway ranks 14th in the world in spending on health care in relation to the size of its economy: about 8% of the country's Gross Domestic Product (GDP) is spent on public and private sector health care, about the same as in many other countries in Europe. But as Norway has the world's fourth largest GDP per person, the amount spent per person is correspondingly high. Moreover, Norway now is upgrading its health care services, in accordance with the World Health Organisation (WHO) strategy calling for "Health for All by the Year 2000".

Overall health care principally is a public service, financed through income taxes and government appropriations. Mostly the municipalities (kommunene) and the counties (fylkeskommunene) support services. The State operates some facilities, such as Rikshospitalet ("The National Hospital") and Det Norske Radiumhospital ("Norwegian Radium Hospital"). Private health care is a growing sector and now accounts for about 5% of all health care services.

The municipal health services (kommune-helsetjenesten) comprise primary health care (primærhelsetjenesten) and include preventive health care, treatment of illness and injury, rehabilitation, nursing and care. Each municipality organises its general medical services, emergency clinics, physiotherapy, nursing, midwives, nursing homes, care facilities and, in a few municipalities, psychology. The services are provided both by municipal out-patient health centres, nursing homes and other facilities and through municipal support of health service professionals in private practice, such as doctors and physiotherapists.

The county health services (fylkeshelsetjenesten) provide specialised health care (spesialisthelsetjenesten) and include hospitals, polyclinics and special services, such as ambulances, rescue services and medical helplines. The counties also provide mental health services (psykisk helsevern) in co-operation with the primary health care and the social services of the municipalities.

For further information on local health care services, contact the municipal services listed under

Helse og sosialetat or Helse og sosialsentre in the Pink Pages under the name of the municipality (kommune) in which you live.

For further information on health care in the county in which you live, contact the County Chief Medical Officer, listed under Fylkeslege in the Pink Pages. For a comprehensive overview of health care, contact the Norwegian Board of Health (Statens Helsetilsyn) ✆ 22248888, 🖷 22249590, ✉ PO Box 8128 Dep, 0032 Oslo, ⊕ http://www.helsetilsynet.no with pages in Norwegian and in English. The best overview is a booklet published by the Norwegian Board of Health: Brief Introduction to Health Services in Norway, order no. IK-2563 (English edition), which is also available on-line from the Board's website.

Abortion (Abort) is of two kinds: spontaneous miscarriage (spontan abort) and induced therapeutic abortion (provosert abort). A miscarriage means that the body separates and expels the contents of the pregnant uterus before the 24th week of pregnancy. There are no statistics on it, but medical estimates indicate that about one pregnancy in ten ends in a miscarriage. A therapeutic abortion involves medical procedures that terminate a pregnancy. Before 1960, therapeutic abortion was a criminal offence with exceptions granted only for medical reasons. The Abortion Act (Lov om svangerskapsavbrudd) of 1960 liberalised the law by permitting therapeutic abortion in cases where there were weighty grounds for it. In December 1978 the Abortion Act was further liberalised and remains the currently valid law. Its principal provisions for a woman who may seek an abortion are:

- The woman has the right to request advice and to reach a decision on her own.
- The doctor who sees the woman must explain the abortion procedure and its medical effects.
- The doctor should tell the woman about the information and social support available, regardless of whether she elects to go through with the abortion or to carry the pregnancy to term.
- The woman has the right to receive birth control information if she so wishes.
- The woman may of her own volition, without substantiating her reason, request an abortion before the 12th week of pregnancy.

Before the 12th week of pregnancy, a woman may

request an abortion simply by visiting a doctor, who will fill out a form entitled *Begjæring om svanger-skapsavbrudd* ("Request to terminate pregnancy") and submit it to the hospital or polyclinic where the abortion will be performed. Some hospitals in larger cities now offer medical abortion using the RU-486 Mifepristone pill developed in 1980 in France, but the legal status of its availability and use are still being debated. Between the 12th and the 18th week of pregnancy, the procedure is the same, but the request is then submitted to a commission consisting of two medical doctors, who must approve it before an abortion can be performed. After the 18th week, an abortion can be granted only if their are weighty grounds for it. If a foetus is viable, an abortion cannot be granted. Each year, some 14,000 therapeutic abortions are performed in Norway, most frequently on women 20 to 24 years old, followed by women 25 to 29 years old and then by teenagers. Less clear than these statistics are the dilemmas and psychological trauma women go through in facing abortion. Assistance on such matters is provided in both the public and private sectors.

Klinikk for seksuell opplysning ("Sexual information clinic") in Oslo has a staff of doctors, nurses and psychologists who provide guidance on matters of sex life, birth control and abortion ✆ 22375114, ✉ Hammerstadgt. 1, 0568 Oslo. *Telefonen for seksuell helse* ("Sexual health help line") is a country-wide service manned by doctors from Monday through Thursday, 8 to 10 pm, to provide advice on birth control, pregnancy and abortion ✆ 81002244 (local rate throughout the country).

Alternativ til Abort i Norge, AAN (Abortion Alternatives of Norway) is an apolitical, non-sectarian private organisation that provides free advice and counselling to women and men on all matters concerned, including pregnancy tests (*graviditetstest*), counselling on choice of whether or not to have an abortion (*rådgivning/valgsamtale*), follow-up counselling (*oppfølgingssamtaler*), couple conferences (*parsamtaler*), information on rights and finances (*informasjon om rettigheter og økonomi*), antenatal and postnatal groups (*gruppetilbud før og etter fødsel*), counselling after abortion (*samtale etter abort*) and practical assistance (*pratisk hjelp*). All AAN material is in Norwegian and almost all the staff are Norwegians. However, all staff members can speak and provide services in English and, if necessary, in other languages using interpreters. You may contact AAN at the nearest of its 19 offices throughout the country, listed under *Viktig telefoner* in the general information in front of the Pink Pages of the telephone directory, or at headquarters: ✆ 22478010, 🖷 22478020, ✉ Dronningensgate 8b, 0152 Oslo, 📧 metorp@online.no, ◉ http://www.sn.no/aan. For further information on all aspects of women's health, you may contact the Norwegian Board of Health in Oslo (*Statens helsetilsyn*) ✆ 22248888, 🖷 22249590, 📧 postmottak@helsetilsynet.dep.telemax.no, ◉ http://www.heltilsynet.no with pages in Norwegian and in English.

Alternative medicine (*Alternativ medisin*) consists of therapies that differ from and are alternative to those of conventional medicine. Many alternative therapies originated in Asian countries, where they are in everyday use and consequently are regarded as commonplace. So the designation "alternative" often implies an approach differing from that of western medicine. There is no complete overview of the alternative therapies and treatments practised in Norway, let alone practised world-wide. In 1998, a Ministry of Health and Social Affairs (*Sosial- og helsedepartementet – SHD*) study of alternative medicine concluded with the publication of a 274-page report, *Alternativ medisin*, NOU 1998:21, ISBN 82-583-0467-4. The therapies described in section 6.3 of that report are listed below, alphabetically by their names in English; you can locate practitioners in the Yellow Pages by looking under the Norwegian names. The Internet probably is the most readily-available source of information on alternative medicine in many languages; one comprehensive database lists many, but not all of the therapies practised world-wide: ◉ http://www.wrf.org.

Acupuncture (*Akupunktur*), originally Chinese, a method of treating various ailments by pricking skin or tissue with needles.

Antroposophic medicine (*Antroposofisk medisin*), practised by doctors, builds on the work of Rudolf Steiner, founder of the Steiner Schools.

Aroma therapy (*Aromaterapi*), use of plant extracts and essential oils in massage.

Ayurveda (*Ayurvedisk medisin*), ancient Hindu art of medicine and of prolonging life.

Biofeedback (*Bioresonansterapi*), use of measuring instrument to monitor body responses and help patient control them.

Biopathy (*Biopati*), uses nutritional approach to improve quality of life.

Craniosacral therapy (*Kraniosakral terapi*), form of osteopathy using extremly light touch to promote healing.

Dietary supplements, vitamins and mineral therapy (*Kosttilskudd, vitamin- og mineralterapi*), treatment using supplements to the diet.

Ear acupuncture (*Øreakupunktur og øremedisin*), the use of acupuncture on the outer ear to treat ailments elsewhere in the body.

Flower remedies (*Blomstermedisin*), use of flower essence to cure; includes Bach flower remedies (*Bachs blomstermedisiner*) and Australian bush flower essence (*Australsk blomstermedisin*).

Fyto therapy and modern herbalism (*Fytoterapi – modern urtemedisin*), use of herbs to cure ailments.

Healing and therapeutic touch (*Healing og håndspåleggelse*), involves transfer of healing energy; includes Spiritual healing (*Fjernhealing*) through prayer, Reiki therapy (*Reiki-healing*), the Japanese method of gentle touch to promote healing, and Shen therapy (*Shen-terapi*), an abbreviation of Specific Human Energy Nexus, entailing physio-emotional release.

Homeopathy (*Homeopati*), use of minute amounts of natural remedies which in larger quantities would reproduce effects of illness treated; leading alternative medicine in Norway, ☞ **Homeopathic medicine**.

Kinesiology (*Kinesiologi*), branch of chiropractic, includes touch for health, biokinesiology, educational kinesiology, stress release, three-in-one, applied physiology, kinesipathy, hyperton-x and professional kinesiology.

Magnetic field therapy (*Magnetfeltterapi*), use of pulsating magnetic fields to promote healing.

Massage and body-oriented therapy (*Massasje og kroppsorienterte terapier*), art of treating body by rubbing, kneading and the like.

Naprapathy (*Naprapati*), massage to correct disorders of connective tissue or ligaments.

Nutrition and health food (*Ernæring og helsekost*), promotes health through judicious choice of foods and supplements.

Osteopathy (*Osteopati*), treatment of ailments through manipulation of the bones, especially the spine.

Photo therapy (*Lysterapi*), use of light, including infrared and ultraviolet, to treat ailments.

Polarity therapy (*Polaritetsterapi*), energy-balancing massage.

Sami folk medicine and traditions (*Samisk folkemedisin og tradisjoner*), traditional practices of the nomadic Sami shaman (*sjamann*).

Tibetan medicine (*Tibetansk medisin*), a combination of herbalism, acupuncture, cauterisation and meditation to promote health and hasten healing.

Therapeutic cupping (*Vacuumterapi og kopping*), the placing on skin of small glass cups on which vacuum is drawn, to promote healing.

Training, exercise and techniques (*Trening, øvelser og teknikker*), including Alexander technique (*Alexander-teknikken*) for good posture, Autogenetic training (*Autogen trening*) involving self-hypnosis, Feldenkrais theory (*Feldenkrais*) involving small movements and including "functional integration" and "awareness through movement", Qigong (*Qi gong*), Chinese gentle exercise for self-healing, Tai chi (*Tai chi*), Chinese self-healing to promote "chi" sense of well-being and Yoga (*Yoga*), the Hindu system of gentle exercises, deep breathing and relaxation.

Unani (*Unani*), the old Greek and now Indian practice of using plants, minerals and massage to cure and promote health.

Vibrational therapy (*krystall- og steinterapi*), use of crystals and stones having vibrational properties to promote healing.

Zone therapy (*Soneterapi*), use of foot massage to treat ailments elsewhere in the body.

Asthma (*Astma*) and related illnesses, including allergies and over-sensitivity affects about 1.5 million people. In the last few years the incidence of asthma amongst children has increased to 10%. Unhealthy climate indoors, and pollution are the main causes for asthma, an important consideration in the increase in childhood cases has been the use of studded ☞ **tyres** (Cars, Roads, Traffic chapter) during the winter, especially in cities. The Norwegian Asthma and Allergy Society (*Norges Astma- og Allergiforbund – NAAF*) offers numerous support services, including pollen warnings, studies of indoor climate, and social groups for young people dealing with asthma. NAAF has groups in all counties; for further information, contact the head office

☏ 22933730 🖷 22933750, ✉ Hegdehaugsveien 31, 0352 Oslo, ⌨ naaf@naaf.no, ⊕ http://www.naaf.no

Autopsy (*Obduksjon*) A post-mortem (after death) medical examination is called an autopsy. An autopsy that involves surgery may be called a necropsy. But in general usage, the two words are synonyms, particularly as most autopsies involve surgery. In Norwegian there is just one word, *obduksjon*, which means a surgical procedure performed on a dead person, usually by a pathologist in a hospital. The results of autopsies clarify the causes of death (*dødsårsak*) and are reported to Norway Statistics (*Statistisk sentralbyrå*); these are the oldest of health statistics in the country, having been recorded since 1853. The Norwegian Board of Health (*Statens helsetilsyn*) regulations and medical practice in the country now distinguish between two categories of autopsy: medical autopsy (*ordinær obduksjon*) and forensic autopsy (*rettsmedisinsk obduksjon*).

Medical autopsies may be performed on all persons who have died in hospital or have been brought there after death. Formal permission is not required, as permission is by presumed consent (*presumert samtykke*). However, patient rights (*pasient rettigheter*) permit exception. Should a person or close relatives object and so inform the hospital, a medical autopsy cannot be performed. Consequently, The Norwegian Medical Association (*Den norske lægeforening*) has six guidelines for medical autopsy:
1. There must be medical reasons for requesting an autopsy.
2. The deceased's closest relatives shall have been notified of the death.
3. At least eight hours shall have passed since death.
4. The deceased or the deceased's relatives have not objected to autopsy.
5. There is no reason to assume that the deceased or the deceased's relatives would object to autopsy on religious or other grounds.
6. Medical autopsy can be performed only if there is no reason to assume that forensic autopsy will be requested (by the police).

Forensic autopsies are requested by the police (*politi*) and may be performed whenever there is reason to suspect that a death was unnatural (*unaturlig dødsfall*). A doctor who suspects unnatural death is obliged to report it (*meldeplikt*) to the police. The Norwegian Board of Health regulations define nine categories of unnatural or apparently unnatural death:
1. Murder, assault or other violence.
2. Suicide or self-inflicted injury.
3. Accidents such as sinking, fire, avalanche, lightning strike, drowning, fall, traffic accident etc.
4. Occupational accident or injury.
5. Fault, negligence or accident in diagnosis or treatment of illness or injury.
6. Narcotics abuse.
7. Unknown cause of sudden or unexpected death.
8. Death in prison or in civilian or military arrest.
9. Find of an unidentified corpse.

Birth control (*Prevensjon*) Most contraceptive devices and systems are available, from pharmacies and as fitted and prescribed by gynaecologists. As elsewhere, the effectiveness of birth control measures are expressed in terms of the Pearl Index (*Pearls indeks*) which is a failure rate equal to the number of unintended pregnancies per hundred women per year, that is, the number of pregnancies in 1200 months of use. The higher the Pearl Index, the less safe the means, though safety also depends on the skill with which a means is used. Ranked in a 1999 study by increasing Pearl Index , the methods used before and during coitus are the Levonorgestrel-releasing intrauterine system (IUS) (*hormonespiral*), sterilisation (*sterilisering*), depot injections (*P-sprøyte*), intrauterine device (IUD) (*kobberspiral*), oral contraceptive pill (*P-pille*), Lady-comp rhythm mini-computer (*Lady-comp*), mini oral pill (*mini-pill*), Persona rhythm mini-computer (*Persona*), condom (*kondom*), cervical cap (*pessar*), and spermicidal cream (*sæddrepende krem*). The Tetragynon (Schering tradename) morning-after pill (*angrepille*) is available on prescription.

Blind and purblind (*Blinde og svaksynte*) Public and private sector organisations offer blind and purblind persons numerous services and support means including training of guide dogs (*førerhunder*), publication and instruction in Braille (*blindeskrift*) and rehabilitation courses (*rehabiliteringstilbud*). The Norwegian Association of the Blind (*Norges Blindeforbund*) is the principal organisation, with a head office in Oslo and offices in all 19 counties as well as liaison with other organisations. Contact the head office for further information ☏ 23215000, 🖷 23215072, ✉ PO Box 5900 Majorstua, 0308

Oslo, @ http://www.blindeforbundet.no with pages in Norwegian and links to other web sites.

Blood banks and donation (*Blodbanker og donasjon*) Every hospital has a facility for taking donations and storing of blood. Blood is kept for five weeks, after which time it is destroyed. You will be accepted as a blood donor only if you were born and brought up in Norway or a Western European country as far south as France. However, if at any time of your life you have lived a year or more in any country other than these, you will not be accepted as a donor. All blood is tested for HIV, hepatitis B and C, HTLV (a variant of HIV), and syphilis. The main blood bank is in Oslo, *Blodbanken*, Ullevål Sykehus ✆ 22118900. If you wish to donate blood, look in the Yellow Pages under *Sykehus* for the telephone number of a hospital near you.

Care of the mentally retarded (*Helsevernet for psykisk utviklingshemmede – HVPU*) was formerly provided at the county level in central institutions. However, in 1991 the overall *HVPU* system was reformed. The responsibility of care was shifted from the counties to the municipalities, and the central institutions were to be phased out. The principal intent was to provide care in smaller, more home-like living units. However, the shift imposed greater financial burdens on the municipalities at a time when many of their budgets already were strained. Consequently, the implementation of the reform measures varies according to a municipality's ability to finance them. Critics claim that the result has been a deterioration of care services. Moreover, many adult patients had lived long in and felt at home in institutions and objected to being moved out of them. Consequently, the *HVPU* reform was and still is a topic of debate, at the local as well as at the national level. For further information on local *HVPU*, contact your municipal social services office.

Chiropractors (*Kiropraktorer*) practise chiropractic, which is concerned with the curing of ailments through manipulation of the structures of body, particularly the spine. Chiropractic has been practised in Norway since 1922, and authorisation of chiropractors began in 1988. All chiropractors who belong to the Norwegian Association of Chiropractors (*Norsk Kiropraktor Forening – MKF*) are authorised and con-

sequently can act as primary contacts with patients. You do not need a referral from a doctor to visit a chiropractor. However, if you are referred by a doctor, part of the chiropractor's fee for treatment can be refunded by the National Insurance Scheme (*Folketrygden*). You may ask your doctor for a referral to a chiropractor. Otherwise, look under *Kiropraktorer* in the Yellow Pages. For information on chiropractic and chiropractors, contact *Norsk Kiropraktor Forening* ✆ 22207890, 🖷 22207895, ✉ St. Olavs pl. 2, 0165 Oslo, @ http://www.kiropraktikk.no

Circumcision (*Omskjæring*) is the cutting round and removal of part or all of the foreskin of the penis. It may be performed for medical reasons or religious reasons. All hospitals can perform medical circumcision, which usually involves a small incision to ease movement of the foreskin. Religious circumcision, as practiced in the Jewish and Muslim faiths, is available on request and is covered by National Insurance (*Folketrygd*) if performed in connection with birth in hospital. In the country, about 600 boys are circumcised each year.

Deaf (*Døve*) Persons with hearing impairment (*hørselshemmede*) are entitled to benefits including refund of the cost of a hearing aid (*høreapparat*) and various support services, such as those of an interpreter (*tolk*); for further details, contact the municipal offices concerned, listed under *Hjelpemiddelsentralen* and *Hørselssentralen* in the Pink Pages. The Folk High School at Ål (*Ål folkehøyskole*) offers a course of studies taught in dactylology (sign language) (*tegnspråk*) ✆ 32082600 voice and 32082651 text, 🖷 32082652, ✉ 3570 Ål. For further information on all matters concerning the deaf and hard-of-hearing, contact the Norwegian Association of the Deaf (*Norges Døveforbund*) ✆ 22111775 voice and 22460691 text, 🖷 22111633, ✉ PO Box 6850 St Olavspl, 0130 Oslo, ✉ norgesdoveforbund@c2i.net, @ http://www.norges-doveforbund.no with pages in Norwegian and links to other related organisations in the country.

Dental care (*Tannhelse*) is performed by three types of professionals. Dentists (*tannleger*) are responsible for the diagnosis, care and treatment of teeth and oral infections. Dental hygienists (*tan-*

npleiere) carry out work in oral hygiene: they clean teeth and mouths and play an educational role in the prevention of tooth decay and gum disease. Dental technicians (tannteknikere) are involved in all aspects of dental technology, including making crowns, dentures and bridge work. Dentists are listed under tannleger in the Yellow Pages. Aside from general practice (almen praksis), the specialities are endodontics (endodonti – rotfylling), oral orthopaedics (kjeveortopedi – tannregulering), oral surgery (oral kirurgi), pedodontics (pedondonti – barnetannpleie), periodontics (periodonti) and prosthodontics and occulision (protetikk og bittfunksjon). Dental hygienists are listed under tannpleiere and dental technicians under tanntekniker in the Yellow Pages. Treatment out of office hours is provided by emergency clinics (tannlegevakt), which usually are public but may be private. If you are regular patient in need of emergency treatment out of hours, call your dentist, who usually has an answer phone message with a telephone number to call. Dental care is primarily private – 2300 of the country's 3600 dentists are in private practice – though children up to age 18 are entitled to free care at public dental clinics. Children under three years old are automatically registered at the nearest local clinic and are sent periodic reminders to come in for dental checks. Both health clinics and dental clinics often are attached to school districts, and accordingly usually have a "school dentist" (skoletannlege). Through its local office (trygdekontor) the national insurance scheme automatically covers children up to age three, who are sent periodic reminders to come to their local clinic for dental checks. For children under 18 and in some cases for adults, national insurance can also refund up to 75% of the expense of private specialist treatment, as for orthodontics; for details, contact your local trygdekontor at the number listed in the Pink Pages. The current trend in dental care is toward group practice clinics, often with several dentists, dental hygienists, dental nurses and dental technicians. And now group practice clinics are banding together in clinic chains. The first and largest chain is Tannhelseklinikken ("Dental care clinics"), now with six clinics in the Oslo area and with plans to incorporate more throughout the country.

Disability aids (Hjelpemidler) Persons with lasting (duration more than two years) disabilities due to injury, defect or illness (skade, lyte eller skydom) are eligible for free rental of or for financial support for buying necessary aids, such as a wheelchair (rullestol), magnifying lamp (lupelampe), aid-call alarm (trygghetsalarm) or personal lift (personløfter). Moreover, support is available for other equipment, as might be needed at work, for special clothing, for computer equipment or for special fittings in cars. For further information, call the nearest disability aids centre listed under Hjelpemiddelsentralen listed in the Pink Pages.

Drugs in combination with alcohol (Legemidler og alkohol) Many drugs interact with alcohol to produce undesirable side effects, ranging from unpleasant to serious. Consequently, if you take a drug and wish to drink, or the other day round, you should know the effects of the combination. There are two ways of finding this information. First, warnings are included in the cautionary rules (forsiktighetsregler) on the packaging of some, but not all drugs that may interact with alcohol. Second, you may look up the drug in a leaflet entitled Preparatliste, which is available free in ☞ **Vinmopolet** (Shopping chapter) wine and liquor shops. In it, drugs are listed by their tradenames in three categories: drugs which cannot be combined with alcohol (legemidler som ikke kan kombineres med alkohol), drugs which may be combined with extremely moderate consumption of alcohol (legemidler som kan kombineres med meget forsiktig alkoholbruk) and drugs which may be combined with moderate consumption of alochol (legemidler som kan kombineres med forsiktig alkoholbruk). Explanations of the interaction of drugs and alcohol are given in a companion brochure entitled Legemidler og alkohol, also available in the Vinmonopolet shops.

Eating disorders (Spiseforstyrrelser) include anorexia, bulimia and compulsive overeating.

Anorexia (Anoreksi) is a diminished appetite. The common form of it regarded as an illness is anorexia nervosa (anoreksia nervosa), which is a personality malfunction characterised by fear of becoming overweight and an aversion to food. It is most common in young women and can result in a weight loss that threatens life.

Bulimia (Bulimi) is erratic overeating. The common form of it regarded as an illness is bulimia nervosa (*bulimia nervosa*). People who suffer from it often have bouts of extreme overeating, followed by self-induced vomiting, use of laxatives or extreme exercise to prevent weight gain.

Compulsive overeating (*Tvangsspising*) is the consumption of food when one is not hungry, principally to satisfy other needs other than hunger. The compulsive eater retains food eaten, but will periodically fast or slenderise to offset weight gained.

Many health services organisations are concerned with these problems, and three associations deal specifically with them:

Interessegruppa for Kvinner med Spiseforstyrrelser ("Advocacy group for women with eating disorders") with a head office in Oslo and local groups in six other cities. For information, contact the head office ✆ 22422222, 🖷 22420795, ✉ PO Box 8877 Youngstorget, 0028 Oslo, ◉ http://www-iks.no

Anorexia/Bulimia Foreningen ("Anorexia-Bulimia Association") with the head office in Bergen and local groups in nine other cities. For information, contact the head office ✆ 55326260, 🖷 55325701, ✉ PO Box 36, 5001 Bergen, ✉ abf@2i.net, ◉ http://www.abf.no

Overeaters Anonymous – OA ✆ 90155748, ✉ Thv Meyers gt 50C, 0552 Oslo, the Norwegian group of the global Overeaters Anonymous ✆+1 505-8912664, 🖷 +1 505-8914320, ✉ PO Box 44020, Rio Rancho, NM 87124-4020, USA, ✉ overeatr@technet.nm.org, ◉ http://www.overeatersanonymous.org with pages in English.

Female genital mutilation (*Kjønnslemlestelse*)

is illegal in Norway. Sometimes referred to as female circumcision, female genital mutilation (FGM) comprises all procedures involving partial or total removal of the external female genitalia or other injury to the female genital organs whether for cultural, religious or other non-therapeutic reasons. FGM is a traditional practice in some societies. The World Health Organization (WHO) estimates that more than 130 million girls and women have undergone some form of FGM. They live in 28 African countries and in a few countries in the Middle East and Asia. FGM is an emerging issue in immigrant communities in Australia, Canada. Europe, New Zealand and the United States. The known reasons for FGM include reduction of female sexual pleasure, identifi-

cation with cultural heritage, traditional aesthetics, myths and religious practice. The religious aspect is not clear. For instance, some Muslim communities practice FGM because they believe it is demanded by their faith, but the practice predates Islam. Whatever tradition or belief is involved, FGM is known to be harmful, with varying degrees of immediate and long-term complications and suffering. It also reinforces inequality suffered by girls and women in the communities in which it is practised. Consequently, FGM is illegal in many countries, including Norway, where it is forbidden by law in the Act prohibiting FGM (*Lov om forbud mot kjønnslemlestelse*) of 15 December 1995. For complete information on FGM, see the World Health Organization Fact Sheet N 153 and other publications, available at some health services facilities and at the WHO Internet web site ◉ http://www.who.int/inf.fs/en for the English version.

If you are a girl or woman threatened with FGM or if you wish to report the practice of it, contact the nearest municipal health services listed under *Helse og sosialetat* or *Helse og sosialsentre* in the Pink Pages. If have cause to fear it, you can discuss your fears in your native language, in one of the network groups supported by the ☞ **MiRA Resource Centre** (Non-government Organisations chapter).

If you have performed FGM or intend to perform it on girls or women, you should know that you are committing a crime which according to Norwegian law is punishable by up to three years in prison or up to six years if the result is an illness or disability lasting more than two weeks or an irreversible disfigurement.

First aid courses (*Opplæring i førstehjelp*) First

aid is the immediate and temporary care given to the victim of an accident or sudden illness until professional medical services can be obtained. First aid skills are essential and useful almost anywhere – in homes, on highways, on beaches, in boats, in wilderness areas, in workplaces and in schools. The easiest route to acquiring first aid skills is to take one of the many courses offered throughout the country. The Norwegian Red Cross (*Norges Røde Kors*) and Norwegian People's Aid (*Norsk Folkehjelp*), offer courses for the public. These two organisations, as well as ambulance services (*Ambulansjetjeneste*) and Norwegian Air Ambulance (*Norsk Luftambulanse*) ☞ **Rescue services, air** (Emergencies chapter) and some colleges offer occupational first aid courses, such as those held by maritime schools (*Maritime skoler*) for fishermen. There are many types of courses, sorting into five general categories:

- Basic courses, usually from 4 to 27 hours in length, for the general public
- Refresher and extension courses for those already trained
- Appointed persons courses, as for safety delegates in workplaces
- Specific skills courses, as for persons working with children
- Rescue services courses, as for ski patrols, mountain rescue teams and the like

In most municipalities (*kommune*), first aid services are provided by volunteer Aid Corps (*Hjelpekorps*). So for information on courses, or for volunteer duty when you are suitably trained, call the local Corps; look under *Norsk Folkehjelp Sanitet* or *Røde Kors Hjelpekorps* in the Pink Pages. First-aid activities throughout the country are co-ordinated by the Norwegian First Aid Council (*Norsk førstehjelpsråd*) ✆ 22054000, 📠 22054040, ✉ PO Box 1 Grønland, 0133 Oslo.

Health care, private (*Private helsetjenester*) is growing and now accounts for more than 5% of all health care services in the country. Most doctors and physiotherapists have private practices, but six in ten have partial public support from municipalities (*kommune*) or city sectors (*bydeler*). Starting in the mid 1980s, comprehensive medical services are offered by private polyclinics (*legesentere*), of which there are some 140 throughout the country. In most cases, the private polyclinics are regarded as a supplement to public health care and consequently have no subsidies. Nonetheless, private medical services are offered at reasonable costs, in line with those elsewhere in Europe. Moreover, some of the larger private polyclinics offer membership arrangements as well as company health plans, which further reduce the costs of individual consultations and treatments. There are several chains of private polyclinics. Volvat is the largest, with 11 polyclinics in seven cities: Oslo, Bergen, Fredrikstad, Hamar, Nøtterøy, Tønsberg and Ålesund, and the largest single private clinic in the country, at Volvat in Oslo, with a staff of more than 90. The Doctors chain has five clinics in the greater Oslo area. The other private polyclinics include:

- Drammen: Klinikk Titterud and St. Joseph BHT
- Elverum: Elverum Legesenter
- Haugesund: Haugesund Gyn. Klinikk
- Jessheim: Gardermoen Medisinske Senter
- Oppdal: Oppdal Medisinske Senter
- Oslo: Brynklinikken, Oslo Akutten, Sinsen-Klinikken, Sjølyst Medisinske Senter and Urologisk Klinikk.
- Strømmen: Romeriksklinikken
- Trondheim: Spesialistlegesenteret
- Ålesund: MEDI3

The leading private polyclinics are members of the Multidisciplinary Medical Centre Association (*Forening for Tverrfaglige Medisinske Sentra – TMS*) ✉ Lørenveien 55, 0580 Oslo. For the addresses and telephone numbers of the private polyclinics near where you live, look under *Leger* in the Yellow Pages or under the name of the polyclinic in the Pink Pages.

Health condition associations (*Foreninger for sykdommer og lidelser*) If you have or seek advice on a health condition or wish to contact others concerned with it, there may be an association specific to your needs, as listed below. Updated listings are available on the Internet at

🌐 http://www.doktoronline.no/organisasjoner/organisasjoner.htm and at

🌐 http://www.fullrulle.no, as well as in the site pages of ☞ **The Norwegian Medical Association** 🌐 http://www.legeforeningen.no/info/pasfor.html. For emergencies, such as potential suicide and domestic violence, see ☞ **Helplines** (Emergencies chapter).

Health screening (*Helseundersøkelse*) is provided countrywide by the National Health Screening Service (*Statens helseundersøkelser*) jointly with the local municipal health services, for tuberculosis (*tuberkulose*), cardiovascular illnesses (*hjerte-karsykdommer*) and pneumoconiosis (*støvlungesykdom*), as well as other illnesses. Usually you will be notified by post when screening is to be done in your municipality. For further details, contact the local health service office, usually listed under *helseetat* or *helsetjeneste* in the Pink Page listings for the municipality. Or for an overall view of screening, contact the head office of the Screening Service ✆ 22242100, 📠 22242101, ✉ PO Box 8155 Dep, 0033 Oslo, 🌐 http://www.shus.no with pages in Norwegian and summary pages in English.

Health Stations (Helsestatsjoner) are local municipal public clinics. The most prevalent health stations offer services to pregnant women, babies and children up to the age of 16. They are staffed by a doctor, nurses, a midwife and sometimes there is also a dental clinic attached, staffed by qualified dental nurses and a dentist. If your children are born in Norway, they are automatically registered in the ☞ **National insurance scheme** (Government and Social Services chapter) and will therefore be registered with the local health station. Your child will be notified to come in for regular development checks, ☞ **vaccination** and hearing and eyesight tests. This service tracks children until they are 16 years old and it is free. Ask your neighbour where the nearest helsestasjon is, alternatively look it up in the Pink Pages in the section for your municipality, the health station name is prefixed with the name of your municipality. Health stations have also been set up for young adults, where they deal with contraception, eating disorders, sexually transmitted diseases and depression. Oslo has a health station near the main railway station for drug addicts and there will soon be one located in the centre of Stavanger.

Homeopathy (Homeopati) is a system of ☞ **Alternative medicine** (this chapter) based on the principle that like cures like. This means that a substance that can produce a certain set of symptoms in a healthy person can cure the same symptoms in an ill person. The homeopathic medicinal substances are produced in a particular way by serial dilution and successions that release curative energies hidden in matter. Homeopathy was developed in the late 18th century in Germany by Dr. Samuel Hahnemann (1755-1843). Thereafter, it spread rapidly: in 1810 it was introduced into India, and toward the end of the 19th century, about one doctor in ten in Europe was a homeopath. But in the early 20th century, conventional medicine replaced homeopathy, and the practice of it declined. Then, starting in 1980 that trend reversed, and there are now some 19,000 doctors in Europe who practise homeopathy. However, in India, there was no decline and subsequent resurgence, but rather steady growth. Now there are 135 homeopathic colleges and half a million registered homeopaths in India. The practice of classical homeopathy starts with the homeopath examining and listening to the patient to outline the symptoms, thoughts and feelings that prompted the consultation. Then the homeopath analyses the entire situation and compares symptoms to known remedies in the homeopathic materia medica list of more than 3,000 medicines, to find a single medicine that best meets the patient's needs. The medicine is then given to the patient with directions on how often it should be taken. Homeopathic medicines are recognised within the European Union (EU) pharmaceutical legislation and approved in countries where homeopaths practise. Homeopathy is now practised world-wide, and in Europe, the National Insurance schemes in France, Germany, the Netherlands and the United Kingdom support homeopathic treatment. For further information on homeopathy, contact the European and International Councils for Classical Homeopathy (ECCH & ICCH) ✆ +44 1953 888163, 🖷 +44 1953 888163, ✉ School House, Market Place, Kenninghall, Norfolk NR16 2AH, UK, 🖃 ecch@gn.apc.org, ⊕ http://www.gn.apc.org/ecch.icch   In Norway, further information on homeopathy is available from the Norwegian Society of Homeopaths (Norske Homeopaters Landsforbund), ✆ 22111299, 🖷 22111303, ✉ Storgt 39, 0182 Oslo, 🖃 petter.viksveen@eunet.no. The Skandinavisk Institutt for Klassisk Homeopati ("Scandinavian Institute for Classical Homeopathy") in Oslo offers a three-year course of studies in homeopathy ✆ 22028062, 🖷 22028064, ✉ Sognsv 75A, 0855 Oslo, 🖃 lims@online.no. There are now more than 400 recognised homeopaths in private practice (homeopathy is not supported by the Norwegian National Insurance scheme). You can locate a homeopath by looking under homeopat in the Yellow Pages.

Hospitals (Sykehus) are operated as a public service, financed through income taxes and government appropriations. Mostly the municipalities (kommunene) and the counties (fylkeskommunene) support services. Hospital capacities are sometimes strained, but the countrywide figure of 13.5 hospital beds per 1,000 population is the fourth highest in the world.

There are three types of hospital, varying by size and the areas they serve: local hospitals (lokalsykehus), central hospitals (sentralsykehus) and regional hospitals (regionsykehus). The country is divided into five health service regions (helseregioner): Region 1:

East, Region 2: South, Region 3: West, Region 4: mid Norway, and Region 5: North. Each Region covers several counties and has its own regional hospital.

The State operates some facilities, such as *Rikshospitalet* ("The National Hospital") and *Det Norske Radiumhospital* ("Norwegian Radium Hospital"). *Rikshospitalet* is the regional hospital for the Southern Region, but it also has national functions, as do other regional hospitals. *Det Norske Radiumhospital* is the national centre for treatment of and research on cancer.

Usually, doctors refer patients to hospitals, and, with the exception of some psychiatric patients, patients enter hospitals voluntarily. All hospitals are obliged to provide immediate help (*øyblikkelig hjelp*) to victims of accidents (*ulykker*) and acute illness (*livstruende sykdommer*) as well as births (*fødsler*) without recommendation from a doctor and regardless of where the patient lives.

Some ☞ **private health care** clinics offer hospitalisation services.

Hospital visits (*Sykehus besøk*) Visitng hours are seldom rigidly fixed, though if in doubt, you should call the hospital in advance. Anything is acceptable as a gift to a patient, though some old wives tales still exist, such as when a new mother takes her flowers home with her from the maternity ward it is said that she will return within a year. Most hospitals have small kiosks in their main entrance halls where you can purchase flowers, sweets, newspapers and magazines.

Medical doctors (*Leger*) There are more than 16,000 doctors in the country, or one for every 303 people, about the same as in Germany. Most are members of ☞ **The Norwegian Medical Association**, and almost all speak English and many speak other languages, as they have been educated abroad. Moreover, one in seven is foreign born.

A general practitioner (GP) is a *spesialist i allmennmedisin*, he is your first point of contact when you are ill. To find a doctor, ask in the neighbourhood where you live, ask someone whose judgement you trust or look in the Yellow Pages under *leger*. Remember to check whether the doctor you plan to see practises privately, their consultation fees will be higher. The ☞ **National Insurance Scheme** (Government & Social Services chapter) provides med-

ical care, although the number of private clinics is increasing.

Municipalities run medical centres (*legesenter*) and ☞ **Health stations** that cater for children and pregnant women, ☞ **Pregnancy** (Family and Children chapter). Appointments can only be made by telephoning at certain times, an answerphone message, in Norwegian, will let you know during which times the telephone is mannned. Medical care for children aged seven and under is free of charge. If you need to see a doctor out of office hours and in the weekend, look for the number of the duty doctor or emergency clinic (*legevakt*) in the Pink Pages under the name of your municipality, in an emergency, call one of the ☞ **emergency numbers** (Emergencies chapter).

You will find specialists under subheadings, in the Yellow Pages, some useful translations: general practice (*allmennmedisin*), anaethetist (*anestesi*), child and youth psychiatry (*barne- og ungdompsykiatri*), ear nose and throat (*øre-nese-halssykdomer*), gynaecology and obstetrics (*fødselshjelp og kvinnesykdommer*), heart specialists (*hjertesykdommer*), pediatrics (*barnesykdommer*), skin specialists (*hudsykdommer*), surgery (*generall kirurgi*). Should you need to see a specialist, your GP will write a letter of referral for you and give you the names of specialists he recommends for your particular illness. It is then up to you to arrange an appointment with the specialist of your choice. When you visit the doctor for the first time, ask for an annual receipt card (*kvitteringskort*) for each member of your family, the amount you pay for consultations (*egenandel*) should be noted on the card and stamped by the doctor's receptionist. A maximum annual amount payable per person is set each year, when you have reached this amount, contact your local benefit office (*trygdekontoret*) who will issue you with a free card (*frikort*), which entitles you to free medical care for the remainder of the year.

For further information about your illness ☞ **health condition associations** may be able to recommend a specialist.

Medicine (*Legemidler*) is sold only at ☞ **pharmacies** as well as at medicine shops (*medisinutsalgene*) operated as subsidiaries by some pharmacies to provide their services in smaller towns and villages. Pharmacies sell both over-the-counter (*reseptfrie*) and prescription (*reseptpliktige*) medicines. You may find them described in the medicine handbook (*Medisinhåndboken*), the condensed version of the ☞ **pharmacopoeia** intended for the public and sold in pharmacies.

Over-the-counter medicines include antacids (link, gaviscon, pepcid, zantac), antihistamines (zyrtec, clarityn), antiseptics (bacimycin, pyrisept to wash out wounds), analygesics (dispril, aspirin, novid), non-aspirin pain relievers (panodil, pamol, paracet, also available in suppositories), children's aspirin (*barneaspirin*), bandages (*bandasje*), cold sore cream (*kamferdråper, lassars pasta*), contraceptive aids (*befruktningshindrende middel, p-piller*), corn plasters (*liktornplåster*), cough medicine (Noskapin, Tuxi), diarrhoea preparations (Imodium) or drink blueberry juice (*blåbærsaft*); ido-form to prevent diarrhoea and gem (mineral and electrolyte replacement), eye allergy (Livostin, Lomudal), eye drops (*øyedråper*), eye wash (*øyebadevann*), fluoride tablets (flux, but if using fluoride toothpaste do not supplement with pills, ask your dentist for advice), gauze (*gas*), hemorrhoids (Scheriproct), hydrocortisone (a small tube up to 1% available over the counter, otherwise on prescription), insect bites and stings (Xylocain), iodine (*jod*), laxatives (Dulcolax, Dulphalac), nasal spray (Otrivin), ovulation kits (*eggløsningstest*), plasters (*plaster*), pregnancy testing kits (*gravidtest*), throat lozenges (*halsepastiller*) and worms (Vermox). Ask the pharmacist (*farmasøyt*) for anything you may need.

Prescriptions can be filled at any pharmacy. If you live far from the nearest pharmacy, you may have your prescriptions filled by post at no charge; call the pharmacy for details.

If you need a prescription medicine to treat a long-term or chronic illness, your doctor will give you a blue discount prescription (*blå resept*) which entitles you to have part of the cost of the medicine covered by ☞ **National insurance** (Government and Social Services chapter). Medicines for children up to age six and for all persons suffering certain illnesses are covered 100%. Otherwise, children seven to 16 and persons 67 or older pay 10% of the cost of the medicine, while other persons, 17 – 66 years old, pay 30%.

The Norwegian Medical Association (*Den norske lægeforening*) is the country's professional medical association. As at 9 September 1999, its membership counted 15,863 doctors as well as 2678 medical students. It publishes the Journal of The Norwegian Medical Association (*Tidsskrift for Den norske lægeforening*) and maintains a central facility, *Legens hus* ("Doctor's House") at Akersgt. 2 in Oslo ✆ 23109000, 🖷 23109010, ✉ PO Box 1152 Sentrum, 0107 Oslo, ✉ legeforeningen@legeforeningen.no, ✎ http://www.legeforeningen.no

Obesity (*Fedme*) According to a report published in 1998 by the ☞ **WHO** (Government and Social Services chapter), obesity is now a global problem that affects more people than does undernourishment. Obesity is now defined by the Body Mass Index (BMI) guideline, which is weight in kilograms divided by the square of height in metres. For instance, a person weighing 80 kg and standing 1.8 metres has a BMI of $80/(1.8x1.8) = 24.7$. A person with a BMI of 25 or more is considered overweight, and a person with a BMI of 30 or more is obese.

In Norway, obesity is increasing most markedly among men. According to figures on 40 to 42 year-old men and women, in 1963-72, the average man had a BMI of 24.8 and 4.3% had a BMI of 30 or more, whilst the average women had a BMI of 24.7 and 9.1% had a BMI of 30 or more. Obesity then was more common among women than among men. But by 1991-95, the situation had reversed. The average man had a BMI of 25.7 and 9.1% had a BMI of 30 or more, whilst the average woman had a BMI of 24.4 and 8.4% had a BMI of 30 or more. Yet Norway still is a slim country compared to many others: in all, less than one adult in ten is obese.

Nonetheless, steps have been taken to reverse the trend. In March 1999, the National Council on Nutrition and Physical Activity (*Statens råd for ernæring og fysisk aktivitet*) was founded with 24 experts who together act as a central resource group for all matters concerning nutrition, physical activity and health. For further information, contact the Council secretariat ✆ 22249061, 🖷 22249091, ✉ PO Box 8139 Dep, 0033 Oslo, ✉ post@ser.no, ✎ http://www.ser.no with pages in Norwegian and in English.

Opticians (*Optiker*) make and sell spectacles and contact lenses. Ophthalmic opticians, also called optometrists, test vision in order to prescribe spectacles and contact lenses. Most opticians and oph-thalmic opticians are in private practice in optical goods shops (*Optiske forretninger* in the Yellow Pages). The larger shops, usually called *synssenter* ("vision centre"), will be associated with an oculist (*øyelege*) or will have one on the staff, and thereby offer a full range of diagnostic services. Some cen-tres offer polyclinic services, including laser treat-ment (*laserbehandling*) of cataracts (*grå stær*). The information department (*Informasjonsavdeling*) of the Norwegian Association of Opticians (*Norges Optikerforbund*) offers many publications on vision, eye care, spectacles, contact lenses and the services of opticians ✆ 67551830, 🖷 67551840, ⊠ PO Box 419, 1302 Sandvika, ✉ synsinfo@optikerforbund.no, ➹ http://www.optikerforbund.no with pages in Norwegian and links to E-Mail addresses for further query.

Organ donation (*Organdonasjon*)

As in many countries, there is a shortage of organs for trans-plantation to patients needing them. According to the Act on Transplantation (*Transplantasjonsloven*) of 1973, a person's organs may be removed after death unless the deceased or the deceased's nearest relatives have declared opposition to removal or there is reason to believe that removal may conflict with their views. So if you are for or against dona-tion, you should inform your relatives, so they may be spared a difficult decision on your behalf. Like-wise, you should know their wishes. In 1998, of the relatives of deceased persons asked for permission to remove organs, 77.5% agreed.

There is no official donor register or donor cards, so family consent is always requested before organs are removed. However, a private association, *Gi Liv* ("Give Life"), issues donor cards ✆ 31283035, ⊠ PO Box 104, 3430 Spikkestad, ✉ ar-iv@online.no, ➹ http://home.sol.no/~aravivers. Most transplants are of organs and tissue from people who die sud-denly, as in an accident or of a brain haemorrhage or who die while in intensive care in one of the 27 donor hospitals. These are hospital who have the expertise and equipment needed to preserve the functions of the organs and who are so authorised. In some cases a living person can donate a kidney to a family member; a third of all kidney transplants are made this way. Seven organs are acceptable for donation, the heart, two lungs, two kidneys, liver and pancreas. Moreover, tissue, including corneas, arteries, veins and skin also may be donated. You can determine which of your organs or tissues you wish to donate. The National Hospital (*Rikshospi-talet*) in Oslo performs all transplants, about 250 a year. A team from the hospital travel to the donor hospitals to remove the organs. For further informa-tion contact the Organ Donation Foundation (*Stif-telsen Organdonasjon*) ✆ 22799292, 🖷 22225037, ⊠ PO Box 4375 Torshov, 0402 Oslo.

Patient Ombudsman (*Pasientombudet*)

In all counties, there is a Patient Ombudsman responsible for ensuring the quality of health care services in the county. As a patient or a close relative of a patient, you may complain to the Ombudsman about hospi-tal or out-patient medical treatment. You may, for instance, believe that your illness requires hospitali-sation but a hospital has refused to admit you, that you have been treated improperly or if you have been discharged from a hospital too early. You may also complain if you find fault with medical exami-nations, medical treatment or therapy, hospital care, faulty diagnosis or insufficient information. The Ombudsman does not charge for services, which, if the case so requires, may include a visit to a hospi-tal. All cases are considered confidential; the details you supply will not be released to any other person or organisation without your permission. You may contact the Ombudsman by post or telephone. The nearest Ombudsman is listed under *Pasientombudet* in the listing for the county in which you live, in the Pink Pages.

Pharmacies (*Apotek*)

are located in all cities and larger towns and villages, while smaller towns and villages may have medicine shops (*medisinutsalgene*) operated as subsidiaries under the direction of the nearest pharmacy. Unlike drug stores and chemists in other countries, and like the pharmacies in some other European countries, an *apotek* sells only pre-scription and over-the-counter ☞ **medicines**, med-ical supplies and some toiletries. The major interna-tional pharmaceutical firms produce most of the medicines sold. However, pharmacists compound 2.5% of the medicine sold, mostly for treating rare illnesses, serving smaller patient groups or meeting special dosage needs. Four pharmacies – Frogner

Apotek in Oslo, Ås Apotek in Akershus County, Haukeland Hospital Apotek in Bergen and Kragerø Apotek in Telemark County – are major producers. Each pharmacy is under the direction of and is staffed by pharmacists (*farmasøyter*), who can advise you on the use of medicines and medical products. Most pharmacies also stock a selection of free brochures on medical topics. You will find pharmacies listed under *Apotek* in the Yellow Pages, and the nearest after hours pharmacies (*Apotekvakt*) listed under *Viktige telefonnummer* in the general information section in front of the Pink Pages.

Pharmacopoeia (*Felleskatalog*) The national consolidated catalogue of pharmaceutical compounds marketed in Norway, with directions for use is entitled *Felleskatalog over farmasøytiske spesialpreparater markedsført i Norge*. Its descriptions are based on those approved by the Norwegian Medicines Control Authority (*Statens legemiddelkontroll*). It is published once a year by a private sector company and is intended for doctors and other healthcare professionals; the 1997-98 edition had some 2200 pages. A condensed version of it, with simplified explanations in everyday non-medical Norwegian, the Medicine Handbook (*Medisinhåndboken*), is published once every two years for the general public and is sold in ☞ **pharmacies** and book shops. The fifth edition of 1997 had 582 pages and listed a total of 2400 over-the-counter and prescription pharmaceutical compounds. Both books are also available in CD-ROM. For further information on the complete pharmacopoeia, contact *Felleskatalogen AS*, ✆ 23161550, 🖷 22417651, ✉ Grev Wedels pl. 9, 0151 Oslo, and on the condensed *Medisinhåndboken*, contact *Elanders Forlag* ✆ 22636400, 🖷 22636590, ✉ PO Box 1156 Sentrum, 0107 Oslo.

Physical therapy (*Fysioterapi*), also called physiotherapy in English and other languages, is the treatment of muscular and skeletal illness, injury and deformity by physical methods including manipulation, massage, remedial exercise, heat and electrical stimulation, but not drugs or other medical procedures. It is available throughout the country, in part because it is a basic health service which all municipalities are required by law to offer to the public. As a consequence, Norway has more physical therapists (*fysioterapeuter*) compared to its population

than do most countries. There are some 8,000 in the country, or about eight for every ten doctors in practice. Another consequence is that Norwegian physical therapy is of high standard; four colleges in the country, at Bergen, Oslo, Trondheim and Tromsø, educate physical therapists, foreign physical therapists come to Norway to train from as far as Australia, and Norwegian physical therapists, including Freddy Kaltenborn and Olaf Evjenth, have written clinical manuals which are used world-wide. The practice of physical therapy can be divided into several specialities, including acupuncture (*akupunktur*), children and youth (*barn- og ungdomsfysioterapi*), ergonomics (*ergonomi*), geriatrics (*gentro- og geriatrisk fydsioterapi*), heart and lung (*hjerte- og lungefysioterapi*), manual therapy (*manuell terapi*), Mensendieck gymnastics (*mensendiecksykegymnastikk*), neurology, orthopaedics and rheumatology (*neurologi, ortopedi og rheumatologi – NOR*), obstetrics and gynaecology (*obstetrisk og gynekologisk fysioterapi*), physical treatment of lymphatitis (*fysikalsk lymfødembehandling*), psychiatric and psychosomatic (*psykiatrisk og psykosomatisk fysioterapi*) and sports (*idrettsfysioterapi*). You need a referral (*henvisning*) from a doctor for physical therapy treatment. Physical therapy is supported by the ☞ **National Insurance Scheme** (Government and Social Services chapter), just as are other medical services, but to be eligible for that support and thereby reduce your own cost as a patient (*pasientens andel*) you must ensure that your physiotherapist has a contract with the municipality,. Physical therapy clinics are listed under *Fysikalske institutter* in the Yellow Pages. The national professional association is the Norwegian Physiotherapists' Association (*Norske Fysioterapeuters Forbund – NFF*), which is a member of the World Confederation for Physical Therapy (WCPT). For further information on physical therapy in Norway, contact NFF ✆ 22933050, 🖷 22565825, ✉ PO Box 2704 St. Hanshaugen, 0131 Oslo, ✉ nff@fysio.no, 🖰 http://www.fysio.no

Psychiatric services (*Psykiatri*) are incorporated in public health services and thereby covered by the ☞ **National Insurance Scheme** (Government & Social Services chapter). Your first point of contact should be your ☞ **medical doctor**. Alternatively you can seek assistance from the local psychiatric polyclinic (*psykiatrisk poliklinikk*) listed in the Pink

Pages. Some useful terms, in alphabetical order: behaviourism (*atferdspsykologi*), psychiatrist (*psykiater*), psychiatry (*psykiatri*), psychoanalysis (*psykoanalyse*), psychoanalyst (*psykoanalytiker*), psychodynamics (*psykodynamikk*), psychologist (*psykolog*), psychology (*psykologi*) and psychotherapy (*psykoterapi*).

Respite care (*Avlastningstiltak*) A person or a family with a greater than normal burden of caring for a handicapped child or other person needing nursing (*pleietrengende*) can request relief from the municipality. There are three forms of relief: respite in the home (*avlastning i hjemmet*) by a professional helper, respite away from home (*avlastning borte fra hjemmet*) by temporarily sending the child to a respite home (*avlastningshjem*) and holiday respite (*ferieavlastning*) by having a professional helper live in the home while the parent(s) go on holiday. For further information, call the municipal office listed under *Avlastningshjem, Avlastningsetat* or *Helse og sosialetat* in the Pink Pages.

Thermometers (*Termometre*) The digital fever thermometer (*digitale termometre*) is now the most common type for home and clinical use. Most are powered by a small battery and have a digital display with readout in 0.1°C increments. They are designed for oral, rectal or under-arm use, and emit a beeping sound when a peak temperature is reached. Old-fashioned mercury thermometers (*kvikksølvtermometre*) are banned, due to the high toxicity of mercury. If you have an old mercury thermometer, you should turn it in at any pharmacy that will in turn send it on to a toxic waste destruction and recycling facility. Mercury thermometers for technical and laboratory uses are exempted from the ban until January 2001. For further information on the regulations on mercury thermometers, see *Forbud mot kvikksølvholdige termometre* ("Ban on thermometers containing mercury"), pamphlet T-1245, ISBN 82-457-0213-7, published by the ☞ **Norwegian Pollution Control Authority** (Climate and Environment chapter).

Urine samples (*Urinprøver*) are used in tests as a part of medical diagnoses. If you are asked for a sample at a doctor's office or other health-care facility, you will be given a container to use. But you may be asked to bring a sample from home. If so, you may use a well-cleaned glass container. The type of container is unimportant. And a wide variety are used, as Dr. Arvid Vatle, a general practitioner at Stord in the western part of the country, found after a year-long cataloguing of the containers used by patients bringing in samples. Writing in the 20 March 1999 issue of the Journal of the Norwegian Medical Association (*Tidsskrift for Den norske lægeforening*), he reported that from May 1997 to May 1998, a total of 164 urine samples were delivered, in an amazing 110 different kinds of containers. Most popular was a small glass jar that originally contained the Stavland brand of tomato paste (*tomatpuré*). Other containers included whiskey bottles and soft drink bottles. Apparently, Dr. Vatle theorised, people use what they have on hand. He found that the choice of container had no effect on the urinalysis tests conducted, as all were properly cleaned.

Vaccinations (*Vaksinasjon*) All children are offered vaccinations against nine diseases: diphtheria (*difteri*), tetanus (*stivkrampe*), whooping cough (*kikhoste*), Haemophilius influenza type b (Hib), poliomyelitis (*poliomyelitt*), measles (*meslinger*), mumps (*kusma*), Rubella (*røde hunder*) and tuberculosis (*tuberkulose*). Vaccination is voluntary, free of charge for children up to the age of 16 and is dispensed in the form of an injection at the health clinic (*helsestasjon*) near where you live or connected to your local school. The vaccination program for children is:

3 months	Diphtheria/tetanus/whooping cough, Hib and polio
5 months	as above
11–12 months	as above
15 months	Measles/mumps/rubella
6–8 yrs	Polio
11–12 yrs	Diphtheria/tetanus
12–13 yrs	Measles/mumps/rubella
senior school	Polio, tuberculosis

Public health services offer the elderly vaccinations against flu in the autumn, usually the local newspaper will carry an advance announcement about it. If you intend to travel to areas of the world where there are health concerns, ring the nearest vaccination centre (*vaksinasjons-poliklinikken*) listed n the Pink Pages under the name of your municipality (*kommune*). They will inform you what vaccinations you require and when to start the vaccination program as some vaccinations require a course of injections. Company health services (*bedriftshelsetjeneste*) often offer a vaccination service, particularly for employees travelling abroad. If you travel abroad, be sure to request a small folder called the International certificate of vaccination, if you do not already have one. Keep it up to date with any vaccinations you receive and carry it with your passport when you travel.

Voluntary euthanasia (*Selvbestemt dødshjelp*) is the bringing about of the gentle death of a terminally ill person at the person's own wishes. Though once a taboo subject, the moral principles and legal status of euthanasia are now being debated. In the late 1990s, there were court cases involving doctors and other health service professionals who had helped suffering patients end their lives, and in a 1999 survey of University of Oslo medical students, more than one in three favoured euthanasia. For further information, contact the Right to Die Society of Norway (*Landsforeningen Mitt Livstestament – Retten til en verdig død*) ✆ & ✉ 22449917, ✉ Inkognitogt 28B, 0156 Oslo.

Historical overview (*Historisk oversikt*)

ca. 9000 BC
First traces of human habitation.

ca. 1500-500 BC
Bronze age; increased contact with countries farther south.

ca. 500-0 BC
Iron age; hunting society, particularly in Northern Norway.

0-ca. 400 AD
Roman influence; first runic writing; trade flourishes.

ca. 500
Area to become Oslo settled.

ca. 800-1000
Viking Age; expeditions abroad on best warships of their time.

ca. 885
Harald Hårfagre wins battle of Hafrsfjord and begins uniting country.

ca. 900
First laws and courts (*lagting*).

995
King Olav I Tryggvason introduces Christianity.

997
Settlement of Nidaros, later city of Trondheim, founded.

1001
Leif Eriksson sent by King Olav I to Christianise Greenland, lands on East coast of North America on return voyage.

1015-1028
King Olav II Haraldsson furthers Christianity throughout country.

1030
Battle of Stiklestad; Olav II killed, canonised to St. Olav.

1050
City of Oslo founded.

1070
City of Bergen founded.

ca. 1100
Bishopric founded at Bergen, Nidaros and Oslo.

1152-53
Archbishop appointed at Nidaros.

1163
First Norwegian coronation of King Magnus Erlingsson.

ca. 1270
Maganus Lagabøte institutes first national laws.

1345
Earth avalanche at Gaudalen kills 250, country's greatest natural disaster ever.

1349-1350
The Black Death kills two-thirds of the population.

1350-1536
Hanseatic League dominates trade, with offices in Bergen, Oslo and Tønsberg.

1380-1814
Norway in union with Denmark.

1397
Kalmar Union, first Scandinavian alliance of Denmark, Norway, Sweden.

1536
Norway becomes a Danish province; the Reformation begins.

1624
Fire destroys Oslo; King Christian IV rebuilds and renames city Christiania.

1647
Postal service starts.

1720-1750
Depression; pietism spreads.

1739
Law passed providing schooling for all.

1763
First newspaper, *Norske-Intelligenz-Seddeler* published in Christiania.

1801
First regular census.

1807-1814
Norway, under Denmark, allied with Napoleon.

1812
University of Oslo founded.

1814
Napoleon defeated; dissolution of union with Denmark; constitution written; liberal for its time save for exclusion of Jews, Jesuits and monks from country.

1814-1905
Union with Sweden.

1815
First national legislative body, the *Storting* ("Pub-

lic Assembly").

1825
Recession; emigration begins.

1851
Constitutional ban on Jews repealed.

1854
First railway, Oslo-Eidsvoll.

1866-1910
Emigration in three great waves, followed by lesser one 1923-1929; in all, 800,000 emigrate, mostly to the USA.

1877
Civil service Norwegianises spelling of capital to Kristiania; municipal authorities adopt spelling in 1897.

1887
Public prostitution banned.

1892
First annual Holmenkollen ski meet, Oslo; women allowed to complete upper secondary school.

1884
Storting becomes parliamentary; women admitted to universities.

1895
First welfare programme, disability compensation for industrial workers.

1897
Constitutional constraint on religious freedom repealed.

1903
Bjørnstjerne Bjørnson awarded Nobel Prize in Literature.

1905
Peaceful dissolution of union with Sweden; Prince Carl of Denmark crowned King Haakon VII.

1910
Norwegian Institute of Technology (NTH) founded at Trondheim.

1911
Roald Amundsen first to South Pole; Anna Rogstad first woman member of *Storting*.

1913
Women granted right to vote and hold public office.

1914-1918
First world war; Norway neutral

1919-1927
Partial prohibition: fortified wine banned until 1923, distilled spirits until 1927.

1920
Norway joins League of Nations; Knut Hamsun awarded Nobel Prize in Literature.

1921
Christian Louis Lange one of two awarded Nobel Peace Prize.

1922
Fridtjof Nansen awarded Nobel Peace Prize.

1925
Old name of Oslo replaces Christiania, or Kristiania in public administration; Svalbard Arctic archipelago becomes Norwegian protectorate; regular radio broadcasting begins.

1928
Sigrid Undset awarded Nobel Prize in Literature.

1939
Gateway airport opened at Fornebu, Oslo.

1940
Germany invades and occupies Norway.

1945
Second world war ends; country free again.

1946
University of Bergen founded.

1946-1953
Trygve Lie first Secretary-General of United Nations; succeeded by Swede Dag Hammarskjöld.

1947
Thor Heyerdahl sails balsa raft Kon-Tiki across Pacific in an attempt to disprove old anthropological theories of island settlement.

1949
Norway one of founding members of NATO.

1951
Scandinavian Airlines founded jointly by Denmark, Norway and Sweden.

1952
Olympic Winter Games held in Oslo.

1956
Constitutional ban on Jesuits repealed; law regulating immigration enacted.

1957
King Haakon VII dies; King Olav V ascends throne.

1960
Regular television broadcasting begins.

1961
Ingrid Bjerkås ordained by Church of Norway, first woman priest.

1964
Woman permitted to retain maiden name in marriage.

1968
Oil discovered offshore in the North Sea; University of Tromsø founded; University of Trondheim founded, incorporates NTH; Lars Onsager awarded Nobel Prize in Chemistry.

1972
EU membership declined by referendum.

1973
Ivar Glæver one of three awarded Nobel Prize in Physics.

1981
Gro Harlem Brundtland becomes first woman Prime Minister.

1985
Bobbysocks group wins Eurovision Song Contest, which then is held following year in Grieg Hall, Bergen.

1987
More than 30,000 immigrants settle in country, causing net immigration (immigration minus emigration) to peak at 15,000.

1988
More than half of all university students are women; all government activities dealing with immigration combined in single Directorate of Immigration.

1990
Royal women born after 1990 given right to ascend throne.

1991
King Olav V dies; King Harald V ascends throne.

1993
Partnership law passed allowing legal bonds for homosexual couples.

1994
Olympic Winter Games held at Lillehammer; law prohibits workplace sexual harassment.

1995
EU membership again declined by referendum.

1995-1996
Major public service governmental agencies privatised, including telecommunications and railways.

1996
Green taxes introduced, penalise use of polluting fuels; Russian passenger aircraft crashes at Svalbard Airport killing 141, country's greatest air disaster ever.

1998
Fornebu Airport closed; new gateway airport opens at Gardermoen 55 km north of Oslo; Gro Harlem Brundtland becomes Director-General of World Health Organization (WHO).

1999
International comparison of 1998 budget surplus or deficit figures in percentage of GDP shows that Norway has world's biggest surplus, 4.1% of its GDP.

Holidays (*Fridager og ferie*)

April fool's day, the first of April, is not a proper holiday, but is observed as it is in many other countries. A trick (*aprilspøk*) sportively imposes to fool others (*aprilsnarr*). Most major newspapers feature at least one contrived story, usually on the front page, of their first of April editions. The classic newspaper *aprilspøk* have included outrageous changes in taxation and unthinkable sales at the governmental Vinmonopol wine and spirits shops. College and university students devise pranks in the spirit of the day. One of the more successful recent April Fool's Day hoaxes was perpetrated by Oslo students in 1997. Dressed as oil exploration crews, groups of students set up surveying in the centre of the city and remarked to those who asked that oil had been discovered there, and they were marking out the location of wells to come. Nearby, other students acted out environmental protest and collected signatures protesting the wells. They collected hundreds of signatures from anxious Osloites, ever fearful for more construction work in the capital. So the rule for the first of April is doubt anything outlandish and then enjoy being knowingly fooled.

Birthdays (*Geburtsdager*) are celebrated much as they are in most western countries. The traditional birthday party for young children – pre-school or primary-school age – is held in the home of the birthday child (*geburtsdagsbarn*) and consists of a light meal and activities. Both the meal and the activities depend on whether the party is held indoors or outdoors. The traditional indoor party meal consists of cakes as well as sweets, usually packed in small white paper bags, one for each child, and a bottle of soft drink, with a straw, one for each child. Usually, ☞ **Children's games** (Family and Children chapter) are played. The traditional outdoor party meal, summer or winter, usually consists of frankfurters (*pølser*) roasted over a bonfire or grill, and served with ketchup and mustard on thin potato bread (*lumpe*), and a bottle of soft drink for each child. The outdoor activities depend on location and season; wintertime ice skating and summertime swimming are favourites. Party times usually are limited to about two hours, such as 4 to 6 pm on a school day or 1 to 3 pm on a holiday. Parents send out simple written invitations in advance, one for each child invited. Most parents now photocopy a standard invitation with a space to write in each child's name, or print out invitations using a word processing program. There are no fixed customs for who to invite, but the trend of the late 1990s is to invite either a very few children, as from a primary school class or kindergarten group, or invite the entire class or group. Each child invited to a birthday party should bring a modest present for the birthday child. Local custom usually involves an unwritten agreement between parents as to the maximum price for a birthday present. If you don't know the local maximum price, ask a staff member of the kindergarten or school or another parent. If you are in doubt as to what to buy for a present, you may simply give cash, taped or clipped to a small birthday card. Increasingly, busy parents with little time to arrange parties have resorted to the parties offered by fast-food outlets, such as McDonalds, and indoor activity facilities, such as swimming pools and bowling alleys. Party goods and novelties are sold in some supermarkets and by speciality shops; look under *Karnevalutstyr* in the Yellow Pages. Birthday parties for older children and adults vary widely, and may or may not be celebrated each year. The most common celebration involves an evening meal at home with one's family and occasionally with invited close friends. For those interested in more extensive events, commercial party organisers offer a wide range of facilities and services; look under *Selskapsarrangement og servering* in the Yellow Pages. The most important birthdays for Norwegian adults are the decades from age 30 on, as well as the half decades from age 65 on. These birthdays are announced, usually on the day, in the *Jubilanter* ("persons celebrating anniversaries") section of the local newspaper. If you subscribe to a newspaper, you will be sent an advance request for information and a portrait photo for your anniversary birthday notice; you may, of course, also request that no mention be made of it.

Public holidays and flag days (*Høytidsdager og flaggdager*) Each year, there are 13 public holidays. Five of these are on fixed dates, and eight are Christian church holidays on variable dates related to the date of Easter Sunday, which is the first Sunday after the first full moon after the vernal equinox (*vårjevndøgn*). There are 13 official flag-flying days, on which the **flag** (Character, Customs, Country chapter) is flown during daylight hours. Six of the public holidays are also flag-flying days.. The fixed and variable holidays are (F means flag-flying day):

Fixed holidays

1 January: New Year's Day (*Nyttårsdag*) (F)
1 May: Labour day (*1. mai*) (F)
17 May: Constitution day (*Grunnlovsdag*) (F)
25 December: Christmas day (*1. juledag*) (F)
26 December: Boxing day (*2. juledag*)

Variable church holidays, with dates in 2000 – 2002

Holiday	2000	2001	2002
Palm Sunday			
(*Palmesøndag*)	16 April	8 April	24 March
Maundy Thursday			
(*Skjærtorsdag*)	20 April	12 April	28 March
Good Friday			
(*Langfredag*)	21 April	13 April	29 March
Easter Sunday			
(*Påskesøndag*) (F)	23 April	15 April	31 March
Easter Monday			
(*2. påskedag*)	24 April	16 April	1 April
Ascension Day			
(*Kristi himmelfartsdag*)	1 June	24 April	9 May
Whitsun			
(*Pinsesøndag*) (F)	11 June	3 June	19 May
Whitmonday			
(*2. pinsedag*)	12 June	4 June	20 May

Flag-flying days that are not public holidays

21 February: HM King Harald's birthday (*Kong Harald V*)
8 May: Liberation day (*Frigjøring*)
7 June: Dissolution of union with Sweden (*unionsoppløsning 1905*)
4 July: HM Queen Sonja's birthday (*Dronniong Sonja*)
20 July: HRH Crown Prince Haakon's birthday (*Kronprins Haakon*)
29 July: St. Olav's Day (*Olsok*)
22 September: HRH Princess Märtha Louise's birthday (*Prinsesse Märtha Louise*)

Religious holidays (*Høytidsdager*) The principal holidays of the Church of Norway are public holidays. If you are a member of a religious faith other than the Church of Norway, you are entitled to two days a year free from work to celebrate its holidays. However, your employer may require that you make up these lost work days at some other time during the year.

Sundays (*Søndager*) are subject to special regulations. The Act on Holidays and Holiday Peacefulness (*Lov om helligdager og helligdagsfred*) of 1995 restricts noisy activities between 1 am and midnight on all Sundays, as well as public holidays that are religious holidays of the Church of Norway. The same rule applies after 4 pm on the eves of Christmas, Palm Sunday and Easter Sunday. Moreover, from 6 am to 1 pm on these days, public assemblies other than religious meetings, exhibitions, contests and sports events are prohibited, with exceptions for major events such as art exhibitions and international sports meets that otherwise would be impractical. Shop ☞ **Opening hours** (Shopping chapter) are restricted on Sundays and public holidays. Most employees have Sundays free. However, in sectors which require work on Sundays, such as transportation, health care and hotels and restaurants, the employees obliged to work on Sundays must be given a free Sunday or public holiday every second or third week.

Vacations (*Ferie*) are yearly breaks from work that are in addition to public holidays (this chapter). All employers are required by law, the Act on Vacations of 1988 (*Ferieloven*), to give employees at least 25 working days of vacation each year. Because Saturdays count as working days, the legal minimum is equal to four weeks plus one day. The additional day was added in May 1981 to the four weeks specified by law in 1964. It was intended as the first step in a planned gradual introduction of a fifth vacation week for all employees. That was during the first tenure of Gro Harlem Brundtland as the country's first woman Prime Minister, so the 25th vacation day popularly is called the "Gro Day" (*Gro-dagen*). Employees age 60 (by September) and older are entitled to at least five weeks of vacation. All employees are entitled to take at least 18 working days (three calendar weeks) of continuous vacation in the principal vacation period (*hovedferieperioden*) from 1 June to 30 September, and to take the remaining seven working days (one calendar week plus the "Gro Day") continuously at any other time of the year, as agreed with employers. The "vacation year" (*ferieåret*) follows the calendar year (*kalenderåret*), but wages or salary paid during a vacation (*feriepenger*) is earned (*opptjent) in the previous "vacation year". Employers are required to set up vacation lists (ferielister) well in advance of the principal vacation period, so they and their employees may agree on vacation dates. Many companies, particularly industries that require nearly full staff to operate, have collective vacation periods (fellesferie) for all employees and then close or have only a skeleton staff. The last three weeks in July are the most common collective vacation period and are so called: fellesferien. Employees are entitled to transfer up to two weeks of vacation not taken to the following "vacation year". Vacation not taken and not transferred to the following "vacation year"

is forfeited. Provided an employer agrees, an employee may take up to four weeks plus one day advance vacation from the following "vacation year" and thereby have a total vacation of up to eight weeks plus two days. The vacation privileges of employees are mutual: if you are entitled to a vacation, you must take it. However, if you have not yet worked long enough for a company to earn vacation pay (feriepenger) and accordingly would lose income if you took a vacation, you may continue to work and take no vacation. But there is an exception to that rule: if the company has a collective vacation period (fellesferie), you must take vacation then.

Housekeeping (Husholdning)

Alarm systems (Alarmsystemer) are of two types: aid-call alarms activated by people in their homes and condition alarms, activated by incidents, such as fire or burglary.

Aid-call alarms (Trygghetsalarm) provide the user, usually an elderly or disabled person, with a small alarm transmitter that can be worn; some resemble a wristwatch or necklace. A person who falls or otherwise needs immediate assistance activates the alarm, which is connected via the home telephone to a manned monitoring centre, which responds by sending help. Local health services, listed under Helseetaten or Helsekontor in the municipal listings in the Pink Pages, often supply Trygghetsalarm. There also is a private service, Trygghetssentralen, a division of the Falken security services company, with a head office in Oslo and five centres elsewhere in the country ✆ 22461310, 🖷 22463740, ✉ PO Box 7063 Majorstua, 🖮 http://www.falken.no with pages in Norwegian and links to other sites.

Burglar alarms (Innbruddsalarm) and fire alarms (Brannalarm) may be either stand-alone systems in a flat or house, or may be connected to an alarm centre. The stand-alone variety consist of sensors, a central unit and indoor and outdoor sirens to warn of activation, such as by break-in or fire. Most have an additional facility such that they may be connected to a remote manned centre for an additional monthly or annual fee. You can find shops, suppliers and installers listed under Alarm og sikringsanlegg in the Yellow Pages.

Allotments (Kolonihage) are small garden plots (parseller) grouped into a village (hageby) near or in a city. The plots are rented, usually from the municipality. Most are about 150 to 300 square metres in area and have a cottage that can be lived in as a holiday or second home during the season, 1 May to 31 October. In all, there are about 1200 allotment cottages in the country. The largest, Solvang kolonihage in Oslo, has 545 cottages. The first was built at Halden in 1896. Now the oldest, Rodeløkka kolonihage in Oslo, was built in 1907. The newest, Klementshaugen kolonihage in Trondheim, was built in 1991. A new 50-cottage village is now planned at Bjerkeskau in Hobøl municipality, south of the E18 highway in Akershus county. For further information, contact Norsk Kolonihageforbund ✆ 22172371, 🖷 22173371, ✉ Grønnlandsleiret 21, 0191 Oslo.

Beds and bedclothes (Seng og sengetøy) Bedding is similar to that used elsewhere in Europe. Various qualities of mattresses (madrasser) of foam or with innersprings are available; water beds (vannsenger) are no longer popular, but are still available at some furniture dealers. Adult bed sizes are standard throughout Scandinavia: 200 cm in length and 80 cm, 90 cm, 120 cm and 160 cm in width. Longer lengths are available on order. There are various children's sizes, in lengths up to 120 cm and widths up to 75 cm. Sheets (laken) are made in sizes to fit the standard beds, and some fitted sheets (formlakken) are available at bedding shops (utstyrsforretninger). Upper sheets and blankets are seldom used; the norm is a duvet (dyne). Duvets and pillows (puter) are available with down (dun), feather (fjær) or synthetic (kunststoff) filling. Traditional down is warmest and most expensive, although some synthetic fills are claimed to be equally as warm. Larger bedding shops offer cleaning and repairing services for duvets and pillows. Most of the duvets and pillows sold are made in Norway, as are the duvet covers (dynetrekk) and pillowcases (putevar) (the leading brand is Høie). But duvets, duvet covers, pillows and pillowcases made in Denmark or Sweden (such as those sold by

Country of manufacture	Duvet (dyne) and duvet cover (dynetrekk) sizes	Pillow (pute) and pillow case (putevar) sizes
Norway	140 X 200 cm standard and 140 X 220 cm extra long	50 X 70 cm and 60 X 80 cm
Sweden	150 X 210 cm	50 X 60 cm
Denmark	140 X 200 cm	60 X 63 cm

the Swedish IKEA home furnishing shops) are also sold. Regrettably for the buyer, sizes differ in Scandinavia, as listed on the previous page. A Danish duvet cover will fit a Norwegian duvet, but neither Swedish nor Danish pillow cases fit Norwegian pillows.

Candles (*Levende lys*) are popular and are used frequently, particular at dinner parties and on festive occasions. In fact, some 250 million are sold each year, about 57 for every resident, the highest figure in the world. Candles are sold in supermarkets, hardware shops, furniture hypermarkets and interior shops, in a wide variety of shapes and sizes, made by domestic and foreign candlemakers. A basic candle vocabulary: beeswax (*bivoks*), candle (*levende lys*), candlestick or candelabrum (*lysestake*), chandler (*lysestøper*), paraffin wax (*paraffin*), short, thick candle (*kubbelys*), snuffer (*lyseslukker*), stearine (*stearin*), tallow (*talg*), taper (*tynt vokslys*), wax (*voks*) and wick (*veke*).

Caretaker services (*Vaktmestertjenester*) deal with all types of maintenance (*vedlikehold*) from cleaning, security services, snow clearing, window cleaning, gardening, high pressure washing, in fact all sorts of odd jobs, look in the Yellow Pages under *vaktmestertjenester.*

Chimney-sweeps (*Feiere*) are sent to your residence once a year by the municipality (*kommune)* in which you live. Their charge is covered by local taxes . You will be notified by a printed note with the following text *Feieren kommer dd/mm, ta forholdsregler* (in other words the chimney-sweep is coming on dd/mm, prepare for the visit). Close all flues and openings in and out of your home, to avoid soot in your living areas. If you live in a house you are required to have a ladder so that the chimney sweep can reach your chimney and have unrestricted access to the chimney. If you live in an apartment, most of the preparation will be taken care of, except for closing openings in your living areas. Should you need a chimney-sweep at any other time of the year, look under *Feievesenet* in the Pink Pages.

Christmas trees (*Juletrær*) are a well-established tradition, both at home and abroad. Some 1.5 million trees are sold at Christmastime, and starting in 1947, a tall Norwegian Christmas Tree is put up every year at Trafalgar Square in London. Most of the ornamental varieties of coniferous trees are sold as Christmas trees, including members of the spruce (genus *picea*), fir (*abies*) and pine (*pinus*) families. The leading sellers are Norway Spruce (*Vanlig gran*), Blue Spruce (*Blågran*), Engelmann Spruce (*Engelmanngran*), Serbian Spruce (*Serbisk Gran*), Alpine Fir (*Fjelledelgran*), Nordmann Fir (*Nordmannedelgran*), Veitch Fir (*Veitchedelgran*), Noble Fir (*Nobelgran*), Silver Fir (*Fageredelgran*) and Scotch Pine (*Vanlig furu*). Christmas trees grown in Norway are increasingly marked and priced into three quality classes according to a national standard (Norwegian Standard 4415): Class 1 (*Klasse 1*) trees have full, uniformly-coloured clusters of needles, straight trunks, a single top tip and branches evenly spaced around the trunk. Class 2 (*Klasse 2*) trees can have trunks out of line and some discoloration of needles, but needle clusters should be evenly spaced around the tree. Class 3 (*Klasse 3*) trees are those that may need special placement to be attractive, such as in a corner of a room, because branches may be missing on one side or needles may be in uneven bunches. About a third of the Christmas trees sold are imported from Denmark, which has large farms producing ornamental trees. Danish trees are classified according to The European Sorting Guidelines issued by the European Christmas Tree Producers Association, valid throughout the EU and, in Denmark, by the Danish Christmas Tree Producers Association (*Dansk juletræsdyrkerforening*). There are three classes, Prime (*Prima*) Standard (*Standard*) and Unclassified (*Uklassificerede*), which correspond approximately to the three numbered Norwegian classes. Trees imported from Denmark are sorted accordingly, as well as into nine height categories, from 40/60 cm to 250/300 cm. Starting in early December, Christmas trees are sold outdoors, most often in supermarket and shopping mall car parks, city and town squares and sports grounds. Prices vary according to type and quality of tree and are usually stated in kroner per metre of tree height. Larger sellers have apparatus to wrap trees in tight plastic netting tubes to temporarily bundle their branches for ease of carrying home, as in an estate care or on a roof rack.

Paint colours (*Farger*) Norway, as well as Spain and Sweden, have standardised on NCS, the Natural Colour System for designating colours. Developed by the Scandinavian Colour Institute (*Skandinaviska Färginstitutet*) in Stockholm and first introduced in 1979, NCS is also used in more than 40 other countries. It designates colours in a Colour Atlas (*fargeatlas*) and is based on the way humans perceive six pure colours, indicated by letters: W for White (*Hvitt*), S for Black (*Sort*), Y for Yellow (*Gul*), R for Red (*Rød*), B for Blue (*Blå*) and G for Green (*Grønn*). Each NCS colour has an alphanumeric code consisting of two parts. The first is the nuance, a four-digit number indicating the degree of blackness and of the maximum colour hue. The second is the hue and consists of two of the four colour letters, Y, R, B or G, separated by a two-digit number. Hues may be viewed as positions on a clock face circle of colours starting with pure yellow at 12 o'clock and proceeding clockwise through red at 3, blue at 6 and green at 9. For instance, deep peach (*fersken*) is designated 2030-Y90R. The 2030 nuance means 20% blackness and 30% chromaticity (of the Y90R hue). The Y90R hue means yellow with 90% redness, about 3:13:30 o'clock on the clock circle of colours. Hues with no yellow, red, blue or green have only nuance numbers followed by the letter N for "Neutral". For instance, 0500-N is white, 2000-N is a light grey and 9000-N is black. In all, there are 1530 colours in the first edition of NCS, used through 1997 and still displayed in many shops. The second edition of 1997, called NCS Edition 2, has 1750 colours. Of these, 261 are new colours and 400 have new designations, because the second edition is based only on pigments that are environmentally approved according to EU guidelines. Moreover, 46 colours of the first edition have been withdrawn, because they cannot be manufactured with environmentally-friendly pigments. A prefix letter S, such as S2030-Y90R distinguishes the second edition colours. NCS is not related to other colour systems, such as Munsell in Japan and the USA and Pantone, as used in graphic arts, but a computer program has been compiled in the UK to equate the various systems to each other. Various coloured paint products are sold by paint and varnish shops (*fargehandel*). Some ready-mixed paints are stocked in colours mixed at the factory. Often these colours are those of the paint companies and are not related to open colour standards. Moreover, almost all paint and varnish shops have a dispensing system that can mix nearly all NCS colours as well as the colours of other colour standard systems. In buying, you can select colours from racks of colour sample cards, so you can take cards home to match and select the colours of your choice. There are two main types of paint and varnish, for exterior use and for interior use. The range of colours available in the exterior products is limited, because many colours cannot be made to tolerate weather. Consequently, manufacturers often supply separate sets of colour cards for their exterior products, to promote sales of only those colours of sufficient weather fastness. Most shops will accept return of unopened cans of factory-mixed standard colours but not shop-mixed colours. So if you are in doubt as to the amount of paint you need, choose either a factory-mixed colour which you can return unopened, or buy slightly less than you think you need of a shop-mixed colour. You can always buy an additional litre if you don't have enough for a job. If you need only a small amount of paint or varnish, choose a ready-mixed colour, because shop dispensing machines in shops work with only half-litre or larger cans of base product. The Scandinavian Colour Institute web site at ✆ http://www.ncscolour.com has further details on NCS, in Swedish and English pages.

Domestic servants (*tjenestefolk*) It is not common in Norway to have live-in domestic help. For help with your children, you may hire ☞ **au pairs and trainees** or ☞ **babysitters** or take your children to ☞ **day care centres** (Family and Children chapter). For help in the household, advertise in the local paper or on the notice boards at the supermarket, your church or the local post office. Be sure to specify what kind of help you require, some useful terms: cleaner (*vaskehjelp*), cook (*kokk*), driver (*sjåfør*), gardener (*gartner*), window cleaner (*vinduvaskehjelp*). Be aware that whenever you employ a person, you are regarded to be an employer and thereby responsible for ensuring that the person is legally employed. If the person is self-employed, you may check with the local tax office (*ligningskontor*) to ensure that he or she is properly registered as a taxpayer. If the person is a foreigner, you also should first ask to see his or her residence and work permit and then check with the tax office, to ensure that you are not employing an illegal alien. You are deemed to know the law, so if the police arrest an illegal alien worker in your employ, you may be fined for having been his or her employer. You can avoid these difficulties by engaging a registered company, which will have an enterprise number (*organisasjonsnummer*) stated on its invoices. There are cleaning companies who will dispatch a team to your home for all types of cleaning activities including carpets and furniture, look in the Yellow Pages under *rengjøringstjenester*.

Drinking water (*Drikkevannet*) If you suspect that the water supplied to your home is of poor quality or is polluted, you may have it analysed by the nearest Food Control Authority. First, call the local office of the Authority (see *Næringsmiddeltilsynet* in the Pink Pages) for test information and prices. Then visit the office to pick up standard test flasks for the water to be tested and order the tests you want. A standard package (*standard-pakke*) of three bacteriological tests and four chemical tests usually is the minimum offered, but you may want additional tests if you suspect specific contaminants. Then take the flasks home, fill them, deliver them to the office and await the results.

You may guard against the hazards of substandard ☞ **water** (Climate and Environment chapter) in two ways. You can buy bottled water in supermarkets or from one of the spring water companies listed under *Kildevann* in the Yellow pages. You also can install a water filter on one or more taps in your home. The most common and least expensive are various varieties of carbon filters (*kull filtere*) which fit on standard household water taps. They are sold by plumbing supply and hardware shops. The most effective are the reverse osmosis filters (*omvendt osmosefiltere*) which have several stages and can even filter the salt out of saltwater. There are several models, from portable countertop boxes to pressure-tank models for fixed installation; all require a drain for wastewater. Specialist filtration companies listed under *Vannbehandling* in the Yellow Pages sell them. You can also find the leading companies listed by the Norwegian Drinking Water Equipment Association (*Norsk Bransjeforening for Drikkevannsutstyr*) online at ✆ http://nettvik.no/foreningesgarden/nbd with pages in Norwegian and links to national and international sites.

Electrical wiring and fixtures (*Elektriske installasjoner*) are similar to those in other European countries, with a few exceptions. ☞ **Lamps** such as the ordinary E14 and E27 screw-thread base incandescent lamps as well as fluorescent lamps and other common household lamps, are identical to those sold elsewhere in Europe. However, plugs and sockets differ from those used in other countries, not because Norway has its own design standards, but because there are so many different standards in Europe. The Norwegian standards are similar to those commonplace in Germany. Plugs are round and have two round pins, 4.8 mm in diameter and 19 mm long, spaced 19 mm from each other. Earthed plugs have an additional pair of side contacts for the earth connection. Sockets are arranged accordingly and many are now fitted with socket guards (*barnevern*) to prevent children sticking objects into them. Lamps and small appliances, such as power supplies for computer and telecommunications devices, are usually fitted with a two-pin, flat "Euro plug" that plugs into a standard ordinary or earthed socket.

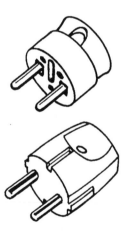

Ordinary (upper) and earthed (lower) plugs; drawings courtesy of Elko.

Most electrical wiring in homes is now concealed (*skjult*) in ducts hidden in walls, ceilings and floors. However, frame houses built before the 1960s and flats built before they were wired may have accessible (*utenpåliggende*) wiring run along baseboards and door and window frames. Most circuits in homes are now fused for 10 Amperes or 16 Amperes, and automatic circuit breakers are now more common than fuses, which were most used in home fuse boxes installed up through the 1970s. Fuses (*sikringer*) are sold in electrical and hardware shops and in many supermarkets. Starting in the 1930s, electrical codes state that only qualified electricians may install wiring and fixtures. Nonetheless, wiring for installation as well as sockets, switches and other fixed installation fixtures are sold in building supply, hardware and electrical shops. Though there is no regulation prohibiting such sale, the Norwegian Electricity Association (*Elforsyningens fellesorganisasjon – EnFO*) advises against non-regulation DIY (Do It Yourself) installation. However, the electrical codes do permit DIY connection of plugs, cord switches, lamp sockets and appliance sockets to flexible cords that are plugged into fixed sockets. Accordingly, EnFO has published a set of assembly instructions (*monteringsveiledning*) that clearly show the steps of connection in large, colour drawings. Contact your local electricity company for a copy (Publication no. 59-1995, ISBN 82-436-0150-3) or view the on-line version: <i class=""></i> http://www.enfo.no

Electricity (*strøm*) in homes is 220 or 230 Volt, 50 Hz alternating current (AC), as it is in most European countries. However, because electric energy consumption is high – many homes are heated electrically – electrical hazards are minimised through standards which in many cases are stricter than those of other countries. There are two principal differences for electricity supply to homes in most parts of the country. First, an IT ("isolated terra") connection is used. It has an isolated neutral (*isolert nullpunkt*) with no neutral wire between the substation and the electrical wiring of a house or block of flats. So there is no direct connection between the "live" parts of apparatus and neutral, and earth connection is local. The advantages of IT are that it ensures electricity supply even in case of one earth fault and that it prevents the type of electrical shock hazard which arises upon failure of a neural line connection to a substation. The disadvantage of IT is that its wires are more easily disturbed by electrical noise and lightning than are those of systems with a through neutral connection. Second, in three-phase supply, as to newer homes, the 220 or 230 Volts is the maximum available, not 380 Volts as it is in some countries. Consequently, three-phase equipment, such as the motors of larger compressors, may need to be reconnected to work in Norway. However, in some areas, principally Rogaland county, the electricity supply system differs from that elsewhere in the country. So when in doubt, contact the local electricity supply company (name of company in the Pink Pages) or an electrical contractor (*Elektroentreprenører* in the Yellow Pages). Electricity is popularly called *strøm*, although that is the technical word for electrical current; the term for "voltage" is *spenning*.

Electricity supply (*Strøm levering*) Some 600 hydroelectric power stations produce more than 99% of the country's electrical energy, and the energy market is competitive. For most homes, price competition applies to about half of the total electric bill exclusive VAT. This is because the overall cost consists of four parts:

1. line rental (*nettleie*) to the local power company (*kraftselskap*): a rate times the number of kilowatt-hours used; some companies also charge a yearly fixed fee (*fastbeløp*).
2. governmental electricity duty (*elavgift til staten*): a rate times kilowatt-hours used.
3. energy consumed (*kraft*): a rate times kilowatt-hours used.
4. Value-Added Tax, VAT (*MVA, 23%*) on the sum of the first three parts

Together, the first two parts, which can be bought only from the local company that owns and maintains the local network, account for slightly less than half of the average household electricity bill, exclusive VAT. The third part, which accounts for slightly more than half the average household bill, exclusive VAT, may be bought from any power company serving the area in which you live. Various pricing schemes are offered. The two most common are floating market price (*flytende markedspris*) or fixed price (*fastpris*) per kilowatt-hour of energy used. If you elect to buy energy from the local power company, you will receive only one monthly or quarterly electricity bill. If you elect to buy energy from another power company, then you will receive two bills, one from it and one from the local company. In short, you can shop around and thereby save on half your electricity bill, but not all of it. The energy used is measured on a kilowatt-hour meter, which usually is installed in the fuse and distribution cabinet inside a house or flat or sometimes in a larger cabinet on each floor of a block of flats. Company readers check meters upon installation or change of owners or renters. When you move into a house or flat, you should agree with the previous owner or renter when the power company should read the meter to terminate the old account and open an account in your name. Upon opening an account, many companies require an advance of about a quarter of the estimated annual bill. Thereafter, there usually are several meter-reading options. You may have the company read your meter, or you may read it yourself, and report readings on specified dates, either by postal card or by calling a company registry number and keying in the reading on a keypad telephone.

Fire protection (*Brannvern*) Norwegian fire protection regulations are strict. Nonetheless, the predominant use of wood in building, a long heating season, high average electric energy consumption and frequent use of candles (on a per-capita basis, Norwegians use more candles than any other country in Europe) are reflected in a high rate of fire damage. Each year, some 60 to 70 people die in fires, most in their own homes, and about 6,000 people sustain burns. Experts believe that almost all home fires are preventable, because very few are caused by unforeseen events such as lightning strikes. Consequently, fire prevention awareness is taught in schools, and fire prevention is a major factor in building design and approval. Starting in 1990, all homes are required to have at least one smoke alarm and either a fire hose or a fire extinguisher (6 kg or larger), and preferably both. Unless an approved storage area is built into a house, the amounts of flammable liquids and gases that may be stored are limited to 5 litres of petrol or alcohol, 20 litres of paraffin oil, 5 litres of propane in disposable cans and 55 litres of propane in refillable containers as used for cooking and lighting. Other regulations concern electrical installations, fireplaces and stoves, chimneys and chimney sweeping, fire walls between attached buildings, fire exits and escape routes, furnace rooms, fire doors and uses of fire retardant materials. The Directorate for Fire and Explosion Prevention (*Direktoratet for brann- og eksplosjonsvern – DBE*) is responsible for preventive measures throughout the country; for further information, contact the nearest fire brigade (*Brannvesenet* or *Brann og Redningsvesen* in the Pink Pages). The Directorate for Product and Electrical Safety (*Produkt- og Elektrisitetstilsynet – PE*) oversees the safety of electrical works

and consumer goods; for further information, contact the your electric power company (*Energiverk* in the Pink Pages). The Norwegian Fire Protection Association (*Norsk Brannvern Forening*) has some ten thousand members throughout the country. Its members provide expertise to insurance companies and builders, and the head office acts as a central source for all public and private sector publications on fires and fire prevention, including rules and regulations, codes of practice and teaching videos. For further details (Norwegian only) contact *Norsk Brannvern Forening* ✆ 22200154, 🖷 22205636, ✉ PO Box 6703 St. Olavs plass, 0130 Oslo, 🌐 http://www.norsk-brannvern-forening.no

Fireplaces and wood stoves (*Peis og vedovn*) are traditional and commonplace. Almost every house has a fireplace and one or more wood stoves, as do many larger flats. Consequently, ☞ **firewood** is readily available, and ☞ **chimney sweeps** come once a year to all dwellings with chimneys. However, the classic wood-burning stove was found to contribute significantly to air pollution, particularly in cities and towns. Consequently, regulations enacted in the late 1990s require more efficient designs. All wood-burning stoves installed after 1 July 1998 must comply with the new regulations. Older stoves in use before that date are exempted, but must comply with the new regulations if refurbished or moved. Open fireplaces are exempted from the new regulations. For further details, contact your local building authority, listed under *Bygningsetaten* in the Pink Pages.

All stoves now being manufactured comply with the new regulations. Among the most efficient are the elegant, tall tiled stoves (*Kakkleovn*) of traditional (and now internally modified) Swedish and Norwegian design, and one of the leading builders of them is Norwegian, *Kakkleovnsmakeriet* ✆ 69313790, 🖷 69314348, ✉ Berggata 11, 1607 Fredrikstad. The world's oldest and largest producer of cast-iron stoves is Jøtul, a Norwegian company founded in 1853 and now global, with sales in more than 20 countries and a total market of about 100,000 stoves a year. The main Jøtul plant is in Fredrikstad, and there are three subsidiary companies, Jøtul USA, Jøtul SA in France and Jøtul Deutschland in Germany. There are Jøtul dealers throughout the country; look under *Ovner og peiser* in the Yellow Pages or view the Jøtul web site

⊕ http://www.jotul.no with pages in Norwegian and in English, as well as an interactive dealer locator map.

Firewood Wood for burning in home fireplaces and stoves (*ved, peisved*) is sold by the litre and by the cubic metre, in cut lengths of 20 cm, 30 cm, 60 cm and 300 cm. The 20 cm and 30 cm lengths are sold in 40 litre, 60 litre and 80 litre sacks, which can be transported in cars. The 60 cm and 300 cm lengths are sold in stacks and usually are transported by truck. There are four quality classes: Extra (*Extra*): birch with no rot: First class (*Klasse 1*): single sort hardwood (not mixed sorts) with dry rot in no more than 10% of pieces; Second class (*Klasse 2*): mixed sorts of hardwood and softwood (*blandingsved*) with dry rot in no more than 15% of pieces;

Third class (*Klasse 3*): all sorts including outside slabs (*bakhun*) and sawmill waste, with no dry rot specification. Sacks and stacks should be clearly marked to show size, sort and quality class. The approximate weights of wood of 20% moisture content in 40, 60 and 80 litre sacks are (below):

Up to 1997, firewood was sold using an older unit of volume, the cord (*favn*), usually, but not always, equal to 2.4 cubic metres, of which 1.66 cubic metres are solid wood. A larger unit, the big cord (*storfavn*) is equal to 12 cubic metres. Wood in sacks is sold at petrol stations, building supply stores and garden centres, as well as by fuel merchants (*Brenselforretninger*) who also sell stack wood in larger quantities. Look under *Ved* (Wood) or *Brenselforretninger* in the Yellow Pages.

Sack volume, litres	Birch (*Bjørk*)	Gray alder (*Gråor*), Pine (*Gran*), Aspen (*Osp*)	Willow (*Selje*), Black alder (*Svartorr*), Fir (*Furu*)	Maple (*Lønn*), Ash (*Ask*), Beech (*Bøk*)	Rowan – Mountain Ash (*Rogn*)
40 litre	15 kg	11 kg	13 kg	16 kg	17 kg
60 litre	22 kg	16 kg	14 kg	23 kg	25 kg
80 litre	30 kg	21 kg	25 kg	31 kg	33 kg

Fittings (*Beslag*) are similar to those used elsewhere in Europe and most now are made to European standards. Consequently, many international companies offer wide ranges of fittings; one of them is Norwegian, Grorud Industrier, part of the Assa Abloy AB group of companies, which is one of the world's largest manufacturers of window and door hardware. In alphabetical order by their names in English, the commonplace fittings, as now sold in plastic packets hung on racks in building supply and hardware shops, are:

Casement handle (for window) *Vindusvrider*
Cover plate *Deksel*
Cylinder lock case *Sylinder falle*
Cylinder locking set *Sylindersett*
Deadbolt *Reile*
Door handle (lever type) *Vrider*
Escutcheon *Langskilt*
Espagnolette *Espagnolett*
Euro hinge *Euro-hengsel*
Fixing plate *Dørdel*
Grille hinge *Sprosserammehengsel*

Guard *barnesikring*
Guide fitting *Glidekloss*
Handle *Håndtak*
Hinge *Hengsel*
Hook *Krok*
Installation bracket *Feste- og justerhylse*
Journal supported hinge *Løftehengsel tappbærende*
Key *Nøkkel*
Knob *Knott*
Latchbolt *Falle*
Lift-off hinge *Løftehengsel*
Lock case *Låskasse*
Lock for interior door *Falle/reilelås*
Lock *Lås*
Make-up wedge *Underlag*
Padlock *Hengelås*
Pivot *friksjonshengsel*
Push bolt *Kantskåte*
Side hung ironmongery *Sidehengsel/løftehengsel*
Side swing ironmongery *Sidehengsel*
Side turn ironmongery *Side turn glidehengsel*
Sliding door gear *Skyvedørbeslag*

Slim vent *Spalteventil*
Snap In Hinge *Snap-in lagerhengsel*
Spring hinge *Fjærhengsel*
Striker plate *Sluttstykke*
Top hung ironmongery *Topphengsel*
Top turn ironmongery *Top turn glidehengsel*
Window hasp and cleat *Vinduslukker*
Window stay *Vindusholder*
Window stop *Vindusholder*

Furniture (*møbler*) can be bought new at one of the furniture ☞ **chain stores** (Shopping chapter) or at independent furniture dealers listed under *møbler (detalj)* in the Yellow Pages. To find somebody to re-upholster (*omtrekking*) or repair your furniture look under *møbeltapsertjenester*. If you want to have something made to your specifications look under *snekkertjenester* for a carpenter. Secondhand furniture can be found at ☞ **flea markets** (Shopping chapter) or ☞ **second-hand shops** (Shopping chapter). Some useful terms: bed *seng,* carpets *tepper,* chair *stol,* chest of drawers *kommode,* coffee table *salongbord,* corner table *hjørnebord,* cupboard *skap,* curtains *gardiner,* desk *skrivebord,* dining table *spisebord,* double bed *dobbelseng,* furnishing fabric *møbelstoffer,* kitchen table *kjøkkenbord,* lamp *lampe,* lampshade *lampeskjerm,* mirror *speil,* night table *nattbord,* shelves *hyller,* sideboard *skjenk,* sofa *sofa,* wardrobe *klesskap.*

Gardening (*hagearbeid*) is popular, in part because the ☞ **climate** (Climate and Environment chapter) is milder than most other countries at comparable northerly latitudes. Nonetheless, summer is shorter than in countries further south. So many gardeners lengthen the season by first planting seeds in sprouting trays kept indoors until the weather is warm enough to permit planting outdoors. A local garden centre (*hagesenter*) will be able to advise you. In the spring, garden centres will be open late in the evening and on Sundays too. To find someone to mow the lawn (*slå gresset*), either put a note up on the noticeboard in your local supermarket or at the nearest garden centre, otherwise look under *vaktmestertjenester* in the Yellow Pages. Winter can damage your plants and pots. Take advice on pruning your roses and fruit bushes and trees. Cover small trees and shrubs with jute sacking in the autumn. Rake leaves from your lawn regularly, once the snow

and frost arrive, it will be difficult to clear and a nuisance in the spring when the snow melts. If you intend to leave your larger pots outside check that the pots are frost resistant. Garden centres also sell decorative containers for inside and out, gardening tools, fertiliser, garden furniture, parasols, barbecues, in fact everything for making life in the garden a pleasure. Some useful terms: bulb *løk,* chalk *kalk,* clay *liere,* compost *kompost,* earth *jord,* fertilizer *gjødsel,* fork *spagreip,* garden shears *hagesaks,* hoe *hakke,* hose *hageslange,* jute sacking *sekkestrie,* lawnmower *plenklipper,* moss *mose,* peat moss *myr,* rake *løvrive,* seeds *frø,* shovel *hagespade,* sprinkler *spreder,* trowel *planteskje,* wheelbarrow *trillebår.*

Gas (*Gass*) is seldom used in homes, though ☞ **gas cookers** (Sports, Recreation, Hobbies chapter) are used whenever electricity is not available, as on board leisure craft, in cabins and cottages and in campers. However, professional chefs in restaurants often prefer gas, as do many gourmet cooks, as cooking with gas permits quicker and often more accurate control of temperature. Several brands of cooktops (*gasstopp*) and cookers (*gass komfyrer*) are imported; Husqvarna of Sweden and Smeg of Italy are two leading brands. Most sales of gas appliances are to professional kitchens, so look under *Storkjøkkenutstyr* in the Yellow Pages to find dealers.

Heating (*oppvarming*) Norway is the world leader in per-capita consumption of electric energy, more than 26,000 kilowatt-hours per year per person. Metals refining and other energy-dependent industries are the big consumers. But abundant hydroelectric power has resulted in most homes being heated by ☞ **electricity** and having heating features that are considered luxuries in other countries, such as heated tiled bathroom floors and heated entrance lobbies to dry out shoes and boots wet with rain or snow. The most common electric heaters are wall-mounted electric panel convectors (*panelovn*) and ceiling-mounted radiant heaters (*stråleovn*). Be careful with these electric heaters; do not regard them as being like hot-water radiators, which can be used for drying wet clothes. Heed the warning usually printed on the top edge of the heater and never drape any wet clothing or other material over it. When air flow through the heater is restricted, its temperature may rise high enough to burn the clothing and start a fire. Modern panel heaters have thermostats that prevent this hazard, but older heaters lack such protection. Many newer buildings have sub-floor electric heating cable (*varmekabel*) and consequently need no panel convectors.

Many older flats and houses were built to be heated by ☞ **fireplaces and wood stoves**, though many subsequently were converted to electric heating or central heating. The first central heating systems, installed up through the 1920s, used coal-fired furnaces, so many older houses still have coal bins. However, oil firing is now more common. Look under *fyringsoljer* in the Yellow Pages for suppliers of heating oil and servicing of your central heating system. Many newer houses are now fitted with heat pumps (*varmepumpe*), though their efficiency is still being debated.

Many modern houses and flats have fireplaces and wood stoves. However, they are mostly for wintertime enjoyment. This is because in terms of the heat it produces, ☞ **firewood** is more expensive than electricity or oil. However, if you cut your own firewood and have a modern wood stove, the heat it produces is inexpensive and nearly non-polluting.

Homemaker assistant (*Husmorvikar*) If the person who usually does the housework in a home is incapacitated, as by illness or giving birth, you may ask the municipal social services office to provide a homemaker assistant (*husmorvikar*) to handle the work. Other similar services include home help for the elderly and disabled (*hjemmehjelp for eldre og uføre*), home nursing (*hjemmesykepleie*) and other assistance (*andre hjelpetiltak*) for persons who need it. The services are provided against a small charge, which depends on your ability to pay. To find out if you are eligible for such assistance, call the *bistand og omsorg servicekontoret* listed under the name of the municipality in the Pink Pages.

Housecleaning (*rengjøring*) is normally done by the family themselves, to save the cost of employing part-time ☞ **domestic servants**. Most houses have wooden floors, ☞ **parquet floors, the care of** and surfaces with ☞ **rugs, care of**. A mop (*mopstativ*) with a frame onto which a 60cm sleeve with mophead fixes, is ideal for washing both wooden and tiled floors after vacuum cleaning. ☞ **window cleaning**.

Instructions (*bruksanvisninger*) The labels on foods produced in Norway are in Norwegian, and the labels on international-brand foods often are in Norwegian and other languages, including English. Other goods are labelled similarly: the instructions on containers of ski wax, for instance, are in Norwegian, English, French and German, and household appliances usually have multi-lingual instruction booklets. Computers and computer equipment may be delivered with either Norwegian or English manuals, depending on buyer preference, and application programs are available in English and Norwegian versions. However, the instruction booklets for some products, such as Japanese cameras, may be delivered in Danish (*betjeningsvejledning*), apparently because the manufacturers regard the Norwegian market as too small to warrant a Norwegian version and because Norwegians can read Danish. Occasionally, instructions may be in Swedish (*bruksanvisning*), which is more difficult for Norwegians to read. Nonetheless, most technological products are made for the international market, so instructions in English and other languages usually are available. Sometimes they are in stock (manuals in Norwegian are usually translated from originals in English). But sometimes English or other language versions must be ordered from the manufacturer. So if you cannot read Norwegian (or Danish or Swedish), you should ask to see the instructions for a product upon buying and, if necessary, request a version in the language of your choice. Simple instructions, such as cooking times for packaged foods imported from abroad, may be in the language of their originating countries only, such as the cooking instructions for pasta imported from Italy being in Italian only, while some are pictorial, with 1-2-3 drawings for preparation. Likewise, the instructions for assembling flat-pack furniture usually have only drawings and no words.

Krafse (*Krafse*) Almost every country has some superior implements. Norway has three tools, used in gardening and construction, which have no peers. The *krafse* (literally "scratcher"), *krafsebrett* ("krafse-pan") and *fyllhakke* ("fill hoe") are unbeatable for working on the surface of the ground, particularly for moving any weight of soil. The *krafse* has a half-moon-shaped blade set oblique to its shaft. Depending on the angle at which it is held, the blade can lightly skim the underlying surface, like a squeegee sweeping water from glass, or can dig deeply, as does a grub hoe. The *krafsebrett*, shaped like a dust pan and fitted with handles on both sides, is used for removing material swept up by the *krafse*. The *fyllhakke* has a pointed blade in the shape of an almond shell, attached obliquely to its shaft just below the rounded end. It is unequalled for digging small furrows, as used for planting a row of seeds or bulbs, and for picking stones out of soil. Anyone who has worked with these three tools in cramped spaces, as in ditches or foundations, realises that they are unique. Simply removing some soil from the bottom of a trench, backbreaking with a spade, is easy with a *krafse* and *krafsebrett*. In fact, hand-powered moving of anything on the ground – spreading gravel, distributing fertiliser, levelling sand – is ergonomically sensible only if you use a *krafse*. This may be why the *krafse* is Norway's most popular gardening and construction hand tool by far, with annual sales equalling the combined sales of all other types of construction spades and shovels. Despite the obvious advantages of the three tools and their predominance in Norway, they have yet to be appreciated elsewhere. Even in neighbouring Sweden, they are virtually unknown.

The tools are indigenously Norwegian, not because they are new, but because they are so old that they have been abandoned elsewhere. Their ancestors were devised in the late Iron Age for iron ore mining in Central Europe. Their present forms first emerged in common mining tools of the 15th and 16th centuries. German miners probably brought the tools to Norway in the mid 16th century, to work the first found iron ore deposits. Norwegians gave the tools descriptive names by their uses: *krafse* means to scratch or scrape and pull towards, and *fyll* means fill or rubble. The tools stayed in the hands of miners for more than three centuries. They first were used for other purposes in the late 19th century. Up until the 1940s, manufacturers apparently felt they owed prospective purchasers some explanation of them: in catalogues, the *krafse* was called *malmkrafse* (iron-ore *krafse*) and the *krafsebrett* was called *malmfat* (iron-ore pan). Modern mining machines have replaced hand tools in mines, and the *krafse* family is now used mostly above and on the ground. In addition to their principal uses, the tools have special applications. Archaeologists have found that they are far superior to the traditional coal spade and scuttle for excavating sites. A skilled sweep of a *krafse* can pull fine layers into a *krafsebrett* for examination. Fishermen use them to quickly clean decks and holds. Day-care centres use them to keep sandboxes tidy. And one teacher of commercial-scale fine baking at a trade school reported that he keeps a *krafse* and *krafsebrett* handy in the apprentice bakery to remove student errors from the floors and walls.

Lamps (*Lamper*) The commonplace electric lamps used in homes and offices are general lighting service (GLS) incandescent light bulbs (*lyspærer*), tubular fluorescent lamps (*lysrør*), compact fluorescent lamps (*energisparepærer*) and tungsten-halogen lamps (*halogenlyspærer*). All are made for 230 V fixtures, except for the tungsten-halogen lamps, most of which are made for 12 V fixtures. GLS light bulbs are by far the most commonly used and are made with two sizes of standard European screw-thread base, the 14 mm diameter E14 and the 27 mm diameter E27, as shown below.

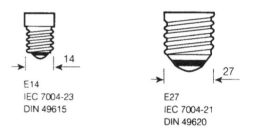

E14
IEC 7004-23
DIN 49615

E27
IEC 7004-21
DIN 49620

There are four leading varieties: standard (*normal*) and round-bulb (*krone*) with an E27 base and candle (*mignon*) and round-bulb (*illum*) with an E14 base, all with either frosted (*matt*) or clear (*klar*) glass envelopes. Compact fluorescent lamps are also fitted with E27 or E14 bases. Tubular fluorescent lamps and tungsten-halogen lamps have pin contacts that plug into their respective standard fixtures. Lamps are sold in supermarkets and food shops, as well as in lighting shops, hardware shops and petrol station shops, in small cartons, usually with one but sometimes with two or three lamps. Carton labelling varies, but usually includes the lamp type along with an outline drawing, voltage (230V or 12V), strength in Watts, glass type (frosted or clear) and base type, and sometimes a description of the socket which the lamp fits, such as large (*stor sokkel*) for E27 bases and small (*liten sokkel*) for E14 bases. Lamps made after 1st January 1996 and marketed internationally also have ☞ **CE Marking** (Measurements and Standards chapter). Most brands of lamps marketed internationally in Europe are sold in shops. The leader is Osram, the company active in more than 110 countries world-wide and the only one actually manufacturing lamps in Norway, at Drammen.

Laundry (*vask*) usually is done at home, and most houses and blocks of flats have laundry rooms. Laundries (*vaskerier*) and dry-cleaners (*renserier*) offer clothes cleaning services. Coin-operated laundries (*selvbetjent vaskerier*) can be found in major cities and towns that welcome people on holiday; most guest harbours for visiting boats will have laundry facilities. Look in the Yellow Pages. Supermarkets stock washing powders (*vaskepulver*) and liquids, fabric softeners (*tøymykner*). Most of the international brands are available, including varieties for sensitive skins. Washing machines (*vaskemaskin*) and tumble driers (*tørketrommel*) can be bought in shops selling ☞ **appliances** (Electrical and Electronic Goods chapter) and rented from ☞ **rentals** companies.

Mending (*reparasjon, stoppetøy*) If you need to mend rips and tears yourself, shops selling ☞ **sewing** notions will stock bonding fabrics and sprays, patches and necessary needles and thread to make the job easier. Stockists of all-in-one snowsuits (*parkdress*) sell repair kits. For professional repairs and alterations ask at the ☞ **dry-cleaning** (Clothing chapter) outlet you use or look under *systuer* in the Yellow Pages.

Municipal fees (*Kommunalegebyrer*) are charged the owner of a property. If you own a flat in a block of flats, you most likely will pay a monthly service fee that will include the municipal fees for the building. If you rent a house, you may or may not pay the municipal fees for it, depending on your rental contract. The fees are set by the utilities (*Kommunalteknisk*) department of each municipality and vary from place to place, even within the same county. The usual fees, which usually are billed together two or four times a year are:

Water and sewage fees (*vann- og kloakkgebyrer*) may be charged together or separately. They are based on volume in cubic metres, either metered (*målt*) or estimated (*estimert*), or for some properties, on the area of the house in square metres. A connection fee (*tilknytningsgebyr*) is charged when you first connect to the municipal water supply or sewage lines.

Refuse collection fee (*renovasjonsgebyr* or *søppeltømmingsgebyr*) depends on the number of collections a week, usually one, and the size of your household. Most municipalities have a fixed fee per sack (*sekk*) sized for the average home. Additional fees are charged for additional sacks or for sacks that must be carried (*bæretillegg*) more than a specified distance. For larger properties, a fee is charged for containers (*containerrenovasjon*) emptied by the volume of the container in cubic metres. Some municipalities offer a fee reduction for reduced volume of refuse, such as when kitchen organic refuse (*kjøkkenavfall*) is composted (*kompostering*) instead of being discarded in the refuse sack to be collected.

Paper for recycling (*papir-gjenvinning*) is collected free by some municipalities, usually once every two weeks, in reusable sacks, most often orange or another bright colour to set them apart from ordinary refuse sacks.

Chimney sweeping fee (*Feieavgift*) depends on the height and size of the chimney and usually covers one sweep a year, in the autumn.

Paint and varnish (*Maling og lakk*) is sold by paint shops (*fargehandel*) as well as by hardware shops (*jernvarer*) and building supply shops (*byggevarer*). The leading brands are Jotun and its subsidiary, Scanox, which together have 70% of the annual market of some 1.7 billion litres of paint and varnish. Star of Drammen sells in the southern part of the country, and there are several smaller special product manufacturers, such as Løvolds exterior oil stains and Treol interior pine stains.

Parquet, the care of (*rengjøring av parkettgulv*) Dust accumulates quickly on wooden floors and surfaces. To keep it looking good, vacuum clean regularly and wash with a weak solution of warm water and ☞ **soft soap**. You need not rinse the floor afterwards. If you have waxed floors, re-wax once a year with floor polish (*gulvpuss*). Remove marks made by shoes with black soles using mineral turpentine (*white spirit*), sold by hardware shops, paint supply shops, petrol stations, building supply merchants and some supermarkets. Stick small felt pads under the legs of tables and chairs to reduce scratching. Hardware shops and furniture and interior shops sell them. A badly marked floor can be resanded and resealed. Look in the Yellow Pages for specialists in parquet treatment (*Parkettsliperi*) or general floor cleaning and treatment (*Gulvbearbeiding*). You can also hire sanders (*Utleiemaskiner*) and do it yourself (DIY). A common practice in most homes is to remove your outdoor shoes when coming in, especially in the winter with snow and grit.

Pest and vermin control (*Skadedyrbekjempelse*) is provided by specialist companies, many of whom also provide services to combat rot (*hussopp*) and condensation damage (*fuktskade*). You will find them listed under *Skadedyrbekjempelse* in the Yellow Pages. A useful vocabulary of pests and vermin: ants *stokkmauer*, black ants *jordmauer*, cockroaches *kakerlakker*, deathwatch beetles *borebiller*, flies *fluer*, larder beetles *fleskeklanner*, longhorn beetles *husbukk*, mealworms *melbiller*, mice *mus*, moths *møll*, pigeons *duer*, rats *rotter*, silverfish *sølvkre*, termites *termitter*, wasps *veps*.

Pine furniture, care of (*rengjøring av furumøbler*) Natural wood furniture can be scrubbed with a weak solution of warm water and ☞ **soft soap**. For stubborn ingrained dirt, add $3/4$ dl domestic bleach (*klorin*) to 5 l of warm water in a bucket; this is particularly effective on garden furniture and teak decking on boats. Caution! Bleach is corrosive (*etsende*); handle it with care; always wear rubber gloves and wear protective glasses when using it. Apply a coat of furniture polish (*møbelpuss*) to indoor furniture and teak oil (*teakolje*) to outdoor furniture.

Plant import (*Innførsel av planter*) The import of plants or parts of plants is subject to restrictions intended to curtail the spread of pests and plant diseases. For instance, the import of chrysanthemums, geraniums and gerbera and the seedlings, but not the seeds, of cucumber, lettuce, strawberry and tomato plants is prohibited without an approved health certificate (*sunnhetssertifikat*) conforming to the international FAO (Food and Agricultural Organization of the United Nations) norm. So if you intend to import plants or receive plants from abroad as gifts, contact the Norwegian Agricultural Inspection Service (*Landbrukstilsyn*) in advance for the relevant regulations, at the Central Administration ✆ 64944400, 🖷 64944410, ✉ PO Box 3, 1431 Ås, 🖳 http://www.landbrukstilsynet.no with pages in Norwegian and in English, or at the nearest Plant Inspection Service (*Planteinspeksjonen*) listed under *Statens landbrukstilsyn* in the Pink Pages for Bergen, Bodø, Kristiansand, Oslo, Stavanger, Trondheim and Tønsberg.

Refuse (*avfall*) If you live in a flat, the building most likely will have a refuse chute (*søppelsjakt*). On each floor, there will be a locking access cover, for which you will have a key. All you need do is pack your refuse in a plastic shopping bag, tie the bag shut, and send it down the chute. The cost of collection is included in your rent or share of the common expenses of the building. But if you live in a house, refuse is collected at the entrance to your property, and the cost of its collection is included in local taxes. The municipality gives each household a roll of refuse bags, which line the large container outside your home. If you have two containers you will receive two rolls of bags, calculated to last you six months. If you do not have a large container outside your home, contact the main office of your municipality at the number listed in the Pink Pages. Refuse packed in other plastic bags may not be collected. Paper, cardboard, glass bottles, tin cans and refillable bottles (for carbonated drinks and beer) are not thrown out but are collected for ☞ **recycling** (Climate and Environment chapter). In most municipalities, paper is collected once or twice a month in special fibre-reinforced plastic sacks. You can discard bottles and tins in recycling containers, usually located at supermarkets and municipal car parks, with sorting by clear (*klar*) and coloured (*farget*) glass. Any larger items like furniture that are in good or repairable condition can be donated to a ☞ **flea market** (Shopping chapter). Larger items like refrigerators and bicycles that are beyond repair can be taken to a municipal refuse tip (*fylling, avfallspark*). Drink containers on which there is a ☞ **deposit** (Shopping chapter) are taken back to shops for refunds. Any clothing or shoes you wish to dispose of are deposited in special containers marked *Freselsarmeen* ("Salvation Army") or UFF, who collect and resell ☞ **used clothing** to finance domestic and foreign aid projects.

Rentals (white and brown goods, TV/radio/computers) (*utleie av hvite- og brun-varer*) White goods are not always provided when renting a house. The largest chain for rentals is the Scandinavian Thorn chain, including shops in Sweden, Denmark (DER name) and Norway, *Thorn Norge* ✆ 22882000, ☎ 22882301, ✉ Brynsengveeien 2, 0667 Oslo, ✇ http://www.thorn.no with an interactive map locator for 30 shops thoroughout the country. Thorn can supply washing machines (*vaskemaskin*), tumble dryer (*tørketrommel*), dishwashers (*oppvaskmaskin*), refirgerators (*kjøleskap*), freezers (*dypfryser*), cookers (*komfyr*), video cameras, video players, televisions (*fjernsyn*), stereo systems (*stereoanlegg*), DVD's. They also stock mobile telephones and computer equipment, but this is for hire purchase (*kjøpe på avbetaling*) only. Look under *Hvitevarer* in the yellow pages for companies that sell and may also rent white goods.

Residents' Associations (*Velforening, Grendelag*) There are some 6000 local residents' associations in the country. Those in cities and towns are called *Velforening*, which usually is shortened to *Vel* and translates to "Benefit Association". Those in rural districts are called *Grendelag*, which translates to "Grange Association", with the word "Grange" used in the older English way, to designate a small group of farms or farm buildings. Each *Vel* or *Grendelag* acts within its locality to preserve the local environment and to act in the collective interest of the local residents, such as in matters concerning road works, developments and municipal or county planning. The larger *Vel* and *Grendelag* also have telephone numbers or offices where the public may obtain free information and advice when having difficulties with the authorities or organisations or when wishing to lodge protest, as against planned buildings, car parks and the like. In a typical city or town, the local *Vel* is most visible through the facilities it provides, such as benches in parks and along woodland paths and hinged-cover sand coffers located along steep uphill stretches of roads and along walkways, ☞ **Sanding and salting**. Indeed, the *Vel* and *Grendelag* deal mostly in practical everyday matters; in many municipalities, the local *Vel* originally was founded for a practical reason, such as to provide street lighting. Each *Vel* and *Grendelag* is supported in part by a subsidy from the Ministry of the Environment (*Miljøverndepartementet*), in part by a subsidy from the local municipality and in part by voluntary annual membership fees paid by the local residents. There is a national association, The Norwegian Coalition for Neighbourhoods (*Norges Velforbund*) with a head office in Oslo. However, if you wish to contact the local *Vel* or *Grendelag*, call or visit the local municipality (*kommune*) for current addresses and telephone numbers of its offices or officers.

Rugs, care of (*Stell av tepper*) Rag rugs (*filleryer*) are popular. Most are made of cotton. So they may be washed in a household washing machine. Use the gentle, low-temperature (40°C) cycle with no centrifuge, and then hang the rug on a sturdy clothesline to drip dry. A traditional trick for wintertime cleaning is to fling a rug upside-down on fresh show, beat it to knock out dust, and then hang it up to dry. Large or expensive rugs are better dealt with by professionals, look under *Teppe- og møbelrensing* in the Yellow Pages. If you want to clean wall-to-wall carpeting, either contact carpet cleaners or hire equipment yourself from them or a ☞ **dry-cleaning** (Clothing chapter) company. You can wash a smaller rug by soaking it in a detergent suitable for wool ☞ **laundry**. All these tasks are most easily done when weather will help to dry the carpets. Always hang a carpet with the underside up, so that the sun will not discolour the fibres.

Sanding and salting (*Strøing*) involves sprinkling sand, salt or grit on driveways, pavements and outdoor steps to improve traction for cars and foothold for pedestrians. Sand (*sand*), grit (*singel*) and salt (*salt*) are used and are sold in various blends by supermarkets, building supply shops and petrol stations. Sand is cheap and affords good traction on sheet ice. But it sticks to soles and consequently is easily tracked indoors, and it blows away when dry. Grit, which is crushed gravel, of 3 – 8 mm grain size, is also cheap and easier to remove in the springtime than sand. But it can slip on hard, sheet ice, unless mixed with salt. Salt helps melt ice by lowering the freezing temperature of water. But it melts ice to a salty slush, which if not removed, sticks to soles and irritates the paws of dogs and cats. Moreover, it pollutes surrounding plants, and when it dries in the spring, it blows about. The Oslo City Roads Administration (*Oslo Vei*), the largest of its sort in the country with the most streets, roads and pavements in its care, uses a mix of equal amounts of sand and grit to which three to four percent salt is added. Large green or bright yellow wooden or fibreglass-plastic, hinged-lid sand coffers are often located along steep uphill roads, at car parks, along walkways in housing complexes, on the platforms of unattended commuter train stations, and the like, for use by the public. These are regularly filled with sand in the wintertime by the local public roads administrations (*Vegvesen*) or a local residents' association (*Vel*), and often are labelled to indicate the organisation responsible, such as *strøsand fra velforeningen* (Sand for sprinkling, from the residents' association).

Sewage (*Avløp*) If you live in a house or flat, the drainage circuit is almost always connected to the municipal sewerage system (*avløpssystem*). If you build a new house, you most likely will be required to connect its drainage to the municipal sewerage. If you build a cabin or cottage (*hytte*) far from a sewerage system, you most likely will be required to provide for sewage treatment on site, because new outdoor toilets are not allowed in most municipalities (though older ones may still be used). There are three approaches. The simplest is the so-called "spin privy" (*snurredass*), named because it resembles an outdoor privy and is fitted with three composting bins fixed to rotate under the seat. The biological lavatory is more advanced. It resembles an ordinary w.c., which is mounted over a composting tank. Builder's merchants (*Byggevarer* in the Yellow Pages) sell these lavatories. Year-round homes away from sewerage systems will be equipped with a septic tank (*septiktank*) in which solid waste is decomposed by bacteria. A septic tank service truck (*Septiktanktømming* in the Yellow Pages) may periodically empty the tank. Alternatively, the tank may drain into a leach field (*filtreringsområde*). For further information, contact the municipal utility section, listed under *Kommunalteknisk* under the name of the municipality in the Pink Pages.

Sewing (*søm*) fabrics (*stoffer*), patterns (*mønsterer*) and notions (*sytilbehor*) can be found at hobby shops selling quilting supplies or shops specialising in fab-

rics; look under *syartikler* or *tekstiler* in the Yellow Pages. Moreover, shops selling sewing machines, listed under *symaskiner og strykemaskiner* in the Yellow Pages, frequently sell sewing materials. Pattern books by Burda, Butterick, Neue Mode Stil and Vogue are available. When looking for a pattern, find out your size ☞ **Clothing sizes** (Clothing chapter). Butterick and Vogue patterns utilise the US sizing standard with the directions written in English and French and fabric requirements in both yards and metres. The other pattern books state sizes in both European and US standards with directions written in Danish/Swedish/Finnish and fabric requirements in metres only. The diagrams are detailed enough for you to be able to construct a garment with a minimum knowledge of the language. You can also order woven ☞ **nametapes** (Clothing chapter). Some useful terminology: bobbins (*symaskin spoler*), buttons (*knapper*), cotton (*bomull*), hooks and eyes (*haker*), dressmaker's workshop (*systuer*), facing (*belegg*), interfacing (*innlegg*), interlining (*mellom for*), needles (*synåler*), pins (*knappenåler*), quilt batting (*bomull vat*), scissors (*sysaks*), sewing machine (*sysmaskiner*), stiffening (*stivning*), thimble (*fingerbøl*), thread (*sytråd*), wool (*ull*), zipper (*glidelås*).

Sizes (*Størrelser*) The sizes of most furnishings are now standardised on basic modules, so that items of different manufacture will work together. For instance, ☞ **beds and bedding** are in standard sizes, so mattresses will fit frames, sheets will fit mattresses, pillowcases will fit pillows, and so on. Likewise, other furnishings that must work together are of standard dimensions. Kitchen counters are 60 cm deep and 85 cm, 88 cm or 90 cm above the floor. Most kitchen appliances, such as cookers, dishwashers and refrigerators, are 60 cm deep and 60 cm wide, though some are 70 cm wide. Doorframes are 190 cm, 200 cm, 210 cm or 220 cm high by 70 cm, 80 cm, 90 cm or 100 cm wide. Window frames are sized in a similar matrix of multiples of 10 cm, but vary widely, according to the age of the building and its exterior architecture.

Snow clearing (*snørydding*) is a widespread public and private wintertime chore; only people living on the southern and south-western coasts may avoid it. Indeed, ☞ **snow** (Climate and Environment chapter) is so much a part of winter life that the means of dealing with it are efficient, swift and routine.

Municipal, Public Roads Administration and private contracted trucks, road machinery and tractors fitted with ploughs (*brøytebiler*) clear roads, streets, pavements, pedestrian precincts and public car parks. Larger companies, shopping centres and the like will clear their car parks and walkways with their own equipment or will contract for clearing services.

If you live in a flat, the building caretaker (*vaktmester*) usually will take care of snow clearing on the grounds. If you live in a house, you may hire services or clear yourself. You will find clearing firms listed under *snørydding* or *vaktmestertjenester* in the Yellow Pages. In rural districts, local farmers and building contractors often keep their tractors and equipment busy through the winter by offering clearing services; your neighbours most likely will know whom to call. However, don't wait until snow falls to call, but call in advance, as those who clear prefer contracts for an entire winter, so they can plan their workloads.

Do-it-yourself clearing is commonplace, and a wide range of implements for it are sold by hardware shops (*jernvareforretninger*), building supply centres (*byggevarer*), garden centres (*hagesentre*) and larger petrol stations (*bensinstasjoner*). You can choose to clear by hand or by using a machine.

Among the hand tools, the snow shovel (*snøspade*) and the larger snow scoop (*snøskuffe*) are the most common, but also the most hazardous to use. The forward bending, twisting and lifting movement of shovelling snow overloads the spine, which is why so many people complain of back pains after a snowfall. Two implements are designed to minimise such overload hazards by allowing you to move snow along the ground without bending and twisting to lift it. There are two principal types. One is the hand snowplough (*snøskyver* or *skyffel*), which has a long handle and a blade similar to that of a snow plough vehicle; you push it to plough snow. The other is the snow mover (*snørydder*), popularly called the southern scoop (*sørlandsskuff*) because it was first devised in southern Norway to move the heavy snows there. It has a large pan resembling an oversized dustpan and fitted with a handle bar similar to that of a garden roller or hand mower. You push the front blade into snow until the pan is full, and then move it by sliding along the snow surface. The *Snedy* model in plastic has accessory wheels that can be fitted in summer, so they may also be used when you rake leaves or grass cuttings.

Motorised snow blowers (*snøfresere*) are increasingly popular, particularly with larger properties or driveways that need to be kept clear. There are many makes and models, from smaller machines that resemble ordinary power lawn mowers, up to mini tractors. In buying, check for features such as the number of blower stages. Single-stage machines work well in light snows, but may clog up in heavy, wet snows. The best machines have two stages (*totrinn*) to prevent clogging: the first impeller at the front cuts into the snow and the second impeller in the throw duct ejects it.

Soft soap, potash soap (*Grønnsåpe*) The traditional European semi-liquid soap used since about 1650 remains in everyday use. It is made from potash lye (potassium hydroxide), vegetable fatty acids, fragrance and water. Several brands, in concentrations of 15% – 30%, are sold in 0.75 – 2.5 litre plastic bottles by grocers, supermarkets and hardware shops throughout the country. The principal fragrances are ordinary (*vanlig*) and pine needle (*furunål*). As in other countries, soft soap is used as a pesticide and in a variety of products, including rubber lubricants and leather preservatives. Its household uses include loosening self-adhesive labels, removing stains and combating the odour of cat urine. It is most widely used for washing floors and wood furniture, using about 50 millilitres of liquid soft soap in a eight-litre household bucket of water. There is also a pharmaceutical grade equivalent to the green soft soap sold in other countries. It is sold by pharmacies, and its medical uses range from traditional cures for minor maladies to clinical treatment of burns and infected fingers.

Timber and woodwork (*trelast*) Wood is the most common building material for homes: most houses are wooden framework and interiors of flats in concrete or masonry buildings are often finished in wood. So a full range of timber and woodwork is available throughout the country, from timber merchants (*trelast*) and builders merchants (*byggevarer*). All architectural drawings and materials are measured in centimetres and millimetres, but tradesmen and merchants still speak of materials in inches (*tommer*), such as a 'two-by-four' (*to-fire*), a common size of plank. However, measurement in inches can be imprecise. In 19th century Europe, the yard, divided into three feet, was defined in many ways. In Norway and Denmark, it was set equal to 94.14 centimetres, so an inch was equal to 26.15 millimetres. That inch was in everyday use up to 1960, when Norway standardised on the international UK yard of 91.44 centimetres. The resultant inch, equal to 25.40 millimetres, is the current standard and is used on the common carpenter's folding rule (tommestokk), which is graduated in both inches and centimetres. However, some older folding rules are still in use, so unless a rule is new, it's best to check its graduations if you measure in inches: if the ten inch mark is at 25.4 cm, it's a new rule; if it is at 26.15 cm, it's an old rule and should not be used. The common names, which you might use in buying timber and woodwork or in describing work for a carpenter, are listed below, alphabetically by their equivalents in English.

architraving *ramtre*	flooring boards *gulv-bord*
balustrade *balustrade*	
bamboo *bambus*	frame *karm*
baseboard *gulvlist*	framework *reisverk*
beading *perlekant*	ground beam *svill*
beam *bjelke*	half round *halvstaff*
beech *bøk*	hand rail *håndlist*
birch *bjerk*	hickory *hikkori*
casing *karmlist, gerikt*	impregnation *impreg-nering*
casing bead *brann-murlist*	
	jamb *sidekarm*
ceiling *tak*	joist *bjelke*
ceiling, panelled *himling*	mahogany *mahogani*
chamfered *høvlet*	moulding *taklist, feielist*
concave moulding *hulkil*	muntin *sprosse*
coping *dekklist*	newel *spindel*
corner *vinkellist*	oak *eik*
door *dør*	panelling *panelprofil*
door sill *terskel*	parapet moulding *bryst-ningslist*
doorsteps *trapp*	
doweling *rundstaff*	parquet *parkett*
fillet *bånd*	picture frame moulding *rammelist*
finished (machined) *justert*	
	pine *furu*
fir *gran*	planed *høvlet*
floor *gulv*	plank *planke*
floor joist *gulvbjelke*	purlin *takås*

quarter round *kvartstaff*	stud *stender*
queen post *hengestav*	teak *teak*
rafter *taksperre*	threshold *terskel*
reveal *smyg*	tongue and groove *not og fjær*
ridgepole *mønsås*	
riser *opptrinn*	trapdoor *lem*
roof *tak*	tread *trappetrinn*
roof truss *takstol*	trellis *espalier*
skirting *gulvlist*	weather bar *vannbrett*
stairs *trapp*	window *vindu*
stile *midtpost*	window sill *karmunder-stikke*
strut *strebebjelke*	

Tools and utensils (*Verktøy og redskap*) are sold by hardware shops, home furnishings shops, supermarkets, automobile supply shops, larger petrol stations and many specialist shops. Many are made in Norway, but most are imported, principally from China, Germany, Japan, Italy, Spain and Sweden. Most are sold from self-serve racks and have international packaging with information in several languages. So if you don't know the name of a tool or utensil in Norwegian, you can probably find it just by looking in shops. Or if you wish, look it up in *Aschehoug og Gyldendals Store Norske Leksikon Visuell Ordbok* (Kunnskapsforlaget, Oslo, 2nd edition 1998, ISBN 82-573-0960-5) which has colour drawings of almost all common tools and utensils, as well as most other everyday items, along with their names and the names of their parts in Norwegian, English, German and French. Most local libraries (*folkebibliotek*) will have the book in their reference rooms (*lesesal*).

Tradesmen (*Håndverkere*)   Most tradesman (Trades chapter) are reliable and honest. But regrettably there are so many exceptions that dealings with tradesmen are at the top of the list of complaints to the ☞ **Consumer council** (Human Rights, Consumer Rights chapter). Consequently the Council and the Heating and Piping Information Bureau (*VVS Informasjon*) suggest precautions that you may take to prevent difficulties:

- Check with the ☞ **Brønnøysund register** (Registrations, Rights, Licences chapter) that the firm is registered.
- Check with the tax authorities to verify that the firm pays its taxes and VAT (*MVA*).
- Call the local office of the Consumer Council (*For-*

brukerrådet in the Pink Pages) to check that there are no outstanding complaints against the firm.
- Ask for references and verify them.
- If the services involve plumbing work, ask to see the firm's certificates [☞**Plumbers** (Trades chapter)].
- Ask if the firm has routines for health, environment and safety – HES (*helse, miljø og sikkerhet – HMS*).
- Have a written contract for services and goods to be delivered, stipulating costs and a schedule for completion of work. Standard contracts are available from the Consumer Council.
- Don't pay in advance.
- Be wary of travelling tradesmen who sell their services unsolicited, door-to-door.

Window cleaning (*Vinduvask*) Many double-glazed windows can be swung round so you may clean the outside panes from the inside. Triple-glazed casement windows usually have frames that can be opened to permit cleaning the panes in the air space between the sealed double pane and the outside panes. Cleaning is easiest and fastest if you use the traditional implements used round the world, a squeegee (*nal*) and a chamois (*pusseskin*); both are sold in supermarkets and hardware shops. Wet the window with a cleaning solution and draw the rubber blade of the squeegee over it to remove the liquid. Use the chamois to clean the blade of the squeegee. Some technique is needed to clean a window without streaks; you can learn it by going to town early in the morning, before shops open, and watching professional window cleaners at work. If you wish, you may mix your own cleaning solution and apply it with a sponge, as do professional window cleaners. But the ready-made glass cleaners sold in supermarkets and petrol stations are more convenient for home use. They usually are in pump-spray plastic flasks labelled *universal, for vinduer, speil og vaskbare flater* ("universal, for windows, mirrors and washable surfaces"). If you prefer not to wash your windows yourself, you can find window washing services listed under *vaktmestertjenester* in the Yellow Pages.

Windows and doors (*Vindu og dør*) are similar to those used elsewhere in Europe, with additional features suiting a cold climate. The casement window, in which the sash opens on hinges that usually are attached to the upright side or the top member of the frame, is the most common type, because it seals well. Modern casement windows usually have a triple glazed sash, with two hermetically-sealed inner panes (*isolérglass*) hinged to a single outer pane with muntins (*sprosser*) to permit cleaning between the inner and outer panes. The double-hung window, which consists of a pair of single-glazed sashes running in vertical grooves in a frame fitted with cords and counterweights, seals poorly and requires external storm windows for weather protection, and consequently is not used in Norway. The traditional, and still most common catch is a hasp on the sash that fits over a cleat on an upright member of the frame. Some modern windows, particularly those in prefabricated houses, are held closed by casement handles that engage strikers in the frame members. Most often, a window sash is held in the open position by a long-shaft hook fixed to the outside of the lower frame member, but some windows are fitted with adjustable casement stays. Some windows, particularly those in blocks of flats, are fitted with nearly fully reversible ironmongery (*husmorvindu*) so they may be reversed, with their outer sides facing inwards, for ease of washing. Most doors are hung on two or three hinges, and are fitted with handles, not knobs. Most houses and the entryways of many blocks of flats are fitted with enclosed porches (*vindfang*) that have two doors, to trap air and thereby cut down on draughts and heat loss in the wintertime. Almost all doors and windows are made to take standard ☞**Fittings**.

Housing (*Bolig*)

Architecture and architects (*Akritektur og arkitekter*) There are some 1.8 million residential buildings in the country, of which more than one million are one-family houses. Moreover, one family in five owns a holiday home, either a seaside cottage or a mountain cabin. Most houses and holiday homes are wooden frame buildings, built to suit the climate. Understandably, there are many architects, more than 3,000 in the country. Fully qualified architects may use the title *sivilarkitekt*, which is reserved for those with degrees from an approved Norwegian or foreign school of architecture. Nearly one architect in three is educated abroad, most in the UK and continental Europe. More than half of all architects are in private practice, one in four works in a private company of architects and one in five is employed by a public agency. Some 14 architectural firms are of international rank, and Norwegian architects won the international competitions for and designed two of the major building projects of the 1990s. *Snøhetta Arkitektur Landskap* of Oslo designed the new library at Alexandria, and *Niels Torp*, also of Oslo, designed the British Airways complex in London.

For further information on architects, contact The National Association of Norwegian Architects (*Norske arkitekters landsforbund*) ☎ 23332500, 🖷 23332501, ✉ Josefines gt 34, 0351 Oslo, ✉ nal@mnal.no, ◉ http://www.mnal.no with pages in Norwegian and in English.

Assessors (*Takstmenn*) are qualified persons who estimate the value of property. The valuation price (*verditakst*), as listed in an advertisement for a house or flat, usually is based on an assessor's appraisal. Other assessor estimates include a property condition report (*tilstandsrapport*), as of a used dwelling put up for sale, a damage appraisal (*skadetakst*) for insurance purposes and various estimates (*skjønn*) made whenever a dwelling is incomplete, as after a fire. You will need the services of an assessor in selling a property, and you may hire an assessor when bidding to buy a property, so as to have an opinion independent to that offered by the seller. Assessors charge for their services in various ways, most often by a fixed fee for the type of service and report provided. You can find an assessor by looking under

Taksering or under *Tilstands- og verdirapportering* in the Yellow Pages, or by contacting The Norwegian Association of Assessors (*Norges Takseringsforbund*) ☎ 22087600, 🖷 22572666, ✉ PO Box 6635 Etterstad, 0607 Oslo, ✉ admin@ntf.no, ◉ http://www.ntf.no with a search locator of all member assessors in the country, by county, company name, surname and type of assessment.

Building and remodelling (*Bygging og ombygging*) must comply with the ☞ **Building codes**. Before you start and as you work, you may need ☞ **building information**. If you wish, you may do most of the work yourself, but you should engage properly-licensed professionals for electrical, plumbing and heating work (Trades chapter). Select ☞ **tradesmen** (Housekeeping chapter) with care; it's often best to hire local firms, as they usually rely on satisfied customers to stay in business. Keep all receipts, not only as proof of payment in case of claim or dispute, but also to show overall expenditure in case the local tax office assesses the value of your work to be more than you actually spent.

The Building code (*Byggeforskrift*) All building is governed by the Planning and Building Act (*Plan- og bygningsloven*). The actual construction of a building is governed by the building code, which comprises Technical Regulations (*Tekniske forskrifter*) that supplement and detail the implementation of the provisions of the Planning and Building Act. The current edition of the Technical Regulations were adopted on 22 January 1997 and include compliance to EEA agreements. The Planning and Building Act and the Technical Regulations are published as separate booklets and are sold by many book shops as well as by the National Office of Building Technology and Administration (*Statens Bygningstekniske Etat*) ☎ 22475600, 🖷 22475611, ✉ PO Box 8742 Youngstorget, 0028 Oslo, ✉ be@bebygg.no, ◉ http://www.bebygg.no with pages in Norwegian and in English. The web site also features access to files of the Act, the Technical Regulations and other relevant documents in Norwegian and in English, all of which may be read on screen and printed out or downloaded in HTML format.

Building information (*Bygge-informasjon*) If you build or remodel a house or flat, you will need information on building products, services and regulations. The easiest way to find it is to contact the leading information centres for building and construction information.

Norwegian Building Centre (*Norsk Byggtjeneste*) is an information clearinghouse for professionals and consumers. It maintains a building product database. It publishes building directory booklets and stocks ☞ **Building codes** and other documents in printed form and on CD-ROM. It is a member of the International Union of Building Centres (*Union Internationale des Centres du Bâtiment – UICB*) and exchanges information internationally, particularly between the Nordic countries. It works jointly with Nordic Building Exhibition (*Bygg Reis Deg*) annual trade fair and permanent exhibition centre at Haakon VIIs gt 5 in downtown Oslo, where its offices are located ✆ 23114400, ✉ 22834233, ✉ PO Box 1575 Vika, 0118 Oslo, ✉ firmapost@byggtjeneste.no, ✇ http://www.byggtjeneste.no with pages in Norwegian and in English.

BA-torget ("Building and construction market") is an online marketplace for the building and construction sector. It is a good starting point for information on products, practices, designs, regulations and the like. Most of the information is available free of charge, and comprehensive commercial services based on subscription and direct sales are available ✆ 22049500, ✉ 22049550, ✉ PO Box 2682 Solli, 0203 Oslo, ✉ firmapost@ba-torget.no, ✇ http://www.ba-torget.no/ba-torget with pages in Norwegian and summary pages in English.

Norwegian Building Research Institute (*Norges byggforskningsinstitutt – Byggforsk*) is the national R&D centre for building and construction. It serves central and local authorities, the construction industry and the public. Its head office and laboratory are in a research park in Oslo, close to other institutes concerned with building and construction ✆ 22965555, ✉ 22699438, ✉ PO Box 123 Blindern, 0314 Oslo, ✉ firmapost@byggforsk.no, ✇ http://www.byggforsk.no with pages in Norwegian and in English and links to all major organisations concerned with building and construction. The *Byggforsk* branch office in Trondheim is on the campus of the Norwegian Institute of Technology ✆ 73593390, ✉ 73593380, ✉ Høgskoleringen 7, 7034 Trondheim.

Cottages and cabins (*hytter*) abound. Many urban families have a seaside cottage or mountain cabin, called *hytte* in Norwegian, which is why a Norwegian may mention it in English as a "hut". But the *hytte* seldom is merely a hut. It may be a holiday home built for the purpose (*vanlig hytte*), a fully-equipped year-round house (*helårs bolig*), a farm house (*våningshus*), a farm outbuilding (*setre*), a rental cottage or cabin (*utleiehytte*), a campground cottage (*campinghytte*) or actually a simple hut or shelter (*koie*). There are more than 400,000 *hytter* in the country, nearly one for every ten residents. Accordingly, there is a business sector devoted to cottages and cabins. If you wish to buy or build a cottage or cabin, look under *Hytter* in the classified sections of newspapers or in the Yellow Pages. Firms specialising in cottage and cabin fittings are listed under *Hytteutstyr* in the Yellow Pages, and those providing caretaker and maintenance services are listed under *Hytteservice*. Some housing rental agencies and some hotels have groups of cottages or cabins (*hyttelandsbyer*) for rental; look under *Hytteutleie og -formidling* in the Yellow Pages. The leading domestic rental company is *Den norske Hytteformidling*, which lists more than two thousand cottages and cabins, publishes an illustrated catalogue ✆ 22356710, ✉ 22719413, ✉ PO Box 3404 Bjølsen, 0406 Oslo, ✇ http://www.hytte.com with pages in Norwegian, in English and in German. The company also has an office in Bergen. *DanCenter*, a Danish company, is the largest rental agent in Scandinavia, has a catalogue offering cottages and cabins in Denmark, Norway and Sweden ✆ 22411935, ✉ 22411939, ✉ Nedre Slottsgt. 13, 0157 Oslo, ✇ http://www.dancenter.com with pages in Danish, English, German, Norwegian and Swedish. DanCentre also has offices in Balestrand, Fåvang and Kristiansand.

Estate agents (*Eiendomsmeglere*) are professional people who deal with the sale of buildings, dwellings and land. For services in connection with a sale, an estate agent will charge the seller 1.5% to 2.5% of the sale price. The buyer must pay the 2.5% ☞ **document fee** (Taxes, Duties, Excise chapter). Most dwellings are now sold by estate agents, particularly as transactions are complex and many regulations must be observed. Consequently, most of the ☞ **housing advertisements** in newspapers are inserted by estate agents, many of whom also maintain Internet web sites of properties for sale. You can locate estate agents by reading the housing advertisements, by looking under *Eiendomsmegling* in the Yellow Pages or by contacting The Norwegian Association of Real Estate Agents (*Norges eiendomsmeglerforbund*) ✆ 22542080, ✉ 22553106, ✉ Inkognitogt. 12, 0258 Oslo, ✉ firmapost@nef.no, ⊕ http://nwttvik.no/naeringsparken/nef with pages in Norwegian, in English and in German and with an interactive map locator to find estate agents throughout the country.

Farms (*Gårdsbruk*) As in other countries from the 1960s on, rural youth has migrated to the cities. So farms stand unworked and vacant all over the country. However, with modern communications and facilities, even the most remote farms are no longer isolated, and young people are again drawn to living on and working the land, often in combination with other trades. Yet finding vacant farms has not been easy, as their owners often have not taken steps to put them up for lease or sale. Three voluntary farming organisations have joined forces in the Let Youth Farm! (*Slipp oss til- ungdom inn i landbruket!*) countrywide project to solve the problem of making vacant farms available to young persons willing to work them:

- Norwegian Farmers and Smalholders Union (*Norsk bonde- og småbrukarlag*) ✆ 22424600, ✉ 22424601, ✉ Øvre Vollgt 9, 0158 Oslo, ✉ info@smabrukarlaget.no, ⊕ http://www.smabrukarlaget.no
- Norwegian Rural Youth (*Norges Bygdeungdomslag*) ✆ 22054800, f ✉ PO Box 9377 Grønland, 0135 Oslo, ✉ post@bygdeungdom.no, ⊕ http://www.bygdeungdom.no
- Nature and Youth (*Natur og ungdom*) ✆ 22364218, ✉ 22204594, ✉ Torggt 34, 0183 Oslo, ✉ natung@online.no, ⊕ http://www.ngo.grinda.no/ngo/nu with pages in Norwegian and in English.

Their efforts are supported in part by the Ministry of Local Government and Regional Development (*Kommunal- og regionaldepartementet – KRD*). The Let Youth Farm! project has an on-line Meeting Place (*Møteplassen*), with general information, advice on how to start farming, and a countrywide listing of available farms and farmhouses, based on data sup-

plied by rural municipalities. So if you are looking for a farm in Norway, look first under the region of your choice in the Meeting Place web site ⊕ http://www.gardsbruk.no. The requirements for buying or leasing a farm are simply that you must live on and work it. Any farm or farmhouse with more than five decares (*mål*) of land – and most are larger than that – cannot be used as a holiday or second home.

The Homeowners' Association (*Huseiernes Landsforbund*) is a national society dedicated to furthering the local and national interests of sole or part owners of houses and business properties. It does this through providing legal, technical and financial advice to its members as well as by politically lobbying for their interests at the local and national levels. It publishes a bimonthly membership magazine, *Hus & Bolig* ("House & Home") which regularly spotlights dishonesty in the building trades as well as injustices imposed by rules and regulations, in addition to its regular articles on refurbishing, rebuilding, building and property transactions. It arranges member discounts on goods and services including electricity, heating oil, insurance, loans, petrol, security services and telecommunications. Its head office is in Oslo, and it has 21 district organisations (*disktriktsorganisasjoner*) throughout the country, with a contact person in each county (*fylkeskontakt*). Its membership fees are reasonable and for many members less than savings realised through its discount arrangements. For further details, contact the head office ✆ 22477500, ✉ 22411990, ✉ Fred Olsensgate 5, 0152 Oslo, ✉ post@huseierhl.no, ⊕ http://www.huseierhl.no

Housing advertisements (*Boligannonser*) Many types of housing are available, and there are listings in the classified advertising pages of newspapers of dwellings for sale (*Eiendomer* or *Eiendoms-markedet*) or rent (*Boligmarked, Bolig tilbys,* or *Boliger til leie*). Property transactions (*eiendomsoverdragelser*) of houses bought and sold usually are listed in a separate column. Most dwellings are described in terms of their total area in square metres (*kvadrattmeter*), number of stories (*etasjer*), number and type of rooms (*rom*) and area of plot. The numbering of floors of a multi-storey building begins with one at ground level. The area of the plot on which a house stands usually is in *mål*, now the everyday term for the decare (1,000 square metres). However, an older *mål*, equal to 984.34 square metres, is still in use, ☞ **measures** (Measurements and Standards chapter). So in advertisements or leaflets issued by ☞ **estate agents**, a *to mål tomt* (two-*mål* plot) can mean 1,968.7 or 2,000 square metres. Consequently, when negotiating purchase, always ask for specification in square metres. The types of dwelling and the principal terms used in describing them in newspaper advertisements are, in alphabetical order in Norwegian (common abbreviations in parentheses):

andel share, usually of ownership or expenses
andelsleilighet co-operative flat
areal area (usually in square metres)
beliggenhet location
blokk block
bolig dwelling
boligareal (BOA) living area
boligtomt plot, usually approved for building a house
borettslag housing cooperative
bruttoareal (BTA) gross area
bygslet leasehold
eiendom property
eierleilighet freehold flat
enebolig one-family house
eneboliger i kjede connected one-family houses
etasje storey
felles gjeld (f.gj.) share of building mortgage, usually for a flat
felles utgifter (f.utg.) share of building running expenses, usually for a flat
feriehus holiday house
finanseringsbistand financing available
fritidsbolig holiday home
frittliggende enebolig detached house
generasjonsbolig multi-generation dwelling
horisontaldelt tomannsbolig house with two dwelling units on separate floors
hybel room, bedsit
hytte cottage, cabin
hybelleilighet bedsit, one-room flat, pied-à-terre
leiegård block of flats
leilighet flat, apartment
lånetakst (LT) loan value
modernisert modernised
obligasjonsleilighet contract leasehold flat
offentlig gebyr (off.geb.) public fees
oppført built

prisantydning (prisant.) estimated price
rekkehus terraced house, undetached house, town house
rom room
selveier freehold
strandlinje private beach
tomannsbolig duplex house
tomannsbolig, halvpart maisonette
tomt lot, plot
utsikt view
vertikaltdeltbolig semi-detached house
verditakst (VT) valuation price
visning showing

Housing cooperatives (*Boligbyggelag*) There are 102 housing cooperatives which together have 600,000 members, provide more than 240,000 dwellings and each year account for some 21,000 sales of new and older dwellings, about a fourth of the property transactions in the country. The largest housing cooperatives are in Oslo: *OBOS* with 140,000 members and *USBL* for young people, with 20,000 members.

The basic principle of the housing cooperatives is similar to that of ☞ **co-operative shops** (Shopping chapter): members holding shares (*andeler*) are entitled to buy flats or houses built or managed by the cooperative. As a shareholder, you are liable for part of the cooperative's joint mortgage (*fellesgjeld*). Consequently, the base price of a cooperative flat or house is the sum of the shares you hold and your part of the joint mortgage. Part of the rent you pay goes to cover interest and repayment of the joint mortgage and the rest covers maintenance, insurance and other common expenses. If you wish, you may sell your share and move out. Many cooperatives have rules that grant members priority in buying (*forkjøpsrett*), but sales are on the open market. Depending on the rules of the individual cooperative, you may sub-let (*framleie*) your flat or house or one or more rooms in it.

You can find housing cooperatives listed under *Boligbyggelag* in the Yellow Pages. For further information on housing cooperatives countrywide, contact the Norwegian Federation of Co-operative Housing Associations (*Norske Boligbyggelags Landsforbund*) ☎ 22403850, 📠 22403920, ✉ PO Box 452 Sentrum, 0104 Oslo, 🖰 http://boligsamvirket.no and ask for its brochures, two of which are in English. For information on housing cooperatives throughout Europe, contact the European Liaison Committee for Social Housing (*Comité Européen de coordination de l'habitat social – CECODHAS*) ✆ +31 356268333, 🖷 +31 356268433, ✉ PO Box 611, 1200 AP Hilversum, Netherlands, ⊕ http://www.cecodhas.org with pages in English, in French and in German.

Housing, owning or renting (*Bolig, eie eller leie*) Fully 86 of 100 households own their homes, whilst 14 of 100 live in private rentals. In comparison with other countries, renting is less common than in Germany, where some 40% of households are renters, but more common than in Britain (8%). Tradition is one cause of the trend. Taxation is another, as owner-occupiers may deduct interest on home ☞ **mortgages** (Banking, Finance, Insurance chapter). Nonetheless, there are more than 380,000 rental homes in the country, most in the cities where population mobility is highest. You can find housing for sale and for rental by contacting ☞ **estate agents** or by reading ☞ **housing advertisements.**

Most rental dwellings (*utleieboliger*) are flats, usually in blocks but sometimes in private houses. They may be furnished (*møblert*) or unfurnished (*ubmøblert*). Some municipalities have rentals (*boliger for utleie*), usually for shorter periods of time or for young people, as under the ☞ **Ungbo** programme. The most common rental accommodation is a bedsit or single room (*hybel*), usually with access to a kitchen and bath in a private home, or in a communal living (*kollektiv*) flat. A slightly larger version, a one-room flat with its own kitchen and bath (*hybelleilighet*) will be located in a block of similar flats, as in a student residence complex (*studentboliger*). Hotels and boarding houses (*pensjonat, hospits*) have rooms for rent, usually on a nightly or weekly basis.

There are four major types of privately-owned dwellings:

- flats or houses in ☞ **housing co-operatives** in which residents own shares.
- shareholding flats (*aksjeleligheter*) in which owner-tenants hold shares in a block and are jointly responsible for its mortgage. In practice, shareholding flats are very much like those in housing co-operatives. They are most common in older

buildings, and may be sold freely on the open market.
- bonded flats (*obligasjonsleiligheter*) in which tenants hold bonds issued by the owner of a block of flats. The contracts involved vary and are complex, so you should consult a lawyer or ☞ **free legal aid** (Law, Lawyers, Courts chapter) before signing a contract.
- privately-owned dwellings (*selveierboliger*) are owned by their occupants. Most one-family houses (*enebolig*) are owned outright, whilst most flats (*leilighet*), terraced houses (*rekkehus*) and the like will also involve an ownership association (*sameie*) and incur joint expenses (*fellesutgifter*), such as for building cleaning and maintenance of a block of flats.

When you consider buying a property, you should check in the property register (*grunnboka*) kept by the ☞ **city recorder or district recorder** (Registrations, Rights, Licences chapter) to see if there is a mortgage on it. In evaluating its overall price, allow an additional 2.5% to cover the ☞ **Document duty** (Taxes, Duties, Excise chapter). Almost all houses and flats are sold by competitive bidding among buyers. Even if a new house or flat is advertised at a fixed price, you may enter a bid for it. Usually a deadline date is set for bids. The seller may assess a bid not only by its total amount, but also on the strength of its proposal for financing purchase and on other factors. For instance, an elderly couple who built and lived in a house for many years may prefer a buyer to their liking. If the seller is not satisfied with any of the bids received, there may be another round of bidding, in which those who have submitted bids will be invited to submit anew. ☞ **Dine Penger** (Media and Information chapter) summarises its advice for bidding in ten rules.

1. Find the price range. The asking price is seldom the same as the final selling price, so you should know worth before you bid.
2. Bid on one only. Refrain from simultaneous bidding on two or more houses or flats, as bids are binding. If more than one of your bids is accepted, you may be in financial trouble.
3. Assess the seller. The reasons for selling may be as vital as your reasons for buying.
4. Don't believe all estate agent statements. Remember, the estate agent is employed by the seller and is interested in finishing a sale so as to

get on to the next.

5. Set your own limit. Resist the temptation to go over your self-set limit, even by "just a little". Those whom you bid against may also go up "just a little", which may make it a lot.

6. There's always another dream house or flat. You may live in a place for 40 years, so you need not be hasty: if you lose out in a bid round, there always will be another chance.

7. State technical conditions only. Arrange financing before you bid, but state your technical conditions, such as requiring that a house put up for sale "as is" (*som besiktiget*) conform to the building codes, as required by *Avhendingsloven*.

8. Start low. Once you have bid, you have shown interest, and will be invited to bid again if the price goes up.

9. Have a margin. Never bid at your limit, as almost all sales involve more than one round of bidding. You should be able to afford to go up slightly for the second round.

10. State a deadline. Adjust the deadline to the seller (rule 3), but make it short enough to convince the seller that you are serious.

The relatively new law on transfers of properties (*Avhendingsloven*), in force since 1 January 1993, sets forth specific requirements for property transactions. Its principal requirements are:

- Sales agreements should be in writing.
- A sales agreement should describe the property and its transfer.
- The property should meet building codes and other requirements, unless otherwise agreed.
- The seller is obliged to disclose all vital facts concerning the property (*opplysningsplikt*).
- Lack of disclosure of vital facts is regarded as a defect (*mangel*).
- The buyer should always examine the property before signing an agreement.
- The buyer may enter claims against delays and defects (*forsinkelser og mangler*) up to five years after purchase.
- Both the buyer and the seller may hold back payment, cancel contract or demand compensation (*erstatning*) if the other party breaks the contract (*avtalebrudd*).

The law requires greater responsibility of the seller than previously was the case. Honest sellers will fulfil their obligations, in part by engaging ☞ **asses-sors** to compile a property condition report (*tilstandsrapport*) and by buying property transfer insurance (*eierskifteforsikring*) to cover any claims that may arise under the five-year rule.

In considering a new or recently-built house or flat, ask to see its certificate of completion (*ferdigattest*) issued by the municipal building control (*bygninsetaten*) to ensure that no legally required works are outstanding. However, in considering an older dwelling, read any certificate put forth, as it applies at the date of completion, not thereafter. Even a recently dated certificate of completion is no guarantee of current worth. It may refer only to improvements required of an owner who neglected to obtain a certificate of completion when a house was built, but years later made the improvements and requested the certificate in order to sell the house.

For complete information on the various aspects of housing, see the specialised publications and view the web sites on it:

- The ☞ **Homeowners' Association** is concerned with all aspects of owning housing and consequently both publishes and advises on housing matters.
- The ☞ **Directorate of Immigration** (Government and Social Services chapter) free 44-page brochure on Housing published December 1994, English edition ISBN 82-427-0272-1, Norwegian edition ISBN 82-427-0262-4, available at most offices dealing with new residents.
- ☞ **Dine Penger** (Media and Information chapter) often publishes articles on housing and has theme sectors on its web site for housing (*bolig*), insurance (*forsikring*) and borrowing (*lån*)
  ⊕ http://www.dinepenger.no
- The ☞ **Consumer Council** (Human Rights, Consumer Rights chapter) has a magazine, *Forbrukerrapporten*, with frequent articles on housing, as well as the *Fakta-blad* series of fact sheets, many of which pertain to housing and are available printed or on-line
  ⊕ http://www.forbrukerradet.no/faktablad

Ungbo, literally meaning "Youth abode", is a service that offers affordable housing to young people in cities in Denmark, Norway and Sweden. It is supported by municipalities, often jointly with ☞ **housing co-operatives**, and differs from other housing services in two ways. First, there are age limits, so only people in their late teens to mid twenties may live in Ungbo flats. Second, Ungbo flats are for rental or short-term co-operative ownership only, whilst otherwise purchase prevails in Scandinavia. In Norway, Ungbo housing is available in Bodø, Oslo and Trondheim and has been proposed elsewhere.

Bodø: Ungbo is a joint undertaking by the Bodø Housing Cooperative (*Bodø Boligbyggelag – BBL*) and the municipality of Bodø. It has 20 two-room flats at Skeidhaugen in the northern part of the city, for ownership through cooperative memberhip for up to five years, for persons less than 30 years old ✆ 75506700, ✉ 75506701, ✉ Sjøgt. 10, 8006 Bodø, ✉ bbl@bblnett.no,
✉ http:/www.boligsamvirket.no/bodo/

Oslo: Ungbo is part of the Municipal Housing and Property Service (*Bolig- og eiendomsetaten*). It houses some 500 young persons, 17 to 23 years old, in rental flats throughout the city. Each flat has four to six private rooms (*hybel*) which share a common living space, kitchen and bath. Some flats primarily are reserved for young families or applicants with special needs. Many flats are in older buildings remodelled by Ungbo. Even the unemployed may apply, as they can work as apprentices in the *APRO* remodelling programme. Ungbo publishes brochures and maintains a public service office at Trondheimsveien 2 in downtown Oslo ✆ 22082870, ✉ 22082871, ✉ PO Box 4753 Sofienberg, 0506 Oslo.

Trondheim: Ungbo is a service of the Municipal Housing Service and Benefit Office (*Boligformidling og bostøtte*) and offers private rooms, most in the central part of the city ✆ 72546133, ✉ 72546614, ✉ Holtermannsv. 1, 7462 Trondheim.

Human rights, consumer rights (*Menneske-rettig-heter, forbruker-rettigheter*)

The Consumer Council (*Forbrukerrådet*) is an organisation dedicated to protecting the interests of all consumers in the country. Its major activities include influencing legislation to benefit consumers, providing information to the public and assisting individuals in filing complaints. It also makes its findings public. For instance, in 1998 the Consumer Council received nearly 150,000 complaints from consumers. Of these, the most frequent, more than 16,000 in all, concerned cars and other motor vehicles, followed by more than 12,000 concerning electrical appliances and more than 12,000 concerning builders and houses. If you believe that you have been misled, deceived or poorly served in any goods or services that you have bought or contracted for, you should, of course, first complain to the supplier of shop involved. If you are not satisfied with the result, you may file a complaint with the Consumer Council, which maintains offices in all 19 counties, principally for that purpose. The Council publishes a no-advertising consumer magazine, *Forbruker-rapporten* ("Consumer Reports"), fact sheets (*Faktablad*) and various booklets and consumer aids, such as the popular family accounts book (*Regnskapsboka*) sold by stationers throughout the country. An overview booklet, "The Consumer Council of Norway", ISBN 82-7166-120-5 is available in English, but otherwise publications are in Norwegian. The Consumer Council is a member of Consumers International (CI), which works for global consumer rights and has member organisations round the world. For further details, contact the nearest *Forbrukerrådet* county office listed in the Pink Pages for Alta, Arendal, Bergen, Bodø, Drammen, Førde, Gjøvik, Hamar, Harstad, Kristiansand, Molde, Oslo, Sarpsborg, Skien, Stavanger, Steinkjer, Tønsberg, Tromsø or Trondheim, or view the Internet web site ☉ http://www.forbrukerradet.no with numerous national and international links. For global consumer organisation information, contact Consumers International ☎ +44 171 2266663, ✆ +44 171 3540607, ✉ 24 Highbury Crescent, London N5 1RX, UK, ✉ consint@consint.org,

☉ http://www.consumersinternational.org with pages in English and in French.

The Consumer Ombudsman (*Forbrukerombudet*) is an independent governmental agency responsible for ensuring adherence to the Marketing Control Act (*Lov om kontroll med markedsføring*) and compliance with regulations on advertising in broadcasting. It also oversees standard contracts (*standardkontrakter*) enforces the regulations on the fiber content and care marking of textiles (*fiber- og vedlikeholdsmerking av tekstiler*). Together with the Marketing Council (*Markedsrådet*), it acts as the public watchdog on fair marketing practices which, for the consumer, are principally:

- Claims made in advertising must be substantiated.
- Offensive or derogatory exploitation of one sex, male or female, is prohibited in advertising.
- TV advertising aimed at children is prohibited.

The Consumer Ombudsman and the Marketing Council can act together to initiate prosecution of offenders. In this respect, the Consumer Ombudsman differs from the ☞ **Consumer Council**, which acts in the interests of consumers but has no formal judicial powers. In practice, most complaints concerning goods and services are made to the Consumer Council. However, if you have a complaint specific to advertising, you may send it either to the Consumer Council, which will forward it to the Consumer Ombudsman, or you may send it directly to the Ombudsman. For further information, contact the head office near Oslo ☎ 67599600, ✆ 67582061, ✉ PO Box 8173 Dep, 0034 Oslo, ☉ http://www.forbrukerombudet.no with pages in Norwegian and in English.

Consumer rights (*Forbrukerrettigheter*) are ensured by three laws:

The Sale of Goods Act (*Kjøpsloven*) principally ensures that the buyer has the right to expect that an item fulfils the claims made for it, as by a salesperson, in advertising or on packaging, without defects or shortcomings (*feil og mangler*). Moreover, the law covers buyer rights to return, replacement, complaint, repair, refund, discount and other aspects of purchase.

The Act relating to a cooling-off period (*Angrefristloven*) applies to agreements for purchase or hire which are entered outside of ordinary shops, such as with travelling salesmen, at exhibitions, by mail order and by telemarketing initiated by the seller. Before or at delivery, the seller is obliged to give the buyer a cooling-off period (*angrefrist*) form that permits annulling an agreement or cancelling purchase.

The Act relating to the sale of goods on credit (*Kredittkjøpsloven*) applies to all goods, except property, that are bought on credit, as with a credit card or as financed by a loan from the seller. Its principal provisions ensure that the buyer be informed of the total credit costs in advance of purchase, that the buyer can refuse to pay for defective goods and that the buyer can demand reduction of credit costs when payments are made before due dates.

These laws not only ensure consumer rights. Many major stores have found that they promote business, as pleased customers usually come back. Most notably, the IKEA home furnishings megastores offer exchange or full refund for any new, full-price, unused goods returned within 30 days.

For more information on these laws, or if you believe that you have been deceived in buying, contact the ☞ **Consumer council**, which has published simplified pamphlets on the laws and advises consumers.

Gender equality (*Likestilling*) means that women and men shall have equal rights in all sectors of society. It is a widespread and recognised principle, promoted by the United Nations, the OECD and other national and international organisations. In Norway, gender equality is specified by the Act on Gender Equality, which is administered by the Ministry of Children and Family Affairs (*Barne og Familiedeparatementet – BFD*), principally through the Gender Equality Ombudsman and the Competence Centre for Gender Equality. The Unions and various NGOs are also involved.

The Act on Gender Equality (*Likestillingsloven*) entered into force in 1979. Initially, its intent was to prevent the discrimination of women in workplaces, so it covered matters such as equal pay and lack of bias in hiring. It was also given a broader scope, to promote equality between the sexes throughout all sectors of society. It is available in both condensed and complete versions, in Norwegian, English and other languages, from the organisations described below, as well as from various municipal social services offices throughout the country.

The Gender Equality Ombudsman (*Likestillingsombudet*) is responsible for interpreting and enforcing the Act on Gender Equality and is empowered to receive and act upon complaints of violations of it. Decisions made by the Ombudsman or by any other authority dealing with gender equality may be brought before the Gender Equality Board of Appeals (*Klagenemda for likestilling*). The services of the Ombudsman include providing a selection of publications in Norwegian, English and other languages, and keeping national and international reference materials at the head office in Oslo ✆ 22242561, ℻ 22249521, ✉ PO Box 8036 Dep, 0030 Oslo.

The Competence Centre for Gender Equality (*Kompetansesenter for likestilling*) is an independent agency that offers guidance and acts as a resource centre for public agencies and private organisations, as well as the general public. It monitors gender equality practices and publishes guidelines and other materials for public and private use. It is located in Oslo ✆ 22242571, ℻ 22249521, ✉ PO Box 8036 Dep, 0030 Oslo, ✉ postmottak@likestilling.no

The ☞ **Unions** (Business and Work chapter) promote gender equality, principally through supporting gender equality ombudsmen at larger workplaces and through processing complaints of sexual discrimination in employment and wages.

The Nordic institute for Women's Studies and Gender Research (*Nordisk institutt for kvinne- og kjønnsforskning*) at the University of Oslo is affiliated with the Nordic Council of Ministers. It serves as a platform for co-operation in women's studies and gender research in the Nordic countries, and promotes relevant measures and research ✆ 22858921, ℻ 22858950, ✉ PO Box 1156 Blindern, 0317 Oslo, ✉ nikk@nikk.no, ◉ http://www.org.no/www-other/nikk with pages in Norwegian and in English and "Women on the Web" links to other web sites.

The Forum for Women and Development (*Forum for Kvinner og Utviklingspørsmål – FOKUS*) co-ordinates the efforts of some 50 women's organisations in development and other international activities ✆ 22209570, ℻ 22209569, ✉ Storgt. 33, 0184 Oslo, ✉ fokuskvinner@online.no, ◉ http://www.fokuskvinner.no with pages in Norwegian and in English.

Human rights (*Menneskerettigheter*) are neither an attitude or a vague ideal. Human rights are a set of commitments, undertaken by many nations, which define norms and standards concerning the rights of individuals. The Norwegian government has undertaken the obligation of fulfilling and respecting those rights. That obligation comprises many legally-binding instruments, including conventions, under the auspices of the United Nations (UN), the Council of Europe and the International Labour Organisation (ILO). It is fulfilled in part by an openness that has made human rights part of free public debate. For instance, in the mid 1990s, inspections by international committees found some human rights abuses in the country, most notably of prisoners in detention, ☞ **torture**. The response of the government was to publish the committee report and its response to the report, and to initiate measures to correct the matters criticised. Moreover, in 1998 the Minister of International Development and Human Rights (*Utviklings- og menneskerettighetsminister*) initiated and released "Human Rights 1998", the first annual report and a comprehensive 120-page, A4-format booklet that covers both national and international issues and is published for free distribution by the Ministry of Foreign Affairs (*Utenriksdepasrtementet*) in Norwegian, English (publication E-595B, ISBN 82-7177-534-0). It also includes a list of the names, addresses and telecoms numbers for more than 40 organisations in the country that are concerned with human rights. Norway is a State party (signing government) of the key United Nations (UN), Council of Europe (CoE) and International Labour Organisation (ILO) conventions on human rights. Norway has long been active internationally in supporting human rights and peaceful negotiation. The ☞ **Norwegian Nobel Committee** (Non-government Organisations chapter) is responsible for selecting the laureate for the annual Nobel Peace Prize. The ☞ **Rafto Prize** (Character, Customs and Country chapter) is awarded each year for human rights achievement. The Norwegian Institute of Human Rights (*Institutt for menneskerettigheter*) was established in 1987 and now has a staff of 40, of which half are engaged in research. The Institute publishes a journal, *Mennesker og rettigheter* ("People and rights") in co-operation with several human rights organisations in the Nordic countries. It also publishes Human Rights Reports and Working Papers, arranges seminars and maintains a library with the largest collection of human rights literature in the country, open to the public. For further details, see the annual "Human Rights" report or contact the Institute of Human Rights ✆ 22842001, ⊠ 22842002, ✉ Universitetsgt. 22-24, 0162 Oslo, ✉ admin@nihr.uio.no, ⊕ http://www.humanrights.uio.no

Personal and confidential data security (*Sikring av personlig og konfidensiell informasjon*) is ensured by the Act on Personal Data Registers (*Personregisterloven*) of 1978. A personal data register is a collection of information on persons that is stored manually or electronically in a way that permit easy access to its contents. The Act applies throughout the public and private sectors and to all individual persons (*personer*) as well as to juristic persons (*juridisk personer*). Typical registers are those in which data is sorted by name. A register sorted by car number plates or telephone numbers also is regarded as a personal data register because it permits identification. The Data Inspectorate (*Datatilsynet*) is responsible for administering and enforcing the Act on Personal Data Registers. It does this principally through requiring a licence (*konsesjon*) before any personal data register can be set up and by monitoring compliance to licences of existing registers. The requirements for a licence cover all aspects of a register, including its maintenance, content and use, as well as who has access to its contents. A licence is also required for any manual register of sensitive personal data, such as the details of race, origin, political views, religious beliefs, criminal record, health, abuse of drugs or alcohol, sex life or family affairs. Moreover, the Data Inspectorate must approve any cross-linking of personal data registers. For further details, contact the Data Inspectorate ✆ 22396900, ⊠ 22422350, ✉ PO Box 8177 Dep, 0034 Oslo, ✉ postkasse@dtatilsynet.no, ⊕ http://www.datatilsynet.no with pages in Norwegian and in English.

Privacy (*Privatliv*) under law is not directly specified but is ensured in numerous ways. Article 110c of the ☞ **Constitution** (Government and Social Services chapter) puts forth a general requirement that the State respect human rights. The Constitution also has other articles relating to the rights of the individual, including the rule of law, freedom of expression, the right to own property and the freedom of religion and political belief. Moreover, Norway is a signatory of principal agreements concerning ☞ **human rights**, including the landmark European Convention for the Protection of Human Rights and Fundamental Freedoms, which entered into force in 1953 and was last amended in 1990. Article 8 of that Convention reads:

- Everyone has the right to respect for his private and family life, his home and his correspondence.
- There shall be no interference by a public authority with the exercise of this right except such as is in accordance with the law and is necessary in a democratic society in the interests of national security, public safety or the economic well-being of the country, for the prevention of disorder or crime, for the protection of health or morals, or for the protection of the rights and freedoms of others.

The prevailing legal opinion holds that Article 8 is binding in matters of personal privacy, as violation of it can be brought before the European Court of Human Rights in Strasbourg, France. Two laws ensure individuals the right of inspection (*innsynsrett*) of public documents concerning themselves: The Public Administration Act (*Forvaltningsloven*) of 1967 and the Act on Public Access to Documents in (Public) Administration (*Offentlighetsloven*) of 1970. Together these laws ensure that you have the right to see any record on yourself kept by any public agency.

Torture (*Tortur*) The European Committee for the Prevention of Torture (CPT) visited Norway in 1993 and in 1997 and concluded that there is little likelihood of a person detained by the police being physically ill-treated. However, the CPT criticised three aspects of police detention: the prolonged remanding in custody (*varetektsfengsling*) of suspects and prisoners awaiting further investigation or trial; the use of incommunicado solitary confinement with a ban on mail and visits (*brev og besøksforbud*) as a means of coercion; and the confinement to security cells (*glattceller*) for periods of more than a few hours. The CPT is a Council of Europe committee and acts under the European Convention for the Prevention of Torture and Inhuman or Degrading Treatment or Punishment signed in September 1987 and put in force in 1989. The first draft of that Convention was put forth by the Association for the Prevention of Torture (APT), a non-government organisation (NGO) founded in 1977 in Geneva, Switzerland. The APT now has members in more than 30 countries round the world and maintains close ties with international and national organisations. The governments of Denmark, Norway, Sweden and Switzerland together support slightly less than a third of the APT budget, whilst the remaining two-thirds are met by membership fees and private contributions. For further information, contact the CPT or the APT:

- The Human Rights Information Centre, Council of Europe ✆ +33 3 888412024, ☏ +33 3 88412704, ✉ F-67075 Strasbourg Cedex, France, ✉ HumanRights.Info@coe.fr, ⊜ http://www.cpt.coe.fr with pages in English and in French.
- The Association for the Prevention of Torture ✆ +41 22 7342088, ☏ +41 22 7345649, ✉ PO Box 2267, CH-1211 Geneva 2, Switzerland, ✉ apt@apt.ch, ⊜ http://www.apt.ch with pages in English.

Information technology (Informasjonsteknologi)

Computers (*Regnemaskiner*) are commonplace. According to figures compiled by the European Information Technology Observatory (EITO), the total market (1999) for desktop computers (*bordmaskiner*) and portables (*bærbare maskiner*) corresponds to more than one resident in ten buying a computer each year. The major international brands, Compaq, Dell and IBM, account for 43% of all sales. Some 25% of all computers sold are made in Norway, by seven companies – AR Data (Molde), Cinet (Oslo), Micronet (Oslo), Mips (Bergen), PS Data (Grimstad), REC (Drammen) and Viking Data (Arendal) – which offer the advantages of personal service and closeness to users. One of them, Cinet, has responded to Norwegian needs by producing and now exporting a moisture and water-resistant maritime model for use on board ships.

Computer programs (*Programvare*) for PCs and Macs are sold in either their original language, usually English, and in Norwegian translation. New computers sold with operating systems and other programs installed almost always have the Norwegian versions. For instance, the Windows98 operating system and the Internet Explorer browser featured in an advertised sale on PCs will be the Norwegian versions, unless otherwise stated. Although the multilingual dictionary for computers and information technology is in its sixth edition and similar dictionaries for other technical fields are also well established, ☞ **Useful books** chapter, the Norwegian terms in translated programs may vary. Moreover, program conflicts may arise if you attempt to install the original English version of an application program on a computer with a Norwegian version operating system. However, most accessory programs compiled in Norway, such as Norwegian encyclopaedias, dictionaries and spell checkers, will work with either English or Norwegian versions of operating systems. Consequently, unless you are familiar with and wish to use Norwegian terminology onscreen, you may prefer the English versions of operating systems and application programs. If so, be sure to specify English when buying a program or a computer with a program installed. Most computer and software importers and wholesalers stock the original English as well as the translated Norwegian versions of programs, though general consumer electronics shops may stock only the Norwegian versions. So computers with English version programs are almost always available, sometimes at a surcharge or a delay in delivery. Software program house (*programvarehus*) shops usually sell both the original US or UK English versions as well as the Norwegian versions of programs. The English versions of new programs, particularly of upgrades, are usually available first, well before Norwegian translations are made. Some high-volume entertainment products, such as computer games, are sold only in their original language, which in most cases is English.

The European Computer Driving Licence – ECDL (*Datakortet*) is an internationally recognised standard of information technology proficiency. It is available to applicants who pass one theoretical and six practical tests, as given at authorised test centres throughout Europe. The ECDL is managed by the ECDL Foundation, which is supported by the EU Commission and has its head office in Dublin, Ireland ☻ http://www.cs.tcd.ie/ECDL with pages in English and links to other sites. The ECDL Foundation was established by the Council of European Professional Informatics Societies (CEPIS) ☻ http://cepis.org with pages in English and links to its member societies. The Norwegian Data Association (*Den Norske Dataforening*) ☻ http://www.dnd.no is responsible for ECDL in Norway, through *Datakortet* ☻ http://www.datakort.no

Internet (*Internett*) When compared to a population, the number of Internet hosts, which are the computers contacted when you key in a web-site address, is a fair indication of the amount of "cyberspace" activity of a country. In 1998, Finland was first among the wired countries of the world, and Norway was second, with one Internet host for every 16 residents, a density just slightly higher than in third-place USA. In 1999, the number of hosts had gone up fastest in the USA, which then placed first, ahead of Finland and Norway. Though Finland and the USA have greater densities of hosts, Norwegians are believed to be the world's leading per-capita users of the Internet. Though the Norwegian figure of 23.1% of all households connected is second to the 24.5% figure for Finland, more homes in Norway have fast (64 kbit/s) ☞ **ISDN** (Telecommunications and Broadcasting chapter) connections, which prompts high usage. Calls to Internet servers now account for more than a quarter of all local telephone line traffic. In step with usage – and as can be seen from the number of Internet addresses identified by the ⊕ symbol in this book – public and private sector organisations have made an enormous amount of information available at Internet web sites, much of it not available elsewhere.

If you need an Internet connection, shop around, as the market is keenly competitive and many different packages of services and connections are offered. All ☞ **telecommunications companies** (Telecommunications and Broadcasting chapter) provide Internet connections, as do many other companies listed under *Datakommunikasjon og nettverk* in the Yellow Pages.

Keyboard (*Tastatur*) The Norwegian keyboard is the national version of the international keyboard for Latin-alphabet languages. It is the same as the English keyboard, except for the locations of punctuation marks and the addition of the last three letters of the Norwegian ☞ **alphabet** (Language chapter) to the right in the middle two rows. It is the standard keyboard delivered with all computers and typewriters. Some suppliers of equipment sold internationally may be able to supply keyboards for other languages.

If you have another PC keyboard and wish to type

The Norwegian keyboard conforms to Standard NS 4115, the national version of the international ISO 8884 standard. On computer keyboards, the function key row at the top, the cursor control and toggle keys to the right and the numerical keypad at the extreme right are the same as on all other Latin-alphabet language computer keyboards.

the Norwegian letters, just hold the ALT key and enter the codes for the letters on the numerical keypad at the right of the keyboard: ALT 145 æ, ALT 146 Æ, ALT 0248 ø, ALT 0216 Ø, ALT 134 å and ALT 143 Å.

Used computers (*Brukt datautstyr*) often are sold as are other used goods, by their owners, through advertisements in the classified sections of newspapers. Sometimes a shop that sells new computers also may sell trade-in computers, but as a rule most do not. There are a few used computer equipment shops, such as *Senter for brukt datautstyr* ("Centre for used computer equipment") in Oslo ✆ 22463688, 🖷 22463641, ✉ Pilestredet 53, 0350 Oslo. Some companies specialise in buying, refurbishing and selling used computers, principally to schools and to used computer shops throughout the country. The leading company in that sector is *Alternativ Data* ("Alternative Data"), founded in 1988 in Oslo. It now sells more than 25,000 computers a year, principally to schools. Some 40% of its sales are exported. The company does not sell directly to consumers, but can recommend reputable used computer shops. For further information, contact the main office in Oslo ✆ 22627300, 🖷 22627320, ✉ PO Box 45 Bogerud, 0261 Oslo, 📧 paal@alternativ-data.no, ⊕ http://www.alternativ-data.no

Web sites (*Web sider*) Many Internet web sites are mentioned in this book, each identified by the ⊕ symbol. Moreover, there are web sites that consist of listings of links to other web sites. The two best for Norway are:

The Norwegian start page

⊕ http://www.startsiden.no in Norwegian with listings of links to sites grouped into themes (*Teamer* A to Å in the Norwegian alphabet), leading domestic sites (*Gode norske*), leading foreign sites (*Gode utenl.*), data and Internett (*Data og nett*), national media (*Riksnyheter*), local newspapers (*Lokalaviser*), weather reports (*værvarsel*), current events (*Aktuelt nå*), news (*Nyheter*) and today's TV (*TV i dag*).

Governments on the web

⊕ http://www.gksoft.com/govt/ with pages in English and with listings of links to sites, in all comprising more than 13,000 entries from 220 countries and territories. The listing for Norway is ⊕ http://www.gksoft.com/govt/en/no.html

Language (Språk)

About Norwegian languages (*Språk*) The ☞ **Scandinavian languages** are Germanic. There are four: one each in Denmark and Sweden and two in Norway. There's some dispute on the nature of the differences between them. In the extreme, the linguistic barriers can cause misunderstandings, which may be why some inter-Scandinavian conferences are conducted in English. But in everyday use, the languages are mutually intelligible and often seem to be dialects of a common "Scandinavian language". Indeed, the crews of SAS aircraft and inter-Scandinavian ferries speak their native languages, both amongst themselves and in speaking with passengers and making PA system announcements. There might well be just one language in Scandinavia, had history not happened. There certainly would be just one in Norway. But that's not the way things are.

The two Norwegian languages are *Bokmål* ("Book Language) and *Nynorsk* ("New Norwegian"). The names imply a dichotomy but that is hardly so. In some respects, Nynorsk is older than Bokmål. Likewise, Bokmål is not restricted to literature and can be viewed as the more vernacular of the two. Few Norwegians other than linguists are concerned with these details. What counts is that Bokmål and Nynorsk are legal equals.

Public documents are published in either of the two languages, and sometimes in both, and common public forms, such as post-office receipts, have both Bokmål and Nynorsk texts. Municipalities are free to elect Bokmål or Nynorsk as a working language, or to remain neutral and accept both. Primary school districts may teach in Bokmål or Nynorsk as the major language. Authors are free to write and publish in either Bokmål or Nynorsk and some popular periodicals are now available in both languages.

Bokmål is the leader. According to official statistics, about 83% of the country's school children are taught in Bokmål versus 17% in Nynorsk. In higher education, Bokmål is even more dominant: college and university figures show that only 3% to 4% of all students declare a preference by requesting matriculation certificates in Nynorsk. These figures imply that Nynorsk is a minority language. If so, it is in an enviable position among the minority languages of Europe in being one of two officially equal to the majority language on a national basis (the other is Swedish in Finland). By regulation, a quarter of the radio and TV programmes sent by NRK (Norwegian Broadcasting) are in Nynorsk.

The most obvious differences between Bokmål and Nynorsk lie in the differing key words in their similar vocabularies. In keeping with official bilingualism, stamps are issued with the name of the country spelled either *Norge* in Bokmål or *Noreg* in Nynorsk. So to the dismay of some stamp collectors abroad, the ge/eg transposition is not a misprint. Milk is sold in cartons labelled either *melk* or *mjølk*, according to the local language preference. Likewise, the catalogues of wines and spirits in Vinmonopolet shops are in either Bokmål or Nynorsk. In many cases, the Bokmål word is closer to Danish and the Nynorsk word is closer to Swedish. The reason lies in history.

At the time of the Reformation in Europe, the Bible was translated from scholarly Latin or the original Hebrew and Greek into the everyday language of many countries. The translations not only made the Bible widely available but also set a norm for written language. Perhaps the most famous such translation was that into German, by Martin Luther, in 1522. An English translation followed, in 1525. In Scandinavia, the Swedish translation was first, in 1526, followed by the Icelandic in 1540 and the Danish in 1550. There was no similar translation of the time in Norway, a failing which was to ultimately result in the present language situation.

For 400 years, up to 1814, Norway was ruled by Denmark. Like it or not, Norwegians read and wrote Danish, then the only written language available to them. In schools, they were taught Danish as *modersmålet*, literally "mother tongue", hardly an apt name, given the circumstances. Four centuries is enough time for something to rub off. It did. The result was *Dano-Norwegian*.

After the dissolution of the union with Denmark, romantic patriotism flourished, and opinion leaders called for eradicating the stamp of Danish and for establishing a more Norwegian written language. There were two ways of going about that task. One was to Norweganise the existing written language. The other was to do what Norwegians had failed to do at the time of the Reformation: write down spoken Norwegian, preferably from areas so remote as to have escaped Danish influence. Both approaches were tried and both were successful.

In the late 19th century, the Norwegianised written language was officially named *Riksmål*, "National Language", to signify the steps that were being taken. The language amalgamated from remote rural dialects was named *Landsmål*, the "Language of the Land" to signify its origins. In 1885, the two were made official equals.

In 1929, the names of the two languages were officially changed to their present forms. *Riksmål* became *Bokmål*. That name was intended to reflect history and to eliminate the connotation of *Riks*, a prefix designation of singular national status, such as *Riksasrkivet*, The National Archives. *Landsmål* became *Nynorsk*, a change aimed both to identify the era when it was compiled from dialects and to remove the agrarian implication of *land*.

Today, Bokmål remains the leading language by far, and there are many speakers of it. Consequently, all the Norwegian words in this book are in Bokmål. Speakers of Nynorsk are few, as it is not a living verbal language, though some rural dialects approach it closely. In most cases, the Nynorsk you may hear in NRK radio and TV programmes is most likely a dialect. Pure Nynorsk remains a written language, a medley of the rural dialects from which it was drawn. Indeed, the motto of *Noregs Mållag*, the organisation that promotes Nynorsk, is *Tal dialekt, skriv nynorsk*, "Speak your dialect, write Nynorsk".

Few Norwegians are without an opinion on their languages. Debate on the subject is ubiquitous, and few walks of life are untouched. Even buying fish can be a linguistic adventure if you don't know that *aure* is Nynorsk for *ørret*, the word for trout in Bokmål.

Abbreviations (*forkortelser*) are commonplace in written Norwegian. The more frequently used abbreviations are listed in ☞ **Dictionaries,** and comprehensive lists are included in books of Abbreviations; (☞ **Useful books** chapter). Abbreviations classify in five broad groups:

Idiomatic expressions are frequently written using their initial letters: *S.u.* on an invitation is the abbreviation of *Svar utbes*, the equivalent of RSVP in English (from the French); *bl.a.* for *blant annet* is the equivalent of "among other things" in English; and *o.s.v.* for *og så videre* is the equivalent of "etc." in English.

Names of organisations are almost always abbreviated, particularly in the media. For Norwegian names, the practice is straightforward: the Norwegian Federation of Trade Unions, *Landsorganisasjonen* is abbreviated to LO. For international names, practice varies, depending on whether the name is used directly or has been translated: the Organization for Economic Cooperation and Development is generally used directly in its abbreviated form, OECD, which is the same as in English and other European languages, whilst the United Nations has been translated to *Forente Nasjoner*, so the abbreviation is *FN*, not UN.

Proper names, particularly men's middle names, are often abbreviated, such as *Chr.* for *Christian*, *Hj* for *Hjalmar* and *Th.* for *Thorvald*.

Suffixes and titles are abbreviated in ways similar to those of other languages. A son named after his father will suffix *d.y.* for *den yngre* ("the younger") to his name. The general title for a man is *Herr*, abbreviated *Hr.*, much as Mister is abbreviated Mr. in English. *Fru* for a married woman is not abbreviated, but *Frøken* for an unmarried woman is abbreviated *Frk.*, the opposite of the practice in English where Mrs. is an abbreviation but Miss is not. The title for a woman which does not divulge whether she is or is not married is *Fr.*, which is equivalent to but much older than Ms. in English. Academic and professional titles follow much the same rules as in English. A professor is abbreviated prof. and a medical doctor is abbreviated Dr. Likewise, suffixes indicating professional membership are used much as they are in English: *MNAL* after an architect's name means *Medlem av Norske Arkitekters landsforbund* ("Member of the Norwegian Association of Architects").

Units are abbreviated following the guidelines of the International Organization for Standardization (ISO): the metre is abbreviated m, the litre l and so on.

Alphabet (*alfabet*) The Norwegian alphabet has 29 letters. The first 26 are the same as in the English alphabet, and the last three are vowels, æ, ø and å. So the Norwegian equivalent of "A to Z" is *A til Å*, as used in telephone directories. dictionaries and other alphabetical listings. These three letters are to the right on the Norwegian keyboard. You also can type them on any PC keyboard by holding down the ALT key and entering the letter code on the numerical keypad at the right of the ☞ **keyboard** (Information Technology chapter).

æ, **Æ**, the 27th letter, is a diphthong of a and e. It comes from Latin, as in Caesar, and is also used in English, as in Encyclopædia Britannica. Typographically, it is called a ligature, or diagraph of a and e, and it is pronounced nearly like the a in "l<u>ai</u>rd" in English.

ø, **Ø**, the 28th letter, is a diphthong of o and e. It comes from Latin and typographically is called a "o slash", to distinguish it from the equivalent letter, ö, Ö, the "o diaeresis" of Swedish and German. It is pronounced nearly like the u in "tr<u>u</u>st" in English.

å, **Å**, the 29th letter, is a short form of the double aa, which was used in Norway until 1917 and in Denmark until 1948; older names are sometimes spelled using aa instead of å, and appear under å in alphabetical listings. Typographically, it is called a "a ring". It is pronounced nearly like the au in "c<u>au</u>ght" in English.

On the Norwegian/Danish ☞ **Keyboard** (Information Technology chapter), these three letters are at the right, in the second and third rows of keys. If you use a computer but don't have a Norwegian keyboard, you may type these letter by using the "foreign characters" features included in most word processing programs. For instance, the keystrokes used in WORD for Windows are:
æ or Æ: CTRL + SHIFT + &, a or A
ø or Ø: CTRL + /, o or O
å or Å: CTRL + SHIFT + @, a or A

Capitalisation in Norwegian may or may not be confusing, depending on your mother tongue. The reason is historical. Languages not using the Latin alphabet, such as Arabic, Chinese, Japanese, Persian, Hebrew, Hindi, Sinhalese, Thai and Urdu, get along well without capitals. But languages written in the Latin alphabet – English and most Western European languages – employ capitals, reflecting their Greco-Roman heritage. But the use of capitals varies. In German, any noun in sight is capitalised. English and Dutch capitalise less, but still insist on capital first letters for all names as well as for words in book and other titles, though opinion is divided on that. Norwegian use is somewhat closer to that of French and the other Romance languages: the first letter of a sentence or a title is capitalised, as are proper names, but not names of nationalities, languages, months or days of the week. The first-person pronoun *jeg* also escapes capitalisation. The reverse in English,

always capitalising "I", complicates the writing of Norwegian using English word processing application programs that have an automatic correction which capitalises any letter "i" between two spaces. In Norwegian, the lone letter "i" is almost never capitalised, but is a frequently-used preposition: "...office on the third floor..." translates to "...kontor i tredje etasje..." (In MicroSoft WORD®, as used to write this book, you can turn off the automatic I capitalisation by selecting AutoCorrect in the menu under Tools; scrolling through the listing and deleting the i-to-I correction.) As is the case for most grammatical rules, there are exceptions, sometimes for practical reasons. The adjective "Norwegian" is *norsk*, which is written with a lower-case "n", even in the name of an organisation, as *Den norske Bank – DnB*, one of the leading commercial banks. However, that rule became increasingly difficult for *Det norske Veritas,* one of the world's leading marine classification societies. So many foreign business contacts misunderstood the name and its abbreviation, *DnV*, that in the early 1990s, the company officially capitalised the N and thereby changed its name to *Det Norske Veritas*. However, the general rules for capitalisation in Norwegian are so simple that the language has no specific word for "capital", though grammarians occasionally may use the rhetorical term, *kapital*, which otherwise means only money. The terms for the cases of letters are the same as in English topography: *store bokstaver* for upper-case letters, and *små bokstaver* for lower-case letters.

Bilingual dictionaries (*ordbøker*) are available for the principal European languages and for some Asian languages. They are of five types:
- **desk dictionaries (*store ordbøker*)** larger reference dictionaries, as used in offices and universities; almost always "one-way" (*enveis*), to or from Norwegian.
- **general dictionaries** having various names, as used in homes and by college students; usually in both "one-way" and combined "two-way" (*toveis*) editions.
- **school dictionaries (*skoleordbøker*)** for pupils in primary and secondary schools; usually in both "one-way" and combined "two-way" editions.
- **student dictionaries (*studentordbøker*)** specifically for university-level students; usually "one-way", to or from Norwegian.

- **pocket dictionaries (*lommeordbøker*)** intended for tourists and travellers; only "two-way".

Some bilingual dictionaries are compiled for Norwegians and consequently do not include the genders of nouns, which children learn along with words. In *Bokmål* ☞ **About Norwegian languages**, a table (*bord*) is neuter (*intetkjønn*), a book (*bok*) is masculine (*hankjønn*) and a cow is feminine (*hunkjønn*). However, Norwegian ☞ **Dictionaries** do list the genders of nouns. So should you have a bilingual dictionary without gender listings, you can supplement it with a Norwegian dictionary with the genders listed ☞ **Useful books** chapter.

Dictionaries (*ordbøker*) Multi-volume, scholarly dictionaries, of the type found in schools, universities and libraries, have long been available. But convenient, single-volume dictionaries for home or office use, similar to the concise Oxford or Webster's dictionaries of English, are relatively recent. Three are now available in book shops, *Aschehoug og Gyldendals Store Norske Ordbok*, a comprehensive dictionary complement to an encyclopaedia, *Escolas Ordbok*, a simple dictionary for middle and upper secondary school use, and *Norsk Ordbok*, with 1000 illustrations, a handy desk dictionary, ☞ **Useful books** chapter.

English (*engelsk*) arguably is Norway's second language. Success in many fields now depends in part on fluency in other languages, particularly English. Primary-school children learn English from the second or third year on. They also pick it up outside school by watching TV, where most feature and serial films shown are in English with Norwegian subtitles. A child with a computer is even more exposed. Though most home computer programs are now available in Norwegian versions, the originals in English usually are in the shops first. Moreover, most computer games are in English. Scandinavian college and university students long have been obliged to cope with foreign languages as a matter of course: in the social sciences, some 90% of all reading material is in English, and in some technical fields, the only texts available are in English. Some curricula, such as the Master of Science in Marketing programme of the Norwegian School of Management (*Bedriftsøkonomisk Institutt – BI*), are taught in Eng-

lish only and are so advertised internationally. English is the language of instruction in the International Baccalaureate (IB) programme offered by some upper secondary schools (*videregåendeskoler*). English is so much the second language of education that schools, colleges and universities require that transcripts of academic work abroad be submitted along with their translations into either Norwegian or English. English is the leading second language for Norwegian web sites on the Internet, such as those listed in this book. All signs at the Oslo Central international railway station, at the Gardermoen gateway airport and on board the airport express trains and in the stations served by them are in Norwegian and English, as is the news on the 27 big video screens at the airport.

So widespread is the understanding of English that it is used in the headlines of advertisements aimed at the general consumer. A full colour, half-page newspaper advertisement for a large American estate car is headlined "Don't you dare call this a Minivan," but the rest of the text is in Norwegian. A restaurant seeking a staff member inserts an advertisement with a headline reading "Food & Beverage Manager" above a text in Norwegian. The English trend is so commonplace that jokes are often told with their punch lines in English. And comedians work English into their routines. One of the most successful TV short serial shows of the mid 1990s was *The Julekalender* ("The Advent Calendar"), in which English and Norwegian dialects were freely mixed, as in the title, with no translation of the English in subtitles. The shows were then put together into a video that became a best seller. Norwegians, it seems, are not only proficient in English, and know it, but also can be foolish, and know that too.

Handwriting (*Håndskrift*) In August 1998, a teacher publicly contended that the teaching of handwriting in primary school could well be dropped in favour of typing on a computer keyboard. That triggered widespread debate in the media. The final consensus was that computers have their place in writing, particularly if pupils learn touch typing, but that handwriting is a necessary skill that will continue to be taught for years to come. The Norwegian school standard for handwriting is cursive longhand (*løkkeskrift*) and resembles most European school standards, save for the three vowels at the end of the alphabet. The capitals and joined lower-case letters look like this:

ABCDEFGHIJKLMNOPQRSTUVWXYZÆØÅ
abcdefghijklmnopqrshuvwxyzaöå

Hints for learning Norwegian (*Tips for å lære norsk*) New residents can learn Norwegian in many ways. Here are some useful hints to ease learning.

Take ☞ **Norwegian language instruction**. If you are not involved in an orientation programme or other schooling, find and sign up for a course of instruction as soon as possible after you arrive.

Read the Donald Duck comics, in the weekly magazine (*Donald Duck & Co*) and the monthly pocketbooks (*Donald Pocket*) or other Walt Disney magazines and comic books sold by ☞ **Newsagents** (Media and Information chapter). Language in comic books is simple, colloquial and correct. In reading, you can draw upon your knowledge of the characters from your mother tongue to understand situations and learn words without translating. In Norway, it's no shame for an adult to be seen reading a comic book, as you may observe by seeing what other passengers read on trams, busses and trains.

If you aim to learn Norwegian via English (because it is your mother tongue or your best second language) and also know some German, you can use it to speed your learning of Norwegian words. In most cases, words that are alike in German and English also are alike in Norwegian. A "locomotive" (English) is "Lokomotiv" (German) and "lokomotiv" (Norwegian); a "flag" (English) is "Flagge" (German) and "flagg" (Norwegian). But in many cases, whenever an English word is completely different from its German counterpart, the Norwegian word is closer to German than to English. A "conductor" (of an orchestra is) is "Dirigent" (German) and "dirigent" (Norwegian); a "college" is "Hochschule" (German) and "høgskole" (Norwegian); a "flower" is "Blume" (German) and "blomst" (Norwegian); "work" is "Arbeit" (German) and "arbeid" (Norwegian).

Listen or view children's programmes on radio and TV. The vocabulary is simple and the actors speak clearly and slowly. Look for the word *barne* (child) in the TV & Radio programme listings in newspapers.

View films on TV with sound in your mother tongue and read the subtitles in Norwegian. The subtitles are not always synchronised with the sound, but their texts will enable you to grasp the concept, as you hear what is said.

Join a course dealing with a hobby you enjoy, such as the many offered by the ☞ **Adult Education Association** (Education chapter). As the other participants most likely will be Norwegians, you will be immersed in the language, in a topic with which you are familiar.

Volunteer for work with a local sports club, rescue service, outdoor association or the like. As you work, you will learn the language in practice.

If you compete in a sport, join the nearest club for it. On a football ground, for instance, few players in a match will bother to translate for your benefit. So you will learn by doing.

If you like pre-school children, take a job caring for them at a local ☞ **Day care centre** (Family and Children chapter), which most likely always is in need of part-time or full-time staff. Children use simple language, and they will tell you when you err.

Immerse yourself as completely as possible in the language. If you are single, mix with Norwegians. As you learn the language, avoid native speakers of your own mother tongue, particularly if it is the language of your home and you must practice Norwegian elsewhere.

Interpreters (*Tolker*) are translators of the spoken word and function principally to extend the linguistic capabilities of persons in the public and private sectors. Interpreters were long classified along with ☞ **Translators**, but from 1997 on, their profession became officially independent and subject to its own specific certification. Most interpreters now provide services in connection with interviews and conferences held by central government and local municipal departments and bureaus. Accordingly, the translator examination (*tolkeprøven*) requires interpretation of monologues and dialogues in health and medicine (*helse og medisin*), law and legal practice (*juss og rettshåndheving*), social services (*sosialforvaltning*) and employment and other major factors in everyday life (*arbeidsliv og sentrale forhold i samfunnsliv*). There are no particular educational requirements for taking the examination, but candidates are expected to have completed secondary school and preferably have some university or college education. The interpreter examination is given only by the University of Oslo. For details, contact *Institutt for lingvistiske fag, Universitetet i Oslo* ✆ 22852918, ⌨ 22856919, ✉ Blindern, 0361 Oslo, 🖳 http://www.hf.uio.no/ilf/info/tolkeautorisasjon. For further information on the work of translators, contact the Certified Translators Association (*Statsautoriserte Translatørers Forening*) ✆ 22443466, ✉ Eil Sundts g 32, 0153 Oslo or the Translators Union (*Norsk Tolkeforbund*) ✆ 23061405, ✉ Youngsgt. 11, 0181 Oslo.

Loanwords (*Lånord*) are common in most languages. In English, most words of foreign origin appear in one of two ways. They can be adopted directly, such as *ski*, a word borrowed from Norwegian. Or they can be respelled, as are many proper names: *København*, the capital of Denmark, is respelled Copenhagen. The same general rules apply in Norwegian. Some English words are used unaltered, as "white spirit". With a tradition of seafaring, Norwegians retain the proper names of cities and places: New York remains New York, not *Ny-York* as it might be if respelled. But the names of deceased monarchs are respelled. To find an entry on one of the famed English kings named Henry in a Norwegian encyclopaedia you look not under Henry, but under *Henrik*, the equivalent Norwegian name. English loanwords are numerous; more than 4,000 have been collected in *Anglisismeordboka, Engelske lånord i norsk* ("Dictionary of Anglicisms, English Loanwords in Norwegian"), by A-L Grædler and S. Johansson, Universitetsforlaget, 1997, 466 pages softcover, ISBN 82-00-22902-5. And English loanword use has become so commonplace as to concern the Norwegian Language Council (*Norsk språkråd*), the governmental guardian of the language. In 1996, the Council proposed that previously unaltered English loanwords be Norwegianized and accordingly compiled a list of phonetic respellings, such as *timvørk* for teamwork and *svetter* for sweater. The proposal triggered debate. Understandably, major newspapers were disinterested, as they favoured a freely evolving language, unaffected by governmental control. Likewise, the Dictionary of Anglicisms reflects the reality of the everyday use of the original English spellings. University of Oslo Prof. Arthur O. Sandved, who also is a member of the Norwegian Academy of Science and Letters (*Det Norske Videnskaps-Akademi*) and the Norwegian Academy of Language and Literature (*Det norske akademi for sprog og litteratur*), agreed with the newspapers. He pointed out that the proposed changes could hardly aid, but certainly would degrade the learning of Norwegian and English as separate languages. Whether governmental regulation or media and academic free evolution of the language will prevail remains to be seen. But however it is spelt in years to come, English is in Norwegian just as certainly as the Scandinavian languages are in English; just ask any *ombudsman* (English word, recently borrowed from Norwegian and Swedish).

Mother tongue education (*Morsmålsopplæring*) is provided in primary schools (*grunnskoler*) throughout the country, to children who have yet to learn enough Norwegian to follow ordinary classes in schools. The languages of mother tongue classes include Albanian, Arabic, Bosnian, English, Farsi, Finnish, French, German, Italian, Japanese, Kurdish, Polish, Punjabi, Russian, Serbo-Croatian, Sign Language, Sámi, Slovenian, Somali, Spanish, Tamil, Turkish, Urdu and Vietnamese. In the 1997-98 school year, more than 33,000 primary-school pupils were taught in these languages. More pupils were taught in Urdu, some 4,618, than any other language, followed by Vietnamese (2,680), English (2,625), Spanish (2,114), Bosnian (1,854), Arabic (1,629), Turkish (1,621) and Somali (1,153). Instruction is in accordance with international agreements, including those of the ☞ **EFTA** and the ☞ **European Social Charter** (Government and Social Services chapter) and are set forth in Governmental memorandum no. 25 of 18 December 1998. For information on mother tongue education near your home, contact your local school department (*Skoletaten* under the name of the municipality) in the Pink Pages. For an country-wide list of schools providing mother tongue education, contact ☞ **SIU** (Education chapter).

The Norwegian Language Council (*Norsk språkråd*) is the governmental regulatory and advisory body on linguistic matters. It regulates the use of language in civil service, reviews several hundred school books a year for linguistic content and monitors language use by NRK, the state broadcasting company. It publishes a periodic journal, *Språknytt* (Language News) as well as reports, pamphlets and books on language and related topics ✆ 22424020, 🖷 22427676, ✉ PO Box 8107 Dep, 0032 Oslo, ⊕ http://www.sprakrad.no with pages in Norwegian, English, French and German.

Norwegian language instruction (*Undervisning i norsk*) You might get along without learning Norwegian, as most Norwegians can speak *to* you in ☞ **English**. However, if you learn their language, they will speak *with* you. Without Norwegian, you will remain an outsider; with it, you participate. Learning the language is wise, even if your residence is temporary. There are several ways to go about it.

If you are a college or university student, you may learn Norwegian as a second language at the University of Bergen ✆ 55213543, 🖷 55231897, ✉ Sydenplass 9N, 5007 Bergen; or the University of Oslo ✆ 22854348, ✉ PO Box 1102 Blindern, 0317 Oslo.

If you wish to learn before you arrive, you may contact one of the nearly 120 colleges and universities in 28 countries that provide courses of ☞ **Norwegian language instruction abroad**.

If you are a child or youth, you will learn in school. If you are enrolled in one of the many ☞ **Mother tongue education** programmes, you will be taught Norwegian as a second language.

If you are an adult, you may attend courses offered by the ☞ **Adult Education Association** (Education chapter); see *Folkeuniversitetet* in the Pink Pages. Other organisations, such as the Worker's Educational Association in Norway (*Arbeidernes Opplysningsforbund – AOF*) also offer courses; see *AOF* in the Pink Pages. Book shops (*bokhandel*) often have the current catalogues of all nearby courses.

If you are an adult and seek certification of fluency in Norwegian, you may wish to stand the Norwegian language test (*Norsk språktest*) administered by the University of Bergen and by the Adult Education Association. For details, contact *Norsk språktest* ✆ 22988822, 🖷 22988801, ✉ Chr. Kroghs gate 34, 0186 Oslo, ✉ norsk-spraktest@sentralt.funorge.no.

If you are a native of and speak the language of another Nordic country, you may consider the NORDKURS programme of courses in Nordic language and literature (*Kurser i Nordens sprog og litteratur*) held each year in Denmark, the Faeroes, Finland, Iceland, Norway and Sweden. NORDKURS is affiliated with the ☞ **Nordliks** (Education chapter) programme, and in Norway courses are held at the Universities of Bergen, Oslo and Trondheim. For further information on NORDKURS, contact the General Secretariat in the Faeroes, Turið Sigurðardóttir in Tórshavn ✆ +298 315304, 🖷 +298 18448, ✉ Fróðskaparsetur Føroya, FR-100 Tórshavn, The Faeroes, ✉ tusig@fmd.fo, or for Norway, view the NORDKURS web site maintained by The University of Oslo ⊕ http://www.hf.uio.no/inl/kurs98

If you are a refugee who has been granted ☞ **Asylum**(Arriving, Settling, Leaving chapter), you will learn Norwegian in classes as part of your overall orientation.

If you feel that you can learn on your own and have Internet access, use one of the popular search engines and key in "learning Norwegian" as a query to view the current sites of many companies and organisations offering textbooks, phrase books, tape and CD-ROM courses and the like, which you can use at home.

If you are an adult or child, you may consider the Berlitz Method® offered by Berlitz Language Centres in 42 countries world-wide. Berlitz is a private enterprise, so instruction may be more expensive than that offered by other organisations, but the range of class structures – individual, semi-private and group – and the Total Immersion® principle employed make it fast and efficient. For further details, contact the nearest Berlitz Centre listed in your local directory, or view the Berlitz Internet site ⊕ http://www.berlitz .com with pages in 16 languages. In Norway, the Berlitz Centre is in Oslo ✆ 22331030, 🖷 22331003, ✉ info@berlitz.no.

Many municipalities (*kommune*) and larger companies co-operate with schools, colleges and language centres to offer Norwegian courses for new residents. Contact the social services (*Sosialetaten*) of your municipality or your employer's personnel officer for details.

Norwegian language instruction abroad (*Norskundervisning i utlandet*) If you do not speak or understand Norwegian, learning the language before you arrive is one of the best preparations for living in Norway. Nearly 120 colleges and universities in 28 countries offer courses in Norwegian; they are listed below, alphabetically by country. For further details, contact the college or university of your choice. An updated list, with addresses, telecommunications numbers and the names of faculty members to contact, is available on the Ministry of Foreign Affairs (*Utenriksdepartementet*) Internet web site; search by year of listing and select "norskweb" ⊕ http://odin.dep.no/ud/publ.

Austria: Universität Graz, Universität Wien

Belgium: Katholieke Universiteit Leuven, Rijksuniversiteit Gent

Bulgaria: Burgas Free University, Universitetet i Plovdiv, Sofia Universitet St. Kliment Ohridski, South West University

Canada: University of Alberta, Augustana University College, University of Victoria

Croatia: Sveuciliste u Zagrebu

Czech Republic: Ustav Germanistiky a Nordistiky, Univerzita Karlovy

Denmark: Københavns Universitet Amager, Odense Universitet, Aarhus Universitet

Estonia: Talinna Pedagoogika ülikool, Tartu University

Finland: Helsingfors Universitet, Tammerfors Universitet, Universitetet i Vasa, Åbo Universitet

France: Université de Caen, Université Lumière LYON II, Université de Paris IV Sorbonne, Université de ROUEN, Université de Strasbourg II

Germany: Humboldt-Universität zu Berlin, Ruhr-Universität Bochum, Friedrich-Wilhelms Universität, Universität Erlangen-Nürnberg, Johannes Wolfgang von Goethe-Universität, Universität Freiburg, Ernst-Moritz-Arndt Universität, Universität Göttingen, Universität Hamburg Germanisches Seminar, Universität Kiel, Universität zu Köln, Johannes Gutenberg-Universität, Universität Mannheim, Universität München, Westfälische Wilhelms-Universität, Universität Tübingen

Hungary: Eötvös Lorand Tudományegyetem, Budapesti Közgazdásagtudományi Egyetem

Iceland: Háskóli Islands

Italy: Università di Bologna, Università degli Studi di Firenze, Università degli Studi di Milano, Università degli Studi, Università degli studi della Tuscia

Japan: Tokai University

Latvia: Latvijas Universitàte

Lithuania: Vilnius University

Netherlands: Universiteit van Amsterdam, Universiteit Groningen

Poland: Uniwersytet Gdanski, Uniwersytet im. Adama Mickiewicza, Uniwersytet M. Kopernika

Romania: Universitetet "Babes-Bolyai" i Cluj-Napoca

Russia: Pomorskij Gosudarstvennyj, Moskovskij Gosudarstvennyj, Moskovskij Gosudarstvennyi, MGI-MO, ul. Germana 3, kv. 67, Leningradskaja 12 – 32, Petrozavodsk University, Gosudarstvennyj Universitet Sankt Petersburga

Slovakia: Univerzita J.A. Komenského

Slovenia: Univerza v Ljubljani

Spain: Universidad Complutense, Instituto de Idiomas

Sweden: Göteborgs Universitet, Lunds Universitet, Stockholms Universitet, Uppsala Universitet

Switzerland: Universität Basel, Universität Zürich

United Kingdom: University of Edinburgh, University of Hull, University College London, University of East Anglia, University of Reading, University of Surrey

USA: Augsburg College, Augustana College, Arizona State University, Brigham Young University, Cameron University, Coastline Community College, Concordia College Moorhead, Foreign Service Institute, Long Island University, Luther College, Mankato State University, Monterey Institute of International Studies, Moorhead State University, New York University, North Park University, Northern Arizona University, Pacific Lutheran University, St Olaf College, University of California Berkeley, University of California Los Angeles, University of California San Diego, University of Chicago, University of Colorado, Boulder, University of Kansas, University of Minnesota Twin Cities, University of North Carolina Chapel Hill, University of North Dakota Grand Forks, University of Oregon, University of Pittsburgh, University of Texas Austin, University of Washington, University of Wisconsin Madison, Weber State University

Yugoslavia: Universitet u Beogradu

Organisations for other languages (*Foreninger, utenlandske språk*)

There are innumerable foreign-language clubs, cultural organisations, educational associations and religious organisations in Norway. Most are specific to countries but many are concerned with a language or group of languages. For names, addresses and telecommunications numbers, look under the name of the organisation in the Pink Pages or contact the relevant ☞ **Embassies and consulates** (Foreigners chapter).

Profanity and vulgarity (*banning og vulgaris-mer*) Many words no longer considered polite come from Old Norwegian (*gammelnorsk*), which has much in common with Old English. But through the centuries, views of words changed. Some Anglo-Saxon words now considered vulgar in English are acceptable in Norwegian, such as "shit"; the Norwegian equivalent with almost the same pronunciation is *skitt*, which is proper and means dirt or filth. The most common modern Norwegian swearwords, in everyday usage and graffiti are:

dritt, equivalent to "shit" in modern English, an insult or expression of distaste.

drittsekk (shit-bag), denigrating insult, most often used in exasperation. On 17 August 1993, at a meeting in Grimstad, Norway, Torbjørn Berntsen, the Norwegian Environmental minister called his British counterpart, John Selwyn-Gummer a *drittsekk* for his refusal to discuss British acid rain over Norway on the grounds of minke whaling. The incident created a minor international political stir and was featured in cartoons in English newspapers.

faen contraction of *fanden*, most used expletive, expresses surprise or anger; equivalent to "damn" in English.

fanden, the devil, combining form in idioms, such as *fanden vet* ("damned if I know"), *det var som fanden* ("damn it all") and *male fanden på veggen* ("paint a dark picture"). Generally considered more polite than the contraction *faen*.

forbannede or *forbanna*, damned, usually an adjective, as in *forbannede idiot* (damned idiot).

Helvete, Hell, used in same contexts as in English: *Dra til Helvete!* (Go to Hell!), *Hva i Helvete?* (What the Hell?), and in combining forms, as *Helvetes...* (Hellish...).

jævel, from *jævelen*, a synonym for *fanden*, the devil, and used in a variety of combining forms.

Words such as these are improper in everyday language; when used against policemen or government officials performing their duties, profanity is considered a misdemeanour and is subject to fines. Blasphemous expletives are direct: *Fader* (God) is from the first word of the title of the Christian Lord's Prayer (*Fadervår*), and *Herregud* (God, our father) is a liturgical word, used in strong expressions of astonishment, equivalent to "Oh, my God!" in English. Norwegian outdoes English in having two words for flatulence: *prump* (low-pitched, rumbling fart) and

fis (high-pitched, squeaky fart). As in other languages, there are innumerable profane synonyms for sex organs and sex acts, some onomatopoeic and some just coarse, too coarse for this book. There are innumerable milder derogatory terms for people, including: *idiot* (idiot), *klovn* (clown), *tufs* (pipsqueak), *tullekopp* (fool, simpleton) and *tulling* (silly fool). Politics abounds with veiled insults. In January 1998, a progressive party politician in Haugesund called a municipal officer a "Stalinist". The officer filed an injury suit, only to have the High Court of Western Norway decide that criticism, even if harshly worded, is part of public life.

Pronunciation (*Uttale*) The ☞ **Norwegian Language Council** recommends standard pronunciation, but it cannot dictate how people speak. Yet for *Bokmål*, the majority language, there is a pronunciation comparable to the Received Pronunciation of English in the UK or to the *Bühnenaussprache* in Germany. The educated dialect of Oslo sets a norm, though every city and region has its own variety. As a new resident from another country, you most likely will be taught in this variety of the language, unless you are a child learning in school and are taught in the local dialect. Spoken Norwegian has three attributes which challenge new speakers:

Vowels (*vokaler*) The three letters at the end of the alphabet, æ, ø and å, as well as the other vowels as found in English – a, e, i, o and u – often distinguish between words. For instance, *love* means "promise"; *låve* means "barn" and *løve* means "lion".

Phonemes (*fonemer*) A phoneme is the smallest segment of speech, which, if changed, would alter the meaning of a spoken word. Together, all the world's languages use no more than 60 phonemes. Each language has its own set. Some languages have few; Hawaiian has just 11. Other languages have many; English has 48 and Norwegian has 44. English and Norwegian share many phonemes. But each also has phonemes not found in the other. This is why phonemes that are close to each other can hinder learning new sounds. For instance, the *kj* (as in *kjemi*, chemistry) and *sj* (as in *sjanse*, chance) phonemes in Norwegian are close to, but not the same as the *sh* (as in shell) phoneme in English. Consequently, an adult English speaker hearing *kjøre* for the first time may believe it to be "shore". The correct pronunciation of *kj* is like the

Ch of *Chemie* in German, and that of *sj* is like the *sh* in "shoe" in English. These rules and those for all the Norwegian phonemes are given an overview table in *Norsk Engelsk Ordbok* by Einar Haugen (Oslo, Universitetsforlaget, 1984 and several subsequent updates ☞ **Useful books** chapter), which is the Norwegian-English dictionary of choice for English speakers, because it originally was compiled for English-speaking learners of Norwegian. But learners are not alone in misusing the phonemes of the language. The speech trend among the young, that began in and grew through the 1990s, includes slurring the *kj* into a *sj*. In 1999, linguistic research among Oslo teenagers showed that most pronounce the word *kjæreste* (loved one) as *sjæreste*. Linguistic purists were shocked. Per Egil Hegge, the polyglot cultural editor of Aftenposten, the national daily newspaper, was not. He reckoned that it could be part of ongoing change, similar to the loss in the middle ages of the *th* phoneme, which was retained in English and in Icelandic.

Inflection (*tonelag*) is the melody, within a word. Known in linguistics as the lexical pitch, it is the alteration of tone that distinguishes a spoken word from an otherwise identical word. Norwegian is one of the few European languages that has it. There are two pitch patterns. Monosyllabic tone (*enkelt* or *enstavelses tonelag*) is a stress in whatever tonal pattern is normal for the dialect spoken. It is used for all single-syllable words and for some multi-syllable words. Polysyllabic tone (*dobbelt* or *tostavelses tonelag*) is a sequence of high-low-high pitch in speaking words of two or more syllables. For instance, the word *årene* means "the years" if pronounced with monosyllabic tone and "the oars" if pronounced with polysyllabic tone. However, confusing the two tones need not be serious; nobody will misunderstand "years" in a sentence such as "The oars are in the boat" (*Årene er i båten*). So context will come to your rescue if you cannot distinguish between monosyllabic and polysyllabic tones.

Scandinavian languages In everyday and official usage, "Nordic" means all countries having flags of similar designs: Denmark, Faroe Islands, Finland, Greenland, Iceland, Norway and Sweden, and "Scandinavia" distinguishes Denmark, Norway and Sweden, as in "Scandinavian Airlines (SAS)". However, the outside world and many international periodicals do not make that distinction, and often refer

English	Danish	Finnish	Icelandic	Norwegian	Swedish
(language)	dansk	suomi	íslenska	norsk	svenska
(inhabitants)	danskere	suomalaiset	Íslendingar	nordmenn	svenskar
English	engelsk	englanti	enska	engelsk	engelska
yes	ja	kyllä	já	ja	ja
no	nej	ei	nei	nei	nej
Aland	Åland	Ahvenanmaa	Áland	Åland	Åland
Denmark	Danmark	Tanska	Danmörk	Danmark	Danmark
Faroe Islands	Færøerne	Färsaret	Færeviar	Færøyene	Färörna
Finland	Finland	Suomi	Finnland	Finland	Finland
Greenland	Grønland	Grönlanti	Grænland	Grønland	Grönland
Iceland	Island	Islanti	Ísland	Island	Island
Norway	Norge	Norja	Noregur	Norge/Noreg	Norge
Sweden	Sverige	Ruotsi	Sví(jóð	Sverige	Sverige
Copenhagen	København	Kööpenhamina	Kaupmannahöfn	København	Köpenhamn
Gothenburg	Gøteborg	Götepori	Gautaborg	Gøteborg	Göteborg
Helsinki	Helsinki*	Helsinki	Helsinki*	Helsingfors*	Helsingfors
Stockholm	Stockholm	Tukholma	Stokkhólmur	Stockholm	Stockholm

* *Helsingfors*, the Swedish name, is also used in Denmark and Iceland; *Helsinki*, the Finnish name, is also used in Norway. Source: INSTA technical report STRÍ TS3

to the six countries as "Scandinavia". The Nordic languages belong to the Germanic branch of the Indo-European family of languages, except for Finnish and Sami (language of the indigenous people of the arctic north) which are in the Finno-Ugric branch, along with Hungarian. Danish, Norwegian and Swedish are sufficiently similar to be mutually intelligible; cabin crews on SAS aircraft work together, even though they speak three different languages. Yet differences exist. For a Norwegian, reading Danish usually is easier than reading Swedish, whilst speaking with a Swede usually is easier than speaking with a Dane. Icelandic is similar to old Norwegian, and is unintelligible to Danish, Norwegian or Swedish speakers. Greenland, which was ruled by Denmark before being given autonomy, has its own language as well as Danish. The Faroe islands speak a language closely related to Danish. Some common words and geographic names in the five majority languages are listed on p. 266.

Translators (*Oversettere*) express the texts of written material in another language. Most translation in the country is to and from Norwegian, but a considerable amount of translation is done between other languages without Norwegian being involved, such as from Asian languages to English. There are two titles associated with the art of translation. Any person who translates is an *oversetter*. A person who has studied translation at the college level and has successfully passed an examination in it is a *translatør*, and may use the title *statsautorisert translatør*, literally "certified translator". If you wish to hire a translator, look under *Oversettere* or *Statsautorisert translatører* in the Yellow Pages. If you wish to study for translator certification, contact one of the six colleges offering translator curricula: Agder College (*Høgskolen i Agder*) in Kristiansand, Stavanger College (*Høgskole i Stavanger*), Volda College (*Høgskolen i Volda*), Østfold College (*Høgskolen i Østfold*) in Halden, the Norwegian School of Economics and Business Administration (*Norges Handelshøyskole*) in Bergen or the University of Oslo (*Universitetet i Oslo*). The translator examination is held only at the Norwegian School of Economics and Business Administration, for details, contact *NHH Studieadministrasjonen* ✆ 55959200, 🖷 55959000, ✉ Helleveien 30, 5035 Bergen-Sandviken, 🖂 stud@nhh.no, 🌐 http://www.nhh.no/stud/spr/transgen with

pages in Norwegian and in English. There are two translator associations. The Norwegian Association of Literary Translators (*Norsk Oversetter Forening*) is concerned with literature (fiction and poetry), and admission to membership is based on an evaluation of two published literary translations. For details, contact the Association at its head office in Oslo ✆ 22334556, 🖂 Rådhusgt. 7, 0151 Oslo, 🌐 http://www.boknett.no/no/index The Norwegian Association of Non-Fiction Writers and Translators (*Norsk faglitterær forfatter- og oversetterforening*) is concerned with translations of non-fiction, and admission to membership is based on an evaluation of at least one hundred pages of texts. For details, contact the Association at its head office in Oslo ✆ 22121140, 🖷 22121150, 🖂 Bygdøy allé 21, 0262 Oslo, 🖂 nffo@online.no, 🌐 http://www.boknett.no/nff.

Transliteration (*Translitterasjon*) The romanized (Latin alphabet) spellings in Norwegian of words originally written in other alphabets follows the general norms of English. For instance, transliteration from Chinese uses the Pinyin (from Chinese; literally "spell-sound") system adopted internationally in 1979. Transliteration from the Russian in the Cyrillic alphabet is listed here, because Russia is close to and has a common border with Norway and Russian names frequently appear in Norwegian media. The current transliteration norm was adopted in 1996. It differs slightly from the International Standards Organisation (ISO9, 1996) norm for scientific works and from the British norm, as indicated in the table on the next page.

Russian letter	Transliteration		
	ISO Scientific	**British**	**Norwegian**
А а	a	a	a
Б б	b	b	b
В в	v	v	v
Г г	g	g	g
Д д	d	d	d
Е е	e	e/ye	e/je*
Ё ё	ë		jo
Ж ж	z	zh	zj
З з	z	z	z
И и	i	i	i
Й й	j	i	j
К к	k	k	k
Л л	l	l	l
М м	m	m	m
Н н	n	n	n
О о	o	o	o
П п	p	p	p
Р р	r	r	r
С с	s	s	s
Т т	t	t	t
У у	u	u	u
Ф ф	f	f	f
Х х	h	kh	kh
Ц ц	c	ts	ts
Ч ч	č	ch	tsj
Ш ш	š	sh	sj
Щ щ	šč	shch	sjtj
Ъ ъ	"	not transliterated	
Ы ы	y	y	y
Ь ь	'	not transliterated	
Э э	é	e	e
Ю ю	ju	yu	ju
Я я	ja	ya	ja

*je initially and after a vowel, otherwise e

Law, lawyers, courts
(Lover, jurister, domstoler)

The Constitution (Grunnlov) has a French connection. During the Napoleonic wars, Scandinavia was polarised, with Denmark, which then ruled Norway, allied with Napoleon. Sweden sided with Great Britain and Russia in the opposing coalition. It was a time of strife, between and on both sides. In 1809, one of Napoleon's marshals, Jean-Baptiste Bernadotte disagreed with his chief and was let go. But he quickly found work. In 1810 Sweden adopted him as Crown Prince Karl Johan. He then had much to do, because his old chief, Napoleon, was defeated three years later. At the peace negotiations at Kiel in January 1814, Bernadotte boldly pushed through measures obliging Denmark to hand Norway over to Sweden. The Norwegians balked; their country was no spoil of war. Congregations throughout the country swore to uphold independence and appointed 112 representatives to a constituent assembly. On 11th April, the assembly convened in the headquarters building of the Eidsvoll Iron Works, the only convenient large hall. While the great powers debated Sweden's claim to Norway, the Eidsvoll delegates worked at record speed for nearly six weeks to draft a comprehensive Constitution of 110 articles. On 17th May they finished and elected their former regent, Prince Christian Frederik of Denmark, as the king of free Norway. The freedom lasted only three months. Sweden invaded. Norway lost and by August was a Swedish subject. That union lasted until it was peacefully disbanded in 1905. The Constitution held throughout the period of Swedish rule and thereafter. It is a remarkable document, as it ensured sovereignty of the people, separation of powers and human rights, the same ideals expressed in the constitutions of the United States of America (1776) and of the French Republic (1791, 1793, 1795). However, the original Constitution of 1814 failed on one count. It made religious intolerance the law of the land. Its Article 2 specified Evangelical Lutheranism as the State religion and commanded immigrant parents to bring up their children in that faith. It also barred Jesuits, monastic orders and Jews from the country. The stipulation of a State Protestant church and the barring of Catholic orders might

have been a descendent of the attitudes of the Reformation, when monasteries and convents had been closed and Catholics banned. The reasons for banning Jews are less clear. In 1998, University of Oslo history professor Øystein Sørensen analysed the mood of 1814 and concluded that three prevalent views of the early 19th century lay behind the ban. First, though religious tolerance was widely accepted, Jews were seen as dissimilar and therefore not worthy of acceptance. Second, Jews were feared to be so culturally different that they could not assimilate with the general population. Finally, the mercantile capabilities of Jewish businessmen were viewed as a threat to native business. Many intellectuals fought the ban, most notably humanitarian poet and author Hendrik Arnold Wergeland (1808 - 1845), whose poem The Jew (Jøden) of 1842 triggered a debate that ended in repeal of the constitutional ban in July 1851. The other intolerant directives were rescinded with the years. Religious freedom was granted in August 1897 and May 1964, and the ban on Jesuits was lifted in November 1956. The version of the Constitution in effect today includes amendments up to July 1995 and has 112 Articles. Article 2 now reads: "All inhabitants of the Realm shall have the right to free exercise of their religion. The Evangelical-Lutheran religion shall remain the official religion of the State. The inhabitants professing it are bound to bring up their children in the same." The current text of the Constitution is available from many sources, both printed and on-line. For instance, ODIN, the governmental on-line service, makes it available in Norwegian and in English translation on the Internet at ⊕ http://odin.dep.no/ud The original constitution of 1814 is a historical document and is replicated in history books, as well as on-line at the University of Oslo web site ⊕ http://www.hist.uib.no/kjelder/const

Courts (Domstoler) The law courts are arranged in three levels, which provides two levels of appeal. Court composition and procedure may differ according to whether a case is criminal (straffeprosess) or civil (sivilprosess). A civil case may start out-of court.

Concilliation board (Forliksråd), for civil cases only; provides out-of-court settlement at the local level, as there are boards in all municipalities in the country.

County or Magistrate's Court (Herred eller

byrett) is the court of first instance for civil cases not resolved out of court as well as for all criminal cases. Civil cases are judged by one professional judge, who may, if one of the parties so wishes, be assisted by two lay judges. Criminal cases are judged by one professional judge and two lay judges and, for some cases, two professional judges and three lay judges. There are 108 County and Magistrate Courts throughout the country.

High court (*Lagmannsrett*) is the court of second instance for appeals. Three judges, who may, if one of the parties so wishes, are assisted by four lay judges judge civil cases. Three judges and a jury of ten judge criminal cases. There are six high court districts, named after the first courts of the country:

Agder lagmannsrett with four circuits: Vestfold county, Telemark county, Aust-Agder county except five western municipalities and Vest-Agder county and the five western municipalities of Aust-Agder county.

Bogarting lagmannsrett with three circuits: Oslo and Akershus counties excluding Romerike, Østfold county and Buskerud county.

Eidsivating lagmannsrett with two circuits: Hedemark and Oppland counties and Romerike district of Akershus county.

Frostating lagmannsrett with two circuits: Møre og Romsdal county and Sør-Trondelag and Nord-Trondelag counties.

Gulating lagmannsrett with two circuits: Rogaland county and Sogn og Fjordane counties.

Hålogaland lagmannsrett with three circuits: Nordland county and two southern municipalities in Troms county, Troms county except two southern municipalities and Finnmark county, as well as the Svalbard archipelago and Jan Mayen island in the Arctic.

Supreme Court (*Høyesterett*) is the highest court of the land. It sits in Oslo and has a Chief Justice and 17 permanent judges. For each case put before the Court, there is a chairman and four judges. The Supreme Court can take cases appealed from a High court and it rules on questions of principle, including interpretation of laws and directives for passing sentence.

Deportation (*Utvisning*), which is also called expulsion, means that a foreign citizen is ordered to leave the country and is not allowed to return. If you

are a foreign citizen, you may be deported if you are convicted of a crime or if you have violated the Immigration Act. The rules regarding deportation are not the same for everyone; they differ, depending on whether you have a residence or work permit or are married to a citizen of an EEA country. Deportation is not the same as extradition (*utlevering*), which is the handing over of a person accused or convicted of a crime in a foreign country to the country in which the crime was committed. Likewise, deportation differs from rejection (*bortvisning*), which requires a foreign citizen to leave the country, such as when an application for a residence or work permit has been refused, but allows re-entry at a later date. The full details of deportation are available as ☞ **free legal advice** in a brochure published by *Juss-Buss* in Norwegian and English versions and available on-line at ✆ http://www.juss-uio/jussbuss/ brosjyrer/utvisning with pages in Norwegian and in English.

Eviction (*Utkastelse*) is the expulsion of a tenant from a property. For instance, if you rent a house or flat and do not move out after the term of the rental contract or fail to observe the terms of the contract, such as by not paying rent, you may be evicted. However, the owner cannot evict you himself. Moreover, he cannot change locks, enter while you are away and remove your possessions, or make the dwelling unliveable, such as by turning off water or electricity. Eviction is a legal procedure that can be performed only by public authorities. When an owner wishes to evict a tenant, he must send an eviction application (*utkastelsesbegjæring*) to the local enforcement authority (*namsmyndighet*), which upon deciding in his favour, will initiate eviction.

Expropriation (*Ekspropriasjon*) is the compulsory transfer of property or legal rights, usually from private individuals or companies to governmental agencies. According to paragraph 105 of the ☞ **Constitution**, a person or company whose property or rights are expropriated is entitled to full compensation.

Free legal advice (*Fritt rettsråd*) may be given by a lawyer as part of ☞ **Free legal aid**. However, if you only seek advice, you may consult one of the advisory services (*rådgivningsinstanser*) operated by law students. They advise but cannot accept cases or provide legal aid as can a lawyer, because they are staffed by students, who have yet to qualify for licences to practise law (*advokatbevilling*). But their services are available to anyone, without the maximum income requirement or application as required for free legal aid. So often they offer the fastest, easiest way to inquire, such as on your rights in a legal matter or whether you should apply for free legal aid. Moreover, they can assist you in legal matters for which a licence to practise law is not required, such as representation at a conciliation board (*forliksråd*). There are five services in the country.

Juss-Buss ("Law Bus"), so named because when founded in 1971 by University of Oslo law students, its first office was mobile, in an old bus. Juss-Buss has four specialist groups, in social and labour law (*sosial- og arbeidsrett*), imprisonment and family law (*fengsels- og familierett*), immigrant law (*innvandringsrett*) and rent and interest law (*husleie- og gjeldsrett*), but also considers other matters. However, it does not deal with inheritance (*arv*), tax (*skatt*), criminal cases (*straff*), property (*fast eiendom*) or business activities (*næringsvirksomhet*). It publishes numerous public information booklets on legal matters, many in English. If you have a legal query, write the main office or call or visit during its consultation hours, Monday 10 am to 3 pm and Thursday 5 to 8 pm ✆ 22851850, ✉ 22851870, ✉ St. Olavs gt. 29, 0166 Oslo, ✉ http://www.jus.uio.no/jussbuss/ with pages in Norwegian and in English.

Juridisk rådgivning for kvinner (JURK) ("Legal advice for women") is operated by women law students at the University of Oslo and specialises in legal matters concerning women. If you have a legal query, write the main office or call or visit during its consultation hours; for calls Monday, Wednesday, Friday 10 am to 3 pm and Thursdays 5 to 8 pm; for visits Tuesday 12 to 3 pm and Thursday 5 to 8 pm ✆ 22859594, ✉ 22859598,✉ Universitetsgt. 22/24, PO Box 6756 St. Olavs pl., 0130 Oslo.

Jussformidling i Bergen ("Legal service in Bergen") is operated by law students at the University of Bergen and deals with a broad range of legal matters. If you have a legal query, write the main office, call for an appointment in advance or visit during its consultation hours, Monday – Thursday 10 am to 2 pm ✆ 55589600, ✉ 55589606, ✉ Mag-

nus Lagabøtes plass 1, 5010 Bergen, ✉ http://www.jur.uib.no/org/jussformidlingen

Jusshjelpa i Nord Norge ("Legal help in Northern Norway") is operated by law students at the University of Tromsø and deals with most legal matters. If you have a legal query, write the main office or call or visit during its consultation hours, Monday-Wednesday 12 noon to 1 pm and Thursday 6 to 7 pm ✆ 77644561, ✉ 77646565, ✉ Breivik senteret, PO Box 635, 9037 Tromsø, ✉ http://www.jus.uit.no/jusshjelpa

Studentjusshjelpa i Trondheim ("Student legal help in Trondheim") is operated by law students at the University at Trondheim and deals with most legal matters, except tax and criminal law. If you have a legal query, write the head office ✉ PO Box 312 sentrum, 7402 Trondheim, or call or visit one of its three offices during their consultation hours, Tuesday 11 am to 2 pm at Bispegt. 9B ✆ 73515250, ✉ 73527280, Wednesday 9 am to 12 noon at the SU office at Dragvoll ✆ 73598241, Thursday 11 am to 2 pm at the SU office at Gløshaugen ✆ 73598325, ✉ http://www.studentjushjelp.org

Free legal aid (*Fri retthjelp*) ensures that the services of lawyers can be made available to persons unable to afford them. There are three types of free legal aid: free legal advice (*fritt rettsråd*), free court aid (*fri sakførsel*) and exemption from standard court fees (*fritak for rettsgbebyr*). You may apply for free legal aid and can qualify for it if your personal finances are under specified limits (*økonomiske grenser*).

Free legal advice is legal help in matters not involving court proceedings (*utenfor rettergang*). Most free advice is given in matters concerning marriage, family, welfare, pensions, rent, compensation and termination of employment, but other matters can be considered. Free legal advice may be extended to include representation at a conciliation board (*forliksråd*) before a summons is issued for a case in a city court (*byrett*) or district court (*herredsrett*). Free legal advice is not available in matters for which other governmental agencies, such as tax offices (*ligningskontorer*) provide advice or in matters for which public application forms and instructions (*søknadsskjemaer og veiledninger*) are available.

Free court aid provides the services of a lawyer

from the time of summons (*stevning*) in a court case.

Exemption from standard court fees means that the court fees are financially supported. In some cases, other direct court costs, such as for witnesses and expert opinion may also be covered.

Free legal aid is provided primarily to individuals. Foreign citizens who apply for free legal aid are assessed on the same grounds as are Norwegian citizens. The Immigration Act (*Utlendingsloven*) includes provisions for foreign citizens to receive free legal aid without consideration of personal finances. Foreign citizens are also entitled to free legal aid in cases of asylum and deportation as well as to free court aid in cases involving questions of their identity or authenticity of their papers. However, there are exceptions. For instance, free legal aid usually is not available in cases of deportation due to criminal activity.

Lawyers in private practice can provide free legal aid. So whenever you contact a lawyer for assistance, be sure to ask if free legal aid is part of the services offered. Many lawyers, particularly commercial and business lawyers, do not provide free legal aid. However, they, as well as any other lawyer not providing free legal aid, are obliged to refer you to lawyers who do provide it. In some cases involving marriage and family law, the court may appoint a lawyer to represent a defendant who fails to appear in court or respond to a summons.

You must apply in writing for free legal aid, to the office of the County Governor of the county in which you live; look under *Fylkesmannen* in the Pink Pages for the address and telecommunications numbers. A lawyer or other service providing ☞ **Free legal advice** can help you submit an application.

Your application must include the figures of your personal finances that show that you cannot afford to pay for legal services. There are limits on annual gross wages (*brutto inntekt*) and net fortune (*formue*), which is the worth of what you own minus your debts. The limits are periodically revised; contact the office of the County Governor for the current figures.

For further information on free legal aid, you may contact a lawyer who offers it. Many lawyers have offices specifically for free legal aid, listed in the Pink Pages under *Fri rettshjelp* or *Rettshjelpkontoret*. In Oslo, there is a municipal office for free legal aid (*Fri rettshjelp, Oslo kommune*) ✆ 22425260, 🖷 22332396, ✉ Storgt. 19, 0184 Oslo. The ☞ **Legal**

first aid offices can also provide information and assist you in applying for free legal aid.

Laws (*Lover*) The oldest known written laws of the country are the Regional Laws (*Landskapslover*), which date from the 12th century. In 1274, King Magnus the Law-Mender (*Magnus Lagabøte*) codified the regional laws into a National Law (*Landslov*), which remained in force for more than 400 years. In 1604, the National Law was revised and translated from Old Norwegian into Danish and renamed Christian IV's Norwegian Law, in honour of the Danish King who then ruled Norway. On 15 April 1687, Christian IV's Norwegian Law was given new codification and remains the oldest law still in force. Since then, law, most notably the ☞ **Constitution**, has been an integral in the development of the country and part of the awareness of its citizens.

Indeed, one of the most-sold references in the country, found in all law and most other public and private sector offices as well as on the bookshelves of homes throughout the country, is the single volume of all current laws, easily recognisable by its red cover with gold lettering and by its size: the current edition weighs nearly 2 kg: *Norges Lover, 1687-1997*, edited by Supreme Court Justice Hans Flock and Prof. Frederik Zimmer, Oslo, 1998, Gyldendal Forlag, 3255 pages hardcover, ISBN 82-417-0910-2. With the exception of the Constitution, which appears first, the laws appear in the book in chronological order by date of initial enactment, and most have a sequence number within the year. For instance, the Immigration Act is the law of 24 June 1988 no. 24.

Individual laws contained in *Norges Lover* as well as laws passed or amended after its most recent edition has been published are available in booklets published by Cappelen Akademisk Forlag and on-line from ☞ **Legal information** (Media and Information chapter).

Many ☞ **translated laws** are available in printed form and on-line, principally into English, for the benefit of the Foreign Service and for international business and trade. If you are a new resident from another country, you most likely will be most interested in two laws:

Immigration Act [Act concerning the entry of foreign nationals into the Kingdom and their presence in the realm] (*Lov om utlendingers adgang til riket og deres opphold her*) enacted 24 June 1988 and most recently amended 30 April 1999. Available in English without updates, on-line and in a booklet published by the University of Oslo in 1991.

Working environment Act [Act relating to worker protection and working environment] (*Lov om arbeidervern og arbeidsmiljø m.v.*) enacted 4 February 1977 and most recently amended 26 June 1998. Available in English with amendments to 28 February 1997 in a booklet published by Cappelen Akademisk Forlag, ISBN 82-456-0387-2.

Lawyers (*Jurister*) are persons properly qualified to practice law. A lawyer in practice is called an *advokat*, a title equivalent to both barrister and solicitor as used in the UK. A lawyer in a civil case is called a legal representative (*prosessfullmektig*). A defending lawyer in a criminal case is called the defence counsel (*forsvarer*). You can find lawyers listed under *advokater* in the Yellow Pages. If you cannot afford the services of a lawyer, you may seek ☞ **free legal advice**, or you may be eligible for ☞ **free legal aid**.

Legal documents and forms (*Juridiske dokumenter og formularer*) are involved in almost all dealings between people, such as those involving family law, wills, inheritance, sale and purchase of property, official registries and business contracts. Consequently, there are many legal documents and forms as well as many sources of them. The most frequently used are collected in a book that is stocked by most major book shops: *Juridiske Dokumenter og Formularer*, by Jan A. Coll & Line M. Coll, Oslo, Cappelen Akademisk Forlag, 11th edition 1998, 344 pages softcover, including an IBM-format disk with the most commonly used forms in WORD6.0 files, ISBN 82-456-0538-7.

Legal first aid (*Advokatvakt*) is provided free by lawyers who are members of the Norwegian Bar Association (*Den Norske Advokatforening*) in 29 cities and towns in 15 of the country's 19 counties. The *advokatvakt* centres are open for consultation for two or three hours, usually one evening during the business week, Monday-Friday; a few every two weeks, monthly or on request. You may seek aid on any legal matter by going to a centre, drawing a queue number (*kølapp*) and waiting your turn to consult with a lawyer for up to one half hour. If your legal problem requires more than one half hour of consultation, you will be referred to a lawyer during ordinary office hours. If other organisations, such as municipal departments, can solve your problem, the lawyer will refer you to them. The lawyer can also assist you in applying for ☞ **Free legal aid** (this chapter). In 1998-99, about half of all legal problems handled by the centres were solved in half an hour or less, and the remaining half required reference to other organisations or for further legal assistance. The centres are located in Oslo (county and city), Akershus county (Sandvika, Kolbotn and Lillestrøm), Østfold county (Moss and Sarpsborg), Hedemark county (Hamar and Elverum), Oppland county (Lillehammer, Gjøvik and Hadeland), Buskerud county (Drammen and Hønefoss), Vestfold county (Horten, Tønsberg, Sandefjord and Larvik), Telemark county (Porsgrunn and Skien), Aust-Agder county (Arendal), Rogaland county (Stavanger and Haugesund), Hordaland county (Bergen, Stord, Bømlo and Kvinnherad), Møre og Romsdal county (Ålesund), Sør-Trøndelag county (Trondheim) and Troms county (Tromsø). In many of these cities and towns, the local library (*bibliotek*) provides a room for the *advokatvakt* and will know about its consultation hours. Local lawyers should also know the location and hours of the nearest *advokatvakt*. A list of *advokatvakt* throughout the country is available on request from the head office of the Norwegian Bar Association (*Den Norske Advokatforening*) ✆ 22035050, 🖷 22115325, ✉ Kr. Augusts g. 9, 0164 Oslo, 📧 dnapost@jus.no, or on-line at 🖳 http://www.jus.no/dna/bruke_advokat/advokatvaktene

The Ministry of Justice and the Police (*Justis- og politidepartementet*) is the country's principal legal entity. Like the other Ministries, has a politically-appointed leadership under a Minister but otherwise consists of career civil servants, with the highest-ranking being the Secretary General (*Departementsråden*). The Ministry is divided into nine departments, each concerned with a branch of the legal system or with related services:
- administration of the Ministry
- civil affairs including the rights of individuals
- ☞ **courts**
- immigration and refugee legislation and legal matters
- legislation resources and drafting of new laws

- polar affairs (the legal aspects of Norwegian Arctic and Antarctic regions)
- ☞ **police** (Crimes, Wrongs, Countermeasures chapter)
- ☞ **prisons** (Crimes, Wrongs, Countermeasures chapter)
- rescue services and emergency planning including ☞ **Civil preparedness** (Defence chapter)

Moreover, an Information Unit (*Informasjonsenhet*) compiles press releases and other external information and responds to enquiries ℡ 22249090, ☎ 22242720, ✉ PO Box 8005 Dep, 0030 Oslo, ✉ postmottak@jd.dep.telemax.no, ⊕ http://odin.dep.no/jd/ including an overview of the Ministry at ⊕ http://odin.dep.no/jd/intro in Norwegian and in English.

Oral agreements (*Muntlige avtaler*) are as binding as written agreements, according to the oldest law still in force, King Christian IV's Norwegian Law of 15 April 1687.

Testifying in court (*Vitneforklaring*) If you are summoned as a witness (*vitne*) in a court case, you must appear. If you have a legitimate reason for not appearing or if circumstances prevent you from appearing, you must notify the court immediately upon receiving the summons. If you are too ill to appear, you should have your doctor send a certificate (*legeattest*) stating the reason. You will not be paid for appearing before the court. However, you are entitled to reimbursement of travel, lodging and food expenses at the normal governmental ☞ **scale of travelling expenses** (Business and Work chapter).

Translated laws (*Lover i oversettelse*) Many laws have been translated, principally into English. Almost all translations are unofficial, as the original Norwegian text of a law is regarded as legally binding.

Few translations have been published. A book of translations into English of selected laws, *Norwegian Laws, Etc., Selected for The Foreign Service* was published in 1980 by The Ministry of Foreign Affairs, 997 pages hardcover; it is out of print but can still be found in some book shops. A translation of the *Immigration Act* was published in 1991 by the University of Oslo but is now out of print; it is available in some libraries. The *Act Relating to Worker Protection and Working Environment* is available in English in a booklet published in June 1997 by Cappelen Akademisk Forlag, ISBN 82-456-0387-2; it is in print and available in book shops.

Almost all translations that have been made to date, into English as well as other languages, are now available on-line at a web site maintained by the Faculty of Law Library at the University of Oslo. As the following example of locating the translation of the Immigration Act shows, it is easy to use:

First, use an Internet browser and key in the address **http//www.ub.uio.no/ubit/ulov/**, which will bring up an opening page in English.

Then key information to start the search. If you know that the Immigration Act was enacted on 24 June 1988, no 24 for the year, key in 19880624 in the Date field and 64 in the Number field. If you don't know those details, simply enter Immigration in the Word in Title field. Finally, point and click on Search, which brings up a display:

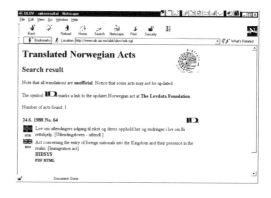

There are four links on which you may point and click. The **LD** logo accesses the updated Norwegian text maintained by ☞ **Legal information (*Lovdata*)** (Media and Information chapter). **BIBSYS** brings up the academic libraries' file reference locator for the printed version in English, whilst **PDF** and **HTML** access on-line versions in those formats.

Measurements and standards (*Måleenheter og standarder*)

CE marking (*CE-merke*) The European Union (EU) and European Economic Area (EEA) countries (including Norway) have an agreement, *Conformité Européenne* (European Conformity), on safety standards and radio noise standards for products including low-voltage (up to household voltages) apparatus and appliances, pressure vessels, toys, construction products, machines, personal protection equipment, non-automatic scales, active implantable medical devices, gas appliances, telecommunications peripheral equipment, hot-water boilers, explosives for civilian uses, medical devices and recreational craft. Subassemblies or finished goods meeting the standards can be marked CE. The CE mark is a declaration by its manufacturer that it meets all applicable standards and can be sold in EU and EEA countries. It is not equivalent to a guarantee, which must be separately stated.

CE mark

Clock (*Klokke*) The time of day is stated in the 24-hour custom, from 01 to 24, for most governmental, business, educational and professional purposes. But in everyday life, the 12-hour clock convention is used. There is no direct equivalent to the a.m. and p.m. of English, so connotation provides the clue as to whether a stated hour is before or after noon: "dinner at seven" clearly means "dinner at 7 p.m.", not "dinner at 7 a.m." The conventions for quarter past (*kvart over*) and quarter to (*kvart på*) the hour are the same as in English. However, the statement of the half hour differs. In Norwegian, "half" (*halv*) means before the hour: *halvsyv* ("half seven") means 6:30, whilst the equivalent statement in English means past the hour: "half seven" means 7:30.

Converting between measurement systems (*Konvertering*) If you are accustomed to the English system of measurement, as used in the USA and still in retail trade in the UK, you may wish to convert.

In length, there are about two and a half centimetre to the inch, so ten centimetres is about four inches, and one meter is a little less than forty inches. A person two metres tall (6 ft. 7 in.) is very tall, but that is a common length of ski for an adult man. One pound is about half a kilogram (500 gr) minus ten percent, so to convert kilograms to pounds, double the number of kilograms and add 10%; to convert pounds to kilograms, divide by two and subtract 10%.

In weight, there are 454 grams to a pound and 2.2 pounds to a kilogram. So to convert from kilograms to pounds, divide by two then subtract ten percent. To convert from kilograms to pounds, multiply by two and add ten percent.

For liquid volumes, as for dairy products and petrol, conversion depends on whether US or UK units are involved, as the Imperial (UK) units are 20% larger than US units. There are 3.785 litres in a US gallon and a US quart is equivalent to 0.95 litre. There are 4.546 litres in an Imperial gallon, and a UK quart is equivalent to 1.14 litre.

For temperature, to convert from Fahrenheit to Celsius degrees, first subtract 32, then divide by 2 and add 10%.

Example: what is 50°F, a typical spring or autumn temperature, in Celsius degrees?
50° − 32° = 18° above freezing
18°/2 = 9°
9° + 10% of 9° = 9.9°C

To convert from Celsius to Fahrenheit degrees, multiply by 2 and subtract 10%, then add 32.
Example: what is -10°C, a chilly winter temperature, in Fahrenheit degrees?
-10° X 2 = -20°
-20° − 10% of -20° = − 18° below freezing
-18° + 32° = 24°F

Remembering a few temperature equivalents also helps mental conversions between the two scales. A comfortable indoor temperature is 20°C (68°F); the body temperature is 37°C (98.6°F); water freezes at 0°C (32°F).

Country codes (*Landskoder*) In addition to the country codes used in placing international telephone calls, countries are assigned letter and number codes for general purposes, letter prefixes for postal codes, letter abbreviations for motor vehicles, codes for data communications, ISBN codes for books and prefix codes for bar-coded items sold in shops. The codes for the Nordic countries are:

Country	two letter	three letter	number	Postal	Vehicles	tele-phone	data comm	ISBN books	bar code prefix
Denmark	DK	DNK	208	DK	DK	45	238	87	57
Finland	FI	FIN	246	SF	SF	358	244	951 & 952	64
Faroe Islands	FO	FRO	234	FR	FR	298	288	87	57
Greenland	GL	GRL	304	DK	DK	299	290	87	57
Iceland	IS	ISL	352	IS	IS	354	274	9979	569
Norway	NO	NOR	578	N	N	47	242	82	70
Sweden	SE	SWE	752	S	S	46	240	91	73
Svalbard & Jan Mayen	SJ	SJM	744	N	N	47	242	82	70

Notes: Faroe Islands and Greenland have some Danish codes. Svalbard and Jay Mayen have some Norwegian codes.
Source: INSTA STRÍ TS3

Dates (*Datoer*) are written in two ways.

The traditional format is DD. MMMM.CCYY (DD = day numerical, MMMM = month spelled out, CCYY = century and year numerical), so 8th November 1999 is written *8.november 1999*. It is also written numerically, such as 08.11.1999 or 8.11.99, or with slash / or hyphen - separators.

The ISO 8601 standard writing is used in the EU and EEA and is favoured in business and government, because it prevents misinterpretation. The full format is CCYY-MM-DD, so 8th November 1999 is written 1999-11-08. It can be shortened to YY-MM-DD: 99-11-08. The full format is best because it prevents misinterpretation of dates for the years 2000 to 2031. For instance, a date written 01.02.03 could be 1st February 2003 in the Norwegian format or 3rd February 2001 in the ISO format, with a point separator instead of the recommended hyphen. The full format avoids misinterpretation by writing 3rd February 2001 as 2001-02-03.

Days (*Dager/døgn*) In banking and finance, as for computing interest, the days of the year are numbered from 001 to 366, with day 001 being 1st January. A day is defined as being a period of time starting at 0000 (HHMM format) and ending at 2400. In Norwegian, a day (*dag*) in the sense of daylight hours or calendar day is distinguished from the full 24-hour day (*døgn*), a convenience with no equivalent in English: "open 24 hours" is written in one word, *døgnåpen*.

ISO 9000 and ISO 14000 are voluntary international standards on quality and on environmental impact. They are among the 10,700 standards issued by the ISO, a leader among ☞ **standards organisations**. Manufacturers certified according to one or more of these ISO standards often so state in their advertisements, such as 'our quality management system is certified to ISO 9001'. Certified Norwegian companies are listed in a *KvalLex* ("Quality Lexicon"). It is available in a printed version (Oslo, 1999, Telenor Media, 150 pages A4 format softcover) as well as on-line at ✉ http://www.kvalex.no. The on-line version has a search facility by company name or by business sector according to the numbering system of the International Standard Industrial Classification of all Economic Activities – NACE (*Nomenclature générale des Activités economiques dans les Communautés Européenes*) devised and maintained by Eurostat, the Statistical Office of the European Communities, and administered in Norway by Norway Statistics (*Statistisk Sentralbyrå*).

Mathematical designations (*Matematiske tegn*) The everyday mathematical designations and conventions common throughout Europe are used:

+	plus sign
–	minus sign
:	division, technical and scientific
/	division or fraction
•	multiplication, technical and scientific
X	multiplication

Moreover, Norway and Denmark also use the ÷ sign to mean 'minus', even though it is the sign for division in most other countries. The reason remains a mystery, though ÷ is known to have been used for minus in medieval times in Germany, Switzerland, The Netherlands and Scandinavia. In Norway, it was used along with the current minus sign but was abandoned in school books and other texts in the late 1930s. Though obsolete, it survives in everyday usage: a sign on a shop window reading '÷ 50%' does not mean 'divide by 50%', but rather 'subtract 50% from all prices'; in other words, a half-price sale is going on. The standard decimal symbol is the comma and the standard three-digit group separator is a space or a dot. So the figure one million, two hundred and thirty-four thousand, five hundred and sixty seven and eighty-nine hundredths is written: 1 234 567,89 or 1.234.567,89.

Measures (Mål) are metric or SI (for *Système Internationale* d'Unités). The basic measures in everyday use are length in metres (m), mass in kilograms (kg), time in seconds (s), electric current in Amperes (A) and temperature in degrees Kelvin (K). Multiples and divisions are indicated by prefixes: milli (m) for one-thousandth, centi (c) for one-hundredth, deca (d) for ten, hecto (h) for one hundred, kilo (k) for one thousand, mega (M) for one million and giga (G) for one billion.

Lengths are stated in different ways. The dimensions of mechanical objects are given in millimetres, body heights in centimetres, house dimensions in metres and road distances in kilometres or tens of kilometres (*mil*). Carpenters speak of prepared timber sizes in inches, such as a "two-by-four" (*to-tom-fire*) with a cross-section of 2 by 4 inches, but a builder's merchant sells the same timber as 49 mm by 98 mm.

Weights are in grams or kilograms for foods, though the hectogram (*hekto*) is often used for expensive foods. Body weights and car weights are in kilograms.

Areas of buildings are in square metres. Land areas are in square kilometres for larger areas and decares (*dekar*), a thousand square metres, for smaller areas, as farms and plots for houses. An older unit of land area, *mål* remains in use for smaller land areas. A *mål* originally was the equal to a quarter barrel (*tønne*), the amount of farmland that could be sewn with a 139 litre barrel of seed. Its area varied, but averaged 984.34 square metres. Today, it is an everyday term for the decare, but the older unit is still used. So the *mål* may be 1,000 or 984.34 square metres.

Volumes of liquids, such as milk, drinks and petrol, as well as capacities, such as of refrigerators, are in litres. Bottles, cans and cartons for drinks, liquid pharmaceuticals and cosmetics are marked in centilitres. The cord (*favn*) is the traditional measure for solid volumes, as for firewood. Its size varies, but it usually is equal to 2.4 cubic metres, of which 1.66 cubic metres are solid wood. A larger unit, the "big cord" (*storvavn*) is equal to 12 cubic metres. In trade, cubic meters replaced the favn in 1997, but it remains the traditional term used by woodsmen and farmers.

NEMKO Electrical products and machinery are tested and certified by NEMKO, a laboratory that has its head office in Oslo and has laboratories in England, Germany, Italy, Taiwan and the USA. A product that has been tested and certified by NEMKO may carry the NEMKO mark, which is a capital letter N in a circle. The other Scandinavian countries have similar marks consisting of letters in circles: Denmark a capital D, Finland capital FI and Sweden a capital S. So electrical goods sold throughout Scandinavia usually carry all four marks, as well as those of Central European laboratories.

NEMKO mark

Paper (Papir) Trimmed paper sizes are according to the ISO 861 standard, which numerically numbers sheet sizes, starting with A0 for a sheet of one square metre in area. Each successive numbered size in the series is half the area of the preceding size and has a long side that is the same length as the short side of the preceding size. A second "B series", based on a 1.414 square metre sheet (size B0) is used principally in the printing industry to provide sizes between those of the A series. The ratio of the long side to the short side of the sheets of the A and B series is always 1.414 (square root of 2). There is also a "C series" for envelopes to suit papers of the A and B series. The most common A series sizes are:

Size number	Dimensions in millimetres
A0	841 X 1189
A1	594 X 841
A2	420 X 594
A3	297 X 420
A4	210 X 297
A5	148 X 210
A6	105 X 148
A7	74 X 105
A8	52 X 74
A9	37 X 52
A10	26 X 37

Broadsheet newspapers are slightly less than A2 size, and many magazines and common letter paper are A4 size. There are two standards for loose leaf binders and accordingly for the holes punched in A4 sheets to be put in them. The most common standard is the international ISO 838 which specifies two holes in a paper sheet, located 80 mm from each other and 12 mm in from the edge of the sheet. The two-hole punching is often extended to four holes (British Standard BS 5097), again at spacings of 80 mm, popularly called "80-80-80".Binders, punched paper and punches for two and four holes are available at stationers. A less common standard, used by companies that deal with or are owned by Swedish companies, is the Swedish "Trio" four-hole/ring standard that specifies hole spacings of 21, 70 and 21 mm, located 10.5 mm in from the edge of the sheet. Binders and punches are available at larger stationers.

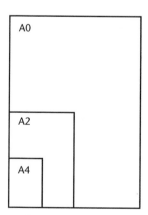

A Series paper sizes. A4 is one-quarter the area of A2, which is one-quarter the area of A0

Standards organisations (*Standardiserings-organisasjoner*) Most standards are related to European standards and to international standards. Each standard aims to ensure uniformity in the goods, services or concepts to which it applies. The principal national body is the Norwegian Standards Organisation (*Norges Standardiseringsforbund (NSF)*, which has its head office in Oslo. NSF co-ordinates the activities of five national standards organisations, each of which is responsible for standards within specific sectors. For details, contact the NSF head office ✆ 22049200, ✏ 22049211, ✉ PO Box 353 Skøyen, 0213 Oslo, ✉ firmapost@standard.no, ⊕ http://www.standard.no with pages in Norwegian and selected pages in English as well as links to national and international standards organisations.

Temperature (*Temperatur*) The Celsius scale common throughout Europe is used. Named for Swedish astronomer Anders Celsius (1701-44), its zero is the freezing point and its 100 degrees is the boiling point of distilled water at sea level. It is sometimes called the "centigrade" (one-hundred degree) scale, though scientifically, there is a very small difference between the Celsius and centigrade scales.

Time zone and summer time (*Tidssoner og sommertid*) ☞ Norway is in the Central European time zone, written GMT + 1, meaning one hour ahead of Greenwich Mean Time (GMT, also called UTC for Universal Time Co-ordinated). The EU practice for summer time is followed: clocks are advanced one hour at 02.00 hours on the last Sunday in March, and turned back one hour at 03.00 hours on the last Sunday in October. Accurate time announcements are made continuously, 24 hours a day, on the time helpline (*Telefonuret*) ✆ 170.

Weeks (*Uker*) The business week and the calendar week both begin on Monday and end on Sunday. In business and government and on all office calendars, the weeks of the year are consecutively numbered, from 01 to 52 or 53, with week 01 being the one that includes the first Thursday of the year. This means that "Week 01" (*uke 01*) of the year starts with a Monday between 29 December and 4 January, and that the last week of the year ends on a Sunday between 28 December and 3 January.

Media and Information
(*Media og informasjon*)

Advertising (*Reklame*), like that elsewhere in Europe, comprises an appreciable business sector, accounting for about 1% of the Gross Domestic Product – GDP (*Bruttonasjonalprodukt – BNP*) and equivalent to about 2.5% of the total household consumption expenditure for the country. In terms of the total amount of money spent, advertising divides roughly equally between printed media and other media, including television, which accounts for more than a third. This is a fairly new distribution. Up to 1981, the government-owned Norwegian Broadcasting Company, ☞ **Broadcasting companies** (Telecommunications and Broadcasting chapter), held a monopoly on radio and television broadcasting and neither accepted nor permitted advertising. It financed and still finances operations in part through the levy of a ☞ **TV licence** (Telecommunications and Broadcasting chapter). However, advertising was and still is permitted in the ☞ **Cinema** (Entertainment and Night Life chapter), where advertising trailers are shown before feature films. So until the mid 1980s, when advertising-financed private television and radio became widespread, Norwegians both paid not to see advertising (on TV) and paid to see it (at cinemas). That situation has changed; advertising is now commonplace in all media. Of the current total expenditure on advertising, newspapers lead with 42%, followed by TV with 36%, and then weekly magazines (7%), professional journals (7%), radio (2%) posters and billboards (2%) and cinema (1%). Advertising is restricted according to the Act on Marketing (*Markedsføringsloven*). Advertising is banned outright for cigarettes and tobacco. Likewise, neither shop signs nor advertising of any other sort may feature alcoholic drink stronger than 2.75% alcohol by volume, which is the upper limit for the B tax class of Light beer (*Lettøl*). This is why you may see a sign for a pub featuring the logo of a well-known brewery and the word *Lettøl*. The sign adheres to the law, though anyone with a thirst for beer reads the message clearly: the pub also serves stronger stuff. Other provisions of the Act on Marketing restrict sexual and racial discrimination and denigration as well as bla-

tantly offensive themes in advertising. Consumers who believe they have been deceived by advertising have several courses of redress, principally the ☞ **Consumer council** (Human Rights, Consumer Rights chapter) and the Marketing Council (*Markedsrådet*). There are 120 some advertising agencies (*reklamebyrå*) in the country, about half of whom are members of the Advertising Agency Association (*Reklamebyråforening*) which, in turn, is a member of the European Association of Advertising Agencies – EAAA. Some 20 marketing associations comprise the Norwegian Marketing Association (*Norges Markedsføringsforbund*). Marketing and advertising education is offered by the Norwegian Marketing College (*Norges Markedshøyskole – NMH*) associated with the Norwegian School of Management (*Bedriftsøkonomisk Institutt – BI*). For information and statistics on advertising, contact the Norwegian affiliate of the global AC Nielsen market research, information and analysis firm ✆ 22583400, 🖷 22583401, ✉ PO Box 100 Kjelsås, 0411 Oslo, 📧 firmapost@acnielsen.no, 🖥 http://www.acnielsen.no

Almanac (*Almanakk*) Like almanacs elsewhere, the Norwegian almanac is an annual calendar of months and days with tables of tides, sunrise and set, moonrise and set and other astronomical data, as well as wind scales, hunting seasons and other general information. Two Oslo publishers offer almanacs in handy A6 (10.5 x 14.8 cm) format with 120 to 148 pages and sold in book shops (*bokhandel*) and newsagents (*kiosk*). Gyldendal offers *Almanakk for Norge* (bokmål) and its counterpart *Almanakk for Noreg* (Nynorsk), and Almanakkforlaget offers *Norsk Almanakk*.

Barcode (*Strekkode*) A barcode is a machine-readable pattern of stripes printed on and identifying an item, such as an article sold in a shop, a piece of airline baggage or a package sent by post or courier. You probably see barcodes most often on articles sold in shops. At a checkout, a clerk moves an article past a window and a laser beam scans the barcode, reading it at any angle. Some shops with small volumes, such as pharmacies, use hand-held laser wands that are aimed at the barcode on an article. Shops selling larger articles, such as furniture or building materials, also have hand-held wands for

ISBN 82-91570-01-9

9 788291 570013

Typical barcode, the ISBN code of this book.

ease of reading barcodes on articles that don't fit on a checkout conveyor. The number read goes to the shop computer, which sends back the name of the item and its price for instant display at the checkout. The computer also adds up the total bill. The laser scanner works in a way similar to the laser pickup of a compact disk (CD) player. It emits a beam of infrared light, which is reflected by the white spaces between the alternating vertical strips of a barcode. The reflected beam comes back, and is converted to an electrical signal that represents the information contained in the barcode. There are many kinds of barcodes. The world's most widespread barcode is called EAN-13, The EAN stands for the European Association for Article Numbering, which has its head office in Brussels, Belgium. The 13 is the number of digits in the code of an item. The format of the EAN-13 code is: PPP XXXXXXXXX C, where:

- PPP is a three-digit number designating a company or organisation. It is assigned by one of the 88 Numbering Organisations covering 90 countries, but does not identify the country of origin of an item. In some cases, the PPP digits are international, such as 977 for ☞ **ISSN** and 978 for ☞ **ISBN**.
- XXXXXXXXX is a nine-digit number assigned to each item.
- C is a check digit computed from the previous 12 digits.

EAN codes are used world-wide, except in the United States and Canada, where barcodes are assigned by the Uniform Code Council (UCC). The barcode of an item identified with a UCC code can be read by EAN-13 optical readers in Norway by inserting a zero in front of its 12 digits. For further information on barcodes, contact EAN International in Brussels ✆ +32 2 2271020, ☏ +32 2 2271021, ✉ rue Royale 145, B-1000 Brussels, Belgium, ✉ info@ean.be, ☻ http://www.ean.be with pages in English. The

EAN Numbering Organisation in Norway is *EAN Norge* ✆ 22971320, ☏ 22655621, ✉ PO Box 454 Økern, 0580 Oslo, ✉ firmapost@ean.no, ☻ http://www.ean.no with pages in Norwegian.

Central Information Service (*Statens informasjonstjeneste*) If you wish to locate an authority or agency within the government or seek a government publication, the Central Information Service is the best place to start. It regularly compiles a catalogue of brochures and pamphlets published by government agencies and some associations, entitled *Brosjyreoversikten*, and maintains a corresponding database on its website, which has pages in Norwegian and in English: ✆ freephone 80030300, ☏ 22249519, ✉ PO Box 8117 Dep, 0032 Oslo, ✉ opplys@si.dep.telemax.no, ☻ http://www.si.dep.no with pages in Norwegian and in English. The Central Information Service does not distribute printed matter, but helps you find sources, such as ministerial distribution offices, where you may order. Your local public library (*folkebibliotek*) or a book shop (*bokhandel*) can also help you find publications via the Central Information Service, sometimes by online search, and may help you order. Or, if you are in Oslo, you can visit the Central Information Service book shop, which does keep a stock of current brochures and pamphlets, and adjoins the Akademika book shop department selling government publications and other books, at Møllergt. 17, with its entrance from Pløensgaten, just south of the Government building complex (*Regjeringskvartalet*) ✆ 22245000.

***Dine Penger* ("Your Money")** was founded in 1983 as the country's first magazine dedicated to the personal finances of the individual, as opposed to the business finances of corporations. The public responded rapidly to the provision of previously inaccessible information, and *Dine Penger* grew to be the sales leader among financial sector magazines. It now has ten issues a year, a circulation of more than 60,000 and a readership of some 470,000, equivalent to about one resident in ten in the country. Each issue features a mix of articles on earning, buying, saving, investing and taxation, as well as on non-financial personal matters, such as what to do if you are arrested, how to safely use fireworks to avoid damage and injury and which birth-control measures are the most effective. The approach is direct and the language is that of everyday speech. If you can read an average Norwegian newspaper, you can read and benefit from *Dine Penger*. The printed edition is sold by news agents throughout the country and by subscription ✆ 22586970, 🖷 22586951, ✉ Media Data AS, PO Box 124 Kjelsås, 0411 Oslo, ✉ abo.service@mediadata.no. The on-line services at ☻ http://www.dinepenger.no include pages duplicating the current printed issue and search facilities for topics in back issues as well as access to information by themes including cars (*bil*), housing (*bolig*), inheritance and law (*arv og jus*), insurance (*forsikring*), loans (*lån*), own business (*firma*), savings and investments (*sparing og pengeplassering*) and taxes (*skatt*) and an on-line interactive calculator for personal finances, interest and investments. A subsidiary company, *Dine Penger Rådgivningstjeneste* provides a wide range of personal finance and investment advisory services ✆ 23276680, 🖷 23276690, ✉ Drammensveien 126A, 0277 Oslo, ✉ radgivni@dinepenger.no. In 1998, *Dine Penger* published three softcover books that detailed the principal aspects of personal finances in the same easily-understood language as used in the magazine:

- *Aksjer og pengeplassering* ("Shares and investments"), by OR Mælingen, R Pedersen and T Staavi, 234 pages, ISBN 82-91618-05-4.
- *Arveoppgjøret trinn for trinn* ("Inheritance step-by-step"), by PJ Haakstad, 232 pages, ISBN 82-91618-07-0.
- *Privatøkonomi 99* ("Private finances 99"), by R Pedersen and T Staavi, 436 pages, ISBN 82-91618-06-2.

Embassies and Mission on the Internet (*Utenriks Internett*) If you have Internet access, you can find information on Norway from around the world, on the web sites maintained by seven Norwegian Embassies and the Permanent Mission of Norway to the United Nations. The most extensive web site is supported by the Norwegian Information Service associated with the Embassy in Washington, with a link from the Mission of Norway to the United Nations site.

Denmark: The Royal Norwegian Embassy, Copenhagen ☻ http://www.norsk.dk/frontpage

Germany: Königlich Norwegische Botschaft, Bonn

☻ http://www.norwegen.org/nbmain

Japan: The Royal Norwegian Embassy, Tokyo ☻ http://www.norway.or.jp

Republic of Korea: The Royal Norwegian Embassy, Seoul ☻ http://bora.dacom.co,kr/~noram

Malaysia: The Royal Norwegian Embassy, Kuala Lumpur ☻ http://www.norway.org.my

UK: The Royal Norwegian Embassy, London ☻ http://www.norway.org.uk

USA: The Royal Norwegian Embassy, Washington ☻ http://www.norway.org/main

UN: Permanent Mission of Norway to the United Nations, New York

☻ http://www.undp.org/missions/norway

Encyclopaedias (*Leksikon*) are widely available in all public libraries (*folkebibliotek*). Typically, the reference room (*lesesal*) of major city library will have encyclopaedias from all the Nordic countries, as well as encyclopaedias in English, French, German and other languages. Encyclopaedias are also sold in most book shops (*bokhandel*). The most comprehensive and largest Norwegian encyclopaedia is the fifteen-volume second edition of *Aschehoug & Gyldendals Store Norsk Leksikon* (Complete Norwegian Encyclopaedia) published in 1990 by Kunnskapsforlaget with subsequent chronological update supplements as well as associated topical books, including Medicine and Health (*Medisin og helse*), a dictionary (*ordbok*) and a pictorial dictionary (*Visuell ordbok*) with terms in Norwegian, English, French and German. The encyclopaedia is also on a CD-ROM, *Fokus 99* released in 1999. *Cap Lex*, published in 1997 by Cappelen is a popular one-volume encyclopaedia; it is also on a CD-ROM, *Caplex 99*, updated through 1998. The 32-volume Ecyclopaedia Britannica in ☞ **English** (Language chapter) is a favourite of scholars. It is available as a reference in most major libraries and is sold by major city book shops. It is also on a CD-ROM, as the Encyclopaedia Britannica CD 99 in both multimedia and standard editions.

Freedom of the press (*Trykkefrihet*) is guaranteed in Article 100 of the ☞ **Constitution** (Government and Social Services chapter). Moreover, the Freedom of Information Act (*Offentlighetsloven*) of June 1970 ensures the right of any person to have access to governmental records, unless the records are protected from disclosure by the exemptions of the Act, which are principally concerned with internal working documents, national security and outdated information. Nonetheless, not all Ministries consistently adhere to the provisions of the Freedom of Information Act, and have been criticised in the press for that lack. In 1995, *Aftenposten*, the major national newspaper, checked 3,000 issues handled by Ministries in 1993 – 1995 and found that that 46.5% of them were not made accessible to the public. That criticism was made public, in Norwegian and in English, by ODIN, part of governmental ☞ **Public information** services. In short, the government made public criticism of itself. In everyday practice, most of the restrictions on the press are self-imposed; most periodicals adhere to the ethical guidelines of The Norwegian Press Association (*Norsk Presseforbund*). There are some 40 specific ethical rules, divided into four groups: role of the press in society, integrity and responsibility, relationships with sources, and publication principles. For further details, contact the Association's Professional Committee (*Pressens Faglige Utvalg*) ✆ 22405040, 🖷 22405055, ✉ Rådhusgt. 17, 0158 Oslo, ⊕ http://www.nal.no with pages in Norwegian and extracts in English.

Free map of Norway (*Gratis kart over Norge*) If you have Internet access, you can download a free map of Norway in colour in a file in Windows Metafile Format (WMF) compatible with most Microsoft Windows applications, from the Norwegian Mapping Authority (*Statens Kartverk*) web site ⊕ http://www.statkart.no by selecting *Gratis data*, then *Gratis kart over Norge* and, finally, selecting *Last Ned* ("Download").

GRID, the Global Resource Information Database, is part of the United Nations Environment Programme (UNEP). There are GRID facilities throughout the world. One of them is in Arendal, with responsibility for environmental information on the Nordic countries with their adjacent seas and on the two polar regions as well as for supporting the global and regional activities of UNEP in environmental. For further information, contact UNEP/GRID-Arendal ✆ 37035650, 🖷 37035050, ✉ PO Box 1602 Myrene, 4801 Arendal, ✉ grid@grida.no, ⊕ http://www.grida.no with pages in English and links to other sites.

The Guinness Book of Records is published every year in a Norwegian edition entitled *Guinness Rekordbok*, by the Schibsted media company in Oslo. The *Guinness Rekordbok* is usually available in book shops (*Bokhandel*) and newsagents (*kiosk*) in the autumn, about the same time as the original UK edition is released and accordingly sold by larger city book shops in Norway. The content of the *Guinness Rekordbok* consists of a Norwegian translation of the English original, with an additional chapter on Norwegian records. The book is a best seller as a Christmas gift, in part because Norwegians hold some standing world records, particularly in sports. By the end of the 1998 Olympic Winter Games in Nagano, Japan, cross-country ski racer Bjørn Dæhlie had won eighteen world championships, including eight Olympic gold medals, more than any other winter sports person ever. Ingrid Kristiansen has held the women's half marathon record since 1987; she also held the women's marathon record for 14 years, until it was bettered in 1998 by Kenyan runner Tegla Loraipe.

ISBN is the abbreviation of the International Standard Book Number (*ISBN – Internasjonalt standard boknummer*) now used on almost all books worldwide, most often on the back cover along with a machine-readable ☞ **Bar code**. An ISBN number consists of ISBN, or its equivalent 978 in bar code, followed by ten digits separated into four parts:
- Group identifier (national, geographic, language, or other convenient grouping). Major languages have group identifiers; English is 0. Smaller countries or language areas have national numbers; Norway is 82.
- Publisher or producer identifier
- Title identifier
- Check digit computed from the previous digits

For instance, the ISBN number of this book, the third edition of *Living in Norway*, is:
82-91570-01-9, where:
82 indicates that the book is published in Norway
91570 is the Palamedes Press publisher identifier
01 identifies the book among those published by Palamedes
9 is the check digit computed from the previous nine digits
ISBN numbers are assigned according to the international ISO 2108:1992 standard, as administered

by the International Standard Book Number Agency at the National Library in Berlin (*Staatsbibliothek zu Berlin*). In Norway, ISBN numbers are assigned and catalogued by the National Library's ISBN office (*ISBN-kontoret Norge*) ℡ 23276217, ℻ 23276010, ✉ PO Box 2674 Solli, 0203 Oslo, ✉ isbn-kontoret@nb.no ⊕ http://www.nb.no/html/isbn.html with pages in Norwegian and in English.

ISMN is the abbreviation of the International Standard Music Number (*ISMN – Internasjonalt standard musikknummer*) now used on almost all sheet music world-wide, frequently on the back cover along with a machine-readable ☞ **Bar code**. An ISMN number consists of ISMN followed by ten digits separated into four parts:

- The letter M to distinguish ISMN from ☞ **ISBN**.
- Publisher identifier. Large-volume publishers have short identifiers; small-volume publishers have longer identifiers.
- Item identifier, including the edition of a work and the items within it, such as full score, miniature score, set of string parts, a violin part and so on.
- Check digit computed from the previous digits

For instance, the ISMN numbers of the three *Microjazz Duets* sheet music books by Christopher Norton, published by Boosey & Hawkes of London are M 060 10680 4, M 060 10681 1 and M 060 10682 8, where:

M indicates the ISMN sytstem
060 is the Boosey & Hawkes publisher identifier
10680, 10681 and 10682 identify the three books among those published by Boosey & Hawkes
4, 1 and 8 are the respective check digits

ISMN numbers are assigned according to the international ISO 10957:1993 standard, as administered by the International Standard Music Number Agency at the National Library in Berlin (*Staatsbibliothek zu Berlin*). In Norway, ISBN numbers are assigned and catalogued by the National Library's ISMN office (*ISMN-kontoret Norge*) ℡ 23276057, ℻ 23276010, ✉ PO Box 2674 Solli, 0203 Oslo, ✉ ismn@nb.no, ⊕ http://www.nob.no/html/ismn.html with pages in Norwegian and in English.

ISSN is the abbreviation of the International Standard Serial Number (*ISSN – Internasjonalt standard-*

nummer for periodika) now used on almost all periodicals world-wide, most often together with a ☞ **Bar code** at a lower corner on the cover. An ISSN number is independent of the country of publication, of the language or alphabet of the periodical, of its frequency or its medium. It consists of ISSN, or its equivalent 977 in bar code, followed by two groups of four characters, of which the first seven are numbers, 0-9, and the eighth may be a number 0-9 or the letter X. The structuring of the numbers is involved, both because some serial publications are short-lived and because there may be several publications of the same title world-wide.

For instance, the ISSN number appearing along with its equivalent bar code at the lower left on 1999 issue six of ☞ **Dine Penger** is

977080011303306, where:
977 is the bar code for ISSN
0800113 is the code for Dine Penger
03 is a price code, which prints out the price when read at a cash point
3 is the bar code check digit computed from the previous digits
06 is the issue number

ISSN numbers are assigned according to the international ISO 3297:1998 standard, as administered by the International Standard Serial Number Centre in Paris. In Norway, ISSN numbers are assigned and catalogued by the National Library's ISSN office (*ISSN Norge*) ℡ 23276179, ℻ 23276010, ✉ ISSN Norge, PO Box 2674 Solli, 0203 Oslo, ✉ issn-norge@nb.no, ⊕ http://www.nb.no/html/issn.html with pages in Norwegian and in English.

Kopinor is the Reproduction Rights Organisation (RRO) of Norway. It administers privileges for photocopying and other secondary uses of printed and published copyrighted works and promotes public respect for the rights attached to copyrighted works. Its authority is based on the Copyright Act (*Åndsverkloven*) and on mandates from the holders of copyrights. In practice, Kopinor enters an agreement with an organisation that allows the photocopying of Norwegian and foreign printed and published works for internal use, within prescribed limits, against a schedule of fees. In turn, Kopinor distributes the income from fees among copyright holder groups in Norway and abroad, based on the extent of copying of their works. Though Kopinor is principally concerned with reproduction rights, it also has a responsibility to encourage the purchase of original works rather than the copying of them. Kopinor is a member of the International Federation of Reproduction Rights Organisations (IFRRO), which is an independent, non-profit, non-governmental organisation. In all, IFRRO membership includes 37 national RROs, including five music RRO, as well as 44 associate members. For further information, contact Kopinor ✆ 22179417, 🖷 22179422, ✉ Stenersgt. 1A, 0050 Oslo, ✉ kopinor.post@kopinor.no, ⊕ http://www.kopinor.no with pages in Norwegian, English, French, German, Italian, Portuguese, Romanian and Spanish. For international details or the addresses of RROs in other countries, contact the IFRRO ✆ +32 2 5510899, 🖷 +32 2 5510895, ✉ Rue do Prince Royal 87, B-1050 Brussels, Belgium, ✉ ifrro@skynet.be, ⊕ http://www.ifrro.org

The international copyright symbol.

Legal information (*Lovdata*) is centralised in The Lovdata Foundation (*Stiftelsen Lovdata*), a non-profit foundation established in 1981 by the Ministry o 🖷 Justice (*Justisdepartementet*) and the Faculty of Law of the University of Oslo. Lovdata creates, maintains and operates systems for legal information and offers general databases of primary legal sources as well as legal texts in machine readable form, to both traditional and electronic publishers. It is host for the English version of Celex, the legal information system of the European Union, which is implemented as a Folio database, *Lovdata CELEX*, on a dedicated server. It provides Norwegian law free on the Internet, including the Supreme Court (*Høyesterett*) decisions of the previous three months, Statutes in force (*Lovene*), central regulations applying to Norway as a whole (*sentrale forskrifter*) and local regulations (*lokale forskrifter*). It maintains *NorLex*, a continuously updated on-line Internet repository of consolidated statutes and regulations in force as well as more than 50,000 legal decisions (*avgjørelser*); an abridged version of it is published on CD-ROM twice a year, as *NorLexCD*. Lovdata also maintains *Norim* via the WinSir® client-server system, to access *NorLex* as well as databases covering EU and EEA law, which comprise

more than 2,000 directives and regulations translated into Norwegian, whilst the EU law section comprises the English version of Celex. For further details, contact Lovdata ✆ 23356000, 🖷 23356001, ✉ PO Box 41, 0101 Oslo, ✉ marked@lovdata.no ⊕ http://www.lovdata.no with pages in Norwegian and in English.

Libraries (*bibliotek*) Norway has more libraries than any other Nordic country, some 1,500 open to the public. More than 1,100 of these are local public libraries (*folkebibliotek*) in cities and towns throughout the country. There are nine national libraries (*nasjonal bibliotek*) and some 220 university and college libraries (*bibliotek ved universiteter og høgskoler*) and nearly 140 special public libraries (*spesialbibliotek, offentlig*), each dealing in a particular field, as well as 33 libraries maintained by non-government organisations (NGOs). For addresses and telecommunications numbers of these libraries, see the Pink Pages. In addition to public libraries, there are innumerable smaller libraries kept by private organisations – companies, associations and clubs – for their employees and members; for further information, call the organisations at numbers listed in the Pink Pages.

Two major national libraries and four city libraries offer extensive specialised services. There is a central facility for the library sciences, a government agency responsible for library matters and an extensive on-line database for library and inter-library referencing and search.

The **National Library** (*Nasjonalbiblioteket*) is the country's principal book and periodical repository and research facility, with facilities in Oslo and Rana. Its tasks are similar to those of other national libraries, such as the British Library or the US Library of Congress and include the assignment of uniform international numbers to Norwegian publications under the ☞ **ISBN** system for books and the ☞ **ISSN** system for periodicals.

The **University of Oslo Library** (*Universitetsbiblioteket i Oslo*) is the country's oldest and largest offering general library services to the public. It maintains numerous special collections of books, periodicals, maps and other graphic materials, photographs and sound recordings, as well as one of Europe's better collections of antique books ✆ 22855050, 🖷 22844050, ✉ PO Box 1085 Blindern, 0317 Oslo, ✉ ubo-fjernlaan@ub.uio.no for lending and ubo-publikasjon@ub.uio.no for ordering publications, @ http://www.ub.uio.no with pages in Norwegian and in English.

The **Environmental Library** (*Miljøbibliotek*) is part of the Steinkjer Public Library (*Steinkjer folkebibliotek*). It keeps an updated stock of printed and electronic reference materials on environmental matters as well as indices and on-line links to search for information elsewhere ℗ 74169356, 🖾 74163959, ✉ PO Box 2502, 7710 Stenkjer, ✉ miljo@steinkjer.folkebibl.no, @ http://www.steinkjer.folkebibl.no/miljo/miljobib.

The **Europa Library** (*Europabibliotek*) is part of the Trondheim Public Library (*Trondheim Folkebibliotek*). It keeps books, periodicals, reports and other publications relating to ☞ **EFTA, EEA and EU** (Government and Social Services chapter), as well as other information concerning European matters ℗ 72547545, 🖾 72547510, ✉ Peter Eggespl 1, 7005 Trondheim, ✉ europa@trondheim.folkebibl.no, @ http://www.tronheim.folkebibl.no/europa

The **Multilingual Library** is a section of the Oslo Public Library (*Deichmanske Bibliotek*), the largest and oldest public library in the country, founded in 1785. It keeps books, newspapers, magazines and other printed materials in 37 languages, has a staff of 25 nationalities and loans to the public as well as to other libraries ℗ 22032905, 🖾 22207214, ✉ Henrik Ibsensgt 1, 0179 Oslo, ✉ innfjern@deich.folkebibl.no, @ http://nyhuus.deich.folkebibl.no

The **North-South Library** (*Nord-sør bibliotek*) is part of the Stavanger Public Library (*Stavanger bibliotek*). It keeps a wide range of books, periodicals and other literature on Norwegian and international aid to developing countries, as well as information on North-South institutes in other countries ℗ 51507922, 🖾 51507015, ✉ PO Box 3101, 4001 Stavanger, ✉ nordsyd@stavnager.kommune.no, @ http://www.stavanger.kommune.no/solvberg/html/body_nord-s_r_biblioteket

The **Library Centre** (*Biblioteksentralen*) in Oslo is the central facility for librarianship and the library sciences. It was first established in 1902 as the Public Library Forwarding Bureau (*Folkeboksamlingens Ekspedisjon*). It was reorganised in 1952 under its present name and now is owned by the municipalities it serves and by the Norwegian Library Association (*Norsk Bibliotekforening*). Consequently, it is the best single source of printed and on-line information on all libraries in the country ℗ 22673489, 🖾 22196443, ✉ PO Box 6142 Etterstad, 0602 Oslo, ✉ bs@bibsent.no, @ http://bibsent.no

The **Norwegian Directorate for Public Libraries** (*Statens bibliotektilsyn*) in Oslo co-ordinates all national and international public library activities in the country ℗ 22832585, 🖾 22831552, ✉ PO Box 8145 Dep, 0270 Oslo, ✉ sb@ bibtils.no, @ http://samson.bibtils.no

The **BIBSYS (***Bibliotek-system***)** on-line database is a shared library system for all Norwegian university libraries, the National Library and several research libraries. It comprises information on books, series, journals and other publications held by these libraries, a total of some 5.4 million entries. It is free to all users, and is available at public terminals at many public libraries (*folkebibliotek*). Users who are registered with BIBSYS with customer IDs may order copies or loan of articles. It is in Norwegian, but has extensive services, including search, in English. It has links to other library databases including the University of Oslo Library (UBO), the Danish Libraries (DANBIB), the British Library (OPAC97), the university libraries in the UK and Ireland (COPAC) and the US Library of Congress (LC) BOOKS (about 3.8 million) and NAMES (about 3.4 million) databases. It also provides access to gateways for searching other databases. The BIBSYS organization that provides on-line and other services is located at the University of Trondheim ℗ 73592097, 🖾 73596848, ✉ Elgeseterg 10, 7034 Trondheim, ✉ bibdrift@bibsys.no, @ http://www.bibsys.no with pages in Norwegian and in English.

Magazines (*Blad***)** Norwegians are among the world's most eager buyers and readers of magazines, which are sold by **newsagents** as well as from racks in supermarkets and petrol stations. *Se og Hør* ("See and Hear", a gossip weekly) tops the list of Norwegian magazines. Some 1200 foreign magazines are increasingly popular, and the top ten sellers countrywide (June 1997 – May 1998) were 1 Bilsport (cars, Swedish), 2 Svensk Damtidning (women's, Swedish), 3 Bravo (teen, German), 4 Daz (cars, German), 5 Lektyr (erotic, Swedish), 6 Match (sport, English), 7 Men Only (erotic, English), 8 Femina (women's, Danish), 9 Classic Motor Magasin (cars,

Swedish) and 10 Auto Motor Und Sport (cars, German). In the capital city of Oslo, news magazines sell well, and the top ten sellers were: 1 Svensk Damtidning (women's, Swedish), 2 Bilsport (cars, Swedish), 3 Femina (women's, Danish), 4 The Economist (news, English), 5 Men Only (erotic, English), 6 Der Spiegel (news, German), 7 Hello (gossip, English), 8 Newsweek (news, American), 9 Time (news, American) and 10 Auto Motor Und Sport (cars, German).

Maps and charts (*Landkart og sjøkart*) and a wide range of cartographic products and services are offered by the Norwegian Mapping Authority (*Statens Kartverk*), which in 1998 celebrated its 225th anniversary and thereby is the oldest continuously-active government agency in the country. Its principal products include land maps (*landkart*), nautical charts (*sjøkart*), digital cartographic products (*digitale produkter*), property information, standards (*standarder*), SATREF for the GPS satellite navigation system, publications (*publikasjoner*) and geodetic products (*geodetic produkter*). Land maps, including the topographic main map series (*Norge 1:50 000*), walking and ski touring maps (*Turkart*), road maps (*vegkart Norge*), hunting and fishing maps (*jakt- og fiskekart*), county maps (*fylkeskart*), map of the country (*Norgeskart*), the Norway Atlas (*Norgesatlas*) and various thematic maps (*Temakart*) of the country and parts of it, highlighting themes such as soils, forestry and farming and the like. These maps are sold by most larger book shops (*bokhandel*). Moreover, there are several types of special-purpose maps, such as the helicopter and light-aircraft charts (HLC) and ICAO (International Civil Aviation Organisation) aviation charts sold by aviation firms. Nautical charts, including the main chart series (*Hovedkartserie*), the harbour chart series (*Havnekartserien*), the coastal chart series (*Kystkartserien*) and the fisheries chart series (*Fiskerikartserien*) are sold by nautical and fisheries supply firms. Two chart series, the small craft chart series (*Båtsportkart* selections from the main series, in 35 x 45 cm format) and the explorer charts (*Opplevelseskart*) are produced specifically for recreational boating and are sold by book shops and boating supply shops in coastal cities and towns. Many maps and charts are sold abroad: land maps in 16 countries and charts in five countries. For lists of shops selling maps and charts at home and abroad and for a full overview of the products and services available, contact the Norwegian Mapping Authority ☏ 32118100, 🖷 32118101, ✉ Kartverksveien 21, 3511 Hønefoss, ✉ firmapost@statkart.no, 🌐 http://www.statkart.no

Newsagents (*kiosker*) Norwegians spend more on books per head than do the people of any other country, and world-wide they rank third in number of newspapers bought. Accordingly, newsagents are located throughout the country; hardly a village, airport, railway station or bus station is without one. The largest by far is Narvesen, founded in 1894 and now with a staff of about 8,500 persons. Narvesen has more than 450 newsagent shops throughout the country and is the country's leading wholesaler of periodicals and paperbacks, serving more than 7,000 shops. Moreover, Narvesen operates more than 100 cafes and restaurants in the Burger King, Peppes Pizza, Carolina and La Baguette and TGI Friday's chains, as well as all cafe and ambulating food services on trains. In all, Narvesen sells some 1300 periodicals, which are listed in a free, 66-page colour illustrated catalogue available at newsagent shops. Foreign newspapers and magazines are in the majority. For instance, the catalogue lists 68 major foreign newspapers: 5 American, 22 British, 7 Danish, 2 Finnish, 3 French, 10 German, 6 Italian, 2 Japanese, 2 Dutch, 2 Spanish, 6 Swedish, and 1 Swiss, as well as more than 1200 foreign magazines. The selection of periodicals at any one newsagent depends on the preferences of its customers. Understandably, downtown city newsagents carry more foreign newspapers and magazines than do those in suburbs or rural villages: Oslo leads the country in buying foreign magazines, with more than half of all fashion magazines and 40% of all lifestyle magazines sold in the country. Any newspaper or magazine in the catalogue may be ordered from a Narvesen newsagent who normally does not stock it, and subscriptions may be placed with all newsagents. Narvesen shops are easily recognised by the square company logo with a stencil block capital N.

Narvesen logo

Newspapers (*Aviser*) are read more avidly than in most countries. The average Norwegian over age 15 spends nearly one hour a day in reading newspapers and magazines. Close to three million copies of newspapers are sold on weekdays, and Norwegian newspaper circulation, in copies per thousand population, ranks highest in Europe and third in the world, behind Macau and first-place Hong Kong. As one Oslo daily editor put it, "the Norwegian press is on the verge of running out of Norwegians". There are newspapers in both of the common European formats: large and broad page broadsheet and smaller page tabloid (half broadsheet format). Both formats have stapled or glued spines, a Scandinavian newsprint tradition, which is convenient in reading because the pages are held together.

Freedom of the press is specifically guaranteed by the Constitution of 1814 and widely exercised. There are more than 200 newspapers in the country. Most are local, and only four, all based in Oslo, are true national dailies: *Aftenposten* with a broadsheet morning and tabloid afternoon edition, *Dagbladet* and *Verdens Gang (VG)*, the leading tabloids, and *Dagens Næringsliv*, the financial tabloid. VG leads in circulation, with an average daily sales of more than 370,000 copies, and the morning edition of *Aftenposten* is in second place with 286,000 (1997 figures). Some newspapers are politically oriented, most notably those with *Arbeiderblad* ("Labour Times") in their names, ☞ **political parties** (Government and Social Services chapter). Three media conglomerates rank among the country's leading companies: *Schibsted* with *Aftenposten*, *VG* and other newspapers; *A-Pressen* with a string of Labour newspapers; and *Orkla Media* with interests in local and national newspapers. More than 90 newspapers have Internet web sites.

For complete lists of newspapers and their post and web addresses, as well as for comprehensive information and statistics in Norwegian and in English on the country's newspapers, contact the Norwegian Newspaper Publishers' Association (*Norske Avisers Landsforening*) ✆ 22861200, ☏ 22422611, ✉ Tollbugt. 27, 0157 Oslo, ✉ nal@nal.no, ✈ http://www.nal.no

NORTRA Before you leave for Norway and after you first arrive, and even thereafter, you will probably want to learn more about the country and see more of it on holidays. You then can benefit from the extensive information provided by NORTRA (acronym for Norwegian Tourist Board), the umbrella organisation that supports, organises and publicises Norwegian tourism world-wide. Many NORTRA publications are in English and other languages; NORTRA books can be indispensable after you arrive and until you learn Norwegian, such as *Adventure Roads in Norway* by Erling Welle-Strand (NORTRA Books, 1996, ISBN 82-90-10371-9), the definitive guide in English to touring by car throughout the country. Consequently, one of your best first sources of information on Norway is at one of the NOTRA bureaux, in Amsterdam, Copenhagen, Hamburg, London, Madrid, Milan, New York, Paris, Stockholm and Tokyo. The head office is in Oslo: ✆ 22925200, ☏ 22560505, ✉ PO Box 2893 Solli, N-0230 Oslo, ✉ norway@nortra.no, ✈ http://www.nortra.no with pages in Norwegian and in English, and with addresses of and links to NORTRA bureaux in other countries.

National Gazette (*Norsk Lysingsblad*) is the government advertisement journal listing civil service announcements, public sector appointments, company registrations, bankruptcies, invitations to tender and other public notices. It is published Monday – Friday, except on public holidays, by the Government Administration Services (*Statens Forvaltningstjeneste*). The Friday edition features an EEA (*EØS*) supplement that includes the week's Tenders Electronic Daily (TED) database listings of international invitations to tender issued in EU and EEA member countries, as well many issued in non-member countries, such as Canada, Israel, Japan, Switzerland and the USA. The Gazette is sold by newsagents throughout the country. For subscriptions, contact *Norsk Lysingsblad* ✆ 76950550, ☏ 76950580, ✉ PO Box 177, 8501 Narvik, ✈ http://norsk.lysningsblad.no with access to a database of civil service vacancies throughout the country.

Phonetic alphabet (*Fonetisk alfabet*) There are two types of phonetic alphabet: code words for letters and characters for sounds. Both are international, and both are used in Norway.

When you call an automatic voice service, you may hear the code words that are used in voice telecommunications to identify letters of the alphabet. They have long been used in radio and other voice communications and now are standardised by the International Telecommunications Union (ITU) in the International Phonetic Alphabet. The Norwegian version is the ITU English version with three additional letters:

A Alfa	P Papa
B Bravo	Q Quebec
C Charlie	R Romeo
D Delta	S Sierra
E Echo	T Tango
F Foxtrot	U Uniform
G Golf	V Victor
H Hotel	W Whiskey
I India	X X-Ray
J Juliet	Y Yankee
K Kilo	Z Zulu
L Lima	Æ Ærlig
M Mike	Ø Østen
N November	Å Åse
O Oscar	

An alphabetic arrangement of separate characters for distinguishable speech sounds is widely used in the study and teaching of languages as well as to indicate the pronunciation of words listed in dictionaries. For further information on this International Phonetic Alphabet, contact the Secretary of the International Phonetic Association: J.H. Esling at the University of Victoria, Canada ☎ +1 2507217423, ⌧ Department o☞ Linguistics, University of Victoria, Victoria, BC V8W 3P4, Canada, ✉ esling@uvic.ca, ⊜ http://www.arts.gla.ac.uk/IPA with pages in English and downloadable files of the alphabet and links to related topics.

Photographic archives (*Fotoarkiv*) are maintained by many organisations in the public and private sectors. The three principal archives are listed below. There are also many commercial bureaux, see under *Bildebyråer* in the Yellow Pages.

The National Photographic Archive (*Nasjonalt fotoarkiv*), a part of the National Library, preserves historical collections and is the country's repository for photographic records of public interest ✆ 81500188, ⊜ http://www.nb.no with pages in Norwegian and in English. It has facilities in Oslo ☎ 23276010, ⌧ PO Box 2674 Solli, 0203 Oslo,

nbo@nb.no and in Mo i Rana ✆ ☎ 75121222, ⌧ 8607 Mo i Rana, ✉ nbr@nb.no

Scanpix Norge is the country's leading supplier of archive and other photographic services to printed media and other sectors. It has agreements with and can supply photographs from more than 80 archives around the world, including those of the major news agencies, AP, Reuters and EPA ✆ 22003200, ☎ 22003210, ⌧ Akersgt 55, 1080 Oslo, ✉ salg@scanfoto.no, ⊜ http://www.sol.no/scanfoto.

Husmo-foto specialises in scenic, cultural and aesthetic photographs, and supplies many of the photographs used in calendars and postal cards ✆ 22134250, ☎ 22060130, ⌧ PO Box 231 Skøyen, 0212 Oslo, ✉ post@husmo-foto.no, ⊜ http://www.husmo-foto.no

Public information (*Offentlig informasjon*) Pamphlets, data sheets and the like are widely available in public services facilities, such as libraries (*bibliotek*), kindergartens (*barnehage*), municipal offices (*kommune-kontorer*) and clinics (*helsestasjoner*). Most are in Norwegian, but many key publications are in English, French or German, as well as Turkish, Urdu or Vietnamese; these usually are made available in areas where language groups need them. The Government Administration Service (*Statens forvaltningstjeneste*) maintains two databases, ESOP and ODIN, which you may access from your own computer or from Internet terminals made available for public use at many public libraries (*folkebibliotek*).

ESOP, an acronym for Electronic Searchable Official Publications (*Elektroniske søkbare offentlige publikasjoner*), is a bibliographic database containing more than 25,000 references to documents released by ☞ **Parliament** and by the ☞ **Ministerial Government** (Government and Social Services chapter). ESOP is in Norwegian only, though some of the documents it lists are in other languages. Use of the site is free, and there are small charges for on-line ordering of printed documents delivered by post ⊜ http://www2.interpost.no/esop

ODIN, an acronym for Official Documentation and Information in Norway (*Offentlig dokumentasjon og informasjon i Norge*), is the central web server for the Ministerial Government, the Office of the Prime Minister and the Ministries. It is mostly in Norwegian, but has general information and news pages in English, French and German. It has links to databases maintained by the Ministries and by major Departments, as well as by Embassies and EU/EEA and UN missions. It also has its own search engine (*søkeverktøy*) and on-line Help (*Hjelp*) in Norwegian and in English ☞ http://odin.dep.no

Public notices (*Kunngjøringer*) are published in the classified advertising sections of newspapers, usually as one of the first categories. *Kunngjøringer* include all local and national government notices to the public as well as announcements and appeals by private organisations. For instance, if water supply or electricity are to be temporarily turned off, as required by construction works, residents are notified by advertisement under *Kunngjøringer*, usually with a map and description of the area affected. The typical topics of *Kunngjøringer* include, alphabetically by their equivalents in English:

Bankruptcies *Konkurs*
Building plans *Bebyggelsesplan*
Electricity *Strøm*
Estate of a deceased person *Dødsbo*
Exhibitions *Messe, Utstilling*
Forced sale by court order *Tvangsauksjon*
Grants *Støtte*
Inquiry *Undersøkelse*
Invitation to tender *Anbud, Tilbud*
Legal notice, as to persons having claims against an estate or bankruptcy *Proklama*
Mushroom check (annual free check by experts, of wild mushrooms picked) *Soppkontroll*
Outage *Stans*
Probate court *Skifterett*
Public display of plans *Offentlig ettersyn*
Public transport *Kollektivtrafikk*
Regional plan *Reguleringsplan*
Road works *Veiarbeid*
Scholarships *Stipend*
Schools *Skoler*
Sewage *Kloakk*
Snow removal *Snørydding*
Summons *Stevning*
Taxes *Skatt*
Telephone *Telefon*
Traffic re-direction *Trafikkregulering*
Water supply *Vann*

Satellite images (*Satellittbilder*) and other aerial photographs of many inhabited areas of the world are now available on-line from Microsoft's TerraServer. The images come from aerial photographs collected by the United States Geological Survey (USGS) and from pictures taken from the Russian Space Agency (SOVINFORMSPUTNIK) satellites. The TerraServer has point-and-click search and a zoom that permits clearly distinguishing buildings and other objects on the ground from each other. As this book goes to press, images of the area of Norway around the Oslofjord are available
☞ http://www.terraserver.microsoft.com

State directories (*Statskalendere*) are annual lists of governmental ministries, departments, agencies as well as of other related information, such as a list of embassies, all with addresses and telecommunication numbers. Two are available:

The official Norwegian Government Yearbook, including lists of State-owned companies, overviews of honorary orders, lists of municipalities by county and an alphabetical index of principal civil servants. In printed form, *Norges Statskalender 1999*, Oslo, Cappelen Akademisk Forlag, 1096 pages hardcover, and on-line at ☞ http://www.odin.dep.no/html/nofovalt/offpub/statskalenderen/1999 with links to all lists.

The public guide to government agencies and services, compiled by the ☞ **Central information service**, indexed and arranged by topic of query, with telecommunications numbers, including E-Mail and Internet addresses, in printed form, *Hvem svarer på hva i staten 1999*, Oslo, Tano-Aschehoug, 486 pages softcover, ISBN 82-518-3751-0.

Subscription (*Abonnement*) to a newspaper or magazine usually is the cheapest way to buy it regularly. Subscription almost always includes home delivery of local newspapers and of national newspapers within the metropolitan areas where they are published and in some other cities. Elsewhere, newspapers are sent by post. Some international newspapers offer delivery in downtown Oslo. Most Norwegian newspapers offer redirection and delivery or posting to summer holiday addresses and accordingly send subscribers temporary address change forms well in advance. Magazines are sent by post. There are two types of subscription agreement, both paid in advance, but differing in renewal practice. The subscriptions to most international newspapers and magazines cease when unpaid. The publisher will send you a renewal notice as well as one or more reminders, well before your subscription expires. If you don't pay, your subscription is cancelled. The subscriptions to many Norwegian newspapers and magazines are valid until cancelled by the subscriber, so renewal notices usually have statements such as *Abonnementet løper til det sies opp* (The subscription continues until you cancel it). If you don't pay, the subscription continues and you will be billed for late payment. The easiest way to subscribe to a newspaper or magazine is to contact its subscriber service (*abonnementsservice*), usually listed in the front or back of each issue, often with a coupon to fill out and return. The most common means of payment is by ☞ **Giro** (Banking, Finance and Insurance chapter).

Museums, exhibitions, fairs (*Muséer, utstillinger, marked, messer, festivaler*)

Art galleries (*Gallerier*) There are hundreds of municipal and private galleries; you will find them listed under *Kunstutstillinger* in the Yellow Pages. There are more than 60 major public and private foundation galleries; you will find them listed under *Muséer og samlinger* in the Yellow Pages as well as in the pages of the *Museumsnett Norge* web site ☻ http://museumsnett.no under the *Art and Applied Art* (English pages) or *Kunst og Kunstindustri* (Norwegian pages) category. Five of these galleries are of true international rank:

Henie-Onstad Art Centre (*Henie-Onstad Kunstsenter*), permanent and visiting exhibitions of modern art, concerts, and the trophies of figure-skating champion and film star Sonja Henie ✆ 67804880, 🖷 67543270, ✉ Sonja Heniesvei 31, 1311 Høvikodden.

The International Museum of Children's Art (*Det Internasjonale Basrnekunstmuseum*), the only one of its kind, an art gallery dedicated entirely to the works of children worldwide ✆ 22468573, 🖷 22692910, ✉ Lille Frøensvei 4, 0369 Oslo.

Munch Museum (*Munch-museet*), the collected paintings, prints and drawings of expressionist painter Edvard Munch ✆ 23241400, 🖷 23241414, ✉ Tøyengata 53, PO Box 2812 Tøyen, 0608 Oslo.

National Gallery (*Nasjonalgalleriet*), the national gallery of fine art with exhibits of international and Norwegian drawings, prints and paintings, including Munch's "Scream", the most famous of all Norwegian paintings ✆ 2200404, 🖷 22361132, ✉ Universitetsgt 13, PO Box 8157 Dep, 0033 Oslo.

Vigeland Museum (*Vigeland-museet*), the studio of sculptor Gustav Vigeland exhibiting sculptures, drawings, woodcuts and models of Vigeland Park, one of the largest collections of statuary anywhere ✆ 22542530, 🖷 22542530, ✉ Nobelsgt 32, 0268 Oslo.

Fairs (*Marked, Messe*) are of two types: the traditional agricultural fair (*marked*), usually held in the autumn and having sales stands and entertainment, and the more modern trade fair (*messe*) exhibiting goods and services, usually of a single business sector. You will find both listed under *Messe- og kongressarrangement* in the Yellow Pages.

Momarkedet ("Mo Fair") is the largest and oldest traditional fair, held each year in late August at Mysen, just south of the E18 highway, about two-thirds of the way between Oslo and the Swedish border, in rolling farmland ✆ 69845600, 🖷 69845601, ✉ Momarkedet, 1850 Mysen, ✉ post@momarkedet.no, ☻ http://www.momarkedet.no

Norway Trade Fairs (*Norges Varemesse*) is the major exhibition organiser, in a large centre at Skøyen at the southwestern border of Oslo (after 2002, at Lillestrøm, northeast of Oslo) ✆ 22439100, 🖷 22431914, ✉ PO Box 130 Skøyen, 0212 Oslo, ✉ nv@messe.no, ☻ http://www.messe.no with pages and descriptions of ongoing and forthcoming exhibitions in Norwegian and English.

Festivals (*Festivaler*) are held throughout the country and throughout the year, but mostly in the summertime. The Bergen International Festival is the major classical musical event of the year. Held each year since 1953, it now is co-ordinated with the Night Jazz festival held at the same time, in late May ✆ 55552020, 🖷 55552025, ✉ PO Box 183, 5001 Bergen, ☻ http://www.fib.no with pages in English. More than 30 other music, art, film and literature festivals are held each year. Programmes, brochures and other information on them are available from the Norwegian festival network, *Norske Festivaler* ✆ 22380066, 🖷 22381116, ✉ Sagveien 23a, 0458 Oslo, ✉ norfest@online.no ☻ http://www.horisont.no/festivaler with pages in Norwegian and in English and with the addresses of and links to all festivals.

Museums (*Museer*) There are more than 800 museums in the country. You can find them listed under *Muséer og samlinger* in the Yellow Pages and in the pages of the *Museumsnett Norge* web site ☻ http://museumsnett.no with pages in Norwegian and in English and links to all museums with web sites. Arguably, eight of the museums are unique:

Alta Museum, an open-air exhibition of the pictographs listed as a UNESCO World Heritage Site ✆ 78456330, 🖷 78456350, ✉ Altaveien 19, 9518 Alta.

Fram Museum (*Frammuséet*), the ship and artifacts of the expeditions that proved the Northwest Passage and first put men at the South Pole ℗ 22438370, ☎ 22550766, ✉ Bygdøynesvn 36, 0286 Oslo.

Kon-Tiki Museum (*Kon-Tiki Museet*), the preserved raft that took ethnographic explorer Thor Heyredahl across the Pacific in an attempt to challenge theories of world settlement ℗ 22086767, ☎ 22086760, ✉ Bygdøynesv 36, 0286 Oslo.

Norwegian Emigrant Museum (*Norsk utvandrermuseum*), a resource centre on the period of major emigration in the late 19th and early 20th centuries ℗ 62574850, ☎ 62574851, ✉ Åkershagan, 2312 Ottestad.

Norwegian Folk Museum (*Norsk Folkemuseum*), one of the largest open-air museums in Europe, with more than 150 historical buildings including the Gol stave church built in 1200 and an extensive summer programme of folk dancing and other events ℗ 22123666, ☎ 22123777, ✉ Museumsvn 10, 0287 Oslo.

Norwegian Glacier Museum (*Norsk Bremuseum*), an exhibition and resource centre on the powers of nature that shaped the country ℗ 57693288, ☎ 57693287, ✉ 5855 Fjærland.

Ski Museum (*Skimuseet*), the world's oldest and largest museum dedicated to the history of skiing, located just below the Holmenkollen ski jump ℗ 22923200, ☎ 22923250, ✉ Kongeveien 5, 0787 Oslo.

Viking Ship Museum (*Vikingskiphuset*), three superbly preserved long ships and other Viking artefacts ℗ 22438379, ☎ 22445581, ✉ Huk Aveny 35, 0287 Oslo.

Non-Government Organisations (*NGOs*)

Amnesty International is a world-wide organisation for the protection of the rights of prisoners of conscience. The General Assembly of the United Nations founded it in London in 1961 and bases its activities on the Universal Declaration of Human Rights, proclaimed in 1948. Round the world, Amnesty International works to promote human rights in many ways, principally to:
- Free all prisoners of conscience detained anywhere for their beliefs or because of their ethnic origin, sex, colour or language – who have not used or advocated violence.
- Ensure fair and prompt trials for political prisoners.
- Abolish the death penalty, torture and other cruel treatment of prisoners.
- End extrajudicial executions and "disappearances".

In 1977, Amnesty International's efforts for humanity were recognised by the Nobel Peace Prize, awarded by ☞ **The Norwegian Nobel Committee**. World-wide, Amnesty International now has more than one million members. In Norway, there are five Amnesty International groups: The Norwegian Section head office in Oslo, the Malaysia Co-ordination Group, the International Student Festival in Trondheim, the Norwegian School of Economics and Business Administration Group in Bergen, and Group 280. These groups work to promote and support Amnesty International activities. For further details on how you may participate or contribute, contact the head office in Oslo ✆ 22402200, ☎ 22402250, ✉ PO Box 702 Sentrum, 0106 Oslo, ✉ admin-no@amnesty.no, ⊕ http://www.amnesty.no with link to the international site at ⊕ http://www.amnesty.org.

AOF is the abbreviation of *Arbeidernes Opplysningforbund* ("The Workers' Educational Association") and is part of the ☞ **labour movement** (Character, Customs, Country chapter). It is a co-ordinating body for 49 national organisations, including trade unions, political groups and cultural and service organisations, such as ☞ **Norwegian People's Aid**. For further information, contact the head office ✆ 23061050, ☎ 23061270, ✉ PO Box 8703 Youngstorget, 0028 Oslo, ⊕ http://thrane.fb.no/aof with pages in Norwegian and summary pages in English.

Bellona is a result-oriented, scientifically-based environmental foundation. It was founded in 1986 in Oslo, the year that the Chernobyl nuclear power plant explosion spread radioactive fallout over Scandinavia. The name Bellona is that of a goddess of Roman mythology, whose domain of power was all of human conflict, both military and diplomatic. The Bellona operations reflect that myth, in that it is both an activist organisation and a conflict mediator. Those roles have increasingly involved it in environmental issues of international concern in Europe, such as the late 1990s activities to draw international attention to the seriousness of the radioactive contamination in Murmansk and Archangel's counties in Russia. Its overall aim is to propose feasible solutions, which have minimal impact on human activity. In 1989, it started regular publication of an environmental affairs magazine, *Bellona Magasin*. In 1996, Bellona Europe was registered as a non-profit organisation in Belgium and an office was then opened in Brussels. Moreover, in 1996 Bellona opened an office in Murmansk and became a member of the Russian Socio-ecological Union (SEU). In additions to these offices abroad, Bellona now has liaison offices in St. Petersburg, Russia and in Washington, DC, USA. For further information on Bellona and its activities, contact the head office in Oslo ✆ 22382410, ☎ 22383862, ✉ PO Box 2141 Grünerløkka, 0505 Oslo, ✉ bellona@bellona.no, ⊕ http://www.bellona.no with pages in Norwegian, English and Russian.

Blue Cross (*Blå Kors*) is an apolitical, non-denominational Christian organisation dedicated to combating alcohol and drug abuse. The International Federation of the Blue Cross was founded in 1877 in Geneva, Switzerland and now is active in more than 40 countries, mostly in Europe and in Africa. In the UK, it is affiliated with Hope UK, and in Sweden with Blue Ribbon, but otherwise it is independent of other organisations. (Blue Cross in Europe has no connection whatsoever with the Blue Cross health insurance company in the USA.) The first Norwegian chapter was founded in 1906 in Oslo, and in 1909 it became a national organisation. It now has 10,000 members, 10 district offices (*kretskontor*), 100 chapters (*hovedforeninger*), 50 women's groups (*kvinneforeninger*) and 20 brotherhoods (*kameratklubber*). It operates 30 centres of various types, including withdrawal stations, polyclinics, long-term treatment and care, rehabilitation, housing assistance, schooling and crisis centres for women. It provides expertise in the care and treatment of alcoholics and addicts, and it operates youth programmes to promote an alcohol-free, drug-free lifestyle. It has 600 employees, most of whom speak English and other European languages, in addition to Norwegian. For information, contact the nearest chapter, see *Blå Kors* in the Pink Pages, the national headquarters in Oslo ✆ 22204269, 🖷 22363101, ✉ PO Box 4793 Sofienberg, 0506 Oslo, ✉ landsadm@blakors.no, ✉ http://nettvik.no/kirkebakken/blaakors, or the international headquarters in Bern ✆ +41 31 3005860, 🖷 +41 31 3005869, ✉ PO Box 6813, CH-3001 Bern, Switzerland, ✉ ifbc.bern@bluewin.ch, ✉ http://www.eurocare.org/bluecross

The Environmental Home Guard (*Miljøheimevernet*) is a joint effort by 17 organisations who directly or indirectly are concerned with environmental matters. They include The Church o🖷 Norway, The Norwegian Confederation of Sports, the YMCA and YWCA and the Folk High Schools, as well as associations concerned with outdoor recreation, farming and health. Its focus is on households and recreational activities, and its aim is to promote individual environmental awareness as well as to organise volunteer activities that benefit the environment ✆ 22715562, 🖷 22717785, ✉ PO Box 2113 Grünerløkka, 0505 Oslo, ✉ miljohv@miljohv.no, ✉ http://www.miljohv.no with pages in Norwegian and in English.

The European Movement (*Europabevegelsen*) is the most important of the organisations created after the second world war to unify the countries of Europe. The first Congress of Europe held in The Hauge in May 1948 resulted in the creation of the Council of Europe in May 1949 and other related organisations soon thereafter. Since 1948, the Euro-

pean Movement has played a vital role in the unification of the European Community. It now consists of two groups of organisations: the national councils, which are active in all EU member countries and in most member countries of the Council of Europe, and non-governmental organisations (NGOs), which support and promote the cause of European unity. Norway's NGO, *Europabevgelsen*, has been active since 1949, with a head office in Oslo and local chapters in Oslo, Akershus and Hedemark counties. For further details on *Europabevegelsen*, contact the head office ✆ 22993600, 🖷 22993601, ✉ Fredensborgveien 6, 0177 Oslo, ✉ eb@europahuset.no, ✉ http://nettvik.no/foreningsgarde...opahuset/europ agevegelsen/org, or for information on the European Movement throughout Europe, contact the headquarters in Brussels ✆ +32 2 5124444, 🖷 +32 2 5126673, ✉ Place du Luxembourg 1, B-1050 Brussels, Belgium, ✉ eruopean.movement@skynet.be, ✉ http://eurplace.org/orga/european.movement with pages in English and in French.

ForUM is a network for some 60 NGOs involved in international environmental and development activities. It facilitates contact between organisations, the media and individuals concerned with the environment and development in other countries. It publishes a monthly newsletter in Norwegian, a quarterly ecological bulletin in Norwegian and a semiannual newsletter in English. Contact the head office for further details and the names and addresses of member and associate NGOs ✆ 22209870, 🖷 22203780, ✉ Storgata 33A, 0184 Oslo, ✉ forum@online.no, ✉ http://disserver.dis.no/forum with pages in Norwegian and in English.

Friendship North-South (*Vennskap Nord/Sør*) is an organisation that helps strengthen international development co-operation through linking communities in southern, developing countries with corresponding communities in northern, developed countries. Its members include some 80 local authorities (*kommuner*), non-government organisations (NGOs) and friendship groups (*vennskapsgrupper*) for Afghanistan, Bangladesh, Cambodia, El Salvador, Eritrea, Ethiopia, Gambia, Guatemala, India, Kenya, Madagascar, Mexico, Mozambique, Namibia, Nepal, Nicaragua, Palestine, South Africa, Tanzania, Uganda and Zimbabwe. For further details and addresses contact the head office ℘ 22994610, ✉ 22994601, ✉ PO Box 6747 St. Olavs plass, 0130 Oslo, ✉ vennskap@online.no, ⊕ http://home.sol.no/~vennskap

Greenpeace is an international organisation that campaigns actively to promote conservation and protect the environment. Its head office is in Amsterdam, The Netherlands, and it has national Greenpeace organisations in 41 countries round the world. On the global scale, it's key campaign goals concern the prevention of climate change, eliminating sources of persistent organic pollutants (POPs) including PVC and chlorine, safeguarding the marine biodiversity of the oceans, protecting future generations from the effects of nuclear contamination, saving the remaining 20% of ancient forests and halting genetic pollution by banning the release of genetically engineered organisms into the environment. For further information, Contact Greenpeace Norge in Oslo ℘ 22205101, ✉ 22205114, ✉ Peder Claussøns gt 1, 0165 Oslo, ✉ info@se.greenpeace.org or the head office of Greenpeace International in Amsterdam ℘ +31 20 5236222, ✉ +31 20 5236200, ✉ Keizersgrach ℘ 176, 1016 DW Amsterdam, The Netherlands, ⊕ http://www.greenpeace.org in English with links to pages in the native languages of the 41 countries having Greenpeace national organisations.

The Ideas Bank (*Idébanken*) is an independent foundation devoted to promoting sustainable development, in accordance with the principles put forth by the United Nations Commission on Sustainable Development (CSD) and Agenda 21, the action plan for the 21st century approved by 171 nations in 1992 at a congress held in Rio de Janeiro, Brazil. The Idea Bank has three principal strategies. First, it promulgates good examples of social innovation that augur sustainable development. The emphasis is on practical approaches rather than on concepts. Second, it promotes and assists creative discussion and dialogue on the aspects of the future, by communities, firms, organisations or other groups. In this effort, it employs the techniques of Future Workshops and SWOT (Strengths, Weaknesses, Opportunities, Threats) analysis. Finally, it prompts future studies to assess potential paths to follow. Idea Bank's programme of activties include courses, publications, study trips and lectures. It maintains a Centre for Future Studies (*Møteplass for framtidsdiskusjon*) in Fredensborgveien 24D in downtown Oslo. The Centre has a library, exhibitions, a workshop and other facilities, including a database for future studies, and is open to the public. For further details, contact the head office ℘ 22034010, ✉ 22364060, ✉ PO Box 2126 Grünerløkka, 0505 Oslo, ✉ idebanken@online.no, ⊕ http://www.idebanken.no with pages in Norwegian and in English.

International Peace Research Institute, Oslo – PRIO (*Institutt for fredsforskning*) was founded in 1959 and conducts research in four principal themes: conditions of war and peace; ethics, norms and identities; foreign and security policies; and conflict resolution and peace building. It publishes two international journals in English, the *Journal of Peace Research* and *Security Dialogue*, as well as a book series. Since 1969, PRIO has been responsible for a six-week course in peace research at the ☞ **International Summer School** (Education chapter) of the University of Oslo. In 1997 it was one of the four founding agencies of ☞ **NISAT**, The Norwegian Initiative on Small Arms Transfers. PRIO now has an international staff of about 50 people. For further information, contact the head office in Oslo ℘ 22547700, ✉ 22547701, ✉ Fuglehauggata 11, 0260 Oslo, ✉ info@prio.no, ⊕ http://www.prio.no with pages in English.

MiRA resource centre (*MiRA ressurssenter*) The full name – the MiRA Resource Centre for Black, Immigrant and Refugee women – points to its being a national facility dedicated to assisting women from abroad, of all nationalities and ethnic origins. In addition to Norwegian, the staff at the MiRA head office in Oslo speak English, Hindi, Punjabi and Urdu as well as several other language. It offers four broad categories of services.

Legal and social counselling: The Centre provides assistance and counselling on legal and social affairs including financial or marital problems, immigration rules and regulations, asylum, deportation and conflict within the family.

Networking: The Centre is the only networking organisation for minority women on an national and Nordic level. It arranges seminars and conferences for minority women where they may discuss issues relevant to their social, economic, political or cultural status.

Information is essential in building the dialogue that promotes mutual understanding in the evolving multicultural society. Accordingly, the Centre has information activities, both for minority women and for Norwegians working with them. It publishes a quarterly magazine, *MiRA*, in Norwegian with a summary page in English, as well as numerous theme pamphlets on relevant current topics. It also holds lectures and gives courses to institutions and organisations seeking greater insight into the problems facing minority women. It maintains and continuously updates archives of information and statistics and acts as a reference source for public agencies as well as private organisations.

Meeting place for young women: The Centre supports a network of young women who arrange meetings on a wide variety of topics and build support groups. In so doing, they elevate awareness and help women take part in the social debates that affect their lives.

The Centre is partly subsidised by the Ministry of Local Government and Regional Development, partly financed by sale of its publications and subscriptions to its magazine, and reliant on volunteers throughout the country. For further details on how you may benefit from MiRA services or contribute to its activities, contact the head office in Oslo ✆ 22116920, ☎ 22364019, ✉ PO Box 1749 Vika, 0121 Oslo, ✉ mira@powertech.no

NISAT – The Norwegian Initiative on Small Arms Transfers

Throughout the 1990s, an estimated six million people have been killed in conflict or "post-conflict" zones round the world. The vast majority of the victims have been civilians. The weapons most commonly-used in conflict and in crime are small arms – automatic rifles, grenades, submachine guns, high-powered pistols and other arms that a single person can easily transport and fire. These arms remain readily available. The end of the Cold War freed copious amounts of them from the former military arsenals of many states, and the black-market thrives. In December 1997, four Norwegian organisations banded together to launch the Norwegian Initiative on Small Arms Transfers (NISAT). NISAT works to:

- formulate and promote standards and agreements by which governments register, control or ban certain kinds of small-arms transfers.
- stimulate and support local and regional initiatives to limit small arms transfers.
- promote a better undersanding of the relationship between security and development.
- develop a suitable research programme to help inform and refine policy goals.

The four partner organisations in NISAT bring together two of the world's largest movements – The Red Cross/Crescent and the Christian Churches and include two key research and foreign policy institutions. Moreover, NISAT has the political and financial backing of the Norwegian government. The NISAT partner organisations are ☞ **The Norwegian Institute of International Affairs** (Government and Social Services chapter), **The International Peace Research Institute, Norwegian Church Aid** and **The Norwegian Red Cross**. For further details on NISAT, contact the International Department of the Norwegian Red Cross ✆ 22054156, ☎ 22054040, ✉ PO Box 1 Grønland, 0133 Oslo, ✉ ole.sunde@redcross.no, ✉ http://www.nisat.org

Norwegian Church Aid (*Kirkens Nødhjelp*) was founded in 1947 in response to need in Europe after the second world war. Now it is one of the country's largest non-governmental humanitarian and development organisations. It operates in many developing countries, supporting projects in Africa, Asia, Europe and Latin America. Its major international partners are national church councils, the World Council of Churches and the Lutheran World Federation. It supports an extensive information service in Norway with the purpose of increasing public awareness of developing countries and of promoting a more just and sustainable international order. It is increasingly active in matters of international concern; in 1997 it was one of the four founding agencies of ☞ **NISAT**, The Norwegian Initiative on Small Arms Transfers. Norwegian Church Aid initially was a ☞ **Church of Norway** (Church and Religion chapter) organisation, but now is Protestant ecumenical (involving all faiths). For further information, contact the head office in Oslo ✆ 22222299, ☎ 22222420, ✉ PO Box 4544 Torshov, 0404 Oslo, ✉ nca_oslo@sn.no, ✉ http://www.nca.no

The Norwegian Nobel Committee (*Den Norske Nobelkomite*) The Nobel Foundation is a private institution established in 1900 on the basis of the will of Swedish industrialist Alfred Nobel. It conducts numerous activities and is best known for its annual awards of the internationally prestigious Nobel Prizes in six fields of endeavour. Four organisations, three in Sweden and one in Norway, are responsible for the nomination and selection of the Nobel Laureates:

- Physics – the Royal Swedish Academy of Sciences
- Chemistry – the Royal Swedish Academy of Sciences
- Physiology or Medicine – the Nobel Assembly at the Karolinska Institute, Sweden
- Literature – the Swedish Academy
- Peace – the Norwegian Nobel Committee
- Economic Sciences [the Sveriges Riksbank (Central Bank) prize in memory of Alfred Nobel] – the Swedish Academy of Sciences

Alfred Nobel did not divulge why he elected to have the Peace Prize awarded by a Norwegian committee, whilst the other Prizes were to be awarded by Swedish Committees. There are three plausible theories which may explain his decision. First, when Nobel drew up his will, Norway and Sweden were united. He may have felt that Swedish organisations possessed the insight to award most of the Prizes, but that Norway should award at least one. Second, Nobel held views on many contemporary problems that were radical for his time. Consequently, he may have been influenced by the actions of the Norwegian Storting, which had promoted mediation, arbitration and peaceful solution as means of settling international disputes. Finally, Nobel admired Norwegian literature and may have been influenced by the works of Bjørnstjerne Bjørnson, and his devotion to the cause of peace.

The Norwegian Nobel Committee comprises five members appointed by the Storting, ☞ **Parliament** (Government and Social Services chapter) and meets at the Nobel Institute in Oslo. It is completely independent and receives neither instructions nor directives on its work. According to the statutes of the Nobel Foundation, its work is not made public, so its members do not take part in public discussions of its decisions. In addition to its work in connection with the annual award of the Peace Prize, The Nobel Institute maintains a library, runs a research programme, co-ordinates Nobel symposia and makes Nobel Foundation materials available to schools, colleges, universities, the media and the public. For further details, contact the Nobel Institute in Oslo ℡ 22443680, 🖷 22430168, ✉ Drammensveien 19, 0255 Oslo, ✉ postmaster@nobel.no, 🖳 http://www.nobel.no with pages in Norwegian and in English and a link to the official website of the Nobel Foundation in Stockholm for information on all the Prizes 🖳 http://www.nobel.se

Norwegian People's Aid (*Norsk Folkehjelp*) was founded in 1939 by the labour movement and now is one of the country's largest non-governmental organisations. It conducts aid programmes within Norway and is involved in more than 30 aid projects in 30 countries. Its domestic activities include:

- Rescue services throughout the country
- First aid and public health information services
- Assistance during natural disasters
- Assistance to the elderly and disabled
- Support of anti-violence programmes and facilities
- Operation of reception centres for asylum seekers

The organisation's international activities include:

- Long-term development assistance within agriculture, environmental activities, production, health care, social assistance, human rights and help to self-help
- Emergency assistance: shelters, rehabilitation, medical aid and mobile clinics
- Mine-clearance and mine-awareness programmes starting in Cambodia in 1992, Mozambique in 1993, Angola in 1994 and Iraq in 1995
- Conflict prevention and resolution

In Norway, *Norsk Folkehjelp* is perhaps most widely recognised for its extensive first aid and rescue services that together have a staff of more than 12,000 volunteers. Centres throughout the country support aid services to the public and offer first-aid courses; look under *Norsk Folkehjelp Sanitet* in the Pink Pages for the address and telecom numbers of the nearest centre. For information on the organisation and its activities, contact the head office in Oslo ℡ 22037700, 🖷 22200870, ✉ PO Box 8844 Youngstorget, 0028 Oslo, ✉ Landmines@npaid.no for information on landmines, No.to.Violence@npaid.no for information on violence against women, npaid@npaid.no for general information, ⊛ http://www.folkehjelp.no with pages in Norwegian and in English.

The Norwegian Red Cross (*Røde Kors*) is part of the International Red Cross/Red Crescent movement. It is among the world's oldest national Red Cross/Red Crescent organisations, founded in 1865, just two years after the first Red Cross organisation was founded in Switzerland. The Norwegian Red Cross now has around 250,000 members, of which 40,000 are actively involved in its voluntary and humanitarian work. It is divided into four branches:- Rescue Corps, Red Cross Youth, Child Relief and Visitor Service. Moreover, it operates four recreational centres for the disabled, a blood transfusion programme and a transit centre for refugees and asylum seekers, and is responsible for operating a third of all ambulances in Norway. It is increasingly active in international humanitarian work, and in 1997 was one of the four founding agencies of ☞ **NISAT**, The Norwegian Initiative on Small Arms Transfers. In November 1997, the President of the Norwegian Red Cross, Astrid Nøklebye Heiberg, was elected president of the International Federation of Red Cross and Red Crescent Societies. For further information, contact the nearest chapter, listed in the Pink Pages under the name of the municipality followed by *Røde Kors*, or contact the head office in Oslo ✆ 22054000, ℻ 22054040, ⊠ PO Box 1 Grønland, 0133 Oslo, ✉ documentation.center@redcross.no, ⊛ http://www.redcross.no

The Norwegian Refugee Council (*Flykt-ningsrådet*) started as Aid to Europe in 1946, just after the second world war, inspired by the work of Norwegian explorer and statesman Fridtjof Nansen after the first world war. Through the 1940s and 1950s, it was mostly concerned in aiding refugees in Europe, but thereafter it extended its sphere of concern to the Middle East and beyond. By the 1990s, it had become a global organisation, capable of providing the United Nations (UN) with expertise on refugee situations at short notice, just 72 hours. Most of its work is in project operations aimed to provide humanitarian assistance to people fleeing their homes and to defend their fundamental rights. The NRC now has offices abroad in Angola, Armenia, Azerbaijan, Bosnia, Burundi, Colombia, Croatia,

Georgia, North Ossetia (Russia), Rwanda, Switzerland, Uganda and Yugoslavia. Another goal is to promote public awareness of the plight and needs of refugees and international displaced persons (IDPs). It publishes several periodicals in Norwegian, and maintains a dedicated library of refugee and migration literature, comprising some 5,000 titles and 200 journals plus video and photo libraries and a press clippings library, all open to the public. Its annual turnover of NOK 300 million is funded by the UN High Commissioner for Refugees, the Norwegian Ministry of Foreign Affairs, and private gifts and donations. For further information, contact the head office in Oslo ✆ 231098090, ℻ 23109801, ⊠ PO Box 6758 St. Olavs plass, 0130 Oslo, ✉ nrc-no@online.no, ⊛ http://www.nrc.no with pages in Norwegian and in English.

Rafto Foundation (*Raftostiftelsen*) Professor Thorolf Rafto (1922-86) of the Norwegian School of Economics and Business Administration (*Norges handelshøgskole*) dedicated much of his professional life as an international human rights activist and was the first western intellectual to call attention to the plight of the Jews of the Soviet Union. The Professor Thorolf Rafto Foundation for Human Rights commemorates his dedication through the Rafto Prize for Human Rights, awarded annually on 4 November, the anniversary of his death. In the spirit of Thorolf Rafto, the Foundation aims to continue his human rights work and promote intellectual freedom, political freedom and freedom of trade. Many recipients of the Rafto Prize have also been nominated for the Nobel Peace Prize, and twice, in 1991 and 1996, successfully, which illustrates a close connection between fundamental human rights and peace. The recipients to date: 1987: Jiri Hajek and "Charter 77" of Czechoslovakia, 1988: Trivimi Velliste of Estonia, 1989: Doina Cornea of Romania and FIDESZ of Hungary, 1990: Aung San Suu Kyi of Burma (awarded 1991 Nobel Peace Prize), 1991: Jelena Bonner of Russia, 1992: Preah Maha Ghosananda of Cambodia, 1993: the People of East-Timor represented by José Ramos-Harta (awarded 1996 Nobel Peace Prize), 1994: Leyla Zana of Khurdistan, 1995: The Soldiers' Mothers Committee in Russia, 1996: Palermo Annu Uno of Italy, 1997: The Romani (Gypsy) People, 1998: End Child Prostitution, Child Pornography and the Trafficking of Children for Sexual Purposes

(ECPAT). For further details, contact the Foundation at its head office ✆ 55210950, ☎ 55210959, ✉ The Rafto House, Olaf Ryes vei 19, 5007 Bergen, ✉ rafto@rafto.no

RORG is an abbreviation for *Rammeavtale ORGanisasjon* ("Framework Agreement Organisations"). It is a collective name for 28 organisations which receive support from ☞ **NORAD** (Government and Social Services chapter) for information and promotion activities in Norway on North-South and other development matters. The organisations include (Norwegian names only): *Arbeidernes Opplysningsforbund, CARE-Norge, Det Kongelige Selskap for Norges Vel, Fellesrådet for Afrika, FOKUS (Forum for Kvinner og Utviklings Spørsmål), Folkehøgskolerådet, FORUT, Framtiden i våre hender, Frikirkens Globale Informajson, Høyres Studieforbund, Idégruppen om Nord/Sør, Internasjonal Reporter, Kirkerådet/MKR, Kr.F's Studieforbund, Landslaget for norske barne- og ungdomsorganisasjoner, Latin-Amerikagruppene i Norge, LO's Internasjonale avdeling, Norsk Fredskorpssamband, Operasjon Dagsverk, Regnskogsfondet, SAIH, Senterpartiets Studiefond, Sosialistisk Opplysningsforbund, Strømmenstiftelsen, Studieforbund Ny verden, Utviklingsfondet, Vennskap Nord/sør* and *Venstres Opplysningsforbund* For further details and addresses of the RORG's, contact the RORG co-ordination office ✆ 22362200, ☎ 22362280, ✉ Osterhausgt. 27, 0183 Oslo, ✉ norg@rorg.no, ✆ http://solidaritetshuset.org/rorg

The Royal Norwegian Society for Development (*Det Kongelige Selskap for Norges Vel*) is a non-government organisation which works to develop sustainable communities. It is involved principally in forage crop production, forage conservation and feeding, developing cost-effective animal production, soil and plant culture, sustainable agriculture, education and agriculture in general. It maintains a research farm at Hellerud and arranges seminars and conferences there, often on rural topics not directly concerned with agriculture, such as the design and building of holiday homes and the preservation of older rural buildings. It is funded both by public sector agencies and private sector companies, and it works closely with the Agricultural University of Norway (*Norges Landbrukshøgskole*) at Ås. It is allied with the co-operative movement and conducts international aid programmes under the auspices of the Norwegian Center for International Co-operative Development (NORCOOP), a joint effort of various co-operative organisations in the country. NORCOOP is now involved in projects in Africa, Central America, the Palestinian areas of the Middle East and Eastern Europe. For further details on the Society and on NORCOOP, contact the head office at Skjetten ✆ 64832000, ☎ 64832001, ✉ PO Box 115, 2026 Skjetten, ✉ norgesvel@norgesvel.no, ✆ http://www.norgesvel.no

The Salvation Army (*Frelsesarmeen*) is an integral part of the Christian Church, although distinctive in its administration and practice. The movement was founded in 1865 in London and spread to many other countries around the world. It is organised in the military style for efficiency in conducting its many evangelistic and social enterprises, and its message is based on the Bible. Today, it works in more than 100 countries using more than 140 languages. The Norwegian national headquarters was set up in 1888, and now there are more than 100 corps throughout the country, in all 19 counties. The headquarters in Oslo also administers the Army's activities in Iceland and the Faeroes, and together some 8,000 Salvationists (as members of the Army are called) are active in the three countries. In Norway, the Army is the leading Non-Government Organisation (NGO) engaged in social activities. It operates the country's largest chain of used clothing outlets, some 57 in all, under the *Fretex* name. It other social activities include 15 centres for alcoholics and drug addicts, 12 children's and youth institutions, four kindergartens, 12 slum centres, eight facilities for the elderly, two facilities in prisons, three facilities for the blind and deaf. It provides one of the ☞ **Folk high schools** (Education chapter) at Jeløy, southeast of Oslo on the Fjord. Salvation Army officers from Norway are active in Bangladesh, Ghana, Haiti, India, Kenya, South Africa and Zimbabwe. For further details on local activities, contact the closest corps (*korps*) listed under *Frelsesarmeen* in the Pink pages. For details on the country as a whole, contact the headquarters in Oslo ✆ 22998500, ☎ 22112063, ✉ PO Box 6866 St. Olavs plass, 0130 Oslo, ✆ http://www.frelsesarmeen.no with pages in Norwegian and in English.

Save the Children (*Redd Barna*) is an independent, voluntary, humanitarian organisation that is politically and religiously neutral. It was founded in 1946 to aid needy children in the aftermath of the second world war. Its first actions included sending packages of food and clothing to children in central Europe and bringing children from other countries to spend holidays in Norway. Through the years, its international activities have expanded, most rapidly after the United Nations (UN) Convention on the Rights of the Child became internationally binding in 1990. It supports an extensive godparent (*fadder*) arrangement whereby a donor contributes financial support for a needy child in one of 23 countries in which *Redd Barna* works in Africa, Asia, Europe and Latin America. It is supported through this arrangement, by donors and by volunteers, some 300,000 people in all, from all sectors of Norwegian society. It now has offices in Bergen, Kristiansand, Oslo, Stavanger, Stokke and Trondheim. For further details on how you may support or work with *Redd Barna*, contact the nearest *Redd Barna* office listed in the Pink Pages. For general information, contact the head office in Oslo ✆ 22990900, 🖷 22990870, ✉ PO Box 6902 St. Olavs plass, 0130 Oslo, ✉ post@reddbarna.no, ➥ http://www.reddbarna.no with pages in Norwegian and summary pages in English.

SOS Children's Villages in Norway (*SOS-barnebyer Norge*) SOS Children's Villages is an independent, private, apolitical and non-denominational welfare organisation. It establishes and operates SOS Children's Villages, which offer abandoned, orphaned and destitute children – regardless of race, nationality or creed – a new and permanent home, to help prepare for an independent life. It was founded in 1949, when Hermann Gmeiner founded the first SOS Children's Village at Imst, Austria. The idea spread: within 20 years there were 70 SOS Children's Villages in 20 countries; there are now more than 380 in 130 countries. There has been widespread public support of the concept, and in 1995 the *Fédération Internationale de Football (FIFA)* – The International Football (Soccer) Association established the "FIFA for SOS Children's Villages" partnership. In Norway, *SOS-barnebyer Norge* funds the building and operation of Villages, and offers an extensive godparent (*fadder*) arrangement in which a donor

can financially support a Village or a child in a specified Village. It also helps support *SOS-Kinderdorf International*, the umbrella organisation for all national associations. For information on how you may contribute to or volunteer for the work of SOS Children's Villages, contact *SOS-barnebyer Norge* ✆ 22479280, 🖷 22479281, ✉ PO Box 733 Sentrum, 0105 Oslo, ✉ sos@sos-barnebyer.no, ➥ http://www.sos-barnebyer.no. For a global overview of SOS Children's Villages or the details of villages and offices in 130 countries, contact *SOS-Kinderdorf International* ✆ +43 512 591800, 🖷 +43 512 580001, ✉ PO Box 645, A-6021 Innsbruck, Austria, ➥ http://www.sos-kd-org with pages in English, French, German and Spanish.

UNICEF in Norway (*UNICEF-komitéen i Norge*) is part of the United Nations Children's Fund, which was founded in 1946 to rescue the starving children of post-war Europe from famine and disease. It then distributed powered milk, began inoculation programmes and promoted education and medical care. By the end of the postwar reconstruction period, its focus had become global. Its major concern remains the provision of basic necessities to the 650 million children of the world who live in poverty. It is now concerned with many other aspects of the lives of children. Starting in 1990, when the United Nations Convention on the Rights of the Child became internationally binding, UNICEF has pursued the dual goals of eliminating child labour worldwide and providing education to ensure decent lives above the survival level. UNICEF in Norway acts both to further public awareness of UNICEF and to help fund UNICEF work. It does this through publishing a quarterly magazine, *FNs Barn* ("The UN's Children"), supporting educational programmes for schools and acting as an information centre for UNICEF activities. It is financed through contributions and sales of UNICEF gifts, including the popular greeting cards sold by the UNICEF Committee in the shop at its head office or by mail order, as well as by Post Offices throughout the country. For further information on UNICEF or on how you may support its efforts while in Norway, contact the head office in Oslo ✆ 22363340, 🖷 22363010, ✉ Møllergaten 24, 0179 Oslo, ✉ unicef@online.no, ➥ http://www.unicef.no

Organisations, societies, clubs (*Organisasjoner, foreninger, klubber*)

Druidism (*Druidorden*) The Ancient Order of Druidism – AOD is devoted to preserving the culture of the Celtic Druids. The Norwegian Order, *Forenede Gamle Druid-Orden* – FGDO has about 2,000 brothers in 42 Lodges, of which three are in Oslo and two are in Iceland. The associated Birgitta Order for women has 21 Lodges, including three in Denmark and one in Germany. For further information, contact the chancellery (kanselliet) ✆ 33474400, ✉ 33474450, ✉ PO Box 1268, 3205 Sandefjord, ✆ http://hope.sol.no/~fgono/formol.html

Foreningen Norden ("The Nordic Association") started in 1919s as an inter-Nordic friendship association. It now is an independent, nonpolitical association that aims to promote inter-Nordic co-operation in jobs, business, education, culture, media, foreign aid and environmental measures. There are national associations in all the Nordic countries and self-governing states – Denmark, the Faroes, Finland, Greenland, Iceland, Sweden and the Åland islands – as well as in Estonia, Latvia, Lithuania, Russia, St. Petersburg, and South Slesvig in Germany. Its members include individuals as well as organisations, schools, libraries and municipalities. In Norway, it has some 8,000 members and 120 local associations. About 100 national associations, including the ☞ **Unions** (Business and Work chapter) and some 600 schools and libraries co-operate with Foreningen Norden. It's activities include the *Klubb Norden* youth club, a youth summer job contact programme and co-operation with ☞ **The Environmental Home Guard** (Non-government Organisations chapter). The international secretariat, *Foreningene Nordens Forbund* ("The Confederation of Nordic Associations") is located in Oslo and can provide the names, addresses and telecommunications numbers of all Foreningen Norden ✆ 22114060, ✉ 22110212, ✉ Akersgata 67, 0180 Oslo, ✉ fnf@norden.no, ✆ http://fnf.norden.no

Freemasons (*Frimurerere*) The first Masonic Lodge was founded in Norway in 1749 and The Norwegian Order of Free and Accepted Masons (*Den Norske Frimurerorden*) was established in 1891. The Grand Lodge is in Oslo and there are three Provincial Lodges, in Bergen, Trondheim and Tromsø, each of which has administrative responsibility for the Lodges of its region of the country. There are five Steward Lodges, in Ålesund, Bodø, Hamar, Sandefjord and Stavanger, as well as 15 St. Andreas Lodges, 51 St. Johannes Lodges and 25 Brother Associations in cities and towns throughout the country. There are 18 Ancillary Groups, and a museum is located at the Grand Lodge. In all, there are now some 17,000 members in Norway, and international contacts are maintained by assigned representatives to 135 Grand Lodges in other countries. For further information, contact the Grand Lodge ✆ 22479500, ✉ 22479521, ✉ Nedrevollgate 19, 0158 Oslo, ✆ http://www.frimurer.no with pages in Norwegian and in English.

Hostelling International Norway (*Norsk Vandrerhjem*) Hostelling was born in 1909 out of the trips taken by German school teacher Richard Schirrmann with his pupils to provide inexpensive, simple overnight accommodations that could help young people of limited means to see the countryside and the cities of the world. Consequently, it was first known as Youth Hostelling. Today, hostels appeal to a far wider age group, and people who stay in them are just as likely to be cost-conscious families who arrive by car as to be young people who arrive on foot with backpacks. There now are now some 4,500 hostels in more than 60 countries, and each year they provide over 31 million overnight stays. There are now some four million hostelling association members world-wide. You need not be a member to stay in a hostel, but non-members must pay a surcharge for an overnight stay. In a few places, young people may be given priority should a hostel be nearly full. In Bavaria, Germany, there is an official age limit of 26. But elsewhere, people of any age may stay in a hostel. The International Youth Hostel Federation (IYHF) now supports an International Booking Network (IBN) and publishes international hostelling directories. Moreover, it also supports the International Communications Network (ICN), which provides international travellers with a variety of communications and information-retrieval facilities at purpose-built kiosks located in major hostels world-wide; in Norway, the *Haraldsheim* hostel in Oslo has an ICN kiosk. *Norsk Vandrerhjem* offers more than 100 hostels throughout the country. Many in the countryside are open in the summer only, whilst those in cities usually are open year-round. Membership is recommended, but limited to residents of the country. However, if you are a resident of another country, you may join its hostelling association and thereby enjoy the privileges of members in Norway. Likewise, if you are a member of *Norsk Vandrerhjem*, you will enjoy member privileges in the hostels of other countries. For further information on *Norsk Vandrerhjem* and on hostels in the country as well as in other countries, contact the head office in Oslo: ☎ 23139300, 🖷 23139350, ✉ Dronningensgt. 26, 0154 Oslo, ⊜ http://www.vandrerhjem.no with pages in Norwegian and in English. For information on international hostelling and links to all national hostelling associations, view the International Youth Hostel Federation (IYHF) web site ⊜ http://www.iyhf.org with pages in English, French, German and Spanish.

IOGT, the International Organisation of Good Templars, is the largest international temperance organisation. The IOGT is well established in Norway, with numerous activities, including owning and operating one of the ☞ **Folk high schools** (Education and Research chapter) at Åsane, having the *Juvente* youth organisation and supporting *FORUT*, an international aid organisation ☎ 23214580, 🖷 23214551, ✉ PO Box 8857 Youngstorget, 0028 Oslo, ✉ iogt@iogt.no, ⊜ http://www.iogt.no with pages in Norwegian; or the international ⊜ http://www.iogt-international.org for information in English, French and German.

IOOF (*Odd Fellow Ordenen*) The first Lodge of the International Order of Odd Fellows (IOOF) was founded in Norway in 1898, and the Order now has 135 IOOF Lodges and 106 Rebecca Lodges for women, with in all nearly 22,000 members ☎ 22839240, 🖷 22832467, ✉ Stortingsgt 28, 0161 Oslo.

Kiwanis is a worldwide humanitarian organisation dedicated to providing aid at the local level. There are 11 Kiwanis Divisions in Norway and the head office of District Norden is in Oslo ☎ 22193510,

✉ Ekebergsvn 45, 0196 Oslo, ⊜ http://www.kiwanis.no with pages in Norwegian, in English and in Swedish.

Lesbian and gay organisation (*Lesbisk og homofil organisasjon*) The National Organisation for Lesbian and Gay Liberation (*Landsforeningen for lesbisk og homofil frigjøring – LLH*) is the principal clearinghouse for lesbian and gay activities throughout the country. LLH is principally a social organisation, though it is politically active in promoting lesbian and gay rights and has lobbied for relevant measures, such as the law on ☞ **registered partnerships** (Family and Children chapter) enacted in 1993. The LLH head office is in Oslo, and it has 15 local associations throughout the country. It is affiliated with similar organisations in Denmark, Finland and Sweden as well as in central Europe. For further details, contact the head office ☎ 22361948, information hotline 82000977, 🖷 22114745, ✉ PO Box 6838 St. Olavs pl, 0130 Oslo, ✉ llh@c2i.net, ⊜ http://www.llh.no

Lions The International Association of Lions provides volunteer services at the local level. There are eight Lions clubs in Norway, which co-ordinate activities, such as support of the Red Feather (*Røde Fjær*). Contact the MD 104 Norway office ☎ 22272980, 🖷 22272952, ✉ Tvetenv 152, 0671 Oslo, ⊜ http://www.lions.no

Nordmanns-Forbundet, with headquarters in Oslo and chapters and members in more than 25 countries, was founded in 1907 with the purpose of strengthening cultural ties between Norway and Norwegians and their descendants living abroad. That is still its primary task. Membership is open to all persons with Norwegian roots or an interest in Norway. Nordmanns-Forbundet publishes a bilingual periodical, *The Norsemann*, five times a year, and offers numerous other member services. His Majesty King Harald V is patron. For further details, contact the home office ☎ 22427514, 🖷 22425163, ✉ Rådhusgt 23B, 0158 Oslo, ✉ norseman@online.no

Rotary Norway has the oldest and largest Rotary organisation in Scandinavia. The first Rotary club was founded in 1922, and there now are 14,000

Rotarians in 335 clubs throughout the country, organised into seven Districts. Each can be contacted through the Governors of the Districts, which are listed in the Rotary web site ⊛ http://home.c2i/hoeyri with pages in Norwegian and in English.

Scouts (*Speidere*) are organised in three associations, which together have some 50,000 members.

The Norwegian Guide and Scout Association (*Norges Speiderforbund*), is the largest of the associations, with about 30,000 boy scout, girl guide and girl scout members. Its groups and troops are organised in 45 local and 6 church divisions (*kretser*) throughout the country, and it has a permanent camp at Ingelsrud, 40 km south of Kongsvinger and 8 km from the Swedish border. It is a member of the World Association of the Scout Movement (WOSM) and the World Association of Girl Guides and Girl Scouts (WAGGGS) and regularly participates in jamborees and other international scouting events. For further information on scouting activities for boys and girls, contact the nearest division head office listed under *Speiderkontoret* in the Pink Pages or contact the association head office for complete address lists ✆ 22862020, ℻ 22862050, ✉ Øvre Vollgt 9, 0158 Oslo, ✉ nsf@scout.no, ⊛ http://www.scout.no with pages in Norwegian and in English and links to national and international scouting associations.

The YMCA Scouts of Norway (*Norges KFUM-Speidere*) are part of the Young Men's Christian Association, ☞ **YMCA** and have about 8,000 members in 19 divisions throughout the country. For further information, contact the nearest YMCA and YWCA office listed under *Norges KFUK-KFUM* in the Pink Pages or contact the association head office for complete address lists ✆ 22115032, ℻ 22203465, ✉ PO Box 6810 St. Olavspl, 0130 Oslo, ✉ forbundskontoret@kfum-speider.no, ⊛ http://www.kfum-speider.no with pages in Norwegian and in English.

The YWCA Guides of Norway (*KFUK-Speidere*) are part of the Young Women's Christian Association, ☞ **YWCA** and have about 7,500 members in 24 divisions throughout the country. For further information, contact the nearest YMCA and YWCA office listed under *Norges KFUK-KFUM* in the Pink Pages or contact the association head office for complete address lists ✆ 22115640, ℻ 22111103, ✉ PO Box 6871 St. Olavsplass, 0130 Oslo, ✉ info@kfuk-speider.no, ⊛ http://www.kfuk-speider.no

YMCA and YWCA (*KFUM og KFUK*) The Young Men's Christian Association (YMCA) and Young Women's Christian Association (YWCA) are well established. The first local *Kristlig forening av unge menn – KFUM* (YMCA) was founded in 1868, the first local *Kristlig forening av unge kvinner – KFUK* (YWCA) in 1887 and a national office for the two, *KFUK-KFUM* in 1880. At the national level, *KFUK* and *KFUM* are non-denominational, but at the local level, activities are closely related to the ☞ **Church of Norway** (Church and Religion chapter). Together, the two associations have some 22,000 members, in addition to as many ☞ **Scouts**. They are organised in local associations throughout the country, and they offer a wide range of activities, from music and drama to sports to youth clubs. *KFUK-KFUM* are involved in education through owning one and being part owner in six ☞ **folk high schools** (Education chapter). They also have overnight hostels for young people in Bergen and in Oslo in the summer. You can find the local association listed under *Norges KFUK-KFUM* in the Pink Pages, or for further information contact the head office ✆ 22204475, ℻ 22204759, ✉ PO Box 6814 St. Olavs plass, 0130 Oslo, ✉ km@kfuk-kfum.no, ⊛ http://www.kfuk-kfum.no with pages in Norwegian and in English.

Pets and animals
(Kjæledyr og dyr)

Cats (katter) Look no further than the notice board in your local supermarket, there are always cats and kittens looking for a new home. The local newspaper will also have advertisements, usually under the heading *kattunger* ("kittens"). If you are interested in pedigree cats, contact The Norwegian National Association of Pedigree Cats (*Rasekattklubbers Riksforbund-NRR*) ℅ 22428889, ☏ 22410248, ⊠ Storgata 23c, 0184 Oslo, ✉ nrrf@online.no, ⊕ http://www.nrr.no with pages in Norwegian and selected pages in English, contact numbers for the 37 pedigree cat clubs associated with it and application forms for the 30 to 40 international cat shows the NRR hosts each year. The NRR is a member of the international Fédération Internationale Féline (FIFe). Norway's national cat is the Norwegian Forest cat (*norsk skogskatt*). If you want to import a cat, ☞ **Pet importation.**

Dogs (hunder) are popular pets and if you go hunting (*på jakt*) in the autumn, you are required to have a dog with you. If you are planning to bring a dog with you to Norway, you will need to know about ☞ **pet importation**. Contact the Norwegian Kennel Club (*Norsk Kennel Klub – NKK*) ℅ 22656000, ☏ 22720474, ⊠ Nils Hansensvei 20, Bryn, 0611 Oslo, ✉ info@nkk.no, ⊕ http://www.nkk.no for information regarding breeds of pedigree dogs. All pedigree clubs are associated with *NKK*. They have a sperm bank where the sperm of dogs can be kept for future use by the owners of that dog. Entry forms for one of the 30 international shows that they organise in Norway every year, are available from their website which has links to other sites including companies that sell pet insurance. If you find a dog, telephone 22648890 stating the ear tattoo number or microchip-ID. You may need the help of a vet or FALKEN (see Pink Pages for their telephone number) to scan the dog.

Leash-law (Båndtvang) There is a national leash-law as well as local leash regulations. The national law, part of the Act on Game (*Viltloven*) requires that dogs be kept on leash while in outdoor areas open to the public, from 1 April to 20 August and be obediently under their owners' control at other times of the year. Otherwise, a dog can run free only if fenced in on its owner's property. A District Governor (*Fylkesmann*) may extend the leash-law to other times of the year and to specific areas. For instance, leash-law is extended through October or November in municipalities in Finnmark county, to protect reindeer, and applies year-round on the Svalbard archipelago in the Arctic. Cities and towns often impose leash-law in parks and recreation areas and accordingly post signs reading *Båndtvang*. Housing co-operatives (*Borettslag*) often permit dogs only by formal application and impose leash-law year-round. Cats usually are permitted if they are kept indoors, and some housing co-operatives have required that they be kept on leash when outdoors.

Pet import (Innførsel av dyr) You may import any breed of cat or any breed of dog other than a Dogo Argentino, Fila Brasilerio, Pit Bull Terrier or Tosa Inu. Breeds of dogs which resemble these prohibited breeds, such as an American Staffordshire Terrier, must be accompanied by an original pedigree certificate and ID-number that proves that the animal is not the offspring of a prohibited breed. Upon import, an animal must be accompanied by a valid Veterinary Certificate on a form approved by the Norwegian Animal Health Authority (*Statens dyrehelsetilsyn*). It must be clearly identified with a readable tattoo or microchip, and its identification number (ID number) must be stated on its Transport Document or Veterinary Certificate. If the microchip does not comply with FECAVA or ISO standards, you must provide a compatible reader. An Import Certificate will be issued for an animal that fulfills the requirements and is legally imported. Norway is free of rabies, so the rules for import depend on the chances that imported animals may have been exposed to rabies. The Norwegian Animal Health Authority (*Statens dyrehelsetilsyn*) distinguishes between six categories for importation of cats or dogs:

Category 1, from Sweden: no restrictions. However, you must keep a valid Veterinary Certificate on hand as proof of legal import.

Category 2: Norwegian and Swedish animals after transit through Finland. A Transit Document, stamped by customs at the first border crossing, is sufficient, provided that the animal has been in Finland less than six hours and has been kept isolated in the transport vehicle so that it has not contacted other animals.

Category 3: From rabies-free EU/EFTA countries (Great Britain, Iceland, Ireland and Northern Ireland). A Veterinary Certificate, comprising a Health Certificate and a Vaccination Certificate, is required and must accompany the animal at a border crossing.

Category 4: From rabies-infected EU/EFTA countries (Austria, Belgium, Denmark, Finland, France, Germany, Greece, Italy, Liechtenstein, Luxembourg, the Netherlands, Portugal, Spain, Switzerland and the Norwegian territories of Svalbard and Jan Mayen). A Veterinary Certificate, comprising a Health Certificate and a Vaccination Certificate, is required and must accompany the animal at a border crossing. All animals must have been vaccinated against rabies: dogs must have been at least three months old at first vaccination, and cats at least 12 months old at first vaccination. A blood sample for confirmation of antibody titre must have been taken not earlier than 120 days, and not later than 365 days, after the last rabies vaccination. Dogs must also have been vaccinated against leptospirosis and against canine distemper. The animal must have lived in the EU/EFTA for the previous six months or more.

Category 5: From rabies-free non-EU/EFTA countries (Australia, Faro Island, state of Hawaii in the USA, Mauritius and New Zealand). A Veterinary Certificate, comprising a Health Certificate and a Vaccination Certificate, is required and must accompany the animal at a border crossing. Dogs must have been vaccinated against leptospirosis and against canine distemper and must have been tested serologically for brucellosis with a negative result prior to importation. The animal must have lived in the rabies-fee country for the previous six months or more.

Category 6: From rabies-infected non-EU/EFTA countries (Countries in North and South America and Asia, as well as other countries not listed in Categories 1 through 5). A Veterinary Certificate, comprising a Health Certificate and a Vaccination Certificate, is required and must accompany the animal at a border crossing. Dogs must have been vaccinated against leptospirosis and canine distemper and must have been tested serologically for brucellosis with a negative result. All animals will be put in quarantine

for at least four months after arrival and be kept isolated at home for at least two months thereafter. There is one approved quarantine station for cats and dogs, located about 70 km from Oslo. You must book a place there 30 days or more before you intend to import an animal. For booking, contact the District Veterinary (*Distriktsveterinæren*) in Mysen and Spydeberg ✆ 69893610, 🖷 69892480, ✉ PO Box 228, 1851 Mysen.

These details are the principal features of the complete rulings, entitled "Information on Requirements for Importation of Dogs and Cats to Norway", valid as this book goes to press. The rulings change with time and their complete details are more extensive than can be included here. Furthermore, other rulings apply to less frequently imported pets. For instance, parrots and endangered species of animals cannot be imported, and a horse may be subject to value added tax (VAT) and import duty, as well as to veterinary control. Moreover, the Norwegian Animal Health Authority may, upon short notice and without compensation to the importer, prohibit importation of animals from certain countries should animal health conditions in them so warrant. Consequently, you should always ask for the most recent edition of the rulings, along with the forms for certificates, all in English as well as Norwegian, from the Norwegian Animal Health Authority Central Unit ✆ 22241940, 🖷 22241945, ✉ PO Box 8147 Dep, 0033 Oslo.

Pets other than dogs and cats (*Øvrige kjæledyr*) include the popular budgie (*undulat*) and canary (*kanari*) birds, hamsters (*hamstre*) and rabbits (*kaninen*) among the animals and tropical fish (*akvariefisk*). You can buy these pets as well as equipment and supplies for them at pet shops; look under *zoologiske forretninger* in the Yellow Pages.

Pets, care of (*stell av kjæledyr*) Find a veterinarian (*veterinær*) either through recommendations by neighbours and friends or look in the Yellow Pages under *Dyrleger, Dyreklinikker* or *Veterinærer*. You can purchase health insurance from the major insurance companies for dogs, cats, larger birds and horses. Your normal visits to the vet will not be covered by insurance but accidents in which the animal has been involved, serious illness and death are covered. Some over-the-counter medication can be purchased from a pharmacy (*apotek*) without a prescription, others will be prescribed by the veterinarian. In the winter, protect the paw pads of dogs with a protective cream that prevents the pads from splitting, the most commonly used cream is *skillaruds salve* and can be purchased from a pet shop; look in the Yellow Pages under *Zoologiske forretningerik* or *Hunder, katter og smådyr*. Pet shops also sell rubber paw boots, which are used when the pad has been damaged and is being treated. Trim away any excess hair near the pads to avoid clumps of ice forming.

Wildlife (*Dyreliv*) The relatively mild climate for its latitude give the country a mix of continental European and Arctic wildlife. On land, animals of the deer family – red deer (*hjort*), roe deer (*rådyr*) and European elk or moose (*elg*) – are found in most woodland areas in the southern part of the country. Herds of reindeer (*rein*) roam the mountainous areas and, in the north, the plateaux. Small animals, such as the badger (*grevling*), beaver (*bever*) and hare (*hare*) live in almost all forests. Native and migratory birds include black grouse (*orrfulgl*), capercaillie (*storfugl*), ducks (*ender*), geese (*gås*), ptarmigan (*fuellrype*) and various sea birds (*sjøfugl*), of which the seagull (*måke*) is most common. There are few predators: about 26 to 55 bears, 500 to 600 lynxes, about 25 wolves (*ulv*) and 130 to 190 wolverines (*jerv*).

Post, shipping and courier
(Post, frakt og kurér)

Courier services (Kurértjenester) divide into two major groups, listed in the Yellow Pages as *Budtjenester* and *Flyfrakt*. *Budtjenester*, or messenger services, include local, city and countrywide messenger delivery and collection services. Inter-city and international mail and express delivery services classify as air freight, even though they also offer surface transport services in urban areas, and are listed under the heading *Flyfrakt*. Most international couriers serve Norway; the four global leaders are DHL, FedEx, TNT and UPS; all with offices in major cities and towns, listed in the Pink Pages. Their headquarters and Internet sites (with pages for Norway) are:

- DHL (for its founders, Dalsey, Hillblom and Lynn), founded in the USA ℚ 81001345, ✆ 67525515, ✉ http://www.dhl.com
- FedEx (Federal Express), founded in the USA ℚ 63940300, ✆ 63940390, ✉ http://www.fedex.com
- TNT (original name Thomas Nationwide Transport), founded in Australia; European headquarters in Amsterdam ℚ 67119500, ✆ 67582000, ✉ http://www.tnt.com
- UPS (United Parcel Service), founded in the USA ℚ 80033470, ✆ 22329998, ✉ http://www.ups.com

Freight and cargo (Frakt og last) Shipping companies offer numerous national and international services. Accordingly, they are listed in varying ways in the Yellow Pages and in transport directories. In alphabetical order, the major categories are:

- Air freight (*Flyftrakt*): The ☞ **Airlines** (Transportation chapter) and air freight lines carry air freight, but for individual shipments by air, independent companies often can offer lower rates, as they combine smaller shipments into containers which then are air freighted at lower cost per kilogram shipped.
- Forwarding and customs clearance agents (*Spedisjon og fortolling*) deal mostly in international shipping by air, rail and road, but also offer national services. Some agents are themselves

shippers, whilst others are brokers who deal with shippers.

- Railway freight is carried by NSB Freight (*NSB Gods*), part of the railway system. NSB Freight offers several services to individuals, including transport of cars in enclosed wagons.
- Road transport is offered by many trucking companies (*lastebiltransport*) which are listed under Transport services (*Transporttjenester*), see ☞ **Trucking** (Transportation chapter). Trucking companies offering services to individuals usually are part of or are associated with ☞ **Removals** (Arriving, Settling, Leaving chapter).
- Sea transport is offered by shipping companies and lines (*Shipsselskaper og ruter*), see ☞ **Shipping** (Transportation chapter). The major companies and lines seldom have services for individuals, so if you wish to ship by sea, you should call a forwarding agent. However, domestic lines, such as ferries on inland waters and along the coast, offer services for small shipments.

Post boxes (Postkasser) Letters and periodicals are delivered in post boxes of regulation designs. A post box for a house is located at the street or road entrance to the property or, for farms or holiday houses away from trafficked roads, along with other boxes in a roadside stand. The most common box is made of green-painted steel, measures 42 cm high by 27 cm wide by 13 cm deep and is fitted with an inner hinged lid with a letter slot and a hasp to take a padlock and an outer hinged lid to cover the letter slot. It is for sale in post offices (*postkontor*) and hardware shops (*jernhandel*). Post boxes for flats are mounted in rows and usually are recessed into a wall near the main entrance door. The most common box is made of green, grey or white painted steel and measures 41 cm high by 29 cm wide by 11 cm deep and has a hinged front door fitted with a cylinder lock. Newspapers usually are delivered at doors of flats, but in the post boxes of houses. If you subscribe to a Norwegian newspaper and wish to avoid overfilling your post box, you may request a newspaper tube (*avisrør*), which many newspapers give free to subscribers. The typical newspaper tube is a rounded 9 by 14 cm rectangle, 38 cm long, made of weatherproof plastic, sealed at one end and open at the other, and fitted with a flange for mounting on a wall or fence. Though there still are some in the doors of older flats, letter slots are no longer used for post, though they may be used for newspaper delivery.

Postal services and postage (*Post og porto*)

There are about 1500 post offices in the country, and Norway Post (*Posten*) now handles about 2.5 billion items per year. Services are similar to those elsewhere in Europe and conform to the guidelines of the Conference of European Postal and Telecommunications Administrations (CEPT). Letter boxes are red and posted items usually are collected from them once a day or more often. In and around the major cities, there are also yellow letter boxes, for items addressed for delivery within the area designated by postal codes stated on the box. Post Office vehicles are red and Post Offices, vehicles and publications carry the Norway Post logo, which is a yellow post horn on a red background.

Most post offices rent Post Office Boxes. But in urban areas, rental usually is restricted to registered public and private sector organisations. Mail is delivered only to one address: an organisation with a street address and a PO Box address receives mail only at its PO Box address. Postage rates are set once a year and are published in a postage brochure available at all post offices, *Priser for å sende brev og pakker inn- og utland* (Postage for letters and packages, domestic and international), in Norwegian only. Postage rates and an interactive postage calculator are available on-line in Norwegian and English at ☺ http://www.posten.no. The principal postal service classes are:

- A Prioritaire The international designation in French for letters, formerly "first class", via air mail, usually one working day delivery within the country; six weight categories from 20g to 1000g domestic and seven from 20g to 2000g international.
- B Economique The international designation in French for letters formerly called "second class"

via surface mail domestic and via air to gateway airport and thereafter surface for international, 3 to 5 working day delivery within the country, same weight categories as for A Prioritaire. B letters must be delivered at post offices, which have slots or bins for them. For letters in weight categories up to and including 100g, you must post at least 20 letters at the same time in order to use the B service, but you may post individual B letters weighing 250g or more.

- C-Post (Domestic Bulk Mail) (*C-Post Adressert*) For company mass mailings of 500 or more items, four weight categories from 100 to 1000g.
- Parcels (*Lettgods*) Various parcel post services from ordinary surface to air expedited overnight service. Private parcels (*Norgespakke*) must be delivered to and upon notice, picked up at a post office. The Business Parcel (*Bedriftspakke*) service offers door-to-door service at a surcharge; it's international version is the Express Mail Service (EMS) for documents and merchandise.
- Swiftpost special delivery (*Ekspressbrev til utlandet*) An international letter service offering overnight delivery throughout Europe.

You should use the blue A Prioritaire and green B Economique self-adhering stickers available at post offices to label international letters. Letters to addresses in Norway are assumed to be A unless stamped "B".

Blue A service and green B service stickers.

Other services, such as Registration (*Rekommandert*), Insurance (*Verdi*), Cash on Delivery (*Postoppkrav*) are available; see the postage brochure or the web site for details. Your local post office will hold mail while you are away, as on holiday; inquire at the counter for details.

Postcodes (*Postnummere*)

consist of a four-digit number before the name of a city or town and separated from it by a space. The country is divided into nine postal zones. As shown in the map below, the first digit, 0-9, designates the zone. A capital letter N (for Norway) and a hyphen are added ahead of the postcode for international post. Moreover, "Norway", spelled in the language of the country to which post is sent, is added after the name of the city or town, separated by a comma and a space or is written on the next line. For instance, the postcode for Palamedes, the publisher of this book, is written:

0028 Oslo for domestic post,

N-0028 Oslo, Norway for post to English-speaking countries, and

N-0028 Oslo, Norvège for post to French-speaking countries.

For all cities, towns and postcodes are assigned as:

- single codes, and sometimes two codes, one for street, road and location addresses (*Gate, vei og stedsadresser*) and one for post office boxes (*postboksadresse*), for smaller cities and towns, or as

- sequences of codes, for postal zones and post office box series, for larger towns and cities, including (in alphabetical order): Alta, Arendal, Asker, Askim, Bergen, Bodø, Bærum, Drammen, Elverum, Fredrikstad, Gjøvik, Grimstad, Halden, Hamar, Harstad, Haugesund, Horten, Hønefoss, Kongsberg, Kongsvinger, Kristiansand S, Kristiansund N, Larvik, Lillehammer, Lillestrøm, Mandal, Mo, Molde, Mosjøen, Moss, Narvik, Notodden, Oslo, Porsgrunn, Sandefjord, Sandnes, Sarpsborg, Skien, Stavanger, Steinkjer, Stord, Tromsø, Trondheim, Tønsberg and Ålesund. In larger cities, some agencies and organisations have dedicated postcodes and consequently need no street or post box address. For instance, the complete address of the Norwegian State Railways is *NSB, 0048 Oslo*.

All postcodes are listed in *Postadressebok for Norge* (Postal address book for Norway) available at post offices; the most recent edition was published in 1999, and continuously updated postcodes are available at the postcode helpline ☏ 81000710. An on-line postcode finder (*Postnummersøk*) in Norwegian and in English is available at the Norway Post Internet web site: ⊕ http://www.posten.no. Frequently updated database files of postcodes, street and road registers on CD-ROM and 3.5 inch disks are available on subscription, ☏ 23148700, 🖷 23148787, ✉ 0645 Oslo, ✉ posten.dm@posten.no Post offices

have these services on-line and can answer queries on postcodes for individual addresses.

The first digit of the postcode designates the postal zone. Map from Postadressebok for Norge 1999.

Redirecting (*Ettersending*) If you move, Norway Post can forward your mail to a new address, which may be temporary – such as a summer holiday home – or permanent, in which case you will not return to your former address. In both cases, you should send a notice of redirection (*Melding om endring av postadresse*) a week or more before you move, using a convenient A6-format (10.5 x 14.8 cm) postal card (number Bl.70.282.03) available at all post offices. On it, you should fill in your new address, the date of first redirection and the date of return if redirection is temporary, as well as the names of everyone in your household, because the post office will not sort items to a single address. Send it to the post office nearest the address from which mail is to be redirected. Redirection services depend on whether your move is within Norway or to another country. If you move within Norway, all A-Post and B-Post, but not C-Post, will be forwarded at no charge for a period of one year, and thereafter returned to the sender; ☞ **Postal services and postage**. Parcels will be forwarded, but additional postage may be charged if you move to a remote postal zone. If you move abroad, only A-Post and B-Post will be forwarded. Items for which the recipient's signature is required, such as some registered mail, will be forwarded with a suitable international post form attached. Cash on Delivery (COD) (*Oppkrav*) items and items which may be subject to customs duty will not be forwarded, but will be returned to the sender with a notice of your new address abroad. The additional postage required for sending an item of domestic mail abroad will be charged to the sender. If there is no return address on an item, the additional forwarding postage will be collected upon delivery. You can avoid the difficulties and delays of forwarding by giving notice of your change of address to all your correspondents and business connections. A convenient way to do this is to fill out and post a change of address card available at all post offices. There are two cards: The domestic card (number Bl.70.282.08) in Norwegian (*Melding om endret postadresse*) can be sent free to addresses in the Nordic countries (Denmark, Finland, Iceland, Norway, Sweden). The international card (number Bl.70.282.24) in English and French ("Change of Address – Changement d'adresse") can be sent free to addresses outside the Nordic countries. If you will be away from your home for a short period of time, up to one month, the post office will hold mail for you until your return. Give notice using the same card as for redirection, and send it to your nearest post office. For further details, consult your local post office (*Postkontor*).

Prices (*Priser*)

Prices fluctuate and change. So in the other 47 chapters of this book, prices are mentioned only if they are likely to remain fixed for several years, as do some government fees. This chapter is an overview of prices that may have changed between press time (October 1999) and the time you read this book.

As indicated by the ☞ **Purchasing Power Parity** for the country, prices are comparatively high. But not all expenditures are higher for all people. As pointed out in the chapters of this book, some goods and services are less expensive than elsewhere, so the average family lives well. At press time, the exchange rates of the Norwegian krone (NOK) against the major currencies used in international comparisons are: NOK 12.69 to one British Pound (GBP, £), NOK 8.25 to one Euro (EUR, €), NOK 4.44 to one German Mark (DEM), NOK 5.16 to one Swiss Franc (CHF) and NOK 7.69 to one US dollar (USD, $).

Price levels (*Priser*) have climbed through the years. But as indicated in the table below, wages have gone up even more, so the time worked to buy essentials has gone down. All figures listed are Norwegian kroner (NOK)

	1899	1949	1974	1989	1999*
1 lt milk	0.11	0.45	1.37	6.51	10.20
1 kg butter	1.75	6.20	10.80	31.06	36.00
1 kg sugar	0.48	0.62	6.96	11.34	10.50
1 kg beef	0.67	3.60	17.13	105.53	168.00
1 kg potatoes	0.59	0.34	1.39	5.37	6.90
1st class postage	0.10	0.25	1.00	3.00	4.00
Hourly industrial wage	0.28	2.85	21.05	87.25	130.97
National budget expenditure	90.6 million	2979 million	43.8 billion	270 billion	431 billion

* Food prices are mid 1999 averages for Oslo area and wage is first quarter average. Prices and wages for other years are yearly averages from "Historical Statistics 1994" published by Statistics Norway and from *Norsk Almanakk 1999* published by Almanakkforlaget.

Prices of housing (*Priser på hus*)

When compared to disposable income, the prices paid for housing are no higher than the average for the European Union. According to an international survey* conducted by Dresdner Kleinwort Benson, a German investment bank, the true cost of housing in a country is best expressed by an affordability index, which is the price of an average house expressed as a multiple of the annual personal disposable income per head. By that measure, housing is most expensive in Japan, where the affordably index is forecast at 26.1 for 1999, and cheapest in the USA, where the index is forecast at 8.3, the lowest of industrialised countries. In Britain, the index was 19.4 in 1989 and is forecast at 13.2 in 1999. For Norway, the index was 15.2 in 1989 and is forecast at 14.3 in 1999.

Price depends on location. In a mid 1999 comparison, NOK 800,00 bought a 22 square metre flat in Oslo, a new 52 square metre flat in Trondheim or a 27 decare farm with three buildings in the Gudbrandsdal valley. As elsewhere, downtown capital city prices are the highest, followed by other cities, and, finally, the rural districts.

* Figures quoted by permission of Dresdner Kleinwort Benson, London office.

Prices for foods and household items (*Priser på dagligevarer*)

Prices on meats vary by cut and season. Prices on fresh fruits and vegetables vary by season. The prices listed below are average for supermarkets in the Oslo area in mid 1999 and may differ elsewhere in the country.

item	NOK
1 lt full fat milk	10.20
1/2 kg butter	18.00
10 eggs	24.90

1 kg sugar	10.50
50 tea bags	29.90
250 g filter coffee	19.90
200g instant coffee	66.90
1 lt orange juice	15.90
Orange squash (makes 6 lt)	18.90
Loaf wholemeal bread	14.50
375g Corn flakes	22.90
400g strawberry jam	24.50
1 kg apples	19.90
1 kg potatoes	6.90
1 kg beef	168.00
1 kg minced beef	79.90
1 kg pork	149.00
1 kg lamb (leg of lamb)	99.00
1 kg cod (fillet)	109.00
1 kg carrots	16.90
Head broc	16.90
cucumber	13.90
Sweet cake (300g)	24.90
1 kg Norvegia cheese	75.50
1 kg chicken breasts	213.00
1/2 lt beer	19.50
1 lt coca cola	14.90
1 lt bottled water	9.90
1 kg tomatoes	29.50
1 kg flour	6.00
1 kg rice	8.00
500g spaghetti	12.90
250 g bag of potato crisps	12.50
Bar of chocolate	22.90
2 lt vanilla ice cream	22.90
850g soap powder	36.90
500ml dishwashing liquid	14.90
6 rolls toilet paper	18.00
200ml bottle shampo	29.90
75ml toothpaste	14.90
Packet of nappies (29, 10–18kg)	74.90

Purchasing power parity (*Kjøpekraftsparitet*)
is a concept that equates the buying power of various currencies. Abbreviated PPP, its main principle is that exchange rates should move toward levels which equalise the prices of goods and services, no matter where they are bought. But prices vary. So PPPs are computed to examine their differences.

The strength of the PPP concept is that it permits currencies to be compared with each other. Its drawback has been that the PPP is difficult to calculate.

Goods differ from country to country, as do the ways of providing services.

There's one increasingly popular exception to that rule. In 1986, The Economist, the renowned British weekly finance and news magazine, instituted a light-hearted guide to PPP by selecting a simple collection – or "basket" as economists call it – of goods consisting of a Big Mac hamburger. The Big Mac is uniform and is produced in more than 100 countries. Its price reflects the costs of local goods – the ingredients – and services – the preparation and serving. The Big Mac PPP is based on the price of a Big Mac averaged over four cities in the USA, its home country. It signals whether each currency is over-valued or under-valued against the US dollar.

The Big Mac PPP index has become a regular annual feature in an April issue of The Economist. It is calculated by comparing the local price at the prevailing exchange rate against the dollar with the average price in the USA. For instance, on 30 March 1999, a Big Mac cost NOK 30 in Norway, which at the day's exchange rate of 7.81, was equivalent to $3.84, compared to an average of $2.43 in the USA. If the exchange rate had been 12.34, the price would have been $2.43 in both countries. Consequently, the Big Mac PPP indicated that the Norwegian krone was 58% overvalued against the dollar. Only in Switzerland was the figure higher, 64%.

In turn, at any one time, the PPPs reflect relative price levels, because exchange rates take time to equalise. PPPs are expressed in percentages, so they can be re-worked to be based on the currency of any country. That is what ☞ **Dine Penger** (Media and Information chapter) did in 1999 by recalculating the Big Mac index compared to Norway:

Hong Kong	-66%
USA	-37%
Spain	-37%
Japan	-37%
Italy	-36%
Netherlands	-32%
Euro	-30%
Germany	-30%
France	-26%
Sweden	-26%
UK	-21%
Denmark	-8%
Switzerland	+2%

Registrations, rights, licences (*Registreringer, rettigheter, sertifikater*)

Birth certificates (*Fødselsattest*) are issued by the offices of the ☞ **National register** to persons born or adopted in Norway, to Norwegian citizens and to citizens of other Nordic countries who are residents of Norway. When a child is born in a hospital or clinic, a notice of birth (*fødselsmelding*) is sent to the nearest National register office. Likewise, when a child is adopted, the office of the County governor (*Fylkesmann*) sends a notice to the National Register office in the municipality where the child will live. The National register office then sends a choice of name (*navnevalg*) form to the parents who must return it within six months, with the choice of ☞ **personal names** (Family and Children chapter) for the child. The National Register office will then issue a birth certificate (*fødselsattest*) with a ☞ **national ID number.**

Brønnøysund Register Centre (*Brønnøysundregistrene*) is a department of the Ministry of Justice and the Police (*Justis- og politidepartementet*) and is responsible for maintaining nine central governmental registers, the contents of which are available to the public:

Annual Reports and Accounts Register (*Regnskapsregisteret*) of the reports submitted as required by all registered stock companies (*aksjeselskaper*), savings banks (*sparebanker*), the post bank (*postbanken*), mutual insurance companies (*gjensidige forsikringsselskaper*) and oil ventures (*petroleumsforetak*) in the country. To date, more than a million reports are held in the Register.

Bankruptcy Register (*Konkursregisteret*) of all bankruptcy estates (*konkursbo*) and forced liquidations (*tvang avviklingsbo*) registered since 1 September 1993.

Business Register (*Foretaksregister*) of some 270,000 businesses in the country. Each business is registered with a name (*firmanavn*) and an enterprise number (*organisasjonsnummer*), sometimes called a company code, and which appear on its certificate of registry (*firmaattest*), a profile document similar to those of other national registries and of the European Business Register (EBR). A Certificate of Registry, also known as a company profile, is necessary in many business transactions, such as opening bank accounts, applying for business loans or requesting a post office box at a city post office.

Chattels Register (*Løsøreregister*) of all moveables on which debt has been recorded. Its major service to the public is an automatic voice-prompt information line for debt on ☞ **Used cars** (Cars, Roads and Traffic chapter).

Debt Settlement Register (*Gjeldsordningsregisteret*) of all voluntary (*frivillige*) and forced (*tvungne*) debt settlements (*gjeldsordninger*) subject to debt negotiations (*gjeldsforhandlinger*) according to the Act on Debt Settlement (*Gjeldsordningsloven*).

Fee Centre (*Gebyrsentralen*) differs from the other eight registers in that it supports the charging of fees by local and national governmental agencies, such as for disbursements (*utlegg*), evictions (*utkastelser*), forced sales (*tvangsauksjoner*) and foreclosures (*utpantinger*).

Marriage Contract Register (*Ektepaktregisteret*) of all antenuptial and postnuptial settlements between spouses from 1928 to date.

Reports Register (*Oppgaveregisteret*) is a central clearing register for all the forms (*skjema*) which are obligatory for businesses (*næringslivets oppgaveeplikter*).

Unified Register (*Enhetsregister*) that co-ordinates the data held in various public registers and makes available the registered details on business owners (*næringsdrivende*) and bodies corporate (*juridiske personer*).

For further details, contact *Brønnøysundregistrene* ✆ 75007000, 🖷 75007505, ✉ 8910 Brønnøysund, 🖳 http://www.brreg.no

The city recorder (*Byfogd*) or district recorder (*Sorenskriver*) is a judge of the city court (*byrettsdommer*) or the court of enforcement (*underdommer på landet*), whose duties also include performing civil marriages (*vigselsmann*), serving as a judge of the probate and bankruptcy court (*skifteforvalter*), acting as a notary public (*norarius publicus*) and providing the functions of the city registrar (*byskriver*) or district registrar (*tinglysningsdommer*).

Fishing licences (*Fiskeravgift og Fiskekort*) Children up to age 15 need no licence to fish, but anyone 16 or older needs licences. There are two types of licence, national and local.

The National Fishing Licence (*Fiskeravgift*) is a fee required of all who wish to fish. It is available in several categories, for individuals and for families, for one week or one year. A folder with a brochure describing the licence in Norwegian, English, Finnish and German and a Giro payment form is published once a year and is available at post offices and at most sport shops that sell fishing gear.

Local fishing licence (*fiskekort*) Fishing rights belong to landowners, so local licences (*fiskekort*) are required for fishing on private lands. Often, several landowners band together for larger areas where they jointly manage fish stocks, rent out fishing areas and sell local licences. Sometimes private fishing rights are rented out to hunting and fishing organisations, who in turn manage fishing and sell licences. Information on and forms for local fishing licences are made available at tourist offices (*turistkontor*), in sport shops and at hotels, as well as at self-serve boxes on bulletin boards and posts near fishing waters. Otherwise, there are a few rules to be observed:

• Don't use live fish as bait.
• File a catch report for any salmon family fish caught with the organisation that issued the local licence.
• If you catch any tagged fish, remove the tags and send them to the Norwegian Institute of Nature Research (NINA) ⊠ PO Box 3727, 7002 Trondheim; a reward will be paid.

Identification (*Legitimasjon*) is required for many daily tasks, such as picking up registered post, opening a bank account and signing for received goods to be invoiced later. You may use a card or other document to identify yourself, provided that it:

• is issued by a State agency or by a company that either is nationally known or is locally familiar.
• has your passport-type photograph and signature and is either signed and stamped by the issuing authority or is photographically reproduced on plastic.
• has your photograph affixed so it cannot be replaced by another, such as by being partly stamped or by being laminated.

There are many types of approved (*godkjente*) identification, including passports, payment cards, Postal identity cards, workplace identity cards, refugee's

travel document and Norwegian driving licences issued after mid 1989. Post offices also recognise the identity card for asylum seekers and others (*Legitimasjonskort for asylsøkere og andre*). Some types of identity cards do not meet the requirements for approved identification, such as upper secondary school, college or university student cards, bus or train season passes, conscript cards and Norwegian driving licences issued before mid 1989.

If you are newly arrived and need an identity card, you may find the Postal identity card (*Postens identitetskort*) convenient, because there are so many post offices in the country where you may obtain it. Apply at any post office, bringing a passport-sized portrait photo of yourself, in black-and-white or colour, without a hat or dark glasses, and recognised identification, such as a Refugee Travel Document (*Reisebevis*), Immigrant's Passport (*Utlendingspass*) or your home country passport stamped by the police to certify that you have a valid residence permit.

Legal registration (*Tinglysning*) is often required for documents to be legally binding.

The ☞ **Brønnøysund Register Centre** is the national registry for bankruptcies, businesses, chattels, debt settlements and ☞ **marriage settlements** (Family and Children chapter).

The ☞ **city recorder or district recorder** keeps the property register (*grunnboka*). Registration is not mandatory when you buy a property, such as a house or holiday home, and you may use your property without it. But it is advisable, because it provides legal protection and the proof of ownership that you may need if you apply for a mortgage. When a lender grants you a mortgage, registration is obligatory. Your mortgaged property (*pantheftelse*) is entered in a security deed (*pantobligasjon*) which is recorded (*tinglyst*) in the property register. A ☞ **Document duty** (Taxes, Duties, Excise chapter) of 2.5% of the property value as well as recording fees (*gebyr*) are charged for registry; the recorder's office will have a list of the applicable rates. When you have paid off the mortgage, the security deed will be returned to you. The property register is a public document. So whenever you consider purchasing a property, you should look it up in the property register to see if it is mortgaged or if there are any other registered agreements concerning it, such as right-of-way, private sewerage and the like.

National Identity Number (*Fødselsnummer*)

Each resident is assigned a National Identity Number (NIN), upon registration of birth in Norway or upon first issue of a residence permit. A NIN is permanent; a person with a NIN, who leaves the country to live abroad, retains that NIN upon later return. The NIN consists of 11 digits in format $D_1D_2M_1M_2Y_1Y_2I_1I_2I_3C_1C_2$. The first six are the date of birth: day D_1D_2 (0-31), month M_1M_2 (01-12) and year Y_1Y_2 (00-99). The following five distinguish between people born on the same day. $I_1I_2I_3$ are the person identity digits. I_3 is even (divisible by 2) for women and odd (not divisible by 2) for men. C_1C_2, are check digits mathematically computed from the first nine digits. C_1C_2 can be re-computed upon each use of a NIN to verify that the it is written correctly or warn if it contains error. The NIN system is valid for 200 years, with no reuse of numbers. When it started in 1964, the oldest resident assigned a NIN was born in 1855, so the system starts with that year. Nearly 500 NINs now can be assigned every day of the year, which is more than twice the combined daily averages of births and immigration and thereby more than adequate for new registrations. However, for immigrants, there are some constraints on 1 January. This is because 1 January is assigned not only to persons born on that day, but also has been assigned to immigrants who arrive from countries that enter only the year of birth in passports and identity papers. The Y digits and I digits of a NIN are related:

Year born	Y_1Y_2 2 digits	$I_1I_2I_3$ Identity digits
1855–1899	55–99	500–749
1900–1999	00–99	000–499
2000–2054	00–54	500–999

Unlike computer programs, which also use two digits for years, the NIN system copes with the turn of the millennium. In February 2004, for instance, a woman born on 1 February 1903, who might have a NIN of 010203 43261, would not be called in for a routine health check of one-year-olds, but a baby girl born on 1 February 2003 will be called in, because the three identity digits of her NIN would be between 500 and 999. If the baby's three identity digits were between 500 and 749, as for persons

born before 1900, there would be no mix up, because the year digits for those persons start with 55. NINs are used mostly for official purposes, including identification in welfare, social services and health records and on driving licences, passports, educational records and the like. Although the only information that can be read from a NIN is the date of birth and sex of the person to which it is assigned, non-official uses are restricted by privacy laws. For further information on NINs, contact the ☞ **National Register** office in the municipality (*kommune*) where you live; see *Folkeregister* in the Pink Pages.

National register (*Folkeregister*)

Each municipality maintains a register of all its residents, primarily as an administrative aid, such as in assigning and maintaining a list of ☞ **National ID Numbers**, as used for taxation purposes. You must notify the local *Folkeregister* (listed in the Pink Pages) upon moving into a municipality. Otherwise, officials will give notice.

Event – who notifies *Folkeregister*

- adoption (*adopsjon*) – County governor (*fylkesmann*)
- birth (*fødsel*) – hospital or clinic; parents for home birth
- change of citizenship (*endring av statsborgerskap*) – County governor (*fylkesmann*) or Directorate of Immigration (*Utlendingsdirektoratet*)
- death (*dødsfall*) – Probate court (*skifterett*) or sheriff (*lensmann*)
- divorce (*skilsmisse*) – County governor (*fylkesmann*) or court (*domstol*)
- guardianship (*vergemål*) – Court (*domstol*)
- marriage (*vigsel*) – Minister/person performing (*vigselsmannen*)
- moving (*flytting*) – You or a family member, within eight days of moving into a municipality; use form RF-0005, available at post offices (*postkontorer*)
- name grant (*navnebevilling*) – County governor (*fylkesmann*) or Ministry of Justice (*Justisdepartementet*)

Patents and inventions (*Patenter og oppfinnelser*)

Patents, designs, trademarks and the like are registered with the Norwegian Patent Office (*Patentstyret*) ℗ 22387300, ☎ 22387301, ✉ PO Box 8160 Dep, 0033 Oslo, http://www.nof.no/patentstyret with pages in Norwegian only. Patent agents and attorneys, listed under *Patentbyråer* in the Yellow Pages, provide assistance in searching and registering. There are two organisations for inventors: The Norwegian Inventors Association (*Norsk oppfinnerforening*) ✆ 22111470, ✇ 22111472, ✉ PO Box 6856 St. Olavs Plass, 0130 Oslo, @ http://www.nof.no/forening and the Inventors' Forum (*Oppfinnerforum*) ✉ Hjaltlandsgt 12, 4009 Stavanger, @ http://www.nof.no

Private pilot licence (*Privatflygersertifikat*)

There are two types of private pilot licence (PPL), PPL-A for fixed-wing aircraft and PPL-H for helicopters. Both conform with the European Joint Aviation Requirement and Flight Crew Licensing (JAR-FCL) rules. The Civil Aviation Administration (*Luftfartsverket*) sets requirements and holds examinations for the licences. An examination for a PPL consists of a practical test of flying skills as well as a theoretical examination. Some 39 ☞ **aeronautical sports** (Sports, Recreation, Hobbies chapter) clubs offer flight training for the PPL. You may also study for the PPL theoretical examination by taking a correspondence course offered by the Aeronautical Correspondence School (*Luftfartsbrevskolen/NAK*) ✆ 23102904, ✇ 23102902, ✉ PO Box 383 Sentrum, 0102 Oslo, ✉ lfb@nak.no, @ http://www.nlf.no/motor/lfb

Registers (*Registere*) are official lists kept by governmental agencies. Those, which you may encounter in your private or working life, are listed below. The agencies keeping the registers are described in this chapter or in other chapters as indicated in parentheses. Registers concerning only businesses, such as the shipping register, are not listed.

Register (agency keeping it

- Annual company accounts (*Regnskapsregisteret*) ☞ Brønnøysund Register
- Bankruptcies (*Konkursregisteret*) ☞ Brønnøysund Register
- Boats/leisure craft (*Småbåtregisteret*) ☞ Directorate of Customs and Excise (Taxes chapter)
- Business enterprises (*Foretaksregisteret*) ☞ Brønnøysund Register
- Convictions of crimes (*Strafferegister*) ☞ Police Department, Ministry of Justice (Law, Lawyers, Courts chapter)
- Debts settlements (*Gjeldsordningsregisteret*) ☞ Brønnøysund Register
- Fee collection (*Gebyrsentralen*) ☞ Brønnøysund Register
- Fines, damages and costs recovery (*Statens innkrevingssentral*) ☞ Ministry of Justice (Law, Lawyers, Courts chapter)
- Legal entities (*Enhetsregister*) ☞ Brønnøysund Register
- Marriage settlements (*Ektepaktregisteret*) ☞ Brønnøysund Register
- Mortgaged movable property (*Løsøreregisteret*) ☞ Brønnøysund Register
- Motor vehicles (*Motorvognregister*) ☞ Directorate of Public Roads (Cars, Roads, Traffic chapter)
- Persons (*Folkeregister*) ☞ National register
- Property (*Grunnbok*) ☞ City recorder or District recorder

Voting rights for resident foreigners (*Stemmerett for utenlandske statsborgere*)

If you are a foreigner who has had a residence permit for three years or more and are age 18 or older at the end of the year, you may vote in county and municipal ☞ **elections** (Character, Customs, Country chapter). Before the election, which is held on a Monday in September, you will receive information in the post enabling you to vote in person or by post. For the complete details of voting, see "If you want to be heard, you have to use your vote", a 16-page brochure in colour published by the ☞ **Directorate of Immigration** (Government and Social Services chapter) in Norwegian, Arabic, English, Finnish, Serbo-Croation, Turkish, Vietnamese, Tamil and Urdu editions. If you wish to vote in your home country while living in Norway, contact your embassy; ☞ **Embassies and consulates** (Foreigners chapter).

Retirement
(Pensjonist tilværelse)

About retirement (Om å være pensjonist) The retirement age is 67. The provisions and facilities provided by the State and the municipalities for retired persons include aid-call alarms (trygghetsalarm), assistance support (hjelpestønad), attendance allowance (omsorgslønn), community nursing (hjemmesykepleie), dental services (tannhelsetjenester), disability pensions (uførepensjon), hearing aids (høreapparater), ☞ **housing and care** (bolig og institusjoner), meal service (ombringing av middagsmat), pedicure and hairdressing (fotpleie og hårpleie), return to home country for foreign citizens (tilbakevending), elderly centres (eldresentere), sheltered housing (trygdebolig), ☞ **State pensions** (alderspensjon), survivor pensions (etterlattepensjon), technical aids (tekniske hjelpemidler), transport assistance (transportordning) and voluntary assistance centres (frivillighetssentral). Moreover, retired persons travel at half price (honnørrabatt) on trains, city public transport, buses, airlines, boats and ferries. Theatres, museums and other places of entertainment also offer discounts to retired persons. Many organisations are involved. For an overview of provisions for the elderly, see the brochure published in 1997 by the ☞ **Directorate of Immigration** (Government and Social Services chapter), Eldre (Norwegian edition, ISBN 82-4270303-5) or Senior Citizens (English edition, ISBN 82-4270311-6). For details on and addresses of organisations, services and facilities, contact The National Council for the Elderly (Statens Eldreråd) ☏ 22248595, 📠 22248272, ✉ PO Box 8102 Dep, 0032 Oslo.

Housing and care for the elderly (Boliger og institusjoner for eldre) divide into five categories. A housing grant (boligtilskudd) can help pay for the improvement of an older flat or house. The State Housing Bank (Husbanken) provides grants to persons whose need for financial assistance can be established; this is called a means test (behovsprøv). A rent allowance (bostøtte) to persons who cannot afford to pay their rent or housing expenses. Also provided by The State Housing Bank and subject to a means test.

Sheltered housing (trygdebolig) are usually complexes of flats or small houses for elderly and disabled persons. The residents look after themselves and may be assisted by home help or community nursing services.

Retirement homes (aldershjem) are intended for elderly persons who can manage well on their own but have difficulty performing housework and need some attention and nursing care.

Nursing homes (sykehjem) are for persons who cannot look after themselves but have no need to be hospitalised.

For further information on all housing and care for the elderly, contact the municipal offices concerned: health and social services (helse- og sosialtjenesten) and rent allowance (bostøttekontor or bostøtteordning).

Private pension plans (Egne pensjonsavtaler) are available, should you wish to contribute to a pension that will supplement your ☞ **State pension**. Private-sector companies usually have collective plans for their employees (private tjenestepensjonsordinger), and public sector employees are covered by the Norwegian Public Service Pension Fund (Statens pensjonskasse). Individuals may also initiate and regularly contribute with tax advantage to their own private pension plans, called Individuelle pensjonsavtaler – IRA ("Individual Retirement Agreements"). IRAs allow you a tax deduction in contributing up to a tenth of your gross income for the previous year, limited by an amount that is set each year. For example, if you had a gross income of NOK 250,000 last year, this year you can contribute up to NOK 25,000 to an IRA and reduce your taxes by 28% of that amount, or NOK 7000. Your contributions to your IRA are locked in until you reach the retirement age of 67. You may take early retirement at age 64, but the payments from your IRA must be paid out over time, at least until you are 77. Banks, insurance companies, mutual funds and unit-linked funds offer IRAs with and without guaranteed yields (med og uten avkastingsgaranti). As you are building your IRA fund, you are not taxed on any yields that may accrue and the amount of the fund is not taxed as part of your estate. However, when you retire and start drawing payments from an IRA, you will taxed as for other retirement income. For further details, contact your bank or insurance company.

State pension (*Alderspensjon*) are paid by the National Insurance Scheme (*Folketrygden*). The retirement age is 67. There is no early retirement under the State pension scheme, but retirement may be postponed until age 70. The State pension is a combination of a basic pension (*grunnpensjon*) and a supplementary pension (*tilleggspensjon*) and in some cases a special increment (*særtillegg*) or provider increment (*forsørgingstillegg*). Pensions are calculated according to the ☞ **basic sum** (Banking, Finance, Insurance chapter).

The basic pension is equal to the basic sum and is paid to everyone, in full to those who have lived in the country at least 40 years after age 16 and in lesser amounts to those who have resided less in the country. Everyone who has resided in the country for three years or more is entitled to some benefits.

The supplementary pension is intended to prevent a decline in standard of living upon retirement. It is paid to everyone who has been in paid employment and has earned pension points (*pensjonspoeng*), which may be accumulated from age 17 to 69. If you elect to continue working and earning past age 67, you may accumulate pension points for two years thereafter. Upon turning 70, you will be eligible for full basic pension, regardless of your income. Pension points are given for all income in excess of the basic sum, as a ratio to the basic sum. For instance, in 1999, the basic sum was NOK 46,950. Consequently, a pensionable income of NOK 175,000 is NOK 128,050 more than the basic amount, which when divided by the basic amount gives 2.7 pension points. The pension points are recorded each year. When you retire, your 20 highest point years, when you earned the most compared to the basic sum, are used to calculate an average point sum (*sluttpoengtall*). The full supplementary pension, according to the average point sum, is paid to to all who have lived in the country at least 40 years, and in lesser amounts to those who have resided less in the country. Everyone who has resided in the country for three years or more and has earned pension points is entitled to some benefits. The supplementary pension was introduced in 1967. So persons born before 1937 cannot fulfil the 40-year requirement before they retire. Consequently, transitional regulations apply to persons born in 1936 or earlier. For instance, a person born in 1918 – 1936 is entitled to a full supplementary pension if he or she has earned pension points each year from 1967 until the year of reaching age 69.

The special increment is paid in place of or in addition to the supplementary pension, to persons who have earned very few points. It is calculated as a percentage of the basic sum and otherwise paid on the same conditions as the basic and supplementary pensions.

The provider increment is half of the basic pension and is paid to persons who must support a spouse or children. You are eligible for the provider increment for your spouse (*ektefelletilleg*) only if he or she receives no income or pension which exceeds the basic amount.

For further details on pensions, contact the nearest National Insurance office, listed under *Trygdekontor* in the Pink Pages.

Shopping (*Innkjøp*)

Antiques (*Antikviteter*) are sold by antique shops (*antikvitetshandlere*), auctions (*auksjon*) and markets (*marked*), most listed under *antikviteter* in the Yellow Pages. The Norwegian Art and Antique Dealers Association (*Norges kunst- og aktikvitetshandleres forening*) lists the leading dealers, including used and rare book shops (*antikvariat*) ☎ & ☎ 22444533, ✉ Skovveien 13, 0257 Oslo,
◉ http://www.cinoa.org/cinoa/nkaf.html with names and addresses in Norwegian and principal goods sold in English. Auctions are also advertised in newspapers, under *Kunngjøringer*. The Antique Net (*Antikknett*) is an Internet web site devoted to free listings of forthcoming auctions, exhibitions and markets ✉ tips@antikknett.no,
◉ http://www.antiknett.no/hvaskjer.html with listings by month. A semimonthly magazine, *Samler & Antikkbørsen* ("Collecting and antique marketplace") carries feature articles on antiques as well as advertisements and now has a paid circulation of more than 16,000 ☎ 32892200, ☎ 32268090, ✉ Torgeir Vraas pl 6, 3044 Drammen.

The export of antiques in any way – by sale, as gifts or in removal goods – is restricted by the Cultural Heritage Act (*Kulturminneloven*). Specifically, permits are required for the export of buildings of all kinds and any parts of buildings as well as other objects of artistic, cultural or personal historic interest that are more than 100 years old. The permits are administered and formally issued by the Ministry of Environment (*Miljøverndepartementet*) and will be required by Norway Customs upon export. Typical objects covered by the law are sculptures, paintings, coins, archives, manuscripts, seals and signets, rare prints, furniture and other inventory or chattels, costumes and weapons. National archives, galleries, libraries and museums in Oslo, Bergen, Hamar, Kristiansand, Trondheim and Tromsø are empowered to issue export permits, each within its own field.

Bargaining (*prute*) Norwegians feel uncomfortable about bargaining, according to Hans Mathias Thjømøe, economist at the Norwegian School of Management. He contends that when shopping, people are overly polite, which is one reason why the prices are high. Custom aside, you need not fear bargaining for goods, as the price of an article is only the starting point for negotiations. The margin on cars is 12-18 %, clothes 100-500%, white and brown goods 20-30%. Also ask for discounts on items like books (*bøker*), building supplies (*byggevarer*), furniture (*møbler*), gold (*gull*), kitchen equipment (*kjøkkenutstyr*), photographic equipment (*fotoutstyr*), shoes (*sko*), spectacles (*briller*), tyres (*bildekk*) and watches (*klokker*), to name just a few. You will have more success if you remain friendly and discrete. Take time to establish good rapport with the salesperson, if you are a regular customer at a sports shop and they know your face, you will more successful. Don't choose to bargain at a busy time.

Beer (*øl*) has been brewed in Norway since Viking times. Until 1994, *Renhetsloven* ("the purity law") required that beer be brewed from malt, hops, yeast and water only. In 1994, EEA agreement invalidated the purity law, but breweries still follow it. There are 11 major breweries, most of whom also produce soft drinks: Ringnes (Oslo), Borg (Sarpsborg), Akershus (Ytre Enebakk), Aass (Drammen), Grans (Sandefjord), Christianssands (Kristiansand), Hansa (Bergen), Hardanger (Bergen), Trio (Skien), Tromi (Trondheim) and Macks (Tromsø). In 1997, domestic beer consumption was about 223 million litres Norwegian beer and 7 million litres imported beer for a total of 230 million litres, equivalent to 53 litres per capita, comparable with Sweden (59) but about half that of the United Kingdom (103). Nonetheless, beer is popular and there is a club for enthusiasts, *Pilsens Venner* ("Lager Friends") ☎ 35070333, ✉ 3895 Edlaug,
◉ http://www.cirkel.no/oscar/pilsens-venner/ with links to other sites in Norway and abroad.

Beer is brewed and sold in seven tax classes by percentage volume alcohol content. Alcohol-free beers (up to 0.7%) may be sold along with soft drinks in kiosks and other stores. True beers (0.7% – 4.75%) may be sold only in food shops holding municipal beer sale licences during specified hours, such as up till 7pm on weekdays and 6pm on Saturdays. Sale stops earlier on some days, including Ascension Day (*Kristi himmelfartsdag*), the eves of Christmas (*jul*), New Year (*nyttårs*), Easter (*påske*) and Whitsunday (*pinse*). Beer cannot be sold on Sundays and public holidays (*offentlige høytidsdager*), 1st and 17th May and on days when voting (*stemmedagen for stort-*

ingsvalg, fylkevalg og kommunevalg) takes place. Strong beers (4.75% – 6.75%) are sold only by the ☞ **Vinmonopolet**. Beer is more heavily taxed than in most other countries and consequently is more expensive. In 1997, for instance, the beer tax on class D lager was nearly five times that of a comparable lager in Denmark. Together, beer tax and VAT account for about 63.4% of the retail price of beer in shops and 38.2% of the price of beer served in eating places and pubs/bars. Standard bottle and can sizes are 0.33, 0.5, 0.7 and 1.5 litre in retail shops, and the price is exclusive of a ☞ **deposit** which is added on in buying and refunded upon container return.

Tax class (skatte-klasse)	% alcohol	popular beers
A	0–0.7%	Non-alcoholic (alkohol-fritt), unfermented malt (vørterøl)
B	0.7–2.75%	Light beer (lettøl)
C	2.75%–3.75%	Light lager (pils)
D	3.75%–4.75%	Lager (pils), dark lager (Bayer), Christmas beer (juleøl)
E	4.75%–5.75%	Imported English ales
F	5.75%–6.75%	Strong pale (lyst sterkøl), Bock (bokkøl), Christmas beer (juleøl)
G	6.75%–7.00%	Imported German Bock and strong Norwegian Bock

Some foreign beers, such as Carlsberg and Tuborg of Denmark, are brewed under licence. Foreign bottled beers are now imported, starting in 1994 as a result of the EEA agreement, and account for about 2% of all beer sold. The popular brands include American Budweiser and Miller, Australian Fosters, Belgian Lindemans Kriek, Czech Budvar, Dutch Grolsch, English Boddington and Newcastle Brown Ale, Irish Guinness, Kilkenny and Murphys Stout, Mexican Corona Extra and Scottish McEwans. Beer is cheaper in Sweden, principally due to lower taxation. So cost-conscious shoppers often buy on trips there and bring it in under their ☞ **duty free quotas** (Travel and Transport chapter). The Swedish sales

rules allow beers of up to 3.5% alcohol content to be sold in supermarkets and other shops, whilst stronger beers are sold only by *Systembolaget*, the Swedish equivalent of the Vinmonopolet. But the selection is good and the price is reasonable. In mid 1999, the Systembolaget catalogue listed 286 beers, and in a price comparison conducted by *Aftenposten* newspaper, the total for ten cans and bottles of different brands was just a little more than half as much as in downtown Oslo shops.

Body piercing (Kroppsmykking), the wearing of jewellery attached to the body through pierced holes in the ears, lips, cheeks, tongue, nipples, navel and other parts, is popular among teenagers and young adults. If you wish to wear a pierce item, check its content of nickel, which is known to cause allergic reaction. Health regulations follow the EU guidelines in limiting the nickel content of any item to 0.05 percent by weight. But items with higher nickel content are sold, which is one cause of the recent rapid rise in nickel allergies throughout Europe. You will find piercing shops listed under *Piercing* in the Yellow Pages. Some piercing shops also offer ☞ **tattooing**.

Books (Bøker) New books are sold principally by bookshops, which are located in all cities and in most towns and villages. By tradition, the trade is regulated and prices are fixed, though change is underway. Most larger bookshops and many kiosks stock books in English and other foreign languages, and all have facilities for ordering books. You can find bookshops listed under *Bokhandlere* in the Yellow Pages; the two leading bookshop chains are *Interbok* and *Libris*. Antiquarian booksellers, listed under *Antikvariat* in the Yellow Pages sell used and antiquarian books. Books, both new and used, are one of the few commodities on which ☞ **MVA** (Taxes, Duties, Excise chapter) is not charged at the retail level.

Border trade (Grensehandel) Prices on most consumer goods are lower in Denmark and Sweden, particularly on tobacco, alcoholic drink, meat and some consumer electronics goods, so you can save by buying when travelling. People who live close to the Swedish border often cross it to shop, and some tour bus companies in Oslo offer shopping trips to Swedish border shops at Svinesund. However, prices fluctuate, so it is wise to check both prices and ☞ **duty-free quotas** (Travel and Transport chapter) before you travel to shop.

Building and do-it-yourself (DIY) supplies (*Byggevarer/gjør-det-selv*) are sold by hardware shops (*Jernhandel*) and builder's merchants (*Byggevarer*) and now mostly by ☞ **chain stores**.

Chain stores (*Kjedeforretninger*) account for an ever increasing portion of non-food retail sales, as do supermarkets for foods. There are chains in almost all retail sectors. Some are subsidiaries of international chains, whilst others are wholly Norwegian. Individual shops and centres may be subsidiaries of, franchised by or owner affiliated with the parent organisation. Some chains, like IKEA home furnishings, have a few mega-stores, whilst others, such as Libris books, have many small or medium-sized shops. By retail sector, the major chains are listed below. Shop locations are listed for ten or fewer shops in a chain; for 11 or more shops, the total number in the country is listed. You may find exact address and telecommunications numbers in the Pink Pages or in the pages of the Internet web sites listed at the ☻ symbol. Most web sites are in Norwegian; other languages are given in parentheses, such as (in English).

Audio, video and hi-fi: *Hi-Fi Klubben*, nine shops, at Bergen, Drammen, Grimstad, Lillehammer, Oslo, Stavanger, Tromsø, Trondheim and Ålesund. ☻ www.hifiklubben.no

Book shops: *Libris*, 130 shops throughout the country

Building supplies: *Byggmakker*, 114 centres throughout the country. ☻ www.byggmakker.no and *Maxbo*, 66 building centres in southern and central parts of the country. ☻ www.maxbo.no.

CDs, computer games and videos: *Akers Mic*, nine shops, at Bergen, Drammen, Kristiansand, Liertoppen, Oslo, Sandnes, Ski, Stavanger and Trondheim. ☻ www.akermic.no

Car accessories and parts: *Biltema*, seven shops, at Arendal, Bergen, Kristiansand, Oslo, Sandnes, Sarpsborg and Troneheim.

Clothing, mens: *Dressmann*, part of Norwegian Varner Group, 100 shops throughout the country and 48 abroad. ☻ http://www.dressmann.com

Clothing, men's, women's and children's: *Benetton*, Italian-based chain of more than 7,000 shops in 120 countries, including more than 30 in Norway. ☻ www.benetton.no for Norway, ☻ www.benetton.com global; *Hennes & Mauritz*, Swedish-based chain of 500 shops in 12 countries, including 51 throughout Norway. ☻ www.hm.com (in English) and *KappAhl*, Swedish-based chain of 152 shops in Scandinavia, including 25 in Norway. ☻ www.kappahl.se (in Swedish)

Clothing, women's and children's fashions: *Cubus*, part of Norwegian Varner Group, 140 shops throughout the country and *Lindex*, Swedish-based chain of 250 shops in Scandinavia and Germany, including 71 in Norway. ☻ http://www.lindex.se

Consumer electronics and household appliances: *Elkjøp*, 102 shops throughout the country and *Expert*, Swiss-based chain of more than 3000 shops in 17 countries, including 217 in Norway. Norwegian ☻ www.expert.no, main ☻ www.expert.org (in English)

Cyberspace entertainment and electronics: *Spaceworld*, focus on youth (7 – 30) market, 27 shops throughout the country. ☻ www.spaceworld.no

Erotic goods: *Kondomeriet*, 10 shops, at Bergen, Bodø, Førde, Kolbotn, Oslo, Sandnes, Strømmen, Tromsø, Trondheim and Verdal. ☻ www.kondomeriet.no

Furniture and home furnishings: *Bohus*, 52 shops throughout the country. ☻ www.bohus.no and *IKEA*, four mega-stores, at Bergen/Åsane, Oslo/Furuset, Oslo/Slependen and Sandnes/Forus. ☻ www.ikea.com (in English, with link to Norway)

Garden centres: *Hageland*, more than 50 centres throughout the country. ☻ www.hageland.no

Hardware and DIY: *Claes Ohlson*, Swedish chain of 10 hardware department and mail-order shops, including three in Norway at Kristiansand, Oslo and Sandnes. ☻ www.claesohlson.no and *Jernia*, 102 shops throughout the country. ☻ www.jernia.no

Medical supplies: *Banda*, 39 shops throughout the country.

Office stationery and related equipment and goods: *Binders*, seven shops, at Begen, Fredrikstad, Oslo/Alnabru, Oslo/Slependen, Stavanger, Tromsø and Trondheim. ☻ www.binders.no and *Tyrbing-Gjedde*, 32 shops throughout the country. ☻ www.tybring-gjedde.com

Plumbing supplies: *Comfort*, 68 shops throughout the country. ✆ www.comfort.no

Sports goods: *G Sport*, more than 230 shops throughout the country. ✆ www.gresvig.no and *InterSport*, world's largest sports good chain, with more than 4000 shops in 25 countries, including 134 in Norway. ✆ www.intersport.com (in English, French or German)

Telecommunication and IT equipment: *KlartSvar*, a subsidiary of the NetCom telecommunications company, 80 shops throughout the country. ✆ www.klartsvar.no and *Telehuset*, a subsidiary of the Telenor telecommunications company, more than 40 shops throughout the country. ✆ www.telehuset.no

Competition (*Konkurranse*) is commonplace. Except for wine and liquor sold by the ☞ **Vinmonopolet** shops, competition is lively in all shopping sectors. However, price and convenience often conflict: you will pay more for food bought in a convenience shop with extended opening hours than in a supermarket with ordinary shop hours. The differences can be extreme: in 1997, an investigative Oslo journalist found that the price per kilogram for clementines was seven times as much in a petrol station convenience shop as in an ☞ **ethnic shop**. Most competitive prices don't vary that much, but price comparison shopping almost always pays. Check newspaper advertisements before you buy, as ☞ **sales** are part of the competitive profile of many shops. Competition and fair trade are ensured by laws enforced by the regional offices of the Norwegian Competition Authority (*Konkurransetilsynet*) in Bergen, Bodø, Hamar, Kristiansand, Oslo, Stavanger, Trondheim and Tromsø. For further information contact one of the regional offices listed in the Pink Pages under *Konkurransetilsynet* or the head office in Oslo ✆ 22400900, ✆ 22420909, ✉ PO Box 8132 Dep, 0033 Oslo, ✆ http://www.konkurransetilsynet.no with pages in Norwegian and in English.

Co-operative shops (*Forbrukersamvirke*) belong to and are supported by co-operative societies. Their aim is the sale of goods at moderate prices and the distribution of any profits among the members. The first co-operative shop was opened in 1844 in Rochdale, England. The concept spread, and in 1895 the International Co-Operative Alliance (ICA) was founded in London. The movement was taken up in other sectors, and there now are co-operative societies in almost all business sectors, including agriculture, banking, energy, industry, insurance, fisheries, housing, tourism and consumer shops. The ICA now has more than 230 member organisations in more than 100 countries, which together have some 730 million members. Today, the co-operative movement is global, aided in part by the Committee for the Promotion and Advancement of Cooperatives (COPAC), of which the ICA is a member, along with two agencies of the United Nations (UN) and four other international agencies. In Norway, the co-operative movement started in the 19th century, and the first co-operative society was founded in Oslo in 1895. There are now four principal country-wide co-operative societies in the country, all members of the ICA, for agriculture (*Landbrukssamvirket*), banking and insurance (*Vår bank og forsikring*), housing (*Norsk Boligbyggelags Landsforbund – NBBL*) [☞ **housing cooperatives** (Housing chapter)] and consumer shops (*Forbrukersamvirket – NKL*). The "NKL" stands for the original name of the organisation, *Norsk Kooperative Landsforening*, founded in 1906. NKL now has some 295 local co-operative societies throughout the country, which together operate nearly 1300 shops. The shops are owned by the local societies and a few are franchised, whilst NKL provides bulk purchasing, distribution and marketing to the 14 name-brand chains. In alphabetical order by name of the chain, followed by the number of shops in parentheses:

- *Bygg & Bo* builder's merchants (23)
- *ByggMix* do-it-yourself (DIY) shops (58)
- *Det norske Møbelsenter* furniture and furnishings (25)
- *Ideel* lamps and electrical appliances (60)
- *Jacobs* colour and interior furnishings (6)
- *KappAhl* clothing (25)
- *Mega* large supermarkets (180)
- *Obs!* hypermarkets (19)
- *Popin* clothing (51)
- *Prix* low-price grocers (259)
- *ProSport* sporting goods and casual wear (14)
- *S-Marked* supermarkets (535)
- *Stilig* home furnishing (7)
- *StraX* kiosk and convenience shops (11)

You may find the nearest shop by looking under the name of the chain in the Pink Pages. All supermarkets and grocers and most of the other shops have brochures that outline the costs and benefits of membership, including dividend arrangements, and include application forms.

Deposit (*Pant*) is added to the price of almost all containers of soft drinks and beer as well as bottles of wines and spirits bottled in Norway, and appears as a separate item, plus deposit (+ *pant*), on cash-register receipts. The deposit is refunded upon return of refillable empty glass and PET (Polyethylene Terepthalate) plastic bottles (*ombruksflasker*), as well as non-refillable plastic bottles (*plastflasker*) and aluminium cans (*bokser*); these containers are marked with a small, red rectangle with white lettering stating the amount of deposit.

All shops selling drinks in deposit containers accept the empties and refund the deposits. Traditionally, this has been done by hand, and still is done by hand in smaller shops, such as drink shops and convenience outlets. However, most supermarkets and larger grocers, as well as the Vinmopolet wine and liquor shops, now have reverse vending machines (*returautomat*) for the purpose. You feed empty beverage containers into the machine; it identifies them, calculates the total deposit due and issues a refund voucher. There are two principal types of reverse vending machine:
- For refillable bottles, which identify the bottles by their shape. These machines usually have a vertical opening and you insert the bottles standing up. Returned bottles are sorted into crates and return to bottlers.
- For non-refillable plastic bottles and aluminium cans, which identify the containers by reading their bar codes. These machines usually have a round opening and you insert the containers horizontal. Returned containers are crushed for transport to recycling plants.

The newest horizontal-insertion machines combine these functions and accept both refillable and non-refillable containers. The containers a machine accepts usually are described in a sign on its front. *Bokser og plastflasker med pantmerke* means "cans and plastic bottles with deposit labels". *Ombruksflasker* means "refillable bottles".

You may redeem the refund voucher in cash or as a deduction on your purchase at the shop cash point. Starting in 1997, some reverse vending machines are fitted with two acceptance buttons to press after you have fed in your last empty container, one green and one yellow. If you press the green button, the machine issues a refund voucher. If you press the yellow button, the total due is donated to one of three charities: the Norwegian People's Relief Association (*Norsk Folkehjelp*), the Norwegian Refugee Council (*Flyktningerådet*) and the Salvation Army (*Frelsesasrmeen*), as stated on the instructions on the machine.

Norway has long had deposit on beverage bottles, which is one reason why a Norwegian company, Tomra, is the world's leading manufacturer of reverse vending machines. Tomra started in 1972 and has grown to be a multinational corporation with business in more than 30 countries. In all, about 29,000 Tomra machines are installed in Europe and 7,000 in North America. If you are interested in reverse vending machines, contact Tomra ✆ 66799100, ✉ 66799111, ✉ PO Box 278, 1372 Asker, ✉ http://www.tomra.no with pages in English.

Discount/customer loaayalty cards (*bonuskorter*) A quarter of a million discount and customer loyalty cards are in circulation in the country. Many people have more than one card, so this is not the same as saying that a quarter of a million people have cards. The leading cards are:

Domino, a customer loyalty card valid in ICA, Rimi and SparMat supermarkets, Statoil petrol stations, Cubus and Dressmann clothing shops, Expert appliance and consumer electronics shops and Telenor private mobile telephone services. Points are awarded upon purchasing, and accumulated points may be redeemed in products or a cheque.

Trumf, a customer loyalty card valid in all Norgesgruppen shops, including AKA, EuroSpar, Joker, Kiwi and Nærmat, as well as Shell petrol stations, Sparebanken NOR, the Byggmakker building merchant chain and the Til Bords interior decoration chain. Points are awarded upon purchasing, and accumulated points may be redeemed in products or a cheque.

Forbrukersamvirket, the discount card for the ☞ **Co-operative shops**, including Domus, Mega, Obs!, Prix and S-Marked supermarkets as well as Den norske Mobelsenter, GullFunn, Ideel and Popin shops. Purchases are periodically totalled, and a refund of up to 3% is made directly to the cardholder.

Duty-free (*Taxfrie*) shopping for travellers in Europe began in 1947 when the first duty-free shop opened at Shannon Airport in Ireland. Duty-free shopping spread world-wide and now is part of international travel. In Europe, duty-free shopping was available for air and sea travel across all of the many borders between countries. On 1 July 1999, duty-free shopping in Europe changed, as it was eliminated for travel across borders between European Union (EU) countries. So now duty-free shopping is available to and from but not within the EU.

Norway is not a member of the EU. So duty-free is available for travellers to and from EU countries, but not between them. Consider, for instance, a round-trip air journey from Oslo to Paris with a change of flights in Copenhagen. France and Denmark are both in the EU, so you cannot buy duty-free for flights between Paris and Copenhagen. This means that on your flight to Paris, you can shop duty-free in Oslo, before entering the EU, but not in the Copenhagen duty-free shop, because your destination is Paris, within the EU. Conversely, on your return flight, you can shop duty-free in Copenhagen, before leaving the EU, but not in Paris on your way to Copenhagen.

However, within the EU, duty-free remains available at some places, including the Canary Islands, the Faeroes, Helgoland island off the north-west coast of Germany, the English Channel islands, Gibraltar and the Åland islands at the southern end of the Gulf of Bothnia between Sweden and Finland. If you fly from Sweden to Finland, you cannot shop duty-free, as both countries are in the EU. But if you take a ferry from Stockholm to Åbo, Finland, it most likely will call at Mariehamn in the Åland islands, so you can shop duty-free.

Ecolabelling (*Miljømerking*) Denmark, Finland, Iceland, Norway and Sweden have a common Nordic environmental labelling scheme. Consumer products that meet set environmental and quality standards are permitted to label their goods with the Nordic Ecolabel, or "Swan label" (*Svanemerket*), so named because its design is based on a swan in flight. The logo may appear with or without text, such as "Nordic Environmental Label" in English or *Miljømerket* in Norwegian. More than 600 products now carry ecolabels, from adhesives to wrapping paper. For further information, contact *Stiftelsen*

Miljømerking i Norge ✆ 22360710, 📠 22360729, ✉ Kr. Augusts g 5, 0164 Oslo, ✉ info@ecolabel.no, 🌐 http://www.ecolabel.no with pages in Norwegian and in English.

Factory outlets (*Fabrikk-utsalg*) are located at or near the factories whose wares they sell and usually offer overstocks, seconds and discontinued lines at discount prices. There are 13 in the country, in alphabetical order:

Aleksander (leather outerwear) at Moi, about 100 km SE of Stavanger on E18 motorway, ✆ 51401200.

Brusletto (sporting knives), at Geilo on highway 7, ✆ 32090200.

Brødrene Øyo (kitchen knives and tools), at Geilo on highway 7, ✆ 32090911.

Dale (knitwear) at Holmedal, 65 km ⊛ of Førde on highway 609, ✆ 56596161.

Figgjo (china and earthenware) at Figgjo, 30 km S of Stavanger on E18 motorway, ✆ 51683500.

Geilo Jernvare (kitchenware) 1 km east of Geilo on highway 7, ✆ 32090155.

Geilo Verktøy (hand tools) 1 km east of Geilo on highway 7, ✆ 32089510.

Gjestdal Spinneri (yarn, knitwear and blankets) at Otedal, 40 km SE of Stavanger at intersection of highways 45 and 508, ✆ 51612210.

Hackman Polaris (pots and pans) at Orstad near Klepp railway station, 25 km SE of Stavanger, ✆ 51423700.

Hadeland Glassverk (glassware) at Jevnaker 12 km N of Hønefoss on highway 241, ✆ 61311000.

Helle Knivfabrikk (sports knives) at Holmedal, 65 km ⊛ of Førde on highway 609, ✆ 57734180.

Høie (bedding and textiles) at Mosby, 10 km N of Kristiansand on highway 12, ✆ 38124400.

Magnor Glassverk (glassware) at Magnor, 30 km S of Kongsvinger on highway 202, ✆ 62837133.

Porsgrund Porselen (china) at Porsgrunn, ✆ 35550040.

Ricco Vero (men's clothing) at Olden, 16 km S of Stryn on highway 60, ✆ 57877080.

Sandnes Uldvare (Yarn and knitting patterns), Foss-Eikeland at Sandnes, 20 km S of Stavanger on E18 motorway, ✆ 51608600.

Sandvika Veveri (textiles and curtains) at Rud, 4

km NE of Sandvika just off E16 motorway, SW of Oslo, ℡ 67153153.

Skjæveland (knitwear) at Ålgård, 30 km S of Stavanger on E18 motorway, ℡ 51617200.

Skogstad Sport (Sportswear) at Olden, 16 km S of Stryn on highway 60, ℡ 57876770.

Svanedal (Yarn and knitwear) at Oltedal, 30 km SE of Stavanger on highway 45, ℡ 51611800.

As yet, there are no "outlet villages" in Norway. The closest is Stockholm Quality Outlet at Järfälla, Sweden, about half an hour's drive N of Stockholm, ℡ +46 8 7952181, @ http://www.retailparks.se.

Farm produce (Gardsmat) Throughout the country, there are some 150 farms that sell their produce directly to customers. Many are seasonal, selling vegetables in the summer, fruits in the autumn and root vegetables and eggs year-round, but some offer meats, poultry, flour, baked goods, dairy products, jams and jellies, preserves and local handicrafts. Many have cafes that are open in season, and some also operate bed and breakfast lodgings. Most are open Saturdays and one or two other days of the week in season, whilst a few have year-round shops. Some offer organic (økologisk dyrket) products. Almost all are members of Norsk Gardsmat ("Norwegian Farm Produce"), a countrywide organisation originally started by the State Bank for Agriculture (Statens landbruksbank) but now owned by the farms. The customer club (Norsk Gardsmat Kundeklubb) offers an information service on produce, special offers and on-line ordering.

See the local Norsk Gardsmat catalogue for the location of the nearest farm produce shop and an overview of its wares. There are nine catalogues: Akershus and Østfold counties, Aust-Agder and Vest-Agder counties, Buskerud, Vestfold and Telemark counties, Hedmark and Oppland counties, Hordaland county, Nordland, Troms and Finnmark counties, Rogaland county, Sogn og Fjordane county and Sør-Trøndelag and Nord-Trøndelag counties. They are available at member farms or on request from Norsk Gardsmat, Statens landbruksbank ℡ 22317300, ℻ 22317317, ✉ PO Box 8183 Dep, 0034 Oslo, or from the Research Park at the Norwegian University of Agriculture at Ås, Forskningsparken i Ås ℡ 64948430, ℻ 64943797, ✉ Saghellinga A, 1432 Ås. The on-line version duplicates the nine printed catalogues and is continuously updated on the web site @ http://www.norsk.gardsmat.org with pages in Norwegian and on-line support of ordering for club members.

Fireworks (Fyrverkeri) are most used at New Year's and are divided into five categories (klasse) which govern their import, sale, storage, transport and use.

Category Ia: Indoor fireworks such as caps (krutlapper) for toy pistols and party crackers (knall bonbon); general shop goods, no restrictions on sale.

Category Ib: Lesser outdoor fireworks such as crackers (bordbomber), party-poopers and electric sparklers (stjerneskudd); general shop goods, sold only to persons 16 years old and older.

Category II: Outdoor fireworks including garden fireworks, smaller Roman candles, Catherine wheels and the like; sold only 27–31 December by shop attendants at fire-regulation-approved counters, to adults only.

Category III: The largest outdoor fireworks that may be sold to the public, including rockets (raketter), bursting charges (luftbomber), larger Roman candles (større romeriske lys), batteries (bombebatterieri) and the like requiring specified safety distances to be observed; sold only 27–31 December by shop attendants at fire-regulation-approved counters, to adults only.

Category IV: Major fireworks for professional displays (display-fyrverkeri); sold by dealers to qualified pyrotechnicians and used only by permit from the local fire marshal (brannsjefen).

When you shop for fireworks, look for banners on or signs in shop windows or on special stalls set up for sales starting 27th December. The business is brisk and competitive, so many shops and stalls advertise fireworks sale in advance in local newspapers.

Flea markets (Loppemarked) are common in cities and usually are held twice a year, in the spring and in the autumn. The principle of the flea market is similar to that of the original Le marché aux puces de Saint-Ouen, which opened in Paris in 1885. Used goods of all sorts, including appliances, books, clothing, furniture, household goods, musical instruments, postal cards, radios, silverware, TVs and sports equipment are put up for sale. However, unlike the marché aux puces in France or the flea markets in other countries, the Norwegian loppemarked is not a commercial undertaking by many stall purveyors, but rather a fund-raising effort by a school band (*korps*), a sports club (*idrettsforening*) or other voluntary or charitable organisation. A few weeks in advance, the organisation will tack posters to market bulletin boards, put flyers into home mail boxes and insert advertisements under *Kunngjøringer* in the classified section of the local newspaper, announcing that the *loppemarked* will be held and asking for contributions of used items for it. Usually, telephone numbers to call are listed, so you may call and arrange to have goods picked up. The voluntary staff, such as the parents of the children in the school band benefited by it, will collect and sort the goods and man the market on sale days, usually at a weekend at a local school. The markets have become so popular and so commonplace that one in five residents in the cities visits them once or twice a year.

Thrift is a common reason for visiting the markets, as one in six visitors is looking for a bargain. But the array of unusual items available is the greatest attraction: one in four visitors comes seeking odds and ends not available elsewhere. And the markets have become social events, where people meet for the entertainment afforded by gathering to shop for the unexpected. The larger markets will have an improvised café serving waffles, coffee, tea, and other snacks and soft drinks. Most *loppemarked* will arrange goods in groups, such as books in one room of the school, clothing in another, children's toys in another, and so on. Sometimes prices are marked on goods, but more often you must ask the salesperson. Bartering is part of the fun of shopping; you can offer; the salesperson can accept or stand firm. Expensive or rare items usually are auctioned, often in the afternoon of the second day of the market.

Foreign/ethnic food shops (*utenlandsk/ ethiskmatvarerbutikker*) are found wherever there is a predominance of foreigners living. In Oslo, the area with a variety of most foreign food shops is Grønland. These shops stock items that are sometimes hard to find in ☞ **supermarkets**, for example unusual vegetables and fruits, bread varieties, tinned and dried goods. They are frequented not only by their own countrymen, but also by people living locally and some who make a special trip for a big shopping expedition. To find out where these shops are in your locality, ask around, there is no section for them in the Yellow Pages.

Gift ideas (*Gave forslag*) For gourmets, an excellent gift is Norwegian fish. The favourites are smoked salmon (*røykelaks*) and marinated salmon (*gravlaks*), sold in vacuum blister packs in the chill counters in ☞ **supermarkets** and fish shops, and pickled herring (*sild*) in jars, flavoured with mustard sauce or tomato sauce. Cheeses, particularly the unique ☞ **goat cheese** (Food and Eating chapter), tempt those who wish to sample Norwegian fare. If you give a block of goat cheese, be sure to include a cheese plane (*ostehøvel*) to slice it wafer-thin. Traditional handicrafts, sold at *Husflid* shops (see the Yellow Pages) travel better than foods and may be shipped easily. The favourites include knitted sweaters, gloves, mittens and caps (*genser, hansker, votter, luer*), felt and fur slippers (*filt, skin tøffler*), carved wooden items (*treskjæring*), sports knives (*sportskniv*), and rose painting (*rosemaling*). Glassware shops (*glass*) offer attractive crystal (*krystall*), and gift shops and departments of larger shops offer useful items of pewter (*tinn*). Books, sold by book shops (*bokhandel*) and newsagents (*kiosk*), are always popular gifts and are easy to send by post; choice titles include *Adventure Roads in Norway* by Erling Welle-Strand, the twenty some titles in the *Tokens of Norway* series published by Aschehoug Press, innumerable cook books, and, of course, this book, *Living in Norway*.

Hardware/ironmonger shops (*Jernhandel*) sell a wide range of goods. A well-stocked shop will offer do-it-yourself goods (*gjør-det-selv*), fittings (*beslagvarer*), garden tools and equipment (*hageredskap*), household goods (*husholdingsprodukter*), interior fixtures (*interiør*), kitchen utensils (*kjøkkentøy*), machine tools (*maskiner*), nails and screws (*spiker og skruer*), paints (*maling*), protective equipment (*verneutstyr*), small electrical appliances (*elektriske artikler*) and tools (*verktøy*). For the location of the nearest shop, look under *Jernvareforretninger* or *Jernvarer* in the Yellow Pages, or contact *Jernia*, the leading hardware shop chain ✆ office 66996600, customer service 81500100, ✆ 66996689, ✉ PO Box 613, 1411 Kolbotn, ✆ http://jernia.no with pages in Norwegian and a list of shops throughout the country.

Health food (*Helsekost*) is sold mostly in health food shops, though some supermarkets and other grocers now offer health foods. Most of the shops

offer a selection of ☞ **Organic foods** (this chapter), vitamins, natural remedies, food supplements, skin care products and other preparations. There are three chains of health food shops. *Helios,* the oldest of the three, was established in the mid 1960s. It has two of its own and 11 franchise shops in the country, and its products are sold by the other health food shops, as the company is a major producer, miller, importer and wholesaler of health foods. *Vitamina Helse & Velvære* ("Vitamina Health and Well-being") is a chain of 20 of its own shops in 12 cities and towns in the southern part of the country. *Sunkost* ("Healthy Diet") is the largest chain, with some 90 shops in cities and towns throughout the country. For the location of the nearest health food shop, look under *Helsekost* in the Yellow Pages or under the names of the chains in the Pink Pages. *Sunkost* has an Internet web site
✉ http://www.sunkost.no

Liquor (*Brennevin*) is sold only by ☞ **Vinmonopolet** shops. Each year, nearly eight million litres are sold; vodka and unflavoured liquors are most popular, accounting for more than three of every ten litres sold, followed by brandies (a quarter of sales) and whiskies (a seventh). Fourth in popularity by volume sold are the domestic and imported brands of aquavit (*akevitt*) – "water of life" – the native Scandinavian drink, distilled from potatoes or cereals and flavoured, usually with caraway seeds. Aquavit accounts for 95% of all liquor exports of more than a million litres per year. A Norwegian favourite type has been aged in casks on a ship that has crossed the equator and accordingly is named *Linje* ("Line"). The movement of the ship sloshes the aquavit in the casks, which is held to add flavour. Liquors are listed in the shop catalogues first by type and then by country of origin. For instance, under the Whiskies (*Whisky*), brands from Canada, Ireland, Scotland and the USA are listed.

Mail order from abroad (*Postordre fra utlandet*) If you wish, you may buy clothing and other personal items from mail order companies abroad, usually in the same way to which you may be accustomed, by filling out and posting or telefaxing an order form along with payment or charge card authorisation. In ordering, be sure to check catalogue prices to see whether or not they include value-added tax (VAT). By international customs agreement, VAT is not to be charged on export orders, because VAT is charged upon import and the same goods cannot be subject to double VAT. American mail-order catalogues usually list prices exclusive VAT ("sales tax" in the USA), because it is charged by the States and not by the federal government. But British mail-order catalogues usually list prices inclusive VAT, which you should request be deducted, as seldom is a space provided on an order form for that purpose. When your shipment arrives in Norway by post, courier or air freight, it will be subject to import duty on the individual items plus Norwegian value-added tax (*MVA*) on the sum of the total for goods, their shipping and the duty levied. You may clear a shipment yourself at the customs house (*tollsted*) at which it is held, or you may have the carrier clear it for you, in which case an administration charge will be added to the total due. A package arriving by post usually is cleared through customs automatically and sent to your local post office, which will send you a notice of the charges due. You then take the notice to the post office, pay the charges, and pick up the package. Couriers and air freight forwarding agents usually notify you of the arrival of a shipment and ask if you or they should clear it through customs. Import duties vary by category of goods and country of origin. As Norway is not a member of the EU, duty is charged on goods imported from EU countries. Duties are listed according to the international harmonisation system (HS) in an annual booklet entitled *Tolltariffen* ("Customs duties") sold in book shops and kept in larger libraries. However, unless you are familiar with importing and customs practices, the easiest way to estimate customs duty on an order is to call the local District Customs House and ask for the current duties (*tollsatser*) on the items you intend to order, see *Distriktstollsted* under *Tollvesenet* in the Pink Pages. If you need to return an item on which you have paid import duty, such as for exchange or repair, ask for a proforma invoice (*proforma faktura*) at the post office. This need not be the local post office that normally deals with your parcels. Fill the form in, so that when your item has been exchanged or repaired and returned, it will be exempt from duties.

Norwegian foods (*Norske matvarer*) in shops increasingly compete with foods from countries with greater agricultural industries, due to the open market conditions imposed by various international agreements within the ☞ **EFTA, EEA and EU** (Government and Social Services chapter). Consequently, in the mid 1990s, *Stiftelsen Godt Norsk* ("The Good Norwegian Foundation") was set up to make Norwegian foods more competitive. Part of that effort has been to promote consumer awareness through marking of foods with the *Godt Norsk* emblem to signify quality. It is not just a nationalistic gesture. Norwegian foods often are of higher quality than the average of imports. For instance, Norwegian fruits and vegetables can be more nutritious and taste better than those grown in more southerly countries. This is because farming is less intensive than that of many other countries and because at the country's high northern latitude, there are comparatively few insects, so insecticides are used sparingly or not at all. The more natural growing and lesser spraying results in higher quality. Thus far, the *Godt Norsk* quality control has awarded the right to display its emblem to more than 1300 foods in six categories: meat and meat products (*kjøtt og kjøttprodukter*), eggs and egg products (*egg og egg-produkter*), fruits and vegetables (*frukt og grønnsaker*), dairy products (*melk og melkeprodukter*), wild (non cultivated) foods (*naturhøstede produkter*) and grains and grain products (*korn og kornprodukter*). For further details, contact *Godt Norsk* ✆ 22317410, 🖷 22317420, ✉ Nedre Vollgt. 11, 0158 Oslo, ✉ stiftelsen@godtnorsk.no, ✇ http://www.godtnorsk.no or ask for a copy of the *Godt Norsk Fakta* ("Godt Norsk Facts") brochure, available in Norwegian or in English.

Godt Norsk emblem

Opening hours (*Åpningstid*) are displayed on building facades and shop windows in a form that indicates six business days, typically 9-21 (10-18), which means that the shop is open from 9 a.m. to 9 p.m. Monday-Friday and 10 a.m. to 6 p.m. on Saturday. Grocers (*dagligvarer*) and supermarkets (*Super*) usually open at 9 a.m., but those in shopping centres and malls (*Kjøpesentere*) usually adhere to centre opening hours. Some convenience shops and larger kiosks (*Storkiosk*) are open from 7 a.m. to 11 p.m., whilst petrol stations with convenience shops may be open day and night. During the major national summer holiday for three weeks in July, the week between Christmas and New Year's and the week before Easter Sunday, opening hours may be shortened or shops may be closed. By an odd linguistic twist, the regulations governing shop opening times were long called *lukningsvedtekter* ("closing regulations"). Consequently, in mid July, a sign on a shop reading *sommerlukning* may mean that the hours of business are less than usual, in which case the hours will be stated, or that the shop is closed for the summer holiday, in which case the dates of closing will be stated. By law, most shops cannot be open on Sundays, except for three weeks during the pre-Christmas shopping rush. Small shops, by ruling less than 100 square metres of floor space (150 square metres for petrol stations), are excepted and may be open after hours and on Sundays. In everyday language, shops limited to this size are now called *Brustad buer* (Brustad booths) after Sylvia Brustad, the member of Parliament (*Storting*) responsible for the specification of smallness when she was Minister of Children and Family Affairs (until October 1997). Two other Norwegian women parliamentarians are also so honoured in the everyday language. In the early 1970s, Christian Democratic Minister of Social Affairs, Bergfrid Fjose, sought to cut alcohol consumption by having the ☞ **Vinmonopol** logo removed from its bottle-sized plastic shopping bags. The word for "bag" in Norwegian is *pose*; hence the term *Fjose-pose* for a logo-less Vinmonopolet bag. In 1981, the government under Prime Minister Gro Harlem Bruntland added an extra day to the statutory four weeks of ☞ **Vacation** (Holidays chapter) for all employees. Though Bruntland later went on to be the director of the World Health Organisation (WHO), the extra free holiday day remained as *Gro-dagen* (Gro day).

Organic foods (*Økologisk mat*) are grown without using chemical or synthetic fertilisers, pesticides, pharmaceuticals or genetic manipulation. Worldwide, there are organic farms and farming associations in more than 35 countries and more than a million hectares of farm land is devoted to organic cultivation. (A hectare is the metric unit of land area, equal to 10,000 square metres or about 2.4 acres.) In Norway, organic farming is modest: of the country's 900,000 hectares of cultivated land, only about 12,000 hectares are devoted to organic farming. However, whilst farming in general is declining, organic farming is now growing at a rate of nearly 30% a year. Most organic foods from Norwegian farms are marketed under the auspices of Debio, the country-wide organic agriculture association. The word Debio is a contraction of Demeter-biological. Demeter, in Greek mythology, the goddess of corn and harvesting, is the name of the world-wide confederation of 19 national associations for organic agriculture. Debio is the Norwegian member, and therefore adheres to the standards and rules set by Demeter, as well as by the International Federation of Organic Agriculture Movements (IFOAM). In shops, the Debio logo on foods indicates that they are from Norwegian organic farms, whilst the Demeter logo indicates that they are imported from organic farms in other countries. Debio and Demeter foods are sold in ☞ **Health food shops** (this chapter) and increasingly in ☞ **Supermarkets** (this chapter). Organic milk, cream and yoghurt, identified by the Debio logo and marketed under the *Dalsgården* brand, are now sold in grocery shops and supermarkets throughout the country. Foods sold directly by organic ☞ **Farm produce** (this chapter) shops may or may not carry the Debio label, depending on whether or not the farm also sells its produce through other shops. For further information on Debio, contact the head office ✆ 63862650, 🖷 63856985, ✉ 1940 Bjørkelangen, ✉ kontor@debio.no, ☻ http://www.debio.no with pages in Norwegian and in English. For further information on Demeter, contact Debio in Norway or the secretariat of Demeter International in the Netherlands ✆ +31 343 512925, 🖷 +31 343 516943, ✉ Kraaybeekerhof, Postbus 17, NL-3970 AA, Driebergen, Netherlands, ✉ krayhof@worldaccess.nl, ☻ http:/www.demeter.ne✆ with pages in English and in German.

Debio logo, based on the letter Ø for Okologisk ("Organic")

Sales (*salg*) occur at least twice a year, in January and August when normal merchandise is marked down significantly. Some things that are not seasonal are seldom on sale, for example souvenirs and crystal, although second-quality crystal can be bought at the factory outlet. Items like bicycles, ski equipment, garden furniture, winter tyres, Christmas and Easter decorations are on special offer (*tilbud*) before their appropriate season, if you don't mind last season's model. Sometimes the current models are on sale when shops are overstocked. For instance, if there is little or no snow before Christmas, little ski equipment is sold, and sports shops will hold sales of ski and other winter sports equipment in January, to make way for springtime stocking of summer sports goods.

Second-hand shops (*Brukthandlere*) are located throughout the country, in almost all cities and towns, and are listed both under *Antikviteter* and under *Brukthandlere* in the Yellow Pages. There are speciality second-hand shops, such as those that sell ☞ **used clothing** (Clothing chapter). But otherwise, the typical second-hand shop is like a small department store: it has everything, from tools and appliances to decorations and art to tableware and period furniture. Some second-hand shops even have linens and costumes, as well as books and records. The attraction of second-hand goods is not their age, because few of them are old enough to classify as ☞ **antiques**. Variety appeals, as does quality, as anything saleable after use certainly has proven its durability. So in general, quality is high and prices are low. For instance, used silverware, even of current patterns, often costs no more than half the price of new. Solid, well-made used furniture seldom costs as much as the cheapest of flat-pack new furniture. Indeed, particularly young people often find that they can furnish a flat more tastefully and at a lower overall cost by spending their time visiting second-hand shops than by working overtime or borrowing to afford to buy new. And often second-hand shopping can be as easy as visiting a shopping mall, as when several shops jointly arrange a second-hand market (*bruktmarked*), usually on a weekend in a convenient local hall; look for advertisements in newspapers.

Second-hand shops are also good places to sell used goods, as the dealers usually know their markets well and often even advertise for certain items. Depending on the item and on the shop's assessment of its market, a shop may buy outright or may accept it on consignment. In any case, if you sell relatively expensive goods that are easily carried, such as silverware, watches or jewellery, the shop may ask for identification in recording the goods received, to ensure that they are not stolen. Most of the goods in shops, however, come from bulk purchases, as of the estates of deceased persons (*dødsbo*) and of goods sold by bankruptcy estates (*konkursbo*).

Sex shops (*Erotiske artikler*) sell sex aids and devices (*sex-hjelpemidler*), contraceptives (*prevensjonsmidler*), erotic underclothing (*undertøy*) and related erotic goods. You can find them listed under *Erotiske artikler* in the Yellow Pages. There is one chain, *Kondomeriet*, with ten shops throughout the country. Some sex shops offer on-line and mail order-shopping.

Shopping bags (*Bæreposer*) were once made of paper. But almost all shopping bags are now made of plastic, usually printed with shop advertising. Some shops give away bags free, while most charge an average of fifty øre for a bag. Most plastic bags are made of a low-density polyethylene plastic (LDPE) which can be recycled, and accordingly most bag manufacturers have an agreement for recycling with *Plastretur AS*, the principal plastics recycling company. However, the greatest reuse of the bags is to pack ☞ **refuse** (Housekeeping chapter) before sending it down a chute in a block of flats or depositing it in the curbside bin in front of a house.

Sports goods (*Sportsutstyr*) are widely available and many domestic brands as well as brands sold internationally are in the shops. Look in the Yellow Pages under *sport og fritidsutstyr* ("Sport and recreational goods"), *kanoer og kajakker*("canoes and kayaks"), *kniver* ("knives"), *sykler* ("cycles"), *ski* ("ski equipment"), *treningsutstyr* ("training equipment") and *fiskeutstyr* ("fishing gear"). There are two sports goods ☞ **chain stores**, *G Sport*, a Norwegian chain with 230 shops and *InterSport*, the leading international chain with 134 shops in the country.

Supermarkets (*Supermarked*) There are more than 4200 self-service markets in the country, vary-ing in size from smaller, local shops to supermarkets to hypermarkets in shopping centres and malls. Most of the markets in the country are organised in one of the four food retailing groups listed below; the number of markets is stated in parentheses after each name. Look under *Dagligvarer, detalj* ("Groceries, retail") in the Yellow Pages or under the name of the market in the Pink Pages for the location of the nearest markets.

Forbrukersamvirket ("Co-operative shops"): 19 OBS!, 180 Mega, 259 Prix and 535 S-Marked

Haakon Gruppen ("Haakon Group", owned by ICA of Sweden): 516 Rimi, 84 ICA, 6 Maxi and 155 SparMat.

Norgesgruppen ("Norway Group"): 300 Aka Spar, 93 Meny/Evensen, 16 Drageset, 14 Fakta-Kjeden, 96 Hedemark Kjøpmenn, 194 Kiwi, 59 Bunnpriskjeden, 50 Fokus Vest, 8 Safari, 233 Kjøpmannskjeden på Vestlandet, 33 CC-Mart'n, 6 Matringen Bikuben, 735 Nærbutikkene Norge and 450 Butikkringen Østlandet.

Reitangruppen ("Reitan Group"): 280 Rema 1000.

Tattooing (*Tatovering*) has a long tradition. The Vikings marked their skin with indelible designs, as have seamen for centuries. Today, tattooing is trendy among teenagers and young adults, women as well as men. You will find tattooing studios listed under *Tatovering* in the Yellow Pages. Some tattooing studios also offer ☞ **body piercing**.

Tax-free shopping involves the refund of ☞ **MVA** (Taxes, Duties, Excise chapter), which is a Value-Added Tax (VAT). Residents of Denmark, Finland, Norway, Sweden and Åland, including citizens and foreign citizens holding ☞ **residence and work permits** (Arriving, Settling, Leaving chapter) cannot claim the refund. But if you are a resident of another country, you may reclaim the *MVA* paid on goods bought in Norway, provided you buy for more than NOK 308 in a shop and you take the goods with you upon leaving the country. There are two ways go about it.

You may do it yourself (DIY). First, obtain an Export Declaration (*Utførselsdeklarasjon*), Form RG-135, from the nearest Customs Office (*Tollsted*) listed under *Tollvesenet* in the Pink Pages. Larger companies who deal in export may have the form on hand, but you should call in advance, as such forms usually are not kept in shops. Then upon buying, fill out the form together with a staff member of the shop, who will enter some details and sign the form. Upon leaving the country, present the goods and the form at the Norwegian Customs office and ask to have the form stamped. Finally, post the stamped form back to the shop where you bought the goods and request a refund of *MVA*. The shop will then write and post a cheque for the refund minus its bank and postal expenses. The DIY approach is time consuming, both for you and for the shop, so much so that most shops will not offer it. And it is expensive: the average cost of issuing and posting a check to you plus the average charge in Europe for cashing a foreign cheque add up to equal the *MVA* on an item with a listed price of close to NOK 1000. So unless you buy relatively expensive goods, *MVA* refund by DIY is not worthwhile.

You may shop at one of the some 3,000 shops displaying the Tax-Free Shopping logo, which indicates association in the Global Refund network for reclaiming *MVA* in countries world-wide. Upon buying goods for NOK 308 or more in a shop, ask for a Tax-Free Shopping voucher with your receipt. The shop will fill in and stamp the voucher, which you should keep along with the receipt for the goods bought. Upon leaving the country, you can claim an immediate cash refund by delivering and signing your voucher(s) at a Cash Refund point. There are nearly one hundred refund points in the country, identified by the same logo as displayed by shops and located at all international airports, on all international ferries and at all major highway border crossings, as well as at other international airports in Europe. The vouchers are issued for up to 18% of the price paid for an item in a shop, or just seven-tenths of one percentage point less than the *MVA* on it. This difference is Global Refund's fee for taking care of all the paperwork and providing you an immediate cash refund. For specific details, ask for a brochure in the shop. For a list of shops offering Tax-Free Shopping, contact Global Refund Norge ✆ 67156010, 📠 67156029, ✉ PO Box 48, 1332 Østerås, ✉ taxfree@no.globalrefund.com, 🌐 http://www.globalrefund.com/norway with pages in English and lists of shops and refund points as well as an on-line ordering form for descriptive leaflets.

Telesales (*Telefon-salg*) are debated. Many, including the ☞ **Consumer council** (Human Rights, Consumer Rights chapter) regard unsolicited telephone sales as an intrusion upon privacy. But telephone salespeople (*telefonselgere*) operate within the law and calls from them are increasingly common. If you wish, you might call the *Reservasjon* number ☎ 81548020 and proceed through the voice-prompt menu (in Norwegian) to bar further distribution of your telephone number and thereby limit access to it by telephone sales firms.

Vinmonopolet As in many other countries, alcoholic drink is sold only by State shops. In Scandinavia, only Denmark does not have State shops: Sweden has *Systembolaget*, Finland has *Alko*, and Norway has *Vinmonopolet* (literally "The wine monopoly") for retail sales of liquors, wine and strong beers. There are 123 *Vinmonopolet* shops in the country; you may find their addresses and telephone numbers in the Pink Pages, or in a brochure entitled *nyttig å vite* ("useful to know") available in the shops. Most of the shops are open during normal shopping hours, Monday through Saturday, but are closed on Sundays, public holidays and days before major public holidays. For opening hours, call ✆ 81500160. In most of the shops, clerks at counters serve customers queued by numbers issued by queuing machines. But self-serve is now being tested and is scheduled for 14 shops, the first of which opened in August 1999 at Vika in Oslo. In all, *Vinmonopolet* sells some 4000 different items, divided into:

- Basic selection (*Basisutvalget*) of about 1400 items listed in a free shop catalogue issued six times a year and sold in shops according to local preference; individual shops may stock from around 400 to nearly 1800 items of the Basic selection.
- On-order selection (*Bestillingsutvalget*) of about 2500 items listed in a free shop catalogue issued six times a year, and which may be ordered at all shops.
- Test selection (*Testutvalget*) of items included in the Basic selection catalogue to test their acceptance by customers and marked with a small, circled capital letter T.
- Lot selection (*Partiutvalget*) of items available in limited quantity and included in the Basic selection catalog and marked with a small, circled capital letter P.

- Additional selection (*Tilleggsutvalget*) of items available seasonally or only in limited quantity and sometimes, but not always, listed in the Basic selection catalogue.

All shops will accept orders, both for pick-up at a later date or for delivery or postal delivery at a surcharge; call the nearest shop for details. As payment, shops accept cash, payment cards and cheques made out to *A/S Vinmonopolet*, but for no more than NOK 2500 when banks are closed and account balances cannot be verified. In comparison with other countries, the prices in *Vinmonopolet* shops are high, principally because of the high taxes on alcoholic drink. For instance, tax accounts for 88% of the NOK 283 price of a bottle of vodka, 81% of the NOK 315 price of a bottle of Cognac, 71% of the NOK 202 price of a bottle of port and 67% of the NOK 70 price of a bottle of wine. For further information, contact the information centre ✆ 22015000, ✆ 22015009, ✉ PO Box 1944 Vika, 0125 Oslo, ✉ postmottak@vinmonopolet.no. *Vinmonopolet* has no Internet web site, because a site would classify as advertising, and advertising for all drink containing more than 2.5% alcohol is prohibited.

Wine (*Vin*) is sold only by the ☞ **Vinmonpolet** shops. As recently as 1980, distilled liquors outsold wine. No more: in 1998, wine accounted for nearly eight litres in ten of the more than 45 million litres of alcoholic drink sold by *Vinmonopolet* shops. Accordingly, the choice is broad, as nearly 3000 different wines are available, from all the major wine-producing countries, including Argentina, Australia, Bulgaria, Chile, France, Germany, Greece, Hungary, Italy, Portugal, Romania, South Africa, Spain and the USA. The catalogues available in all *Vinmonopolet* shops list wines according to their main types: natural wine (*vin*), sparkling wine (*musserende*) and fortified wine (*sterkvin*). The natural wines are grouped together, first according to whether they are red (*rød*), white (*hvit*) or rosé (*rosé*), and then alphabetically by country or origin. Each wine in the catalogue is described briefly in text and by three small circles, shaded to show the extent of body (*fylde*), acidity (*garvestoffer*) and bouquet (*fruktighet*). There are also small symbols indicating recommended dishes suiting the wine: *aperitiff* ("aperitif"), *skalldyr* ("seafood"), *fisk* ("fish"), *kylling, kalkun, gris* ("poultry and pork"), *storfe*("beef"), *småfe* ("mutton and lamb"), *småvilt –hare,fugl* ("small game – rabbit and birds"), *storfilt – rein, elg, hjort, rådyr* ("big game – reindeer, elk, red deer and roe deer"), *gryterett* ("with casseroles"), *grillmat* ("grilled foods"), *orientalisk mat* ("oriental foods"), *ost* ("cheese"), *koldtbord, snitter* ("cold dishes and small sandwiches"), *dessert, kake, søt frukt* ("desserts, cakes, sweet fruit) and *terrasevin* ("sipping wine"). The maturity of the wine is indicated by one of three symbols showing a bottle. A vertical bottle means that the wine is mature and should not be aged; an inclined bottle means that it is mature but still can be aged and a horisontal bottle indicates that it is well developed but further ageing is recommended.

Sports, recreation, hobbies (*Sport og fritid*)

Aeronautical markings (*Kjennetegn*) consist of five capital letters in the English alphabet (Æ, Ø and Å are not used). The first two letters are the national code, LN for Norway. The third, fourth and fifth letters are assigned in sequences by the Norwegian Civil Aviation Administration (*Luftfartsverket*) and apply to all aircraft registered in the country, both commercial and private. They have no meaning, with four exceptions: the third letter is C for balloons, G for gliders, O for helicopters and Y for microlight and ultralight aircraft.

Aeronautical sports (*Luftsport*) include ballooning (*ballong*), motorised flying (*motorfly*), gliding (*seilfly*), hanggliding and paragliding (*hang- og paragliding*), microlight flying (*mikrofly*), aero-modelling (*modell*) and parachuting (*fallskjerm*). There are more than 270 aeronautical sports clubs in the country, the greatest number for motorised flying – 76 clubs with some 4000 members in all. Of these clubs, 39 are certified for flight training for private pilot licences (*privatflygersertifikat*). For further information on all aspects of aeronautical sports in the country as well as the addresses of clubs, contact the Norwegian Aero Club (*Norsk Aero Klubb*) ✆ 23102900, ✇ 23102901, ✉ PO Box 383 Sentrum, 0102 Oslo, ✉ nak@nak.no, ⊕ http://www.nif.no

Amateur radio (*Amatørradio*) operators in Norway are identified by the LA prefix in their call signs. Throughout the country, more than 80 amateur radio groups are affiliated with the Norwegian Radio Relay League (*Norsk Radio Relæ Liga*) ✆ 22213790, ✇ 22213791, ✉ PO Box 20 Haugenstua, 0915 Oslo, ✉ nrrl@online.no, ⊕ http://home.sol.no/~nrrl with pages in Norwegian and pages for international operations in English.

Norway has implemented CEPT (Conference of European Postal and Telecommunications Administrations) recommendation T/R 61-01. Consequently, a radio amateur from another country, which also has implemented T/R 61-01, may stay in Norway and use his or her call sign prefixed with LA for up to one year. A radio amateur from another country, which has not implemented T/R 61-01, may apply for permission to operate from Norway for up to one year, provided that there is a reciprocal agreement between his/her home country and Norway. Foreign radio amateurs need special permission to operate from Norwegian polar territories, including Svalbard, Bjørnøya and Jan Mayen in the Arctic and Peter I Island in the Antarctic. Contact NRRL for further details.

Boat number signs (*Båtskilter*), identify leisure craft, just as ☞ **Car number plates** (Cars, Roads, Traffic chapter) identify cars. Boat numbers are listed in the boat register (*Småbåtregister*) maintained by Norwegian Customs and Excise (*Tollvesenet*) for motorboats and motorless sailboats longer than 4.5 metres that have a home port in Norway or are owned by residents of the country. Boats in other registries, such as the Ship Register, boats owned and operated by the armed forces, motorless boats shorter than 4.5 metres and boats longer than 4.5 metres that are powered neither by motor or sail are excepted from registration. Each newly-registered boat is assigned a six-character number that appears on a self-adhering number sign (*nummerskilt*) affixed to the boat and on its credit-card-sized registration card (*båtkort*). The number is permanent and stays on the boat as long as it is registered in Norway. It consists of three letters followed by three numerals. The first letter indicates the county in which the owner lives at first registration, as listed below, and the following two letters and three numerals are assigned sequentially. Older boats, not yet registered after the *Småbåtregister* was implemented in 1998, may have other numbers which they can retain until re-registered. For further information and for registering boats, contact the nearest Customs Office, listed under Tolldistrikt or *Tollsted* in the Pink Pages. The registration form, entitled *Melding om nyregistrering av småbåter*, is number RD 0015 and is available in *Bokmål* or *Nynorsk* on-line and can be downloaded from ⊕ http://www.toll.no/baat, point and click on *Skjemaer*.

County letter, county: **A** Oslo, **B** Østfold, **C** Akershus, **D** Hedemark, **E** Oppland, **F** Buskerud, **H** Telemark, **I** Aust-Agder, **K** Vest-Agder, **L** Rogaland, **P** foreign address, **R** Hordaland, **S** Sogn og Fjordane, **T** More og Romsdal, **U** Sør-Trøndelag, **V** Nord-Trøndelag, **W** Nordland, **X** Troms, **Y** Finnmark and **Z** Vestfold.

Boating and yachting (*båtsport*) is popular, mostly in the summertime along the coast, on the fjords and on inland lakes and watercourses. In all, there are more than 400,000 boats over 4.5 m in length, and an untold number of smaller boats in the country. Most are motor boats, though sailing is popular on the fjords and as a competitive sport. All motor boats as well as sail boats over 4.5 m in length carry ☞ **boat number signs**.

For some people who own summer cottages (*hytter*) on islands not connected to the mainland by bridge or ferry, small boats are the only means of transport, to and from the island. Usually the first weekend after Easter (the customary end of the skiing season) the boating season commences with frenetic work being done on boats prior to putting them back into the water. Most boats are stored ashore during the winter, covered by tarpaulins pitched like a tent to ease the snow off. The tarpaulins are weighed down with used plastic, five-litre containers that have been filled with water. Some yachts and larger boats are kept in the water in a bubble berth (*boblehavn*). A *boblehavn* is an area of the marina reserved for larger yachts and boats, with a network of rubber hosing which has been weighted down on the seabed which is usually between two and three metres deep at that point. The hosepipe has small holes out of which compressed air escapes creating disturbed water circulation around the boat preventing ice from forming. The added benefit is that upward flow of the air bubbles keeps the temperature around the boat at a constant 0-4°C, which helps stop condensation. Having your boat in a bubble berth saves you from hauling it out of water and taking the mast down in the autumn.

If you intend to skipper a motor boat, you should attend a basic course (*båtførerkurs*) and stand an examination (*båtførerprøven*) to get your certificate (*båtførerbevis*). The certificate is not compulsory, but is recommended by all boating organisations. If you wish to skipper a larger yacht, over 15 m long or over 25 gross register tons (GRT) or both, you will need a recreational boat captain's licence (*fritidsbåtskippersertifikat*). It is issued upon successful completion of a course of study and of an examination given by a person who holds a higher rank of certification according to the regulations of the Maritime

Directorate (*Sjøfartsdirektoratet*). For information on courses, examinations and rules, contact the Royal Norwegian Boating Association (*Kongelig Norsk Båtforbund – KNBF*) ✆ 22356800, ☎ 22356811, ✉ Vågebyvn 23, 0569 Oslo, ✉ knmf@online.no, ✆ http://www.baat.aller.no/reklamenmf with pages in Norwegian only.

If you'd like to learn to row (*ro*) or sail (*seil*), look under *foreninger og forbund, sport- og fritidsforeninger* in the Yellow Pages, to find a club near you. To buy a boat, either look in the newspaper or in the Yellow Pages under *båter,* you will also have to register the boat if it is new, telephone the customs in your municipality, look under *tollvesenet* in the Pink Pages. To buy boating equipment, look under *båtutstyr;* to charter a boat, look under *båtutleie* in the Yellow Pages. For any other information about boats, call *Båtbransjensopplysingstelefon* ✆ 82080027.

Card games (*kortspill*) Most European games are played. Some games retain their English or French names, including Baccarat, Boston, Bridge, Canasta, Cribbage, Napoleon, Pinochle, Poker, Rummy and Trente et Quarante (Rouge et Noire), while some are re-named in Norwegian, including Blackjack or Twenty-one (*Tjueet*), Casino (*Kasino*), Faro (*Hasardspill*), Old Maid (*Svarteper*), Ombre (*L'hombre*), Solitaire (*Kabal*) and Tarot (*Tarokk*). Both Norwegian-made and imported decks of 52 cards or more with joker(s), usually in 6 by 9 cm format, are sold in book shops and game shops. The four suits have Norwegian names: spades (♠ *spar*), clubs (♣ *kløver*), hearts (♥ *hjerter*) and diamonds (♦ *ruter*). Bridge is the most popular game; there are bridge columns in newspapers. The Norwegian Bridge Federation (*Norsk Bridgeforbund* ✆ 22431356, ☎ 22551701, ✉ PO Box 2828 Solli, 0204 Oslo ✆ http://www.bridgefederation.no, has about 15,000 members in 600 clubs throughout the country, and publishes a member magazine, *Norsk Bridge* (Norwegian Bridge). Contact the Federation for names and addresses of clubs; all publications are in Norwegian only, but the Oslo office staff and officers of most clubs speak English and other European languages. There is also an independent magazine, *Bridge i Norge* (Bridge in Norway).

Chess (Sjakk) Archeological excavations in Oslo, Bergen and Trondheim have shown that chess has been played in Norway since the 13th century. The Norwegian Chess Federation (*Norges Sjakkforbund* ✆ 22151241, 🖷 22710007, ✉ Frennings vei 3, 0588 Oslo, ✉ sjakkfor@online.no, ❀ http://home.sol.no/~sjakkfor, was founded in 1914, and Norway is now in Zone 1.3 (Scandinavia) of FIDE (*Fédération Internationale des Échecs*). More than 50 major and local newspapers have chess columns, and the Federation publishes a member magazine, *Norsk Sjakkblad* (Norwegian Chess Magazine), and co-ordinates the activities of some 130 clubs in the country. Publications and information are in Norwegian only, but officers of the Federation and of most clubs speak English and other European languages. Most of the clubs meet weekly or more frequently to play chess, and there are four grandmasters in the country. The Norwegian Correspondence Chess Association (*Norges Postsjakkforbund*) is associated with the ICCF (International Correspondence Chess Federation). Its members may be contacted through ICCF associate clubs in other countries or via the Association's Internet home page ❀ http://home.sol.no/@sjoel/npsf/info.htm

Coin collecting (*Myntsamling*) is a popular hobby, due in part to the country being well-off and to there being no ☞ **MVA** (Taxes, Duties, Excise chapter) on collectable coins. Moreover, the history of the country suits it well to coin collecting. The seafaring ☞ **Vikings** (Character, Customs, Country chapter) brought back coins from afar. The oldest known mint in Europe, dating from the early 16th century, was uncovered by archaeologists in Trondheim and now is a museum. Some of the largest coin transactions ever, worthy of listing in the ☞ **Guinness Book of Records** (Media and Information chapter), have been made by Norwegian coin dealers. Accordingly, the selection of collectable coins is large and the average prices reasonable compared to elsewhere in Europe. You can find coin dealers listed under *Mynthandlere* in the Yellow Pages. The leading dealer is *Oslo Mynthandel* ✆ 23100000, 🖷 23100025, ✉ Øvre Slotts gt 6, PO Box 355 Sentrum, 0101 Oslo, ❀ http://www.oslocoin.com with pages in Norwegian and in English.

The Norwegian Confederation of Sports (*Norges Idrettsforbund*) and The Norwegian Olympic Committee (*Norges Olympiske*

***Komite*)** are the governing and co-ordinating bodies for sports. The Confederation of Sports is organised into the individual sport associations (*særforbund*) and into 17 districts (*krets*) covering the country. The Olympic Committee is responsible for the country's involvement in the Olympic Games and Olympic Winter Games. For further information on the confederation or the committee, contact the joint head office ✆ 67154600, 🖷 67132989, ✉ Hauger Skolevei 1, 1351 Rud, ✉ fellesadm@nif.idrett.no, ❀ http://www.nif.idrett.no with pages in Norwegian and with links to the individual sport association web sites, many of which also have pages in English. For further information on the individual sports, contact the associations listed below.

Sport: *Association name in Norwegian*

Aeronautical sports: *Norges Luftsportsforbund*

American football: *Norges Amerikansk Fotballforbund (NoAFF)*

Archery: *Norges Bueskytterforbund*

Athletics (track and field): *Norges Fri-idrettsforbund (NFIF)*

Badminton: *Norges Badminton Forbund*

Bandy: *Norges Bandyforbund (NBF)*

Baseball and softball: *Norges Softball og Baseball Forbund*

Basketball: *Norges Basketballforbund (NBBF)*

Biathlon: *Norges Skiskytterforbund (NSSF)*

Billiards: *Det Norske Biljardforbund*

Bobsleigh and Luge: *Norges Ake-og Bobforbund (NABF)*

Bowling: *Norges Bowlingforbund (NBF)*

Boxing (amateur): *Norges Bokseforbund (NBF)*

Budo: *Norges Budo Forbund*

Canoeing: *Norges Padleforbund*

Casting: *Norges Castingforbund*

Climbing: *Norges Klatreforbund (NKF)*

Company sports: *Norges Bedriftidrettsforbund (NBIF)*

Curling: *Norges Curlingforbund*

Cycling: *Norges Cykleforbund (NCF)*

Dance sport: *Norges Danseforbund (ND)*

Diving: *Norges Dykkeforbund*

Equestrian sports: *Norges Rytterforbund (NRYF)*

Fencing: *Norges Fekteforbund (NF)*

Football: *Norges Fotballforbund*

Frisbee: *Norges Frisbeeforbund*

Golf: *Norges Golf forbund (NGF)*

Gymnastics: *Norges Gymnastikk-og Turnforbund*

(NGTF)

Handball: *Norges Håndballforbund (NHF)*

Handicapped sport: *Norges Funksjonshemmedes Idrettsforbund (NFI)*

Ice hockey: *Norges Ishockeyforbund (NIHF)*

Judo: *Norges Judoforbund*

Kick boxing: *Norges Kickboxing Forbund (NKBF)*

Motorcycle sports: *Norges Motorsykkelforbund (NMF)*

Orienteering: *Norges Orienteringsforbund (NOF)*

Power boating: *Norges Båtsportforbund*

Power lifting: *Norges Styrkeløftforbund (NSF)*

Rowing: *Norges Roforbund (NR)*

Rugby: *Norges Rugbyforbund*

Sailing: *Norges Seilforbund (NSF)*

Shooting: *Norges Skytterforbund (NSF)*

Skating: *Norges Skøyteforbund (NSF)*

Skiing: *Norges Skiforbund (NSF)*

Sled dog racing: *Norges Hundekjørerforbund (NHF)*

Snowboarding: *Norges Snowboardforbund*

Squash: *Norges Squash Forbund (NSQF)*

Swimming: *Norges Svømmeforbund (NSF)*

Table tennis: *Norges Bordtennisforbund (NBTF)*

Tennis: *Norges Tennisforbund*

Triathlon: *Norges Triathlonforbund NTF)*

University sports: *Norske Studenter Idrettsforbund (NSI)*

Volleyball: *Norges Volleyballforbund (NVBF)*

Walking: *Norges Gang- og Turmarsjforbund (NGF)*

Water skiing: *Norges Vannskiforbund*

Weight lifting: *Norges Vektløfterforbund (NVF)*

Wrestling: *Norges Bryteforbund*

Extreme sports (*Extrem-sport*) are outdoor activities that are seldom competitive but almost always entail high risk. Norway has ample wilderness which offers many places to practise extreme sports including bungy jumping (*strikkhopp*), canyoning (*juvvandring*), ice climbing (*isklatring*), mountaineering (*fjellklatring*), off-piste skiing (*off-piste kjøring*), river boards (*elvebrett*), river kayaking (*kayakpadling i elv*), rock climbing (*klatring*), snowboarding (*snowboarding*), whitewater rafting (*rafting*) and wilderness adventure (*villmarksopplevelse*). Two centres, both located in the south central mountain ranges, offer extreme sports as well as other wilderness recreations that vary by season. Both offer guided tours, instruction and various degrees of the sports, and many of their instructors and leaders speak English and other languages, including French and German.

For further details and programmes, contact the centres: Norwegian Wildlife and Rafting ✆ 61238727, ✍ 61238760, ✉ Randsverk, 2680 Vågå, ✉ nwr@nwr.no, ✇ http://www.nwr.no with pages in Norwegian, English and German; Opplev Oppdal ✆ 72404180, ✍ 72404181, ✉ Rute 7 Stølen, 7340 Oppdal, ✉ opplevoppdal@online.no, ✇ http://www.opplev-oppdal.no

Fitness and workout clubs and centres (*Trenings foreninger og sentere*) Outdoor recreation, including walking, cross-country skiing, cycling and jogging remains the most common form of exercise, but is dwindling as the country becomes more urbanised. Accordingly, fitness and workout clubs and centres in cities and towns now provide supervised exercise. You can find them listed under *Trening* in the Yellow Pages. *Friskis & Svettis*, a fitness association founded in Sweden in the early 1980s, now has clubs throughout the country; you can find them listed in the Pink Pages as well as on the association web site ✇ http://www.friskissvettis.no with links to the sites of clubs throughout the country. The *Sport-Aerobic-Treningsenter (SATS)* chain of more than 60 centres is the largest in the country; you can find SATS centres listed in the Yellow Pages and in the Pink Pages, as well as on the SATS web site ✇ http://www.sats.no

Folk dance (*Folkedans*) is the general name for all dances of national or ethnic origin. Folk dance groups are active throughout the country. Many practice dances from other countries, but by far the most popular are Norwegian rural dances, song dances and figure dances. Two rural youth organisations, *Bygdelagssamskipnaden (BLS)* and *Bondeungdomslaget (BUL)*, arrange folk dances and courses in cities and towns; you can find their local clubs listed in the Pink Pages. The oldest and most active are two BUL groups, *Leikarringen* ("fiddler ring") in Oslo ✆ 23214160, ✍ 23214166, ✉ Rosenkrantz gt 8, 0159 Oslo, ✉ Leikarringen@bul.oslo.no, ✇ http://bul.oslo.no/Leikarringen with pages in Norwegian and links to other BUL activities in the Oslo area, and *Leikarlaget* ("fiddler club") in Trondheim ✆ 73514258, ✍ 73514260, ✉ PO Box 18 Dragvoll, 7055 Dragvoll, ✉ leikar-s@kraft.iet.hist.no, ✇ http://www.hist.no/~herman/bul/ with pages in Norwegian, English, French and German.

Gas cookers (*Gasskokeapparater*), as used on boats and in caravans and holiday homes, conform to the European Directive 90/396/EEC standard and burn propane, as supplied in 2 kg, 5 kg or 11 kg refillable tanks and other sizes of containers made of metal or fibreglass-reinforced plastic. If you intend to bring in a gas cooker, as in the galley of a motor or sailing boat or for use in a holiday home, you should ensure that it meets the European standard, both because Norwegian fire safety regulations require that it must and because only propane in tanks conforming to the standard is sold. Butane is not sold in refillable tanks for cookers and heaters, although it is sold in disposable cartridges to lightweight fuel camping stoves and lamps, as sold by sports shops and hardware shops. The reason is that butane loses its pressure at about 0°C, so appliances fueled by it will not work below that temperature, while propane burns well down to -30°C. Most cookers sold internationally can burn either butane or propane, because they provide about the same amount of heat. If you have a cooker fuelled by butane, you need not alter its burners (*bluss*), unless they are of an older type made to operate at a lower pressure than the current 30 mbar European standard. Some cooker burners are made to work on two different pressures, a lower pressure as well as 30 mbar. They can be adapted by inverting the air control sleeve inside the burner (refer to manufacturer's instructions). If you are converting from butane to propane, you must replace the regulator, because the gas pressures differ. Moreover, you also must replace the regulator if it is not of the clip-on (*påtrykks*) type that fits European-standard tanks. If you replace the regulator, you should also replace the hose (*slange*) and its fittings, to ensure tight seals at the cooker and the regulator.

Guns and gun controls (*Skytevåpen og våpenloven*) The selling, buying and use of guns are regulated by law. You must be at least 18 years old to buy a shotgun (*haglegevær*) or air gun (*luftvåpen*). To buy a revolver, pistol or other handgun (*håndvåpen*), you must be at least 21 years old and must have a gun permit (*våpenkort*) issued by the police. Moreover, you should be trustworthy, should not have an alcohol or drug problem and should be able to prove that you need a gun, such as for hunting or for shooting as a sport. The police can withdraw permits and confiscate firearms from persons no longer considered fit to bear arms. They may also search homes to ensure that weapons and ammunition are stored according to regulations. There is a general ban on bearing firearms in public places without just cause. In general, people own guns for sport, not for protection. Even the police do not bear arms when on daily duty, though they may be armed when pursuing an armed fugitive. In 1998, a tightening of the gun control law provided for the establishment of a central weapon register. It will replace the local police registers, which now list some 720,000 firearms, and require registration of previously unregistered firearms, including an estimated 500,000 shotguns. Compared to some other countries, these rules and the recent tightening of them may seem strict. But one of their benefits is undeniable: the annual murder rate is less than one per 100,000 population, among the lowest in the world, and seldom are more than a third of all murders committed with firearms.

Hash House Harriers, the international association of imbibing runners, has five clubs in Norway. Of these, three are in the Oslo area: Kolbotn Grand HHH, Oslo Full Moon HHH and Oslo HHH. Additionally the Scandi Hooligans HHH is in Kristiansand, and the Troll HHH is in Stavanger. Runs and get-togethers are held weekly, or almost so, by most of the clubs. As elsewhere, English is the HHH written and spoken language. For run announcements and other information, contact the Norwegian Hash Trash editor Frode Dahlseng ✉ Dælingengt- 3b. 0567 Oslo, or view HHH on-line
🔊 http://users.aol.com/GTstraydog/gtidxn.html

Hunting (*Jakt*) is as varied as the terrain. The chief species hunted in the autumn are European elk (*elg* in Norwegian, *Alces alces* in Latin), red deer (*hjort, Cervus elaphus*) and roe deer (*rådyr, Capreolus capreolus*). Reindeer (*rein, Rangifer tarandus*) is hunted in the winter. The more common game birds include willow grouse (*lirype, Lagopus lagopus*), ptarmigan (*fjellrype, Lagopus mutus*), black grouse (*orrfugl, Lyrurus tetrix*), large European grouse, or capercaillie (*storfugl, Tetrao urgallus*) and hazel grouse (*jerpe, Testrastes bonasia*). Some wading birds, including duck (*ender*), geese (*gjess*) and sea birds (*sjøfugl*) are hunted, as are small mammals such as hare (*hare*) and beaver (*bever*). All first-time hunters (*førstegangs jegere*) must pass a hunting proficiency test (*jegerprøven*), for which the minimum age is 14. Hunting equipment (*Jaktutstyr*) and arms and ammunition (*Våpen og ammunisjon*) shops often hold courses for taking the proficiency test. All hunters must have a valid yearly (1 April to 31 March) licence, paid to the Wildlife Fund (*Viltfondet*), whether they hunt on private or public land. On private land, the owner holds the exclusive hunting rights and may charge a hunting fee or may lease a tract of land for hunting. On public land, permits may or may not be required. The arms and ammunition permitted depend on whether the hunting is for big game (*Storviltjakt*) or small game (*Småviltjakt*) and on the species of animal hunted. Hunting seasons (*jakttider*) are set each year by governmental authorities, but private landowners (*grunneiere*) may set shorter seasons. A concise overview of all relevant rules and regulations is given in Norwegian and in English in a 16-page brochure published by the Directorate for Nature Management (*Direktoratet for naturforvaltning*) and available at municipal offices, post offices and hunting equipment or arms and ammunition shops (see under *Jaktutsryr* or *Våpen og ammunisjon* in the Yellow Pages). For laws, regulations, registration, proficiency test information, seasons and the details of permission to hunt by the sea and fjords, contact *Direktoratet for naturforvaltning* ✆ 73580500, 📠 73915433. For permission to hunt on state-owned land and for information on local seasons, contat *Statskog SF* ✆ 74270500, 📠 74270540 or the Ministry of Agriculture (*Landbruksdepartementet*) ✆ 22349090, 📠 22349555. For the particulars of hunting on private land, conact the Norwegian Forest Owners Federation (*Norges Skogeierforbund*) ✆ 22010550, 📠 22834047. For general information on hunting, contact the Norwegian Association of Hunters and Anglers (*Norges Jeger- og Fiskerforbund*), which offers services to hunters and anglers and has a membership magazine, *Jakt og Fiske* (Hunting and Fishing) ✆ 66792200, 📠 66901587, ✉ http://www.njff.no

Indoor facilities for outdoor sports (*Innendørs sportsanlegg*)

Indoor sports facilities were once exclusively for indoor competitive sports, such as ball games, gymnastics and swimming. But now there are indoor facilities for outdoor sports and recreation, such as climbing, go-cart, golf, scuba diving and shooting. There are public and private facilities throughout the country; you can find them listed under *Idrettsanlegg* in the Yellow Pages and by asking others who practice the sport of your interest.

Lifejackets (*Redningsvester*) are available in three basic types: permanent buoyancy lifejackets, inflatable lifejackets and buoyancy aids.

Permanent buoyancy lifejackets (*Redningsvester*) are the traditional type, and consist of a vest filled with blocks of plastic foam and fitted with a buoyancy collar and a harness devised to keep an unconscious person face-up in water. They are recommended for small children and general safety wear, as when working or fishing near water.

Inflatable lifejackets (*Oppblåsbar redningsvester*) are slimmer than permanent buoyancy lifejackets and consequently are favoured in boating. The basic design resembles that of the lifejackets on board commercial airliners and lifejackets are available for manual inflation or automatic inflation (*automatisk oppblåsbar*) from a compressed carbon-dioxide cartridge.

Buoyancy aids (*Flyttevester*) for active water sports are designed to help a conscious wearer stay afloat in water.

Up to eight sizes of lifejackets are available, from baby (0-20 kg) up to large adult (over 70 kg). In buying, be sure that a lifejacket has ☞ **CE marking** (Measurements and Standards chapter), which indicates that it is manufactured according to European standards. There are four CE categories, according to the buoyancy force of a lifejacket measured in Newtons (abbreviated N; 10 Newtons is about one kg).

- 50 N buoyancy aid, suitable for capable swimmers; provides only support to a conscious wearer.
- 100N lifejacket, suitable for swimmers; for use in relatively calm waters; not guaranteed to self-right an unconscious wearer in rough water.
- 150N lifejacket, suitable for swimmers and non-swimmers in all but the most severe weather conditions.
- 275N lifejacket, suitable for swimmers and non-swimmers in severe conditions when heavy waterproof clothing is worn.

Lifejackets are sold by sports shops, boating supply shops and insurance companies as well as by some newspapers in connection with summertime water safety campaigns. Two of the leading brands are Helly Hansen of Norway and Crewsaver of the UK. If you seldom need a lifejacket, you may consider renting one: in cities and towns along the coast, the fire brigade stations (*Brannstasjoner*) have lifejackets available for rental.

Light tracks and head lamps (*Lysløyper og hodelykter*) enable cross-country skiers to enjoy their sport in the late afternoon and evening, even though the winter sun sets early. There are innumerable maintained ski tracks illuminated as are streets, with lamps fixed to poles. Many lead to woodland lodges that are open in the evenings and on weekends to serve refreshments to skiers, and all are free for public use. Accordingly, they are marked on local street maps as well as recreational maps, by red lines with small round dots at intervals of about half a centimetre. Not even the Norwegian Mapping Authority knows how many light tracks there are in the country, but some estimates place the total at several hundred, with a total length of several thousand kilometres. In surveys of the accessibility of leisure activities conducted by Norway Statistics, light tracks are as nearby as are swimming pools. For the average resident throughout the country, the nearest light track is no more than 6 km away, and for city dwellers, the figure is 4.3 km. The greater Oslo area has the country's greatest concentration of light tracks, some 190 km in all. Skiers who wish to ski beyond the light tracks after dark can light their own way using battery-powered head lamps. Several models of high-tech head lamps fitted with tungsten-halogen bulbs are available in sport shops throughout the country; the two leading brands are Mila and Silva.

Marina (*marinaer, lystbåthavn*) There are innumerable islands and harbours along the coast, so you need not tie on at a marina for an overnight stop unless you need to be ashore for shopping, sightseeing, laundry, charging the batteries or visiting a restaurant. Marinas are found in coastal towns and cities where boat owners keep their boats. Boat owners are usually members of a *båtforening* (boat club). Activities at these clubs take place mainly during the week with sailing lessons and competitive races. Most boat owners live relatively close to where they keep their boats and the working day and long summer evenings make boating a popular evening activity during the season. At weekends boats leave the marina to spend the weekend at a favourite bay or just exploring. Rates and facilities at marinas with visitors berths (*gjestehavn*) vary with most supplying electricity, water, shower, toilet and laundry facilities. During the summer months the marinas with guest berths can get very busy and it is common to raft up, sometimes even several boats deep. Remember to take your ensign down by 9 pm or sunset, whichever is the earliest. Holding tanks are emptied out in open water. Look under *foreninger og forbund (sport- og fritidsforneinger)* for sailing clubs or *marinaer* (marinas) in the Yellow Pages or alternatively ask the tourist information office (*turistinformasjon*) in the places you wish to visit for recommendations. If you are sailing on a unusually large vessel, it is advisable to check beforehand whether there are mooring facilities available.

Mountain climbing and walking (*Fjellsport*)
Three-quarters of the area of the country is wilderness, much of it mountainous. Though as rugged as mountains anywhere, the ranges differ from those elsewhere in their lower altitude. The highest peak, Galdhøpiggen, which also ranks as Scandinavia's loftiest, has a summit elevation of 2,469 metres, puny on the customary scale of mountain might. But many peaks tower 1,000 to 1,500 metres from their bases, which puts them on a par with the Alps of central Europe or the Rocky Mountains of North America. The advantage in Norway is that you can wander above timberline at elevations of 800 to 1,200 metres and enjoy scenery available elsewhere only at twice to thrice the altitude. Closer to timberline, in the surrounding valleys or along the railway lines that cut through the wilderness, there are thousands of cabins and lodges. The mountains are both wild and accessible, a paradise for walkers. There are thousands of kilometres of marked trails, most with red letter "T"s painted on rocks. The "T"s stand for *Den Norske Turistforening* (DNT), the outdoor wilderness recreation organisation that marks the trails that meet and meander between *hytte*, which translates as "hut". But *hytte til hytte*, or "hut to hut" as Norwegians put it, doesn't mean that you rough it. Pic-

ture a "hut" with 128 to 185 bunks in two-, four- and eight-person rooms, hot showers, toilets, a staffed dining room, a snack bar and several lounges, and you have four of the larger *hytte*, Finsehytta, Gjendesheim, Glitterheim and Rondvassbu run by DNT. In all, DNT has 14 staffed and 64 self-service *hytter* (the plural) in mountain ranges throughout the country, and together they have some 2,700 bunks. Membership is not required for staying in DNT *hytte*, but is a good investment, as the cost is more than offset by the accumulated member discounts of two nights stay. For opening dates, prices, membership, addresses of affiliated associations throughout the country, addresses of membership agents in Belgium, England, Germany, the Netherlands and the USA, or further information, contact DNT ✆ 22822800, 📠 22822801, ✉ PO Box 7 Sentrum, 0101 Oslo ✉ http://www.dnt.org with pages in Norwegian and in English. There are more than 40 mountaineering and rock climbing clubs in the country. The oldest is the Norwegian Alpine Club (*Norsk Tindeklub – NTK*), founded in 1908. NTK publishes a magazine, *Norsk Fjellsport* as well as climbing guides and operates three mountaineering lodges, Giklingdalshytta in Innerdalen, Skaadalshytta in the western part of the Jotunheimen range and Vengedalshytta near the Romsdalshorn peak. For details, contact NTK ✆ c/o Egil Fredriksen 22505466, ✉ PO Box 7 Sentrum, 0101 Oslo, ✉ Egil.fredriksen@ntk.no, ✉ http://home.sol.no/~ntk. The Norwegian Climbing Association (*Norges Klatreforbund – NKF*) is part of the Norwegian Confederation of Sports (*Norges Idrettsforbund*) and is a member of the international climbing association, *Union Internationale des Associations d'Alpinisme (UIAA)*. NKF has 92 member clubs throughout the country and arranges indoor wall and outdoor rock climbs, as well as competitive climbing meets. For further details and local club addresses, contact NKF ✆ 67154834, 📠 67132989, ✉ Hauger skolevei 1, 1351 Rud, ✉ klatring@nif.idrett.no, ✉ http://www.nif.idrett.no/klatring. The oldest and arguably most active rock climbing club is *Kolsås Klatreklubb*, named for the rock outcroppings at Kolsås just west of Oslo near the terminus of the Kolsås tram line ✆ c/o Magnus Berntsen 22507646, 📠 22507646, ✉ Veslekroken 4, 0379 Oslo, ✉ http://www.dmbb.no/KKK/KKK.html

National parks (*Nasjonalparker*), preserves and other protected areas together comprise more than a tenth of the area of the country. There are 21 national parks that are part of the ☞ **cultural and natural heritage protection** (Character, Customs, Country chapter) programme. Eighteen are on the mainland: *Ånderdalen, Børgefjell, Dovrefjell, Femunden, Gressåmoen, Gutulia, Hardangervidda, Jostedalsbreen, Jotunheimen, Omtjernkampen, Øvre Anarjåkka, Øvre Dividal, Øvre Pasvik, Rago, Reisa, Rondane, Saltfjellet-Svartisen*, and *Stabbursdalen*. Three are on Spitzbergen island in the Svalbard Arctic archipelago: *Forlandet, Nordvest Spitsbergen* and *Sør Spitsbergen*. New national parks are planned at seven locations: *Kvinnherad, Leirne, Nordreisa, Røros, Saltdal, Svanvik* and *Tinn*. The ☞ **public right of access** ensures that the Parks may be used for recreation. Indeed, the four in the south central part of the country – *Hardangervidda, Jotunheimen, Jostedalsbreen* and *Rondane* – are the principal mountain recreation areas. Brochures on and maps of the parks are available at nearby tourist information centres, and countrywide overviews are available from The Directorate for Nature Management (*Direktoratet for naturforvaltning*) ✆ 73580500, 📠 73580501, ✉ 7485 Trondheim, ✉ direktoratet@naturvorvaltning.no, ✉ http://www.naturforvaltning.no with pages in Norwegian and lists of publications, some in English. An overview map with links to websites for all the Parks is available on the ☞ **GRID** (Media and Information chapter) website ✉ http://www.grida.no/nor/soeno95/biodiv/prot/prot.html

Public right of access (*Allemannsretten*) is part of the cultural heritage of the country and now is embodied in law by the Outdoor Recreation Act (*Friluftsloven*) of 1957. It sets forth the relationships between recreational and commercial uses of land, and, with few restrictions, it permits the public to roam the countryside, the forests and the mountains even though much of the land may be privately owned. The restrictions distinguish between cultivated land (*innmark*) and uncultivated land (*utmark*). Cultivated land includes all tilled land, fields, meadows, gardens, house plots, farmyards and forest planting areas. These areas need not be fenced, but their owners control access to them. Uncultivated land is all other land. The public has the right of access to uncultivated land and, in winter, to frozen or snow-covered tilled land, fields and meadows. This means that you may walk or hike across the land in the summer and ski across it in the winter. In season, on uncultivated land, you may pick wild berries. You may rest, put up a tent, or camp overnight. You may swim, or travel by boat. The right also imposes obligations. You must not damage trees, land or other natural features or buildings, fences and the like. You may build a fire if you wish, but not between 15 May and 15 September, except in the mountains, above timberline. Dogs must be kept on leash from 1 April to 20 August. You can use offroad motor vehicles or snowmobiles only by special permit and not for recreation.

Skiing (Skisport) is so much a part of the life and history of the country that there is no word that sets the sport apart in Norwegian: *skisport* literally means "the sport of skiing".

Cross-country skiing is the basic sport, in two varieties: recreational ski touring (*turskiløping*) and racing (*langrenn*). Almost all cities and towns have nearby outdoor recreation areas with trails marked for summertime walking and wintertime cross-country skiing, in all about 30,000 kilometres in length. And there are some 2,500 illuminated trails (*lysløyper*) for skiing after sundown, which is early at the northerly latitude of the country.

Alpine skiing, the prevalent form of the sport in central Europe and North America is called *Alpint* to distinguish it from the more prevalent cross-country. There are now Alpine ski resorts and slopes throughout the country, in all with four gondolas, 425 lifts and 250 smaller tows, many illuminated for nighttime skiing and the larger ones with snow-making equipment.

Ski jumping is principally a competitive sport, but children jump for fun. There are more than 600 ski jumps in the country, from small jumps for neighbourhood use to international-standard ski jumping and ski flying hills.

There are more than 150 ski playgrounds, which are areas specifically devised to let terrain teach skiing skills. A typical playground will have a small jump, several slalom runs, a cross-country circuit and a mogul run. Children play in the area using ordinary touring skis, and learn skiing skills by negotiating its features.

Oslo unquestionably is the world's leading capi-

tal city in skiing skills and facilities and the only major city in which Olympic Winter Games and World Ski Championships have been held. A large woodland recreation area adjoins the city. Known as *Oslomarka* (literally "Oslo's fields"), it is an assemblage of nine contiguous woodlands totalling some 1,700 square kilometres (370,500 acres), about the area of greater London or twice the area of New York City. Here there are 2,500 km of ski trails marked with red painted slashes on trees and rings round sign poles at trail intersections. The total length of the summertime walking trails is even longer; they are marked in blue, the difference being that red-marked trails can cross lakes and marshes frozen in the winter, whilst blue-marked trails cannot. Some 110 km of ski trails are illuminated with their trail heads at car parks or tram stations, for ease of after-dark access. All the illuminated trails, as well as some 500 km of other trails are regularly maintained with tracks set by machine. Trail use is free, as cross-country skiing is regarded as part of public recreation. Along the trails, there are some 20 staffed lodges with lounges, cafeterias and toilets; most are open on weekends and during school holidays, and some along the light tracks are open evenings. There are also 16 Alpine skiing lift hills and 48 ski jumps. In *Nordmarka* just north of the city, lies the *Holmenkollen* ski jump and arena, where ski meets have been held for more than 100 years. *Skiforeningen*, Oslo's largest skier service organisation, has four of the trailside lodges, the Holmenkollen meets and facilities, including the world's largest ski museum, and numerous programmes, including ski schools for children. For details, contact Skiforeningen ✆ 22923200, 🖷 22923250, ✉ Kongeveien 5, 0390 Oslo, ✉ skif@skiforeningen.no, 🖳 http://www.sn.no/skif The Oslo Municipal Forestry Service (*Skogvesen*) maintains trails, operates the illuminated trails and 11 of the trailside lodges ✆ 22082200. Wintertime snow reports and trail conditions (*føremelding*) for the Oslo area are recorded once a day at ✆ 82052020; other cities have similar lines; look under *Friluftstelefonen* under *Nyttige telefoner* in the general information pages in the Pink and White Pages directory.

Most mountain resort towns have networks of marked ski trails, and lodge-to-lodge skiing in mountain ranges at Eastertime is popular. Each year, depending on snow conditions, some 1,400 to 2,000 kilometres of mountain ski trails are marked with branches or poles stuck in the snow, and the trails interconnect the same lodges that serve summer walkers and mountaineers, most operated by DNT ☞ **Mountain climbing and walking**.

Snowmobiles (*Snøscootere*) Each year, some 3,500 snowmobiles are sold, mostly in northernmost counties and in the Svalbard archipelago in the Arctic. However, sales in the southern part of the country are climbing, despite restrictions on the recreational use of snowmobiles. Five makes account for almost all snowmobile sales: Arctic Cat, Lynx, Polaris, Ski-Doo and Yamaha. Look in the Yellow Pages under *Snøscootere* to find the nearest dealer of a particular make. In some parts of the country, such as in the Oslo area, few snowmobiles are sold and there are no separate listings in the Yellow Pages. You should then look under *Motorsykler og Mopeder*. If you fail to find a dealer or seek a dealer for a make of snowmobile not advertised in the Yellow Pages, contact the Snowmobile Importers Association (*Snøscooterimportørenes forening*), which maintains an updated list of dealers ✆ 66849711, ✇ 66849788, ✉ Østre vei 76, 1315 Nesøya.

Spark (*Spark*) In the countryside in winter, some children still ski to school, and many people go about their daily errands on self-propelled sledges. It is these sledges that mark the scene as Nordic in general and Norwegian in particular. More of them are made and used in Norway than anywhere else, and even city centre sport shops stock and sell them along with other winter sports gear. The full name *sparkstøtting* ("kick and stand") is descriptive and tells how the *spark*, the usual abbreviation, is used. The user stands on one foot on one of the two runners and kicks rearwards on the snow between the runners to propel the *spark* forward. So abroad, the *spark* is sometimes called a "kick sled". For kicking on hard snow or ice, the kicking foot can be shod with a small pad of spikes for grip, but otherwise, using a *spark* requires no special skills or additional equipment. A *spark* is steered just as is a traditional children's sledge, by leaning to the side and twisting the handlebars. Likewise, it's slowed and stopped by dragging the feet. Though a *spark* can be used for fun, it is no toy. It's the ultimate simple, basic winter vehicle. It has spring steel runners and a sturdy birch frame fitted with handlebars and a combined seat

and baggage platform. Its history is not known exactly. Sledges antedate skis by several thousand years; the oldest known, found in Heinola, Finland, dates from 6500 BC. A variety of types evolved; every village had its sledgemaker, and sledges differed as much as did English carts and wagons. The *spark* probably evolved from simultaneous invention in different places. But most experts credit the first modern design to Sweden. Although the *spark* may have been invented in Sweden, its tradition has been best preserved in Norway. Two of the world's four *spark* manufacturers are Norwegian: Nansen Produkter of Vegårshei and Norø Industri of Tynset. Together, the two make and sell some 30,000 to 35,000 *sparks* a year, about twice as many as the combined sales of motorcycles, motorbikes and snowmobiles, but only a fifth as many as the sales of new cars. *Sparks* are so much a part of the winter scene that one poster for the 1994 Olympic Winter Games, held in Norway at Lillehammer, featured the girl and boy mascot figures, Kristin and Håkon, gliding along on a *spark*, she kicking, he riding. *Sparks* are even exported in small quantities, to Canada, Germany, Sweden and the USA. Before cars became commonplace in Norway, *sparks* were sales leaders: in 1950, close to 100,000 were manufactured and sold, half again as many as the total number of cars then registered in the country. Like skis, *sparks* are made in sizes to suit the user. Size is stated in two ways. Fridtjof Nansen Standard sparks are sized in the traditional way, by the length of a runner, measured from the tail at the rear, along the straight section and around the front upturn of the bow. There are four sizes, stated in feet: $4^1/_2$, 6, $6^3/_4$ and $7^1/_2$ feet, the smallest for children and the largest for adult men. Norø's traditional Rapp sparks and sturdy steel-frame Tarzan sparks are made in two lengths, 194 cm and 152 cm, but with four sizes of frame and seat, to suit adults and children. All models now made can be demounted and packed flat, for ease of transport and summer storage. The *spark* is basically a workhorse, but it can be a racehorse as well. Up to the late 1930s, *sparkkjøring*, a race between *sparks* dawn by horses, was a popular winter sport. And unofficial Norwegian *spark* speed championships are still held, on a closed road between Ustaoset and Geilo in the south central mountain range.

Typical spark

Competitive sports (*Idrett*) are a leading pastime. So in Norwegian there are two words for sport: *idrett* for competitive sports in which human performance is decisive, and *sport* for all sport as well as sports determined by other factors. For instance, a human foot race round a track is *friidrett*, whilst a car race (*bilsport*) or horse race (*hestesport*) round a track is *sport*, but not *idrett*. An estimated one-tenth of the population is involved in *idrett*, either as competitors, coaches or trainers, club officials or helpers at matches and races. All competitive sports are organised in associations, which comprise the ☞ **Norwegian Confederation of Sports;** for information on a particular sport, contact its association. For a competitive sport without its own association, contact a related association, as the water skiing association for wakeboarding, and the budo or judo associations for other martial arts.

Square dance is a dance, similar to a quadrille, usually with four couples, arranged in a square, facing inward. It became popular in pioneer America and evolved to be a major form of folk dancing there. In Norway, there are clubs devoted to American square dancing in five cities: The *Fjord Frolickers Square Dance Club* in the Bærum suburb of Oslo, the *West Coast Square Dancers* in Haugesund, the *Horten og Omegn Square Dancers* in Horten, the *Oslo Square Dance Club* in Oslo and the *Stavanger Squares* in Stavanger. All the clubs invite new members, hold dances and give instruction. For further information and addresses of the clubs and their officers, view the *Square Dance in Norway* web site ☻ http://home.sol.no/~lholland/sqDance with pages in Norwegian and in English.

Stamp collecting (*Frimerkesamling*) More than 100,000 Norwegians collect postage stamps, some 30,000 of them as earnest hobbyists or professional collectors. There are more than 50 stamp shops in the country, from larger international dealers to small counters at newsagents, and stamp collecting is a leading indoor hobby, with a total annual turnover (1997) of about NOK 100 million. There are stamp clubs in all cities and most towns; contact the Norwegian Philatelic Association (*Norsk Filatelistforbund* ✆ 22416140, ⊠ 22424812, ⊠ PO Box 875 Sentrum, 0104 Oslo for addresses and names of contact persons. Publications are in Norwegian only, but Association officers speak English and other European languages. The Oslo Philatelist Club (*Oslo Filatelistklubb*) publishes an large (400 pages in 1998) annual, colour-illustrated Catalogue of The Postage Stamps of Norway (*Norgeskatalogen*), with texts in Norwegian and English. It is sold at most stamp shops or may be ordered from *Oslo Filatelistklubb Norgeskatalogen* ⊠ PO Box 298 Sentrum, 0103 Oslo. The Norwegian Post office has a philatelic service (*Postens frimerkertjeneste* ⊠ PO Box 9350, 0135 Oslo, which sells collectable Norwegian stamps, mostly mail-order, regularly publishes brochures on them, with texts in Norwegian, English, French and German and also issues a periodically updated CD-ROM catalogue of Norwegian stamps.

Tall ships (*Fullriggere*) The three Norwegian fully rigged steel sailing ships are the *Statsraad Lehmkuhl*, the *Sørlandet* and the *Christian Radich*. All originally served as maritime cadet training vessels, are now owned by foundations that offer sail training and have taken part in international tall ships race, including the famed Cutty Sark Tall Ships race.

Statsraad Lehmkuhl is the oldest and largest of the three ships and one of the world's oldest sailing vessels still in service. She was launched in 1914 as the *Grossherzog Friedrich August,* a training ship for the Germany merchant marine. In 1923, the ship was bought by a Norwegian group and named after Minister (*Statsraad*) Kristofer Lehmkuhl, who promoted the use of training ships. Bergen is her home port ✆ 55301700, ⊠ 55301701, ⊠ Brandbenken, 5003 Bergen, ✉ lehmkuhl@lehmkuhl.no, ☻ http://www.lehmkuhl.no with pages in Norwegian and in English and links to other tall ship sites.

Sørlandet was launched in 1927 as a maritime training vessel. In 1933, she became the first Norwegian training ship to cross the Atlantic, when she sailed to the World's Fair in Chicago. Kristiansand is her home port ℱ 38029890, ✆ 38029394, ✉ Gravene 6, 4610 Kristiansand, ✉ stiftelsen@full-riggeren-sorlandet.no, ⊕ http://www.fullriggeren-sorlandet.no with pages in Norwgian and in English.

Christian Radich was launched in 1937 as a replacement for *Statsraad Erichsen*, then 79 years old. In 1956 she was chartered for six months for the filming of *Windjammer* in Cinemiracle, a cinematic system using three synchronised cameras, and is still remembered by many as the film-star tall ship. Oslo is her home port ℱ 22478270, ✆ 22478271, ✉ PO Box 666 Sentrum, 0160 Oslo, ✉ kontoret@christian-radich.no, ⊕ http://www.christian-radich.no with pages in Norwegian and in English.

Veteran cars and other vehicles are popular, and there are clubs for almost all makes and types of vehicles, as well as a countrywide organisation of the larger clubs, *Landsforbundet av Motorhistoriske Kjøretøyklubber (LMK)* ("National association of historical motor vehicle clubs") ℱ 22670795, ✆ 22670795, ✉ PO Box 652 Sentrum, 0106 Oslo. A magazine, *Norsk Motorveteran* ℱ 66910656, ✆ 66910657 ✉ PO Box 210, 1450 Nesoddtangen, published 10 times a year and sold by news agents and on subscription, is devoted to all veteran vehicles, and regularly carries advertisements of firms specialising in parts, restoration and import of veteran cars, motorcycles and other motor vehicles. According to current regulations, a veteran vehicle is defined as one more than thirty years old; it may be imported free of import duty and may be registered on "historic" number plates (One letter plus three or more numerals) and is not subject to annual number plate fees. Insurance companies, some in association with LMK, offer veteran car insurance at discount rates, contingent upon limited driving per year. There are more than 100 veteran car and vehicle clubs in the country. Alphabetically, by makes and areas of interest, the major clubs that are members of LMK are:

- Adler: Adlerklubben Norge ✉ PO Box 86, 4875 Nedenes.
- Alfa Romeo: Klubb Alfa Romeo Norge ✉ PO Box 7170 Majorstuen, 0307 Oslo.
- Alvis: see British cars, Albion.
- American cars: American Car Club Lillehammer ✉ PO Box 350, 2601 Lillehammer; American Cruisers Club Eidsvoll, ✉ PO Box 27, 2092 Minnesund; American Drivers Club – Blaker ✉ PO Box 196, 1920 Sørumsand; Eight Amcars Club ✉ PO Box 36, 1990 Sørum;.Gjøvik Amcarclub ✉ PO Box 223, 2801 Gjøvik; Genland Veteranvogn Klubb ✉ PO Box 92, 3701 Skien; Hallingdal Veteranvogn Klubb, ✉ PO Box 259, 3550 Gol; Street and Crusin Club of Halden ✉ PO Box 566 Busterud, 1754 Halden; West Side Cruisers ✉ Løxaven. 2, 1351 Rud.
- Austin 7/10: see British cars, Albion.
- British cars: Alvis, Austin 7/10, Daimler, Ford, Humber, Jaguar, MG, Morris, Riley, Rover, Standard, Triumph, Vauxhall, Wolseley: Albion, Norsk Britisk Bilhistorisk Forening, ✉ Svartolderveien 11, 2300 Hamar.
- Buick: Buick Club of Norway ✉ PO Box 6565 Etterstad, 0606 Oslo.
- Busses: Rutebilhistorisk Forening ✉ PO Box 36, 6830 Sande i Sunnfjord.
- Chrysler: Walter P. Chrysler Club of Norway ✉ PO Box 57 Bekkelaget, 0137 Oslo.
- Citroën B-11/B-15 ✉ Traction Norvége, ✉ PO Box 72 Vinderen, 0319 Oslo.
- Citroën DS/ID: Citroën DS/ID Klubb Norge ✉ c/o Henrik Schibsted, Østre vei 47, 1315 Nesøya.
- Corvette: Corvette Club Norway ✉ PO Box 55 Bryn, 0611 Oslo.
- Daimler: see British cars, Albion.
- Datsun/PMC: Datsun/PMC-Registeret ✉ PO Box 80, 3371 Vikersund.
- DKW Union: Norsk DKW Union ✉ PO Box 602, Stasjonssiden, 2201 Kongsvinger.
- Fiat: Norsk Fiat Register ✉ PO Box 64, 1321 Stabekk.
- Ford Model A :Norsk A Modell Klubb ✉ PO Box 1930 Vika, 0215 Oslo.
- Ford, British: see British cars, Albion.
- Ford, early V8 models: Early Ford V8 Club – Norway ✉ PO Box 3253 Bjølsen, 0406 Oslo.
- Ford: Ford M Klubb Norge ✉ PO Box 138, 5610 Øystese.
- Honda: Classic Honda Club Norway ✉ c/o Lars Chr. Dahl, Solveien 112, 1162 Oslo.
- Hudson-Essex-Terraplane: Norsk Hudson-Essex-Teraplane Klubb ✉ c/o Eivind Daldorff, Levrev. 6, 1346 Gjettum.
- Humber: see British cars, Albion.

- Jaguar: see British cars, Albion; Norsk Jaguar Klubb ⊠ PO Box 1748 Vika, 0121 Oslo.
- Japanese motorcycles: Klassisk Japansk Motorsykkelklubb ⊠ Ørneveien 6, 1476 Rasta.
- Lancia: Lancisti Norvegesi ⊠ c/o Bilservice, Sagveien 11G, 0458 Oslo.
- Land Rover: Norsk Land-Rover Klubb ⊠ PO Box 6047 Etterstad, 0601 Oslo.
- Mercedes-Benz: Mercedes-Benz Klubben Norge ⊠ PO Box 170, 4033 Forus.
- MG: see British cars, Albion; Norsk MG Klubb ⊠ Engveien 20, 0487 Oslo.
- Military vehicles: Historiske Militære Kjøretøyers Forening ⊠ PO Box 51 Blindern, 0313 Oslo; Møringen Forsvarskjøretøyers Union ⊠ PO Box 241, 3192 Horten; Norsk Militærtransporthistorisk Forum ⊠ c/o Harald Ulvestad, Frognersetervn. 40B, 0387 Oslo.
- Mini Cooper: Norsk Mini Cooper Club ⊠ PO Box 450, 1322 Høvik.
- Morgan: Norsk Morgan Klubb ⊠ Malmøgaten 7, 0566 Oslo.
- Morris Minor: Nordisk Morris Minor Klubb ⊠ PO Box 37 Hovseter, 0705 Oslo.
- Morris: see British cars, Albion.
- Motorcycles: Classic Bike Owners Club ⊠ PO Box 2392, 5037 Solheimsviken; Norsk Veteran Motorsykkel Club ⊠ PO Box 594 Sentrum, 0106 Oslo.
- Opel: Opelregisteret ⊠ PO Box 29 Haugenstua, 0915 Oslo.
- Peugeot: Norsk Peugeot Klubb ⊠ c/o Eddie Bruvoll, Grenaveien 22, 5500 Haugesund.
- Porsche 356: Porsche 356 Klubb Norge ⊠ c/o Einar Harboe, Skogvn. 99, 1320 Stabekk.
- Porsche: Porsche Klubb Norge ⊠ PO Box 83 Lilleaker, 0216 Oslo.
- Renault: Club Renault Norvége ⊠ c/o Olaf Danielsen, Strindheimvn. 6, 7045 Trondheim.
- Riley: see British cars, Albion.
- Rootes: Rootes Car Club Norway ⊠ PO Box 2, 3520 Jevnaker.
- Rover: see British cars, Albion.
- Saab: Gammelsaabens Venner ⊠ PO Box 2384 Strømnsø, 3003 Drammen.
- Sports cars: Norsk Sportsvogn Klubb ⊠ PO Box 13 Sentrum, 0101 Oslo.
- Standard: see British cars, Albion.
- Triumph: see British cars, Albion; Triumph Owners MCC, Norway ⊠ c/o Rolf Haukeberg, Vestvn. 48, 0284 Oslo.
- Trucks: Transporthistorisk Forening ⊠ PO Box 1340, 3001 Drammen.
- Vauxhall: see British cars, Albion.
- Veteran cars, general: Agder Motorhistoriske Klubb ⊠ PO Box 4551 Grim, 4602 Kristiansand S.; Bergen Veteranvogn Klubb ⊠ Klostergt. 28, 5005 Bergen; Gammelbilens Venner ⊠ PO Box 3029 Mariero, 4004 Stavanger; Horten og Omegn Veteranvogn Klubb ⊠ Kirkebakken 1C, 3184 Horten; Jotunheimen Veterankjøretøyklubb ⊠ c/o Jan Randen, Bismo, 2690 Skjåk; Kvam Veteranvogn Klubb ⊠ c/o Jan A. Augestad, 5600 Norheimsund; Køyretøy Historisk Klubb Voss ⊠ PO Box 408, 5701 Voss; Larvik-Sandefjord Veteranvognklubb ⊠ PO Box 2139, 3255 Larvik; Lillehammer Veteranvogn Klubb ⊠ PO Box 1106 Skurva, 2601 Lillehammer; Motorhistorisk Lubb – Drammen ⊠ PO Box 2193 Strømsø, 3003 Drammen; Motorhistorisk Klubb- Nord Østerdal ⊠ PO Box 180, 2501 Tynset; Motorhistorisk Klubb Ringerike og Omegn ⊠ PO Box 1019 Flattum, 3501 Hønefoss; Motorveteranene Hedemark ⊠ PO Box 1090, 2301 Hamar; Narvik Automobilselskap ⊠ PO Box 468, 8501 Narvik; Nome Motorhistorisk Forening ⊠ c/o Erik Stoa, 3745 Ulefoss; Nordfjord Motorhistoriske Klubb ⊠ PO Box 218, 6771 Nordfjordeid; Nordmøre og Romsdal Kjøretøyhistorisk Klubb ⊠ PO Box 2006, 6401 Molde; Nord-Trøndelag Motorhistorisk Forening ⊠ c/o Svein Holmstad, Fr. Nilssensv. 12, 7650 Verdal; Norsk Veteranvogn Klubb ⊠ PO Box 5379 Majorstuen, 0304 Oslo; Oppdal Gammel Teknisk Forening ⊠ c/o Johan Vindal, Morkelveien 2, 7340 Oppdal; Romerike Gammelbil Klubb ⊠ c/o Ivar Olsen, Hasler, 2072 Dal; Storfjordens Automobil Klubb ⊠ PO Box 30 Sentrum, 6001 Ålesund; Sunnfjord Veteranvogn Klubb ⊠ PO Box 376, 6801 Førde; Søre Sunnmøre Motorhistoriske Klubb ⊠ PO Box 117, 6060 Hareid.; Toten Gammelbilklubb ⊠ PO Box 109, 2851 Lena; Tromsø Veteranvognklubb ⊠ PO Box 244, 9001 Tromsø; Trøndelag Veteranvognklubb ⊠ PO Box 2196, 7001 Trondheim; Tønsberg Automobilklub ⊠ PO Box 110, 3140 Borgheim; Valdres Veteranvogners Venner ⊠ PO Box 133, 2901 Fagenes; Vest-Telemark Motorhistoriske Klub ⊠ PO Box 106, 3840 Seljord; Veteranvogn-

klubben Østra & Volda ✉ c/o Oddvin Aasen, Fonnavn. 12, 6150 Ørstra; Østfold Veteranvogn Klubb ✉ PO Box 47, 1740 Borgenhaugen.
- Volkswagen: Veteran VW Klubben ✉ Røsslyngveien 23, 3030 Drammen; Volkswagen Auto Club Bergen ✉ PO Box 37, 5363 Ågotnes.
- Volvo 164/P1800: Norsk Volvo 164/P1800 Klubb ✉ PO Box 73, 1790 Tistedal.
- Volvo Amazon: Norsk Volvo Amazon Klubb ✉ PO Box 1528 Framnes, 3206 Sandefjord.
- Volvo PV: Norsk Volvo PV Klubb ✉ PO Box 299, 3051 Mjøndalen.
- Wolseley: see British cars, Albion.
- Z1: Z1 Owners Club Norway ✉ PO Box 97 Veitvet, 0518 Oslo.

Veteran railways (*Museums jernbaner*) operate at many locations. Some are narrow gauge, which means that the distance between the inner heads of the rails is less than the normal 1435 mm, the standard in most countries in Europe and in North America. There are five veteran railways that offer scheduled rail excursion services in the summertime:

Gamle Vossebanen, the first part of the original Bergen Line opened in 1883 and now trafficked by steam locomotives drawing teak carriages on a normal-gauge (1435 mm) line near Bergen ✆ 55249100, ✉ PO Box 638, 5807 Bergen.

Krøderbanen, steam locomotives draw teak carriages on a 26 km stretch of line that was part of the main rail network from 1872 to 1985, between Krøderen and Vikersund southeast of Noresund in Buskerud county ✆ 32147603, ✆ 32148505, ✉ 3535 Krøderen.

Setesdalsbanen, steam locomotive draws teak carriages on a 15 km stretch of 1067 mm narrow-gauge track at Vennesla, 15 north of Kristiansand in Vest-Agder county ✆ 38156482, ✆ 38156721, ✉ Grovane, 4700 Vennesla.

Tramshavbanen, Norway's first and now the world's oldest electrified railway, operating on a 19 km stretch of 1000 mm narrow-gauge track between Løkken Verk and Fannrem, south of Orkanger in Sør Trøndelag county ✆ 72499095, ✆ 72499101, ✉ Turistkontoret, 7332 Løkken Verk.

Urskog-Høplandsbanen, trains drawn by the *Teritten* steam locomotive on a 4 km stretch of 750 mm narrow-gauge track between Sørumsand and Skulerud south of Lillestrøm in Akershus county

✆ 63826970, ✆ 63827121, ✉ PO Box 59, 1920 Sørumsand.

Moreover, the Norwegian Railway Club (*Norsk Jernbaneklubb – NJK*) operates Heritage Trains (*Museumstog*) jointly with NSB railways, the Norwegian National Rail Administration (*Jernbaneverket*), the Norwegian Rail Museum (*Norsk Jernbanemuseum*) and the Technical Museum (*Norsk Teknisk Museum*). These trains may be chartered for excursion trips. For details on them, as well as on all veteran railway activities, contact the Club ✆ 22270010, ✆ 22271600, ✉ PO Box 1492 Vika, 0116 Oslo 🖥 http://www.njk.no with pages in Norwegian and in English and links to other veteran railway sites.

Veteran steamships (*Veteran dampskip*) are a part of living culture, understandable for maritime Norway.

The *Skiblander* is the world's oldest paddlewheel steamship still in service. Named after a sailing ship of Nordic mythology and built in 1854-56 by the Motala Shipyard in Sweden as a passenger launch, it entered service in 1856 on Lake Mjøsa, as an extension of the railway which then ended at Eidsvoll. It has been restored several times, most recently in 1983, is 165 feet long and is registered to carry 230 passengers. It now has regularly scheduled tours on Lake Mjøsa six days a week in the summertime. Contact Skiblanderkontoret for information and schedules ✆ 62527085, ✆ 62533923, ✉ Parkgata 2, 22300 Hamar, ✉ skiblander@online.no, 🖥 http://www.hamarnett.no/skiblander

The *Engebret Soot* is the world's oldest propeller-driven steamship still in service. Named after the man who designed the canal system branching out from Halden and built in 1861-62 by the Nyland Shipyard in Norway as its No. 1 ship, it entered service in 1862 as a tug towing timber on the canals. It was fully restored in 1989-94, is 79 feet long and is registered to carry 50 passengers in its new configuration as an excursion launch. It now has periodic tours on the inland lakes around the Halden Canal system locks at Ørje on the E18 highway close to the Swedish border, starting from the locks just east of town and south of E18. Contact the Halden Waterways Canal Museum there for information and schedules ✆ 69811021, ✆ 69811266, ✉ Storg. 31, 1870 Ørje, or visit the museum, the only one in the country dedicated to canals, open 11 am – 4 pm from late June through early August.

Water skills (*Badevett/båtvett/sjøvett*) are vital, because many outdoor activities are on or near water. Each year, some 150 people drown. That figure is doubly tragic, as almost all drowning can be prevented by learning basic water skills and observing simple water safety rules, including:

- Learn to swim and observe swimming safety. Most swimming pools, listed under *Svømmehaller og bad* in the Yellow Pages, teach swimming, as do many schools, children's summer camps and the like. The sports consultant (*Idrettskonsulent*) in your local municipality will have the details.
- Learn and practise artificial respiration; ☞ **first aid courses** (Health Care chapter) teach it.
- No alcohol or drugs, before or when swimming or boating. About a third of all adult men who drown are inebriated.
- Careful on ice in the wintertime; learn to recognise and avoid dangerously thin ice.
- Watch small children; they love to play in water, but have yet to appreciate its dangers.
- Learn boat safety rules.
- Wear a ☞ **life jacket** if you cannot swim, if you are in a boat or if you fish alone from shore or a pier.

For more information, see "We and the water" (*Vi og vannet*), a well-illustrated colour brochure on water skills, published in 1999 by ☞ **Norwegian People's Aid** (NGOs chapter) in Norwegian, Arabic, English, German and Serbo-Croatian versions and distributed free by municipalities, refugee reception centres and water sports organisations.

Statistics and polls (*Statistikk og meningsmålinger*)

The Norwegian Road Federation (*Opplysningsrådet for Veitrafikken*) is a private organisation that compiles motor vehicle and road statistics. It is a member of the International Road Federation and of the European Road Federation. Its publications include a broad range of current and historical motor vehicle and road statistics, which it makes available on a subscription basis to member companies and organisations involved in road traffic. However, individual publications may be bought from the head office in Oslo ✆ 22403240, ✉ 22403232, ✉ PO Box 88 Sentrum, 0101 Oslo, ✉ firmapost@ofv.no, ✉ http://www.ofv.no

OECD Statistics (*OECD statistikk*) and other national and comparative publications relating to member countries are listed in the OECD web site, ✉ http://www.oecd.org and can be located using SWISH, the site's search engine. In Norway, all in-print OECD publications may be ordered from the head office of the Narvesen newsagent chain ✆ 22573300.

Opinion polling (*Meningsmåling*) started in 1944, and in 1946, the Norwegian Gallup Institute (*Norsk Gallup AS*) was set up to systematise polling, using the principles developed by George Gallup in the USA in the 1930s. As elsewhere, opinion polls in Norway attempt to assess national opinion on matters by putting questions to samples of the population, usually 800 to 2000 persons, by telephone, personal interview or filling out forms. Norway Statistics (☞ **Statistics**) conducts polls for governmental purposes, and four polling institutes offer services to public and private sector clients: ACNielsen (✆ 22583400, ✉ 22583401), Markeds- og Mediainstituttet, MMI (✆ 22954700, ✉ 22954850), Scan-Fact (✆ 22473500, ✉ 22473501) and Opinion (✆ 22688801, ✉ 22681185). Moreover, international polling companies often include Norway in polls, such as in the World Poll conducted by the international Angus Reid Group. In mid 1998, for instance, the "Angus Reid World Poll of Citizens' Ratings of Quality of Life and Hope for the Future, across 29 countries" ranked Norwegians high in satisfaction with current quality of life, but in 25th place in outlook for the future; details are available on the Internet at ✉ http://www.angusreid.com

Statistics (*Statistikk*) are compiled by Statistics Norway (*Statistisk sentralbyrå, SSB*), an independent bureau of the Ministry of Finance and Customs, and published as the Official Statistics of Norway (*Norges offisielle statistikk, NOS*), a series comprising some 80 publications a year. The annual Statistical Yearbook of Norway (*Statistisk årbok*) is the most comprehensive and widely-available NOS compilation. It has more than 500 tables of national statistics as well as more than 40 international comparison tables and is published in both Norwegian and English editions. Annual statistics through the years are summarised in Historical Statistics (*Historisk statistikk*), a bi-lingual (Norwegian and English) lexicon featuring tables, graphs and overview articles on 25 major groups of statistics, some including data from the early 19th century on. Other NOS publications include topical and thematic compilations and reviews, many available in both Norwegian and English editions. The Weekly Bulletin of Statistics (*Ukens statistikk*) is the principal SSB periodical and contains current tabulations and articles in Norwegian, with summaries in English on SSB's web site ✉ hppt://www.ssb.no. The home page of the web site has a link to its English version, which has extracts and selected tables, both from annual publications and from weekly statistics. A CD-ROM, Statistics Across Borders (*Statistikk uten grenser*), with the principal statistics of the Nordic countries is issued once a year. The Statistical Yearbook and other major publications are stocked in larger book shops. The CD-ROM and all publications in print are available on order from Statistics Norway, Sales and Subscription Office ✆ 62885500, ✉ 62885595, ✉ PO Box 1260, 2201 Kongsvinger, or from Akademika, Official Publications Department ✆ 22116770, ✉ 22420551, ✉ PO Box 8134 Dep, 0033 Oslo, and are stocked along with other governmental publications by the Akademika book shop at ✉ Møllergata 17, Oslo.

Taxes, duties, excise
(Skatt, toll, avgifter)

Capital gains tax (Gevinstskatt) For companies as well as for private persons holding shares, gains (gevinst) realised upon sale of shares are subject to the 28% capital gains tax. Likewise, losses (tap) are deductable on tax returns. The gain or loss in a sale is in principle equal to the difference between the initial cost of the shares, including fees, and the price upon sale. However, in some cases, gains could be taxed twice. Consider investors who chose the general partnership form to found a company with the required minimum share capital of NOK 100,000. In its first year, the company does well and declares a profit of NOK 100,000, which is taxed at 28%. The company then is worth NOK 172,000. Suppose that the investors then elect to sell their shares to others, who are willing to pay NOK 172,000. On paper, the original investors have realised a gain of NOK 72,000, the difference between the selling price and their original investment. But if that gain is taxed, the money that created it has been taxed twice.

A system to avoid such double taxation was introduced as part of the tax reform of 1992. It is called **RISK (Regulering av aksjens Inngangsverdi med Skattelagt kapital)** ("Adjustment of the cost price of taxed capital") and applies only to shares held in Norwegian companies. The effect of RISK computation is to adjust the original cost of shares by the net change in a company's taxed capital, for the period of time that the shares are held. After closing their accounts for a tax year, usually in the autumn of the following year, companies having shares perform their RISK calculations and notify their shareholders of the RISK amount per share (RISK-beløp pr. aksje), which is valid for the calendar year after the tax year for which it was computed. Shareholders then use the RISK amount per share in computing gains or losses from any sales of shares to enter in their tax returns (selvangivelser). This means that unrealised gains are not taxed and unrealised losses cannot be deducted.

Customs (Avgift ved innførsel) is a tax payable on goods from other countries, collected by ☞ **Norwegian Customs and Excise**. If you import goods from abroad, such as by ☞ **mail order from abroad** (Shopping chapter), you will be charged customs when you collect the goods, such as a package at a post office. The total customs taxation on an item consists of three parts: import duty (toll), special duty (særavgift) and value-added tax (MVA).

Import duty (toll) usually is based on the declared value (tollverdi) at the point of import, but for some goods is based on weight.

Special duties and other duties and fees (Særavgifter og andre avgifter/gebyrer) are charged on selected categories of goods including alcohol in essences (alkohol i essenser), batteries (batterier), beer (øl), boat motors (båtmotorer), cassettes for sound and video recording (uinnspilte kassettbånd), chocolate and sweets (sjokolade- og sukkervarer), coal and coke (kull og koks), foodstuffs (næringsmiddel), liquor and wine (brennevin og vin), lubricants (smøreolje), motor vehicles (motorvogner) ☞ **car import** (Cars, Roads, Traffic chapter), packaging for drinks (emballasje til drikkevarer), ☞ **petrol** and ☞ **diesel** (Cars, Roads, Traffic chapter), petroleum products (mineralolje), plants and parts of plants (planter og plantedeler) ☞ **plant import** (Housekeeping chapter), radio and TV receivers and accessories (radio- og fjernsynsmateriell), soft drinks (alkoholfrie drikkevarer), sugar (sukker), tobacco products (tobakkvarer) and tyres (dekk).

Value-added tax (MVA) is charged, with few exceptions, on all imported goods. As a general rule, the exceptions include goods exempt from ☞ MVA within the country, such as books for private use and not to be re-sold.

For rates and other details, contact the nearest Customs office (tollsted) listed under tollvesenet in the Pink Pages.

Document duty (Dokumentavgift) is imposed on registrations of property transactions by the ☞ **City recorder or District recorder** (Registrations, Rights, Licences chapter). It was introduced in 1976, is equivalent to the stamp duty in the UK and the transfer tax in the USA, and is charged at 2.5% of the sale price of the property registered.

Excise (Avgift) is a tax levied on goods or services within the country of origin or on certain licences. Excises on the following goods and services are collected by ☞ **Norwegian Customs and Excise**: ☞

Air travel tax (Transport chapter) (*Avgift på flyging*), beer (*øl*), carbonated soft drinks (*kullsyreholdige, alkoholfrie drikkevarer*), chocolate and sweets (*sjokolade og sukkervarer*), coal and coke (*kull og koks*), diesel fuels for motor vehicles (*autodiesel*), documents listed with ☞ **City/district recorder** (Registration, Rights, Licences chapter) (*Dokumentavgift*), electric energy consumption (*elektrisk kraft*), heavy motor vehicles annual weight fees (*vektårsavgift*), initial motor vehicle registration (*engangsavgift på motorvogner*) as upon ☞ **Car import** (Cars, Roads, Traffic chapter), liquor and wine (*brennevin og vin*), lubricants (*smøreoljer*), motor vehicle annual licence fees (*årsavgift*), motor vehicle re-registration (*omregistering*), motor vehicles built in Norway (*motorvogen bygd opp her i landet*), non-carbonated soft drinks (*kullsyriefrie, alkoholfrie drikkevarer*), petrol (*bensin*), petroleum products (*mineralolje*), radio and TV receivers and accessories (*radio- og fjernsynsmateriell*), recordable audio/video cassettetes (*kassetter*), refuse processing and tipping (*sluttbehandling av avfall*), sugar (*sukker*) and tobacco products (*tobakkvarer*).

Foreign tax affairs (*Skatt – utenlandssaker*) In principle, you are subject to taxation as soon as you start earning income in Norway, regardless of your citizenship. However, Norway has tax treaties with more than 80 countries, principally for the avoidance of double taxation and to prevent tax evasion. Consequently, the taxation of your income may depend on various circumstances, such as the length of your stay in Norway, whether your employer is a foreign company and whether you have a permanent home in Norway. In short, your tax status depends on the particular tax treaty between Norway and the country in which you are or were a resident before arriving in Norway, as well as the particular circumstances in your case. However, in general, income from employment will in most cases be taxable in Norway if your stay exceeds 183 days during a 12-month period or a calendar year. The tax treaties are available in Norwegian and English editions, as well as French and Spanish editions for some countries. A list of the treaties is available on-line ☻ http://www.finans.dep.no in Norwegian (click on *Skatteavtaler* under *Skatter og avgifter*) and in English (click on *Tax treaties* under *Taxes*). The treaties are available in print from the *Akademika* publication service ✆ freephone 80080960, ✉ Møllergt 17, 0179 Oslo. Treaties not stocked by *Akademika* are available from the archive service of the Ministry of Finance (*Finans og Tolldepartementet*) ✆ 22244193. For further information and interpretation of treaties, contact your local tax office (*Likningskontor*) or The Central Office for Foreign Tax Affairs (*Sentralskattekontoret for utenlandssaker*) ✆ 51969600, ✇ 51678559, ✉ Prinsens vei 1, 4300 Sandnes, ✉ postkassessu@skattetat.no

Import restrictions (*Innførselsrestriksjoner*) apply to the categories of goods listed below. The restrictions range from requiring a licence for goods to be sold to totally barring import, such as of CFCs or child pornography. For further details, contact the nearest office of the Customs Service, listed under *Tollvesenet* in the Pink Pages.

- Alcohol (*Alkohol*), including alcoholic drink and industrial/scientific alcohols.
- Asbestos (*Asbest*)
- Bees, beehives and beeswax products (*Bier, voksbygninger, presset bivoks*)
- Cattle feeds (*Kraftfôr*)
- Chloro-flurocarbons – CFCs (*Klorfluorokarboner – KFK*)
- Cosmetics containing alcohol and/or isopropanol (*Kosmetikk, med innhold av spirit og/eller isopropanol*)
- Earth, turf, bark, compost and natural fertiliser (*Jord, torv, bark, kompost og naturlig gjødsel*)
- Eggs (*Egg*)
- Essences containing alcohol (*Essenser, spiritholdige*)
- Explosives and flammable materials (*Eksplosiver og brannfarlige stoffer*)
- Fish and fish products (*Fisk og fiskeprodukter*)
- Foods (*Næringsmidler*)
- Fruits (*Frukt*)
- Grains and flours (*Korn og melvarer*)
- Grass, hay, straw and alfalfa (*Gras, høy, halm og lucerne*)
- Live mammals and birds (*Pattedyr og fugler, levende*)
- Meat (*Kjøtt*)
- Medicines (*Legemidler*)
- Milk and dairy products (*Melk og melkeprodukter*)
- Narcotics (*Narkotika*)
- Plants, parts of plants and pesticides (*Planter,*

plantedeler og plantevernmidler)
- Poisons, chemicals and products posing health hazards (*Gifter, kjemiske stoffer og produkter som kan medføre helsefare*)
- Pornography (*Pornografi*)
- Potatoes (*Poteter*)
- Seeds for crops (*Såvarer*)
- Semen, embryos and eggs (*Sæd, embryoner og egg fra dyr*)
- Skins and leathers (*Huder og skinn*)
- Soil conditioners (*Jordforbedringsmidler*)
- Stuffed animals (*Dyr, utstoppede*)
- Telecommunications equipment (*Teleteknisk brukerutstyr*)
- Textiles and clothing (*Tekstiler og klær*)
- Timber (*Tømmer*)
- Used farm machinery and animal transport crates/cages (*Jordbruksmaskiner og transportkasser/bur til dyr, brukte*)
- Vegetables (*Grønnsaker*)
- Weapons, weapon parts and ammunition (*Våpen, våpendeler og ammunisjon*)

Income tax (*inntektsskatt*) now is calculated from two tax bases: ordinary income and personal income.

Ordinary income (*alminnelig inntekt*) is a net income tax base and is equal to the total income from employment, pensions and all types of capital income, less tax deductions (*fradrag*). The principal deductions are tax-deductible interest on debts and a basic tax allowance on employment and pension income, excluding self-employment income. Moreover, travel expenses to and from work in excess of NOK 7000, trade union fees, documented expenses for childcare and other legitimate expenses are deductible. A class allowance (*klassefradrag*) is deducted according to the class to which the taxpayer belongs.

Personal income (*Personinntekt*) is a gross income tax base and is equal to the sum of gross employment and pension income, from which social security taxes and surtax are calculated. Employment income is a broad term that is defined as the sum of wages, income from self-employment that is related to labour input and fringe benefits such as company cars, free phone, free stock options and the like.

There are two tax categories, Class 1, mostly for single people, and Class 2, principally for joint tax returns. Married couples may elect to file separately in Class 1 or be taxed jointly in Class 2, whichever results in the lowest total tax. Couples with one income usually elect Class 2, whilst couples with two incomes usually file two Class 1 returns. Single parents are taxed in Class 2. The principal tax differences between the categories are that in Class 2, the class allowance is twice the amount allowed in Class 1, so surtax thresholds are higher.

The marginal tax on employment income is currently 49.3%. The marginal tax rate for self-employed persons is 52.2%, due to higher social security contributions.

Taxpayers living in the northernmost two counties, Nord-Troms and Finnmark, are generally taxed at lower rates and enjoy higher surtax thresholds. Wealth, or estate tax is generally paid on net worth minus a standard deduction. It is paid at the municipal level, now 0.7%, and at the national level, now 0.4%.

Tax returns (*Selvangivelser*) are filed by 1 April for the previous tax year ending 31 December and submitted to the nearest tax office (*Ligningskontor*). Taxes are then computed, and taxpayers notified within five to six months, usually in September.

MVA is the abbreviation of *Merverdiavgift*, the country's Value-Added Tax (VAT) of 23%. It is imposed on businesses at each stage of production or turnover of goods and services. It applies mostly to turnover (*omsetning*), so it is sometimes called *Moms*, which is the abbreviation of *Meromsetningsavgift* the Danish word for VAT. MVA is collected by adding 23% to prices. Prices in shops include it. For instance, if the pre-tax retail price of an item is NOK 50, its listed price in a shop will be NOK 61.50, which is NOK 50 plus 23% of NOK 50. When you buy an item costing NOK 61.50, you can compute the MVA by taking 18.7% of NOK 61.50, which is NOK 11.50.

MVA always applies to final prices. So if you order an item from a catalogue, MVA will be charged on the total of its price plus packing and shipping charges. By international agreements preventing double taxation, MVA is not collected on exports. But it is collected on imports and applies to the total cost of an import, including all customs duties. Some goods and services are exempted from MVA, including:
- Art sold by the artist or the artist's agent

- Articles sold by charities
- Bank safe-deposit box rentals
- Books, newspapers and some magazines sold retail
- Film rights, except advertising films
- Medical and dental care
- Postage stamps, bank notes and coins
- Postal services, except courier services
- Property and dwelling transactions
- Used cars

Norwegian Customs and Excise (Tollvesenet) collects duties and excises, acts to prevent the illegal import and export of goods and combats drug trafficking and economic crime. It comprises the central Directorate of Customs and Excise (Toll og Avgiftsdirektoratet) and the Regional Customs Administration (Distriktsforvaltning), which serves the public through 11 Customs Regions (Tolldistrikter), 34 Customs Offices (Tollsteder) and 10 Anti-smuggling and/or Customs Clearance Units (Ekspedisjons- eller kontrollenheter). It also maintains the leisure craft registry that issues ☞ **Boat number signs** (Sports, Recreation, Hobbies chapter) and a narcotics watch hotline ☞ **Helplines** (Emergencies chapter). You may call the nearest office, listed under Tollvesenet in the Pink Pages for information and advice on customs matters. Common queries include:
☞ **Car import** (Cars, Roads, Traffic chapter).
Customs regulations in 15 countries with which Norway has agreements.
EU and EFTA forms and regulations.
☞ **Excise**.
Import and export regulations and procedures.
☞ **Import restrictions**.
☞ **Pet import** (Pets and Animals chapter).
☞ **Plant import** (Housekeeping chapter).

The Revenue Service (Skatteetaten) collects taxes and other duties and provides other services, including the National register. The Revenue Service is past of the Ministry of Finance and Customs and comprises the Directorate of Taxes (Skattedirektoratet), 19 county tax offices (Fylkesskattekontor), 18 tax collector's offices (Skattefogdkontor), 436 local tax offices (Likningskontor) and National register offices (Folkeregister), the Central Office for Taxation – Large-Sized Companies (Sentralskattekontoret for storbedrifter), the Central Office – Foreign Tax Affairs (Sentralskatekontoret for utenlandssaker) and the Petroleum Tax Office (Oljeskattekontoret). As an individual taxpayer, you principally will be concerned with the ☞ **National register** (Registrations, Rights, Licences chapter) and with the local tax office (Likningskontor) in connection with your ☞ **income tax**. If you are a citizen of a foreign country, you may be concerned with ☞ **foreign tax affairs**. For further information on The Revenue Service, see the brochure published by the Directorate of Taxes, Veiviser til skatteetten (Norwegian edition, September 1998) or Guide to the Norwegian revenue service (English edition, October 1998) available from many local tax offices as well as from the Directorate's information service ✆ 81500799, ☏ 22077108, ✉ PO Box 6300 Etterstad, 0604 Oslo. The complete texts of the Norwegian and English editions also are available on-line ⊜ http://www.skatteetaten.no with pages and navigation guides in Norwegian and in English.

The Norwegian Taxpayers Association (Skattebetalerforening) is an independent public watchdog and consultant in tax and duty matters. It has a staff of six tax lawyers, two tax consultants and eight others at its headquarters in Oslo, and serves 24,000 individual and company members. It publishes a magazine, Skattebetaleren ("The Taxpayer"), two yearly guides to income tax returns, Skatte-nøkkelen ("Tax Key") for personal income taxpayers and Nærings-nøkkelen ("Business-Key") for company taxpayers, an inter-Scandinavian tax guide, Skatt i Norge, Sverige og Finland ("Tax in Norway, Sweden and Finland") with texts in Norwegian, Swedish and Finnish, and several booklets on special tax topics. It is a member of the International Fiscal Association (IFA) and of the Taxpayers Association International (TAI), which has 20 member organisations in 18 countries on five continents, including Australia, Austria, Belgium, Brazil, Canada, Croatia, Estonia, Finland, France, Hungary, Germany, Japan, The Netherlands, Norway, Slovakia, Sweden, the UK and the USA. TAI holds annual conferences, principally to promote greater uniformity in taxation; as this book goes to press, the last, in September 1999, was held in Berlin, Germany. For further details, contact Skattebetalerforening ✆ 22420727, ☏ 22337180, ✉ PO Box 213, 0103 Oslo, ⊜ http://www.skattehjelp.no

Telecommunications and broadcasting
(*Telekommunikasjon og kringkasting*)

Broadcasting companies (*kringkastingsselskap*) There are five national broadcasting companies – NRK, TV2, TV3, TVNorge and P4 – as well as numerous local broadcasting stations. They are listed below, along with the logos used on TV screens and in the programme pages of newspapers and magazines.

NRK *(Norsk Rikskringkasting)* is the former governmental monopoly. In 1988, the broadcasting market was deregulated, and NRK accordingly was reorganised to compete with new private broadcasting companies. It now has two TV channels, NRK 1 and NRK 2

and three radio channels, P1, P2 and P3:

as well as the classical radio (*NRK alltidklassisk*) and news (*alltidnyheter*) channels in major cities and the Sami-language service (*Sami radio*) in Finnmark county, the most northern in the country.

TV2 is the principal national private, advertising-financed competitor to NRK, with its headquarters and major studios in Bergen. It started operations in 1992 and now provides coverage throughout the country.

TV3 is a national private broadcaster owned by Modern Times Group, a Scandinavian media company. TV3 Norway began operations in 1989, and transmits programs via satellite and cable, but not on conventional TV broadcast channels. Its main studios

in London originate programs for its three national channels, for Denmark, Norway and Sweden.

TVNorge is an advertising-financed, satellite, cable and local TV broadcaster owned by an American company, Scandinavian Broadcasting Systems (SBS), and by TV2. It started operations in 1988. Its programme profile is "young, modern and entertaining". TVNorge was the first TV channel to regularly broadcast an all-Norwegian soap opera drama series.

P4 is the country's first and only national private radio channel, with offices and studios in Bergen, Lillehammer, Oslo, Tromsø and Trondheim. It started operations in 1993 and now transmits a mix of music and news, 24 hours a day.

Cable TV (*Kabel-TV*) is available in almost all cities and towns throughout the country. If you live in a house with a view of the southern horizon, you may choose between mounting an outside dish antenna for satellite TV or putting in a cable for cable TV. But if your house has no view of the southern horizon or if you live in a block of flats where individual outside antennas are not permitted, cable TV is the only way you may receive channels in addition to those broadcast locally. Houses and flats in smaller blocks usually will connect to a local network of cables strung on poles or run underground like telephone cables, whilst larger blocks of flats may be fitted with satellite TV receivers and their own cable distribution networks. Cable TV operators offer a variety of installation and subscription services for both ordinary broadcast channels and pay-TV channels, for which decoders usually are fitted. The two major cable TV companies are Telenor Avidi, with about 270,000 subscribers throughout the country, and United Pan-European Communications (UPC), with about 323,000 subscribers in the major cities in the southern part of the country. See the Pink Pages for the local offices of these companies, or their web sites: Telenor Avidi ☻ http://www.telenor.no/avidi with pages in Norwegian only, or UPC ☻ http://www.upc.no with pages in Norwegian and in English. You can find local operators listed under *Kabel-TV* or *Antenner* in the Yellow Pages.

Call-back telephone services (*call-back*) aim to offer low rates for international calls by routing them through telephone exchanges in the USA, currently the country with the world's lowest rates for international calls. Procedures vary, but all involve dialling a call-back service access number at a telephone exchange in the USA using a personal identity number, hanging up, and then waiting a few seconds for the exchange to call back and provide a dialling tone to place a call. Depending on how the call-back feature is implemented, the initial ordering call may be charged at the Norwegian telecommunication company's international rate. Otherwise, call costs are at the rates offered by the call-back company. Because the companies send invoices from offices in the USA, they do not charge Norwegian VAT (*MVA*). Some call-back companies have agents in Norway and several advertise in international weekly news magazines, including The Economist and the European edition of Newsweek. The call-back companies currently active include Justice, Kallback, Maxtel, Newworld, Telegroup and United World Telecom.

Cellular telephone (*mobilkommunikasjon*) services are available throughout the country. There are two systems, the analogue Nordic Mobile Telephone (NMT) system and the digital Global System for Mobile (GSM). When it started in 1981, the NMT system, developed jointly by the Scandinavian telecommunications ministries, was one of the world's most modern and the first in Europe to feature roaming, allowing the same cellular phone to be used in any of the Nordic countries (Norway, Sweden, Denmark, Finland and Iceland). There are now two varieties of it, the original system, now called NMT 450 because it uses radio frequencies around 450 MHz, and, starting in 1986, NMT 900 (for 900 MHz frequency). In the late 1980s, the advanced features of the two varieties of NMT resulted in Norway having more cellular phones per hundred population than any other country; it now is in second place world-wide, with 38.3 mobile telephones per 100 people, behind first-place Finland with 41.9. NMT technology is used in the analogue cellular systems of other countries, including Austria, Belgium, Cyprus, France, Spain and Turkey. NMT 450 is used in the main cellular network in Switzerland, and NMT systems now are common throughout eastern Europe. Nonetheless, the Norwegian NMT systems are scheduled to be shut down on 31 December 2001, as digital GSM is more efficient and offers more services. There are two varieties of GSM that differ by radio frequency, the original GSM, now called GSM 900 (for 900 MHz), and, starting in 1997, GSM 1800 (for 1800 MHz). GSM 900 is now common throughout Europe, and GSM 1800 is being implemented, starting in high-population-density areas such as major cities. "Dual-band" GSM cellular phones are now available to work with both GSM 900 and GSM 1800. GSM offers extensive international roaming: a GSM phone registered in Norway can be used throughout Europe and as afar as Australia. Likewise, GSM cellular phones registered elsewhere may be used in Norway. There are two Norwegian cellular operators, Telenor (NMT and GSM) and NetCom (GSM), but only dealers actually sell or service cellular phones; see under *Mobilkommunikasjon* in the Yellow Pages. There are many price schemes, including various packages of phones and Telenor or NetCom subscriptions. Both companies offer cash cards (*kontantkort*) for prepaid amounts of phone use in Norway only (not valid abroad). In some public places, cellular phone use is politely restricted, so that others not be disturbed, such as in churches and theatres. Warning signs are posted whenever use might disturb navigational instruments, as on board commercial aircraft, or sensitive equipment, as in hospitals, banks and post offices, cellular phone use is prohibited and warning signs are posted.

Ex-directory number (*Hemmelig nummer*) Slightly less than 2% of all telephone numbers are ex-directory. Consequently they do not appear in any directory, they are not available at Enquiries (180), they are not made available in lists for telephone and postal sales and they are not forwarded for screen display at a called number. Any subscriber may order an ex-directory number against a surcharge. An ex-directory subscriber may also elect not to receive the telephone directory, which otherwise is distributed once a year to all subscribers in each of the 12 telephone regions. For further information: ℡ 140.

Freephone (*Grønt nummer*) Calls dialled to numbers starting with **800** are free for the caller. Some organisations can be dialled free from abroad using an International Freephone number (*Internasjonalt Grønt nummer*) in each of the 35 countries where the service is offered or an Universal Freephone number (*Universelt Grønt nummer*) that is the same in all countries. Other numbers starting with 8 involve charges to the caller:

810 general services with shared costs, usually with the caller paying only the local call rate (*lokaltakst*).

815 Internet servers.

820-829 various charges for billed services via telephone (*telefonfakturerte tjenester*), such as for information services and donations.

82947-82949 opinion poll voting, as for TV talk shows.

Home billing (*Norge direkte*) permits calling from abroad to numbers in Norway and having charges reversed, billed to your home number in Norway or debited to your TeleKonto charge card. The procedure involves dialling a specific number in each country, which often is a freephone number, and requesting further connection when a Norwegian operator answers. The service is now offered from more than 60 countries. For further details, see *Norge Direkte* in the general information section of the Pink and White Pages directory, or call Telenor's customer service freephone ☏ 140.

Internet telephony (*Internet-telefoni*) allows calls to be made between multimedia-equipped computers connected to the Internet or between computers and telephones. The services offered are according to the International Telecommunications Union (ITU) H.323 standard issued in February 1998. The advantage of Internet telephony is its low price, as callers pay only for calls to their local Internet servers and consequently can call internationally at rates lower than possible with conventional telephone circuits. The disadvantage is that the Internet does not carry voice signals, but rather digitised and compressed speech, so the quality of connection is not as good as that of a telephone circuit. In 1998, the major telecommunications company, Telenor initiated the *Interfon PC* services through its Nextel subsidiary. Otherwise, American companies, including Delta Three and Net2Phone also offer services, as do various independent private operators. For fur-

ther details, call the nearest Telenor Nextel office at the number listed in the Pink Pages or view its web site ☞ http://www.nextel.no/interfon/pc.

ISDN lines (*ISDN linjer*) Since its invention, the telephone has transmitted speech using an analogous electrical signal. Traditional telephone systems and most of the world's telephones that they serve, are therefore said to be analogue. Starting in the early 1960s, telephone companies have increasingly digitised their networks, using technologies similar to those of computers and CD audio recording. More recently, telephone companies have adopted the Integrated Services Digital Network (ISDN), which is a universal international standard for the design and operation of digital telephone systems. Throughout Europe, ISDN services have been increasingly available to subscribers since the mid 1990s. In Norway, ISDN services have been available to subscribers since May 1994. An ISDN telephone has several advantages over a traditional analogue telephone. Even though it uses a two-wire connection as does an analogue telephone, an individual subscriber connection can carry two circuits that can carry simultaneous calls; if you are speaking on the telephone, you can also send or receive a fax or E-Mail message. With an ISDN line, a computer connection to the Internet needs no modem, because the connection is 'all-digital. Communication is also far faster, at least twice the speed of the fastest modem. If you wish, you may have as many as ten separate telephone numbers, instead of just one, as with an analogue telephone. Unless you specifically request that it be cancelled, your ISDN telephone displays both the numbers you call and the numbers from which incoming calls are made. ISDN telephones and installations currently are more expensive than for analogue, but prices are falling. ISDN calls are charged by the second, as are analogue calls. The typical ISDN installation consists of a network termination box. Called 'NT1', the box provides at least two and as many as eight digital lines and, if ordered, up to two analogue lines. So if you have a traditional analogue telephone and a telefax, you can connect them to the analogue ports of an NT1 box or adapter, yet have one or more digital lines available for your computer(s). ISDN telephones and equipment are sold in telecommunications and electronics shops. For the details of installations and subscription prices, call Telenor Customer Service (*Telenor Kundeservice*) at freephone ✆ 140.

The Norwegian Post and Telecommunications Authority (*Post- og teletilsynet*) is responsible for many regulation and monitoring tasks in telecommunications and postal services. All equipment to be connected to fixed telecommunications lines must be approved either by the Authority or by an equivalent authority in an EEA country, to ensure that it conforms to international standards and thereby will work correctly when connected. For further information, contact the head office of the Authority ✆ 22824600, 🖷 22824640, ✉ PO Box 447 Sentrum, 0104 Oslo, ✆ http://www.npt.no with pages in Norwegian and selected pages in English.

Paging (*Personsøking*) is a mobile communications system in which tones or alphanumeric messages are sent to pocket terminals. A pager (*personsøker*) is cheaper than a cellular telephone to buy and operate and provides a low-cost way to stay in touch when on the move. The two cellular telephone companies, Telenor Mobil and NetCom, have countrywide paging systems. The simplest pagers have a small screen that displays only numerals, as keyed in from a keypad telephone. More advanced pagers have screens that also can display letters, as keyed in from the keyboard of a computer connected via a modem or ISDN to the telephone network. Subscriptions can be arranged for reception of text information, such as news, stock market figures, foreign exchange rates and weather reports. Pagers and subscriptions for their use are sold in mobile communications shops, see under *Mobilkommunikasjon* in the Yellow Pages.

Phone cards (*telekort*) resemble plastic credit cards and are used to place calls at phones with international standard ☞ **Telephone keypads** that have asterisk * and hash mark # keys. There are several types of cards, differing according to:
- When you pay: prepaid (*forhåndsbetalt*) before calling or on credit (*kreditt*), against a bill (*faktura*).
- The phones used: all telephones (fixed and cellular mobile) or only public pay phones (*betalingstelefoner*) that accept cards (*kort-telefoner*)
- Where the call account is kept: in a memory chip

on the card ("smart card") or in a database at a specific telephone exchange ("remote memory")
- Period of use: the card is meant to be discarded after a prepaid amount is used up ("throwaway"), may be "recharged" with another prepaid amount, or offers continuous credit.

Three types of cards are available in Norway: prepaid smart cards, prepaid international cards and credit calling cards.

Prepaid smart card (*TeleKort*) Prepaid, payphone, throw-away smart card for use in any Norwegian card pay-phone. The Telenor *TeleKort* cards are sold with 22, 65 or 150 message units, by Narvesen newsagents, Mix kiosks, Post Offices, Government cafeterias (*Statens kantiner*), *Telehus* Telenor equipment shops and kiosks near card phones. More than 80% of the country's pay phones are now card phones; coin-box phones are in the minority. The faces of the cards feature photographs and artwork in designs that are frequently changed, so the cards have become collectable and are now sold at auctions. Telenor offers a service to card collectors, freephone ✆ 80031180.

Prepaid international phone card (*Reis og ring*) Prepaid, all-phone, throw-away ordinary card which may be used in any country supporting the service. This is a simple card of a type first used in 1974-76 in Italy and now common round the world. A card has a specified amount of prepaid call time, which you activate by scraping off a latex film to reveal a Personal Identity Number (PIN) code, just as you scrape the latex film off the play area of a lottery scratch card. Calls are placed by dialling a ☞ **Freephone** number and then keying in the PIN to get the dialling tone to place the call. Most cards are valid only to specified countries, usually listed on their reverse sides or in attachments to them. The cards are sold by kiosks, newsagents and other shops, and the more popular brands include GlobalOne, MCI, OnlineTelecom and Unitel.

Credit calling card (*TeleKonto*) Credit, allphone, continuous credit until its date of expiration, ordinary card which may be used in any country supporting the service. Calls are placed by dialling a freephone (800) number, waiting for a voice prompt, and then entering the PIN number to get a dialling tone to place a call. Voice prompts often are in English, but some companies offer a selection of languages. Bills for calls are sent regularly to subscribers, just as are ordinary phone bills for fixed-line telephone or cellular phone use. Some cards involve prepayment of calls and billing for each prepayment; they are sometimes called "rechargeable prepaid phone cards". In most cases, the cards are valid directly to a specified list of countries and sometimes to other countries using a ☞ **Callback** option. The Telenor TeleKonto card may be used in Norway and in 60 other countries, and calls made using it have voice prompts in Norwegian. For details, call freephone ✆ 80081088. Other companies offering cards in Europe include BT, FT, DT, MCI and OnlineTelecom.

Radio and TV broadcasting stations (*Kringkastingsstasjoner*) There are about 2,700 radio and TV broadcasting stations in Norway, most owned and operated by Norkring, the countrywide broadcasting service. Up to five radio channels and five TV channels are broadcast (see below):

The channels listed above are now technically called *terrestrial*, which means that they are broadcast by traditional wireless transmitters sending their signals through the atmosphere. This sets them apart from cable channels, which are wired, and from satellite channels which require special parabolic "dish" antennas for reception. However, most of the terrestrial broadcasting channels are also available via satellite at 1°W or via cable or both satellite and cable. An additional channel, TV3, is available via satellite or cable but is not broadcast. TV broadcasting is in the VHF (Very-High Frequency) Band I (48 – 68 MHz, Channels 2-4), VHF Band III (175-230 MHz, Channels 5-12), UHF (Ultra-High Frequency) Band IV (470-621 MHz) and UHF Band V (622-790 MHz,

Channels 40-60). FM broadcasting is in UHF Band II (87.5 – 108 MHz). In addition, there are six AM radio stations in the country, broadcasting in the Long, Medium and Short-Wave bands from transmitters in Bodø, Finnmark, Kvitsøy, Longyearbyen (Svalbard), Sveio and Vigra. As elsewhere in Europe except in France, TV broadcasting uses the PAL (Phase Alternating Line) colour system and digital NICAM (Near Instantaneous Companded Audio Multiplex) sound. All FM broadcasting is in stereo and all countrywide FM broadcasting includes RDS (Radio Data System) digital information that facilitates automatic tuning of radio receivers and presentation of station details on radios that have suitable displays. DAB (Digital Audio Broadcasting) is scheduled to be available in the southern part of the country in mid 1999 and countrywide by the year 2002. In addition to providing CD-quality audio, DAB channels carry programmes in Sámi and other minority languages, as well as round-the-clock classical music and news. Newspapers list daily and weekly overviews of Norwegian programmes, and in areas where they can be received, local newspapers also list Swedish, Danish or Finnish programs. Radio station frequencies and TV station channels are seldom listed in newspapers. However, there is a countrywide listing, *Kringkastingsstasjoner i Norge* ("Broadcasting stations in Norway") with tabulations of all stations and maps of their locations, published in a booklet available free from Norkring, ✆ 22893100, 🖷 22893200 and available at the Norkring web site: ⊕ http://www.norkring.no. Norkring also supports the countrywide helpline, ✆ 124; call it to report irregularities or failures of radio or TV broadcasting transmitters (but not satellite or cable channels, for

Channel	Service	Coverage	Programmes
NRK 1	TV	countrywide	General, news and entertainment
NRK 2	TV	countrywide	General, news and entertainment
TV 2	Commercial TV	95% countrywide	News and entertainment
TV Norge	Commercial TV	80% countrywide	Entertainment
Local TV	Commercial/Public TV	local	Local and district
NRK P1	FM radio	countrywide	General and district, 24 hour/day
NRK P2	FM radio	countrywide	Culture, 24 hour/day
NRK P3	FM radio	countrywide	Youth entertainment, 24 hour/day
P4	Commercial FM radio	countrywide	Entertainment, 24 hour/day
Local	Commercial FM radio	local	Entertainment and news

which you must cll their operators). To report interference or radio or TV noise, call the nearest office of *Radiostøykontrollen* ("Radio noise inspectorate") listed in the Pink Pages.

Satellite telephones (*Satellitt telefon*) In 1976, Norway became the first country in the world to implement satellite communications in its telephone network, for long-distance circuits between the mainland and the Svalbard archipelago in the Arctic. And in 1978, Norway was one of the first countries to implement satellite communications for ships, in the predecessor of the Inmarsat system. The Eik earth station, south of Stavanger on the west coast, now has the world's greatest volume of satellite communications traffic. The earth station at Nittedal, north of Oslo, is one of the leading stations in Europe in supplying VSAT-based business communications. NERA, a Norwegian company, is a world leader in building large satellite earth stations and in manufacturing mobile satellite communications terminals for use on land and at sea. Consequently, satellite communications are well developed and widespread. In fact, satellite communications are so commonplace that they are listed in Telenor telephone directories as an everyday service, available to users just as are cellular telephony and international direct-dialling. Users may now choose between two satellite communications systems, Inmarsat and Iridium. Inmarsat was so named as an acronym for International Maritime Satellite, because it was first developed to serve ships at sea. It became fully operational in 1982 and now uses four third-generation satellites spaced round the globe in the geostationary earth orbit (GEO) 35,786 km above the equator. In this orbit, the satellites travel eastward, or anti-clockwise as seen from the North Pole, and circle the earth once a day. So they appear still in the sky, which is why the orbit is called geostationary. The GEO is also used by broadcast satellites, such as those that provide satellite TV coverage. Communications to and from mobile terminals is in the 1,600 MHz band of frequencies. Small mobile terminals, about the size of a laptop computer, are now available; the world's smallest is made by NERA. You may buy a NERA marine or land mobile terminal and use it along with subscriber services supplied by Telenor Satellite Services (TSS), just as you can buy a telephone instrument and use it along with an ordinary telephone

subscriber line. Or, if you wish, you may you may subscribe to Mobiq, a satellite communications package including the NERA terminal of your choice and the subscription for its use, offered jointly by Telenor and British Telecom (BT). Iridium was so named because the original plan was to have 77 satellites (the number of electrons in an atom of the element Iridium) in low earth orbit (LEO) at an altitude of 780 km. Later, that number was reduced to 66, which, to be consistent in naming after the elements, would be Dysprosium. But the name Iridium was retained, and the system started operation in late 1998. Like Inmarsat, its terminals communicate to and from satellites in the 1,600 MHz band of frequencies. Unlike GEO satellites, LEO satellites travel across the sky, and at night they are visible in flares about as bright as the planet Venus. Because they move, communications are transferred between them, using technologies similar to those used in GSM mobile telephone systems when a mobile phone moves between adjacent cells. Because LEO satellites are far closer than GEO satellites, hand-held terminals can communicate with them. Two types of hand-held terminal are now available: a single-mode terminal that communicates only with Iridium satellites and a dual-mode terminal that works as a GSM 900 cellular telephone when within range of GSM stations, and automatically switches over to Iridium satellites when out of GSM range. Further details on Inmarsat and Iridium are available on the Internet at ⊛ http://www.inmarsat.org and at ⊛ http://www.iridium.com For details of the systems and the terminals available in Norway, see Inmarsat or Mobiq in the general information section of the Pink and White Pages of directories, or call Telenor Satellite Services or Telenor Mobil at the number listed in the Pink Pages, or view the Telenor web site at ⊛ http://www.telenor.no

Satellite TV broadcasting (*Satellitt kringkasting*) Over Europe, two types of geostationary satellites (see **Satellite telephones**) are used for TV broadcasting: higher-power Direct Broadcasting Satellites (DBS), and telecommunications satellites. Signals from the DBS are in the 11.7 – 12.5 GHz band and are intended primarily for reception directly by home viewers using parabolic 'dish' antennas. Signals from the telecommunications satellites are in the 10.95 – 11.2 GHz and 12.5 – 12.71 GHz bands and are intended primarily for reception by ground stations that distribute them further by cable, but they may also be received by suitably fitted home antennas. The 15 satellites whose signals can be received in Norway are listed in the following table.

Satellite	Position (degrees longitude)
Astra 1A, 1B, 1C, 1D & 1E	19.2°E
Eutelsat II-F1	13°E
Hot Bird I	13°E
Intelsat 707	1°W
Orion	37.5°W
Sirus	5°E
Thor I, II & III	1°W
TV-SAT	1°W

The Astra satellites, operated by Societe Europeenne des Satellites (SES) of Luxembourg and the Thor satellites, operated by Telenor of Norway, broadcast the most TV and radio programmes. As seen from Norway, the satellites appear at an elevation of 3° to 5° above the southern horizon. So to receive broadcasts, you must have clear view of the sky to the south toward the satellite of your choice. More than 100 TV and radio channels are available, at different frequencies, broadcasting systems and encoding. Some channels are free whilst there are charges for others. Various subscription schemes involving decoder purchase or rental and programme cards are offered. There are two satellite broadcasting companies, Telenor CTV, part of the Telenor telecommunications group of Norway (about 80 channels), and SF Vision, a subsidiary of the Bonniers media group of Sweden (about 30 channels). For companies that sell and install dish antennas and offer viewing subscriptions, see *Satellittanlegg, Antenner* or *Radio og TV* in the Yellow Pages. Equipment, channels, satellites and other aspects of broadcasting are covered in a satellite trade magazine, *Tele-satellite International*, which has articles in German and English and is available at newsagents and at
@ http://www.Tele-satellite.com.

Telecommunications charges (Telekom priser)

consist of installation (*tilkobling*), line rental (*faste avgifter*) and call charges (*samtaleavgifter*). Of three competing companies (see Telecommunications

companies), only Telenor can install or move a telephone line and rent it to a subscriber. All three, Telenor, Telia and Tele2 offer services on lines installed by and rented from Telenor. Call charges depend on the duration of a call in seconds, the time of day (8 am to 5 pm most expensive; 5 pm to 8 am least), day of the week (Monday-Friday most expensive; weekends least) and type of call: local rate (*lokaltakst*), regional (*innenfor landsdel*), domestic long-distance (*fjerntakst*), international (*til utlandet*) or to mobiles (*til mobil*). For Telenor installation, line rental and call charges, look under *Priser* in the general information section of the Pink and White pages directory. For Telia and Tele2 call charges, contact the companies at telephone numbers listed in the Pink Pages. In mid 1998, *Dine Penger* magazine published a comparative call charge survey in which Telenor was found cheapest for local calls, Telia cheapest for regional calls and Tele2 cheapest for domestic long-distance, international and to mobile calls. Because neither Telia nor Tele2 charge for initiating a subscription on a line already installed by Telenor, the survey concluded with the recommendation that cost-conscious users have subscriptions with all three companies.

Telecommunications companies (Telekommunikasjon)

As in other countries where telecommunications evolved as a government service, three groups of companies now compete.

A 'first operator' is either a government organisation or its privatised successor and usually still supplies the fixed-line connections to subscribers. In Norway, the first operator is **Telenor**, the successor of the Telecommunications Directorate (*Teledirektoratet*), privatised 1 January 1995 and now the country's seventh largest company, offering all telecommunications services.

A 'second operator' is a company permitted to compete with the government organisation in the initial privatisation of telecommunications. A 'third operator' is a company that comes in later to compete with the established first and second operators. In Norway, privatisation began in 1989 and telecommunications were completely de-regulated starting 1 January 1998. The result is that five companies now compete with Telenor.

Mobile phone use is similar for all companies who offer it, because each company operates its own base stations to provide the mobile connections. However, fixed-line use differs, because first-operator Telenor still installs the lines. There are two ways to access the fixed line services of the other four companies. You may subscribe and, when you dial a call, access services by first dialling a four-digit prefix. Or you may have a full subscription, in which you are connected by a "fixed preselect" (*fast forvalg*) feature, so you can dial numbers the four-digit prefixes. The five companies are listed below. For further information, contact them at numbers listed in the Pink Pages.

ElTele is a third operator of fixed-line services in six regions of the country: East and Oslo (*Øst*), Østfold, Hallingdal, Rogaland, West (*Vest*) and North (*Nord*) and principally offers high-capacity fibreoptic network services for corporate communications. It was established in 1996 and is owned by several Norwegian electricity companies and by France Telecom. The ElTele prefix is 1505.

GlobalOne is a third operator of fixed-line services, including business communications. It was established in 1996 and is part of the international Global One organisation backed by Deutsche Telekom, France Telecom and Sprint. The GlobalOne prefix is 1501.

NetCom is the second operator for GSM digital cellular telephone. It was established in 1993 and is an affiliate of NetCom Systems of Sweden, which is part owner, along with companies in Norway, the USA and Singapore. It offers all GSM digital cellular telephone services throughout the country and now has about a third of the total market.

Tele2Norge, the Norwegian subsidiary of NetCom Systems of Sweden, which also operates Tele2 in Denmark and Sweden. Tele2 was established in Norway in 1995 as the third operator of fixed-line services, including Internet. The Tele2 prefix is 1502.

Telia, the privatised successor of the Swedish Telecommunications Directorate, established in Norway in 1995 as the second operator of fixed-line services, including Internet, and in mid 1999 as the third operator of GSM digital cellular telephone. The Telia prefix is 1516.

Just as this book went to press in late 1999, Telenor and Telia merged, and the effect of the merger on services to subscribers had not yet been made known to the public.

Telecommunications numbers Almost all telephone numbers, including those for telefax terminals and computers connected via modem or ISDN line to access Internet servers, have eight digits [there are no national destination or "area" codes]. There are two exceptions:
- three-digit emergency and helpline numbers starting with 1, as 110 fire and 180 enquires.
- five-digit short numbers starting with 0 and in range 02000-09999, principally for businesses requiring countrywide numbers.

The eight digits of most numbers are most often written in groups of two digits: NN NN NN NN NN or in a three-three-two grouping: NNN NNN NN [N is a number, 0-9, except that the first N cannot be 0 or 1.] The national prefix for Norway is 47, which is written with a plus sign, +47, ahead of the eight-digit number. Many European countries now use a double zero to access an international number, so from abroad, a Norwegian number most often is dialled 0047 NN NN NN NN. The prefixes for the public telephone, data and telex networks in the Nordic countries are:

Country	Telephone	Data	Telex
Denmark	45	238	55
Finland	358	244	57
Iceland	354	274	501
Norway	47	242	56
Sweden	46	240	54

Prefixes for countries world-wide are listed in the telephone, data communications and telex directories. Within the country, the initial digits of eight-digit telephone and telefax numbers are assigned to counties.

Telefax (*Telefaks*) Any fixed or mobile telephone connection may also be used for telefax communications. Telefax terminals communicate using one of four Groups, which are protocols, or rules for transmission. The older Group 1, which transmitted a page in about six minutes, and Group 2, which transmitted a page in about three minutes, are obsolete and no longer available. Group 3, which transmits a page in about one minute via a conventional analogue telephone line, is now the most used. Group 4, which transmits a page in a few seconds via an ☞

Svalbard 790

Finnmark
78

Troms
77

Nordland
75, 76

Nord-Trøndelag 74

Møre og Romsdal
70, 71

Sør-Trøndelag
72, 73

Hedmark
62

og Fjordane
57

Oppland
61

Hordaland
53, 55, 56

Buskerud
31, 32

Akershus
63, 64, 66, 67

Oslo 22, 23

Telemark
35

Østfold 69

Aust-Agder
37

Vest-Agder
38

Vestfold 33

52

*Initial digits
assigned by
counties.
Source:
Telenor Media*

Telephone (*Telefon*) Norway is among the leading ten countries in the world in the number of telephones compared to its population, with just 1.8 people per telephone line, only slightly more than the United States (1.6 people per line), Sweden (1.5) and first-place Bermuda (1.4). Three ☞ **telecommunications companies** compete in supplying services, but only one of them, Telenor actually installs telephone lines; for further information on installation, call Telenor *Kundeservice* ✆ 140. Both conventional analogue and digital ☞ **ISDN** lines are available. A telephone brought in from another country may be used only if it meets the requirements of the ☞ **Norwegian Post and Telecommunications Authority**. Some older dial telephones are still in use, but are no longer sold, because the ☞ **telephone keypad** now is standard. Telephones are sold upon installation by Telenor as well as by other ☞ **telecommunications equipment** (Electrical and Electronics Goods chapter) shops.

Telephone and telefax directories (*telefon/telefax-katalog*) The telephone and telefax directories are published by Telenor Media. The telephone directory is divided into the White Pages (*Hvitesider*) listing of private subscribers by surname, the Pink Pages (*Rosasider*) A-to-Å (A-to-Z plus three additional letters, Ø, Æ, Å) listing of public and private sector businesses and organisations by registered name and the Yellow Pages (*Gulesider*) classified and indexed listing of businesses and organisations. Listings are alphabetical, by surname or company name, then by first name(s), title or occupation, address, post code and telephone number. For directory assistance, call 180 for national numbers or 181 for international numbers. Further details on directory use are given in English, German, French and Spanish in the general information section of the Pink and White Page directory. There are 12 numbered regional directories. Most are in two parts, the alphabetical Pink and White Pages and the classified Yellow Pages, but less populous areas may have a combined directory. The numbered regions and initial digits of numbers listed are: 1 Oslo (22 & 23), 2 Akershus (63, 64, 66 & 67), 3 Østfold (69), 4 Hedmark (62) and Oppland (61), 5 Buskerud (31 & 32) and Vestfold (33), 6 Telemark (35), Aust-Agder (37) and Vest-Agder (38), 7 Rogaland (51 & 52), 8 Hordaland (53, 55 & 56), 9

ISDN line, is now replacing Group 3, though terminals for it are more expensive. A telefax terminal purchased abroad may be used only if it meets the requirements of the ☞ **Norwegian Post and Telecommunications Authority**. Mains and telephone line connectors vary from country to country, so telefax terminals brought into Norway should also should be checked for compatibility with the mains power points and telephone line jacks. A separate line and number for a telefax terminal is preferable to a fax/phone switch connected to the same line as a telephone, particularly if telefaxes are to be received from abroad. This is because telefax protocols include waiting times, which are sufficient to cope with the delays in most international connections, but may be exceeded if a fax/phone switch introduces further delay.

Sogn & Fjordane (57) and Møre & Romsdal (70 & 71), 10 Sør-Trøndelag (72 & 73) and Nord-Trøndelag (74), 11 Nordland (75 & 76) and 12 Troms (77), Finnmark (78) and Svalbard (790). There is one telefax catalog for the country, with an alphabetical listing of subscribers. The 12 Pink and White Pages directories are also available on a CD-ROM that is updated four times a year and is sold at book shops. The Yellow Pages are available on-line at ☺ http://www.gulesider.no (see page 396).

Telephone keypad (*telefon tastatur*) The international standard keypad recommended by the International Telecommunications Union (ITU) is used throughout the country, on all telephone instruments, mobile telephones and telefax terminals, as well as on other devices for keying in numbers, such as ATM and credit-card verification terminals. It has ten number keys and two symbol keys, as shown below. The number keys do not have letters, as do the keys of the North American version of the international standard keypad. The keypads of some models of telefax terminals and digital telephone instruments have letters to facilitate keying in information for alphanumeric display. Because these letters are not used for dialling, their arrangement may or may not agree with that of the North American keyboard. So if you call a number in North America that is listed by its letters only, you will need to know the letter positions on the standard keypad. They are: ABC on 2, DEF on 3, GHI on 4. JKL on 5. MNO on 6, PRS on 7, TUV on 8 and WXY on 9; there is no Q or Z.

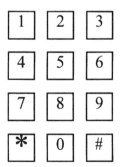

International standard touch-tone keypad (adapted from ITU-T Recommendation Q.23, 1988).

TV Licence fee (*NRK lisens*) As in other European countries, the governmentally-owned Norwegian Broadcasting Corporation (*Norsk Rikskringkasting – NRK*) levies an annual license fee on all households using a television set. A VCR with a TV receiver function counts as a television set. The licence fee must be paid in advance for six months at a time, and is due 1 March and 1 September or 1 May and 1 November, depending on where you live in the country. A television set is subject to the licence fee from and including the month of its purchase or import to Norway, as household goods. No reductions are granted for less than six months use or for lack of use due to mains failure or television set failure. A household may have more than one television set registered for one licence, including a television set at a temporary second home, such as a summer cottage., without paying another licence. If you are not registered with a licence and buy a new television set, tell the shop when you purchase it. An application form will be submitted for you along with notification of its sale. If you buy a used television set or bring one into the country, you must apply for a licence to the Licence Office: NRK Lisenskontoret, ☞ PO Box 600, 8601 Mo i Rana, ✆ 75122250. You may pay your licence fee via ☞ **Giro** (Banking, Finance, Insurance chapter), and once you have a licence, you will receive a notice of payment due, with a giro form attached, a month in advance of the due date. A surcharge is added for late payment, and a licence not paid within one month of its due date is subject to debt collection (*innkasso*) and the charges it incurs. Non-payment of a licence fee is a misdemeanour, subject to fine. Nonetheless, an estimated 12% of all television sets in the country are without licence. Throughout the country, some 55 licence controllers visit users to verify licences and who have technical equipment to detect sets in use. For further details, contact the Licence Office, which has brochures in Norwegian and in English, or view the NRK web site for licences ☺ http://www.nrk.no/info/publik

Television standards (*TV standard*) Norwegian television, like that of other western European countries, except France, uses the PAL (Phase Alternating Line) system. So TV receivers brought in from the American continent and in Japan and other Asian countries, which use the NTSC (National Television

System Committee) standard or from France or some eastern European countries, which use the SECAM (*Sequential Couleur Avec Memorie*) system cannot be used. There are two reasons for this. First, the way of encoding the signals that make up the TV picture differ between the three systems. Second, the NTSC system, first implemented in 1953 in the USA, has 30 picture frames per second, compatible with the 60 Hz mains frequency, whilst the PAL and SECAM systems, first implemented in Europe in the 1960s, have 25 frames per second, compatible with the 50 Hz mains frequency of Europe. TV receivers brought in from a country using the PAL systems can be used, although some may need adjustment to suit the versions of PAL used in the Norwegian VHF and UHF TV bands.

Videos and VCRs (*Video*) Video cassettes from abroad may not always play on VCRs (Video Cassette Recorders) in Norway, and Norwegian video cassettes may not play on VCRs abroad. This is because there are three methods of transmitting and recording colour television signals: NTSC (National Television Standards Committee) developed in 1953 in the USA and now used in North America and many Asian countries, including Japan, PAL (Phase Alternating Line) developed in the early 1960s and widely used in Europe, except in France, and SECAM (*Sequential Couleur Avec Memoire*) developed in the early 1960s and used in France and some countries in the Middle East. There are two principal ways of recording TV programs on the magnetic tape in cassettes: VHS (Video Home System), developed in 1976 by JVC and Matsushita of Japan and now used worldwide, and Betamax, developed in 1975 by Sony of Japan, and now obsolete, though a professional version, Betacam is used in broadcasting and high-qual-

ity professional TV recording. Throughout most of Europe, including Norway, video cassettes and VCRs use VHS recording of PAL colour. There are two ways of playing cassettes not compatible with PAL VHS. First and usually cheapest, many video conversion specialists, in or near larger cities, can convert and copy between the various systems; see under *Videokonvertering* in the Yellow Pages. Second, starting in the late 1980s, some VCRs implemented for PAL VHS also have features that permit them to play NTSC or SECAM VHS cassettes; check features upon buying.

Video conferencing (*Videokonferanse*) is the telecommunications service that links two or more places together using audio and video to replace face-to-face meetings. There are two major types of video conferencing systems: group and desktop. Group systems connect fixed conference room studios to each other. For instance, Telenor offers various sizes of video conferencing studios, accommodating two to twenty persons, in all major cities and many larger towns. For further details and reservations, call the number listed for *Telenor Bedrift* in the Pink Pages. Moreover, Telenor Satellite Services (TSS) operates the *Norsat* satellite communications system, part of which provides private networks, including video conferencing, for businesses and other high-volume telecommunications users; see *Telenor Satellite Systems* in the Pink Pages. Desktop systems use computers or video monitors and cameras, microphones and relevant software to connect different places via local area networks (LANs) or the Internet. Several companies sell or lease the equipment and software, see *Videokonferanseutstyr* in the Yellow Pages.

Trades (*Håndverk*)

About the trades (*Om håndverk*) Craftsmen (*håndverkere*) practise their trades as they do in other countries. Their certification and titles are regulated by law. A person begins in the trades as an apprentice (*svenn*), and, after acquiring the basic skills, can gain certification by examination (*svenneprøv*). The craft certificate permits the apprentice to work with a master (*mester*). After having had a craft certificate and having worked at the craft for two years, the apprentice may stand an examination for master (*mesterprøv*), which includes a test of skills in leadership, marketing and finance, in addition to capabilities in the craft involved. A succefully passed examination confers a master certificate (*Mesterbrev*). With the master certificate, the craftsman can operate independently in the craft, start a business offering services in the craft and use the title *mester*, such as *snekkermester* ("Master joiner") and the master seal, which is round and has three hammers inside a gear with the word *MESTER* underneath. For further information, contact the Master Certificate Council (*Mesterbrevnemnda*) ✆ 23088000, ✍ 23088001, ✉ PO Box 5250 Majorstua, 0303 Oslo, ⊕ http://www.mesterbrevnemnda.no

Carpenters (*Snekkere*) There are two principal trades in carpentry and woodworking: structural carpenters (*tømrere*), who work on buildings, and joiners (*snekkere*), who make furniture and light woodwork. The trades overlap: structural carpenters are also called *bygningssnekkere* ("structural joiners"), and specific woodworking trades have their own names: cabinet makers are called *møbelsnekkere*. You can find all these trades listed under *Bygningssnekkere og tømere* or *snekkertjenester* in the Yellow Pages.

Electricians (*Elektrikere*) Traditionally, the electrical trades have been divided into two groups: *sterkstrøm* ("electrical power") and *svakstrøm* ("electronics"). The two terms are still used in everyday speech and in electrical contractor advertisements. However, more specific terms now are commonplace in describing the work electricians perform, including *boligbygg* ("residences"), *kontorbygg* ("offices"), *industrianlegg* ("industrial buildings"), *datasystemer* ("computer systems"), *telekommunikasjon* ("telecommunictions") and *brannalarmer* ("fire alarms"). You can find electrical contractors listed under *Elektroentrepenører* in the Yellow Pages.

Locksmiths (*Låsesmed*) can be found under *låser and låsesmedtjenester* ("locks and locksmith services") in the Yellow Pages. They offer services from simply opening your home or car if you've locked your keys in, repairs after burglaries, supplying safety locks and cutting copies of keys. Most instant ☞ **shoe repair** outlets cut keys too.

Masons (*Murere*) Traditionally, masons have been tradesmen who built with stone. However, most masons now work with more modern materials, and those who work with stone are called *steinhoggere* ("stone masons"). There are specialities within the services provided by masons, including fireplace building (*peismuring*), foundation wall building (*grunnmuring*) and tiling (*flislegging*). You can find masons listed under *Murmestere og murere* in the Yellow Pages.

Painters (*Malere*) who paint buildings are distinguished from artists, who are called *kunstmalere* ("art painters"). Most painters offer interior and exterior painting services (*malertjenester*). Specialist painters (*dekorasjonsmalere*) may offer sign painting, decorative painting and theatre scene painting. You can find painters listed under *Malertjenester* in the Yellow Pages.

Plumbers (*Rørlegere*) are in the *VVS (Vann, Varme og Sanitær)* sector of the building trades. *VVS* translates literally to "Water, Heating and Sanitation" and is equivalent to the "HP" of HPAC (Heating, Piping and Air Conditioning) in English, but without the air conditioning, which is a separate field in Norway. So plumbers work with all household plumbing, including water supply, sewage and water-borne heating, as from a furnace (*sentralfyr*). Accordingly they are listed under *Rørinstallasjon – varme og sanitær* ("Piping installation – heating and sanitation") in the Yellow Pages. Many plumbing firms provide complete services for building and rebuilding bathrooms and laundry rooms, collectively called "wet rooms" (*våtrom*), which require specific sealing methods and wall and floor construction techniques according to the "wet-room standard" (*Byggbransjens våtrom-*

snorm – BVN). Countrywide in homes, the damage caused each year by water leakage and moisture penetration from older and substandard bathrooms costs as much as do fire damages. For homeowners, these water damages are costly, because home insurance covers sudden pipe breaks but not damages that accumulate over time. Consequently, hiring a properly-qualified professional plumber to build or rebuild a bathroom or laundry usually saves money in the long term. Many VVS firms now offer a ten-year quality guarantee (*kvalitetsgaranti*) for complete building or rebuilding of a "wet room". For further details on the VVS Kvalitetsgaranti or for other plumbing matters, contact the plumbing trades information centre, *VVS Informasjon* ℅ 23084280, ✆ 23084281, ✉ PO Box 6726 Rødderløkka, 0503 Oslo, ✉ vvsinfo@online.no, ⊛ http://www.vvsinformasjon.no

Shoe repair (*Skoreperasjon*) There are very few traditional shoemakers (*skomakere*) who will make shoes to order as well as repair footwear and other leather goods. However, there are many shoe repair services, often combined with key making (*sko-reperasjon & nøkkelservice*) or with dry cleaning (*rens & sko*) services. The word *flikk* ("patch") in the name of a shoe repair shop indicates that it has a while-you-wait service for heels and other small repairs. You can find shoe repair shops listed under *Sko-reperasjon* in the Yellow Pages.

Tinsmiths (*Blikkenslagere*) provide services for cladding, guttering and other exterior as well as interior metalwork on buildings. Tinsmiths now work almost exclusively with galvanised steel, though many work with other metals. Those who work with copper are known as coppersmiths (*kobberslagere*). Those who specialise in roofing are said to offer *tak-tekkingstjenester*. You can find tinsmiths and coppersmiths listed under *Blikk- og kobberslagertjenester* in the Yellow Pages.

Travel and transport
(*Reise og transport*)

Air travel (*Flyreiser*) The direct airline distance from the country's southernmost airport at Lista to its northernmost at Mehamn is as long as from Lista to Rome. The coastline is the second longest in Europe, after Russia, and the interior is mountainous. Geography and topography combine to favour air travel. Though 29th in population in Europe, Norway ranks 8th in passenger arrivals and departures at its airports. It is a nation of air travellers.

Air travel tax (*Avgift på flyging*) is an excise duty on the carriage of passengers by air. It popularly called "seat tax" (*seteavgift*) because it is charged per passenger seat. In March 1998 it was set at:
- NOK 106 per seat for travel from Norwegian airports to destinations abroad.
- NOK 53 per seat for travel between Oslo and four other cities: Bergen, Kristiansand, Stavanger and Trondheim.

Complete details are available on-line at the Customs and Excise web site
- http://www.woll.no/engelsk/S-14-fly-eng with pages in English.

Airlines (*Flyselskaper*) Four airlines based in Norway offer scheduled domestic and international services. For information and schedules, see the English or Norwegian versions of the web sites listed below or call the numbers listed in the Pink Pages or under *Flyselskaper* in the Yellow Pages for the airlines. Most travel bureaux stock schedules, and a single booklet, *Flyruter i Norge* (Airline routes in Norway) lists all domestic flights.

Braathens started as the subsidiary of a shipping company, Braathens SAFE (South American and Far East), and is now the leading competitor to SAS on domestic routes, principally between cities. Braathens has international routes, and in an alliance with KLM and Northwest, it offers connections to more than 400 destinations world-wide
- http://www.braathens.no

Coast Air operates a fleet of five turboprop aircraft and serves domestic routes between west-coast cities as well as one international route, between Haugesund and Aberdeen, Scotland
- http://www.coastair.no

SAS (Scandinavian Airlines) was founded in 1946 when Danish, Norwegian and Swedish domestic airlines amalgamated to start international services. Now SAS, together with Air Canada, Air New Zealand, Ansett Australia, Lufthansa, Thai, Varig, United Airlines and (from October 1999) All Nippon Airways, is a member of the Star Alliance network that covers more than 720 destinations in 110 countries. SAS serves domestic routes between cities in Norway and carries the bulk of the inter-Scandinavian traffic in the Oslo-Copenhagen-Stockholm triangle - http://www.sas.no and
- http://www.star-alliance.com

Widerøe started in the 1930s with taxi and ambulance flights, training and aerial photography; an affiliate, Fjellanger-Widerøe now leads in aerial photography. Scheduled passenger services began in the 1950s, to seaplane ports in the north. Widerøe now serves 39 destinations countrywide, including STOL (Short Take Off and Landing) ports, and destinations abroad - http://www.wideroe.no

The international airlines offering scheduled services between Norwegian gateway airports and destinations abroad include: Aeroflot, Air France, Alitalia, British Airways, CSA Czech Airlines, Delta, Finnair, Gulf Air, Iberia, Icelandair, KLM, LOT, Lufthansa, Maersk, Malév, Pakistan International, Royal Air Maroc, Sabena, Singapore, Swissair and TAP.

Airports (*Lufthavn*) Some 55 airports serve more than 27 million domestic and international scheduled airline flight passengers per year and are located near all major cities and towns on the mainland as well as on Spitzbergen in the Svalbard arctic archipelago. Oslo's Gardermoen airport is the country's newest and is the major international gateway, but other airports, including those at Bergen and Stavanger, also serve international flights. All airports have ample car parks and taxi ranks, and most have car hire services. The five major airports, their locations relative to the centres of the cities they serve and the public ground transport services available are:
- Bergen: Flesland, 19 km to the south, bus service.
- Oslo: Gardermoen, 51 km to the northeast, bus and airport express train service.
- Stavanger: Sola, 14 km to the southwest, bus service.

- Tromsø: Langnes, 5 km to the west, bus service.
- Trondheim: Værnes, 32 km to the east, bus service.

The location of Gardermoen well away from Oslo follows the general trend of locating new airports far from cities. Many other capital city airports are equally far from city centres: Arlanda is 40 km north of Stockholm, Sweden; Keflavik is 51 km west of Reykjavik, Iceland; Narita is 66 km east of Tokyo, Japan; Chaing Kai-Shek International is 40 km from Taipei, Taiwan; and Dulles International is 43 km west of Washington, DC, USA.

B&B (*overnatting med frokost*) is available at campsites (*campinplasser*), farms (*bondegårder*), fisherman's shacks (*rorbuer*), hotels (*hoteller*), holiday homes and cabins (*feriehus og hytter*), holiday resorts (*feriesenterer*) and youth hostels (*vandrerhjem*). Ask at your local tourist information office (*turistkontoret*) for detailed information about the B&B possibilities in the area you wish to visit, look for their telephone number in the Pink Pages. Alternatively use the Internet specifying '*overnatting med frokost*'.

Boat travel (*Båtreiser*) is common, in part because Norway has Europe's second-longest coastline (after Russia) and a tradition of some ten centuries of seafaring. Many highways, particularly along the west coast, include car ferry (*bilferge*) connections. Scheduled passenger ships (*rutebåter*) provide services along the coast and on inland waters. Larger ferry liners (*ferger*), mostly on international routes, carry cars and trucks on ro-ro ("roll-on, roll-off") decks and passengers in cabins and, for the budget-minded, reclining seats, and usually have restaurants, cafeterias, duty-free shopping and entertainment, particularly on overnight sailings. The principal companies are listed below, with company booking numbers (you may also book at travel agencies):

- Color Line, the largest ferry liner company, serves Oslo-Kiel, Oslo-Hirsthals, Kristiansand-Hirsthals, Bergen-Stavanger-Newcastle and Larvik-Fredrikshavn, as well as Larvik-Fredrikshavn under the Color Scandi Line name ✆ booking 81000811, ⊕ http://www.colorline.com with pages in Norwegian and in English and featuring on-line booking.
- DFDS Seaways, a Danish line serving Oslo-Helsinborg-Copenhagen, Kristiansand-Gothenberg and Kristiansand-Newcastle ✆ booking 22419090, ⊕ http://www.scansea.com with pages in Danish, English, German and Norwegian.
- Fjord Line serving Bergen-Haugesund-Stavanger-Newcastle and Bergen-Egersund-Hanstholm ✆ booking 55548800 Bergen, 51494900 Egersund 52726799 Haugesund or 51843450 Stavanger, ⊕ http://www.fjordline.no with pages in Norwegian and in English.
- Fylkesbaatane i Sogn og Fjordane serving Bergen-Sogn and Bergen-Nordfjord, as well as ferries in Sogn ✆ booking 55907070, ⊕ http://www.fylkesbaatene.no with pages in Norwegian, English, French and German.
- HSD serving the west coast, principally around Bergen ✆ booking 55596400, ⊕ http://www.hsd.no with pages in Norwegian and in English
- Hurtigruten, the scenic west coast express line from Bergen around the North Cape to Kirkenes, owned by Ofotens og Vesteraalens Dampskibsselskab ✆ booking 76967696, and Troms Fylkes Dampskipsselskap ✆ booking 77648200, one web site ⊕ http://www.hurtigruten.com with pages in Norwegian and in English.
- Møre og Romsdals Fylkesbåter, the largest domestic ferry services operator with 30 routes along the west coast ✆ 71219501 , ⊕ http://www.mrf.no
- Stena Line, a Swedish line serving Oslo-Fredrikshavn ✆ booking 23179000, ⊕ http://www.stenaline.com with pages in Swedish and in English and booking in Danish, Dutch, English, German, Norwegian and Swedish.

Bus travel (*Bussreise*) Buses account for about 1% of all motor vehicles in the country and carry about 7% of all passenger traffic, some 4.5 billion passenger-kilometres a year. Aside from the buses of ☞ **public transport** systems in and around the cities, buses operate on routes interconnecting almost all cities and towns throughout the country, as well as destinations abroad.

More than 20 "Train-Bus" (*TogBuss*) routes serve railway stations with co-ordinated schedules that conveniently extend ☞ **train travel**; their schedules are included in train timetables.

Intercity express buses usually are modern, air-conditioned coaches, many equipped with toilets and warm drink dispensers, and some with passenger telephones. *NOR-WAY Bussekspress*, the leading long-distance bus service, operates more than 250 buses on a network of express routes extending as far north as Namsos and offers a customer card (*kundekort*) useful for frequent travellers. For information and schedules, contact the head office in Oslo ✆ 81544444, ✉ http://www.nor-way/no with pages in Norwegian and in English. Europe's longest bus route, more than 2000 km long, connects Oslo and Hammerfest via Sweden and Finland, and is trafficked by a bus company in Alta in Finnmark county, fittingly named Express 2000 ✆ 78444090, ✉ http://sarah.trollnet.no/express 2000/html.

There are eight airport express bus routes (*Flybussekspressen*) serving the Gardermoen gateway airport, from Asker, Bekkestua, Drammen, Fredrikstad, Hamar, Hønefoss, Kongsvinger, Oslo downtown, Sarpsborg and Ski and points in between. For schedules and prices, call *Flybussekspressen* at the above number for *Nor-Way Bussekspress*.

For other bus services, call the companies listed under *Rutebiler* in the Yellow Pages or call the local bus terminal, such as *Busstasjon* in Bergen ✆ 55559090, *Bussterminalen* in Oslo ✆ 23002400 and *Buss-senteret* in Trondheim ✆ 73965500.

Containers (*Containere*) are large, rectangular metal receptacles for the transport of goods, designed to be transferable from one form of transport to another. You may use one in moving your household possessions, as ☞ **Removals** (Arriving, Settling, Leaving chapter) are increasingly containerised, particularly whenever transport by sea is involved. There are two standard sizes of container, 20-foot and 40-foot. The 20-foot container is just over 6 metres long, has a capacity of 30 cubic metres and weighs about 2.2 tons empty. All national and international containerised transport is measured in terms of Twenty-foot Equivalent Units (TEU). The 40 foot container is equal to 2 TEU, is just over 12 metres long, has a capacity of 60 cubic metres and weighs about 3.8 tons empty. The purpose-built ships that carry containers are called LO-LO ships (for "Lift-on, Lift-off"). There are several specialised ports (*container-havn*) for containers, and there are extensive land transport facilities for them, including by rail (*container-tog*) and road (*container-bil*).

Cycling (*Sykling*) is popular, despite the northerly climate of the country. Traffic experts estimate that one in twenty commuters travels by cycle, sometimes year-round: in Trondheim, fully a third of summertime cyclists also cycle through the harsh winter. There are more than 2,000 km of cycle and pedestrian pathways (*gang- og sykkelveier*) along the national roads, or about one kilometer for every 14 km of road. The cities of Drammen, Oslo, Sandnes, Stavanger and Trondheim have cycle lanes (*sykkelfelt*) in many downtown streets. In city suburbs, commuter rail stations have cycle racks, as do many larger companies and public agencies. There are no accurate figures on the number of cyclists in the country, though Oslo is estimated to have some 300 thousand, or close to half as many as the population of its urban area. Many cycles are used only on pleasure trips, and almost all woodland recreation areas have cycle paths and maps.

If you cycle regularly, you may wish to have copies of the countrywide Cycle Norway (*Sykkel-Norge*) compilation of 12 tour maps, as well as the Tunnel Guide for Cyclists (*Tunnelguide for syklister*), both in Norwegian and English and published by the ☞ **Public roads administration** (Cars, Roads, Traffic chapter) for free distribution.

If you cycle in traffic, you must obey the rules for motor vehicles and may cycle along all roads except those marked with a round sign with a red ring and diagonal slash on a white background with a black drawing of a cycle, meaning "cycling prohibited" (*forbudt for syklende*). Unless prohibited locally, you may cycle pedestrian pavements (*fortau*), provided that you give way to pedestrians and are cautious in cycling near them. However, if you cross a street or road at a zebra crossing (*fotgjengerovergang*), you must act as a pedestrian and be on foot: you must get off the cycle and wheel it across, as cycling there is prohibited.

Doors and stop signals on transport vehicles (*dører, kollektivtrafikk*) Bus drivers manually control bus doors. Bus or tram passengers signal wish to alight at the next stop by pulling a cord or pushing a button, most often labelled *stopp*, which triggers illumination of a red sign near the driver reading *stopp* or *stopper* (will stop) or of roof-mounted red lamps. If the sign or lamps are lit as you approach a stop, you need not signal. Doors on trams and commuter train carriages are usually controlled at stops from the outside by push buttons beside the door, labelled *Døråpner* (Door opener); pushing the button opens the door. From the inside, these doors are usually controlled by pairs of push buttons, one red labelled *åpne* (open) and one black labelled *lukke* (close). Some exit doors on older trams in Oslo are opened at stops by pushing hand rails fitted on their inner sides. Through train carriages have a variety of door opening mechanisms. Older carriages have mechanical lever handles that will open the doors of a stopped train. Newer carriages have levers or *døråpner* push buttons on the outside and pairs of red *åpne* (open) and black *lukke* (close) push buttons on the inside to control doors.

Duty-free quotas (*Toll- og avgiftsfri innførsel*)
Upon entering the country from abroad you need not pay duty on limited amounts of goods brought with you, provided that:
- You hand carry the goods, as through the "green channel" at an airport, or have them with you, as in the boot of your car. You cannot send duty-free goods in unaccompanied baggage, unless you claim it before clearing customs.
- The total value of the goods is no more than NOK 2,000 if you have been out of the country less than 24 hours, or no more than NOK 5,000 if you have been out of the country longer. You cannot claim duty free for an item costing more than NOK 2,000 (or 5,000); you cannot "divide" it up between several trips or several persons.

There are four groups of quotas:
- Liquor, wine and tobacco (*brennevin, vin og tobakksvarer*): If you are 18 or older, you may bring in up to two litres of beer (2.5% or more alcohol) and up to two litres of wine or fortified wine (up to 22% alcohol). You may also bring in up to 200 cigarettes, 250 g of other tobacco products and 200 RYO (roll-your-own) cigarette papers if you are a resident of a European country, or double those amounts if you are a resident of a country outside Europe. If you are 20 or older, you may substitute one litre of liquor (up to but not more than 60% alcohol) for one of the two litres of the wine quota. If you are a resident of Norway, you must have been out of the country for more than 24 hours to bring goods in duty-free, or you must show a receipt to prove that

you bought them with full duty paid in Denmark, Finland or Sweden.
- Sugar, chocolate and sweets (*Sukker, sjokolade og sukkervarer*): Up to 5 kg of sugar and up to 1 kg of chocolate or sweets.
- Fuel (*drivstoff*): Up to the normal amount in a vehicle tank, though not more than 200 l, or up to 600 l for a vehicle registered to carry nine or more persons. Private motorcycles and motor vehicles can also carry a spare tank (*reservekanne*) of up to 10 l, but have no more than 200 l total.
- Other goods (*andre varer*), including repairs made to a motor vehicle.

These regulations may change, so always check quotas before departing; a comprehensive Norway Customs leaflet is available at all international airports, ports and border crossings. Duty-free shops abroad also have lists of the current quotas. If you shop ☞ **duty-free** (Shopping chapter) on land in or on a ferry from Denmark, Finland or Sweden on your way to Norway, you will be allowed to buy no more than your duty-free quota.

Helicopter services (*Helikoptertjenester*) are available throughout the country. In some cases, as transport between land and North Sea platforms, the only practical way to travel is by helicopter. You can find helicopter services listed under *Helikoptertjenester* in the Yellow Pages.

The Helicopter Services Group of Norway is one of the world's leading operators and the largest in terms of annual turnover. It comprises Helikopter Service in Stavanger, Bond Helicopters in the UK, Lloyd Helicopters in Australia and Court Helicopters in South Africa. It provides helicopter services in Norway, Sweden, the United Kingdom, Ireland, Ausralia, the Philippines, Thailand, South Africa, Angola, Nigeria and Namibia. Its main activity is helicopter support to the offshore oil and gas industry. It also operates ambulance and rescue services. For further information, call local services listed in under Helikopter Service, or its subsidiary, Lufttransport AS in the Pink Pages. The head office is in Oslo ✆ 22423270, 🖷 22424001, ✉ PO Box 531 Sentrum, 0105 Oslo, ⊕ http://www.hesgrp.com with pages in English.

Hotels (*hoteller*) can be found in the Yellow Pages under *hoteller og andre overnattingssteder* ("Hotels and other overnight lodgings"). Most of the international and Scandinavian hotel chains have hotels and motels in the larger cities, and most chains now have central booking services which you may call at numbers listed in the Yellow Pages.

Lifts (*Heiser*) Up to the 1950s, there were few lifts in the country, principally because there were few buildings higher than four storeys. Thereafter, taller blocks of flats, office complexes, hotels and other buildings were built, and more lifts were installed. There are now more than 27,000 lifts (*heiser*), escalators (*rulletrapp*) and moving pavements or travelators (*rulle-fortau*) in the country. Designs now conform to international European standards, and there are many modern variations, such as the glass-enclosed lift cars (*heisstoler*) fitted to the inside walls of multi-storey shopping malls. However, many older lifts lack modern features, such as centre-opening two-leaf doors and an inner door on the lift car in addition to an outer lift shaft door on each floor (*etasjedør*). Moreover, a vintage Norwegian semi-automatic lift control system is still in use, principally for lifts in older blocks of flats that have not yet been modernised. Its control buttons are not for your wishes for lift use, but for directions to the lift. Pushing the *Ned* ("Down") button does not bring the lift so you may descend, but rather sends it all the way down to the ground floor. The button to press, if you wish to go up or down, is marked *Hit* ("Here"). When the lift is in motion, a signal lamp marked *I Fart* ("In Motion") will light, indicating that the lift is obeying your command. These older lifts will remain in use as long as they are safe, but will be phased out with newer lifts as buildings are remodelled. Lifts, escalators and travelators in most municipalities are subject to monitoring and inspection by the Norwegian Lift Inspection Foundation (*Norsk Heiskontroll – HHK*), which also acts as a central resource centre for all relevant national and international information ✆ 22965950, ✆ 22608570, ✉ PO Box 99 Blindern, 0314 Oslo.

Public transport (*Kollektivtrafikk*) is extensive in all urban areas. All cities have public transport services that operate buses within the city and on commuter lines to and from it. Oslo also has trams (*trikk*) and an underground (*T-bane*). ☞**Train travel** includes commuter services (*lokaltrafikk*), and cities on the coast also have commuter boat services. Most

cities have a co-ordinated transport arrangement whereby tickets and season passes are valid throughout the city and its surroundings on all services. The largest is *Stor-Oslo Lokaltrafikk – SL* ("Greater Oslo Public Transport") which co-ordinates all bus, boat, commuter train, tram and underground services in the Oslo area. Departure times are posted at all bus and tram stops (*holdeplass*), at all train and underground stations (*stasjoner*) and at all ferry and passenger launch terminal quays (*kai*). Complete schedules are available at ticket booths and at offices of the transport companies, and most cities have a schedule information telephone; look under *Ruteopplysning* in the introductory pages of the Pink and White Pages directory. SL of Oslo also has an Internet site ☻ http://www.sol.no/trafikanten with an interactive schedule information service as well as an information centre, *Trafikanten* at the plaza in front of the Oslo S railway station.

Roadside cafés (*Veikroer*) are located throughout the country. Most started as local family eating places or, more recently, as convenience cafés for people travelling by car. Unlike the transport cafés or truck stops of other countries, few, if any roadside cafés in the country began business by serving hauliers, principally because road freight haulage became a major transport sector only after motor vehicle import restrictions were rescinded in the early 1960s. There now are more than 100 roadside cafés in the country, most along major highways and in or near towns and villages, sometimes near petrol stations, and always with ample car parks. Nearly one in five of them belongs to one of two chains, *Veikroer* and *By the Way*, which have cafés along the E6 and E18 E-roads as well as the Rv7 and Rv51 national highways in the more heavily populated south-eastern part of the country. Both *Veikroer* and *By the Way* feature cafeteria-style self-serve and take-away, as well as restaurant á la carte meals on short order, and all have licences to serve beer and wine. Four of the *By the Way* cafés also have motels.

Taxi (*Drosje*) Countrywide, there are about 5500 taxis, most owned by their drivers. In cities and towns, taxis are organised through a dispatcher (*sentral*), whilst local taxi ranks have their own telephone numbers. In rural areas, taxi owners may list their home or mobile telephone numbers. "Taxi" is the current word, though the older *drosje* (from the Russian *drogi* for 'work vehicle') is still used in everyday speech and in listings, ✆ under *drosjer* in the Pink or Yellow Pages. A proper taxi has a roof lamp with one or more letters, which indicate the county and dispatcher area, and several numerals, which together are the taxi's medallion number. The lamp is lit when the taxi is free and out when it is engaged or not in service. Beware pirate taxis without roof lamps; not only are they often more expensive and of lower quality, but they increasingly are involved in assault and other street crime.

Traditionally, a taxi has a standard-delivery colour chosen by its owner, so without a roof lamp, it looks like a private car. Starting in 1998, *Norgestaxi*, a countrywide fleet, has yellow taxis, now some 350 on the streets of Bergen, Oslo, Stavanger and Trondheim. The uniform, highly-visible colour was borrowed with permission from the famed Yellow Cabs of New York, though it is more reddish. *Norgestaxi* has a single countrywide dispatcher number, displayed on the sides of the vehicle the five-digit ✆ 08000.

You may flag down a taxi (roof lamp lit), provided you are more than 100 metres from the nearest taxi rank; if you are closer, you must go to the rank and wait if there is a queue. You may call a dispatcher or a taxi rank and order immediate service or pick-up at a specific time, provided you call in advance, such as the evening before an early-morning departure to an airport. Most taxis are saloon and estate cars, but you may order larger estates (*stasjonsvogner*) or mini-buses (*maxi-taxi*) that take 9 to 15 passengers. Most taxis have safety equipment to fit children. You can order taxis fitted for wheelchairs or cycle racks or taxis guaranteed to be non-smoking (*røykfritt*) and free of animal hair (*astmabiler*). Ordinary taxis have five seats, and consequently can take four passengers, which are included in the trip cost shown on the meter. Larger taxis, for five or more passengers, have higher rates, usually less per passenger than hiring two ordinary taxis. Children are regarded as individual passengers, entitled to their seats and counted in the capacity of a vehicle. Traffic regulations require passengers, but not the driver, to wear ☞ **seat belts** (Cars, Roads, Traffic chapter) when fitted in a vehicle. The driver is responsible for ensuring that children up to 14 years old wear seat belts, whilst children of 15 or more are regard-

ed as adults, who may be subject to fine should a taxi be stopped in a seat-belt control. When a taxi enters your service, the driver starts its meter, for a flagged taxi at a fixed initial fee (*påslag*) that depends on the time of day and whether it is an ordinary workday or a holiday, or for an ordered taxi, at a pick-up fee (*fremmøtetakst*). Thereafter, the meter charges by distance driven and time elapsed. You may request a receipt upon paying. Most city taxis are now fitted with meters integrated into digital dispatch systems and can automatically print out a trip receipt. These taxis also can accept credit cards. As in shops, card validation is required, so to save time at the end of your trip, give the driver your card when the trip starts, so it can be validated during the trip. Hand baggage that you take into the vehicle is free, but there is a small surcharge for baggage put in the boot or on a roof rack. Most taxis can carry skis, prams, cycles, dogs or cats, but it's best to inquire in advance, as when ordering by telephone. Anything you may leave in a taxi will be turned in to the nearest police station's lost and found property office (*hittegodskontor*). In addition to everyday taxi trips, you may order a taxi for courier service, at standard rates, or for sightseeing, at a rate agreed upon with the driver. In addition to Norwegian, most taxi drivers speak English, and some speak other languages.

Train travel (*Togreise*) NSB ("Norwegian State Railways") trains run on rails and serve stations operated by the Norwegian National Rail Administration – NNRA (*Jernbaneverket*) in a network of more than 4000 km, of which 2450 km are electrified. The main lines branch out from the 67 km Trunk Line (*Hovedbanen*) between Oslo and Eidsvoll and run through splendid scenery, which is one of the joys of train travel. Most known is the 471 km Bergen Line (*Bergensbanen*) over the high plateau between Oslo and Bergen, with more than 100 km of it above timberline. Its highest station, Finse, seems a world apart, in a landscape of glaciers and nigh year-round snows. Seemingly uninhabitable yet readily accessible, Finse was the setting for the filming of the ice-planet scenes of "The Empire Strikes Back", the sequel to the original "Star Wars". A branch off the Bergen Line at Myrdal, the 20 km Flam Line (*Flåmsbana*) winds downhill to Flåm on the Aurlands Fjord and affords one of the world's most scenic railway journeys. The 586 km Southern Line (*Sørlandsbanen*) that links Oslo, Kristiansand and Stavanger offers the maritime scenery of the coast it follows. The 551 km Dovre Line (*Dovrebanen*) connecting Oslo and Trondheim through the Gudbrandsdal valley provides inland scenery, from farmlands to high mountains. The 114 km Rauma Line (*Raumabanen*) branches off from the Dovre Line at Dombås and runs north-west to Åndalsnes, through terrain rivalling that of the Flåm Line. The 431 km Røros Line (*Rørosbanen*) is an alternate route between Oslo and Trondheim, through valleys farther east. The 729 km Nordland Line (*Nordlandsbanen*) between Trondheim and Bodø is the country's longest and one of the few in the world to cross the Arctic Circle. Shortest and not connected to the other parts of the network, the Ofot Line (*Ofotbanen*), the world's northernmost railway, runs eastward from Narvik to the Swedish border, connecting to the Swedish line to Kiruna and on southward to Stockholm. From Oslo, the 169 km Eastern Norway Line (*Østfoldbanen*) from Oslo and south-east to the Swedish border is the main line to Gothenburg, Copenhagen and continental Europe. An eastern spur of the Trunk Line connects to the Swedish line eastward to Stockholm. The high-speed rail link to the Gardermoen gateway airport (*Gardermobanen*) stretches from Asker, south-west of Oslo to the airport, 55 km north of the city. It is a separate service with its own trains and, north of Oslo, its own line, but its trains stop and its tickets are sold at NSB stations.

NSB trains are comfortable, clean and punctual. Schedules meet passenger needs and are co-ordinated at travel junctions with the local bus (*TogBuss*) and boat (*TogBåt*) services. If, for instance, you arrive at a station to travel onward on a *TogBuss* service, the bus will be waiting for the train, and on your return journey, the bus will arrive a few minutes before the scheduled train departure. There are three major groups of train services:

- *Puls* short-distance (*kortdistanse*) services, mostly for trips of up to 45 minutes, and including the commuter services in the Oslo, Bergen, Stavanger and Trondheim areas. Economy service only.
- *Agenda* medium-distance (*mellomdistanse*) services, mostly for trips of 45 minutes to three hours, typically as served by InterCity trains. First and economy-class seats are available and seat reservations usually are required.

- *Signatur* long-distance (*langdistanse*) services, for trips of more than three hours, such as between major cities and including overnight trains. First and economy-class seat and sleeper reservations are required, and sleeping cars have two or three bunks in each compartment, but you may reserve one only against a surcharge. Single and two-bunk compartments with WC and shower are available on some lines.

Medium and long-distance trains have food services, either café carriages (*bistrovogn*) or ambulating trolleys (*salgsvogn*), as well as telephones that accept cards (*Telefonkort*) sold in stations and on board. Most trains have special compartments for parents travelling with infants up to two years old (*småbarnkupé*) as well as compartments and facilities for passengers in wheelchairs (*rullestolbrukere*). Many long-distance trains have a carriage specifically for children (*barnetoget*), with two compartments, one a playroom (*lekestue*) and one with reclining-seats (*hvilestoler*).

Ticket prices vary according to class (first or economy) and type of service, and several discount schemes are offered. For commuter travel, there are day, week and season passes. For instance, in the greater Oslo area, SL ("Greater Local") offers monthly season passes valid on trains, buses, trams, underground and some boats. For travel outside the commuter zones, NSB offers several discounts, most for journeys on "green departure" (*grønne avganger*) off-peak days, as indicated by green dots in rows for the days of the week at the bottom of each schedule table. You save more by departing on days marked with green dots.

The NSB Customer Card (*NSB Kundekort*) is valid for one year and grants you a 50% discount on green departure days and a 20% discount on other days on all economy-class tickets. Many organisations have agreements with NSB which offer their members a discount on NSB Customer Cards, so before buying, check any memberships you may have to see if you are entitled to a discount. Other discounts include Family discounts (*Familietilbud*) for children travelling with adults, Mini-price (*Minipris*) tickets with advance booking and payment, Group discounts (*Grupperabatt*) for at least ten persons travelling together, Student discounts (*Studentrabatt*) for trips of 150 km or more, Senior citizen and disabled person discounts (*Honnørrabatt*) and Military dis-

The rail network; map courtesy of NSB

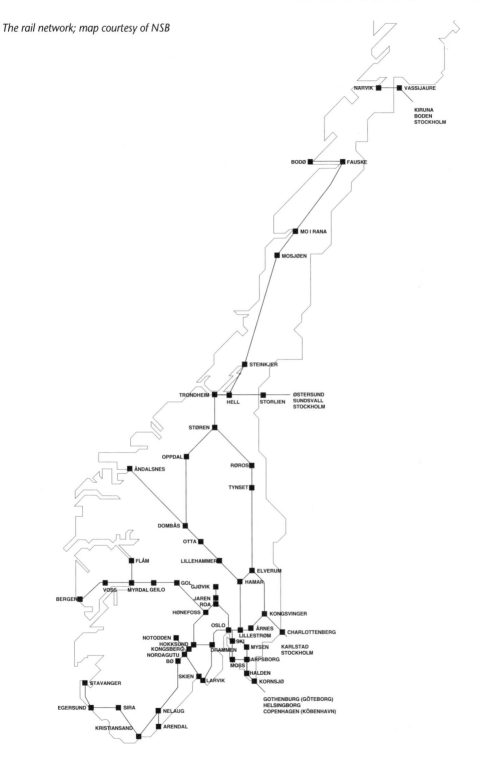

counts (*Militære rabatter*) for recruits (*vernepliktige*) and cadre (*befal*). ScanRail passes are available for five to 21 days of travel within Scandinavia. Inter Rail tickets are available for up to one month of travel throughout Europe, except in the country of your residence, at prices depending on your age (under or over 26) and the extent of your travels. Further information and booking are available at NSB railway stations, listed under *NSB* in the Pink Pages. Or you may call the NSB customer helpline (*kundetelefon*) ℡ 81500888 where the operators will speak Norwegian, English and sometimes other languages, or view the NSB web site ☺ http://www.nsb.no with pages in Norwegian and in English.

Travel Bureaux (*Reisebyråer*) deal with flights, hotel bookings, package holidays and of course the business market. There are some 500 travel bureaux and tour operators in the country; you can find them listed under *Reisebyråer* in the Yellow Pages. If you seek or wish to verify the integrity of a travel bureau, you may contact The Norwegian Travel Trade Association (*Den norske reisebransjeforening*) ℡ 22546000, ☎ 22546001, ✉ PO Box 2924 Solli, 0230 Oslo, ☺ http://www.dnr.no with updated lists of all member bureaux and tour operators. Travel bureaux charge for their services at varying rates, which a bureau is obliged to state when you inquire about prices for specific types of bookings. If you are just looking for a single least-price airline ticket, it may be worth your while to contact the airlines (*flyselskaper*) directly; look under *flyselskaper* in the Yellow Pages.

Useful books
(Referanseverk)

Books related to specific topics are listed in the entries for those topics; for instance, the publications of Norway Statistics are listed under **Statistics**. Other general reference books are listed below, each with its year of publication and its International Standard Book Number (ISBN) that can help you find it in a book shop or library. These books and other useful references are listed in the continuously updated Norwegian libraries database available online in English as well as Norwegian at ⊕ http://www.bibsys.no

Abbreviations
Books with comprehensive lists of Norwegian and international abbreviations:
Forkortingsboka, S. Løland & V. Leira, Norwegian Language Council (*Norsk Språkråd*), Cappelens, Oslo, 1997, ISBN 82-02-16419-2.
Forkortingsordbok, anonymous, Norwegian Council for Technical Terminology (*Rådet for teknisk terminologi*), book no. RTT 67, Oslo, 1997, ISBN 82-7566-033-5.

Comparative rankings of countries
The economic and social statistics of countries are compared in many ways by international organisations, such as ☞ **EU, EFTA and EEA**, (**OECD** and ☞ **WHO**. The volume of material available is enormous and spread in hundreds of publications and Internet web sites. Fortunately, there are two small annual summaries of the comparative rankings of countries world-wide. You can use them to compare life in Norway with the life you know in your home country, by finding where your home country and Norway rank in almost any aspect of life that can be expressed as a statistic.
   Pocket world in figures, The Economist in association with Profile Books, London, pocket diary sized hardcover, 1999 edition ISBN 1-86197-110-9.
   Pocket Europe in figures, The Economist in association with Profile Books, London, pocket diary sized hardcover, 1999 edition ISBN 1-86197-093-5.

Dictionaries, Bilingual
Desk, General, School and Student editions. "One-

way" general dictionaries are not listed, because they usually contain the same material as "two-way" editions. Pocket dictionaries are listed only when they are not available from a publisher in larger format. Multimedia and CD-ROM editions are not listed, as they duplicate material in printed editions. Each listing includes the summary details: to, from or to/from Norwegian (abbreviated N.), *abbreviated title in Italics*, type (as above), author(s)/editor(s), publisher and year published.
Chinese
to N, *Kinesisk-norsk*, Desk, H. Rekkedal & others, Kunnskapsforlaget, 1998, ISBN 82-573-0759-9.
Danish & Swedish
to/from N, *Skandinavisk*, Desk, B. Lindgren & others, Kunnskapsforlaget, 1994, ISBN 82-573-0630-4.
English
to/from N, *English-Norwegian, Norwegian-English Dictionary*, staff of Berlitz Guides, Lausanne & Oslo, Gyldendal, 1998, hardcover, ISBN 2-8315-0948-3.
from N, *Collins English-Norwegian Dictionary*, L.S. Knight & H. Hasselgård, Glasgow, Harper Collins, 1998, ISBN 0-00-470705-2.
to N, *Stor ordbok*, Desk, H. Svenkerud Cappelen, 1996, ISBN 82-02-10823-3.
to N, *Stor ordbok*, Desk, W.A. Kirkeby, Kunnskapsforlaget, 1996, ISBN 82-573-0727-0.
from N, *Stor ordbok*, Desk, W.A. Kirkeby, Kunnskapsforlaget, 1997, ISBN 82-573-0275-9.
to/from N, *Ordbok*, School, H. Svenkerud Cappelen, 1997, ISBN 82-02-16990-9.
to/from N, *Lingua*, General, anonymous, Universitetsforlaget, 1998, ISBN 82-00-12768-0.
to/from N, *Blå ordbok*, General, W.A. Kirkeby, Kunnskapsforlaget, 1993, ISBN 82-573-0618-5.
to/from N, *Lingua, Skoleordbok*, School, anonymous, Universitetsforlaget, 1998, ISBN 82-00-12765-6.
to/from N with gender of nouns, *Skoleordbok*, School, Ø. Ek, Kunnskapsforlaget, 1992, ISBN 82-573-0484-0.
from N with gender of nouns, *Studentordbok*, Student, E. Haugen, Universitetsforlaget, 1996, ISBN 82-00-22722-7.
to N, *Studentordbok*, Student, W.A. Kirkeby, Universitetsforlaget, 1996, ISBN 82-00-22463-5.
to N., *Eng\elsk-Norsk Ordbok på Newsweek* (vocabulary above basic, as used in Newsweek maga-

zine), Lærerbokforlaget, 1998, ISBN 82-91821-10-0.

Farsi (Persian)

to N, *Store ordbok*, Desk, M. Amarloui, Universitetsforlaget, 1998, ISBN 82- 00-02975-1.

Finnish

to N, *Mellomstore*, Desk, T. Farbregd & H. Seppinen, Universitetsforlaget, 1994, ISBN 82-00-21765-5.

to/from N, *Lommeordbok*, Pocket, T. Farbregd & A Kämäräinen, Kunnskapsforlaget, 1996, ISBN 82-573-0616-9.

French

to N, *Store ordbok*, Desk, L.O. Grundt, Universitetsforlaget, 1994, ISBN 82-00-21977-1.

to/from N, *Blå ordbok*, General, A. Elligers & F. Reichborn-Kjennrud, Kunnskapsforlaget, 1995, ISBN 82-573-0717-3.

to/from N, *Lingua*, General, anonymous, Universitetsforlaget, 1998, ISBN, 82-00-12767-2.

to/from N, *Ordbok*, General, H. Svenkerud & U. Parnemann, Cappelen, 1997, ISBN 82-02-16988-7.

to/from N, *Skoleordbok*, School, E.H. Gabrielsen, Kunnskapsforlaget, 1998, ISBN 82-573-0905-2.

to/from N, *Lingua skoleordbok*, School, anonymous, Universitetsforlaget, 1998 ISBN 82-00-12764-8.

German

to N, *Store ordbok*, Desk, T.Hustad, Universitetsforlaget, 1998, ISBN 82- 00-22365-5.

to/from N, *Blå ordbok*, General, G. Paulsen, Kunnskapsforlaget, 1998, ISBN 82-573-0909-5.

to/from N, *Ordbok*, General, H. Svenkerud & H. Parnemann, Cappelen, 1997, ISBN 82-02-16989-5.

to/from N, *Lingua*, General, anonymous, Universitetsforlaget, 1998 ISBN 82- 00-12766-4.

to/from N, *Lingua skoleordbok*, School, anonymous, Universitetsforlaget, 1998, ISBN 82-00-12762-1.

to/from N, *Skoleordbok*, School, Ø. Ek Kunnskapsforlaget, 1998, ISBN 82- 573-0904-4.

Greek

to/from N, *Lommeordbok*, Pocket, B. Braaten & E. Theophilakis, Kunnskapsforlaget, 1997, ISBN 82-573-0005-5.

Icelandic

from N, *Mellomstore*, Desk, H. Einarsson, Universitetsforlaget, 1995, ISBN 82- 00-22700-6.

Italian

to/from N, *Blå ordbok*, General, M. Ulleland & D. Haakonsen, Kunnskapsforlaget, 1998, ISBN 82-573-0907-9.

Latin

to N, *Ordbok*, General, Johanssen, Nygaard & Schreiner, Cappelen, 1998, ISBN 82- 02-15499-5.

Polish

to/from N, *Lommeordbok*, Pocket, Z.W. & H.H. Soleng, Kunnskapsforlaget, 1997, ISBN 82- 573-0797-1.

Portugese

from N, *Mellomstore*, Desk, K. Nilsson, Universitetsforlaget, 1994, ISBN 82- 00-21129-0.

Russian

to N, *Store ordbok*, Desk, V. Berkov, Universitetsforlaget, 1994, ISBN 82- 00-21975-5.

to/from N, *Lommeordbok*, Pocket, E. Tuv & B. Morken, Kunnskapsforlaget, 1994, ISBN 82- 573-0496-4.

Serbo-Croatian

from N, *Mellomstore*, Desk, B. Bakker & others, Universitetsforlaget, 1995, ISBN 82- 00-22357-4.

to/from N, *Lommeordbok*, Pocket, M. Sesseng, Kunnskapsforlaget, 1995, ISBN 82- 573-0207-4.

Spanish

from N, *Mellomstore*, Desk, K. Nilsson, Universitetsforlaget, 1997, ISBN 82- 00-22508-9.

to/from N, *Blå ordbok*, General, S. Loennicken & C.A. Blomdal, Kunnskapsforlaget, 1998, ISBN 82- 573-0726-2.

to/from N, *Skoleordbok*, School, S. Flydal-Blichfeldt & M.L. Villanueva Aasen, Kunnskapsforlaget, 1990, ISBN 82- 573-0409-3.

Swedish

from N, *Stor ordbok*, Desk, B. Fowler, Kunnskapsforlaget, 1992, ISBN 82- 573-0480-8.

Turkish

to N, *Mellomstore*, Desk, B. Brendemoen & Y. Tanrikut, Univesitetsforlaget, 1997, ISBN 82- 00-22903-3.

Veitnamese

from N, *Mellomstore*, Desk, N.Q. Khanh & others, Universitetsforlaget, 1993, ISBN 82- 00-21869-4.

Dictionaries, Norwegian

Single-volume dictionaries, similar to the concise Oxford or Webster's dictionaries of English, with definitions and including genders of nouns:

Aschehoug og Gyldendals Store Norske Ordbok, Oslo,

1991, Kunnskapsforlaget, hardcover, ISBN 82-573-0312-7 (red), 82-573-0397-6 (burgundy), 82-573-0396-8 (black); binding matches that of second edition of 15 volume encyclopaedia (1991).

Escolas Ordbok, Bokmål, Indre Arna, 1993, Escola forlag, hardcover, ISBN 82-7423-001-9.

Norsk Ordbok, Oslo, 1998, Kunnskapsforlaget, hardcover, ISBN 82-573-0497-2; binding matches that of second edition of 15 volume encyclopaedia (1991).

Norsk ordbok, Oslo, 1996, Cappelen, hardcover, ISBN 82-02-15304-2.

Dictionaries, pictorial bilingual and multilingual

Single-volume pictorial dictionaries, similar to the Oxford-Duden series in English but more richly illustrated with large drawings in colour with relevant vocabulary directly on each.

Ord i Bilder, Norsk og engelsk billedordbok, Oslo, 1991, Kunnskapsforlaget, hardcover, ISBN 82-573-0420-4; terms in Norwegian and English; book is out of print but can be found in old/rare book shops (*antikvariat*).

Aschehoug og Gyldendals Store Norske Visuell ordbok, Oslo, 1998, Kunnskapsforlaget, hardcover, ISBN 82-573-0973-7 (red), 82-573-0962-1 (burgundy), 82-573-0974-5 (black); terms in Norwegian, English, German and French; binding matches that of second edition of 15 volume encyclopaedia (1991).

Dictionaries, topical

Dictionaries of professional fields are usually arranged in one of three ways. Some are bilingual, either to Norwegian or from Norwegian, or both to and from Norwegian. Some have terms in alphabetical order in Norwegian with translations into English (*engelsk*), French (*fransk*), German (*tysk*), and other languages in the entries for all words. Others have definitions in Norwegian with bilingual lists to/from Norwegian in the back of the book. The Norwegian Council for Technical Terminology (*Rådet for teknisk terminologi – RTT*), a governmental organisation, compiles and publishes an extensive series of topical dictionaries; for the latest catalogue or information on individual topics, contact RTT, PO Box 41 Blindern, 0313 Oslo, ✆ 22198040, 🖷 22198041. Topical dictionaries currently avail-

able in shops are listed below.

Administration and government
Norsk-engelsk administrativ ordbok, P. Chaffey, Universitetsforlaget, 1988, ISBN 82-00-07758-6.

Business and finance
Norsk-fransk økonomisk ordbok, T. Selmer, Universitetsforlaget, 1st edition 1993, ISBN 82-00-41149-4.

Bedre engelsk forretnings-språk, E. Hansen, Bedriftsøkonomers Forlag, 3rd edition 1995, ISBN 82-7037-845-3.

Cars and traffic
Bil- og trafikk-teknisk ordbok, Norsk-engelsk/Engelsk-norsk, W.A. Kirkeby, Kunnskapsforlaget, 1979, ISBN 82-573-0079-9.

Computers and information technology
Norsk dataordbok, S. Løland & P. Scott, 6th edition 1997, Universitetsforlaget, ISBN 82-00-22506-2.

Economics
Norsk-engelsk økonomisk ordbok, J. Aagenæs, Kunnskapsforlaget, 1993, ISBN 82-573-0548-0.

Electrical installations in buildings
Norsk-engelsk, engelsk-norsk ordbok, Hjelpebok, S. Hauge, Elektroinstallatørenes Landsforbund & Universitetsforlaget, 1985, ISBN 82-7345-041-4.

English loanwords
Anglisismeordboka, Engelske lånord i norsk, A-L Gradler & S. Johansson, Universitetsforlaget, 1st edition 1997, ISBN 82-00-22902-5.

Health care and medicine
Medisinsk engelsk-norsk/norsk-engelsk ordbok, E. Kåss & G. Marthilm, Kunnskapsforlaget, 1993, ISBN 82-573-0558-8.

Heating, Ventilation and Sanitary Systems
Engelsk-norsk norsk-engelsk VVS ordbok, Norsk VVS energi- og miljøteknisk Forening, Norsk VVS, 1992, softcover, ISBN 82-90033-18-4.

Insurance
Forsikrings-ordbok, norsk-engelsk/engelsk-norsk, Å. Lind, Kunnskapsforlaget, 1989, ISBN 82-573-0314-3; out of print but may be available in used book shops (*Antikvariat*).

Law
Anglo Scandinavian Law Dictionary (English, Norwegian, Swedish, Danish), R.J.B. Anderson, Universitetsforlaget, 1979, ISBN 82-00-02365-6.

Store norske-engelsk juridisk ordbok, R. Craig, Universitetsforlaget, 1st edition 1999, ISBN 82-00-12923-3.

Law, business and contract
Norsk-engelsk juridisk ordbok, R. Craig, Universitets-forlaget, 1st edition 1992, ISBN 82-00-21327-7.
Law, criminal
Norsk-engelsk juridisk ordbok, Strafferett, straffepros-ess og andre juridiske termer, P. Chaffey & R. Wal-ford, Universitetsforlaget, 2nd edition 1977, ISBN 82-00-22602-6.
Maritime technology
Norsk-engelsk maritim-teknisk ordbok, P. Askim, Grøn-dahl & Søn Forlag, 11th edition 1984, ISBN 82-504-0500-5; still the only book of its kind and therefore valuable in nautical work, but now out of print, and current publisher Cappelen plans no new edition; occasionally can be found new in book shops and used in old/rare book shops (*antikvariat*).
Metalworking
Metallurgisk ordbok, anonymous, Norsk teknologi standardisering, 1976, ISBN 82-90204-00-0, now out of print but occasionally can be found in book shops; 2nd revised edition published mid 1999.
Military
Engelsk-norsk militær ordbok, Ministry of Defence, Grøndahl Dreyer/Cappelen Fakta, 1996, hard-cover, ISBN 82-50402195-7.
Norsk-engelsk militær ordbok, Ministry of Defence, Cappelen, 1998, hardcover, ISBN 82-02-17058-3.
Oil industry
Illustrated glossary of process equipment, English, Français, Norsk, B.H. Paruit, Elf Aquitaine Norge & Gulf Publishing, 1982, ISBN 82-991067-0-2.
Petroleumsordliste engelsk-norsk/norsk-engelsk, Norsk termbank U. Bergen, Kunnskapsforlaget, 1988, ISBN 82-573-0308-9.
Socio-economics
Engelsk-norsk samfunnsøkonomisk ordbok, E. Hansen, Universitetsforlaget, 1st edition 1992, ISBN 82-00-21546-6.
Sports
Den store idrettsordboka, O. Hem, Universitetsfor-laget, 1st edition 1998, ISBN 82-00-12781-8.
Sports, winter
Norsk-engelsk/engelsk-norsk ordbok for vinteridretter, O. Hem, Universitetsforlaget, 1st edition 1996, ISBN 82-00-22775-8.
Technology, general
Norsk-engelsk teknisk ordbok, J. Arnsteinsson & O. Reiersen, Bruns Forlag, 4th edition 1994, ISBN 82-7028-496-3.
English-Norwegian technical dictionary, J. Arnsteins-son, Bruns Forlag, 6th edition 1994, ISBN 82-7028-495-5.
Engelsk-norsk Teknisk Ordbok, Jan E. Prestesæter, For-matic 1998, ISBN 82-90431-16-3
Tysk-norsk Teknisk Ordbok, Jan E. Prestesæter, For-matic 1998, ISBN 82-90431-14-7
Transportation
Ordbok for transportfag, norsk, engelsk, fransk, E.T. Garder, Yrkeslitteratur, 1996, ISBN 82-584-0175-0.

First names in Norwegian
A listing of first names and the frequency of their use from 1880 to 1997, a good guide to recognising and spelling, in Norwegian only:
Fornavn i Norge, J.E. Kristiansen & J. Ouren, Ad Notam division of Gyldendal, 1998, ISBN 82-417-0945-5.

Glossaries
Forlaget Fag & Kultur publishes schoolbooks, includ-ing texts, workbooks, cassettes, glossaries and teach-ing aids for courses of instruction in Norwegian as a second language, for native speakers of 21 lan-guages. The materials are divided into two levels: the beginning level *Ny i Norge* ("New in Norway") by G. Manne and the advanced learner level *Bo i Norge* ("Live in Norway") by G. Manne and K.E. Engen. These materials are used in schools and in Norwegian language courses for adults. The soft-cover glossaries from Norwegian to other languages are listed below.

Albanian and Turkish *Ny i Norge* 1990, 8th print-ing 1996, ISBN 82-11-00137-3, *Bo i Norge* 1991, 2nd printing 1994 ISBN 82-11-00171-3.

Arabic *Ny i Norge* 1990, 2nd printing 1991, ISBN 82-11-00395-3, *Bo i Norge* 1989 ISBN 82-11-00155-1.

Chinese *Ny i Norge* 1990, 2nd printing 1991 ISBN 82-11-00150-0.

English *Ny i Norge* 1990, 10th printing 1996 ISBN 82-11-00135-7, *Bo i Norge* 1990, 7th printing 1997 ISBN 82-11-00154-3.

Farsi *Ny i Norge* 2nd edition 3rd printing 1991 ISBN 82-11-00167-5, *Bo i Norge* 1990 ISBN 82-11-00191-8.

French *Ny i Norge* 2nd edition 1991, ISBN 82-11-00178-0.

German and Italian *Ny i Norge* 1991, 5th printing 1997 ISBN 82-11-00163-2.

Hindi and Punjabi *Ny i Norge* 1991 ISBN 82-11-00169-1.

Kurdish *Ny i Norge* 1991 ISBN 82-11-00152-7, *Bo i Norge* 1994 ISBN 82-11-00258-2.

Polish *Ny i Norge* 1990, 2nd printing 1991 ISBN 82-11-00147-0, *Bo i Norge* 1993 ISBN 82-11-00228-0.

Portugese *Ny i Norge* 1995 ISBN 82-11-00316-3.

Russian *Ny i Norge* 1991, 4th printing 1994 ISBN 82-11-00198-5, *Bo i Norge* 1994 ISBN 82-11-00259-0.

Serbo-Croatian *Ny i Norge* 1992, 10th printing 1996 ISBN 82-11-00193-4, *Bo i Norge* 1994 ISBN 82-11-00256-6.

Somali *Ny i Norge* (with English) 1990, 8th printing 1998 ISBN 82-11-00168-3, *Bo i Norge* 1990 ISBN 82-11-00157-8.

Spanish *Ny i Norge* 1990 ISBN 82-11-00144-6.

Tagalog from N. *Ny i Norge* 1995 ISBN 82-11-00260-4.

Tamil *Ny i Norge* 1991, 2nd printing 1991 ISBN 82-11-00153-4, *Bo i Norge* 1990, 3rd printing 1993 ISBN 82-11-00172-1.

Thai *Ny i Norge* (with English) 1990 ISBN 82-11-00358-9.

Tigrinya *Ny i Norge* 1996 ISBN 82-11-00315-5.

Urdu *Ny i Norge* 1991 ISBN 82-11-00170-5, *Bo i Norge* 1993 ISBN 82-11-00227-2.

Vietnamese *Ny i Norge* (with English) 1990 ISBN 82-11-00143-8, *Bo i Norge* 1994 ISBN 82-11-00257-4.

Medicines and drugs

Consumer information on medicines and drugs sold over the counter and by prescription in pharmacies, in Norwegian only:

Medisin Håndboken, H.M. Tørisen, Elanders Forlag, 5th edition 1997, ISBN 82-90545-70-3.

Society

A comprehensive, one-volume overview of all current national and local governmental rules, regulations and practices that affect the daily lives of residents, in Norwegian only:

Samfunnsboka 1999/2000, Statens Informasjonstjeneste and Universitetsforlaget, 9th edition 1999, ISBN 82-00-12847-4.

An overview of multicultural life in the country and the integration of immigrants into the society, written principally for professionals in health and social services but also useful for anyone interested in the topic, in Norwegian only:

Flerkulturell Håndbok, G. Neegaard, Kommuneforlaget, 1998, ISBN 82-446-05380-8.

Glossary of British English – American English words

The spelling conventions of British English and American English differ, most famously in the s-z differences in spellings, as in *recognise* (British) and *recognize* (American). Moreover, American English tends to be more phonetic – *esthetic* (American) is spelled more closely to the way it is spoken than is *aesthetic* (British). These and other differences in spelling are minor; they often escape reader notice, though word processing spell checkers highlight them. However, some words are problematic, because their meanings differ. The following two lists – British to American, useful in reading, and American to British, useful in finding topics in the index – are of the differing words used in this book. For a comprehensive guide to the differences, see *American and British English*, Part II of *The Economist Style Guide*, 1998 edition, The Economist in association with Profile Books, London, 154 pages hardcover, ISBN 1-86197-111-7.

British: American

aerial: antenna
anti-clockwise: counterclockwise
autumn: fall
baby's dummy: pacifier
banknote: bill
caravan: house trailer
cheque: check
chips: French fries
cooker: stove
crisps: chips
curtains: drapes
district: neighborhood
doctor: physician
driving licence: driver's license
estate agent: real-estate agent
estate car: station wagon
flat: apartment

football: soccer
garden: yard
gearbox: transmission
greengrocer: vegetable market
grill: broil
ground floor: first floor
handbrake: emergency brake
high street: main street
motorway: freeway
nappy: diaper
number plates: license plates
pants: underpants
pavement: sidewalk
permanent way: railway
petrol: gasoline
petrol station: gas station
pitch (football): field

post (verb): mail
refuse: garbage
railway: railroad
ring road: beltway
road surface: pavement
spanner: wrench
shareholder: stockholder
sweets: candy
terraced house: row house
toilet: bathroom, restroom
transport: transportation
trousers: pants or slacks
trunk call: long-distance call
tyre: tire
underground: subway
walk: hike
wardrobe: closet

American: British

antenna: aerial
apartment: flat
bathroom, restroom: toilet
beltway: ring road
bill (currency): banknote
broil: grill
candy: sweets
check: cheque
chips: crisps
closet: wardrobe
counterclockwise: anti-clockwise
diaper: nappy
drapes: curtains
driver's license: driving licence
emergency brake: handbrake
fall (season): autumn
field (playing): pitch

first floor: ground floor
freeway: motorway
French fries: chips
garbage: refuse
gas station: petrol station
gasoline: petrol
hike: walk
house trailer: caravan
license plates: number plates
long-distance call: trunk call
mail (verb): post
main street: high street
neighborhood: district
pacifier: baby's dummy
pants or slacks: trousers
pavement: road surface
physician: doctor

railroad: railway
railway: permanent way
real-estate agent: estate agent
row house: terraced house
sidewalk: pavement
soccer: football
station wagon: estate car
stockholder: shareholder
stove: cooker
subway: underground
tire: tyre
transmission: gearbox
transportation: transport
underpants: pants
vegetable market: greengrocer
wrench: spanner
yard: garden

Yellow Pages
Alphabetised English index to Norwegian Yellow Pages *(Gule sider)*

The English classifications below are based on the those commonly used in the UK. For American classifications, see the American-to-British glossary on page 380. The Norwegian classifications are those used in the Yellow Pages *(Gule Sider)* throughout the country. Business and government in Norway are organised differently than in the UK, so some classifications in one language may have several equivalents in the other, while others may exist in one language only: there are no ski factories in England, and no kilt shops in Norway. Likewise, in Norway many municipal and governmental services, such as the police and fire brigades, are not listed in the Yellow Pages, but are listed alphabetically in the Pink Pages *(Rosa Sider)*, so each such listing is identified by 'in Pink Pages'. Some classifications have sub-divisions, as listed below.

Sub-divisions of listed classifications

Agencies/Distributors *Agentur*
Authorised *Registrerte*
Certified (by governmental agency) *Statsautoriserte*
Distribution (of periodicals) *Distribusjon*
Editorial Staff (of publishers) *Redaksjon*
Export *Eksport*
Hire *Utleie*
Import *Import*
Licensed (workshops) *Godkjente* or *Offentlig godkjente*

Makers *Makere*
Manufacturers *Produksjon*
Master (trades) *Mestere*
Other *Øvrige*
Producers (of foodstuffs) *Produsenter*
Retailers, Shops *Detalj*
Sales *Salg*
Service *Service*
Wholesalers *En gros*

A-Z of Yellow Pages

Each classification consists of the English term in bold face followed by the Norwegian term in italics:
English term *Norwegian term.*

Abattoir eqpt *Slakteriutstyr*
Abattoirs *Slaktere*
Abrasive products *Slipemaskiner og -utstyr*
Accountants *Regnskapstjenester*
Acoustic engineers *Akustikk*
Actors *Skuespillere*
Actuaries *Aktuarer*
Acupuncture- practitioners *Akupunktur*
Adhesives & glues *Lim*
Adoption (Social Services) *Adopsjonstjenester*
Advertising agencies *Reklamebyråer*
Advertising consultants *Reklamekonsulenter*
Advertising - media *Annonsesalg*
Aerial surveys & photographers *Flyfotografering*
Aerosols *Trykkfylling*

Agricultural buildings *Driftsbygninger, landbruk*
Agricultural machinery - sales *Landbruksmaskiner og -redskaper*
Agricultural machinery - service *Landbruksmaskinverksteder*
Air compressors *Kompressorer*
Air conditioning eqpt & supplies *Luftkondisjonering*
Air purification *Luftrensing*
Aircraft fittings *Fly og flyutstyr*
Aircraft sales *Fly og flyutstyr*
Airfreight services *Flyfrakt*
Airlines *Flyselskaper*
Airports *Flyplasser*
Air-raid shelters *Tilfluktsrom*

Alcoholism advice *Rusvern*
Alternative & complementary medicines/
therapies *Biopati*
Aluminium fabrications *Aluminium og aluminiums-
varer*
Aluminium products *Alulminium og aluminiums-
varer*
Ambulance *Ambulanse (Medisinsk nødtelefon)* in
Pink Pages
Animal feed (fur-bearing animals) *Pelsdyrfôr*
Animal feeds *Fôr og gjødningsstoffer*
Animal welfare organisations *Dyrebeskyttelsen* in
Pink Pages
Antique dealers *Antikviteter*
Antique repair & restoration *Restaurering*
Aquarium supplies *Zoologiske forretninger*
Arcade machines *Lotteri- og spilleutstyr*
Architects *Arkitekter*
Armed services *Forsvaret* in Pink Pages
Armed services, reserve forces *Heimevernet* in Pink
Pages
Arms & ammunition *Våpen og ammunisjon*
Aromatherapy *Aromaterapi*
Art dealers *Kunsthandlere og -formidling*
Art galleries *Kunstutstillinger*
Art restorers *Malerikonservatorer* or *Restaurering*
Artisans *Kunsthåndverkere*: Glassworkers *Glass*, Je-
wellers *Smykker*, Leatherworkers *Lær og skinn*,
Potters *Keramikk*, Textile artists *stofftrykk og
håndmalte tekstiler*, Weavers *Vev*, Wood crafts
Tre
Artists' materials *Kunstnerutstyr*
Asbestos removal *Asbestsanering*
Asphalt & macadam suppliers *Asfalt*
Assessors *Taksering*
Astrologers *Astrologi*
Auctioneers & valuers *Auksjonsforretninger*
Audiologists *Audiopedagogikk*
Audio-visual eqpt & supplies *Audiovisuelle hjelpe-
midler*
Audio-visual eqpt, production & presentation
Lydmedia
Auditors *Revisjonstjenester*
Auto electricians *Bilelektriske verksteder*
Automation systems & eqpt *Automasjon*
Automotive consultants *Bilkonsulenter*
Awnings *Solskjerming*
Baby goods *Barneutstyr*
Badges & emblems *Emblemer og medaljer*
Bags, plastic *Poser*
Bait merchants *Agn*
Baker & confectionery supplies *Bakeri- og
konditorvarer*
Bakers & confectioners *Bakerier*
Bakery eqpt mfrs & supplies *Bakeri- og konditori-
maskiner*
Ball bearing stockists *Maskiner og rekvisita*

Ballet *Ballett*
Balloons - party, promotional *Ballonger*
Balustrades & balconies *Balkonger*
Bands - music *Artister og artist formidling*
Bands - packaging *Emballasje*
Bankrupcy *Gjeldsrådiving*
Banks *Banker*
Banqueting rooms *Selskapslokaler*
Bar code products & services *Butikkdata*
Bar fixtures & fittings *Storkjøkkenutstyr, hotell-
innredninger og -utstyr*
Barbers *Frisør, herrefrisør*
Bark & bark products *Bark og barkeprodukter*
Barometers *Måleinstrumeter*
Barristers *Advokater*
Bathroom eqpt & fittings *Baderomsinnredninger*
Bathroom fixtures - mfrs *Armatur*
Battery mfrs & supplies *Batterier*
Battery servicing *Batterier*
Bearing mfrs & stockists *Maskiner og rekvisita*
Beauticians' supplies *Kosmetikk*
Beauty centres *Kroppspleie*
Beauty salons & consultants *Hudpleie*
Bedding *Utstyrsforretninger*
Bee farmers & beekeepers *Birøktere og birøkterut-
styr*
Beekeeper supplies *Birøktere og birøkterutstyr*
Belt (clothing) mfrs *Beltefabrikker*
Belting (machinery) *Reimer*
Billiards & pool halls *Biljard*
Binocular supplies & repairs *Optiske forretninger*
Biotechnology *Bioteknologi*
Biscuit mfrs *Kjeksproduksjon*
Blacksmiths *Smeder*
Blast cleaning *Fasaderengjøring*
Blinds, awnings & canopies *Solskjerming*
Blood donor services *Blodbanken* in Pink Pages
Boat builders & repairers *Båtslip*
Boat charter, rental & leasing *Båt utleie*
Boat eqpt & accessories *Båtutstyr*
Boat storage *Båtopplag*
Boat trips & excursions *Turkjøring (båt)*
Boats - new & used *Båter*
Boilers - servicing eqpt *Kjelerensingsutstyr*
Boilers - servicing *Kjelerensing*
Bolt & nut stockists *Skruer, nagler og bolter*
Book publishers *Forlag*
Book shops *Bokhandlere*
Bookbinders *Bokbinderier*
Books - rare & second-hand *Antikvariater*
Bottle & jar mfrs *Glass, steintøy og porselen,
produksjon*
Bowling centres *Bowlingbaner*
Brake service *Bremseservice*
Brake service centres *Bilbremseverksteder*
Brass & copper stockholders *Jern, stål og metaller*
Brewers *Bryggerier*

Brewers eqpt & services *Bryggerimaskiner og -utstyr*
Brick mfrs *Teglverk*
Bridal shops *Brudeutstyr*
Bridalwear *Klær - brudeklær*
Broadcasting services (local) *Lokalradio og -TV*
Brushes & art brushes *Børster og pensler*
Builders' merchants - mfrs *Byggevareprodusenter*
Builders' merchants *Byggevarer*
Building facade contràctors *Fasadeentrepenører*
Building facade treatment *Fasadebehandling*
Building services *Byggforvaltning*
Buildings - portable (plastic) *Plasthaller*
Buildings - relocatable *Brakker*
Buildings, industrial & storage *Industri- og lager-bygg*
Bunkers *Bunkers*
Burglar alarms & security systems *Tyverivern*
Bus & coach operators & stations *Rutebiler og godsruter*
Business & trade organisations *Foreninger og forbund*
Business enterprise agencies *Næringsetablering og -utvikling*
Butchers (meat & game) *Kjøtt og vilt*
Buttons & buckles *Knapper*
Cabinet makers *Møbler, produksjon*
Cable & wire suppliers *Kabler og kraftledninger*
Cable cars, gondolas & ski lifts *Fjellheiser*
Cable TV services *Kabel-TV*
Cafes & cafeterias *Kafeer*
Cafeteria services *Kantinetjenester*
Calendar mfrs *Kalendere*
Calibration services *Kalibrering*
Calorimeters *Varmemålere*
Camping eqpt *Sport og fritidsutstyr*
Camps & camp schools for children *Leirskoler og leirsteder*
Candles *Stearinlys*
Canneries & canned goods agents *Hermetikk-fabrikker og -agenter*
Canoes *Kanoer og kajakker*
Car accessories & parts *Bildeler og rekvisita*
Car body repairs *Biloppretting*
Car breakdown recovery *Redningstjeneste*
Car breakers & dismantlers *Bilopphogging or Biloppsamlingsplasser*
Car customising specialists *Påbyggerverksteder*
Car dealers *Bilforretninger*
Car hire - chauffeur driven *Limousinutleie*
Car hire - self drive *Bilutleie*
Car importers *Bilimportører*
Car instruments *Bilinstrumenter*
Car painters & sprayers *Billakkering*
Car parking & garaging *Parkering*
Car radiator servicing & repairs *Radiatorer*
Car radio dealers *Bilstereo*

Car repairs *Bilverksteder*
Car security *Bilalarmer*
Car servicing *Bilservice*
Car springs *Bilfjærer*
Car testing centres *Trafikkstasjon* under *Statens Vegvisen* in Pink Pages
Car undersealing *Bilunderstellsbehandling*
Car valeting *Bilpleie*
Car washing & polishing eqpt & supplies *Bilvaskanlegg og -maskiner*
Caramel *Sukkerkulør*
Caravan dealers *Campingbiler og vogner*
Caravan parks *Campingplasser*
Career guidance services *Karrierrådgiving*
Career guidance services *Yrkesveiledning*
Caretaker services *Vakmestertjenester*
Cargo brokerage *Fraktmegling*
Carpenters & joiners *Snekkertjenester*
Carpet, curtain & upholstery cleaners *Teppe- og møbelrensing*
Carpets & rugs - mfrs & distributors *Tepper, Agen-tur og produsenter*
Carpets & rugs - shops *Tepper, detalj*
Carpets & rugs wh'sale *Tepper, engros*
Cartographers *Kart og karttegnere*
Cartons & packaging *Esker og kartonger*
Cash registers *Butikkmaskiner og -utstyr*
Castings (iron) *Støpegods*
Caterers *Catering*
Catering eqpt *Storkjøkken utstyr*
Catering products - disposable *Engangsservice og -bestikk*
Catering supplies - food *Selskapsmat*
Catteries *Hunder, katter og smådyr*
Cattle breeders *Stutterier*
CCTV & video eqpt *TV-overvåking*
Ceiling contractors *Bygg- og tømrermestere*
Cemeteries & crematoria *Gravlund* and *Kirkegård* under *Kirken* in Pink Pages
Central government *Staten* and *Deparatementene* in Pink Pages
Central heating - installation & servicing *Fryingsanlegg*
Central heating eqpt (oil) *Oljefyringsanlegg*
Ceramic supplies & services *Keramikk*
Cerographic printing *Serigrafisk trykk*
Certification bodies *Standardiseringsforbund* in Pink Pages
Chain mfrs & supplies *Kjettinger og ståltau*
Chambers of commerce *Handelskammer* in Pink Pages
Chandlers *Skipshandlere og -proviant*
Charities & voluntary organisations *(name of or-ganisation)* in Pink Pages
Chemical mfrs *Teknisk-kjemiske produkter*
Chemicals - distributors & wh'sale *Kjemikalier og kjemiske varer*

Chemicals & allied products *Teknisk-kjemiske produkter*
Chemists - dispensing *Apotek*
Chemists, dispensing *Apotek* in Pink Pages
Child care department *Barnevern*
Child safety *Barnesikring*
Children's & infant's wear *Barneklær*
Children's entertainers *Barneunderholdning*
Chimney builders & repairers *Skorsteinsarbeid*
Chimney sweeps *Feiervesen* in Pink Pages
China & glassware repairers *Porselensrestaurering*
China & glassware shops *Glass, steintøy og porselen*
China decorating *Porselens- og emaljemaling*
Chiropodic eqpt *Fotpleieutstyr*
Chiropodists *Fotpleie*
Chiropractors *Kiropraktorer*
Chocolate & sweets, wh'sale *Sjokolade, drops og sukkervarer*
Christmas trees & goods *Julepynt og juletrær*
Churches (Norwegian state churches) *Kirker* in Pink Pages
Churches (other than Norwegian State Church) *Kirker og trosamfunn*
Cinema eqpt *Kinoteknisk utstyr*
Cinemas *Kinoer*
Circuses *Sirkus*
Clairvoyants & palmists *Spåtjenester*
Cleaning eqpt *Rengjøringsmaskiner*
Cleaning materials - suppliers *Rengjøringsprodukter*
Cleaning services *Rengjøringstjenester*
Clinics *Sykehus og klinikker*
Clock & watch supplies & repairs *Urmakere og -forretninger*
Clothing & fabrics - mfrs *Konfeksjonsfabrikker*
Clothing wh'sale *Klær*
Clubs & associations *Foreninger og forbund*
Clutch service *Bilverksteder*
Coach hire *Turkjøring*
Cod-liver oil *Tran*
Coffee machines *Kaffetraktesystemer*
Coffee merchants (roasters) *Kaffebrennerier*
Cog carpentry *Lafting*
Coin & bank note machines *Mynt- og seddelmaskiner*
Coin & medal dealers *Mynthandlere*
Colleges, higher education *Universitetet* in Pink Pages
Colleges, technical & agricultural *Høgskolen* in Pink Pages
Colour therapy baths *Fargeterapibad*
Commercial kitchen eqpt *Storkjøkkenutstyr*
Commercial kitchen services *Storkjøkkentjenester*
Commercial vehicle body building & repairing *Karosserifabrikker og -verksteder*
Commercial vehicle fittings *Bilinnredninger*
Community centres *Bydelshus* (city) or *Samfunnshus* (town/village) in Pink Pages
Company registrar *Brønnøysundregistsrene* (one for entire country) in Pink Pages
Computer & data processing eqpt *Datamaskiner og -utstyr*
Computer & data processing services *Datadrift*
Computer aided design service *Data- og IT-konsulenter, DAK*
Computer consultants *Data- og IT-konsulenter*
Computer games *Data- og TV-spill*
Computer maintenance & repairs *Dataservice og vedlikehold*
Computer security *Datasikkerhet*
Computer systems & software development *Dataprogramvare og -utvikling*
Computer training *Dataopplæring*
Concrete - products *Betong og betongvarer*
Concrete - ready mixed *Betong og betongvarer*
Concrete machines & eqpt *Begongmaskiner og -utstyr*
Concrete repairing services *Betongvedlikehold* or *Overflatebehandling, Betong*
Concrete sawing & drilling *Betongsaging og -boring*
Conference organisers *Møte- og konferansearrangører*
Conference rooms & centres *Kurs og konferanselokaler*
Conference services *Kongress-service*
Conservatories *Utestuer og vinterhager*
Construction contractors - general *Entrepenører*
Construction machine contractors *Maskinentrepeniører*
Construction machinery *Anleggsmaskiner*
Consulates & embassies *Ambassader og konsulater*
Consultants and consulting engineers *Konsulenter og rådgivende ingeniører*: **Accounting technologies** *regnskapsteknikk*, **Acoustic** *akustikk*, **Agricultural engineers** *landbruksspørsmål*, **Automation** *automasjon*, **Boiler technology** *kjeleteknikk*, **Building** *byggøkonomi*, **Building** *byggteknikk*, **Business & management** *bedriftsmegling, bedriftsorganisa sjon, bedriftsutvikling, bedriftsøkonomi*, **Car park planning** *parkeringsplanlegging*, **Cartography & land surveying** *kartlegging og oppmåling*, **Chemical engineers** *kjemiteknikk*, **Cleaning** *renholdsteknikk*, **Construction management** *byggeledelse-byggadministration*, **Consultants - Industrial** *forskjellige ingeniørtjenester*, **Damp & dry rot control** *hussopp-spørsmål*, **Data processing** *databehandling*, **Disinfection** *desinfisering*, **Electrical engineers** *elektroteknikk*, **Electronic engineers** *elektronikk*, **Energy conservation** *energi*, **Environmental -engineers** *miljø*, **Explosives - engineers** *fjellsprengingsteknikk*, **Export** *eksport og internasjonalisering*, **Factory planning** *fabrikkplannlegging*, **Filing and archives** *akivteknikk*, **Financial** *økono-*

mi, **Fire protection -**
engineers brannteknologi, **Food technologists**
næringsmiddelindustri, **Geological & geophysical**
geofysikk, geologi, geoteknikk, **Heating** varme-
ventilasjons- og sanitæranlegg, **Hospital** sykehus-
konsulenter, **Hydrogeology** hydrogeologi, **Instru-**
mentation engineers måleteknikk, **Language**
språk, **Lifts** heiser, **Lighting** lysteknikk, **Loading**
and unloading Ships laste- og losseteknikk, **Long-**
range planning langtidsplannlegging, **Mainte-**
nance vedlikehold, **Marine engineers** maritim teknologi, **Marketing** markedsføring, **Materials ad-**
ministration materialadministrasjon, **Materials**
technologies masterialteknikk, **Mechanical eng-**
ineers maskinteknikk, **Naval architects** skipstek-
nikk, **Organisation** organisasjon, **Patent services**
patentspørsmål, **Petroleum facilities** oljeanlegg,
Product development produktutvikling,
Production technologies produksjonsteknikk,
Project management prosjektadministrasjon,
Property management eiendomøkonomisk rådgivning, **Public relations** informasjon, **Rationali-**
sation rasjonalisering, **Refrigeration** kjøleteknikk,
Relocation bedriftsflytting, **Restaurant/large kit-**
chens storkjøkkenanlegg, **Road & traffic plan-**
ning veg- og trafikkplanlegging, **Roads, bridges &**
tunnels veg, bro og tunnel, **Safety** sikkerhet, **State**
analysis & rehabilitation tilstandsanalyse og rehabilitering, **Strategic planning** strategisk planleg-
ging, **Telecommunications** telekommunikasjon,
Textile technologies tekstilteknikk, **Town plan-**
ning by og regionplannlegging, **Transport** sam-
ferdsel, transportøkonomi, transportrasjonalisering,
Utilities kommunalteknikk, **Warehouse systems**
lagerrasjonalisering, **Water supply & Sewage**
vannkraftanlegg, vannverk og kloakkanlegg, **Wel-**
ding sveiseteknikk, **Workplace safety** verneteknik-
ke
Consumer organisations Forbrukerkontorer
Container hire & transport Containere
Conveyors & conveyor belts Transmisjoner og
transportbånd
Co-operative shops Samvirkelag
Copying & duplicating services Kopiering
Copying services Lys- og fotokopiering
Cork products Kork
Corporate entertainment Underholdningsbyråer
Corrosion prevention & control Overflate-
behandling
Cosmetic surgery Leger, kirurgi, kosmetisk
Costumes Bijouterivarer
Cottage & cabin fittings Hytteutstyr
Cottage & cabin rentals & management
Hytteutleie og -formidling
Cottage & cabin services Hytteservice
Cottages & cabins Hytter
Counselling & advice, family Familierådgivning

Courier services Budtjenester
Credit reference agencies Inkasso og kreditt-
opplysning
Crispbread producers Flatbrød- og knekke-
brødproduksjon
Curtain cleaners Renserier, gardin
Curtains Gardiner og gardinutstyr
Customs & excise consultants Tollspørsmål
Cycle mfrs & wh'salers Sykkelverksteder og
-fabrikker
Cycle shops Sykler
Dairies Meierier
Dairy eqpt suppliers Meirimaskiner og -utstyr
Damp proofing & control Skadebegtrensning og
-sanering
Dance & ballet wear Ballettutstyr
Dancing schools Danseskoler
Data communication services Datakommunikasjon
og nettverk
Day care centre development Barnehageutbygging
Deaf services, interpreters Døvetolker
Debt collection agencies Inkasso og kredittopplys-
ning
Decorators' merchants Dekorasjonsmateriell
Delicatessens Deiktasseforretninger
Delivery services Varetaxi
Demolition & dismantling contractors Gård-
nedriving og demontering
Demolition Sprengningstjenester
Demonstration sales promotion Demonstrasjons-
salg
Dental eqpt & supplies Tannlege- og tann-
teknikerrekvisita
Dental hygienists Tannpleiere
Dental technicians Tannteknikere
Dentists Tannleger: **Endodontics** endodonti (rotfyl-
ling), **General practice** allmenn praksis, **Oral ot-**
hopaedics kjeveortopedi (tannregulering), **Oral**
surgery oral kirurgi, **Pedodontics** pedodonti (bar-
netannpleie), **Periodontics** periodonti (tannkjøtt-
sykdommer), **Prosthodontics and occulision** pro-
tetikk og bittfunksjon
Department stores Kjøpesentere
Design consultants Designere
Designers - graphic Grafiske formgivere
Desk top publishing Dastaprogramvare og
-utvikling
Detective agencies Privat etterforskning
Diamond tools Diamantboreverktøy
Die sinkers & stampers Stansefabrikker
Diesel engine eqpt & services Bildieselverksteder
Dieticians & nutritionists Kosholdskonsulenter
Direct mail (addressing services) Adressering
Direct mail (advertising) Direkte reklame
Disabled aids Hjelpemidler for funksjonshemmede
Disco eqpt Diskotekutstyr
Discos Diskotek og dansesteder

Dishwashing machines - servicing *Elektroverksteder*
Dishwashing machines (home) *Elektirske artikler*
Disinfecting *Desinfeksjon*
Display fittings & fixtures *Displaymarteriell*
Disposable products *Engangsservice og -bestikk*
Distribution services *Budtjenester*
Divers *Dykking*
Docks, floating *Flytebrygger og flåter*
Doctors *Leger:* **Anaesthesiology** *Anestesi,* **Cardiologists** *Hjertesykdommer,* **Cosmetic surgeons** *Plastikkirurgi,* **Ear, nose & throat** *Øre- nese- halssykdommer,* **General medicine** *Almennmedisin,* **General practice** *Almen praksis,* **Immunologists** *Immunhematologi,* **Internists** *Indremedisinske sykdommer,* **Lung diseases** *Lungesykdommer,* **Medical biochemists & physiologists** *Medisinsk biokjemi og fysiologi,* **Medical microbiologists** *Medisinsk mikrobiologi,* **Neurologists** *Nerrologi,* **Neurosurgeous** *Nevrokirurgi,* **Obstetrics & gynecology** *Fødselshjelp og kvinnesykdommer,* **Ophthalmologists** *Øyesykdommer,* **Orthopaedic surgeons** *Ortopedisk kirurgi,* **Pathologists** *Patologi,* **Paediatric surgeons** *Barnekirurgi,* **Paediatricians** *Basrnesykdommer,* **Physiology & rehabilitation** *Fysikalsk medisin og rehabilitering,* **Psychiatrists** *Psykiatri,* **Radiologists** *Medisinsk radiologi,* **Rheumatic illnesses** *Revmatiske skydommer,* **Skin & veneral diseases** *Hud- og veneriske sykdommer,* **Sports medicine** *Idrettsmedisin,* **Surgeons** *Kirurgi,* **Urologists** *Urologi*
Document processing systems *Elektronisk dokumentutveksling*
Documentation *Dokumentasjon*
Dog breeders *Hunder, katter og smådyr*
Dog trainers *Hunder, katter og smådyr*
Dolls & dolls' houses *Dukkemakere*
Domestic services *Vikarbyrå*
Doors & windows *Dører og vinduer*
Drain & pipe cleaning *Høytrykksrengjøring*
Draughtsmen & drawing services *Tekniske tegnere*
Drawing office eqpt & materials *Tegneutstyr*
Dressmakers *Systuer*
Drilling contractors *Boretjenester*
Driving schools *Trafikkskoler*
Drums, kegs, barrels & casks *Tønner*
Dry cleaners *Renserier*
Dry cleaning eqpt *Renserimaskiner*
Dust extraction & ventilation *Innemiljø*
Ear piercing services *Piercing*
Educational equpt & supplies *Skolemateriell*
Educational services *Kurs*
Egg merchants *Egg en gros*
Electric motor sales & service *Elektromotorer og -aggregater*
Electrical appliance repairs *Elektroverksteder*
Electrical assessors *Eltaksering*
Electrical goods - mfrs *Elektroteiniske fabrikker og produkter*
Electrical goods *Elektirske artikler* or *Hvitevarer*
Electricians & electrical contractors *Elektro-entrepenører*
Electricity companies *Energiforsyning*
Electrochemical/metallurgical Industries *Elektrokjemisk og metallurgisk industri*
Electronic component mfrs & distributors *Elektronikk komponenter*
Electronic eqpt *Elektronisk utstyr*
Electronic/low-voltage Installation *Svakstrømsanlegg*
Electroplating & metal finishing services *Overflatebehandling, Stål og metaller*
Embroidery designers & mfrs *Broderier*
Employment & recruitment agencies *Arbeidsformidling*
Employment service *Arbeidskontoret* in Pink Pages
Enamelling *Emaljeringsarbeid*
Energy brokers *Energimeglere*
Energy conservation consultants *Energiøkonomisering*
Engine mfrs & distributors *Motorer*
Engines, overhauling *Motoroverhaling*
Engraving & chaser eqpt *Gravør og siselørutstyr*
Engraving *Gravører og siselører*
Entertainers & entertainment agencies *Artister og artistformidling*
Entertainment agencies *Underholdningsbyråer*
Entertainment centres - concert halls *Konsertlokaler*
Entertainment centres *Kulturhus*
Envelopes - mfrs *Konvoluttproduksjon*
Environmental consultants & engineers *Miljøteknologi*
Environmental consultants *Miljøvern*
Environmental products & supplies *Miljøvennlig produkter*
Equestrian supplies *Hester og -utstyr*
Erotic goods *Erotiske artikler*
Essence manufacturers *Essensfabrikker*
Estate agents *Eiendomsmegling*
EU questions *EU-spørsmål*
Evening Classes *Friundervisningen* in Pink Pages
Exhibition & trade centres *Utstillinger og utstillingslokaler*
Exhibition services *Messe og utstillinger* or *Messebyråer*
Explosives *Sprengstoffer*
Fabrics - importers & wh'salers *Tekstiler, Agentur og en gros*
Fabrics - shops *Tekstiler, Detalj*
Facilities management *Gårdsbestyrelse*
Facsimile machines *Telefonapparater og -systemer*
Factoring & invoice discounting *Faktureringstjenester*
Farm holidays *Gårdsturisme*

Farm services *Landbrukstjenester*
Fashion agents *Modelbyråer*
Feldenkrais therapy *Feldenkraispedagoger*
Felt & felt products *Filt og filtvarer*
Fence, gate & barrier supplies *Gjerder og porter*
Ferries *Ferjer*
Fertilisers *Fôr og gjødningsstoffer*
Fibre optics *Fibreoptikk*
Filing systems & supplies *Arkivmateriell*
Film - showing *Film, framvising*
Film - sound technicians *Film, lydteknikere*
Film directors *Film, regissører*
Film eqpt *Film, utstyr*
Film institutes *Film, institutter*
Film libraries *Film, utleie*
Film processors *Film, laboratorier*
Film production services *Film, produsenter*
Film props *Film, dekorasjon*
Film studios *Film, studio*
Film texting & translation *Film, teksting - oversetting*
Filtration systems & services *Filter og filterutstyr*
Financial advisers *Økonomisk rådgivning*
Financial institutions *Finansieringsforetak*
Financial services *Finansiell information*
Fire & water damage - services & restoration *Skadebegrensing og -sanering*
Fire protection consultants & engineers *Brannsikring*
Fire stations *Brannvesenet* in Pink Pages
Firefighting eqpt *Brannslukkingsutstyr*
Fireplaces *Ovner og peiser*
Fireproofing products *Ildfaste materialer*
Firewood *Brenselforretninger*
Firework display technicians *Fyrverkeri*
Firework stockists *Fyrverkeri*
Fish farming eqpt *Fiskeoppdrettsutstyr*
Fish farms & hatcheries *Fiskeoppdrett*
Fish merchants - wh'sale *Fiskesalgslag*
Fish oil & meal machines *Sildolje- hvalolje- og fiskemelmaskiner*
Fisheries *Fisking*
Fishing & angling eqpt *Fiskeutstyr*
Fishing shanty rentals *Rorbutleie*
Fishmongers *Fisk og fiskeprodukter*
Fitness centres *Treningssenter*
Fitness eqpt *Treningsutstyr*
Fitting & installing services *Montering*
Fixings, locks & hinges *Beslag, hengsler og låser*
Flags, banners & bunting *Flagg og flaggutstyr*
Flagstaffs *Flaggstenger*
Flight simulators *Flysimulatorer*
Floor cleaning & polishing eqpt *Rengjørings-maskiner*
Floor coverings *Gulvbelegg*
Flooring services *Gulvbearbeiding*
Flooring, parquet *Parkett*

Floral displays - rental & leasing *Planteinnredning og -stell*
Florists - wh'sale & supplies *Blomser en gros*
Florists *Blomster- og kranseforretninger*
Flour & cereal producers *Mel og kornvarer*
Flowers - dried (florists) *Tørkede blomster*
Flowers & shrubs, artificial *Kunstige blomster og plants*
Flying schools *Skoler*
Foam products - rubber & plastic *Skumplast*
Food products *Næringsmidler*
Forest assessment *Skogtaksering*
Forestry consultants *Skogspørsmål*
Forestry eqpt *Skogbruksmaskiner og -utstyr*
Forestry services *Skogbruk*
Fork lift trucks *Transportutstyr*
Formwork *Forskaling*
Foundations (organisations) *Stiftelser*
Foundries - brass (bells) *Klokkestøperier*
Foundries (iron, steel) *Jern-, stål- og metallstøperier*
Foundries, bronze *Kunststøperier*
Fountains & eqpt *Fontener og -utstyr*
Franchise services *Franchising*
Free-range associations *Allmeninger*
Freight forwarding *Spedisjon og fortolling*
Frozen foods - wh'sale *Frysevarer*
Fruit & vegetables - wh'sale *Frukt, bær og grønnsaker*
Fruit preservation *Fruktkonservering*
Fruit storehouses *Fruktlager*
Fuel dealers *Brenselforretninger*
Fumigation services *Skadedyrbekjempelse*
Fund management *Fondsforvaltning*
Funeral directors & services *Begravelses- og kremasjonsbyråer*
Fur retailers *Pels- og skinnvarer*
Fur-bearing animal farms *Pelsdyroppdrett*
Furniture - repairing & restoring *Møbelrestaurering*
Furniture - repairing *Møbelverksteder*
Furniture - retail *Møbler*
Furniture - used *Brukthandel*
Furniture, steel *Stålmøbler*
Furriers (dressers of furs) *Pelsbrederier*
Galvanising, electrolytic *Forsinking, elektrolystisk*
Galvanising, hot-dip *Forsinking, varm*
Game dealers *Vilt*
Games shops *Spill og spillkort*
Garage doors - suppliers & installers *Garasjer og porter*
Garage eqpt *Bilverksdsutstyr*
Garage services *Bilverksteder*
Garden & patio furniture *Hage- og parkmøbler*
Garden centres & nurseries *Hagesentre*
Garden sheds *Utestuer og vinterhager*
Garden tools *Hageredskaper og -utstyr*
Gardening services *Gartnere og gartnerier*

Gas - industrial & medical suppliers *Gasser og gassutstyr*
Gas analysis & measurement *Gassanalyse og -målinger*
Gas stockists *Gasser og gassutstyr*
Gaskets *Pakninger og tetninger*
Gates & railings *Gjerder og porter*
Genealogists & family historians *Slektsforskning*
Generators - sales & service *Elektromotorer og -aggregater*
Giftware *Gaveartikler*
Glass merchants *Glassindustri*
Glass products - mfrs *Glassverk*
Glassworkers *Glassblåserier*
Glaziers *Glassarbeid*
Glove shops *Hansker*
Goldsmith tools *Gullsmedverktøy*
Goldsmiths & silversmiths *Gull- og sølvvarer*
Goldsmiths *Gullsmeder og juvelerer*
Golf courses & clubs *Golf*
Graffiti removers *Grafittifjerning*
Graphic artists *Billedkunstnere, Grafikere*
Graphic arts materials *Grafisk utstyr*
Graphologists *Skriftsakkyndige*
Greeting card mfrs & wh'salers *Kunstforlag*
Grilles *Grill og grillutstyr*
Grinding & abrasive machinery *Slipemaskiner og -utstyr*
Grinding & sharpening services *Slipeverksteder*
Grocers *Dagligvarer*
Grouting work & eqpt *Fugarbeid og -utstyr*
Guide agencies, travel *Reiselederformidling*
Guide services *Guidetjenester*
Gunsmiths *Våpen og ammunisjon*
Gut *Tarmindustri*
Guttering *Blikkvarer*
Haberdashers *Kortevarer*
Hair transplants *Hårbehandling*
Hairdressers & hair stylists *Frisører* or *Hårbehandling*
Hairdressers' eqpt & supplies *Friséartikler*
Hairpieces & wigs *Parykker og løshår*
Handbags *Reiseeffekter*
Handicrafts *Brukskunst*
Hard metal tools *Hardmetallverktøy*
Hardware - wh'sale & mfrs *Skruer, nagler og bolter*
Hardware merchants & ironmongers *Jernvarer og kjøkkenutstyr*
Hardware mfrs & agents *Spiker og trådstifter*
Hat shops *Hatter og luer*
Haulage, road & sea *Transporttjenester*
Hazardous goods consultants *Farlig gods*
Health & safety consultants *Helse- og arbeidsmiljøtjenester*
Health authorities *Helserådet, Helsetjenesten* or *Helsestasjoner* (sometimes prefixed by city or town/village name) in Pink Pages

Health centres *Helse- og kursteder*
Health foods & products *Helsekost*
Health insurance *Trygdekontor* (national insurance) or name of private company in Pink Pages
Hearing aids *Høreapparater*
Heat exchangers *Varmepumper og -vekslere*
Heating consultants *Fyringsteknikk*
Heating eqpt *Varme-sanitæranlegg og -utstyr*
Heating, floor *Gulvvarme*
Helicopter hire *Helikoptertjenester*
Heneries *Hønserier*
Herbalists *Helsekost*
Herring oil, whale oil & fish meal *Sildolje, hvalolje og fiskemel*
Hide & skin merchants *Pels- og skinnvarer*
Hire - ladies & men's wear *Selskapsklær*
Hire - tools & equpt *Utleie*
Hobby supplies *Hobbyvarer*
Holding companies *Holdningsselskaper*
Home crafts shops *Husflid*
Homeopathic practitioners *Homøopati*
Horse breeders & dealers *Hester og -utstyr*
Horse breeders *Stutterier*
Horse supplies *Hester og -utstyr*
Horse trainers *Travtrenere*
Horse-drawn vehicles - hire *Hesteskyss*
Hoses, tubing & fittings *Slanger*
Hospital eqpt & supplies *Syke- og helsepleieartikler*
Hospitals *Sykehus og klinikker*
Hotel & restaurant eqpt *Hotellinnredninger og -utstyr*
Hotels & hostels *Hoteller og andre overnattingssteder*
House builders *Bygg- og tømrermestere* or *Hus*
Housing associations, societies & co-operatives *Boligbyggelag*
Hydraulic systems & eqpt *Hydraulikk-Pneumatikk*
Hygiene & cleansing services *Hygienetjenester*
Ice cream *Iskrem*
Ice merchants *Is*
Identification cards *Plastkort*
Illustrators *Billedkunstnere, Tegnere* or *Illustrasjonsasrbeid*
Industrial designers *Industriadesignere*
Industrial doors & gates *Industriporter*
Industrial protective clothing *Yrkesklær*
Insolvency practitioners *Gjeldsrådgiving*
Insulation contractors, installers, materials *Isolering*
Insurance agents & companies *Forsikringstjenester*
Insurance brokers *Forsikringsmegling*
Interior designers & fiurnishers *Interiørtjenester*
Interior furnishers *Interiørforretninger*
Internationalisation *Internasjonalisering*
Internet services *Internett og multimedia*
Interpreters *Tolker:* **Albanian** *Albansk,* **Arabic** *Arabisk,* **Chinese** *Kinesisk,* **Czech** *Tsjekkisk,* **Dutch**

Nederlandsk, **English** *Engelsk*, **Finnish** *Finsk*, **French** *Fransk*, **German** *Tysk*, **Greek** *Gresk*, **Italian** *Italiensk*, **Japanese** *Japansk*, **Multi-lingual** *Flere språk*, **Persian** *Persisk*, **Polish** *Polsk*, **Portuguese** *Portugisisk*, **Russian** *Russisk*, **Sami** *Samisk*, **Serbo-Croatian** *Serbokroatisk*, **Somali** *Somali*, **Spanish** *Spansk*
Introduction agencies *Kontaktformidling*
Investment consultants *Investeringserådgivning*
Irrigation systems & eqpt *Vanningsanlegg*
Janitorial supplies *Rengjøringsprodukter*
Jewellers *Gullsmeder og juvelerer*
Joiners & carpenters *Bygningssnekkere og tømere*
Journalists *Journalister og fotografer*
Juke boxes *Automater*
Karaoke *Diskotek og nattklubber*
Kayaks *Kanoer og kajakker*
Kennels *Hunder, katter og smådyr*
Kinesipathy *Kinesiologi*
Kitchen planners & furnishers *Kjøkkeninnredninger*
Kitchen ware *Jernvarer og kjøkkenutstyr*
Knitting machines *Symaskiner og strikkemaskiner*
Knitwear - mfrs *Strikkeproduksjon*
Knitwear *Trikotasje*
Knives *Kniver*
Labels & tags *Etiketter*
Laboratories *Laboratorier*
Laboratory eqpt *Laboratorieutstyr*
Laboratory instruments *Instrumenter*
Lace *Bånd og lisser*
Ladder hire *Stiger og stillaser*
Ladies tailors *Dameskreddere*
Ladieswear *Dameklær*
Laminating services *Trykkerier*
Lamps & lampshades *Lamper*
Landscape architects & designers *Landskapsarkitekter*
Landscape architects & designers *Landskapskonsulenter*
Landscape contractors *Anleggsgartnertjenester*
Language consultants *Språkkonsulenter*
Language schools *Språkundervisning*
Laser eqpt *Laser*
Laser medical treatment *Laserbehandling*
Laundries & laundrettes *Vaskerier*
Laundry & dry cleaning supplies *Vaskeri- og renserirekvisita*
Laundry eqpt *Vaskerimaskiner*
Lawnmowers & garden machinery *Hageredskaper og -utstyr*
Lawyers *Advokater*
Leather garments & repairs *Skinnklær og reperasjoner*
Leather goods shops *Skinn og lær*
Leather repairs *Skinnreparasjoner*
Ledger mfrs *Protokollfabrikker*
Legal services *Advokater* or *Rettshjelpere*

Leisure centres *Foreninger og forbund, barne- og ungdom*
Letting agents *Boligutleie*
Libraries *Biblioteker*
Life assurance & pension companies *Forsikringstjenester*
Lifting gear *Kraner og løfteutstyr*
Lifts *Heiser*
Lighters & barges *Lektere*
Lighting *Belysning*
Lighting fittings *Belysningsarmatur*
Lighting hire *Lysanlegg*
Lime mfrs & distributors *Kalkverk*
Linen shops *Utstyrsforretninger*
Lingerie *Undertøy*
Lithographers *Reproduksjon, litografering*
Lithographic plate makers *Reporduction, litografmester*
Livestock carriers *Dyretransport*
Local government *(name of municipality/town/village) in Pink Pages*
Lockers *Oppbevaringsbokser*
Locksmiths *Lås- og nøkkelservice*
Loft conversions *Bygg- og tømremestere*
Logistics *Logistikk*
Looms & reeds *Vevstoler og vevskjeer*
Lotteries *Lotterivirksomhet*
Lubricants *Smøremidler*
Lubricating eqpt *Smørepumper og -apparater*
Lubrication services *Smøreteknikk*
Luggage *Reiseeffekter*
Machine shops *Mekaniske verksteder*
Machine tools *Verktøymaskiner*
Machinery - industrial & commercial *Maskiner og rekvisita*
Magicians (entertainers) *Tryllekunstnere*
Magnets *Magneter*
Mailing houses *Adressering*
Mail-order & catalogue shopping *Postordre*
Maps & charts *Kart og karttegnere*
Marble specialists *Fliser og mosaikk*
Margarine *Margarin*
Marinas, boat moorings *Marinaer*
Marine electronic eqpt *Skipselektronikk*
Marine engines *Båtmotorer*
Marine eqpt & supplies *Skipsutstyr*
Marine instruments *Nautiske instrumenter*
Marine salvage services *Bergningsselskaper*
Marine services - ship classification *Skipsklassifisering*
Marine surveyors *Havaribyåer og -agenter*
Market garden eqpt *Gartneriutstyr*
Market research *Markedsundersøkelser*
Marketing consultants *Markedsføring*
Marking & pricing eqpt *Pris- og merkemaskiner*
Masonry, acid-resistant *Syrefast muring*
Massage treatment *Klassisk massasje*

Match factories *Fyrstikkfabrikker*
Materials handling eqpt *Transportanlegg* or *Transportutstyr*
Maternity courses *Svangerskapskurs*
Maternity homes *Barne- og mødrehjem*
Maternity wear *Mammaklær*
Mats & matting *Matter*
Mattresses *Madrasser*
Measuring, analysing & controlling instruments *Måleinstrumenter*
Meats, cured *Spekemat*
Media monitoring & clipping services *Mediaovervåking*
Medical eqpt & instruments *Medinisk teknisk utstyr*
Medical instruments *Instrumenter*
Mensendieck therapy *Mensendieck*
Menswear *Herreklær*
Metal industries - primary *Metallurgisk industri*
Metal netting mfrs *Metalldukproduksjon*
Metal strapping *Patentbånd*
Metal workers *Driere, metaldriere*
Microfilming services *Mikrofotografering*
Midwives *Jordmødre*
Milliners *Hatter og luer, dame*
Mills & millers *Mølls*
Mining companies *Gruveforretninger*
Mirrors & decorative glass *Glassiliperier og speilfabrikker*
Mirrors, glass plate *Speil- og vindusglass*
Mobile phones *Mobilkommunikasjon*
Model agencies *Modellbyråer*
Model makers (architectural & engineering) *Modellverksteder*
Monumental masons *Gravmonumenter*
Mortgage brokers *Låneformidling*
Motels *Moteller*
Motor caravans *Campingbiler og vogner*
Motor cycles - service *Motorsykkel- og mopedverksteder*
Motor cycles *Motorsyker og mopeder*
Motor sports *Motorsport*
Mountain lodges *Fjellstuer*
Multimedia services *Internett og multimedia*
Museums & art galleries *Muséer og samlinger*
Music publishers *Musikkforlag*
Music teachers *Musikk- og sangundervisning*
Music therapy *Musikkterapi*
Musical instruments & sheet music *Musikkhandlere Musikkinstrumenter*
Musical instruments repairs & servicing *Musikkinstrumenter*
Musicians *Musikere og sangere*
Nail technicians *Negldesignere*
Nappy delivery *Bleieservice*
Naprapathy *Naprapati*
National costumes (Norwegian) *Bunader*
Natural therapies *Naturterapi*

Needlecraft shops *Borderier*
Needlework & reweaving *Kunststopperier*
Netting - trawls & seines *Notbøterier*
News & photo agencies *Nyhetsbyråer* or *Pressebyråer*
Newsagents (kiosks) *Kiosker*
Newspaper & magazine publishers *Aviser, blader og tidsskrifter*
Night clubs *Barer, puber og nattklubber*
Noise control & measurement *Støydemping og støymåling*
Notaries public *Byfogden* (city) or *(name of municipality) heredsrett* (town/village) in Pink Pages
Nurseries & creches *Barnehager og Parker*
Nursery & creche fittings *Barnehageinnredninger*
Nurserymen - trees & shrubs *Planteskoler*
Nurses' agencies *Syke- og barnepleie*
Nursing homes *Alders- og sykehjem*
Occupational health *Arbeidsmiljø*
Occupational therapists *Ergoterapi*
Office cleaners *Rengjøringstjenester*
Office furniture & eqpt *Kontormøbler og -innredninger*
Office machinery *Kontormaskiner og -utstyr*
Office rental *Kontorutleie*
Office stationery supplies *Kontorrekvisita*
Oil & gas extraction (offshore) *Offshore*
Oil changes (road vehicles) *Oljeskift*
Oil companies *Oljeselskaper*
Oil field eqpt *Oljeindustriutstyr*
Oil fuel distributors *Fryingsoljer*
Oil recycling & disposal services *Oljerensing*
Oil spill clean-up services *Oljevern*
Oil well drilling eqpt *Oljeboringsutstyr*
Oils - edible *Oljer (animalske og vegetabilske)*
Optical goods *Optiske instrumenter og varer*
Opticians - dispensing *Optiske forretninger*
Opticians - optometrists *Synsklinikker*
Organic foods *Helsekost*
Ornamental metalwork *Kunstsmeder*
Orthopaedic care eqpt *Orthopediske verksteder*
Orthoptists *Ortoptister*
Osteopaths *Osteopati*
Ostrich farms *Strutseoppdrett*
Outboard motors *Båtmotorer, påhengsmotorer*
Ovens, industrial *Industriovner*
Packaging & wrapping eqpt & supplies *Emballeringsmaskiner og -utstyr*
Packaging materials *Emballasje*
Packers *Pakketjenester*
Paint spraying eqpt & accessories *Malerutstyr*
Painters & decorators *Dekorasjonsmalere, Dekoratører* or *Malertjenester*
Painters (artists) *Billedkunstnere, Malere*
Painting & decorating supplies *Fargehandlere*
Paints & varnishes *Maling og lakk*
Pallets, crates & packing cases *Lastesystemer*

Paper & board *Papir*
Paper & pulp mills *Papirindustri*
Paperhangers *Byggtapetsere*
Parachuting *Fallskjermhopping*
Paragliding & hang gliding *Paraglidning*
Park & municipal fittings & eqpt *Utemiljø*
Partitions & cubicles *Systeminnredninger*
Party goods & novelties *Karnevalsutstyr*
Party organisers *Selskapsarrangement og
-servering*
Passenger boat services *Skyssbåter*
Patent agents *Patentbyråer*
Patent services *Patentutnytting og -formidling*
Paving (stone) *Belegningsstein*
Pensions *Trygdekontoret* (national) or name of private fund in Pink Pages
Perfume & toilertry supplies *Parfyme- og toalettartikler*
Personnel consultants *Personalutvelgelse*
Personnel training & administration *Personaladministrasjon og opplæring*
Pest & vermin control services *Skadedyrbekjempelse*
Pet foods & supplies *Hunde- og kattemat og
-utstyr*
Pet shops *Zoologiske forretninger*
Petrochemical industries *Petrokjemisk industri*
Petrol filling stations *Bensinstasjoner*
Petroleum products *Petroleumsteknologi*
Pewter & tinware *Tinnvarer*
Pharmaceutical mfrs & distributors *Farmasøytiske
varer*
Pharmacies *Apotek*
Photocopiers *Kontormaskiner og -utstyr, lyskopiering*
Photograph libraries *Bildebyråer*
Photographers - advertising & commercial
Reklamefotografer
Photographers - film *Film, filmfotografer*
Photographers - general (news/events) *Journalister og fotografer*
Photographers - general *Fotografer*
Photographic eqpt & supplies *Fotoutstyr*
Photographic processors *Fotolaboratorier*
Physiotherapists *Fysioterapeuter*
Physiotherapy clinics *Fysikalske institutter*
Piano & organ tuners *Piano- og orgelstemmere*
Pianos & accessories *Pianoer, flygler og orgler*
Picture & photo framing services *Rammer*
Pig breeders & dealers *Svineavl*
Pipe inspection *Rørinspeksjon*
Pipe marking *Rørmerking*
Pipes & fittings *Rør- og rørleggerartikler*
Pitch, tar, hemp & hards *Bek-, tjære, drev- og stryprodukter*
Pizza *Pizza*
Places of worship *Kirker og trosamfunn*
Planning systems *Planleggingssystemer*

Plant & machinery hire *Utleie*
Plant protection & insecticides *Plantevernmidler*
Plasterers *Gipsmakere og modellører*
Plastics - consultants *Plastkonsulenter*
Plastics - machinery & eqpt *Plastmaskiner*
Plastics - raw materials *Plastråstoffer*
Plastics - repairs *Plastreparasjoner*
Plastics - stockists & supplies *Plastvarer*
Playground eqpt *Lekeapparater og -utstyr*
Playgroups & day centres *Barnehager og parker*
Playgroups & pre-school education *Basrnehager* in
Pink Pages
Pleating *Plissering*
Plumbers' merchants *Varme-sanitæranlegg og
-utstyr*
Plumbers *Rørleggere*
Pneumatic despatch eqpt *Rørpostanlegg*
Pneumatic systems & eqpt *Trykkluftsutstyr*
Podiatrists *Fotterapeuter*
Police *Politiet* (city) or *Lensmannen* (rural districts) in
Pink Pages
Political parties *(name of party)* in Pink Pages
Pollution control *Miljøverntjenester*
Ports, docks & harbours *Havnevirksomhet*
Post office services *Posten* in Pink Pages
Potato flour mills *Potetmelproduksjon*
Potato merchants & supplies *Poteter*
Poultry wh'salers *Fjørfe*
Power tool supplies & repairs *Verktøy*
Precious stones *Edelstenhandel*
Printed matter *Trykksaker*
Printed media consultants *Trykksak-konsulenter*
Printers - textile *Tekstiltrykkerier*
Printers' services *Reproduksjon*
Printers *Trykkerier*
Printing ink mfrs *Trykkfargefabrikker*
Prisons *(name of prison)* in Pink Pages
Process control & automation *Posesskontroll og
automasjon*
Promotional items *Reklameartikler*
Promotional items, fabrics *Reklametekstiler*
Property & estate management *Eiendomsforvaltning og -utvikling*
Property developers *Eiendomsforvaltning og
-utvikling*
Protective coating eqpt *Overflatebehandlingsutstyr*
Psychologists *Psykologer*
Psychotherapists *Psykoterapeuter*
Public address & music systems *Høytaleranlegg*
Public houses, bars & inns *Barer, puber og nattklubber*
Public relations consultants *Informasjonsrådgivere*
Public relations consultants *Public relations*
Publishers *Forlag*
Pulp (wood) *Treull*
Pumps *Pumper*
Quality consultants *Kvalitetssikring*

Quaries Steinbrudd, -huggerier og -sliperier
Queue systems Køsystemer
Quit smoking Røykeavenning
Racecourses & tracks Veddeløpsbaner
Radio communications eqpt Radiokommunika-
sjonsutstyr
Radio stations (private) Radiostasjoner
Radio telephone services Radiokommunikasjon
Rafting Rafting
Railway eqpt Jernbanemateriell
Railways NSB in Pink Pages
Rainwear Regntøy
Raw materials, industrial Råvarer for industrien
Record, tape & CD mfrs CD produksjon
Recording services - sound Lydproduksjon
Records, tapes & CDs CD-plater, plater og musikkas-
setter
Records, tapes & CDs Plater og musikkassetter
Recruiting, armed forces Forsvarets rekruttering in
Pink Pages
Recycling centres - paper Returpapir
Recycling centres Avfallsbehandling og gjenvinning
Refineries Oljeraffinerier
Reflective product mfrs Refleksutstyr
Reflexology Refleksologi
Refrigeration contractors Kuldeentrepeniører
Refrigeration eqpt - commercial Kjøle- og frysean-
legg
Refrigerators & freezers - service & repairs
Elektroverksteder
Refrigerators & freezers (home) Elektirske artikler
Refuse collection Renovasjon
Rehabilitation institutions Attføringsinstitusjoner
Religious furnishings & supplies Kirke- og presteut-
styr
Religious organisations Kirker og trosamfunn
Removals & storage Flyttetjenester
Rescue eqpt Redningsutstyr
Research organisations Forskning og utvikling or
Forskningsråd
Rest & retirement homes Alders- og sykehjem
Restaurants (overview) Restaurant oversikt:
American Amerikansk, **Beef** Biffrestauranter, **Cafés**
Kafeer, **Chinese** Kinesisk, **Creole** Kreolsk, **Cypriote**
Kypriotisk, **Danish** Dansk, **Fish and Seafood** Fis-
kerestauranter, **French** Fransk, **German** Tysk, **Gre-
ek** Gresk, **Hamburger/fast food** Hamburgerres-
tauranter, **Hungarian** Ungarsk, **Indian** Indisk, **In-
donesian** Indonesisk, **International** International,
Iranian Iransk, **Irish** Irsk, **Italian** Italiensk, **Japane-
se** Japansk, **Korean** Koreansk, **Lebanese**
Libanesisk, **Lunch Restaurants,** Lunsjrestauranter,
Mexican Meksikansk, **Mongolian** Mongolsk, **Norwegian** Norsk, **Pakistani** Pakistansk, **Pizza** Pizza,
Spanish Spansk, **Swiss** Sveitsisk, **Thai** Thailandsk,
Turkish Tyrkisk, **Vegetarian** Vegetarrestauranter,
Vietnamese Vietnamesisk, **Yugoslavian** Jugoslavisk

Retouching Retusjører
Retraining institutes Opptreningsinstitusjoner
Riding schools Rideopplæring
Road haulage services Rutebiler og godsruter
Road marking Oppmerking
Road surfacing eqpt Veivedlikeholdsmasker
Road toll stations Bompengerstasjoner
Roller shutters Gardiner og gardinutstyr, rulle-
gardiner
Roof trusses Takstoler
Roofing materials Taktekking- og takstein
forretninger
Ropes & hawsers Tauverk og hyssing
Rosettes & pins Pins
Rubber products Gummi og gummivarer
Rubber stamps Stempler
Rustproofing services Rustbehandling
Sacks & bags Sekker
Saddlers & harness makers Salmakere
Safes & vaults Verdiskap
Safety eqpt & clothing Verne- og sikkerhetsutstyr
Sailmakers & repairers Seilmakere
Sales promotion consultants Media- og reklamefor-
midling
Salt suppliers Salt en gros
Sand blasting eqpt Overflatebehandlingsutstyr
Sand blasting Overflatebehandling or Sandblåsing
Sand, gravel & other aggregates Sand, pukk og
grus
Sandwiches Smørbrød
Sanitary goods Hygienevarer
Sanitary towels Sanitetsbind
Satellite television - eqpt & services Satellittanlegg
Saunas - mfrs Badsuer og badstuovner
Sausage mfr eqpt Pølsemakerimaskiner
Sausage mfs Slaktere og pølsemakerier
Sawmill & planing mill technology Sagbruk- og
høvleriteknikk
Sawmills Sagbruk og høvlerier
Scaffolding & work platforms Stiger og stillaser
Scales & weighing eqpt Vekter og mål
Schools - local authority Skoleetaten under name
of township kommune in Pink Pages
Schools & colleges Skoler, kurs og utdanning
Scrap merchants Avfallsforretninger
Sculptors Billedkunstnere, billedhoggere
Seals Plomber
Searchlights & outdoor illumination Lykter og lys-
kastere
Seaweed & sea tangle products Tang- og tarepro-
dukter
Second-hand clothing Brukte klær
Second-hand shops Brukthandel
Secretarial & typing services Avskrivningskontorer
or Kontor- og sekretærservice
Security & intruder alarm systems Alarm og
sikringsanlegg

Security eqpt Alarm og sikringsanlegg
Security services Kontrolforretninger or Vaktselskaper
Seed merchants Frø og frørensing
Septic tank services Septiktanktømming
Sewing machines & accessories Symaskiner og strikkemaskiner
Sheet metal work Blikk- og kobberslagertjenester
Shell sand Skjellsand
Shellfish farming Skalldyroppdrett
Shelving & racking Butikk innredninger og -utstyr
Sheriff's officers Lensmenn in Pink Pages
Ship & boat illumination Skips- og båtlysanlegg
Ship breakers Skipsopphogging
Ship brokers Skipsmeglere
Ship builders, repairs & fittings Skipsbyggerier og -verft
Ship design Skipskonstruksjoner
Ship fittings Skipsinnredninger
Ship forwarding Skipsekspedisjoner
Ship machinery Skipsmaskineri
Ship maintenance Skipsvedlikehold
Ship operations Skipsdrift
Shipbuilding materials Skipsbyggingsmateriell
Shipping companies Skipsrederier or Skipsselskaper og -ruter
Shoe repairing Skoreparasjon
Shoe shops Skotøy
Shoemaker eqpt Skomakerutstyr
Shop fixtures & fittings Butikkinnredninger og -utstyr
Shop machines & eqpt Butikkmaskiner og -utstyr
Shopping centres Kjøpesentere
Shower units & accessories Baderomsinnredninger
Shredding eqpt Makuleringsmaskiner og -utstyr
Sign makers Skilt- lys- og dekorreklame
Silicones Silikoner
Silversmiths Sølvsmeder
Singers & prologues Sanger og prologer
Site & lot companies Tomteselskaper
Ski lifts & gondolas Ski- og fjellheiser
Ski workshops Skiverksted
Skip hire Containere, avfallscontainere
Skis & sledges Ski og kjelker
Slimming products & services Slanking
Small enterprises Småindustri
Smelters & refiners Smelteverker
Smokehouses & salt curers Røykerier og salterier
Smokers' requisites Piper og røykeartikler
Snow removal eqpt Snøryddingsutstyr
Snow removal services Snørydding
Snowmobiles Snøscootere
Soaps, detergents & polishing materials Såpe-, vaske- og pusseartikler
Social planning & studies Sosialplanlegging og utredning
Social security Trygdekontor in Pink Pages
Social services Helse og sosialkontorer under name

of township kommune in Pink Pages
Social services Trygdekontor
Soft drinks - mfrs Mineralvannfabrikker
Soft drinks - shops Mineralvannutsalg
Soils & soil conditioners Jord og jordforbedring
Solar energy eqpt Solenergipaneler
Solariums & tanning eqpt Solariumsutstyr
Solariums & tanning salons Solarium
Soles Såler
Solicitors Advokater
Sound eqpt installations Lydutstyr
Sound eqpt systems Lydutstyr
Soundproofing Støydemping og støymåling
Souvenirs Suvenirer
Speech therapists Logopeder
Spices Krydder
Sports goods shops Sport og fritidsutstyr
Sports grounds & stadiums Idrettsanlegg
Sports management & promotion Sponsormegling og rådgivning
Sportsground & gymnasium eqpt Idretts-anleggsutstyr
Spray painting & coating Lakkering
Spraying eqpt Sprøytemaleutstyr
Springs Fjærer
Stables Rideopplæring
Stainless steel stockists Rustfritt stål
Staircase mfrs Trapper
Stamp dealers Frimerker
Standards organisations Standardiserings-organisasjoner
Stationery Papir, detalj
Steam plants & boilers Dampanlegg og kjeler
Steam technology Kjeleteknikk
Steel & aluminium buildings Stål- og aluminiumshaller
Steel fabricators & erectors Stålkonstruksjoner
Steel mfrs Jern- og stålverk
Steel stockholders Jern, stål og metaller
Steel windows, walls & doors Stålvinduer, -vegger og -dører
Steel wool Stålull
Steeplejacks Klatring
Stockbrokers Aksje- og fondsmegling
Stockings & socks Strømper og sokker
Stone merchants Steiner og mineraler
Stone products Steinbrudd, -huggerier og -sliperier
Stonemasons Murmestere og murere
Storage & shelving systems Lagerinnredninger og -utstyr
Storage services Lagringstjenester
Storage services, archives Arkivlagring og -tjenester
Stoves, electric (home) Elektirske artikler
Sub-sea contractors Undervannsentreprenører
Sub-sea eqpt Undervannsutstyr
Surveying instruments & eqpt Oppmålings- og

stikningsutstyr
Surveyors - land Oppmålingstjenester
Swimming pool contractors & eqpt Svømmebasseng
Swimming pools - public Svømmehaller og bad
Swimming pools, public, babies Babysvømming
Tailors Skreddere
Take away food shops Gatekjøkken
Tank supplies & installers Varme-sanitæranlegg og - utstyr
Tapes Tape
Tarpaulins Presenninger
Tattooing Tatovering
Tax consultants Skattespørsmål
Taxidermists Utstopping av dyr
Taxis Drosjer
Tea & coffee merchants Kaffe og te
Tea rooms Konditorier
Telecommunications eqpt & systems Tele-kommunikasjonsutstyr or Telematikk
Telecommunications installers Teleinstallatører
Telecommunications services Telekommunikasjon
Telemarketing Telefonmarkedsføring
Telephone answering services & message centres Telefonvakt
Telephone cleaning Telefonrensing
Telephone eqpt Telefonapparater og -systemer
Television broadcasting services TV-selskaper
Television production services TV-produksjon
Television stations (private) TV-kanaler
Television, video & radio dealers & mfrs Radio & TV, agentur, en gros og produksjon
Television, video & radio servicing Radio & TV, verksteder or Radio og TV-reparasjon
Television, video & radio shops Radio & TV, detalj
Temps - agencies Vikarformidlking
Temps - bureaux Vikarbyrå
Tennis courts Tennis baner og -haller
Tents Telt
Terrazzo flooring Terrazzoarbeid
Textile artists Billedkunstnere, Tekstil kunstner
Textile machinery & eqpt Tekstilmaskiner og -utstyr
Textile mfrs Tekstil fabrikker
Textile raw materials Tekstilråstoffer
Textile treatments Tekstilbehandling
Theatres Teater
Theatrical agencies Konsert- og teaterbyråer
Theatrical eqpt & supplies Teaterutstyr
Theme parks Fornøyelsesparker
Therapists Psykoterapi
Thermographic surveys Termografi
Thermostats Termostater
Ticket agencies Billettformidling
Tickets & ticketing machines Billetter og billettmaskiner
Ties & neckwear Slips

Tiles Fliser og mosaikk
Tiling contractors Flisleggere
Timber merchants Trelast
Timber preservation services Impregnering
Time & motion studies Tids- og arbeidsstudier
Time recording machines Tidsregistreringsutstyr
Time recording systems Uranlegg
Tinsmith & coppersmith eqpt Blikk- og kobberslagerutstyr
Tinsmiths & coppersmiths Blikk- og kobberslagertjenester
Tobacco importers & distributors Tobakk, Agentur og engros
Tobacco products - mfrs Tobakk, Production
Tobacconists Tobakk, Detalj
Toning studios Farge analyse
Tool merchants Verktøy
Tour operators Reisearrangører
Tourism consultants Reiselivskonsulenter
Tourist information Turistinformasjon
Towel supply & washroom services Håndkleutleie
Towing services & eqpt, ship Slepetjenester og -utstyr
Towing, car Borttauing
Toy libraries Lekotek
Toy shops Leker
Trade mark agents Patentbyråer, varemerker
Trade unions Landsorganisasjonen i Norge in Pink Pages
Traders Varemeglere
Traffic management systems Trafikksikring
Trailers & towing eqpt Biltilhengere og -utstyr
Train stations & information NSB and Opplysninger in Pink Pages
Transformers Transformatorer
Translators Oversettere, Translatører: **Arabic** Arabisk, **Bulgarian** Bulgarsk, **Chinese** Kinesisk, **Czech** Tsjekkisk, **Danish** Dansk, **Dutch** Nederlandsk, **English** Engelsk, **Esperanto** Esperanto, **Estonian** Estisk, **Finnish** Finsk, **French** Fransk, **German** Tysk, **Greek** Gresk, **Hungarian** Ungarsk, **Italian** Italiensk, **Japanese** Japansk, **multiple languages** Flere språk, **Persian** Persisk, **Polish** Polsk, **Portuguese** Portugisisk, **Rumanian** Rumensk, **Russian** Russisk, **Sami** Samisk, **Serbo-Croatian** Serbokroatisk, **Spanish** Spansk, **Swedish** Svensk, **Thai** Thailandsk
Travel agents Reisebyråer
Trawler workshops Trålverksteder
Tree work Trefelling
Trimmings & trimmers Possementprodukter
Trophies, medals & rosettes Premier
T-shirt printers Kopieringstjenester- T-skjorter
Turbine mfrs Turbiner
Turbo chargers Turboladere
Turf supplies Torv og torvstrø
TV & radio aerials Antenner

TV & radio rental *Radio og TV, utleie*
TV, film & video production services *Video, produksjon, kopiering, distribusjon*
Typesetters *Setterier*
Tyre dealers *Bilgummi*
Umbrellas & parasols *Paraplyer og parasoller*
Uniforms & staff wear *Uniformer og militæreffekter*
Upholsterers *Møbeltapetserere* or *Møbelverksteder*
Upholstery *Møbelstoffer*
Used electrical appliances *Elektroverksteder*
Vacuum cleaners - industrial & commercial *Rengjøringsmaskiner*
Vacuum cleaners (home) *Elektirske artikler*
Valuers *Tilstands- og verdirapportering*
Valuers, car *Biltaksering*
Valve mfrs & supplies *Ventiler*
Van & lorry hire *Bilutleie*
Vehicle inspection service *Trafikkstasjon* under *Statens Vegvesen* in Pink Pages
Vending machines *Automater*
Veneer mfrs *Finér og kryssfinér*
Ventilation contractors *Ventilasjons-varmtluftanlegg og lufteknikk*
Veterinary clinics *Dyreklinikker*
Veterinary surgeons & practitioners *Veterinærer*
Video conferences *Videokonferanse*
Video conversions (PAL-NTSC-SECAM) *Video, konvertering*
Video tape shops *Video, salg, utleie*
Vitamins *Vitaminpreparater*
Volunteer services *Frivillighetssentraler*
Wallpapers & wall coverings *Tapeter*
Wardrobe furnishings *Garderobeinnredninger*
Washing machines *Vaskemaskiner*
Waste disposal eqpt *Renovasjonsutstyr*
Waste disposal, special *Spesialavfall*
Waste products - reclaimers *Avfallsforretninger*
Water authorities *Vann og avløpsverket* or *Vann, avløp, renovasjon* under *(name of municipality) kommune* in Pink Pages
Water coolers *Vannforsyning*
Water suppliers - bottled *Kildevann*

Water suppliers *Vannforsyning*
Water treatment eqpt & service *Vannrensing*
Wedding services *Bryllupsbyråer*
Welders *Sveise verksteder*
Welding eqpt - sales & services *Sveiseutstyr*
Wheels & castors *Hjul*
Winches, capstans & blocks *Vinsjer, spill og taljer*
Window cleaners *Rengjøringstjenester, vinduspuss*
Window film mfrs *Dekorasjonstjenester*
Windscreen services *Bilglass*
Wine & spirits *Vinmonopolet* in Pink Pages
Wines & spirits importers, mfrs & wh'sale *Vin og brennevin*
Wire products - mfrs *Trådvarefabrikker*
Wire products (iron & steel) *Jern- og ståltråd*
Wire rope mfrs & suppliers *Kjettinger og ståltau*
Wood craftsmen *Treskjærere*
Wood preservation services *Overflatebehandling, treverk*
Wood processing *Treforedling*
Wood products except furniture *Trevarer*
Wood stripping, lye *Luting*
Wood turning & machining *Driere, tredreiere*
Wood-burning stoves *Ovner og peiser*
Workshop fittings *Verkstedinnredninger*
Workwear *Yrkesklær*
Wreath ribbon printers *Kransebåndtrykkerier*
Writers - technical & commercial *Forfattervirksomhet*
X-ray services *Røntgen*
Yarn supplies *Garn*
Yeast *Gjær*
Youth clothing *Undomsklær*
Youth exchange programmes *Ungomsutveksling*
Youth hostels *Hoteller og andre overnattingssteder*
Youth organisations & centres *Ungdoms- og idrettsorganisasjoner*
Zinc white mfrs *Sinkhvittfabrikker*
Zip fasteners *Glidelåser*
Zone therapy *Soneterapi*
Zoos *Dyreparker*

Yellow Pages on-line (Gule Sider on-line) The Yellow Pages for the entire country are available together at the Telenor web site w http://www.gulesider.no/ with pages in Norwegian Bokmål and Nynorsk as well as in English.

The site has its own search engine that supports search by business category or keyword or by company name, by districts or by counties. The Norwegian Bokmål version is shown below, as it appears on screen. The buttons at the upper right are for selecting the Nynorsk and English versions. You can go directly to the English version at ☺ http://www.gulesider.no/eng/

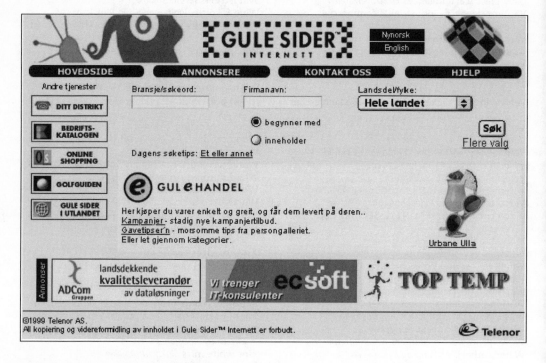

Reproduction of on-line opening page courtesy of Telenor Media.

Index, English

Index, Norwegian